Principles of Supply Chain Management

A BALANCED APPROACH

3e

Joel D. Wisner
University of Nevada, Las Vegas

•

Keah-Choon Tan
University of Nevada, Las Vegas

•

G. Keong Leong
University of Nevada, Las Vegas

SOUTH-WESTERN
CENGAGE Learning

Australia • Brazil • Japan • Korea • Mexico • Singapore • Spain • United Kingdom • United States

SOUTH-WESTERN
CENGAGE Learning™

**Principles of Supply Chain Management,
Third edition**
Joel D. Wisner, Keah-Choon Tan,
G. Keong Leong

Editorial Director: Jack W. Calhoun

Sr. Acquisitions Editor: Charles
McCormick, Jr.

Developmental Editor: Daniel Noguera

Editorial Assistant: Nora Heink

Marketing Manager: Adam Marsh

Media Editor: Chris Valentine

Manufacturing Buyer: Miranda Klapper

Production Service: PreMediaGlobal

Sr. Art Director: Stacy Jenkins Shirley

Cover Designer: Lou Ann Thesing

Cover Image: iStock Photo

Library of Congress Control Number: 2010943343

ISBN 13: 978-0-538-47546-4

ISBN 10: 0-538-47546-3

South-Western
5191 Natorp Boulevard
Mason, OH 45040
USA

Cengage Learning products are represented in Canada by Nelson Education, Ltd.

For your course and learning solutions, visit **www.cengage.com**
Purchase any of our products at your local college store or at our preferred online store **www.cengagebrain.com**

Printed in the United States of America
1 2 3 4 5 6 7 15 14 13 12 11

To CJ, Hayley and Blake.

JOEL D. WISNER

To Shaw Yun, Wen Hui and Wen Jay.

KEAH-CHOON TAN

To Lin and Michelle.

G. KEONG LEONG

Brief Contents

On the Companion Website

Cases in Supply Chain Management
Student and Instructor Materials

Contents

On the Companion Website

Cases in Supply Chain Management

Part 2 Cases
Part 3 Cases
Part 4 Cases
Part 5 Cases

Student and Instructor Materials

Preface

Welcome to the third edition of *Principles of Supply Chain Management: A Balanced Approach*. The practice of supply chain management is becoming widespread in all industries around the globe today, and both small and large firms are realizing the benefits provided by effective supply chain management. We think this text is unique in that it uses a novel and logical approach to present discussions of this topic from four perspectives: purchasing, operations, logistics and the integration of processes within these three vitally important areas of the firm and between supply chain trading partners. We think this book is somewhat different than the other supply chain management texts available, since we present a more balanced view of the topic—many of the texts available today concentrate primarily on just one of the three areas of purchasing, operations or logistics.

The objective of the book is to make readers think about how supply chain management impacts all of the areas and processes of the firm and its supply chain partners, and to show how managers can improve their firm's competitive position by employing the practices we describe throughout the text. Junior- or senior-level business students, beginning MBA students, as well as practicing managers can benefit from reading and using this text.

There are a number of additions to this third edition that we hope you will find interesting and useful. There is a greater emphasis on environmental sustainability throughout the text. In addition, each chapter contains new Supply Chain Management in Action, e-Business Connection, and Global Perspective features, along with new references throughout and new or additional end-of-chapter discussion questions and exercises. Other specific additions and changes to the text are described below.

The textbook also comes with a dedicated website containing dozens of teaching cases split among each section of the book. Most of the case companies and situations are real, while others are fictional, and the cases vary from easy to difficult and short to long. Also on the website is a guide to supply chain management videos along with the YouTube Website addresses for each video. Finally, Power Point lecture slides are available for downloading. Part of the website is protected and for instructors only, and this site contains sample syllabi, case teaching notes, answers to all of the end-of-chapter questions and problems, and a test bank. In the Chapter 1 Appendix, there is a discussion of the Beer Game, with inventory tracking sheets to allow instructors to actually play the game with their students. Finally, there are quantitative as well as qualitative problems and questions, Internet exercises and Excel problems spread throughout most of the chapters.

Part 1 is the overview and introduction of the topic of supply chain management. This chapter introduces the basic understanding and concepts of supply chain management, and should help students realize the importance of this topic. Core concepts such as the bullwhip effect, supplier relationship management, forecasting and demand management, enterprise resource planning, transportation management and customer relationship management are discussed. There is also a new section on current trends in supply chain management.

Part 2 presents supply issues in supply chain management. This very important topic is covered in three chapters, building from an introduction to purchasing management, to managing supplier relationships and then to ethical and sustainable sourcing. Within these chapters can be found sections on government purchasing, global sourcing, e-procurement, software applications, supplier development and green purchasing.

Part 3 includes four chapters regarding operations issues in supply chain management. This section progresses from topics on forecasting, resource planning and inventory management to lean production and Six Sigma. New sections in Part 3 include a greater emphasis on collaborative planning, forecasting, and replenishment (CPFR); discussions of distribution requirements planning (DRP) and radio frequency identification (RFID); and finally discussions of the latest lean production and Six Sigma programs.

Part 4 presents distribution issues in supply chain management and consists of four chapters. Chapter 9 is a review of domestic U.S. and international logistics and contains new sections on green transportation, international logistics security and reverse logistics. This is followed by chapters on customer relationship management, global location decisions and service response logistics. New content in these chapters includes new software application discussions, trends in customer relationship management, new location trends in the global economy and cloud computing services.

The final section is Part 5, which presents discussions of the integration issues in supply chain management and performance measurements along the supply chain. While cooperation and integration are frequently referred to in the text, this section brings the entire text into focus, tying all of the parts together, first by discussing integration in detail, followed by a discussion of traditional and world-class performance measurement systems. New material here includes the topics of supply chain risk management and expanded coverage of performance measurement models.

We think we have compiled a very interesting set of supply chain management topics that will keep readers engaged and we hope you enjoy it. We welcome your comments and suggestions for improvement. Please direct all comments and questions to:

Joel D. Wisner: joel.wisner@unlv.edu (primary contact),

Keah-Choon Tan: kctan@unlv.nevada.edu, or

G. Keong Leong: keong.leong@unlv.edu

Acknowledgements

We greatly appreciate the efforts of a number of fine and hard-working people at Cengage Learning/South-Western College Publishing. Without their feedback and guidance, this text would not have been completed. The team members are Charles E. McCormick, Jr., Senior Acquisitions Editor; Adam Marsh, Marketing Manager; and Daniel Noguera, our Associate Developmental Editor and day-to-day contact person. A number of other people at Cengage Learning and South-Western also need to be thanked including Stacy Shirley, Chris Valentine and Libby Shipp. We also would like to thank Katy Gabel and her people at PreMediaGlobal who put the manuscript into final copy form.

Additionally, we would like to thank all of the case writers who contributed their cases to this textbook. Their names, along with their contact information, are printed with each of the cases on the website. As with any project of this size and time span, there are certain to be a number of people who gave their time and effort to this textbook, and yet their names were inadvertently left out of these acknowledgments. We apologize for this and wish to thank you here.

About the Authors

Joel D. Wisner is Professor of Supply Chain Management at the University of Nevada, Las Vegas. He earned his BS in Mechanical Engineering from New Mexico State University in 1976 and his MBA from West Texas State University in 1986. During that time, Dr. Wisner worked as an engineer for Union Carbide at their Oak Ridge, Tennessee facility and then worked in the oil industry in the wet and green Louisiana Gulf Coast area and also in the dry and sandy West Texas area. In 1991, he earned his PhD in Operations and Logistics Management from Arizona State University. He holds certifications in transportation and logistics (CTL) and in purchasing management (C.P.M.).

He is currently keeping busy teaching undergraduate and graduate courses in supply chain management at UNLV. His research and case writing interests are in process assessment and improvement strategies along the supply chain. His articles have appeared in numerous journals including *Journal of Business Logistics, Journal of Operations Management, Journal of Supply Chain Management, Journal of Transportation, Production and Operations Management Journal,* and *Business Case Journal.* More information about Dr. Wisner can be found at his website: http://faculty.unlv.edu/wisnerj.

Keah-Choon Tan is Professor of Operations Management and Chair of the Marketing Department at the University of Nevada, Las Vegas. He received a BSc degree and an MBA from the University of South Alabama, and a PhD in Operations Management from Michigan State University. He is a certified purchasing manager of the Institute for Supply Management, and is certified in production and inventory management by the APICS. He has published articles in the area of supply chain management, quality, and operations scheduling in academic journals and magazines. Prior to academia, Dr. Tan was a hospital administrator and an account comptroller of a manufacturing firm. He has served as co-track chair and on various committees for the Decision Sciences Institute. He has also served as editor, co-guest editor and on the editorial boards of academic journals. Dr. Tan has received several research grants and teaching awards, including the UNLV Foundation Distinguished Teaching Award.

G. Keong Leong is Professor and Chair of the Management Department in the College of Business at the University of Nevada, Las Vegas. He received an undergraduate degree in Mechanical Engineering from the University of Malaya and an MBA and PhD from the University of South Carolina. He was previously a member of the faculty at Ohio State University and a visiting faculty at the Thunderbird School of Global Management.

His publications appear in academic journals such as *Journal of Operations Management, Decision Sciences, Interfaces, Journal of Management, European Journal of Operational Research* and *International Journal of Production Research,* among others. He has co-authored three books including *Operations Strategy: Focusing Competitive Excellence* and *Cases in International Management: A Focus on Emerging Markets* and received research and teaching awards including an Educator of the Year award from the Asian Chamber of Commerce in Las Vegas. He has been active in the Decision Sciences Institute, serving as President, Editor of *Decision Line,* At-Large Vice-President, Chair of the Innovative Education Committee, Chair of the Doctoral Student

Affairs Committee and Manufacturing Management Track Chair. In addition, he served as Chair of the Professional Development Workshop and Chair of the Operations Management Division, Academy of Management. Professor Leong is listed in *Who's Who Among American Teachers, Marquis Who's Who in the World, Who's Who in America,* and *Who's Who in American Education.*

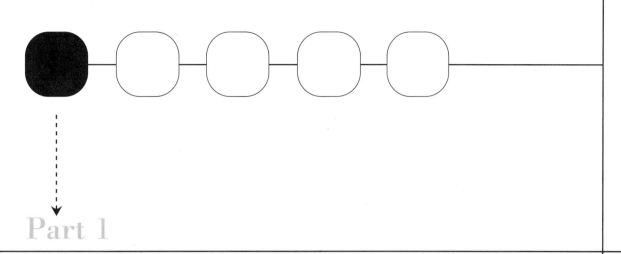

Part 1

Supply Chain Management: An Overview

Chapter 1

INTRODUCTION TO SUPPLY CHAIN MANAGEMENT

Given how quickly and continuously everything is changing these days, it is essential to understand analytically the functioning of supply chains and to be able to know what strategies will produce the best results. This requires greater attention to creating supply chain solutions that are effective and efficient.[1]

Growth is our mantra as an organization. We know that if you're not growing, you're dying. So we have to make sure that in the supply chain organization, we're positioning ourself for that growth.[2]

Learning Objectives

After completing this chapter, you should be able to

- Describe a supply chain and define supply chain management.
- Describe the objectives and elements of supply chain management.
- Describe local, regional and global supply chain management activities.
- Describe a brief history and current trends in supply chain management.
- Understand the bullwhip effect and how it impacts the supply chain.

Chapter Outline

Introduction

Supply Chain Management Defined

The Importance of Supply Chain Management

The Origins of Supply Chain Management in the U.S.

The Foundations of Supply Chain Management

Current Trends in Supply Chain Management

Summary

Supply Chain Management in Action   *Where Does the Coal Go?*

At the same time most every year my dad would be asking, "But where does the coal go?" We'd be on our family vacations on Lake Erie, and as a lover of ships, he'd closely observe the comings and goings of the big freighters that moved iron ore, coal, coke and other materials east and west across the Great Lakes. He'd explain to me why certain ships rode heavy (low in the water and very slow) or light (high in the water and very fast), and what materials were in the ones coming from the west, where they came from and what part they played in making steel—and in turn, what was carried in the bowels of these giant ships, some of them 1,000 feet long.

One of those cargoes was coal, and the coal-bearing freighters would always pull in and unload at the harbor three miles east of us. But the one piece of this shipping and transfer and delivery and supply puzzle that my dad couldn't quite figure out was what happened to the coal after it was unloaded at the harbor in Conneaut, Ohio.

Oh, he knew what its ultimate fate would be and the role it would play in making steel or other products, but he couldn't figure out the physical steps involved with the movement of that coal inside the harbor, and that really bugged him.

He and I would try to find secluded roads leading into the back of this enormous industrial harbor so we could see where the coal went, but we'd always be caught short by fences bearing grim warnings. We tried hiking in from the far shore, hacking our way through thick woods, but always the fence would stop us.

So I took my fellow seeker on a surprise outing. We parked at the little airport in Erie, Pennsylvania, where I'd chartered a private plane. For the next couple of hours, the pilot flew us all over Lake Erie, swooping down over the decks of some of the freighters as they made their way across the lake and circling a few times over the Conneaut harbor.

I'll never forget the sight or sound of my dad triumphantly laughing and slapping his knee as he looked out the window at the massive expanse of the harbor that we'd never been able to see from the ground as he said, "Now I see where the coal goes!" We had to go a half mile up in the air to get the perspective we needed, but we got it.

He saw the railroad shunt that moved the coal from the ships to huge machines that transferred it to a massive web of railroad cars that linked up with rail lines heading south and thence all over the country. I suspect at some level he always knew this is what went on, but he had to see it; he had to really know; he had to be able to tangibly put into place that last piece of the puzzle that ran across thousands of miles of water and rail lines and touched hundreds of industries.

I've been thinking about this a lot recently because companies of all sorts seem to be striving for the same kind of end-to-end view of their businesses, from their farthest-flung suppliers through their partners to their customers and even out to their customers' customers. The need to know, to really know and to have end-to-end vision, is becoming increasingly vital in this business world that moves and changes so rapidly.

Thanks for indulging me in this mostly personal tale of end-to-end vision. I'd like to close by adding that several weeks after our plane ride, my dad died quite unexpectedly. But before he left us, he got to see where the coal went.

Source: Evans, B., "Remembering My Dad," *InformationWeek*, July 26, 2010: 6–7. Used with permission. Bob Evans is senior VP and director of *InformationWeek's* Global CIO unit.

Introduction

Operating successfully today requires organizations to become much more involved with their suppliers and customers. As global markets expand and competition increases, making products and services that customers want means that businesses must pay closer attention to where materials come from, how their suppliers' products and services are designed, produced and transported, how their own products and services are produced and distributed to customers, and what their direct customers and the end-product consumers really want.

Over the past twenty-plus years, many large firms or conglomerates have found that effectively managing all of the business units of a **vertically integrated firm**—a firm whose business boundaries include former suppliers and/or customers—is quite difficult. Consequently, firms are selling off many business units and otherwise paring down their organization to focus more on core capabilities, while trying to create alliances or strategic partnerships with suppliers, transportation and warehousing companies, distributors and other customers who are good at what they do. This collaborative approach to making and distributing products and services to customers is becoming the most effective and efficient way for firms to stay successful—and is central to the practice of supply chain management (SCM).

Several factors require today's firms to work together more effectively than ever before. Communication and information exchange through computer networks using enterprise resource planning (ERP) systems (discussed further in Chapter 6) and the Internet have made global teamwork not only possible but necessary for firms to compete in most markets. Communication technology continues to change rapidly, making global partnerships and teamwork much easier than ever before. Competition is expanding rapidly in all industries and in all markets around the world, bringing new materials, products, people and resources together, making it more difficult for the local, individually owned, "mom-and-pop" shops to keep customers. The recent global economic recession has made customers more cost-conscious while simultaneously seeking higher levels of quality and service, which is requiring organizations to find even better ways to compete. New markets are opening up as governments change and as consumers around the world learn of new products from television, the Internet, radio and contact with tourists. Customers are demanding more socially responsible and environmentally-friendly activities from organizations. Considering all of these changes to the environment, it is indeed an exciting time for companies seeking to develop new products, find new customers and compete more successfully. New jobs and opportunities are opening up in the areas of purchasing, operations, logistics and supply chain management as firms build better competitive infrastructures.

As you read this textbook, you will be introduced to the concepts of supply chain management and how to use these concepts to become better managers in today's global economy. We use examples throughout the text to illustrate the topics discussed; and we provide online cases for each section of the textbook to enable you to test your problem-solving, decision-making and writing skills in supply chain management. We hope that by the end of the text you will have gained an appreciation of the value of supply chain management and will be able to apply what you have learned, both in your profession and in future courses in supply chain management.

In this chapter, the term *supply chain management* is defined, including a discussion of its importance, history and developments to date. The chapter ends with a look at some of the current trends in supply chain management.

Supply Chain Management Defined

To understand supply chain management, one must begin with a discussion of a **supply chain**; a generic one is shown in Figure 1.1. The supply chain shown in the figure starts with firms extracting raw materials from the ground—such as iron ore, oil, wood and food items—and then selling these to raw material suppliers such as lumber companies, steel mills and raw food distributors. These firms, acting on purchase orders and specifications they have received from component manufacturers, turn the raw materials into materials that are usable by these customers (materials like sheet steel, aluminum, copper, lumber and inspected foodstuffs). The component manufacturers, responding to orders and specifications from their customers (the final product manufacturers) make and sell intermediate components (electrical wire, fabrics, plumbing items, nuts and bolts, molded plastic components, processed foods). The final product manufacturers (companies like Boeing, General Motors, Coca-Cola) assemble finished products and sell them to wholesalers or distributors, who then resell these products to retailers as their product orders are received. Retailers in turn sell these products to us, the end-product consumers.

Consumers buy products based on a combination of cost, quality, availability, maintainability and reputation factors, and then hope the purchased products satisfy their requirements and expectations. The companies, along with their supply chains, that can provide all of these desired things will ultimately be successful. Along the supply chain, intermediate and end customers may need to return products, obtain warranty repairs or may just throw products away or recycle them. These **reverse logistics activities** are also included in the supply chain, and are discussed further in Chapter 9.

Figure 1.1	A Generic Supply Chain

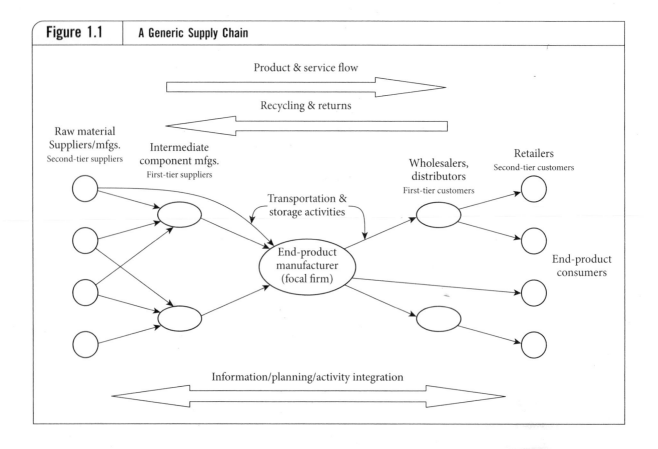

Referring again to Figure 1.1, the firm in the middle of the figure is referred to as the *focal firm,* and the direct suppliers and customers of the focal firm are first-tier suppliers and customers. The first-tier suppliers' suppliers are thus the focal firm's second-tier suppliers, and the first-tier customers' customers are the focal firm's second-tier customers. Some supply chains, such as an automobile supply chain, might have many tiers, while others such as a law office, might have very few tiers. While the focal firm is presented here and in other chapter discussions as an end-product assembly firm, it can be any of the firms involved in the supply chain, depending on the frame of reference of the manager viewing the diagram.

Thus, the series of companies eventually making products and services available to consumers—including all of the functions enabling the production, delivery and recycling of materials, components, end products and services—is called a supply chain. Companies with multiple products likely have multiple supply chains. All products and services reach their customers via some type of supply chain—some much larger, longer and more complex than others. Some may involve foreign suppliers or markets. With this idea of a supply chain in mind, then, it is easy to come to the realization that there really is only one true source of income for all supply chain organizations—the supply chain's end customers. Steve Darendinger, vice president of advanced sourcing and supply chain strategy for Cisco Systems of California, says the key to developing effective supply chain management programs is *keeping the customer in mind.* "The things that we do within our supply chain are driven around customer success," he says. "We provide opportunities and solutions for customers."[3] When individual firms in a supply chain make business decisions while ignoring the interests of the end customer and other chain members, these suboptimal decisions transfer risks, costs and additional waiting time along the supply chain, ultimately leading to higher end-product prices, lower supply chain service levels and eventually lower end-customer demand.

A number of other companies are also indirectly involved in most supply chains, and they play a very important role in the eventual delivery of end products to customers. These are the many service providers, such as trucking and airfreight shipping companies, information system providers, public warehousing firms, freight forwarders, agents and consultants. These service providers are extremely useful to the primary firms in most supply chains, since they can help to get products where they need to be in a timely fashion, allow buyers and sellers to communicate effectively, allow firms to serve outlying markets, enable firms to save money on domestic and global shipments, and in general allow firms to adequately serve their customers at the lowest possible cost.

So now that a general description of a supply chain has been provided, what is **supply chain management (SCM)**? A number of definitions are available in the literature and among various professional associations. A few of these are provided here from three organizations connected to the practice of supply chain management:

- The Council of Supply Chain Management Professionals (CSCMP) defines supply chain management as: "The planning and management of all activities involved in sourcing and procurement, conversion and all logistics management activities. Importantly, it also includes coordination and collaboration with channel partners, which can be suppliers, intermediaries, third-party service providers and customers."[4]
- The Institute for Supply Management (ISM) describes supply chain management as: "The design and management of seamless, value-added processes across organizational boundaries to meet the real needs of the end customer."[5]

- The Singapore-based Logistics & Supply Chain Management Society defines supply chain management as: "The coordinated set of techniques to plan and execute all steps in the global network used to acquire raw materials from vendors, transform them into finished goods, and deliver both goods and services to customers."[6]

Consistent across these definitions is the idea of coordinating or integrating a number of goods- and services-related activities among supply chain participants to improve operating efficiencies, quality and customer service among the collaborating organizations. Thus, for supply chain management to be successful, firms must work together by sharing information on things like demand forecasts, production plans, capacity changes, new marketing strategies, new product and service developments, new technologies employed, purchasing plans, delivery dates and anything else impacting the firm's purchasing, production and distribution plans.

In theory, supply chains work as a cohesive, singularly competitive unit, accomplishing what many large, vertically integrated firms have tried and failed to accomplish. The difference is that independent firms in a supply chain are relatively free to enter and leave supply chain relationships if these relationships are no longer proving beneficial; it is this free market alliance-building that allows supply chains to operate more effectively than vertically integrated conglomerates.

For example, when a particular material or product is in short supply accompanied by rising prices, a firm may find it beneficial to align itself with one of these suppliers to ensure continued supply of the scarce item. This alignment may become beneficial to both parties—new markets for the supplier leading to new, future product opportunities; and long-term continuity of supply and stable prices for the buyer. Later, when new competitors start producing the scarce product or when demand declines, the supplier may no longer be valued by the buying firm; instead, the firm may see more value in negotiating with other potential suppliers for its purchase requirements and may then decide to dissolve the original buyer–supplier alignment. As can be seen from this example, supply chains are often very dynamic or fluid, which can also cause problems in effectively managing them.

While supply chain management may allow organizations to realize the advantages of vertical integration, certain conditions must be present for successful supply chain management to occur. Perhaps the single most important prerequisite is a change in the corporate cultures of all participating firms in the supply chain to make them conducive to supply chain management. More traditional organizational cultures that emphasize short-term, company-focused performance in many ways conflict with the objectives of supply chain management. Supply chain management focuses on positioning organizations in such a way that all participants in the supply chain benefit. Thus, effective supply chain management relies on high levels of trust, cooperation, collaboration and honest, accurate communications.

Purchasing, operations, logistics and transportation managers not only must be equipped with the necessary expertise in these critical supply chain functions but also must appreciate and understand how these functions interact and affect the entire supply chain. Rebecca Morgan, president of Fulcrum Consulting Works, an Ohio-based supply chain management consulting firm, says too many companies go into agreements they call partnerships and then try to control the relationship from end to end. "A lot of the automotive companies did this in the beginning," she says. "They issued a unilateral ultimatum: you will do this for me if you want to do business with me, no matter what it means for you."[7] This type of supply chain management approach can lead to distrust, poor performance, finding ways to "beat the system" and ultimately loss of customers.

Boundaries of supply chains are also dynamic. It has often been said that supply chain boundaries for the focal firm extend from "the suppliers' suppliers to the customers' customers." Today, most firms' supply chain management efforts do not extend beyond those boundaries. In fact, in many cases, firms find it very difficult to extend coordination efforts beyond a few of their most important direct suppliers and customers (in one survey, a number of firm representatives stated that most of their supply chain efforts were with the firm's *internal* suppliers and customers only!).[8] However, with time and successful initial results, many firms are extending the boundaries of their supply chains to include their **second-tier suppliers and customers**, logistics service companies, as well as non-domestic suppliers and customers. Some of the firms considered to be the best at managing their supply chains have very recognizable names: Procter & Gamble, Cisco Systems, Wal-Mart, Apple Computers, PepsiCo and Toyota Motor.

The Importance of Supply Chain Management

While all firms are part of a chain of organizations bringing products and services to customers (and most firms operate within a number of supply chains), certainly not all supply chains are managed in any truly coordinated fashion. Firms continue to operate independently in many industries (particularly small firms). It is often easy for managers to be focused solely on their immediate customers, their daily operations, their sales and their profits. After all, with customers complaining, employees to train, late supplier deliveries, creditors to pay and equipment to repair, who has time for relationship building and other supply chain management efforts? Particularly within this most recent economic downturn, firms may be struggling to just keep their doors open.

Many firms, though, have worked through their economic problems and are encountering some value-enhancing benefits from their supply chain management efforts. Firms with large system inventories, many suppliers, complex product assemblies and highly valued customers with large purchasing budgets have the most to gain from the practice of supply chain management. For these firms, even moderate supply chain management success can mean lower purchasing and inventory carrying costs, better product quality and higher levels of customer service—all leading to more sales.

According to the *U.S. Census Bureau's Annual Survey of Manufactures,* the total cost of all materials purchased in 2008 exceeded $3.2 trillion among U.S. manufacturers, up from $2.2 trillion in 2000. Additionally, fuel purchases among manufacturers in the U.S. totaled $63 billion, up 10 percent from just the previous year due to rising fuel prices.[9] Thus it can easily be seen that purchasing, inventory and transportation cost savings can be quite sizable for firms utilizing effective supply chain management strategies. In fact, in a *2009 Global Survey of Supply Chain Progress* conducted by Michigan State University, almost two-thirds of the respondents reported the existence of an "official" supply chain management group within the firm with jurisdiction over activities like logistics, sourcing and performance measurement. Additionally, about 70 percent of the respondents reported that their supply chain initiatives had either reduced costs or improved revenues.[10] In some cases firms hire a company knowledgeable in supply chain management activities to help the firm develop its own capabilities, and to get the benefits much faster. The Global Perspective feature describes global security system

Global Perspective	*How Diebold Learned to Manage Its Supply Chains*

In 2006, the senior management at Diebold established an aggressive set of cost savings goals as part of its Smart Business 200 program. And the Canton, Ohio, company's supply chain organization was expected to contribute a significant portion to the $200 million savings goal through consolidation, optimization and process improvements. "We knew the opportunity was there but we didn't have the scale of resources or the access to industry best practices" to meet those goals, says Paul Dougherty, strategic procurement manager in Diebold's global procurement organization.

In short, he knew Diebold needed outside help and brought in a fourth-party logistics provider (4PL), Menlo Logistics, to do a full supply chain assessment.

"We actually used to have a map on the wall in one of our procurement conference rooms that depicted each known storage location marked with a pin. There were literally hundreds of excessive, disparate stocking locations with limited or no real-time visibility of inventory positioning, turnover cycles or valuation," says Dougherty.

Based on evaluation of this core mission alignment and a mandate to achieve aggressive savings goals, Diebold chose to have the infrastructure services provided by a 3PL and the more strategic initiatives developed and implemented by a 4PL. To guide its 4PL implementation, Diebold established a Logistics Directorate team with extensive experience across the supply chain. "Today, the map we used to have on the wall is gone and we have consolidated most of that inventory into two distribution centers using a warehouse management system with detailed visibility at the transaction level," says Dougherty.

The primary objective of Menlo's 4PL work is to drive bottom line, year-over-year net cost reductions to Diebold while improving its service levels, which is no small task. "There was a lot of low hanging fruit at the outset and the initial emphasis was consolidating inventory and establishing a flexible, cost-effective, distribution network," says Dougherty.

Gradually, Diebold placed increased reliance on its internal expertise to manage its regional warehousing while looking to Menlo 4PL for continuous engineering improvements to the supply chain network design. The allocation of specific duties is a collaborative effort based on constantly evolving requirements. To date, Menlo has successfully achieved its annual savings goals.

Source: Hannon, D., "Signs that Your Company May Need a 4PL Intervention," *Purchasing,* V. 139, No. 2 (2010): 16. Used with permission.

manufacturer Diebold's choice of a company to do just that, with great and quick success. Today, they still use their **fourth-party logistics provider (4PL)** company (a company hired to manage all of a firm's logistics and supply chain management capabilities) but have also developed internal skills in managing their supply chains.

Managers must realize that their supply chain management efforts can start small—for instance, with just one key supplier—and build through time to include more supply chain participants such as other important suppliers, key customers and logistics services. Finally, supply chain management efforts can include second-tier suppliers and customers. So why are these integration activities so important? As alluded to earlier, when a firm, its customers and its suppliers all know each others' future plans and are willing to work together, the planning process is easier and much more productive, in

---

Example 1.1   Grebson Manufacturing's Supply Chain

The Pearson Bearings Co. makes roller bearings for Grebson Manufacturing on an as-needed basis. For the upcoming quarter, they have forecasted Grebson's roller bearing demand to be 25,000 units. Since Grebson's demand for bearings from Pearson has been somewhat erratic in the past due to the number of bearing companies competing with Pearson and also the fluctuation of demand from Grebson's customers, Pearson's roller bearing forecast includes 5,000 units of safety stock. The steel used in Pearson Bearings' manufacturing process is usually purchased from Rogers Steels, Inc. Rogers Steels has, in turn, forecasted Pearson's quarterly demand for the high-carbon steel it typically purchases for roller bearings. The forecast also includes safety stock of about 20 percent over what Rogers Steels expects to sell to Pearson over the next three months.

This short description has exposed several problems occurring in most supply chains. Because Pearson does not know with full confidence what Grebson's roller bearing demand will be for the upcoming quarter (it could be zero, or it could exceed 25,000 units), Pearson will incur the extra costs of producing and holding 5,000 units of safety stock. Additionally, Pearson risks having to either scrap, sell or hold onto any units not sold to Grebson, as well as losing current and future sales to Grebson if their demand exceeds 25,000 units over the next quarter. Rogers Steels faces the same dilemma—extra materials, labor costs and warehouse space for safety stock along with the potential stockout costs of lost present and future sales. Additionally, Grebson's historic demand pattern for roller bearings from its suppliers already includes some safety stock, since it uses roller bearings in one of the products it makes for a primary customer.

---

terms of cost savings, quality improvements and service enhancements. A fictitious example is provided in Example 1.1.

Example 1.1 illustrates some of the costs associated with independent planning and lack of supply chain information sharing and coordination. Grebson's safety stock, which they have built into their roller bearing purchase orders, has resulted in still additional safety stock production levels at the Pearson plant. In fact, some of the erratic purchasing patterns of Grebson are probably due to their leftover safety stocks causing lower purchase quantities during those periods. This, in turn, creates greater demand variability, leading to a decision at Pearson to produce an even higher level of safety stock. This same scenario plays out between Pearson and Rogers Steels, with erratic buying patterns by Pearson and further safety stock production by Rogers. If the supply chain were larger, this magnification of safety stock, based on erratic demand patterns and forecasts derived from demand already containing safety stock, would continue as orders pass to more distant suppliers up the chain. This supply chain forecasting, safety stock and production problem is known as the **bullwhip effect**. If Grebson Manufacturing *knew* its customers' purchase plans for the coming quarter along with how their purchase plans were derived, it would be much more confident about what the upcoming demand was going to be, resulting in little, if any, safety stock required. And consequently it would be able to communicate its own purchase plans for roller bearings to Pearson. If Grebson purchased its roller bearings from only Pearson and, further, told Pearson what their quarterly purchase plans were, and if Pearson did likewise with Rogers, safety stocks throughout the supply chain would be reduced drastically, driving down the costs of purchasing, producing and carrying roller bearings at each stage. This discussion also sets the stage for a supply chain management concept called *collaborative planning, forecasting and replenishment,* discussed further in Chapter 5.

The result includes lower supply chain costs and better customer service (remember, there would be few, if any, stockouts if purchase quantities were decided ahead of time and shipping companies delivered on time; additionally, production quantities would be less, reducing purchase costs and production time). Trade estimates suggest that the bull-whip effect results in excess costs on the order of 12 to 25 percent at each firm in the supply chain, which can be a tremendous competitive disadvantage.

Lower costs resulting from reducing the bullwhip effect can also result in better quality, since potentially higher profit margins mean more investment into materials research, better production methods and use of more reliable transportation and storage facilities. Additionally, as working relationships throughout the supply chain mature, suppliers will feel more comfortable investing capital in better facilities, better products and better services for their customers. With time, customers will share more information with suppliers and suppliers will be more likely to participate in their key customers' new product design efforts, for instance. These, then, become some of the more important benefits of a well-integrated supply chain. In the following chapters, other associated benefits will also become apparent.

The Origins of Supply Chain Management in the U.S.

During the 1950s and 1960s, U.S. manufacturers were employing mass production techniques to reduce costs and improve productivity, while relatively little attention was typically paid to creating supplier partnerships, improving process design and flexibility,

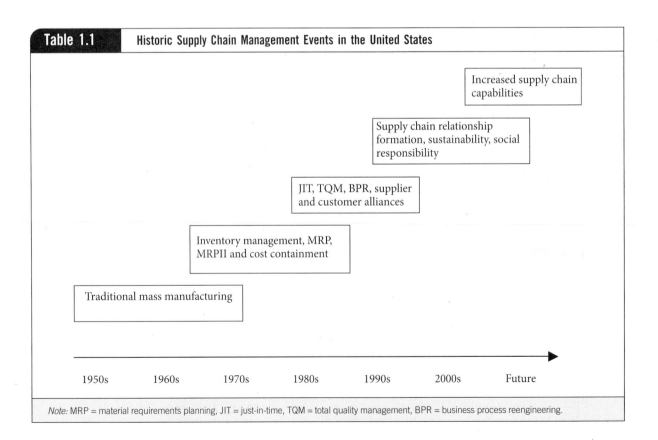

| Table 1.1 | Historic Supply Chain Management Events in the United States |

Note: MRP = material requirements planning, JIT = just-in-time, TQM = total quality management, BPR = business process reengineering.

or improving product quality (see Table 1.1). New product design and development was slow and relied exclusively on in-house resources, technologies and capacity. Sharing technology and expertise through strategic buyer–supplier partnerships was essentially unheard of back then. Processes on the factory floor were cushioned with inventory to keep machinery running and maintain balanced material flows, resulting in large investments in work-in-process inventories.

In the 1960s and 1970s, computer technologies began to flourish and material requirements planning (MRP) software applications and manufacturing resource planning (MRPII) software applications were developed. These systems allowed companies to see the importance of effective materials management—they could now recognize and quantify the impact of high levels of inventories on manufacturing, storage and transportation costs. As computer capabilities grew, the sophistication of inventory tracking software also grew, making it possible to further reduce inventory costs while improving internal communication of the need for purchased parts and supplies.

The 1980s were the breakout years for supply chain management. One of the first widely recorded uses of the term *supply chain management* came about in a paper published in 1982.[11] Intense global competition beginning in the 1980s (and continuing today) provided an incentive for U.S. manufacturers to offer lower-cost, higher-quality products along with higher levels of customer service. Manufacturers utilized just-in-time (JIT) and total quality management (TQM) strategies to improve quality, manufacturing efficiency and delivery times. In a JIT manufacturing environment with little inventory to cushion scheduling and/or production problems, firms began to realize the potential benefits and importance of strategic and cooperative supplier-buyer-customer relationships, which are the foundation of SCM. The concept of these partnerships or alliances emerged as manufacturers experimented with JIT and TQM.

As competition in the U.S. intensified further in the 1990s, accompanied by increasing logistics and inventory costs and the trend toward market globalization, the challenges associated with improving quality, manufacturing efficiency, customer service and new product design and development also increased. To deal with these challenges, manufacturers began purchasing from a select number of certified, high-quality suppliers with excellent service reputations and involved these suppliers in their new product design and development activities as well as in cost, quality and service improvement initiatives. In other words, companies realized that if they started giving only their best suppliers most of their business, then they, in return, could expect these suppliers to help generate more sales through improvements in delivery, quality and product design and to generate cost savings through closer attention to the processes, materials and components they used in manufacturing their products. Many of these buyer–supplier alliances have proven to be very successful.

Interestingly, the general idea of supply chain management had been discussed for many years prior to the chain of events shown in Table 1.1. Back in 1915, Arch W. Shaw of the Harvard Business School wrote the textbook *Some Problems in Market Distribution*, considered by many to be the first on the topic of what we now refer to as supply chain management (Shaw never used this term). The text included discussions of how best to purchase raw materials, transport products, locate facilities and analyze productivity and waste. He espoused a "laboratory point of view" or systematic study of supply chain issues.[12] And business school professors today continue to discuss these topics with students and business managers. According to C. John Langley, Jr., professor of supply chain management at the Georgia Institute of Technology and longtime logistics and supply chain management educator and consultant, "The idea that companies ought to work together and coordinate activities has always been around, but ask people today what one of the biggest problems with supply chains are today, and they say companies don't work very well together." And Langley continues, "It takes a period of time to identify new ideas. It takes a lot longer to implement them."[13]

Business process reengineering (BPR), or the radical rethinking and redesigning of business processes to reduce waste and increase performance, was introduced in the early 1990s and was the result of a growing interest during this time in the need for cost reductions and a return to an emphasis on the key competencies of the firm to enhance long-term competitive advantage. As this "fad" died down in the mid- to late 1990s (the term became synonymous with downsizing), supply chain management rapidly increased in popularity as a source of competitive advantage for firms.

Also during this time, managers, consultants and academics began developing an understanding of the differences between logistics and supply chain management. Up until then, supply chain management was simply viewed as logistics outside the firm. As companies began implementing supply chain management initiatives, they began to understand the necessity of integrating key business processes among the supply chain participants, enabling the supply chain to act and react as one entity. Today, logistics is viewed as one important element of the much broader supply chain management concept.

At the same time, companies also saw benefits in the creation of alliances or partnerships with their customers. The focal firm became the highly valued and heavily used supplier to its customers. Developing these long-term, close relationships with customers meant holding less finished product safety stock (as discussed earlier in the bullwhip effect example) and allowed firms to focus their resources on providing better products and services to these customers. In time, when market share improved for its customers' products, the result was more business for the firm.

Thus, supply chain management has evolved along two parallel paths: (1) the purchasing and supply management emphasis from industrial buyers and (2) the transportation and logistics emphasis from wholesalers and retailers. The increasing popularity of these alliances with suppliers and customers (and suppliers' suppliers and customers' customers) in the latter part of the 1990s and continuing today has also meant a greater reliance on the shipping, warehousing and logistics services that provide transportation, storage, documentation and customs clearing services to many firms within a typical supply chain. Relationship building has also occurred increasingly with many of these **third-party logistics providers (3PLs)** and the firms that use them to ensure a continuous, uninterrupted supply of goods. The need to assess the performance of these relationships periodically has also accompanied the growth of supply chain management. One of the challenges faced today by many firms involved in supply chain management is how to adequately assess overall performance in often extremely complex, global supply chains.

For the wholesaling and retailing industries, the supply chain management focus is on location and logistics issues more often than on manufacturing. Supply chain management in these industries has often been referred to as quick response, service response logistics or integrated logistics. The advancement of electronic data interchange (EDI) systems, bar coding, Internet systems, logistics software applications and radio frequency identification (RFID) technologies over the past two decades has greatly aided the evolution of the integrated supply chain concept. Organizations in the retail industry have utilized supply chain management to meet the ever-increasing uncertainty and complexity of the marketplace and to reduce inventory throughout the supply chain.

Most recently, the rapid development of client/server supply chain management software that typically includes integrated supply chain management and electronic commerce components has aided in the evolution and adoption of supply chain management. Sharing information with supply chain partners through the Internet has enabled firms to integrate stocking, logistics, materials acquisition, shipping and other functions to create a more proactive and effective style of business management and customer responsiveness.

Today, there is an emphasis being placed on the environmental and social impacts of supply chains. Customers are demanding that companies and their supply chains act in an ethically and socially responsible manner. This includes attention to how suppliers are hiring and training employees, how they are harvesting plants and other materials, how their activities impact the environment and what sorts of sustainability policies are being utilized. With these practices in mind, supply chain managers today must also cope with maintaining the most flexible supply chain possible to take advantage of new markets, new sources of supply and new customer demands.

The Foundations of Supply Chain Management

The foundation elements of supply chain management are introduced in this section. These elements essentially make up the table of contents for this textbook and are shown in Table 1.2 along with the chapters where they are discussed.

Supply Elements

Traditional purchasing strategies emphasized the use of many suppliers, competitive bidding and short-term contracts. This often created adversarial buyer–supplier relationships with a focus primarily on the product's purchase price instead of the capabilities of the suppliers and how they can contribute to the long-term competitiveness of the buying organization. Over the past fifteen or twenty years, there has been a gradual shift toward a more strategic approach to purchasing, and this broader approach is more commonly referred to as supply management. Effective supply management has resulted generally

Table 1.2	Important Elements of Supply Chain Management	
SUPPLY CHAIN MANAGEMENT ELEMENTS	**IMPORTANT ISSUES**	**CHAPTERS**
Supply	supply base reduction, supplier alliances, SRM, global sourcing, ethical and sustainable sourcing	2, 3, 4
Operations	demand management, CPFR, inventory management, MRP, ERP, lean systems, Six Sigma quality	5, 6, 7, 8
Logistics	logistics management, CRM, network design, RFID, global supply chains, sustainability, service response logistics	9, 10, 11, 12
Integration	barriers to integration, risk and security management, performance measurement, green supply chains	13, 14

in smaller supply bases and the development of more long-term supplier relationships to achieve the competitive benefits described earlier. Purchasing and the strategic concepts of supply management are one of the foundations of supply chain management, since incoming material quality, delivery timing and purchase price are impacted by the buyer–supplier relationship and the capabilities of suppliers. Chapters 2, 3 and 4 cover the topics associated with supply management.

Harvey Kaylie, president of Mini-Circuits, a New York-based manufacturer of microwave components, sees the supply chain as a relay team, with each link like a runner handing off a baton to the next in line. "It's a challenge, having a process to work with suppliers as partners to achieve the goal of a smooth hand-off," he says. "If we truly want to be world-class, we have to be in tune with our suppliers. If we cannot respond because we don't have the right materials at the right time, we will fail," he adds.[14]

The recent economic downturn has added another problem to the supply side of businesses, namely how the focal firm will continue to produce when several key suppliers go out of business. "One of the lessons learned was that we often do a very good job of looking at the creditworthiness of our customers and their ability to pay us, but we don't do as good a job looking at the financial wherewithal of our suppliers," says Tom Murphy, executive vice president of manufacturing and wholesale distribution at Georgia-based RSM McGladrey, a professional services firm.[15] Thus, supply chain managers are busy building better visibility into their supply chains to spot these problems before they become unmanageable.

One of the most crucial issues within the topic of supply management is **supplier management**. Simply put, this means encouraging or helping the firm's suppliers to perform in some desired fashion, and there are a number of ways to do this. This involves assessing suppliers' current capabilities and then deciding if and how they need to improve them. Thus, one of the key activities in supplier management is **supplier evaluation**, or determining the current capabilities of suppliers. This occurs both when potential suppliers are being evaluated for a future purchase and when existing suppliers are periodically evaluated for ongoing performance purposes. A closely related activity is **supplier certification**. Certification programs can either be company designed and administered, or they can be internationally recognized and standardized programs like the ISO 9000 series of quality certifications. Supplier certification allows buyers to assume the supplier will meet certain product quality and service requirements covered by the certification, thus reducing duplicate testing and inspections and the need for extensive supplier evaluations.

Iowa-based Wells' Dairy, Inc., for example, recently built an ice cream manufacturing facility in Utah. The company is dedicated to providing the highest-quality product on time to its customers. Consequently, it has a very detailed supplier certification program. It includes a thorough review of each supplier's insurance, food quality, government registration and guarantee documents, as well as the completion of the Wells' food safety questionnaire. In addition, each supplier is required to furnish a third-party food safety audit along with any corrective actions taken. Wells' has also instituted a verification site-visit program.[16]

Over time, careful and effective supplier management efforts allow firms to selectively screen out poor-performing suppliers and build successful, trusting relationships with the remaining top-performing suppliers. These suppliers can provide tremendous benefits to the buying firm and the entire supply chain. As discussed in greater detail in Chapter 2, higher purchase volumes per supplier typically mean lower per unit purchase costs (causing a much greater impact on profits than a corresponding increase in sales), and in many cases higher quality and better delivery service. These characteristics are viewed as strategically important to the firm because of their impact on the firm's competitiveness.

Suppliers also see significant benefits from the creation of closer working relationships with customers in terms of long-term, higher-volume sales. These trading partner relationships have come to be termed **strategic partnerships** and are emphasized throughout this text as one of the more important aspects of supply chain management. Florida-based radio manufacturer Harris Corp., for example, has been trying recently to improve their strategic sourcing capabilities. Part of their plan has been "working very closely with our supply base to pick the right few, and then get much deeper within the relationship with those critical few," explains Janis Lindsay, vice president of supply chain operations at Harris.[17] Chapter 3 explores these and other topics associated with supplier relationship management.

Recently, the supply management discipline has come to include a closer emphasis on **ethical and sustainable sourcing**, or purchasing from suppliers that are governed by environmental sustainability and social and ethical practices. Companies are realizing that suppliers can have a significant impact on a firm's reputation and carbon footprint, as well as their costs and profits. Supply chain managers must therefore learn how to develop socially responsible and environmentally friendly sourcing strategies that also create a competitive advantage for the company. These topics along with other supplier management topics are discussed in detail in Chapter 4.

Operations Elements

Once materials, components and other purchased products are delivered to the buying organization, a number of internal operations elements become important in assembling or processing the items into finished products, ensuring that the right amount of product is produced and that finished products meet specific quality, cost and customer service requirements. After supply management, operations management is considered the second foundation of supply chain management and is covered in Chapters 5 through 8.

During a calendar year, seasonal demand variations commonly occur. Firms can predict when these variations occur, based on historic demand patterns, and use forecasting techniques to guide weekly or monthly production plans. If demand does not occur as forecasted, then the focal firm is left with either too much inventory (or service capacity) or too little. Both situations are cost burdens to the firm and can result in permanent lost future business if a stockout has occurred. To minimize these costs, firms often rely on **demand management** strategies and systems, with the objective of matching demand to available capacity, either by improving production scheduling, curtailing demand, using a back-order system or increasing capacity.

Controlling or managing inventory is one of the most important aspects of operations and is certainly value enhancing for the firm. Firms can and typically do have some sort of **material requirements planning (MRP)** software system for managing their inventory. These systems can be linked throughout the organization and its supply chain partners using **enterprise resource planning (ERP)** systems, providing real-time sales data, inventory and production information to all business units and to key supply chain participants. These system configurations vary considerably, based on the number and complexity of products and the design of the supply chain. Retailers like Wal-Mart, for example, scan the barcodes of the products purchased, causing the local store's MRP system to deduct units from inventory until a preset reorder point is reached. When this occurs, the local

e-Business Connection	Black & Decker's Global POS System

With manufacturing and distribution facilities in the U.S., Canada, Mexico and China, Black & Decker Hardware manages offshore and on-shore supply chains, often resulting in long lead times. The company knew their old communication system was reactive and poorly integrated, resulting in a delayed understanding of changes in supply or demand. "When we looked at our pain points within our supply chain, we decided we needed to address manufacturing first," says Scott Strickland, vice president of information systems. "The supply chain forecasts were inaccurate and there was no planning capability at the customer's distribution center or store."

Black & Decker has a 12- to 14-week lead time on all of its products manufactured in China. The manufacturer needed a better view of consumer demand as soon as the products were coming off the shelves. With Lowe's and Home Depot as major retail partners, their new software enhanced communication system was configured to incorporate the retailers' point-of-sale (POS) data. "We can now look at this information at any time and determine what the POS off-take is at one of their stores, and how that off-take is accounted for at our distribution centers," says Strickland. "We're able to quickly understand the demand changes."

With the new system, the company can compare forecasts, shipment history, as well as POS and order history for any of its SKUs at any given time. This resulted in a ten percent improvement in forecast accuracy. The forecast development cycle time improved from five days to two days. The manufacturer has improved order fill rates to its retail partners while holding less inventory than competitors.

Wilfred Eijpen, director of supply chain systems, says, "The planning cycle time for each manufacturing facility usually took two days. This can now be accomplished in four hours. We have seen a major shift from putting out fires on a daily basis to proactively managing inventory reductions across the supply chain."

Source: Anonymous, "Bringing Plants and Purchases Closer Together," *Modern Materials Handling*, 64(11), 2009: 40. Used with permission.

computer system automatically contacts Wal-Mart's regional distribution center's MRP system and generates an order. At the distribution center, the order is filled and sent along with other orders to the particular Wal-Mart. Eventually, the inventory at the distribution center needs replenishing, and at that time, the distribution center's MRP system automatically generates an order with the manufacturer who sells the product to Wal-Mart. This order communication and **inventory visibility** may extend farther back up the supply chain, reducing the likelihood of stockouts or excess inventories. The e-Business Connection feature profiles Black & Decker's use of a point-of-sales software application with hardware retailers Lowe's and Home Depot to improve forecasting and order fill rates.

Indeed, inventory visibility may be quite difficult to achieve along the supply chain. Ohio-based Sterling Commerce, a subsidiary of AT&T and one of the world's largest providers of business process management software, points out that in order to convert point-of-sale data into valuable intelligence along the supply chain, it must be cleansed, harmonized, contextualized, unified and connected with business operations data from the customer relations management, ERP and SCM applications. Additionally, the data, hardware and software configuration of trading partners has to be recognized, aligned and optimized to achieve any strategic advantage.[18]

Another common form of inventory management is through use of a **lean production system** (lean production is also referred to as just-in-time or the Toyota Production System). Implementing this type of system takes time but usually results in faster delivery times, lower inventory levels and better quality. "Lean is a major restructuring that involves doing business differently," says Anand Sharma, CEO of North Carolina-based lean experts TBM Consulting Group. "Companies that do it right get delayered. They get closer to the customer and they break large enterprises into small, entrepreneurial teams that are focused on customers. They have the agility of a start-up and yet they have the security of a large company with capital and market savvy," he adds.[19]

An important aspect of a lean production system is the quality of the incoming purchased items and the quality of the various assemblies as they move through the various production processes. This is due to the characteristically low inventory levels of purchased goods and work in process in lean-oriented facilities. Thus, firms and supply chains employing concepts of lean usually have a **Six Sigma quality** or a total quality management strategy in place to ensure continued quality compliance among suppliers and with internal production facilities. The type of inventory control system used is especially important when considering the design of the supply chain (for instance, where to construct distribution centers, what transportation services to use and how big to make the various production facilities and warehouses).

Considering both lean and Six Sigma systems, one aspect considered very important is the use of a continuous stream of small ideas from front-line employees. These ideas create employee involvement, are somewhat easy to implement, face little resistance and are easy to gain management approval. South Carolina-based Milliken & Company, for example, averages about 100 implemented ideas per employee per year on a global basis. At Milliken Denmark, several looms, each of which had several hundred small ideas applied to it, were operating at speeds two to three times faster than the original design speeds. Additionally, the looms were capable of making special weaves the designers had thought impossible.[20]

Logistics Elements

When products are completed, they are delivered to customers through a number of different modes of transportation. Delivering products to customers at the right time, quality and volume requires a high level of planning and cooperation between the firm, its customers and the various logistics elements or services employed (such as transportation, warehousing and break-bulk or repackaging services). For services, products are produced and delivered to the customer simultaneously in most cases, so services are extremely dependent upon server capacity and successful service delivery to meet customer requirements. Logistics is the third foundation of supply chain management, and these topics are presented in Chapters 9 through 12.

Logistics decisions typically involve a trade-off between cost and delivery timing or customer service. Motor carriers (trucks), for example, are typically more expensive than rail carriers but offer more flexibility and speed, particularly for short routes. Air carriers are yet more expensive but much faster than any other transportation mode. Water carriers are the slowest but are also the least expensive. Finally, pipeline transportation is used to transport oil, water, natural gas and coal slurry. Many transportation services offer various modal combinations, as well as warehousing and customs-clearing services. In a typical integrated supply chain environment where JIT deliveries are the norm, third-party logistics services, or 3PLs, are critical to the overall success of the supply chain. In many cases, these services are considered supply chain partners and are viewed as key value enhancers for the supply chain. California-based clothing company

Anchor Blue, for example, was having many problems a few years ago with its distribution center and inventory management system, leading to problems stocking its retail stores. Consequently, they outsourced their logistics function to UPS Supply Chain Solutions, resulting in a 40 percent decrease in unit processing costs and a 37 percent increase in merchandise pieces moved per year. According to Richard Space, senior vice president for logistics at Anchor Blue, "We have increased delivery to stores and seen better fill rates. What used to take ten days from DC to stores now takes two. And that means improved cash flow." In the end, Space says the keys to a successful outsourcing arrangement are communication and trust.[21]

The desired outcome of logistics is better customer service. In order to provide a desired level of customer service, firms must identify customer requirements and then provide the right combination of transportation, warehousing, packaging and information services to successfully satisfy those requirements. Through frequent contact with customers, firms develop **customer relationship management** strategies regarding how to meet delivery due dates, how to successfully resolve customer complaints, how to communicate with customers and how to determine the logistics services required. From a supply chain management perspective, these customer activities take on added importance, since second-tier, third-tier and end-product consumers are ultimately dependent on the logistics outcomes at each stage within the supply chain. New York-based online grocer FreshDirect uses customer relationship management as a way to stay competitive in a tough economic environment. They survey customers in depth weekly on key metrics for success, loyalty aspects, several key product categories and relevant "issues of the day" such as the economy. Given this data, FreshDirect has been able to develop initiatives that respond to customer needs.[22]

Designing and building a **distribution network** is one method of ensuring successful product delivery. Again, there is typically a trade-off between the cost of the distribution network's design and customer service. For example, a firm may utilize a large number of regional or local warehouses in order to deliver products quickly to customers. The transportation cost from factory to warehouse, the inventory holding cost and the cost to build and operate warehouses would be quite high, but the payoff would be better customer service. On the other hand, a firm may choose to operate only a few highly dispersed warehouses, saving money on the inbound transportation costs from factories (since they would be delivering larger quantities at one time) and the warehouse construction and operating costs, but then having to be content with limited customer service capabilities, since the warehouses would be located farther from most customers. Customer desires and competition levels play important roles in this network design decision. Building a dependable distribution network can often mean higher profits. A study performed by AMR Research, an independent company of supply chain experts headquartered in Massachusetts, found that a three percent improvement in **perfect order fulfillment** (orders arriving on time, complete and damage free) led to a one percent improvement in profits.[23] This might be an argument for more local warehouses.

When firms operate globally, their supply chains are more complex, making global location decisions, the topic of Chapter 11, a necessary aspect of supply chain management. The increasing demand for products in emerging global markets like Russia and China and the growing foreign competition in domestic markets, along with low production costs in many Asian countries, have made overseas business commonplace for many companies. Firms must understand both the risks and advantages of operating on a global scale and the impact this may have on their **global supply chains**. Some of the advantages include a larger market for products; economies of scale in purchasing and production; lower labor costs; a supply base of potentially cheaper, higher-quality suppliers; and the generation of new product ideas from foreign suppliers and employees. Some of the risks include fluctuating exchange rates affecting production, warehousing and purchasing and selling prices, or **operating exposure**; government intervention or political instabilities causing supply disruptions, security concerns and potential changes in subsidies, tariffs and taxes; and, finally, failure to identify foreign customer needs and local reactions to products.

Firms can successfully react to these problems by building flexibility into their global supply chains. This is accomplished by using a number of suppliers, manufacturing and storage facilities in various foreign locations. As product demand and economic conditions change, the supply chain can react to take advantage of opportunities or cost changes to maximize profits. "Obviously, those with production capability in multiple regions and/or countries present a lower risk than a single location or a cluster of facilities in a single region or country," says Mark Taylor, vice president at North Carolina-based Risk International Services. "Even if you source 90 percent from the primary, by maintaining a second or third qualified (supplier), you've substantially shortened your lead time in making a change."[24]

For service products, the physical distribution issue is typically much less complex. Making sure services are delivered in a timely fashion is the topic of Chapter 12. Services are, for the most part, delivered by a server when customers request service. For instance, consider an example in which a customer walks into a bank in search of a loan for a used automobile. He may contact three separate bank employees during this transaction but eventually will complete a loan application, wait for loan approval and then receive funds, assuming his loan is approved. He will leave, satisfied with the service products he received, provided that a number of things occurred: he got what he came for (the loan); he got the type of service he expected to get (a fairly short waiting period and knowledgeable servers); and he got his product at a reasonable price (a good interest rate for the right period of time).

Thus, successful service delivery depends on service location (service providers must be close to the customers they are trying to serve), service capacity (customers will leave if the wait is too long) and service capability (customers must be able to trust what servers are telling them or doing for them). Hard goods producers must also be concerned with the delivery of service products for their customers, such as providing warranty repairs and information, financing, insurance and equipment troubleshooting and operating information.

Integration Elements

Thus far, three of the foundations of supply chain management have been discussed: supply, operations and logistics activities occurring among the firm and its various tiers of customers and suppliers. The final foundation topic—and certainly the most difficult one—is to coordinate and integrate these processes among the focal firm and its key supply chain trading partners. Supply chain **process integration** is discussed in the final two chapters of the text.

Processes in a supply chain are said to be integrated when members of the supply chain work together to make purchasing, inventory, production, quality and logistics decisions that impact the overall profits of the supply chain. If one key activity fails or is performed poorly, then the flow of goods moving along the supply chain is disrupted, jeopardizing the effectiveness of the entire supply chain. Successful supply chain process integration occurs when the participants realize that effective supply chain management must become part of each member's strategic planning process, where objectives and policies are jointly determined based on the end consumers' needs and what the supply chain as a whole can do for them.

Ultimately, firms act together to maximize total supply chain profits by determining optimal purchase quantities, product availabilities, service levels, lead times, production quantities, use of technology and product support at each tier within the supply chain. This integration process also requires high levels of internal functional integration of activities within each of the participating firms, such that the supply chain acts as one entity. This idea of supply chain integration can run contrary to the notion among many potential supply chain participants of their firm's independent profit-maximizing objectives, making supply chain integration a very tough sell in many supplier-buyer-customer situations. Thus, continued efforts are required to break down obstacles, change cultural norms, change adversarial relationships, knock down silos, reduce conflict and bridge functional barriers within and between companies if supply chain integration is to become a reality. When John Bradshaw, for instance, was hired by Belgium-based Godiva Chocolatier as vice president of global procurement, his changes had everything to do with integration. "Each function was doing its work in isolation and throwing the results over the wall for the next function," remarked Bill Kornegay, senior vice president of global supply chain for Godiva. "He had everyone work through touch points in the process, such as who should be communicating with whom and when, helping tear down walls that built up over time," he added. Bradshaw's strategies were recently projected to save the company over $10 million in 2010.[25]

One additional integration topic is the use of a **supply chain performance measurement** system. Performance measurements must be utilized along supply chains to help firms keep track of their supply chain management efforts. It is crucial for firms to know whether certain strategies are working as expected—or not—before they become financial drains on the organizations. Firms work together to develop long-term supply chain management strategies and then devise short-term tactics to implement these strategies. Performance measurements help firms decide the value of these tactics and should be developed to highlight performance within the areas of purchasing, operations, logistics and integration.

Performance measures should be designed around each important supply chain activity and should be detailed performance descriptors instead of merely sales or cost figures. High levels of supply chain performance occur when the strategies at each of the firms fit well with overall supply chain strategies. Thus, each firm must understand its role in the supply chain, the needs of the ultimate customer, the needs of its immediate customers, and how these needs translate into internal operations requirements and the requirements being placed on suppliers. Once these needs and the products and services themselves can be communicated and transported through the supply chain effectively, successful supply chain management and its associated benefits will be realized. University of Massachusetts professor Larry Lapide, for example, points out that paying attention to second- and third-tier supplier performance can play a predictive role for the focal firm's supply chain. "If a second- or third-tiered supplier is having difficulty supplying a company's first-tier suppliers, then their performance will eventually degrade over time as well," he states.[26]

Current Trends in Supply Chain Management

The practice of supply chain management is a fairly recent phenomenon, and many organizations are beginning to realize both the benefits and problems accompanying integrated supply chains. Supply chain management is a complex and time-consuming undertaking, involving cultural change among most or all of the participants, investment and training in new software and communication systems, the building of trust between supply chain members and a change or realignment of the competitive strategies employed among at least some of the participating firms. Further, as competitors, products, technologies and customers change, the priorities for supply chains also must change, requiring them to be ever more flexible to respond quickly to these changes. As we look at the most recent practices and trends in supply chain management, a number of issues present themselves as areas that need to be addressed including the expansion (or contraction) of the supply chain, increasing supply chain responsiveness, creating a sustainable supply chain and reducing total supply chain costs.

Expanding (and Contracting) the Supply Chain

As potential markets for firms are identified, their supply chains must grow to accommodate new production and logistics networks. Today, firms are increasing their partnerships with foreign firms and building foreign production facilities to accommodate their market expansion plans and increase their responsiveness to global economic conditions and demand. The supply chain dynamic today is changing, and companies are working with firms located all over the globe to coordinate purchasing, manufacturing and logistics activities. For many years now, computer maker Hewlett-Packard (HP) has been expanding with the help of a third-party logistics company. As Tom Healy, worldwide supply chain strategy manager for HP, said recently, "In a globalized environment, there isn't a single part of the world we are not trying to dominate."[27]

While these global expansions of supply chains are occurring, firms are also trying to expand their influence and control of the supply chain to include second- and third-tier suppliers and customers. This supply chain expansion is occurring on two fronts: increasing the *breadth* of the supply chain to include foreign manufacturing, sales offices and retail sites, along with foreign suppliers and customers; and increasing the *depth* of the supply chain to include the influencing of second- and third-tier suppliers and customers.

Today, some firms are also finding that their foreign markets are contracting. Logistics costs are escalating, security concerns are growing and there is increasing awareness that it might be time to concentrate on doing what the firm does best to protect its most profitable and loyal customers in domestic markets. Much of this supply chain contraction emphasis was born with the recent economic downturn. Some have come to refer to these contraction activities as **right-shoring**. Right-shoring is the combination of on-shore, near-shore and far-shore operations into a single, flexible, low-cost approach to supply chain management. Foreign suppliers in many cases have simply shut their doors as orders dried up, forcing companies to seek other suppliers. A recent survey conducted by Georgia-based MFG.com, for instance, found that 44 percent of their respondents experienced a significant supply chain disruption that forced them to find an alternative supplier. As a result, companies like Caterpillar and General Electric have announced plans to repatriate some of their production to new factories in the U.S.[28]

Additionally, firms that had identified low-cost Asian suppliers several years ago began seeing labor cost increases as more and more firms were contracting their manufacturing needs to the same Asian suppliers. When adding up the total costs of manufacturing and transporting goods from these far-flung locations to U.S. or European markets, for instance, it simply no longer made economic sense. This, in turn, significantly reduced the amount of transportation dollars being collected by ocean-going vessels. "Although virtually every company involved in the supply chain cut costs and increased productivity, this precipitous drop (in 2009 logistics spending) was caused more by the rapid decline in shipments and the cutthroat rate environment," says Roslyn Wilson, a logistics industry consultant.[29] As a matter of fact, since so many companies have pulled out of China today, dramatic excess capacities can be found at some manufacturing sites. Consequently, buyers can once again be found moving back to Chinese suppliers to take advantage of quick turnaround times and cheap ocean transportation.[30] So today, both expansion and contraction of supply chains can be seen.

With advances and improvements in communication technology, manufacturing and transportation, more and more companies around the globe have the capability to produce and sell high-tech parts and products and move these quickly to world markets as demand develops. The many trade agreements such as the European Union, the World Trade Organization and the North American Free Trade Agreement have also facilitated the production and movement of goods between countries; and this has enabled firms to more easily expand their supply bases and their markets. New software applications bring buyers and suppliers together in e-marketplace settings, helping to expand supply chains considerably and more easily, using the Internet. A rapid expansion of the global e-marketplace is occurring, and this pace should continue as new market enablers, producers and customers come into the global picture.

As firms become more comfortable and experienced with their supply chain trading partner relationships, there is a tendency to expand the depth or span of the supply chain by creating relationships with second- and third-tier suppliers and customers. This span expansion phenomenon is now occurring in many industries and should continue to increase as the practice of supply chain management matures.

Increasing Supply Chain Responsiveness

Agile manufacturing, JIT, mass customization, lean manufacturing and quick response are all terms referring to concepts that are intended to make the firm more flexible and responsive to customers' changing requirements. Particularly with the tremendous levels of competition in almost all avenues of business, firms (and their key supply partners) are looking today at ways to become more responsive to customers. To achieve greater levels of responsiveness, supply chains must identify their end customers, determine their needs, look at what the competition is doing and position their supply chain's products and services to successfully compete; then finally, consider the impact of these requirements on each of the supply chain participants. Once these requirements have been adequately identified among the firms in the supply chain, additional improvement in responsiveness comes from designing more effective information and communication systems, and faster product and service delivery systems as products and information are passed through the supply chain. Supply chain members must also continuously monitor changes occurring in the marketplace and then use this information to reposition supply chain member capabilities and outputs to stay competitive.

Mobile technologies, for example, have now improved to the point that they are used in many supply chain applications where real-time data transfers can improve responsiveness. "Modern manufacturing warehouse facilities are hundreds of thousands of square feet in size," says Reik Reed, an industry analyst at Wisconsin-based Robert W. Baird & Co. "Having real-time mobile capability from any point in these facilities allows companies to track both people and assets. The manufacturing and warehousing environments are dynamic and change constantly. With optimization through real-time mobile communications, the instantaneous changes can be delivered to drivers. It allows greater visibility into the manufacturing process."[31]

Improving **supply chain responsiveness** requires firms to reevaluate their supply chain relationships, utilize business process reengineering, reposition and automate warehouses, design new products and services, reduce new product design cycles, standardize processes and products, empower and train workers in multiple skills, build customer feedback into daily operations and, finally, link together all of the supply chain participants' information and communication systems using the latest technologies. So, very quickly, it is seen that achieving high levels of customer satisfaction through responsiveness requires potentially significant changes not only in firm culture but also in the technical aspects of providing products, services and information throughout the supply chain. This remains a significant and ongoing challenge for successful supply chain management. Automotive sector companies, for instance, have been heavy users of product life-cycle management systems to connect supply chain management members. "Tires used in specific models may need to be recalled, for example," explains Sath Rao, industry manager at Texas-based research and consulting company Frost & Sullivan. "So, systems must be able to find customers who need to be informed of the recall. And managers want to determine if the problem can be traced back to a design flaw or a manufacturing error."[32]

The Greening of Supply Chains

Purchasing, producing, packaging, moving, storing, repackaging, delivering and then returning or recycling products can pose a significant threat to the environment in terms of discarded packaging materials, scrapped toxic materials, carbon monoxide emissions, noise, traffic congestion and other forms of industrial pollution. As the practice of supply chain management matures, governments along with firms and their supply chain partners are working harder to reduce these environmental problems. Many governments, for example, are enacting environmental regulations that restrict inbound shipments of products containing hazardous materials. Following the European Union, which enacted restrictions in July of 2006, China established the first stage of their restrictions in March of 2007. Eventually, exporters to China will be prohibited from shipping any items containing lead, mercury, cadmium and several other hazardous materials.

Many green or **sustainable supply chain** initiatives continue to be launched, and David North, consumer and government director at U.K.-based Tesco, a large supermarket group, says there is a strong commercial reason for succeeding in these initiatives. "The supply chain is the big prize," he says. "We think that in the future many of our customers are going to care about this. We think this will be an area of competitive advantage." It is now aiming for a 30 percent reduction in carbon emissions among suppliers by 2020, while helping their customers to halve the emissions arising from their purchases by the same date.[33]

Probably the biggest supporter and enabler of sustainable supply chains is Wal-Mart, the behemoth retailer. Since 2007 and their Sustainability 360 initiative, wherein Wal-Mart began moving the company's emphasis to its suppliers, customers and their communities, they have shown tremendous commitment to green practices. Because of their enormous size and influence in their supply chains, they have created a significant change in the way their suppliers, logistics companies and customers think about environmental sustainability. One very small example typifies the way Wal-Mart views sustainability—a number of stores as of 2010 are using the waste oil from their deep-fryers to fuel Wal-Mart trucks. Wal-Mart is hip to biodiesel? You bet.[34]

Staples, too, the global office supply retailer, has been driving costs out of and environmental responsibility into their supply chains using green practices for a number of years. Today, its products contain about 30 percent recycled paper content. It buys products only from paper mills that do not accept old-growth trees. Additionally, they are working with the Forest Stewardship Council to encourage small landowners to certify their forests as sustainable by creating a market for products from sustainable forests. "Our challenge," says Mark Buckley, vice president of environmental affairs at Staples, "is being able to [extend sustainability] practices from the shelf to the stump."[35]

In fact, relationships between companies in a well-managed supply chain are much more conducive to taking a more proactive approach to reducing the negative environmental consequences of producing, moving and storing products as they wend their ways through the supply chain. Over time, consumer sentiment toward environmentally friendly processes and the prevention of global warming has tended to increase, making this topic one of concern for companies managing their supply chains. Unfortunately, this growing demand for green products has led to what is termed **greenwashing**, or making environmental claims for products that are exaggerated or misleading. Companies today are flooding the market with green products—a 79 percent increase from 2007 to 2009, according to environmental marketing company TerraChoice, based in Canada. As a matter of fact, a study by TerraChoice of 2,219 products claiming to be green found 98 percent carried exaggerated or misleading claims.[36]

Added to this increasing concern and awareness among the general public for environmentally friendly business processes is the growing cost of natural resources such as wood products, oil and natural gas. Strategies to successfully compete under these conditions include using recyclable materials in products; using returnable and reusable containers and pallets; using recyclable and reusable packaging materials; managing returns along the supply chain efficiently; designing effective transportation, warehousing and break-bulk/repackaging strategies; and using environmental management systems from initial producer to final consumer in the supply chain. The benefits of these activities will include lower system-wide costs, fewer duplicate activities, marketing advantages, less waste and, ultimately, greater customer satisfaction.

Reducing Supply Chain Costs

Considering again the objectives of supply chain management, cost reduction is clearly high on this list of priorities, and the economic hardships of the past few years have likely moved cost reduction even higher on most firms' priority lists. Cost reduction can be achieved throughout the supply chain by reducing waste as already described, by reducing purchasing and product distribution costs and by reducing excess inventories and non-value-adding activities among the supply chain participants. As supply chains become more mature, they tend to improve their performance in terms of these cost reduction activities through use of continuous improvement efforts, better supply chain communication and inventory visibility capabilities and a further integration of processes. Interestingly, a recent survey of Chicago, Illinois, CEOs found that, while 75 percent said their company's overall focus was on top-line growth, 82 percent said their company's current supply chain initiatives were directed at cost reduction. "Cutting costs via the supply chain and being much more closely connected, umbilically connected, to customers are absolutely the driving principles of our supply chain," says Doug Ramsdale, CEO of Home Products International, a consumer housewares product manufacturer based in Illinois.[37]

As time passes, supply chain costs continue to decrease due to trial and error, increased knowledge of the supply chain processes, use of technology to improve information flow and communication, **benchmarking** other successful supply chains to copy what they are doing well and continued performance measurement and other process improvement efforts. Sometimes it just means looking for ways to economize. Shipping a 50-pound package on FedEx from Minneapolis, Minnesota, to New York City, for instance, costs about $190 overnight but only about $80 for two-day delivery—a savings of over 60 percent every time a shipment such as this is made.

Firms are also employing better software applications to streamline their supply chains and hiring third-party spend management consultants to reduce supply chain costs. According to Greg Aimi, research director at Boston-based business research specialist AMR Research, less than 40 percent of companies are using a transportation management system (TMS) software application right now. "If you don't have a TMS, and if you're using spreadsheets and fax machines to handle the routing and shipping, then a large portion of the savings identified at procurement will evaporate and never materialize," says Adrian Gonzalez, director of Massachusetts-based ARC Advisory Group's Logistics Executive Council. Leading European seafood supplier MWBrands has hired Ariba, a leading spend management advisor, to fuel an aggressive cost reduction initiative using technology, expertise and market intelligence. "The key to success in the post-recession world will be agility," says Charles Royon, vice president at Ariba. "By tapping Ariba's expertise, MWBrands can quickly enable this agility, advance its cost reduction efforts and accelerate the results they deliver."[38]

As discussed here and in later chapters, the purchasing function will continue to be viewed as a major strategic contributor to supply chain cost reduction through better supplier evaluation techniques, value engineering and analysis in product design and production, standardization and reduction of parts and materials and through make-or-buy decisions. Finally, the logistics function will also play a major role in cost reduction along the supply chain through better design of distribution networks, use of software applications and use of third-party logistics service providers.

SUMMARY

Supply chain management is the integration of trading partners' key business processes from initial raw material extraction to the final or end customer, including all intermediate processing, transportation and storage activities and final sale to the end-product customer. Today, the practice of supply chain management is becoming extremely important to reduce costs and improve quality and customer service, with the end objective of improving competitiveness. Many firms are just now becoming aware of the advantages of supply chain integration. Supply chain management is an outgrowth and expansion of lean and Six Sigma activities and has grown in popularity and use since the 1980s. The foundations of supply chain management can be found in the areas of purchasing, production, logistics and process integration or collaboration between trading partners. Finally, as markets, political forces, technology and economic conditions change around the world, the practice of supply chain management must also change and grow.

KEY TERMS

benchmarking, 26

bullwhip effect, 11

business process
    reengineering (BPR), 14

customer relationship
    management, 20

demand management, 17

distribution network, 20

enterprise resource planning
    (ERP), 17

ethical and sustainable
    sourcing, 17

fourth-party logistics
    providers (4PLs), 10

global supply chains, 20

greenwashing, 26

inventory visibility, 18

lean production system, 19

material requirements
    planning (MRP), 17

operating exposure, 21

perfect order fulfillment, 20

process integration, 21

reverse logistics activities, 6

right-shoring, 23

second-tier suppliers and
    customers, 9

Six Sigma quality, 19

strategic partnerships, 17

supplier certification, 16

supplier evaluation, 16

supplier management, 16

supply chain, 6

supply chain management
    (SCM), 7

supply chain performance
    measurement, 22

supply chain responsiveness,
    25

sustainable supply chain, 25

third-party logistics providers
    (3PLs), 14

vertically integrated firm, 5

DISCUSSION QUESTIONS

1. Define the term supply chain management in your own words, and list its most important activities.

2. Can a small business like a local sandwich or bicycle shop benefit from practicing supply chain management? What should they concentrate on?

3. Describe and draw a supply chain for a bicycle repair shop.

4. What roles do collaboration and trust play in the practice of supply chain management?

5. What are the four foundation elements of supply chain management? Describe some activities within each element.

6. What does the bullwhip effect refer to, and what causes it? How, then, would you try to reduce the bullwhip effect?

7. What are the benefits of supply chain management?

8. Can nonprofit, educational or government organizations benefit from supply chain management? How?

9. What does the term third-tier supplier mean? What about third-tier customer? What about the focal firm? Provide examples.

10. Could a firm have more than one supply chain? Explain.

11. When did the idea and term supply chain management first begin to be thought about and discussed?

12. Do you think supply chain management is simply the latest trend in management thinking, and will die out in a few years? Why or why not?

13. Is the use of a large number of suppliers a good idea? Why?

14. Do you think the proper way to choose a supplier is to always find the one that will give the lowest price? When might this not be a good idea?

15. Why don't firms just buy out their suppliers and industrial customers, forming conglomerates, instead of practicing supply chain management?

16. What is the difference between an MRP system and an ERP system?

17. What role do information systems play in supply chain management? Give some examples.

18. Briefly describe the terms lean and Six Sigma.

19. What are 3PLs and what role do they play in SCM?

20. What does process integration mean, and what does this have to do with SCM?

INTERNET QUESTIONS

1. Visit the websites of companies like Wal-Mart, Dell and Home Depot, and see if you can find discussions of their supply chain management activities. List information you can find on purchasing/supplier issues, logistics, information systems, quality and customer service.

2. Search on the term supply chain management. How many hits did you get? Describe five of the websites found in your search.

3. Go to www.agrichain-centre.com (or a similar website found when searching on New Zealand supply chain management), and discuss the current state of supply chain (or value chain) management in New Zealand.

4. Search for the term bullwhip effect, and write a paper on the impacts of the bullwhip effect and the companies profiled in the papers you find.

5. Search on the term supply chain management software applications, and write a paper about how companies use these to improve their financial performance.

6. Search on green supply chains, and write a paper regarding the global regulatory status of environmental legislation and how it is impacting supply chain management.

APPENDIX 1.1
The Beer Game[39]

The Beer Game has become a very popular game played in operations management and supply chain management courses since being developed by MIT in the 1960s. The game simulates the flow of product and information in a simple supply chain consisting of a retailer, a wholesaler, a distributor and a manufacturer. One person takes the role of each supply chain partner in a typical game. The objective is to minimize total supply chain inventory and back order costs. In this way, a class can be separated into any number of four-person supply chains—each supply chain competing against the others. The game is used to illustrate the bullwhip effect, and the importance of timely and accurate communications and information with respect to purchases along the supply chain (in this game, no one is allowed to share any information other than current order quantities, as might be found in unmanaged or unlinked supply chains).

© 2007 Ted Goff

"Do you know anything about the system resources being overloaded by some kind of game?"

Each supply chain participant follows the same set of activities:

1. Each participant fills customer orders from current inventory and creates back orders if demand cannot be met.

2. Participants forecast customer demand and then order beer from their supplier (or schedule beer production if the participant is the manufacturer), which then takes several weeks to arrive.

3. Each participant attempts to manage inventories in order to minimize back order costs (stockouts) and inventory carrying costs.

Figure A1.1 illustrates the beer supply chain, showing the transportation and information delays. There is no product transportation or order delay between the retailer and the end customers. For the other supply chain members, there is a one-week delay

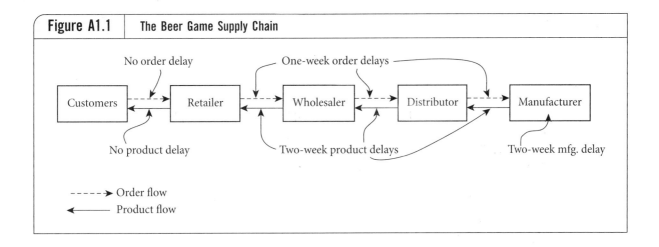

Figure A1.1 | **The Beer Game Supply Chain**

between customer order and supplier acceptance, and a two-week transportation delay from the time a customer's order is received until that order reaches the customer. It also takes two weeks to complete a production order at the factory, such that beer will be ready to fill customer orders.

Here is how the game progresses:

Starting conditions. At the start of the game (Week 0), each supply chain member (except the manufacturer) has twelve cases of beer in ending inventory (see Table A1.1), four cases in the second week of inbound transportation delay, four cases in the first week (updated) of inbound transportation delay and four cases in the beginning of the first week of inbound transportation delay. The manufacturer has twelve cases of beer in ending inventory, four cases of beer in the second week of production lead time, four cases in the first week of production lead time and four cases at the beginning of the first week of production lead time. Each player also has an *outgoing order* of four cases sitting in their outgoing order box (or production order box). The retailer must begin with twenty weeks of customer demand information provided by the game coordinator or instructor, such that the retailer can only view one week's demand at a time (these can be written on the underneath side of twenty sticky note pads for each retailer, for example).

Step 1. Each member *updates their beer inventories.*

- Move the cases of beer from the second week of inbound delay for the previous period and add to the ending inventory of the previous period, putting the total in the beginning inventory column of the current period (see Week 0/Week 1 of Table A1.1). For the manufacturer, this is a production delay.

- Move inventory from the first week of inbound delay (updated column) to the second week of delay (see Table A1.1).

- Move inventory from the first week of inbound delay (beginning column) to the first week of inbound delay (updated column) (see Table A1.1).

Step 2. Each member *fills their customer orders.*

- The retailer uncovers and reads the current week's customer demand slip, and then places the slip face down in the discard area, **such that it cannot be seen by the wholesaler**.

Table A1.1	Inventory Record Sheet

Your supply chain role:

Your name: Team name:

Incoming demand from supply chain customer	Discard area		Outgoing orders to supply chain supplier, OR production orders for manufacturer

Week	Ending Inventory	Beginning Inventory	Back Orders	Second Week Inbound Delay	First Week Inbound Delay	
					Updated	Beginning
0	12		0	4	4	4
1		16		4	4	
2						
3						
4						
5						
6						
7						
8						
9						
10						
11						
12						
13						
14						
15						
16						
17						
18						
19						
20						
Totals						

Amount of outgoing order received

Note: Ending inventories must be zero when you have a back order. If ending inventory is greater than zero, backorders must equal zero. Back orders equal previous period back orders plus incoming order minus current inventory.

At end of game: Sum *ending inventory* column and *back orders* column and determine total cost as—[Total ending inventories × $1] + [Total back orders × $2] = $_____. Then sum total costs for all supply chain members. Total supply chain costs = $_____.

- The retailer then fills this order (after first satisfying any back orders) and subtracts demand from beginning inventory. This amount then becomes the ending inventory amount. If ending inventory is negative, then a back order of this amount is created, and ending inventory becomes zero.
- Next, the retailer places last week's outgoing order on the wholesaler's incoming demand order box.
- Finally, the retailer forecasts future demand and orders beer from the wholesaler by writing an order on the slip provided and places it face down in the retailer's outgoing order box, *such that it cannot be seen by the wholesaler*. (This order will go to the wholesaler next week—remember the one-week delay).

The wholesaler follows the same steps as above: it reads the incoming demand order slip, discards it, satisfies any back orders and fills as much of the incoming order as possible from beginning inventory. At this point, the wholesaler must tell the retailer how much of the order it can satisfy, and the retailer records this amount in the first week beginning delay for the current period. The wholesaler then updates its ending inventory and back order quantities, sends last week's outgoing order to the distributor's incoming demand, and then decides how much to order and places the order sheet face down in the wholesaler's outgoing order box, *such that it cannot be seen by the distributor*.

The distributor goes through the same steps as the wholesaler when it gets an incoming order from the wholesaler.

The manufacturer follows the same steps also, except instead of sending last week's outgoing order somewhere, it reads the outgoing order and fills the production request by transferring that number of cases from its raw materials storage area to the first week's beginning production delay (it simply creates the cases needed for the order).

Step 3. Repeat steps 1 and 2 until the game limit is reached. Calculate total costs at game's end.

A typical game progresses in this fashion for twenty weeks (this is usually sufficient to introduce the bullwhip effect into the game). The game is played with sticky note pads for beer orders, using Table A1.1 to keep track of inventories, orders and back orders. Players must take care **not to talk** to the other players during the game **or to show what orders they are receiving or planning** for the next week. The retailer must **not look at future customer demand data**, provided by the instructor. Remember, this game is meant to illustrate what happens when *no communication* about future orders or order strategies occurs between supply chain members.

At the end of twenty weeks (or shorter if time does not permit), players determine the total cost of their inventories and back orders on the inventory record sheet (back orders cost $2 per unit per week, and inventories cost $1 per unit per week). Given these costs, the basic strategy should be to attempt to avoid stockouts or back orders, while also somewhat trying to minimize total inventory carrying costs. This requires attempting to forecast future demand accurately (as time progresses, firms should use their inventory record sheet demand information for forecasting purposes). The winning team is the team with the lowest total supply chain costs.

BEER GAME QUESTIONS AND EXERCISES

1. All players but the retailer should answer this question. What do you think the retailer's customer demand pattern looked like? How did your customer orders vary throughout the game?

2. What happened to the current inventory levels as we move backward, up the supply chain from retailer to manufacturer? Why?

3. How could the supply chain members reduce total inventory and back order costs in the future?

4. Go to http://beergame.mit.edu and try playing the Internet version of the game from MIT. Report on your experiences playing the game.

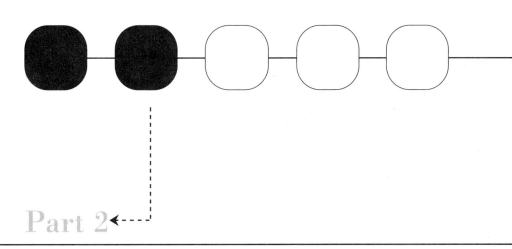

Part 2

Supply Issues in Supply Chain Management

Chapter 2

PURCHASING MANAGEMENT

The primary function of the Purchasing Department is to assist our university with the identification, selection and acquisition of required materials and services. Purchasing strives to accomplish this as economically as possible, within acceptable standards of quality and service, while utilizing professional ethics and best business practices throughout the process.[1]

Total cost of ownership can be determined for a wide variety of corporate initiatives, but when it comes to sustainability—and, especially, social responsibility—hard numbers aren't always clear.[2]

Learning Objectives

After completing this chapter, you should be able to

- Understand the role of supply management and its strategic impact on an organization's competitive advantage.
- Have a basic knowledge of the traditional purchasing process, e-procurement, public procurement and green purchasing.
- Understand and know how to handle small value purchase orders.
- Understand sourcing decisions and the factors impacting supplier selection.
- Understand the pros and cons of single sourcing versus multiple sourcing.
- Understand centralized, decentralized and hybrid purchasing organizations.
- Describe the opportunities and challenges of global sourcing and understand how globalization impacts supply management.
- Understand and compute total cost of ownership.

Chapter Outline

Supply Chain Management in Action

The Key to an Effective Purchasing System: Is It Technology or Supplier Relationship Management?[3]

Las Vegas based Harrah's Entertainment Inc., founded in 1937, is one of the world's largest providers of branded casino entertainment. The company has expanded rapidly through the development of new properties, expansions and acquisitions. On January 28, 2008, Harrah's was acquired by private-equity firms TPG Capital and Apollo Global Management. Harrah's operates 52 casinos in six countries and had a net revenue in excess of $9 billion in 2009. Harrah's owns the famous World Series of Poker and eight properties in Las Vegas—Bally's, Caesars Palace, Flamingo, Harrah's, Paris, Rio, Bill's and Imperial Palace.

Harrah's operates multiple restaurants in each property. Since foods and beverages account for at least 25 percent of the costs of restaurant sales, it is imperative that Harrah's has a well-designed supply management system that maintains tight control of the purchasing process and yet provides maximum service to the chefs and other users of the system. Moreover, the system must ensure that suppliers are treated fairly and professionally. Supply management effectiveness impacts not only the operating costs of a restaurant, but more importantly its quality, customer service and ability to introduce new menus quickly.

The Las Vegas division of Harrah's uses a centralized-decentralized or hybrid purchasing structure that stresses contemporary management philosophy to enable buyers to purchase foods, beverages and operating supplies efficiently and effectively. Contrary to the traditional adversarial approach that forces suppliers to bid on each purchase or contract to achieve lowest purchase cost, Harrah's purchasing system stresses long-term, mutually beneficial buyer–supplier relationships, trust and single sourcing to achieve lowest total acquisition cost.

Harrah's uses a centralized structure to negotiate blanket orders at the national and regional level, whereas a decentralized structure is used to release orders by buyers at each property. The regional purchasing office selects the best supplier, and negotiates a blanket order for each item based on quality, reliability, delivery and total costs of acquisition. Estimated usage, price and delivery terms along with the corresponding tolerance for each performance measure are negotiated for each blanket order. The blanket orders are then made available to the buyers at each property, called property buyers, via a computer database. Property buyers purchase goods by issuing order releases against the appropriate blanket orders without the need to re-negotiate prices and delivery terms. Once an order is released, suppliers must deliver the products according to specified terms.

Harrah's uses a single source for most of its products to achieve purchase volume concentration, low cost and high quality service. However, competing suppliers' terms are listed side-by-side to the single source so that the single source's performance can be monitored and benchmarked against current market conditions. Besides, this information allows the company to locate an alternate source quickly if problems arise with its single source.

The hybrid purchasing system has many benefits, including cost and time savings by eliminating duplicate bidding by each property for the same product. Moreover, the system allows the regional purchasing office to fully utilize its contracted suppliers, national contracts, regional contracts and other programs. Most notably, the regional office preserves the four fundamental purchasing rights to *select the supplier, use whichever pricing method is appropriate, question the specifications* and *monitor contacts with potential suppliers*.

Introduction

In the context of supply chain management (SCM), The **purchasing** profession can be defined as the act of obtaining merchandise; capital equipment; raw materials; services; or maintenance, repair and operating (MRO) supplies in exchange for money or its equivalent. The purchasing profession can be broadly classified into two categories: **merchants** and **industrial buyers**. The first category, merchants, includes the wholesalers and retailers, who primarily purchase for resale purposes. Generally, merchants purchase their merchandise in volume to take advantage of quantity discounts and other incentives such as transportation economy and storage efficiency. They create value by consolidating merchandise, breaking bulk and providing the essential logistical services. The second category is the industrial buyers, whose primary task is to purchase raw materials for conversion purposes. Industrial buyers also purchase services; capital equipment; and maintenance, repair and operating supplies. The typical industrial buyers are the manufacturers, although some service firms such as restaurants, landscape gardeners and florists also purchase raw materials for conversion purposes.

An effective and efficient purchasing system is crucial to the success of a business. Indeed, the *Annual Survey of Manufactures*[4] shows that the total cost of materials exceeded value added through manufacturing in the U.S. Thus, it is not surprising that purchasing concepts and theories that evolved over the last two decades focused on industrial buyers' purchases of raw materials and how purchasing can be exploited to improve competitive success.

The primary focus of this chapter is the industrial buyer. The chapter describes the role of purchasing in an organization, the processes of a traditional purchasing system and the common documents used, how an electronic purchasing system works, various strategies for handling small order problems, the advantages and disadvantages of centralized versus decentralized purchasing systems, purchasing for nonprofits and government agencies, sourcing issues including supplier selection and other important topics affecting the role of purchasing and supply management in supply chain management.

A Brief History of Purchasing Terms

Purchasing is a key business function that is responsible for acquisition of the required materials, services and equipment. However, acquisition of services is widely called *contracting*. The increased strategic role of purchasing in today's business setting has brought a need for higher levels of skill and responsibility on the part of the purchasing professionals. Consequently, the term **supply management** is increasingly being used in place of purchasing to describe the expanded set of responsibilities of the purchasing professionals. The traditional purchasing function of receiving requisitions and issuing purchase orders is no longer adequate, but a holistic and comprehensive acquisition strategy is required to meet the organization's strategic objectives.

The Institute of Supply Management (ISM) defines supply management as the "identification, acquisition, access, positioning and management of resources an organization needs or potentially needs in the attainment of its strategic objectives."[5] Key activities of supply management have expanded beyond the basic purchasing function to include negotiations, logistics, contract development and administration, inventory control and management, supplier management and other activities. However, purchasing remains the core activity of supply management. Although *procurement* is frequently used in place of purchasing, procurement typically includes the added activities of specifications development, expediting, supplier quality control and some logistics activities; hence it is widely used by government agencies due to the type of purchases and frequent service contracting they made with government suppliers. However, it is difficult to clearly distinguish where purchasing activities end and the supply management function begins. Moreover, many organizations are still using these terms interchangeably. In many parts of this book, we have retained the traditional term "purchasing" in place of "supply management" to emphasize the term's original meaning.

The Role of Supply Management in an Organization

Traditionally, purchasing was regarded as being a service to production and corporate executives paid limited attention to issues concerned with purchasing. However, as global competition intensified in the 1980s, executives realized the impact of large quantities of purchased material and work-in-process inventories on manufacturing cost, quality, new product development and delivery lead time. Savvy managers adopted new supply chain management concepts that emphasized purchasing as a key strategic business process rather than a narrow specialized supporting function to overall business strategy.

The *Annual Survey of Manufactures* (Table 2.1), conducted by the U.S. Census Bureau, shows that manufacturers spent more than 50 percent of each sales dollar (shown as "value of shipments") on raw materials (shown as "cost of materials") from 1977 to 2006. Purchases of raw materials actually exceeded value added through manufacturing (shown as "manufacture"), which accounted for less than 50 percent of sales. Purchases as a percent of sales dollars for merchants are expected to be much higher since merchandise is primarily bought for resale purposes. Unfortunately, aggregate statistics for merchants are not readily available.

However, individual information can easily be obtained from the annual reports of publicly traded companies, either directly or from the U.S. Securities and Exchange Commission (SEC). For example, Wal-Mart Stores, Inc., reported that its cost of sales was more than 75 percent of its net sales for the three most recent fiscal years ended January 31, 2008, 2009 and 2010. This ratio shows the potential impact of purchasing on a company's profits. Therefore, it is obvious that many successful businesses are treating purchasing as a key strategic process.

The primary goals of purchasing are to ensure uninterrupted flows of raw materials at the lowest total cost, to improve quality of the finished goods produced and to maximize customer satisfaction. Purchasing can contribute to these objectives by actively seeking better materials and reliable suppliers, working closely with and exploiting the expertise of strategic suppliers to improve the quality of raw materials, and involving suppliers and purchasing personnel in product design and development efforts. Purchasing is the crucial link between the sources of supply and the organization itself, with support coming from overlapping activities to enhance manufacturability for both the customer and the supplier. The involvement of purchasing and strategic suppliers in concurrent engineering activities is essential for selecting components and raw materials that ensure that requisite quality is designed into the product and to aid in collapsing design-to-production cycle time.

Table 2.1   Cost of Materials as a Percentage of the Value of Shipments

YEAR	VALUE OF SHIPMENTS $ MILLIONS	COST OF MATERIALS $ MILLIONS	%	MANUFACTURE $ MILLIONS	%	CAPITAL EXPENDITURES $ MILLIONS	%
2006	$5,015,553	$2,752,904	54.9%	$2,285,929	45.6%	$135,801	2.7%
2005	$4,742,077	$2,557,601	53.9%	$2,210,349	46.6%	$128,292	2.7%
2004	$4,308,971	$2,283,144	53.0%	$2,041,434	47.4%	$113,793	2.6%
2003	$4,015,387	$2,095,279	52.2%	$1,923,415	47.9%	$112,176	2.8%
2002	$3,914,719	$2,022,158	51.7%	$1,889,291	48.3%	$123,067	3.1%
2001	$3,967,698	$2,105,338	53.1%	$1,850,709	46.6%	$142,985	3.6%
2000	$4,208,582	$2,245,839	53.4%	$1,973,622	46.9%	$154,479	3.7%
1999	$4,031,885	$2,084,316	51.7%	$1,954,498	48.5%	$150,325	3.7%
1998	$3,899,810	$2,018,055	51.7%	$1,891,266	48.5%	$152,708	3.9%
1997	$3,834,701	$2,015,425	52.6%	$1,825,688	47.6%	$151,510	4.0%
1996	$3,715,428	$1,975,362	53.2%	$1,749,662	47.1%	$146,468	3.9%
1995	$3,594,360	$1,897,571	52.8%	$1,711,442	47.6%	$134,318	3.7%
1994	$3,348,019	$1,752,735	52.4%	$1,605,980	48.0%	$118,665	3.5%
1993	$3,127,620	$1,647,493	52.7%	$1,483,054	47.4%	$108,629	3.5%
1992	$3,004,723	$1,571,774	52.3%	$1,424,700	47.4%	$110,644	3.7%
1991	$2,878,165	$1,531,221	53.2%	$1,341,386	46.6%	$103,153	3.6%
1990	$2,912,227	$1,574,617	54.1%	$1,348,970	46.3%	$106,463	3.7%
1989	$2,840,376	$1,532,330	53.9%	$1,325,434	46.7%	$101,894	3.6%
1988	$2,695,432	$1,444,501	53.6%	$1,269,313	47.1%	$84,706	3.1%
1987	$2,475,939	$1,319,845	53.3%	$1,165,741	47.1%	$85,662	3.5%
1986	$2,260,315	$1,217,609	53.9%	$1,035,437	45.8%	$80,795	3.6%
1985	$2,280,184	$1,276,010	56.0%	$1,000,142	43.9%	$91,245	4.0%
1984	$2,253,429	$1,288,414	57.2%	$983,228	43.6%	$80,660	3.6%
1983	$2,045,853	$1,170,238	57.2%	$882,015	43.1%	$67,480	3.3%
1982	$1,960,206	$1,130,143	57.7%	$824,118	42.0%	$77,046	3.9%
1981	$2,017,543	$1,193,970	59.2%	$837,507	41.5%	$83,767	4.2%
1980	$1,852,668	$1,093,568	59.0%	$773,831	41.8%	$74,625	4.0%
1979	$1,727,215	$999,158	57.8%	$747,481	43.3%	$65,797	3.8%
1978	$1,522,937	$877,425	57.6%	$657,412	43.2%	$58,346	3.8%
1977	$1,358,526	$782,418	57.6%	$585,166	43.1%	$51,907	3.8%

Source: "2006 Annual Survey of Manufactures," *Annual Survey of Manufactures*, U.S. Census Bureau, November 18, 2008.

The Financial Significance of Supply Management

Undoubtedly, purchasing has become more global and gained strategic corporate focus over the last two decades. The increasing use of outsourcing noncore activities has further elevated the role of purchasing in a firm. In addition to affecting the competitiveness of a firm, purchasing also directly affects profitability. Next, we discuss the financial significance of purchasing on a firm.

Profit-Leverage Effect

Purchase spend is the money a firm spends on goods and services. The **profit-leverage effect** of purchasing measures the impact of a change in purchase spend on a firm's profit before taxes, assuming gross sales and other expenses remain unchanged. The measure is commonly used to demonstrate that a dollar decrease in purchase spend directly increases profits before taxes by the same amount. However, it is important to remember that a decrease in purchase spend must be achieved through better purchasing strategy that enables the firm to acquire materials of similar or better quality and yield at a lower total acquisition cost. The profit-leverage effect example in Table 2.2 shows that if a firm manages to lower its purchase spend on materials by $20,000, profits before taxes increase by $20,000 because purchase spend on materials is a part of the cost of goods sold. Indeed, the reduction in purchase spend has an identical impact on gross profits. Table 2.2 shows that gross profits also increased by $20,000 from $500,000 to $520,000. The direct effect of purchasing on a firm's profitability is a key reason that drives business executives to continually refine the sourcing function. Boosting sales and cutting costs are not the only ways to increase profits. An often overlooked but very efficient means to improve profits is through smarter purchasing.

Return on Assets Effect

Return on assets (ROA) is a financial ratio of a firm's net income in relation to its total assets. The ratio is also referred to as **return on investment (ROI)**. In the context of accounting, total assets consist of current and fixed assets. Current assets include cash, accounts receivable and inventory, whereas fixed assets include equipment, buildings and real estate. ROA indicates how efficiently management is using its total assets to generate profits. A high ROA suggests that the management is capable of generating large profits with little investment.

Assuming the firm in Table 2.2 has total assets of $500,000, its ROA is ten percent ($50,000 ÷ $500,000). If the firm reduces its purchase spend on materials by $20,000 through a more effective purchasing strategy, its ROA increases to fourteen percent ($70,000 ÷ $500,000). The $20,000 reduction in purchase spend on materials is also likely to result in a lower raw material inventory (and thus lower total assets).

Table 2.2	**Profit-Leverage Effect**		
		SIMPLIFIED PROFIT & LOSS STATEMENT	REDUCE MATERIAL COSTS BY $20,000
Gross Sales/Net Revenue		$1,000,000	$1,000,000
– Cost of Goods Sold (Materials + Manufacturing Cost)		–$500,000	–$480,000
Gross Profits		$500,000	$520,000
– General & Administrative Expenses (45%)		–$450,000	–$450,000
Profits Before Taxes		$50,000	$70,000

However, its effect on ROA is difficult to quantify because the portion of a firm's raw material inventory to its total assets, and the ratio of materials cost to its total cost of goods sold, vary widely depending on the firm and industry.

Inventory Turnover Effect

Inventory turnover shows how many times a firm's inventory is utilized and replaced over an accounting period, such as a year. There are numerous ways to compute the inventory turnover ratio, but a widely used formula is the ratio of the cost of goods sold over average inventory at cost. In general, low inventory turnover indicates poor sales, overstocking and/or obsolescence. Through a more effective sourcing strategy, purchasing can help to reduce inventory investment, and thus improve the firm's inventory turnover.

The Purchasing Process

The traditional purchasing process is a manual, paper-based system. However, with the advent of information technology, personal computers, local area networks and the Internet, many companies are moving toward a more automated, electronic-based system. The goal of a proper purchasing system is to ensure the efficient transmission of information from the users to the purchasing personnel and, ultimately, to the suppliers. Once the information is transmitted to the appropriate suppliers, the system must also ensure the efficient flows of the purchased materials from the suppliers to the users and the flow of invoices from the suppliers to the accounting department. Finally, the system must have adequate operational or **internal control** to prevent abuse of purchasing funds. For example, purchase orders (POs) should be pre-numbered and issued in duplicate and buyers should not be authorized to pay invoices. Pre-numbered purchase orders make it easier to trace any missing or unaccounted-for purchase orders. A duplicate purchase order should be issued to the accounting department for internal control purposes and to inform the department of a future payment or commitment of resources.

The Manual Purchasing System

Figure 2.1 shows a simplified traditional manual purchasing system. While some manual systems may look slightly different than what is shown in Figure 2.1, it captures the essential elements of a good purchasing system that is easy to use and yet exerts adequate internal control of the process. The manual purchasing system is slow and prone to errors due to duplications of data entries during various stages of the purchasing process. For example, similar information on the material requisition, such as the product description, is reproduced on the purchase order.

The Material Requisition

The purchasing process starts when the material user initiates a request for a material by issuing a **material requisition (MR)** in duplicates. A **purchase requisition**, instead of a material requisition, is used in some firms. The product, quantity and delivery due date are clearly described on the material requisition. The number of duplicates issued depends on the internal accounting control system of the organization. Generally, the issuer retains a copy and the warehouse receives the original plus a duplicate. The duplicate accompanies the material as it moves from the warehouse to the user. This copy also provides the essential information for the accounting department to charge the appropriate user or department for the material.

While most requisitions are transmitted through the generic material requisition, a **traveling requisition** is used for materials and standard parts that are requested on a recurring

Figure 2.1 | Traditional Manual Purchasing System

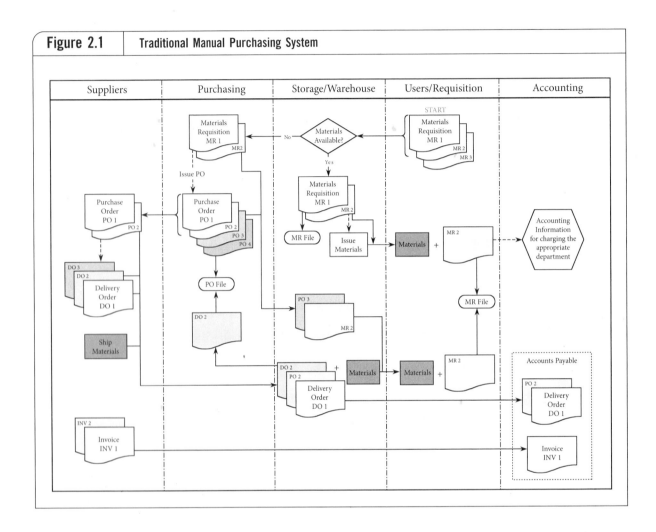

basis. Instead of describing the product on the generic material requisition, the product description and other pertinent information, such as delivery lead time and lot size, are pre-printed on the traveling requisition. When a resupply is needed, the user simply enters the quantity and date needed and submits it to the warehouse. Once the resupply information is recorded, the traveling requisition is returned to the user for future requests.

Planned order releases from the material requirements planning (MRP) system or a bill of materials (BOM) can also be used to release requisitions or to place orders directly with the suppliers. This approach is suitable for firms that use the same components to make standard goods over a relatively long period of time.

If the requested material is available in the warehouse, the material is issued to the user without going through the purchasing department. Otherwise, the requisition is assigned to a buyer who is responsible for the material. If there is a better substitute for the material, purchasing recommends and works with the user to explore whether it is a viable substitute. However, purchasing personnel should not change the specifications of the materials or parts without the user's knowledge and agreement. While it is the right and responsibility of purchasing personnel to select the appropriate supplier, the user in many cases may suggest a list of potential suppliers when requesting new material. A sample material requisition is shown in Figure 2.2.

Figure 2.2 | Sample Purchase Requisition

BabiHutan Inc.	**Purchase Requisition**	RX #: 6334554
523 Las Vegas Blvd		
Las Vegas, NV89154		
Tel: 702-123-4567		

Requestor: _____   Department: _____

Phone #: _____   Account #: _____   Date: _____

Suggested Vendor: _____

Address: _____   Phone: _____

No.	Description	Price	Quantity

Special instructions: _____
_____
_____

Approval Authority: _____   Date: _____

Distribution: White-Purchasing/Yellow-Purchasing (return to requestor)/Pink-Department

---

The Request for Quotation and the Request for Proposal

If the material is not available in the warehouse, the material requisition is routed to the purchasing department. If there is no current supplier for the item, the buyer must identify a pool of qualified suppliers and issue a **request for quotation (RFQ)**. A **request for proposal (RFP)** may be issued instead for a complicated and highly technical component part, especially if the complete specification of the part is unknown. An RFP allows suppliers to propose new material and technology, thus enabling the firm to exploit the technology and expertise of suppliers.

A growing trend among firms that practice supply chain management is **supplier development**. When there is a lack of suitable suppliers, firms may assist existing or new suppliers to improve their processing capabilities, quality, delivery and cost performance by providing the needed technical and financial assistance. Developing suppliers in this manner allows firms to focus more on core competencies, while **outsourcing** noncore activities to suppliers.

The Purchase Order

When a suitable supplier is identified, or a qualified supplier is on file, the buyer issues a **purchase order (PO)** in duplicates to the selected supplier. Generally, the original purchase order and at least a duplicate are sent to the supplier. An important feature of the purchase order is the terms and conditions of the purchase, which is typically preprinted on the back. The purchase order is the buyer's offer and becomes a legally binding contract when accepted by the supplier. Therefore, firms should require the supplier to acknowledge and return a copy of the purchase order to indicate acceptance of the order. A sample purchase order is shown in Figure 2.3.

Figure 2.3	Sample Purchase Order

BabiHutan Inc.
523 LasVegas Blvd
Las Vegas, NV89154
Tel: 702-123-4567

Purchase Order

PO#: 885729

Date: _____

Vendor:	Required Delivery Date: _____
	Payment Terms: _____
	FOB Terms: _____
	Price Agreement No.: _____
Ship To:	Include PO # in all packages, invoice, shipping papers & correspondence. Mail original and one copy of invoice attached to second copy of Purchase Order for payment.

No.	Description	Unit Price	Quantity	Total Price
		Total $ of Order		

Buyer: _____   Phone: _____   Fax: _____

Buyer Signature: _____   Requisition No.: _____

SEE REVERSE FOR TERMS & CONDITIONS

Distribution: White-Vendor/Yellow-Vendor(return with invoice)/Pink & Blue-Purchasing/Green-Fixed Assets

The supplier may offer the goods at the supplier's own terms and conditions, especially if it is the sole producer or holds the patent to the product. Then a supplier's **sales order** will be used. The sales order is the supplier's offer and becomes a legally binding contract when accepted by the buyer.

Once an order is accepted, purchasing personnel need to ensure on-time delivery of the purchased material by using a **follow-up** or by **expediting** the order. A follow-up is considered a proactive approach to prevent late delivery, whereas expediting is considered a reactive approach that is used to speed up an overdue shipment.

The **Uniform Commercial Code (UCC)** governs the purchase and sale of goods in the U.S., except in the state of Louisiana. Louisiana has a legal system that is based on the Napoleonic Code.

Electronic Procurement Systems (e-Procurement)

Electronic data interchange (EDI) was developed in the 1970s to improve the purchasing process. However, its proprietary nature required significant up-front investments. The rapid advent of Internet technology in the 1990s spurred the growth of more flexible Internet-based e-procurement systems. Proponents of e-commerce argued that Internet-based systems would quickly replace the manual system, as we saw many e-commerce service providers rise rapidly in the late 1990s. Since then, there has been a shake-up among these companies as they have struggled to find a sustainable market. A large number of e-commerce firms saw their share values plummet in the early 2000s and many are no longer in business after the dot-com bubble burst in 2000. Critics argued that growth in e-commerce had been overinflated and the savings for users were inadequate to justify their time and investments. Today, though, many well-managed e-commerce firms are beginning to thrive as users realize the benefits of their services.

Figure 2.4 describes the Internet-based electronic purchasing system used by the University of Nevada, Las Vegas. The database that drives the e-procurement system resides on a server, but the software is installed on workstations. The e-procurement system is also accessible via the Internet. The e-procurement system allows users to submit their purchase requisitions to the purchasing department electronically and enables buyers to transmit purchase orders to suppliers over the Internet, fax or mail.

The material user initiates the e-procurement process by entering a purchase request and other pertinent information, such as quantity and date needed, into the purchase requisition module. The material user may recommend suppliers or potential sources for the requisition. Next, the purchase requisition is approved and transmitted electronically to a buyer at the purchasing department. The buyer reviews the purchase requisition for accuracy and appropriate approval level and determines the value of the requisition. If the amount is below $25,000, the buyer extracts details of the purchase requisition stored in the database to prepare an electronic purchase order. Next, the buyer assigns a preferred supplier from the e-procurement database, or uses a supplier from the purchase requisition. If the amount of the purchase requisition is between $25,000 and $50,000, two formal requests for quotation are needed before a purchase order can be released. However, if the amount exceeds $50,000, a supplier must be chosen by means of a formal bidding process. At the specified time and place, bids are opened publicly. The purchase is awarded to the lowest responsible bidder whose bid conforms to all requirements of the solicitation. Then an electronic purchase order (or formal contract for purchase of services) is prepared and transmitted or mailed to the selected supplier.

Figure 2.4	Internet-based Electronic Purchasing System

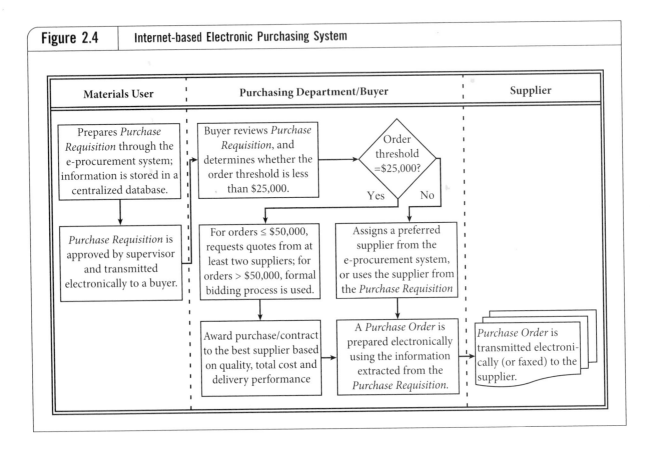

Advantages of the e-Procurement System

The traditional manual purchasing system is a tedious and labor-intensive task of issuing material requisitions and purchase orders. Although EDI solved some of these problems, its proprietary nature requires a high start-up cost, making it inaccessible to small firms with limited budgets. Internet-based e-procurement systems have changed the infrastructure requirement, making it readily affordable to most firms. Benefits derived from implementing an e-procurement system include:

1. *Time savings*: E-procurement is more efficient when (a) selecting and maintaining a list of potential suppliers, (b) processing requests for quotation and purchase orders and (c) making repeat purchases. Individual buyers can create preferred supplier lists for each category of products and services. For example, a small tools supplier group may consist of fifteen suppliers of small tools. The buyer uses this group to purchase small tools. The list can be edited and shared with all buyers in the firm. Supplier performance data can be updated quickly and made available online in real time. Collecting, sorting, reviewing and comparing RFQs are labor-intensive and time-consuming processes. Using the manual purchasing system, a typical firm may have to sort and match hundreds of bids on a daily basis. E-procurement eliminates these non-value-adding collection and sorting activities. Duplicate data entry on the purchase order is eliminated since the information can be extracted from the RFQ, originally entered by the user. Also, an e-procurement system minimizes the need for interdepartmental routing of paper purchase requisitions, streamlines the approval process and automates purchase order issuance.

Some e-procurement systems can be programmed to handle automatic bidding of frequently ordered items on a fixed interval, such as daily or weekly—a practice used by some casino hotels in Las Vegas. The ability to submit automatic bidding is invaluable for handling perishable goods, which must be ordered in small lot sizes and other frequently purchased items where the specifications are known.

2. *Cost savings*: Buyers can handle more purchases and the manual task of matching bids to purchase requisitions is reduced. Other cost savings include lower prices of goods and services since more suppliers can be contacted, reduced inventory costs due to the ability to purchase on a more frequent basis, fewer buyers, lower administrative costs, elimination of the need for preprinted purchase requisition forms and faster order fulfillment.

3. *Accuracy*: The system eliminates double-key inputs—once by the materials users and then once again by the buyers. The system also enhances the accuracy of communications between buyers and suppliers. More up-to-date information on suppliers, with goods and services readily available online, allows users to assess their options before preparing a purchase requisition.

4. *Real time*: Buyers have real-time access to the purchase requisition once it is prepared. Once the purchase requisition is processed, the buyer can post the bid instantly, instead of waiting to contact all the suppliers individually to alert them of the bids. The system enables buyers to initiate bids and suppliers to respond in real time on a 24/7 basis.

5. *Mobility*: The buyer can submit, process and check the status of bids, as well as communicate with suppliers regardless of the buyer's geographical location and time of day. Thus, the e-procurement system is highly flexible.

6. *Trackability*: The e-procurement system allows submitters and buyers to track each purchase requisition electronically through the process—from submission, to approval and finally conversion to a purchase order. Moreover, audit trails can be maintained for all transactions in electronic form. Tracing an electronic bid and transaction is much easier and faster than tracking paper trails. Buyers and suppliers can ask for additional information online, leave comments, or indicate whether they are interested in bidding.

7. *Management*: The system can be designed to store important supplier information, including whether suppliers are minority or locally owned, thus allowing the buyers to support such businesses. Summary statistics and supplier performance reports can be generated for management to review and utilize for future planning.

8. *Benefits to the suppliers*: Benefits include lower barriers to entry and transaction costs, access to more buyers and the ability to instantly adjust to market conditions, thus making e-procurement attractive to most suppliers.

Small Value Purchase Orders

The administrative costs to process an order can be quite substantial. It has been estimated that the cost of placing an order using the manual purchasing system could be as high as $175.[6] The figure could be higher when we consider the salary of senior purchasing personnel and other indirect costs incurred by purchasing personnel. It is not uncommon to find that the cost to process a purchase order exceeds the total dollar value of the order itself. While *small dollar value* is a relative term depending on the size of the firm, $500 to $1,000 can be considered a reasonable cutoff point.

e-Business Connection

Apple's iFortress[7]

Secrecy permeates Apple's corporate culture. Former employees speak of information being parceled out on only a "need-to-know" basis and of heavily secured product-testing rooms. Others report that executives regularly disseminate false information, making it easier for Apple to trace and fire workers suspected of leaking information. However, not only is this obsession with secrecy present in the iPod maker's corporate headquarters, it has also trickled down to the very factory workers that assemble their products.

In fact, Apple has its own "Forbidden City" in southern China: a sprawling, walled compound in Longhua operated by Foxconn, a division of Taiwan's Hon Hai Precision Industry. Inside the compound walls, employees assemble Apple products such as the hugely successful iPod. But there's more: within the compound are also dormitories, a hospital, a swimming pool, grocery stores and a fire brigade. There's even an in-house television network and multiple canteens to feed the complex's over 200,000 employees. Though living conditions are Spartanlike, such basic amenities give employees little reason to venture beyond the compound's walls, and thus, little opportunity to leak product information to outsiders.

To enter the compound, workers must swipe security cards at the gate. Vehicle occupants are scanned with fingerprint recognition devices before they are granted entrance. Metal detectors ensure that employees cannot smuggle devices—or even parts of devices—out of the factory. Security is of the utmost importance here: one Reuters reporter who journeyed to a similar nearby complex that also manufactured iPod components was roughed up by factory security guards. The guards tried to drag him inside and the dispute was eventually settled by the police.

The secrecy shrouding the complex parallels the mystique with which Apple's executives operate. It's embedded in Apple's supply chain. While other companies prefer to "one-stop shop," obtaining parts from one manufacturing firm, Apple opts to order from multiple manufacturers such as Hon Hai who are tasked with producing different components. Sometimes they are asked to produce custom-designed parts, requiring manufacturers to reconfigure factory equipment.

Even workers in the Longhua compound—workers who labor up to 15 hours each day for as little as $50 a month—know little about the products they assemble. They too understand Apple's culture of silence, and this silence, one worker reports, is largely self-enforced in the Longhua iFortress. Yet this silence comes at a price: one employee who allegedly smuggled an iPhone out of the complex jumped to his death after being interrogated by his superior.

by Wen Hui Tan

Small value purchases, particularly in a manual purchasing system, should be minimized to ensure that buyers are not overburdened with trivial purchases that may prevent them from focusing on crucial purchases. Due to the efficiency of the e-procurement system, buyers are less likely to be overburdened by small value purchases. Nevertheless, all firms should have a system in place to handle small value purchases. To control unnecessary administrative costs and reduce order cycle time, purchasing managers have various alternatives to deal with small value purchases. Generally, the alternatives are used for purchase of office supplies and other indirect materials. Let us review the alternatives.

Procurement Credit Card/Corporate Purchasing Card

Procurement credit cards or **corporate purchasing cards** (**P-cards**) are credit cards with a predetermined credit limit, usually not more than $5,000 depending on the organization, issued to authorized personnel of the buying organization. American Express, Diners Club, MasterCard and Visa cards are commonly used for this purpose. The card allows the material user to purchase the material directly from the supplier, without going through purchasing. Usually, the user must purchase the needed materials from a list of authorized suppliers. Procurement credit cards have gained popularity over the last decade, especially among government agencies, because of their ease of use and flexibility.

When authorized, the card can also be used to pay for meals, lodging and other traveling expenses, thus eliminating the need to process travel expenses in advance for the user. At the end of the month, an itemized statement is sent to purchasing, the cardholder's department, or directly to the accounting department. Generally, the purchasing department is responsible for managing the overall program, but the individual unit is responsible for managing its cardholder accounts. To ensure appropriate internal control of the procurement credit card system, a supervisor should be assigned to review the monthly statement of each cardholder to prevent unauthorized use of the procurement card. Cardholders should maintain proper supporting documents and records for each purchase.

Despite the success of the P-card program, there are unique challenges in expanding the program globally. The Global Perspective feature highlights the challenge of expanding a firm's P-card program across international boundaries.

Blanket or Open-End Purchase Orders

A **blanket purchase order** covers a variety of items and is negotiated for repeated supply over a fixed time period, such as quarterly or yearly. The subtle difference of an **open-end purchase order** is that additional items and expiration dates can be renegotiated. Price and estimated quantity for each item, as well as delivery terms and conditions, are usually negotiated and incorporated in the order. A variety of mechanisms, such as a **blanket order release** or production schedule, may be used to release a specific quantity against the order. Blanket or open-end purchase orders are suitable for buying maintenance, repair and operating (MRO) supplies and office supplies. At a fixed time interval, usually monthly, the supplier sends a detailed statement of all releases against the order to the buying firm for payment.

While blanket purchase orders are frequently used to handle small value purchases, the company discussed in the Supply Chain Management in Action feature at the beginning of this chapter demonstrates that when used in conjunction with blanket order releases, cooperative supplier relationships and single sourcing, blanket purchase orders are a formidable tool to handle the complex purchasing needs of a large, multidivision corporation.

Blank Check Purchase Orders

A **blank check purchase order** is a special purchase order with a signed blank check attached, usually at the bottom of the purchase order. Due to the potential for misuse, it is usually printed on the check that it is not valid for over a certain amount, usually $500 or $1,000. If the exact amount of the purchase is known, the buyer enters the amount on the check before passing it to the supplier. Otherwise, the supplier enters the amount due on the check and cashes it after the material is shipped. Nevertheless, purchasing managers are embracing the use of procurement credit cards and phasing out blank check purchase orders.

Stockless Buying or System Contracting

Stockless buying or **system contracting** is an extension of the blanket purchase order. It requires the supplier to maintain a minimum inventory level to ensure that the required items are readily available for the buyer. It is stockless buying from the buyer's perspective because the burden of keeping the inventory is on the supplier. Some firms require suppliers to keep inventory at the buyer's facilities to minimize order cycle time.

Petty Cash

Petty cash is a small cash reserve maintained by a midlevel manager or clerk. Material users buy the needed materials and then claim the purchase against the petty cash by submitting the receipt to the petty cashier. A benefit of this system is that the exact reimbursement is supported by receipts.

Standardization and Simplification of Materials and Components

Where appropriate, purchasing should work with design, engineering and operations to seek opportunities to standardize materials, components and supplies to increase the usage of standardized items. For example, a car manufacturer could design different models of automobiles to use the same starter mechanism, thus increasing its usage and reducing storage space requirements while allowing for large quantity price discounts. This will also reduce the number of small value purchases for less frequently used items.

Simplification refers to reduction of the number of components, supplies or standard materials used in the product or process. For example, a computer manufacturer could integrate the video card directly onto the motherboard instead of using different video card modules for different models. Thus, simplification can further reduce the number of small value purchases while reducing storage space requirements, as well as allowing for quantity purchase discounts.

Accumulating Small Orders to Create a Large Order

Numerous small orders can be accumulated and mixed into a large order, especially if the material request is not urgent. Otherwise, purchasing can simply increase the order quantity if the ordering cost exceeds the inventory holding cost. Larger orders also reduce the purchase price and unit transportation cost.

Using a Fixed Order Interval for a Specific Category of Materials/Supplies

Another effective way to control small orders is to group materials and supplies into categories and then set fixed order intervals for each category. Order intervals can be set to biweekly or monthly depending on usage. Instead of requesting individual materials or supplies, users request the appropriate quantity of each item in the category on a single requisition to be purchased from a supplier. This increases the dollar value and decreases the number of small orders.

Sourcing Decisions: The Make-or-Buy Decision

While the term *outsourcing* originally referred to buying materials or components that were previously made in-house, it is now also commonly used to refer to buying materials or components from suppliers instead of making them in-house. In recent years, the trend has been moving toward outsourcing combined with the creation of supply chain relationships, although traditionally firms preferred the make option by means of backward or forward vertical integration. **Backward vertical integration** refers to acquiring upstream suppliers, whereas **forward vertical integration** refers to acquiring downstream customers. For example, an end-product manufacturer acquiring a supplier's operations that supplied component parts is an example of backward integration. Acquiring a distributor or other outbound logistics providers would be an example of forward integration.

Whether to **make or buy** materials or components is a strategic decision that can impact an organization's competitive position. It is obvious that most organizations buy their MRO and office supplies rather than make the items themselves. Similarly, seafood restaurants usually buy their fresh seafood from fish markets. However, the decision on whether to make or buy technically advanced engineering parts that impact the firm's competitive position is a complex one. Do you think the Honda Motor Company would rather make or buy the engines for its automobile manufacturing facilities? Why?

Traditionally, cost has been the major driver when making sourcing decisions. However, organizations today focus more on the strategic impact of the sourcing decision on the firm's competitive advantage. For example, Honda Motor would not outsource the making of its engines because it considers engines to be a vital part of its automobiles' performance and reputation. However, Honda may outsource the production of brake drums to a high-quality, low-cost supplier that specializes in brake drums. Generally, firms outsource noncore activities while focusing on core competencies. Finally, the make-or-buy decision is not an exclusive either-or option. Firms can always choose to make some components or services in-house and buy the rest from suppliers.

Reasons for Buying or Outsourcing

Organizations buy or outsource materials, components and/or services from suppliers for many reasons. Let us review these now:

1. *Cost advantage*: For many firms, cost is an important reason for buying or outsourcing, especially for supplies and components that are nonvital to the organization's operations and competitive advantage. This is usually true for standardized or generic supplies and materials for which suppliers may have the advantage of **economies of scale** because they supply the same item to multiple users. In most outsourcing cases, the quantity needed is so small that it does not justify the investment in capital equipment to make the item. Some foreign suppliers may also offer a cost advantage because of lower labor and/or materials costs.

2. *Insufficient capacity*: A firm may be running at or near capacity, making it unable to produce the components in-house. This can happen when demand grows faster than anticipated or when expansion strategies fail to meet demand. The firm buys parts or components to free up capacity in the short term to focus on vital operations. Firms may even subcontract vital components and/or operations under very strict terms and conditions in order to meet demand. When managed properly, **subcontracting** instead of buying is a more effective means to expand short-term capacity because the buying firm can exert better control over the manufacturing process and other requirements of the components or end products.

3. *Lack of expertise*: The firm may not have the necessary technology and expertise to manufacture the item. Maintaining long-term technological and economical viability for noncore activities may be affecting the firm's ability to focus on core competencies. Suppliers may hold the patent to the process or product in question, thus precluding the make option, or the firm may not be able to meet environmental and safety standards to manufacture the item.

4. *Quality*: Purchased components may be superior in quality because suppliers have better technologies, processes, skilled labor and the advantage of economies of scale. Suppliers' superior quality may help firms stay on top of product and process technologies, especially in high-technology industries with rapid innovation and short product life cycles.

Reasons for Making

An organization also makes its own materials, components, services and/or equipment in-house for many reasons. Let us briefly review them:

1. *Protect proprietary technology*: A major reason for the make option is to protect proprietary technology. A firm may have developed equipment, product or processes that need to be protected for the sake of competitive advantage. Firms may choose not to reveal the technology by asking suppliers to make it, even if it is patented. An advantage of not revealing the technology is to be able to surprise competitors and bring new products to market ahead of competition, allowing the firm to charge a price premium. The e-Business Connection feature highlights the unique challenge of protecting proprietary technology when a firm chooses the buy option.

2. *No competent supplier*: If suppliers do not have the technology or capability to produce a component, the firm may have no choice but to make an item in-

house, at least for the short term. The firm may use supplier development strategies to work with a new or existing supplier to produce the component in the future as a long-term strategy.

3. *Better quality control:* If the firm is capable, the make option allows for the most direct control over the design, manufacturing process, labor and other inputs to ensure that high-quality components are built. The firm may be so experienced and efficient in manufacturing the component that suppliers are unable to meet its exact specifications and requirements. On the other hand, suppliers may have better technologies and processes to produce better-quality components. Thus, the sourcing option ensuring a higher quality level is a debatable question and must be investigated thoroughly.

4. *Use existing idle capacity:* A short-term solution for a firm with excess idle capacity is to use the excess capacity to make some of its components. This strategy is valuable for firms that produce seasonal products. It avoids layoff of skilled workers and, when business picks up, the capacity is readily available to meet demand.

5. *Control of lead-time, transportation and warehousing cost:* The make option provides better control of lead-time and logistical costs since management controls all phases of the design, manufacturing and delivery processes. Although raw materials may have to be transported, finished goods can be produced near the point of use, for instance, to minimize holding cost.

6. *Lower cost:* If technology, capacity and managerial and labor skills are available, the make option may be more economical if large quantities of the component are needed on a continuing basis. Although the make option has a higher fixed cost due to initial capital investment, it has a lower variable cost because it precludes suppliers' profits.

Make-or-Buy Break-Even Analysis

The current sourcing trend is to buy equipment, materials and services unless self-manufacture provides a major benefit such as protecting proprietary technologies, achieving superior characteristics, or ensuring adequate supplies. However, buying or outsourcing has its own shortcomings, such as loss of control and exposure to supplier risks. While cost is rarely the sole criterion in strategic sourcing decisions, **break-even analysis** is a handy tool for computing the cost-effectiveness of sourcing decisions when cost is the most important criterion. Several assumptions underlie the analysis: (1) all costs involved can be classified under either fixed or variable cost, (2) fixed cost remains the same within the range of analysis, (3) a linear variable cost relationship exists, (4) fixed cost of the make option is higher because of initial capital investment in equipment and (5) variable cost of the buy option is higher because of supplier profits.

Consider a hypothetical situation in which a firm has the option to make or buy a part. Its annual requirement is 15,000 units. A supplier is able to supply the part at $7 per unit. The firm estimates that it costs $500 to prepare the contract with the supplier. To make the part, the firm must invest $25,000 in equipment and the firm estimates that it costs $5 per unit to make the part.

COSTS	MAKE OPTION	BUY OPTION
Fixed Cost	$25,000	$500
Variable Cost	$5	$7
Annual Requirements = 15,000 units		

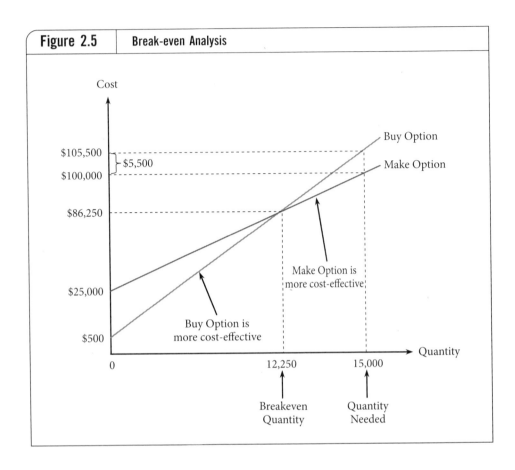

Figure 2.5 | **Break-even Analysis**

Break-even Point, Q

The break-even point Q is found by setting the total cost of the two options equal to one another and solving for Q (see Figure 2.5):

Total Cost to Make	= Total Cost to Buy
$25,000 + \$5Q$	$= \$500 + \$7Q$
$\Rightarrow 7Q - 5Q$	$= 25,000 - 500$
$\Rightarrow 2Q$	$= 24,500 \text{ units}$
$\Rightarrow \text{Break-even point, Q}$	$= 12,250 \text{ units}$

$$\text{Total Cost for both options at the Break-even Point, } TC_{BE} = \$25,000 + (\$5 \times 12,250)$$
$$= \$86,250$$

For the annual requirement of 15,000 units:

$$\text{Total Cost for the Make Option, } TC_{Make} = \$25,000 + (\$5 \times 15,000)$$
$$= \$100,000$$
$$\text{Total Cost for the Buy Option, } TC_{Buy} = \$500 + (\$7 \times 15,000)$$
$$= \$105,500$$
$$\text{Cost Difference} = TC_{Buy} - TC_{Make}$$
$$= \$105,500 - \$100,000$$
$$= \$5,500$$

The analysis shows that the break-even point is 12,250 units. Total cost at the break-even point is $86,250. If the requirement is less than 12,250 units, it is cheaper to buy. It is cheaper to make the parts if the firm needs more than 12,250 units. With small purchase requirements (less than 12,250 units), the low fixed cost of the buy option makes it attractive. With higher purchase requirements (greater than 12,250 units), the low variable cost of the make option makes this option more attractive. The analysis shows that the firm should make the item since the quantity is large enough to warrant the capital investment.

Roles of Supply Base

The **supply base** or **supplier base** refers to the list of suppliers that a firm uses to acquire its materials, services, supplies and equipment. Firms engaging in supply chain management emphasize long-term strategic supplier alliances by reducing the variety of purchased items and consolidating volume into one or fewer suppliers, resulting in a smaller supply base. For example, both Xerox and Chrysler reduced their supply bases by about 90 percent in the 1980s. An effective supply base that complements and contributes to a firm's competitive advantage is critical to its success. Savvy purchasing managers develop a sound supply base to support the firm's overall business and supply chain strategies, based on an expanded role for suppliers. It is thus vital to understand the strategic role of suppliers.

Besides supplying the obvious purchased items, key or preferred suppliers also supply:

1. product and process technology and expertise to support the buyer's operations, particularly in new product design and value analysis;
2. information on the latest trends in materials, processes or designs;
3. information on the supply market, such as shortages, price increases or political situations that may threaten supplies of vital materials;
4. capacity for meeting unexpected demand; and
5. cost efficiency due to economies of scale, since the supplier is likely to produce the same item for multiple buyers.

When developing and managing the supply chain, preferred suppliers are found or developed to provide these services and play a very important role in the success of the supply chain.

Supplier Selection

The decision to select a supplier for office supplies or other noncritical materials is likely to be an easy one. However, the process of selecting a group of competent suppliers for important materials, which can potentially impact the firm's competitive advantage, is a complex one and should be based on multiple criteria. In addition to cost and delivery performance, firms should also consider how suppliers can contribute to product and process technology. Factors that firms should consider while selecting suppliers include:

1. *Process and product technologies*: Suppliers should have competent process technologies to produce superior products at a reasonable cost to enhance the buyer's competitive edge.

2. *Willingness to share technologies and information*: With the current trend that favors outsourcing to exploit suppliers' capabilities and to focus on core competencies, it is vital that firms seek suppliers that are willing to share their technologies and information. Suppliers can assist in new product design and development through **early supplier involvement (ESI)** to ensure cost-effective design choices, develop alternative conceptual solutions, select the best components and technologies and help in design assessment. By increasing the involvement of the supplier in the design process, the buyer is free to focus more attention on core competencies.

3. *Quality*: Quality levels of the purchased item should be a very important factor in supplier selection. Product quality should be high and consistent since it can directly affect the quality of the finished goods.

4. *Cost*: While unit price of the material is not typically the sole criterion in supplier selection, total cost of ownership is an important factor. **Total cost of ownership** or **total cost of acquisition** includes the unit price of the material, payment terms, cash discount, ordering cost, carrying cost, logistical costs, maintenance costs and other more qualitative costs that may not be easy to assess. An example of a total cost of ownership analysis is provided in Example 2.1 at the end of the chapter. The total cost analysis demonstrates how other costs beside unit price can affect the purchase decision.

5. *Reliability*: Besides reliable quality level, reliability refers to other supplier characteristics. For example, is the supplier financially stable? Otherwise, it may not be able to invest in research and development or stay in business. Is the supplier's delivery lead time reliable? Otherwise, production may have to be interrupted due to a shortage of material.

6. *Order system and cycle time*: How easy to use is a supplier's ordering system and what is the normal order cycle time? Placing orders with a supplier should be easy, quick and effective. Delivery lead time should be short, so that small lot sizes can be ordered on a frequent basis to reduce inventory holding costs.

7. *Capacity*: The firm should also consider whether the supplier has the capacity to fill orders to meet requirements and the ability to fill large orders if needed.

8. *Communication capability*: Suppliers should also possess a communication capability that facilitates communication between the parties.

9. *Location*: Geographical location is another important factor in supplier selection, as it impacts delivery lead-time, transportation and logistical costs. Some firms require their suppliers to be located within a certain distance from their facilities.

10. *Service*: Suppliers must be able to back up their products by providing good services when needed. For example, when product information or warranty service is needed, suppliers must respond on a timely basis.

There are numerous other factors—some strategic, others tactical—that a firm must consider when choosing suppliers. The days of using competitive bidding to identify the cheapest supplier for strategic items are long gone. The ability to select competent strategic suppliers directly affects a firm's competitive success. Strategic suppliers are trusted partners and become an integral part of the firm's design and production efforts.

Example 2.1   Total Cost of Ownership Concept

Total cost of ownership is more than just the purchase price; other qualitative and quantitative factors, including freight and inventory costs, tooling, tariffs and duties, currency exchange fees, payment terms, maintenance and nonperformance costs must be considered. Firms can use total cost analysis as a negotiation tool to inform suppliers regarding areas where they need to improve.

AN EXAMPLE

Kuantan ATV, Inc., assembles five different models of all-terrain vehicles (ATVs) from various ready-made components to serve the Las Vegas, Nevada, market. The company uses the same engine for all its ATVs. The purchasing manager, Ms. Jane Kim, needs to choose a supplier for engines for the coming year. Due to the size of the warehouse and other administrative restrictions, she must order the engines in lot sizes of 1,000 each. The unique characteristics of the standardized engine require special tooling to be used during the manufacturing process. Kuantan ATV agrees to reimburse the supplier for the tooling. This is a critical purchase, since late delivery of engines would disrupt production and cause 50 percent lost sales and 50 percent back orders of the ATVs. Jane has obtained quotes from two reliable suppliers but needs to know which supplier is more cost-effective. She has the following information:

Requirements (annual forecast)	12,000 units
Weight per engine	22 pounds
Order processing cost	$125/order
Inventory carrying rate	20 % per year
Cost of working capital	10 % per year
Profit margin	18 %
Price of finished ATV	$4,500
Back-order cost	$15 per unit

Two qualified suppliers have submitted the following quotations:

UNIT PRICE	SUPPLIER 1	SUPPLIER 2
1 to 999 units/order	$510.00	$505.00
1,000 to 2999 units/order	$500.00	$498.00
3,000 + units/order	$490.00	$488.00
Tooling Cost	$22,000	$20,000
Terms	2/10, net 30	1/10, net 30
Distance	125 miles	100 miles
Supplier Quality Rating (defects)	2%	3%
Supplier Delivery Rating (late delivery)	1%	2%

Jane also obtained the following freight rates from her carrier:

Truckload (TL $\geq$ 40,000 lbs): $0.80 per ton-mile
Less-than-truckload (LTL): $1.20 per ton-mile
Note: per ton-mile = 2,000 lbs per mile

The total cost analysis (see Figure 2.6) shows that Supplier 1 is more cost-effective, although its unit price and tooling costs are slightly higher than those of Supplier 2. The cash discount, quality cost and delivery performance set Supplier 1 apart from Supplier 2. Using unit cost as the sole criterion to select a supplier would have cost the company $138,926.67 ($6,265,060.00 − $6,126,133.33).

Figure 2.6	Total Cost Analysis

Description	Supplier 1		Supplier 2	
1. Total Engine Cost	12,000 units × $500	$6,000,000.00	12,000 units × $498	$5,976,000.00
2. Cash Discount				
n/30	$6,000,000 × 10% × 30/360 $50,000.00		$5,976,000 × 10% × 30/360 $49,800.00	
1/10	N/A		$5,976,000 (10% × 10/360 + 1%) $76,360.00	
2/10	$6,000,000 (10% × 10/360 + 2%) $136,666.67		N/A	
Largest discount		$(136,666.67)		$(76,360.00)
3. Tooling Cost		$22,000.00		$20,000.00
4. Transportation Cost (22,000 lb LTL)	125 miles × 12,000 units × 22 lb × $1.20/2000	$19,800.00	100 miles × 12,000 units × 22 lb × $1.20/2000	$15,840.00
5. Ordering Cost	(12,000/1000) × $125	$1,500.00	(12,000/1000) × $125	$1,500.00
6. Carrying Cost	(1000/2) × $500 × 20%	$50,000.00	(1000/2) × $498 × 20%	$49,800.00
7. Quality Cost	$6,000,000 × 2%	$120,000.00	$5,976,000 × 3%	$179,280.00
8. Delivery Rating				
Backorder (50%)	12,000 × 1% × 50% × $15	$900.00	12,000 × 2% × 50% × $15	$1,800.00
Lost Sales (50%)	12,000 × 1% × 50% × $4500 × 18%	$48,600.00	12,000 × 2% × 50% × $4500 × 18%	$97,200.00
TOTAL COST		$6,126,133.33		$6,265,060.00

How Many Suppliers to Use

The issue of how many suppliers to use for each purchased item is a complex one. While numerous references propose the use of a single source for core materials and supplies to facilitate cooperative buyer–supplier partnerships, single sourcing can be a very risky proposition. Although Xerox and Chrysler had substantially reduced their supply base in the 1980s, it was not documented that they resorted to single sourcing for their vital materials and components. However, the company featured in the Supply Chain Management in Action feature relied on a single source for most of its materials. Nonetheless, current trends in sourcing favor using fewer sources, although not necessarily a single source. Theoretically, firms should use single or a few sources whenever possible to enable the development of close relationships with the best suppliers. However, by increasing reliance on one supplier, the firm increases its risk that poor supplier performance will result in plant shutdowns or poor quality finished products. Although **sole sourcing** and **single sourcing** have been used interchangeably, sole sourcing typically refers to the situation when the supplier is the only available source, whereas single sourcing refers to the deliberate practice of concentrating purchases of an item with one source from a pool of many potential suppliers. A comparison follows of some of the reasons favoring the use of a single supplier versus using two or more suppliers for a purchased item.

Reasons Favoring a Single Supplier

1. *To establish a good relationship*: Using a single supplier makes it easier for the firm to establish a mutually beneficial strategic alliance relationship with the supplier, especially when the firm can benefit from the supplier's technologies and capabilities.

2. *Less quality variability*: Since the same technologies and processes are used to produce the parts when using a single source, variability in the quality levels is less than if the parts are purchased from multiple suppliers.

3. *Lower cost*: Buying from a single source concentrates purchase volume with the supplier, typically lowering the purchase cost per unit. Due to the large purchase volume, the supplier is more likely to ensure that it meets all of its performance goals to keep the business. Single sourcing also avoids duplicate fixed costs, especially if the part requires special tooling or expensive setups.

4. *Transportation economies*: Because single sourcing concentrates volume, the firm can take advantage of truckload (TL) shipments, which are cheaper per unit than the less-than-truckload (LTL) rate. By moving up to full truckloads, the firm has the option of using both rail and motor carriers. Rail carriers are more efficient for hauling heavy loads over long distances.

5. *Proprietary product or process purchases*: If it is a proprietary product or process, or if the supplier holds the patents to the product or process, the firm has no choice but to buy from the sole source.

6. *Volume too small to split*: If the requirement is too small, it is not worthwhile to split the order among many suppliers. Single sourcing is a good approach for acquiring supplies and services that do not contribute to the firm's core competencies.

Reasons Favoring Multiple Suppliers

1. *Need capacity*: When demand exceeds the capacity of a single supplier, the firm has no choice but to use multiple sources.

2. *Spread the risk of supply interruption*: Multiple sources allow the firm to spread the risk of supply interruptions due to a strike, quality problem, political instability and other supplier problems.

3. *Create competition*: Using multiple sources encourages competition among suppliers in terms of price and quality. While modern supplier management philosophy opposes the use of multiple sources simply to create competition, this may still be the preferred approach for sourcing non-vital items that do not affect the firm's competitive advantage. Using a single source to develop alliances for these types of purchases may not be cost-effective.

4. *Information*: Multiple suppliers usually have more information about market conditions, new product developments and new process technologies. This is particularly important if the product has a short product life cycle.

5. *Dealing with special kinds of businesses*: The firms, particularly government contractors, may need to give portions of their purchases to small, local or women- or minority-owned businesses, either voluntarily or as required by law.

The number of suppliers to use for one type of purchase has changed from the traditional multiple suppliers to the use of fewer reliable suppliers and even to the extent of using single supplier. Relationships between buyers and suppliers traditionally were short-term, adversarial and based primarily on cost, resulting in mutual lack of trust. Buyer–supplier relationships, particularly in integrated supply chain settings, have evolved today into trusting, cooperative and mutually beneficial long-term relationships. Firms today reduce their supply base to only the best suppliers.

Purchasing Organization

Purchasing organization within the firm has evolved over the years as the responsibilities of the purchasing function of firms changed from a clerical, supporting role to an integral part of corporate strategy that directly affects the competitiveness of the firms. In addition to the actual buying process, purchasing is now involved in product design, production decisions and other aspects of a firm's operations. The decision of how to organize purchasing to best serve its purpose is firm and industry specific and dependent on many factors, such as market conditions and the types of materials required. Purchasing structure can be viewed as a continuum, with centralization at one extreme and decentralization at the other. While there are few firms that adopt a pure centralized or decentralized structure, the benefits of each are worth a closer examination. The current trend is toward purchasing centralization for the vital materials where firms can take advantage of economies of scale and other benefits.

Centralized purchasing is where a single purchasing department, usually located at the firm's corporate office, makes all the purchasing decisions, including order quantity, pricing policy, contracting, negotiations and supplier selection and evaluation. **Decentralized purchasing** is where individual, local purchasing departments, such as at the plant level, make their own purchasing decisions. A discussion of advantages and disadvantages to each of these purchasing structures follows.

Advantages of Centralization

1. *Concentrated volume*: An obvious benefit is the concentration of purchase volume to create quantity discounts, less-costly volume shipments and other more favorable purchase terms. This is often referred to as **leveraging purchase volume**. A centralized system also provides the buying firm more clout and bargaining power. Suppliers generally are more willing to negotiate, give better terms and share technology due to the higher volume.

2. *Avoid duplication*: Centralized purchasing eliminates the duplication of job functions. A corporate buyer can research and issue a large purchase order to cover the same material requested by all units, thus eliminating duplication of activities. This also results in fewer buyers, reducing labor costs.

3. *Specialization*: Centralization allows buyers to specialize in a particular group of items instead of being responsible for all purchased materials and services. It allows buyers to spend more time and resources to research materials for which they are responsible, thus becoming specialized buyers.

4. *Lower transportation costs*: Centralization allows larger shipments to be made to take advantage of truckload shipments, and yet smaller shipments still can be arranged for delivery directly from suppliers to the points of use.

5. *No competition within units*: Under the decentralized system, when different units purchase the same material, a situation may be created in which units are competing among themselves, especially when scarce materials are purchased from the same supplier. Centralization minimizes this problem.

6. *Common supply base*: A common supply base is used, thus making it easier to manage and to negotiate contracts.

Advantages of Decentralization

1. *Closer knowledge of requirements*: A buyer at the individual unit is more likely to know its exact needs better than a central buyer at the home office.

2. *Local sourcing*: If the firm desires to support local businesses, it is more likely that a local buyer will know more about local suppliers. The proximity of local

suppliers allows materials to be shipped more frequently in small lot sizes, and is conducive to the creation of closer supplier relationships.

3. *Less bureaucracy*: Decentralization allows quicker response, due to less bureaucracy and closer contact between the user and the buyer. Coordination and communication with operations and other divisions are more efficient.

Thus, while centralized purchasing may result in lower costs and better negotiating power, the centralized system may also be too rigid and even infeasible for large, multiunit organizations consisting of several unrelated business operations. For these reasons, a **hybrid purchasing organization** may be warranted. Large multiunit organizations may use a **decentralized-centralized purchasing structure** to decentralize purchasing at the corporate level, but centralize the procurement function at the business unit level. Conversely, a firm may utilize a **centralized-decentralized purchasing structure** to negotiate national contracts at the corporate level, but decentralize buying at the business unit level, like the example discussed in the Supply Chain Management in Action feature. The hybrid purchasing organization allows the firm to exploit the advantages of both the centralized and decentralized systems.

International Purchasing/Global Sourcing

International agreements aimed at relaxing trade barriers and promoting free trade have provided opportunities for firms to expand their supply bases to participate in **global sourcing**. Indeed, world merchandise exports and commercial services trade reached $15.717 trillion and $3.780 trillion, respectively in 2008.[9] In 2008, the U.S was the world's largest importer for merchandise trade ($2.170 trillion) and the world's largest importer and exporter for commercial services (imports were $368 billion; exports were $521 billion). The world's top three merchandise trade exporters were Germany ($1.462 trillion), China ($1.428 trillion) and the U.S ($1.287 trillion). While global sourcing provides opportunities to improve quality, cost and delivery performance, it also poses unique challenges for purchasing personnel. Engaging in global sourcing requires additional skills and knowledge to deal with international suppliers, logistics, communication, political, cultural and other issues not usually encountered in domestic sourcing. The total cost of ownership example shown in Example 2.1 can also be used to compare the cost-effectiveness of domestic versus global sourcing.

Various methods are employed for global sourcing. It is not limited to setting up an international purchasing office or using the existing purchasing personnel to handle the transactions in-house. An **import broker** or **sales agent**, who will perform transactions for a fee, can be used. Import brokers do not take title to the goods. Instead, title passes directly from the seller to the buyer. International purchasers can also buy foreign goods from an **import merchant**, who will buy and take title to the goods and then resell them to the buyer. Purchasing from a **trading company**, which carries a wide variety of goods, is another option.

There are numerous international trade organizations designed to reduce tariff and nontariff barriers among member countries. A **tariff** is an official list or schedule showing the duties, taxes or customs imposed by the host country on imports or exports. **Nontariffs** are import quotas, licensing agreements, embargoes, laws and other regulations imposed on imports and exports. A discussion of major international trade organizations follows.

1. The *World Trade Organization (WTO)* is the largest and most visible international trade organization dealing with the global rules of trade between nations. It replaced the *General Agreement on Tariffs and Trade (GATT)* on January 1, 1995. Its primary goal is to ensure that international trade flows smoothly, predictably and freely among member countries. The WTO Secretariat is based in Geneva, Switzerland. It has 153 member countries as of January 2010.

2. The *North American Free Trade Agreement (NAFTA)* was implemented on January 1, 1994. Its goal is to remove trade and investment barriers among the U.S, Canada and Mexico. Under NAFTA, all nontariff agricultural trade barriers between the U.S and Mexico were eliminated. Most tariffs affecting agricultural trade between the U.S. and Canada were removed by 1998. NAFTA was fully implemented as of January 1, 2008. Ten years after its implementation (from 1994 to 2004), studies showed that NAFTA had only a modest positive effect on the U.S. and Mexican economies.[10]

3. The *European Union (EU)* was set up on May 9, 1950, and was comprised of Belgium, France, Luxembourg, Italy, the Netherlands and Germany. The United Kingdom, Denmark and Ireland joined the EU in 1973. As of January 2010, the EU has 27 member countries. Three more countries have applied for EU membership. One of the primary goals of the EU is to create a single market without internal borders for goods and services, allowing member countries to better compete with markets like the U.S.

Reasons for Global Sourcing

Firms expand their supply base to include foreign suppliers for many reasons. These can include lower price, better quality, an overseas supplier holding the patent to the product, faster delivery to foreign units, better services and better process or product technologies.

A primary reason that many firms purchase from foreign suppliers is to lower the price of materials. As stated earlier, price generally is an important factor when purchasing standard materials and supplies that do not impact the competitive position of the firm. Many factors can contribute to cheaper materials from overseas suppliers—for example, cheaper labor costs and raw materials, favorable exchange rates, more efficient processes, or intentional dumping of products by foreign suppliers in overseas markets.

Additionally, the quality of overseas products may be better due to newer and better product and process technologies. Further, while foreign suppliers may be located farther away, they may be able to deliver goods faster than domestic suppliers due to a more efficient transportation and logistical system. Foreign suppliers may even maintain inventory and set up support offices in the host country to compete with domestic sources and to provide better services.

Firms may buy from foreign suppliers to support the local economy where they have subsidiaries, or they may be involved in **countertrade**, in which the contract calls for the exchange of goods or services for raw materials from local suppliers. While foreign purchasing may provide a number of benefits to the buyer, some problems may also be encountered.

Potential Challenges for Global Sourcing

Over the last few decades, global sourcing has surged due to many factors, such as the improvement of communication and transportation technologies, the reduction of international trade barriers and deregulation of the transportation industry. However, global sourcing poses additional challenges that purchasing must know how to handle effectively. For example, the complexity and costs involved in selecting foreign suppliers and dealing with duties, tariffs, custom clearance, currency exchange and political, cultural, labor and legal problems present sizable challenges for the international buyer.

Unlike dealing with domestic suppliers, the costs involved in identifying, selecting and evaluating foreign suppliers can be prohibitive. If the foreign supplier is in a distant location, custom clearance, transportation and other logistical issues may render delivery lead time unacceptable, especially for perishable goods.

In addition to the Uniform Commercial Code (UCC), which governs the purchase and sale of goods in the U.S (except the state of Louisiana), global purchasers must also know the United Nations' **Contracts for the International Sale of Goods (CISG)**. The CISG applies to international purchases and sales of goods, unless both parties elect to opt out. The UCC allows either party to modify the terms of acceptance for the purchase contract, but the terms of acceptance cannot be modified under the CISG.

Global purchasers must also deal with more complex shipping terms than domestic buyers. The International Chamber of Commerce created a uniform set of rules, called **incoterms (International Commercial Terms)**, to simplify international transactions of goods with respect to shipping costs, risks and responsibilities of buyer, seller and shipper. However, incoterms do not deal with transfer of title of the goods. Incoterms are often used in conjunction with a geographical location. There are currently thirteen incoterms, grouped into four categories.

Countertrade

Global sourcing may involve countertrade, in which goods and/or services of domestic firms are exchanged for goods and/or services of equal value or in combination with currency from foreign firms. This type of arrangement is sometimes used by countries where there is a shortage of hard currency or as a means to acquire technologies. Countertrade transactions are more complicated than currency transactions because goods are exchanged for goods.

The various forms of countertrade include barter, offset and counterpurchase. **Barter** is the complete exchange of goods or services of equal value without the exchange of currency. The seller can either consume the goods or services or resell the items. **Offset** is an exchange agreement for industrial goods or services as a condition of military-related export. It is also commonly used in the aerospace and defense sectors. Most of the offset packages are divided into direct and indirect offsets. **Direct offset** usually involves coproduction, or a joint venture and exchange of related goods or services; whereas **indirect offset** involves exchange of goods or services unrelated to the initial purchase. **Counterpurchase** is an arrangement whereby the original exporter agrees to sell goods or services to a foreign importer and simultaneously agrees to buy specific goods or services from the foreign importer. Many developing countries mandate the transfer of technology as part of a countertrade or offset arrangement.

Procurement for Government/Nonprofit Agencies

Public procurement or **public purchasing** refers to the management of the purchasing and supply management function of the government and nonprofit sectors, such as educational institutions, hospitals and the federal, state and local governments. Although public procurement is subjected to political pressure and public scrutiny, its goals are similar to the private sector. However, public procurement is subjected to special rules and regulations that are established by the federal, state and local governments. For example, all U.S. federal government purchases must comply with the **Federal Acquisition Regulation (FAR)**. Consequently, the procedures for public procurement differ from the private sector—in addition to ensuring that purchases for goods and services are in strict compliance with statutes and policies, public procurement procedures are generally designed to **maximize competition**. The e-procurement system described in Figure 2.4 is an example of a public procurement system. In addition to the typical operations control, the e-procurement system in Figure 2.4 requires additional treatments of purchases exceeding $25,000.

In the U.S., the **General Services Administration (GSA)**, passed by the 81st Congress and signed into law by President Harry Truman in 1949, is responsible for most federal purchases. The GSA, based in Washington, D.C., has eleven regional offices in Boston, New York, Philadelphia, Atlanta, Chicago, Kansas City, Fort Worth, Denver, San Francisco, Auburn (Washington) and Washington, D.C. It is one of the world's largest purchasing entities. The **Department of Defense (DOD)** is the other major public procurement entity in the U.S.

Characteristics of Public Procurement

A unique characteristic of public procurement is the preference to use competitive bidding to encourage competition among suppliers. For example, a government agency may implement procurement procedures that require a written quote for purchases that are more than $2,500 but less than $10,000; two written quotes for purchases that are less than $25,000; three written quotes for purchases less than $100,000; and purchases over $100,000 must be competitively bid.

In competitive bidding, the contract is usually awarded to the **lowest-priced** bidder determined to be **responsive** and **responsible** by the buyer. A responsive bid is one that conforms to the invitation to bid, and a responsible bid is one that is capable and willing to perform the work as specified.

The bidding process is usually very time-consuming and not cost-efficient for small purchases. On October 13, 1994, U.S. President Bill Clinton signed the **Federal Acquisition Streamlining Act (FASA)** to remove many restrictions on government purchases that do not exceed $100,000. Instead of using full and open competitive bidding, government agencies can now use simplified procedures that require fewer administrative details, lower approval levels and less documentation for soliciting and evaluating bids up to $100,000. **Micro-purchases**, government purchases of $2,500 and below, can now be made without obtaining competitive quotes. Additionally, all federal purchases between $2,500 and $100,000 are now reserved for small businesses, unless the buyer cannot obtain offers from two or more small businesses that are competitive on price, quality and delivery. A small business is defined as a business with less than 100 employees in the U.S.

Government agencies are required to advertise all planned purchases over $25,000. When the requirements are clear, accurate and complete, the government agency usually uses an **invitation for bid (IFB)** to solicit **sealed bids**. The specifications for the proposed purchase, instructions for preparation of bids, and the conditions of purchase, delivery and payment schedule are usually included with the IFB. The IFB also designates the date and time of bid opening. Sealed bids are opened in public at the purchasing office at the time designated in the invitation, and facts about each bid are read aloud and recorded. A contract is then awarded to the lowest responsible and responsive bidder.

Generally, bidders are also required to furnish bid bonds to ensure that the successful bidder will fulfill the contract as stated. There are three basic types of bid bond: **bid** or **surety bonds** guarantee the successful bidder will accept the contract; **performance bonds** guarantee the work of the successful bidder meets specifications and in the time stated; and **payment bonds** protect the buyer against any third-party liens not fulfilled by the bidder.

Another characteristic of public procurement is the **Buy American Act** that mandates U.S. government purchases and third-party purchases that utilize federal funds to buy domestically produced goods, if the price differential between the domestic product and an identical foreign-sourced product does not exceed a certain percentage amount. However, the U.S. President has the authority to waive the Buy American Act.

While **green purchasing** is not a new sourcing concept, there is a push to expand green purchasing requirements in the public sector. There are at least five federal statutes and more than a dozen Presidential Executive Orders requiring federal purchasing officials to include environmental considerations and human health when making purchasing decisions.[11] Public procurement advocates the purchase of more energy efficient products, bio-based products, recycled content products, non-ozone-depleting substances, green power and other environmentally friendly products. The term **green power** refers to electricity products that include large proportions of electricity generated from renewable and environmentally preferable energy resources, such as wind and solar energy.[12]

SUMMARY

Over the last decade, the traditional purchasing function has evolved into an integral part of supply chain management. Purchasing is an important strategic contributor to overall business competitiveness. It is the largest single function in most organizations, controlling activities and transactions valued at more than 50 percent of sales. Every dollar saved due to better purchasing impacts business operations and profits directly. Purchasing personnel talk to customers, users, suppliers and internal design, finance, marketing and operations personnel, in addition to top management. The information they gain from all this exposure can be used to help the firm to provide better, cheaper and more timely products and services to both internal and external customers. Savvy executives are thus turning to purchasing to improve business and supply chain performance.

KEY TERMS

backward vertical integration, 53

barter, 65

bid or surety bonds, 67

blank check purchase order, 51

blanket order release, 51

blanket purchase order, 51

break-even analysis, 55

Buy American Act, 67

centralized purchasing, 62

centralized-decentralized purchasing structure, 63

Contracts for the International Sale of Goods (CISG), 65

corporate purchasing cards (P-cards), 51

counterpurchase, 65

countertrade, 64

decentralized purchasing, 62

decentralized-centralized purchasing structure, 63

Department of Defense (DOD), 66

direct offset, 65

early supplier involvement (ESI), 58

economies of scale, 54

expediting, 47

Federal Acquisition Regulation (FAR), 66

Federal Acquisition Streamlining Act (FASA), 66

follow-up, 47

forward vertical integration, 53

General Services Administration (GSA), 66

global sourcing, 63

green power, 67

green purchasing, 67

hybrid purchasing organization, 63

import broker, 63

import merchant, 63

incoterms (International Commercial Terms), 65

indirect offset, 65

industrial buyers, 39

internal control, 43

inventory turnover, 43

invitation for bid (IFB), 66

leveraging purchase volume, 62

lowest-priced, 66

make or buy, 53

material requisition (MR), 43

maximize competition, 66

merchants, 39

micro-purchases, 66

nontariffs, 63

offset, 65

open-end purchase order, 51

outsourcing, 46

payment bonds, 67

performance bonds, 67

petty cash, 52

planned order releases, 44

procurement credit cards, 51

profit-leverage effect, 42

public procurement, 65

public purchasing, 65

purchase order (PO), 46

purchase requisition, 43

purchase spend, 42

purchasing, 39

request for proposal (RFP), 45

request for quotation (RFQ), 45

responsible, 66

responsive, 66

return on assets (ROA), 42

return on investment (ROI), 42

sales agent, 63

DISCUSSION QUESTIONS

1. Describe the steps in a traditional manual purchasing system.

2. Describe the e-procurement system and its advantages over the manual system. Are there any disadvantages to the electronic system? Do you think the e-procurement system will ultimately replace the manual system? Why or why not?

3. How can purchasing help to improve the competitive edge of an organization?

4. What is the profit-leverage effect of purchasing? What is the return-on-assets effect of purchasing?

5. How does a merchant differ from an industrial buyer?

6. Describe the purpose of a material requisition, a purchase order, a request for quotation and a request for proposal. Does the material requisition serve the same purpose as the purchase order?

7. Why are small value purchase orders problematic? How can purchasing more effectively deal with this problem?

8. Should unit price be used as the sole criterion for selecting suppliers? Why or why not?

9. Explain backward vertical integration. What are the advantages of outsourcing compared to backward vertical integration?

10. When should a firm outsource instead of making the items in-house?

11. What factors should be considered while choosing suppliers?

12. What are the reasons to use a single supplier? Is this the most efficient way to purchase materials in general?

13. Describe centralized and decentralized purchasing and their advantages.

14. Describe how the hybrid purchasing organization works.

15. Describe how blanket orders and blanket order releases can be used to manage the procurement system of a business that owns a dozen large restaurants in a city.

16. How does public procurement differ from corporate purchasing?

17. Describe the different types of bid bonds.

18. What are micro-purchases? How can they be used to improve public procurement?

19. Why do firms purchase from foreign suppliers? What are the risks involved in global sourcing?

20. What is countertrade? Describe the various types of countertrade.

21. Describe how a typical government bidding process is conducted.

22. How can global sourcing enhance a firm's competitiveness?

23. Describe the disadvantages of global sourcing and how it can adversely affect a firm's competitiveness.

INTERNET QUESTIONS

1. Go to the World Trade Organization's website and use the information to write a report that includes (a) the functions of the WTO, (b) the latest number of membership countries, (c) its relationship with GATT, (d) the number of countries that had originally signed the GATT by 1994 and (e) the last five countries that became members of the WTO.

2. Go to the Institute of Supply Management's website and use their "ISM Glossary of Key Supply Management Terms" to explain these terms: (a) supply management, (b) materials management, (c) procurement, (d) purchasing, (e) sourcing, (f) acquisition, (g) sole sourcing and (h) single sourcing. If you are not an ISM member, you will need to register and create an account before you can access the glossary page.

3. Go to the U.S. General Services Administration website and use the information to write a report on the GSA SmartPay program.

4. Go to the European Union's website and use the information to write a report that includes its brief history, membership countries and the euro.

5. Utilize the Internet to search for the thirteen incoterms. Write a report to explain the primary purpose of the terms in general and then describe each of the thirteen terms individually.

6. Go to the General Services Administration's Web site and use the information to write a brief report to summarize the roles of GSA. Additionally, discuss the roles of the Federal Acquisition Regulation (FAR), Federal Management Regulation (FMR) and the Federal Travel Regulation (FTR).

7. Use Internet resources to write a report on the results achieved by NAFTA in promoting trade among the U.S, Canada and Mexico since its implementation in 1994.

8. Use Internet resources to write a report on green purchasing efforts in public procurement.

9. Use Internet resources to write a report on green purchasing efforts in the private sector.

10. Use Internet resources to write a report on renewable energy efforts in the U.S. and the European Union.

SPREADSHEET PROBLEMS

1. If a firm's net income (profits before taxes) is $120,000 and it has total assets of $1.5 million, what is its return on assets?

2. If a firm is able to sustain the same level of operations in terms of sales and administrative expenses but reduces its materials cost by $50,000 through smarter purchases, what is the profit-leverage effect on gross profits? What is the profit-leverage effect on profits before taxes?

3. If a firm's cost of goods sold is $2.5 million and its average inventory is $500,000, what is the inventory turnover?

4. You are given the following information:

COSTS	MAKE OPTION	BUY OPTION
Fixed Cost	$125,000	$5,000
Variable Cost	$15	$17

a. Find the break-even quantity and the total cost at the break-even point.

b. If the requirement is 150,000 units, is it more cost-effective for the firm to buy or make the components? What is the cost savings for choosing the cheaper option?

5. You are given the following information:

COSTS	MAKE OPTION	BUY OPTION
Fixed Cost	$25,000	$3,000
Variable Cost	$8	$12

a. Find the break-even quantity and the total cost at the break-even point.

b. If the requirement is 4,500 units, is it more cost-effective for the firm to buy or make the components? What is the cost savings for choosing the cheaper option?

c. If the requirement is 6,000 units, is it more cost-effective for the firm to buy or make the components? What is the cost savings for choosing the cheaper option?

6. Ms. Jane Kim, Purchasing Manager of Kuantan ATV, Inc., is negotiating a contract to buy 20,000 units of a common component part from a supplier. Ms. Kim has done a preliminary cost analysis on manufacturing the part in-house and concluded that she would need to invest $50,000 in capital equipment and incur a variable cost of $25 per unit to manufacture the part in-house. Assuming the total fixed cost to draft a contract with her supplier is $1,000, what is the maximum purchase price that she should negotiate with her supplier? What other factors should she negotiate with the suppliers?

7. A Las Vegas, Nevada, manufacturer has the option to make or buy one of its component parts. The annual requirement is 20,000 units. A supplier is able to supply the parts for $10 per piece. The firm estimates that it costs $600 to prepare the contract with the supplier. To make the parts in-house, the firm must invest $50,000 in capital equipment and estimates that the parts cost $8 per piece.

a. Assuming that cost is the only criterion, use break-even analysis to determine whether the firm should make or buy the item. What is the break-even quantity and what is the total cost at the break-even point?

b. Calculate the total costs for both options at 20,000 units. What is the cost savings for choosing the cheaper option?

8. Given the following information, use total cost analysis to determine which supplier is more cost-effective. Late delivery of raw material results in 60 percent lost sales and 40 percent back orders of finished goods.

Order lot size	1,000
Requirements (annual forecast)	120,000 units
Weight per engine	22 pounds
Order processing cost	$125/order
Inventory carrying rate	20% per year
Cost of working capital	10% per year
Profit margin	15%
Price of finished goods	$4,500
Back order cost	$15 per unit

ORDER SIZE	SUPPLIER 1	SUPPLIER 2
1 to 999 units/order	$50.00 per unit	$49.50 per unit
1000 to 2,999 units/order	$49.00 per unit	$48.50 per unit
3,000 + units/order	$48.00 per unit	$48.00 per unit
Tooling cost	$12,000	$10,000
Terms	2/10, net 30	1/10, net 30
Distance	125 miles	100 miles
Supplier Quality Rating	2%	2%
Supplier Delivery Rating	1%	2%

Truckload (TL ≥ 40,000 lbs): $0.85 per ton-mile

Less-than-truckload (LTL): $1.10 per ton-mile

Note: per ton-mile = 2,000 lbs per mile

9. A buyer received bids and other relevant information from three suppliers for a vital component part for its latest product. Given the following information, use total cost analysis to determine which supplier should be chosen. Late delivery of the component results in 70 percent lost sales and 30 percent back orders of finished goods.

Order lot size	2,000
Requirements (annual forecast)	240,000 units
Weight per engine	40 pounds
Order processing cost	$200/order
Inventory carrying rate	20% per year
Cost of working capital	10% per year
Profit margin	15%
Price of finished goods	$10,500
Back order cost	$120 per unit

ORDER SIZE	SUPPLIER 1	SUPPLIER 2	SUPPLIER 3
1 to 999 units/order	$200.00 per unit	$205.00 per unit	$198.00 per unit
1,000 to 2,999 units/order	$195.00 per unit	$190.00 per unit	$192.00 per unit
3,000 + units/order	$190.00 per unit	$185.00 per unit	$190.00 per unit
Tooling Cost	$12,000	$10,000	$15,000
Terms	2/10, net 30	1/15, net 30	1/10, net 20
Distance	120 miles	100 miles	150 miles
Supplier Quality Rating	2%	1%	2%
Supplier Delivery Rating	1%	1%	2%

Truckload (TL ≥ 40,000 lbs): $0.95 per ton-mile

Less-than-truckload (LTL): $1.20 per ton-mile

Note: per ton-mile = 2,000 lbs per mile

Chapter 3

CREATING AND MANAGING SUPPLIER RELATIONSHIPS

"If you are only measuring your procurement department on what has been saved, you're missing out on half of what suppliers can do. They're not just cost centers anymore; they are partners. Suppliers can bring new technology, innovation and process improvement suggestions that can reduce time to market or improve the value you deliver to customers. These are opportunities that can drive incremental revenue in some direct or indirect way."

Jonathan Hughes, Vantage Partners[1]

"We knew that driving supplier performance and improving the total value of acquisition would require a greater level of supplier integration. Over the past three years, Cessna has been driving a collaborative approach linked to our supplier relationship management process with a vision to be the customer of choice. We firmly believe that having world-class suppliers requires being a good customer to them. This vision has been driven by various collaborative strategies, with the supply base working together for the betterment of the supply chain. Trust between Cessna and its suppliers is the cornerstone of these collaborative strategies. It really comes down to this: Do what you say you will, and work to address suppliers' interests."

Brent E. Edmisten, Director, Strategic Sourcing & ISC Strategies, Cessna Aircraft Company[2]

Learning Objectives

After completing this chapter, you should be able to

- Explain the importance of supplier partnerships
- Understand the key factors for developing successful partnerships
- Develop a supplier evaluation and certification program
- Explain the importance of a supplier recognition program
- Understand the capabilities of Supplier Relationship Management
- Explain the benefits of using SRM software to manage suppliers

Chapter Outline

Introduction

Developing Supplier Relationships

Supplier Evaluation and Certification

Supplier Development

Supplier Recognition Programs

Supplier Relationship Management

Summary

Supply Chain Management in Action   *Xerox Takes Supplier Audits Seriously*

At Connecticut-based Xerox Corp., a potential new supplier is sent documentation that lays out Xerox's expectations and requirements before any auditor visits the supplier.

"As part of the process, we send a supplier assessment survey to suppliers ahead of time and we ask them to do a self assessment," says Bradley Bulger, manager of the global procurement engineering organization. "Once we receive the self-assessment, we schedule a time for us to go and do a survey on site at the supplier's location."

Xerox's audits assess effectiveness of the company's quality management and environment management systems. The audit also covers how the supplier manages its sub-tier suppliers, as well as adherence to supply chain standards and the Electronics Industry Citizenship Coalition (EICC)'s code of conduct, which provides guidelines on how workers should be treated. If audits reveal deficiencies in quality management or manufacturing processes, Xerox gives suppliers a corrective action plan, which must be implemented before the supplier can be qualified for consideration for Xerox business. "For Xerox we do audits on an as-need basis," says Bulger. "With the economic downturn, we have done a lot more audits than we have previously concerning suppliers' financials," he says.

Besides quality issues, Xerox will also audit a current supplier if the supplier relocates a manufacturing facility or if there are changes in the supplier's senior management team or ownership. Bulger says various departments at Xerox are involved in audits, depending on the types of audit. "If it deals with new supplier assessment, environmental management, quality management systems, the audit will be led by the supplier quality engineering organization," he says.

If the audit is a business assessment to understand the financial resources of a supplier's production capacity or business resources needed to fulfill requirements, it will be led by supplier managers or supplier quality engineers. "If the audit is an assessment of a potential supplier with a new technology, it would be led by the design organization." says Bulger. He adds technology assessment audits are a collaborative effort across design, manufacturing, engineering, supplier quality engineering and supplier managers within global purchasing.

Many companies that are moving manufacturing and sourcing to low-cost countries are doing corporate social responsibility audits. Some companies in emerging low-cost areas use child labor, or force workers to work long hours and provide substandard working conditions for employees. "We did roughly 40 social responsibility audits last year and some follow-up audits in addition to that," says Barbara Ceglinski, manager of global purchasing business operations at Xerox. She says Xerox focuses on the top 50 suppliers by spend and on suppliers that are in "high-risk areas" such as Southeast Asia.

With social responsibility, Xerox has a no-tolerance policy for certain EICC infractions in its audits, but is flexible with lesser issues. "For instance, if a supplier has issues with child labor or inhumane treatment of workers we have zero tolerance," he says. "But if we had an instance where documentation of a process was insufficient, that would be different. It may be a management process that would have been in nonconformance that could be negotiable," she says.

Source: Carbone, J. "Supplier Audits Dig Deeper," *Purchasing*, V. 139, No. 4 (2010): 24. Used with permission.

Introduction

In today's competitive environment, as companies focus on their core competencies, the level of outsourcing will continue to rise. Increasingly, companies are requiring their suppliers to deliver innovative and quality products not only in just-in-time (JIT) fashion, but also at a competitive price. In the last few decades we have learned that good supplier relations can provide many benefits such as flexibility in terms of delivery, better quality, better information, and better material flows between buyers and suppliers. Many companies believe strongly that better supplier partnerships are important to achieving competitive corporate performance. As such, companies are realizing the importance of developing win-win, long-term relationships with suppliers. It is critical that customers and suppliers develop stronger relationships and partnerships based on a strategic rather than a tactical perspective and then manage these relationships to create value for all participants. Successful partnerships with key suppliers can contribute to innovations and have the potential to create competitive advantage for the firm. Selecting the right supply partners and successfully managing these relationships over time is thus strategically important; it is often stated that "a firm is only as good as its suppliers." Xerox for example, takes the management and cultivation of their supplier relationships very seriously, as discussed in the chapter opening Supply Chain Management in Action feature.

According to the Institute for Supply Management's glossary of terms, a supplier partnership is defined as: "A commitment over an extended time to work together to the mutual benefit of both parties, sharing relevant information and the risks and rewards of the relationship. These relationships require a clear understanding of expectations, open communication and information exchange, mutual trust and a common direction for the future. Such arrangements are a collaborative business activity that does not involve the formation of a legal partnership."[3] Ford Motor Company uses their Aligned Business Framework (ABF) program to provide "intensified annual reviews of commodity suppliers, which are made available to all car making organizations; a supplier evaluation system of eleven financial and nonfinancial metrics by which potential suppliers can be judged by buyers; a five-year supplier training plan that will provide a basis for ongoing cooperation in areas of corporate social responsibility."[4] This rigorous framework is beneficial to Ford since it enables the company to reduce costs and obtain suppliers' innovative technologies. At the same time this arrangement also benefits the suppliers who get a long-term commitment that will significantly improve their forecasting and planning. According to Tony Brown, group vice president of global purchasing at Ford, "Strong supplier relationships are embedded in the principles of the automaker's strategic plan. By increasing our ABF network, Ford is building a strong foundation of suppliers."[5] Good supplier relationships are just one ingredient necessary for developing an end-to-end integrated supply chain.

Developing Supplier Relationships

According to Kenichi Ohmae, founder and managing director of Ohmae & Associates, "Companies are just beginning to learn what nations have always known: in a complex, uncertain world filled with dangerous opponents, it is best not to go it alone."[6] Building strong supplier partnerships requires a lot of hard work and commitment by both buyers and sellers. Developing true partnerships is not easily achieved, and much has to be done to get the partnership to work. Several key ingredients for developing successful partnerships are discussed below.

Building Trust

Trust is critical for any partnership or alliance to work. It must be built not just at the senior management level but at all levels of the organization. Trust enables organizations to share valuable information, devote time and resources to understand each other's business, and achieve results beyond what could have been done individually. Jordan Lewis, in his book *Trusted Partners,* points out that "Trust does not imply easy harmony. Obviously, business is too complex to expect ready agreement on all issues. However, in a trusting relationship conflicts motivate you to probe for deeper understandings and search for constructive solutions. Trust creates goodwill, which sustains the relationship when one firm does something the other dislikes."[7] With trust, partners are more willing to work together; find compromise solutions to problems; work toward achieving long-term benefits for both parties; and in short, go the extra mile. In addition, there is goodwill developed over time between the partners. This can be beneficial when one partner gets into a difficult situation and the other partner is willing to help out.

Shared Vision and Objectives

All partnerships should state the expectations of the buyer and supplier, reasons and objectives of the partnership, and plans for the dissolution of the relationship. According to Lenwood Grant, sourcing expert with Bristol-Myers-Squibb, "You don't want a partnership that is based on necessity. If you don't think that the partnership is a good mix, but you do it because you have to—possibly because that supplier is the only provider of that material in the market, because you've signed an exclusive contract in the past, or for some other reason—it's not a true partnership and is likely to fail."[8] Both partners must share the same vision and have objectives that are not only clear but mutually agreeable. Many alliances and partnerships have failed because objectives are not well aligned or are overly optimistic. The focus must move beyond tactical issues and toward a more strategic path to corporate success. When partners have equal decision-making control, the partnership has a higher chance of success.

Personal Relationships

Interpersonal relationships in buyer-supplier partnerships are important since it is people who communicate and make things happen. According to Leonard Greenhalgh, author of *Managing Strategic Relationships,* "An alliance or partnership isn't really a relationship between companies, it's a relationship between specific individuals. When you are considering strategic alliances of any kind, the only time the company matters is in the status associated with it [strategic alliance]. Whoever is interfacing with the other company, they are the company."[9]

Mutual Benefits and Needs

Partnering should result in a win-win situation, which can only be achieved if both companies have compatible needs. Mutual needs not only create an environment conducive for collaboration but opportunities for increased innovation. When both parties share in the benefits of the partnership, the relationship will be productive and long lasting. An alliance is much like a marriage: if only one party is happy, the marriage is not likely to last.

Commitment and Top Management Support

First, it takes a lot of time and hard work to find the right partner. Having done so, both parties must dedicate their time, best people, and resources to make the partnership succeed. According to author Stephen R. Covey, "Without involvement, there is no commitment. Mark it down, asterisk it, circle it, underline it. No involvement, no commitment."[10] Commitment must start at the highest management level. Partnerships tend to be successful when top executives are actively supporting the partnership. The level of cooperation and involvement shown by the organization's top leaders is likely to set the tone for joint problem solving further down the line.

Successful partners are committed to continuously looking for opportunities to grow their businesses together. Management must create the right kind of internal attitude needed for alliances to flourish. Since partnerships are likely to encounter bumps along the way, it is critical that management adopt a collaborative approach to conflict resolution instead of assigning blame.

Change Management

With change comes stress, which can lead to a loss of focus. As such, companies must avoid distractions from their core businesses as a result of the changes brought about by the partnership. Companies must be prepared to manage change that comes with the formation of new partnerships. According to author Stephen Covey, "The key to successful change management is remaining focused on a set of core principles that do not change, regardless of the circumstances."[11] Whirlpool attributed the success of their global outsourcing initiative to the change management involved. Steven Rush, Whirlpool's vice president of North American region procurement, noted that "Since outsourcing was a politically charged term, the department needed an effective communication program in order to build alignment within the organization; not only at the senior management level, but to make sure that there was buy-in throughout the organization."[12] Thus a company must ensure that the reasons why certain processes are being outsourced are communicated to those affected by the change. Thus, effective internal communications is one of the keys to successfully managing change.

Information Sharing and Lines of Communication

Both formal and informal lines of communication should be set up to facilitate free flows of information. When there is a high degree of trust, information systems can be customized to serve each other more effectively. Confidentiality of sensitive financial, product and process information must be maintained. Any conflict that occurs can be resolved if the channels of communication are open. For instance, early communication to suppliers of specification changes and new product introductions are contributing factors to the success of purchasing partnerships. Buyers and sellers should meet regularly to discuss any change of plans, evaluate results and address issues critical to the success of the partnerships. Since there is free exchange of information, nondisclosure agreements are often used to protect proprietary information and other sensitive data from leaking out. It is not the quantity but rather the quality and accuracy of the information exchanged that indicates the success of information sharing.

While collaboration has many positives, there is also the fear of the loss of trade secrets when sensitive information is shared between partners. According to the U.S.

Economic Espionage Act of 1996, 18 U.S.C. § 1839 (3), the definition of trade secrets is: "All forms and types of financial, business, scientific, technical, economic, or engineering information, including patterns, plans, compilations, programmed devices, formulas, designs, prototypes, methods, techniques, processes, procedures, programs, or codes, whether tangible or intangible, and whether or how stored, compiled, or memorialized physically, electronically, graphically, photographically, or in writing."[13] Trade secrets tend to be more critical in the high technology sector where the unique technique or process used in the company's business can provide it with tremendous competitive advantage. Vendors have been known to steal or misappropriate trade secrets, terminate the partnership and become competitors. One of the most basic and successful approaches for protecting trade secrets is to require employees and vendors to sign a nondisclosure agreement.

Capabilities

Organizations must develop the right capabilities for creating long-term relationships with their suppliers. In a recent study on world-class procurement organizations, the Hackett Group found that one of the two best practices for top-performing companies is using cross-functional teams to achieve common objectives.[14] As such, companies aspiring to be world class must develop cross-functional team capabilities. In addition, the employees must not only be able to collaborate successfully within the company in a cross-functional team setting but have the skills to do so externally. Key suppliers must have the right technology and capabilities to meet cost, quality and delivery requirements. In addition, suppliers must be sufficiently flexible to respond quickly to changing customer requirements. Before entering into any partnership, it is imperative for an organization to conduct a thorough investigation of the supplier's capabilities and core competencies. Organizations prefer working with suppliers who have the technology and technical expertise to assist in the development of new products or services that would lead to a competitive advantage in the marketplace. A survey carried out by global management consulting company Accenture "demonstrates that leaders in SRM [Supplier Relationship Management] have turned their investment in more sophisticated collaboration capabilities into hard dollars—achieving an average of $79 million savings from postcontract award activities—far in excess of the survey average of $22 million. Many believe they can increase those savings by as much as 20 percent in the near term."[15]

Performance Metrics

The old adage "You can't improve what you can't measure" is particularly true for buyer-supplier alliances. Measures related to quality, cost, delivery and flexibility have traditionally been used to evaluate how well suppliers are doing. Information provided by supplier performance will be used to improve the entire supply chain. Thus, the goal of any good performance evaluation system is to provide metrics that are understandable, easy to measure and focused on real value-added results for both the buyer and supplier.

By evaluating supplier performance, organizations hope to identify suppliers with exceptional performance or developmental needs, improve supplier communication, reduce risk and manage the partnership based on an analysis of reported data. FedEx not only has performance scorecards for their suppliers but has also developed a Web-based "reverse scorecard" that allows suppliers to provide constructive performance feedback to the company to enhance the customer–supplier relationship.[16] After all, it is not unusual that the best customers want to work with the best suppliers. Additionally, the best suppliers are commonly rewarded and recognized for their achievements. Supplier awards will be discussed later in this chapter.

Although price/cost is an important factor when selecting suppliers, other criteria such as technical expertise, lead times, environmental awareness and market knowledge must also be considered. In the electronics industry, which pioneered the Six Sigma revolution, quality is the prime supplier selection criteria due to its strategic importance. Thus quality and the ability of suppliers to bring new technologies and innovations to the table, rather than cost, are often the key selection drivers. A multicriteria approach is therefore needed to measure supplier performance. Examples of broad performance metrics are shown in Table 3.1.

Over the past several years, **total cost of ownership (TCO)**, a broad-based performance metric, has been widely discussed in the supply chain literature. As mentioned in Chapter 2, TCO is defined as "the combination of the purchase or acquisition price of a good or service and additional costs incurred before or after product or service

---

Table 3.1	**Examples of Supplier Performance Metrics**[17,18,19,20]

1. Cost/Price
- Competitive price
- Availability of cost breakdowns
- Productivity improvement/cost reduction programs
- Willingness to negotiate price
- Inventory cost
- Information cost
- Transportation cost
- Actual cost compared to: historical (standard) cost, target cost, cost-reduction goal, benchmark cost
- Extent of cooperation leading to improved cost

2. Quality
- Zero defects
- Statistical process controls
- Continuous process improvement
- Fit for use
- Corrective action program
- Documented quality program such as ISO 9000
- Warranty
- Actual quality compared to: historical quality, specification quality, target quality
- Quality improvement compared to: historical quality, quality-improvement goal
- Extent of cooperation leading to improved quality

3. Delivery
- Fast
- Reliable/on-time
- Defect free deliveries
- Actual delivery compared to promised delivery window (i.e., two days early to zero days late)
- Extent of cooperation leading to improved delivery

delivery". Costs are often grouped into **pretransaction**, **transaction** and **posttransaction costs**.[21] These three major cost categories are described as follows.

- *Pretransaction costs:* These costs are incurred prior to order and receipt of the purchased goods. Examples are the cost of certifying and training suppliers, investigating alternative sources of supply and delivery options for new suppliers.

Table 3.1	**Examples of Supplier Performance Metrics[17,18,19,20] (Continued)**

4. Responsiveness and Flexibility

- Responsiveness to customers
- Accuracy of record keeping
- Ability to work effectively with teams
- Responsiveness to changing situations
- Participation/success of supplier certification program
- Short-cycle changes in demand/flexible capacity
- Changes in delivery schedules
- Participation in new product development
- Solving problems
- Willingness of supplier to seek inputs regarding product/service changes
- Advance notification given by supplier as a result of product/service changes
- Receptiveness to partnering or teaming

5. Environment

- Environmentally responsible
- Environmental management system such as ISO 14000
- Extent of cooperation leading to improved environmental issues

6. Technology

- Proactive improvement using proven manufacturing/service technology
- Superior product/service design
- Extent of cooperation leading to improved technology

7. Business Metrics

- Reputation of supplier/leadership in the field
- Long-term relationship
- Quality of information sharing
- Financial strength such as Dun & Bradstreet's credit rating
- Strong customer support group
- Total cash flow
- Rate of return on investment
- Extent of cooperation leading to improved business processes and performance

8. Total Cost of Ownership

- Purchased products shipped cost-effectively
- Cost of special handling
- Additional supplier costs as the result of the buyer's scheduling and shipment needs
- Cost of defects, rework and problem solving associated with purchases

- *Transaction costs:* These costs include the cost of the goods/services and cost associated with placing and receiving the order. Examples are purchase price, preparation of orders and delivery costs.
- *Posttransaction costs:* These costs are incurred after the goods are in the possession of the company, agents or customers. Examples are field failures, company's goodwill/reputation, maintenance costs and warranty costs.

TCO provides a proactive approach for understanding costs and supplier performance leading to reduced costs. However, the challenge is to effectively identify the key cost drivers needed to determine the total cost of ownership.

Continuous Improvement

The process of evaluating suppliers based on a set of mutually agreed performance measures provides opportunities for continuous improvement. As discussed in Chapter 8, continuous improvement involves continuously making a series of small improvements over time, resulting in the elimination of waste in a system. Both buyers and suppliers must be *willing to continuously improve their capabilities in meeting customer requirements of cost, quality, delivery and technology.* Partners should not focus on merely correcting mistakes, but work proactively toward eliminating them completely. For continuous improvement to work, employees must first identify areas that are working to understand the improvements made. These improvements provide the basis for implementing improvements in other processes, which in turn will lead to even more success. In today's dynamic environment, staying ahead of change means that you have to practice continuous improvement. Companies must work with suppliers on continuous improvement programs to ensure that products and services are meeting customer requirements.

Key Points

It must be noted that developing supplier partnerships is not easy. All the factors mentioned above have to be in place for the supplier relationship to be successful. While in numerous instances supplier partnerships work well, there are also examples where the relationship did not turn out as expected. In 2007, Mattel pulled more than 18 million toys off the shelves due to product safety concerns.[22] A failure on the part of Mattel to properly monitor the quality of the goods they purchased from Chinese suppliers created a "moral hazard" within their supply chain. In China, production costs are increasing and intense pressures to reduce prices are making it more difficult for suppliers to maintain their profit margins. As a result, without a good quality verification program, it is easy for suppliers to compromise on quality and to deliver substandard products. The importance of supplier relationships cannot be overstated, and cultivating these relationships is an essential part of doing business in China. According to Ryan Finstad, director of operations at California-based supply chain solutions provider Cathay Solutions, "Companies that have long-standing relationships with their manufacturers have naturally become more lax over time. As these firms searched for ways to cut costs, they may have reduced or eliminated monitoring of manufacturers that had historically performed well."[23] However, the problem can be avoided if companies have better two-way communications, a quality assurance program in place, sound performance metrics and trust built into the relationship.

Supplier Evaluation and Certification

Only the best suppliers are targeted as partners. Companies want to develop partnerships with the best suppliers to leverage their expertise and technologies to create a competitive advantage. Learning more about how an organization's key suppliers are performing can lead to greater visibility, which can provide opportunities for further collaborative involvement in value-added activities. Many organizations are tracking product and service quality, on-time deliveries, customer service efforts and cost-control programs as part of the supplier rating system. This information can be used to develop supplier programs that will help eliminate problems or improve supply chain performance.

A supplier evaluation and certification process must be in place so that organizations can identify their best and most reliable suppliers. In addition, sourcing decisions are made based on facts and not perception of a supplier's capabilities. Providing frequent feedback on supplier performance can help organizations avoid major surprises and maintain good relationships. For example, Honeywell has developed a supplier portal, which allows "Honeywell's internal Integrated Supply Chain professionals to share information, interact/collaborate, and ultimately form closer relationships with Honeywell's external supply base."[24] In addition, the company has the Honeywell Supplier Scorecard Training module. The purpose of the scorecard is to communicate to Honeywell the supplier's overall performance in terms of quality (parts per million defective) and on-time delivery for the last month, last three months and last twelve months. [25] The website also enhances supplier relationships since the Web-based technology has resulted in improvements in efficiency and productivity for Honeywell and the suppliers because faster decisions can be made as a result of speedier transmission of information. The Global Perspective feature profiles Pitney Bowes and their streamlined spending capability.

Global Perspective	*Pitney Bowes Saves Millions with Streamlined Spending*

Through its mailstream technology, Pitney Bowes Inc. helps organizations manage the flow of information, mail and packages. To free working capital to meet its growth objectives, the firm had to streamline and automate its purchasing practices and gain visibility into its spending. Implementing a set of processes based on the SAP® Supplier Relationship Management application has saved costs in many ways. Customization is at a minimum in the solution, because 98.5% of requirements are satisfied "out of the box."

"SAP software provides a robust, integrated transaction platform for our requisition-to-payment process that has enabled us to realize a number of business benefits in sourcing and procurement."

Laura K. Taylor, Vice President Procurement Operations, Pitney Bowes Inc.

MAILSTREAM INDUSTRY LEADER UNIFIES PROCUREMENT PROCESSES

Once known as the postage meter company, Pitney Bowes Inc. has emerged through innovation and acquisitions as the leader in the fast-growing field of mailstream, helping customers through the entire process of creating, producing, distributing and managing mail, documents, and packages. Since 2002 Pitney Bowes has run its business with SAP® software, including the SAP ERP application and the business-to-business procurement functionality now found in the SAP Supplier Relationship Management (SAP SRM) application. This software served as the basis for process improvements that helped the company cut many kinds of costs, including spending on direct and indirect materials. But the firm knew it could save even more through improved supplier management, especially by unifying procurement processes across its business units. So it recently added the entire SAP SRM application, with functionality that enabled additional cost improvements and offered tighter integration with existing SAP applications.

STRICT RESTRICTIONS MINIMIZE CUSTOMIZATION

Pitney Bowes employed a number of implementation best practices, notably a requirement for very strict justification for any customization. This policy was so successful that the company satisfied 98.5% of its requirements with standard SAP software, a very high rate for a large firm with established business processes.

AUTOMATION, VISIBILITY AND TIGHTENED PROCESSES SAVE MILLIONS

To recognize labor savings, Pitney Bowes's IT experts used the new software to build 15 electronic catalogs for purchasing; employees now enter orders online instead of using paper-based processes. Pitney Bowes gained visibility into its global spend on a supplier-by-supplier basis, providing intelligence to build spend category strategies and leverage for negotiating enterprise-wide agreements. By broadly communicating the benefits of using these preferred vendors, the firm achieved over 80% compliance—greatly reducing maverick spending in these areas. Using the SAP NetWeaver® Business Intelligence (SAP NetWeaver BI) component, Pitney Bowes built functionalities to manage its suppliers for ontime delivery, cost, product quality and stakeholder satisfaction. This tracking also expedites sourcing projects by helping determine the most viable candidates to fulfill requirements. In invoice processing and payment, the original SAP implementation, along with process improvements and reporting enhancements utilizing SAP NetWeaver BI, has helped introduce efficiencies that halved the prevalence of aging invoices, which too often resulted in late fees and unhappy suppliers. Prompt payment discounts have replaced penalties. These supplier management improvements have helped Pitney Bowes accrue $250 million in spend reduction over the last five years. With the additional functionality that SAP SRM brings to the table helping to further automate preferred supplier management, requisitions and purchase order processing, the firm is saving even more through efficiency improvements and enterprise-wide spend leverage. "SAP software has provided an end-to-end requisition-to-pay platform, which has enabled us to realize the operational benefits and compliance requirements of an integrated process. SAP's solution set has rapidly evolved with the industry and has helped us to deliver process innovation through technological adoption," states Joseph Santamaria, VP enterprise business applications at Pitney Bowes.

EXPANDED USE OF SAP SRM WILL DELIVER EVEN MORE SAVINGS

Next Pitney Bowes will finalize its global rollout of SAP SRM to the entire company, expanding its user base by 1,500 people to a total of 4,500. It will also extend the application's use to automate contract life-cycle management, implement e-sourcing functionality for RFP creation and process management, integrate with user-friendly portal and desktop applications, and enable collaboration with suppliers. In these ways, SAP SRM will continue to help Pitney Bowes transform its highly decentralized purchasing model to an integrated global sourcing and procurement organization.

Source: "Pitney Bowes: Customer Success Profile"; available from www.sap.com/solutions/business-suite/srm/customers/index.epx.

Table 3.2	Criteria Used in Certification Programs[26]

- No incoming product lot rejections (e.g., less than 0.5 percent defective) for a specified time period
- No incoming non-product rejections (e.g., late delivery) for a specified time period
- No significant supplier production-related negative incidents for a specified time period
- ISO 9000/Q9000 certified or successfully passing a recent, on-site quality system evaluation
- Mutually agreed set of clearly specified quality performance measures
- Fully documented process and quality system with cost controls and continuous improvement capabilities
- Supplier's processes are stable and in control

One of the goals of evaluating suppliers is to determine if the supplier is performing according to the buyer's requirements. An extension of supplier evaluation is **supplier certification**, defined by the Institute of Supply Management as "an organization's process for evaluating the quality systems of key suppliers in an effort to eliminate incoming inspections."[27] The certification process implies a willingness on the part of customers and suppliers to share goals, commitments and risks to improve their relationships. This would involve making visits to observe the operations at the supplier organizations. For example, dirty bathrooms and messy shop floors could indicate that an emphasis on quality is lacking in the production facility. A supplier certification program also indicates long-term mutual commitment. For example, a certification program might provide incentives for suppliers to deliver parts directly to the point of use in the buyer firm, thus reducing costs associated with incoming inspection and storage of inventory.

Implementing an effective supplier certification program is critical to reducing the supplier base, building long-term relationships, reducing time spent on incoming inspections, improving delivery and responsiveness, recognizing excellence, developing a commitment to continuous improvement and improving overall performance. Supplier certification allows organizations to identify the suppliers who are most committed to creating and maintaining a partnership and who have the best capabilities. Table 3.2 presents criteria generally found in many certification programs.

The Weighted Criteria Evaluation System

One approach toward evaluating and certifying suppliers is to use the weighted criteria evaluation system described below:

1. Select the key dimensions of performance mutually acceptable to both customer and supplier.

2. Monitor and collect performance data.

3. Assign weights to each of the dimensions of performance based on their relative importance to the company's objectives. The weights for all dimensions must sum to 1.

4. Evaluate each of the performance measures on a rating between zero (fails to meet any intended purpose or performance) and 100 (exceptional in meeting intended purpose or performance).

5. Multiply the dimension ratings by their respective importance weights and then sum to get an overall weighted score.

6. Classify vendors based on their overall scores, for example:
   - Unacceptable (less than 50)—supplier dropped from further business
   - Conditional (between 50 and 70)—supplier needs development work to improve performance but may be dropped if performance continues to lag
   - Certified (between 70 and 90)—supplier meets intended purpose or performance
   - Preferred (greater than 90)—supplier will be considered for involvement in new product development and opportunities for more business
7. Audit and ongoing certification review.

An example of the above evaluation and certification process is shown in Table 3.3.

Federal-Mogul is an example of a company that uses a weighted scorecard to evaluate their suppliers. The company has a Global SupplyNet Scorecard website (www.federal-mogul.com/en/Suppliers/SupplyNet/Scorecard/) that provides the Supplier Rating Criteria and rates suppliers on three main categories, with the weights shown in parenthesis: quality (40 percent), delivery (40 percent) and supplier cost-saving suggestions (SCSS) (20 percent).The quality score is based on two equally weighted components: parts per million (ppm) defective and quality of supplier corrective action requests (SCARs) issued. The delivery score is computed as "line items received on time divided by the number of line items due by the supplier for the month." The total score ranges from 0 to 100. Suppliers are considered "preferred" if they score between 90 and 100. Preferred suppliers are those that Federal-Mogul will work with on new product development, approve for new business, and assist in maintaining a competitive position. An acceptable supplier rating is between 70 and 89. In this category, the supplier is required to provide a plan to Federal-Mogul on how to achieve preferred status. A score of 0 to 69 means that the supplier has a developmental supplier rating. Here, Federal-Mogul "requires corrective action if the supplier is rated at this level for three consecutive months during the calendar year" (see Table 3.4).

Today, external certifications such as ISO 9000 and ISO 14000 have gained popularity globally as a natural extension of an organization's internal supplier evaluation and certification program. Let's briefly discuss these next.

Table 3.3	Supplier Scorecard Used for the XYZ Company			
PERFOMANCE MEASURE	**RATING**	**× WEIGHT**	**=**	**FINAL VALUE**
Technology	80	0.10		8.00
Quality	90	0.25		22.50
Responsiveness	95	0.15		14.25
Delivery	90	0.15		13.50
Cost	80	0.15		12.00
Environmental	90	0.05		4.50
Business	90	0.15		13.50
Total score		1.00 ✓		88.25

Note: Based on the total score of 88.25, the XYZ Company is considered a certified supplier.

Table 3.4	Federal-Mogul's Supplier Rating Criteria

Road to Supplier Performance Excellence
Supplier Rating Criteria Overview

Introduction
Federal-Mogul Corporation uses the following criteria to rate the performance of our suppliers for all Federal-Mogul manufacturing and distribution facilities.

Purpose
Identification of continuous improvement and cost-savings opportunities
Promote and encourage improved communication on performance issues
Provide objective data for use in supplier management and sourcing decisions
Recognition of exceptional supplier performance

Terminology
Category: These are the main groupings by which suppliers will be measured. The initial set of categories for which measurements will be compiled are Delivery, Quality and Supplier Cost-Saving Suggestions (SCSS). Each category has assigned weighting, which is rolled into the overall score. Category scores range from 0 to 100 points.

Overall Rating: The Overall Rating is a description of the performance level of supply as viewed by Federal-Mogul. Scores for each category are multiplied by the weighting, and the summation entails the overall score for the supplier. Overall Ratings associated to the overall score are as follows:

Overall Rating Weighted Point Score:
Preferred: 90 to 100
Acceptable: 70 to 89
Developmental: 0 to 69

"Preferred" Supplier Rating:
1. Federal-Mogul will work with these suppliers on new product development.
2. Federal-Mogul will assist these suppliers in maintaining a competitive position.
3. Federal-Mogul will maintain a listing of "Approved for New Business" suppliers.

"Acceptable" Supplier Rating:
1. Federal-Mogul will require a plan from the supplier outlining how to achieve preferred status.
2. Federal-Mogul will monitor supplier improvement.

"Developmental" Supplier Rating:
1. Federal-Mogul requires corrective action if the supplier is rated at this level for three consecutive months during the calendar year.
2. The supplier must provide plans to improve performance to an acceptable level.
3. Federal-Mogul will look at alternative sources if performance does not improve.

Supplier Rating Qualifications: The rating system will entail any supplier deemed appropriate by the Federal-Mogul Manufacturing/Distribution Purchasing Team.

Supplier Scores and Category Weighting

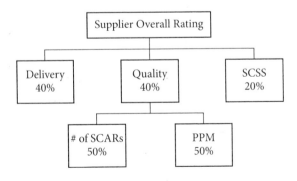

As illustrated above, there are three main categories by which suppliers are measured:

> Delivery 40 percent
> Quality 40 percent
> Supplier Cost-Saving Suggestions (SCSS) 20 percent

A value is displayed in each category on the Global Scorecard for every Federal-Mogul facility receiving product(s) or service(s) from the supplier.

Quality Category: Rating Criteria
The Quality category is comprised of two components:

> Parts Per Million (PPM) 50 percent
> Quantity of supplier corrective action requests (SCARs) issued 50 percent

PPM is based on SCARs. Both the number of SCARs and PPM are reported monthly. SCAR responsiveness does not factor into the supplier's Overall Score. Currently, it is only displayed on the Scorecard.

PPM	COUNT POINTS	# OF SCARS	POINTS
0	100	0	100
1 – 25	90	1	70
26 – 50	80	2 – 4	40
51 – 100	60	5+	0
101 – 250	40		
251 – 500	20		
501+	0		

Delivery Category: Rating Criteria
On-time delivery: The delivery score is based on the average percentage across using plants for the current month. On-time delivery percentage has a window of one day early and zero days late to the due date and +/- 5 percent of order quantity. The on-time delivery percentage is determined by line items received on time divided by the number of line items due by the supplier for the month.

Consignment programs receive a 100 percent delivery percentage unless a stockout is caused. The score is reduced by 10 percent for each day of the stockout.

SCSS (Supplier Cost-Saving Suggestions): Rating Criteria
5 percent target performance: SCSS are targeted at 5 percent of the year's forecasted dollars spent. The supplier must make SCSS submittals to the plant or the commodity manager.

SCORE	SCSS MEASUREMENT
100	5% and above
85	4% to 4.9%
70	3% to 3.9%
40	2% to 2.9%
20	1% to 1.9%
0	0.9% and below

Source: http://www.federal-mogul.com/en/Suppliers/SupplyNet/Scorecard/ Reproduced with permission from Federal-Mogul.

ISO 9000

In 1987 the global network of national standards institutes called the International Organization for Standardization (ISO) developed **ISO 9000**, a series of management and quality assurance standards in design, development, production, installation and service. The European Union in 1992 adopted a plan that recognized ISO 9000 as a third-party certification; the result is that many European companies prefer suppliers with ISO 9000 certifications. Thus, U.S. companies wanting to sell in the global marketplace are compelled to seek ISO 9000 certifications. Note that while we refer to this family of quality standards as ISO 9000, their most commonly recognizable name, the quality standards have actually been revised a number of times over the years and most recently are called ISO 9001:2008. To minimize confusion, we'll stick with the original name of ISO 9000.

There are eight quality management principles on which the quality management system standards of the ISO 9000 series are based:[28]

- *Principle 1—Customer focus:* Organizations depend on their customers and therefore should understand current and future customer needs, should meet customer requirements and strive to exceed customer expectations.
- *Principle 2—Leadership:* Leaders establish unity of purpose and direction of the organization. They should create and maintain the internal environment in which people can become fully involved in achieving the organization's objectives.
- *Principle 3—Involvement of people:* People at all levels are the essence of an organization, and their full involvement enables their abilities to be used for the organization's benefit.
- *Principle 4—Process approach:* A desired result is achieved more efficiently when activities and related resources are managed as a process.
- *Principle 5—System approach to management:* Identifying, understanding and managing interrelated processes as a system contributes to the organization's effectiveness and efficiency in achieving its objectives.
- *Principle 6—Continual improvement:* Continual improvement of the organization's overall performance should be a permanent objective of the organization.
- *Principle 7—Factual approach to decision making:* Effective decisions are based on the analysis of data and information.
- *Principle 8—Mutually beneficial supplier relationships:* An organization and its suppliers are interdependent and a mutually beneficial relationship enhances the ability of both to create value.

The ISO Survey 2008[29] shows that 982,832 ISO 9000 certificates were awarded in 176 countries in 2008. This represents an increase of 49 percent compared to 2004. In the U.S., 32,400 certificates were issued in 2008, representing 4.2 percent of the worldwide total. Not surprising, China had the largest number of ISO 9000 certificates in 2008—224,616. The ANSI (American National Standards Institute)/ISO/ASQC (American Society for Quality Control) Q9000 standards are the U.S. equivalent of ISO 9000. Obtaining the ISO 9000 certification however, provides verification to a global audience that the company has an established quality management system in place.

ISO 14000

In 1996, **ISO 14000**, a family of international standards for environmental management, was first introduced. In 2004, it was revised to make the standards easier to understand and emphasized compliance and compatibility with ISO 9000 for businesses that wanted to combine their environmental and quality management systems (and again for simplicity, we will stick with the term ISO 14000, even though the actual number has changed slightly due to the revisions). Companies that implemented ISO 14000 benefitted from cost savings (conserving materials, reduced water and energy use), better public image and decreased liability due to reduced waste cleanup costs. According to the 2008 survey conducted by ISO, there were 4,974 ISO 14000 certificates issued in the U.S. in 2008, representing only 2.6 percent of the 188,815 certificates issued globally in 155 countries.[30] According to the same study, China and Japan were the top two countries obtaining ISO 14000 certificates. As shown here, the annual number of ISO 14000 certifications issued pales in comparison with those for ISO 9000. The benefits of investing in an **Environmental Management System (EMS)** based on ISO14000 standards include reduced energy and other resource consumption, decreased environmental liability and risk, reduced waste and pollution and improved community goodwill. As such, investment in environmental management systems is likely to increase in the future. Additionally, as more organizations are certified in ISO 14000, they are likely to pass this requirement on to their suppliers in the future.

ISO's standards for quality and environmental management systems are playing an increasingly positive role in the world in the following areas:[31]

- a unifying base for global businesses and supply chains—such as the automotive and oil and gas sectors
- a technical support for regulation—as, for example, in the medical devices sector
- a tool for major new economic players to increase their participation in global supply chains, in export trade and in business process outsourcing
- a tool for regional integration—as shown by their adoption by new or potential members of the European Union
- the rise of services in the global economy—nearly 32 percent of ISO 9000 certificates and 29 percent of ISO 14000 certificates in 2007 went to organizations in the service sectors, and
- the transfer of good operating practices to developing countries and transition economies.

Supplier Development

Supplier development is defined as "any activity that a buyer undertakes to improve a supplier's performance and/or capabilities to meet the buyer's short- and/or long-term supply needs."[32] Supplier development requires financial and human resource investments by both partners and includes a wide range of activities such as training of the supplier's personnel, investing in the supplier's operations and ongoing performance assessment. As companies outsource more and more parts, a larger portion of costs lie outside the company in a supply chain, and it becomes increasingly difficult to achieve further cost savings internally. One way out of this dilemma is for companies to work with their suppliers to lower the total cost of materials purchased. Companies that are able to leverage their supply base to impact their total cost structure will have a competitive advantage in their markets.

A seven-step approach to supplier development is outlined below:[33]

1. *Identify critical goods and services.* Assess the relative importance of the goods and services from a strategic perspective. Goods and services that are purchased in high volume, do not have good substitutes or have limited sources of supply are considered strategic supplies.

2. *Identify critical suppliers not meeting performance requirements.* Suppliers of strategic supplies not currently meeting minimum performance in quality, on-time delivery, cost, technology or cycle time are targets for supplier development initiatives.

3. *Form a cross-functional supplier development team.* Next, the buyer must develop an internal cross-functional team and arrive at a clear agreement for the supplier development initiatives.

4. *Meet with top management of suppliers.* The buyer's cross-functional team meets with the suppliers' top management to discuss details of strategic alignment, supplier performance expectations and measurement, a time-frame for improvement and ongoing professionalism.

5. *Rank supplier development projects.* After the supplier development opportunities have been identified, they are evaluated in terms of feasibility, resource and time requirements, supply base alternatives and expected return on investment. The most promising development projects are selected.

6. *Define the details of the buyer-supplier agreement.* After consensus has been reached on the development project rankings, the buyer and supplier representatives jointly decide on the performance metrics to be monitored such as percent improvement in quality, delivery and cycle time.

7. *Monitor project status and modify strategies.* To ensure continued success, management must actively monitor progress, promote exchange of information and revise the development strategies as conditions warrant.

Intel's Supplier Continuous Quality Improvement (SCQI) program is a "corporate wide program that utilizes critical Intel supplier management tools and processes to drive continuous improvements in a supplier's overall performance and business."[34] Their SCQI program was started in the 1980s with the objective of improving supplier quality and minimizing the time needed to inspect incoming products. According to Intel, the SCQI program accomplishes the following[35]:

- Establishes aligned goals, indicators and metrics
- Enables benchmarking of supplier's performance
- Identifies potential quality issues before they impact Intel
- Drives supplier's agility and ability to provide leading-edge products and services
- Matures critical Intel-supplier relationships
- Encourages collaborative agreements, team problem resolution and two-way continuous learning
- Encourages continuous improvement throughout the year
- Provides data to support supplier recognition

With the SCQI program, Intel was able to reap valuable benefits from their suppliers. Additionally, as the quality of the suppliers' products improves, greater opportunities exist for making further improvements.

By tracking supplier performance over time, Honeywell is able to observe trends and to catch problems early. Honeywell has implemented their Six Sigma Plus program aimed at eliminating variations in processes to meet required specifications with no more than 3.4 parts per million defective and to apply lean manufacturing techniques to eliminate waste and to synchronize suppliers' activities. At Honeywell, Six Sigma

Plus is an "overall strategy to accelerate improvements in all processes, products and services, and reduce the punitive cost of poor quality through elimination of waste and reduction of defects and variations."[36]

In summary, it is critical that an organization has an active supplier development program. The program should be managed such that it can meet both current and future needs. With a proactive supplier development program, suppliers are forced to stay on top of today's dynamic environment, so that customers are not stuck with products or services that are not leading edge.

Supplier Recognition Programs

While a large percentage of companies track supplier performance, only about half recognize excellent performance with supplier awards and appreciation banquets. Today, it is not sufficient just to reward your best suppliers with more business; companies need to recognize and celebrate the achievements of their best suppliers. As award-winning suppliers, they serve as role models for a firm's other suppliers. Boeing understands that supplier performance excellence is critical to its success. The company's Performance Excellence Award and Supplier of the Year Award are presented annually to recognize "suppliers who achieve the high performance standards necessary to meet customer expectations and remain competitive in the global economy."[37] The winners, selected from more than 12,000 active global suppliers, have been located in Germany, India, Japan and the United States, and are judged on "quality, delivery performance, cost, environmental initiatives, customer service and technical expertise."[38] Ray Conner, Boeing enterprise leader of Supplier Management and vice president and general manager of Supply Chain Management and Operations said, "Boeing and our suppliers are more interconnected now than ever before—combining our talents and capabilities to create the most innovative products and services for our customers and the aerospace industry worldwide."[39]

As part of Intel's SCQI Program (see discussion in the preceding section), there are three recognition awards: Certified Supplier Award (CSA), Preferred Quality Supplier (PQS) Award and Supplier Continuous Quality Improvement (SCQI) Award. The CSA is given to suppliers who consistently meet Intel's expectations and have a proven commitment to continuous improvement. Intel's PQS award is for outstanding commitment to quality, excellent performance and excellence at meeting and exceeding high expectations and tough performance goals. The SCQI Award, which is the most prestigious of Intel's three recognition awards, is given to suppliers who consistently perform at world-class levels, provide outstanding strategic contribution and deliver cost reduction. Nikon Precision Equipment Company is a recent recipient of the SCQI award, and Kazuo Ushida, Nikon's president, said, "We set a goal to achieve Intel's highest supplier quality designation. We were awarded the Preferred Quality Supplier (PQS) award in 2007 and now have received the SCQI award for 2008. Nikon is honored to be recognized by Intel as an SCQI Supplier, which reflects our commitment to continuous support of Intel's technology needs, flawless ramp support and systematic improvements in equipment availability. This is a credit to our worldwide Nikon team and to Intel for their continued support."[40]

Hormel Food Corporation's No. 1 Award program differs from other programs because they only give awards once every five years. Hormel gave out its first award in 1996 for suppliers whose relationships span from 1991 to 1995. The next award will be presented in 2011 for 2006 to 2010. To qualify for the No. 1 Award, a supplier must have met the following criteria:[41]

- Have a Supplier Rating Index of 98 percent or better in the fourth calendar quarter of the reporting year.
- The average of the five-year Supplier Rating Index must be equal to or greater than 98 percent.
- Must be a recipient of the Spirit of Excellence Award—an annual award given by Hormel Foods—for a minimum of four times over the past five consecutive years.
- The trend of the Supplier Rating Index must be even or positive over the five-year period.
- Must meet certain requirements as far as number of products sold by the supplier to Hormel Foods; dollars of exposure and deliveries to Hormel Foods; number of Hormel Foods locations serviced; and stage of Hormel Foods' Quality Improvement Process.

To receive the Spirit of Excellence Award, suppliers must achieve a minimum Supplier Rating Index score of 92 over a twelve-month period. The criteria for the Supplier Rating Index include an ability to meet requirements, make timely deliveries, provide accurate administrative support and maintain inventories. Additional criteria such as customer support, awareness of environmental concerns, and sales representative performance are considered but are not a requirement for the award. Melanie A. Faust, director of purchasing at Hormel Foods, said, "The Spirit of Excellence Awards [is] a great way to thank our suppliers for helping Hormel Foods continue to build upon our heritage of innovation and quality. Each year, we look forward to presenting this award as a way of showing appreciation to our suppliers."[42]

Supplier Relationship Management

Supplier relationship management (SRM) has garnered increasing attention among firms actively practicing supply chain management. SRM is an umbrella term that includes "extended procurement processes, such as sourcing analytics (e.g., spend analysis), sourcing execution, procurement execution, payment and settlement and—closing the feedback loop—supplier scorecarding and performance monitoring."[43] According to global consultant Accenture, SRM "encompasses a broad suite of capabilities that facilitate collaboration, sourcing, transaction execution and performance monitoring between an organization and its trading partners. SRM leverages the latest technology capabilities to integrate and enhance supplier oriented processes along the supply chain such as design-to-source, source-to-contract and procure-to-pay."[44] In addition, SRM "strives to help companies determine their most important suppliers. It also reveals how best to focus time and energy to create and maintain more effective, strategic relationships with suppliers, thus maximizing the positive impact the supply base has on costs, quality, delivery and innovation within an organization."[45] In a nutshell, SRM involves streamlining the processes and communication between the buyer and supplier and using software applications that enable these processes to be managed more efficiently and effectively. Table 3.5 lists several SRM software companies and some of their customers.

Definitions of what is included in these SRM software modules vary widely, with Texas-based software company i2 Technologies claiming to have coined the SRM term in collaboration with AMR Research. The success of e-procurement, which has a

Table 3.5	Examples of Companies Offering SRM Software

EcVision (www.ecvision.com/)

Customers: JC Penney, MAST Industries, Inc. (buying arm for The Limited family of stores including Express, Lerner New York, Lane Bryant, Limited Stores, Structure and Henri Bendel)

JDA Software Group, Inc. (www.jda.com/)

Customers: Samsung Electronics Company, Nippon Steel Corporation, Dana Corporation, Ashland Inc., eLSG.SkyChefs, Airbus, PEMSTAR Inc., Hitachi Global Storage Technologies, Honeywell

(Acquisition of Manugistics in July 2006; i2 Technologies in January 2010)

Oracle (www.oracle.com/)

Customers: Dartmouth-Hitchcock Medical Center, Gwinnett County Public Schools, Sprint, The Hackett Group, City of Los Angeles

(Acquisition of PeopleSoft in 2005)

SAP (www.sap.com/)

Customers: Lockheed Martin, Mercedes-Benz Espana (Spain), Deutsche Bank, Kimberly Clark, Proctor and Gamble, Royal Dutch/Shell

SAS Institute (www.sas.com/)

Customers: BayerCropScience, Schneider Electric.

SupplyWorks (www.supplyworks.com/)

Customers: BorgWarner Morse TEC, Ingersoll-Rand, Associated Spring

predominantly internal focus, created the need for SRM solutions for managing the supply side of an organization's supply chain. SRM software automates the exchange of information among several layers of relationships that are complex and too time-consuming to manage manually and results in improved procurement efficiency, lower business costs, real-time visibility, faster communication between buyer and seller and enhanced supply chain collaboration.

Many organizations are investing in SRM software modules due to the wealth of information that can be derived from these systems. SRM software can organize supplier information and provide answers to questions such as:

- Who are our current suppliers? Are they the right set of suppliers?
- Who are our best suppliers and what are their competitive rankings?
- What are our suppliers' performances with respect to on-time delivery, quality and costs?
- Can we consolidate our buying to achieve greater scale economies?
- Do we have consistency in suppliers and performance across different locations and facilities?
- What goods/services do we purchase?
- What purchased parts can be reused in new designs?

According to global software developer SAS, an effective SRM solution "provides real supplier intelligence—the ability to understand and predict the value of supplier relationships—through an enterprisewide, integrated view of a company's suppliers and the commodities or services they provide. It enables businesses to collect, analyze and leverage all aspects of their supplier data and purchasing history, providing vital insights into the supply base and purchasing history."[46]

In general, SRM software varies by vendors in terms of capabilities offered. AMR Research has identified five key tenets of an SRM system:[47]

- **Automation** of transactional processes between an organization and its suppliers.
- **Integration** that provides a view of the supply chain that spans multiple departments, processes and software applications for internal users and external partners.
- **Visibility** of information and process flows in and between organizations. Views are customized by role and aggregated via a single portal.
- **Collaboration** through information sharing and suppliers' ability to input information directly into an organization's supply chain information system.
- **Optimization** of processes and decision-making through enhanced analytical tools such as data warehousing and online analytical processing (OLAP) tools with the migration toward more dynamic optimization tools in the future.

There are two types of SRM: transactional and analytic. **Transactional SRM** enables an organization to track supplier interactions such as order planning, order payment and returns. The volume of transactions involved may result in independent systems maintained by geographic region or business lines. Transactional SRM tends to focus on short-term reporting and is event driven, focusing on such questions as: What did we buy yesterday? What supplier did we buy from? What was the cost of the purchase? On the other hand, analytic SRM allows the company to analyze the complete supplier base. The analysis provides answers to questions such as: Which suppliers should the company develop long-term relationships with? Which suppliers would make the company more profitable? Analytic SRM enables more difficult and important questions about supplier relationships. Thus, we can see that transactional SRM addresses tactical issues such as order size, whereas analytic SRM focuses on long-term procurement strategies. With analytic SRM, an organization can assess where it was yesterday, where it stands today and where it wants to go in the future to meet its strategic purchasing goals.

The challenges in any SRM software implementation are assembling all the data needed for an SRM application to work and employee training. For example, analysis of supplier information requires access to applications containing data about suppliers, as well as enterprise resource planning (ERP), material requirements planning (MRP), accounting and existing supplier information databases. Before SRM implementation, buyers typically spend 10 percent of their time on supplier relationship development, 40 percent on expediting and 50 percent on order processing/tracking. After SRM implementation, the buyer's time allocation is estimated to be 50 percent on collaborative planning, 30 percent on supplier relationship development, 10 percent on expediting and 10 percent on exception management.

Until recent years, purchasing professionals did not have the right technologies to help them accomplish their jobs effectively. Automating procurement activities can lead to significant cost savings as buyers move toward managing processes by exception. This effectively frees buyers to focus on more strategic and value-added activities such as collaborative planning. In addition, purchasing professionals can work effectively on maximizing the return on their relationships with suppliers. Greater procurement visibility from using SRM software also translates into smoother processes, faster cycle times, reduced new product development, improved time to market, streamlined purchasing and reduced inventory costs. The supplier relationship management application at Siemens is profiled in the e-Business Connection feature.

e-Business Connection

Supplier Relationship Management at Siemens Global Shared Services

Siemens AG is one of the leading global players in the energy, healthcare and industrial sectors. The company wanted to centralize and automate procurement to improve visibility, increase efficiencies and drive down costs. To do this, Siemens Global Shared Services implemented the SAP® Supplier Relationship Management application as a shared service, allowing users across the enterprise to access centralized e-procurement functionality.

"With the SAP Supplier Relationship Management application supporting e-procurement as a shared service, we've successfully reduced process costs, increased productivity, and optimized overall spend."

Drake Paben, Manager of Procurement Processes and Tools,
Siemens Global Shared Services

CENTRALIZING THE PROCUREMENT PROCESS AT SIEMENS

From manufacturing small electronic appliances to building power stations, Siemens AG is a global powerhouse. But its size provided a challenge for efficient procurement. For the most part, Siemens relied on decentralized procurement and manual processes that impeded transparency and increased costs. The company had to fight maverick buying and enforce contract compliance. It also struggled to gain insight into buying patterns, which made it difficult to optimize spend. Siemens is a longtime SAP customer; groups within the company had been successful doing e-procurement with local implementations of the SAP® Supplier Relationship Management (SAP SRM) application. After interviewing these groups to discover best practices and analyzing requirements throughout the company, Siemens Global Shared Services decided to extend this success across the enterprise.

The objective was to implement SAP SRM as part of a shared service approach to procurement, allowing employees throughout the company to access centralized purchasing functionality.

KEEPING IT SIMPLE

Executive leadership at Siemens threw its full weight behind the project and communicated effectively to emphasize its importance. To ensure adoption, the company streamlined implementation and designed simplicity into the purchasing approval process. This meant relying on training to bring users up to speed rather than customization to accommodate diverging preferences. Siemens involved users early on, providing training in a variety of formats.

MORE NEGOTIATING POWER

Today, Siemens enjoys a globally available e-procurement process that increases efficiency, enforces compliance and optimizes spend. Automated approval workflow minimizes maverick buying. Standardization and integration into the SAP ERP application ensures that all data is captured and stored for tracking and analysis, yielding greater insight into spend patterns. With increased data transparency and greater ease in shifting spend to preferred suppliers, Siemens now negotiates from a position of strength, able to consolidate spend with specific suppliers and negotiate larger discounts. Siemens' suppliers, such as MSC Industrial Supply Co. Inc., see the benefits as well. Today the supplier (also an SAP partner) manages its high volume of orders with Siemens via electronic data interchange (EDI), creating efficiencies on both sides of the equation.

LOWER PROCESS COSTS, HIGH PRODUCTIVITY

For both Siemens and its preferred suppliers, the SRM platform is a key enabler of procurement automation. The implementation of SAP SRM has resulted in a 20% reduction in overall process costs.

Centralizing the shared services model and automating the entire procurement process has helped increase productivity, doubling the number of purchasing transactions per employee without increasing the number of hours worked. Electronic catalogs and automated approval workflows allow for a "touchless" purchase order and self-service ordering, similar to shopping on the Internet. Suppliers benefit from having a complete electronic and real-time ordering interface with Siemens. Orders, confirmations and invoices are exchanged electronically, streamlining the ordering process and improving order-to-receipt response times by 50%. A centralized help desk for all commercial and technical inquiries was critical to the success of the program and its adoption by the procurement community. Based on this positive experience, Siemens is now evaluating additional functionality within SAP SRM as part of ongoing efforts to improve supplier relationships, drive down procurement costs and compete even more effectively on the global stage.

Source: "Siemens Global Shared Services"; available from www.sap.com/solutions/business-suite/srm/customers/index.epx. Used with permission of SAP.

SUMMARY

Over the past two decades we have seen the buyer-supplier relationship evolve from an arms-length/adversarial approach to one favoring the development of long-term partnerships. Significant competitive advantage can be achieved by organizations working closely with their suppliers. Without a shared vision, mutual benefits and top management commitment, partnerships are likely to be short-lived. Other ingredients necessary for developing and managing lasting supplier relationships are trust, creating personal relationships, effective change management, sharing of information and using performance metrics to create superior capabilities. Mutually agreeable measures to monitor supplier performance provide the basis for continuous improvement to enhance supplier quality, cost and delivery. Supplier certification ensures that buyers continue to work with their best suppliers to improve cost, quality, delivery and new product development to gain a competitive advantage. Finally, supplier relationship management software automates the exchange of information and allows for improved efficiency and effectiveness in managing supplier relationships and improving performance. Organizations that successfully implement supplier relationship management can improve quality, reduce cost, access new technologies from their suppliers, increase speed-to-market, reduce risk and achieve high performance.

KEY TERMS

analytic SRM, 94

automation, 94

collaboration, 94

environmental management
    system (EMS), 89

integration, 94

ISO 9000, 87

ISO 14000, 88

optimization, 94

pretransaction, transaction
    and posttransaction
    costs, 80

supplier certification, 84

supplier development, 89

supplier relationship
    management (SRM), 92

total cost of ownership
    (TCO), 79

transactional SRM, 94

visibility, 94

DISCUSSION QUESTIONS

1. Why should an organization be concerned with supplier relationships?

2. Compare and contrast the arm's-length or adversarial approach to the partnership approach to building customer-supplier relationships.

3. How can an organization manage its suppliers effectively?

4. What are the key factors that contribute to a lasting buyer-supplier partnership?

5. It has often been pointed out that 60 percent of strategic alliances fail. What are the reasons for this?

6. What are the criteria used in evaluating a supplier?

7. Discuss how an organization develops a supplier evaluation and certification program.

8. Why should an organization invest in supplier development programs? What are the challenges of supplier development activities?

9. What are the benefits of ISO 9000 certification?

10. Are environmental concerns impacting purchasing decisions? What are the benefits of ISO 14000 certification?

11. Research ISO's website (www.iso.ch) and discuss the growth of ISO 9000 and 14000 certifications by regions of the world such as Africa/West Asia, Central and South America, North America, Europe, Far East and Australia/New Zealand.

12. What are the key capabilities of supplier relationship management software?

13. Why do organizations have supplier awards programs?

14. Why do organizations use supplier certification? What are its benefits?

15. What are the similarities and differences in capabilities of SRM software offered by i2, Oracle and SAP?

16. What are the advantages of using SRM solutions to manage suppliers?

17. What are the differences between transactional and analytic SRM?

18. **Discussion Problem:** The Margo Manufacturing Company is performing an annual evaluation of one of its suppliers, the Mimi Company. Bo, purchasing manager of the Margo Manufacturing Company, has collected the following information.

PERFORMANCE CRITERIA	SCORE	WEIGHT
Technology	85	0.10
Quality	95	0.25
Responsive	90	0.15
Delivery	80	0.15
Cost	90	0.20
Environment	75	0.05
Business	95	0.10
Total score		1.00

A score based on a scale of 0 (unsatisfactory) to 100 (excellent) has been assigned for each performance category considered critical in assessing the supplier. Different weights are assigned to each of the performance criteria based on its relative importance. How would you evaluate the Mimi Company's performance as a supplier?

Chapter 4

ETHICAL AND SUSTAINABLE SOURCING

*Starbucks bought 385 million pounds of coffee in 2008. Seventy-seven percent of that—
295 million pounds worth—was responsibly grown and ethically traded, meeting
Starbucks Shared Planet™ ethical sourcing principles for coffee.[1]*

*Each year roughly 32 million acres of forestland—an area the size of Louisiana—are
lost to logging and agricultural conversion. And during the next four decades, the
human population is expected to grow from 6.8 billion to more than 9 billion, putting
even greater pressure on forests around the world. These statistics prove that it has
never been more important to manage our remaining natural resources wisely.[2]*

Learning Objectives

After completing this chapter, you should be able to

- Understand and appreciate the trends in ethical and sustainable sourcing.
- Define and describe the terms fair trade products, green purchasing, social sustainability, supply base rationalization, VMI, supplier co-location, and collaborative negotiations.
- Describe how ethical and sustainable sourcing strategies are developed and implemented.
- Understand the use of environmental supplier certifications.
- Define outsourcing and how it differs from purchasing.
- Discuss the importance of developing strategic alliances.
- Define benchmarking and discuss how it is used in strategic sourcing.
- Understand the benefits of using 3PL suppliers.

Chapter Outline

Ethical and Sustainable Sourcing Defined

Developing Ethical and Sustainable
  Sourcing Strategies

Supply Base Rationalization Programs

Ethical and Sustainable Supplier
  Certification Programs

Outsourcing Products and Services

Early Supplier Involvement

Strategic Alliance Development

Use of e-Procurement Systems

Rewarding Supplier Performance

Benchmarking Successful Sourcing Practices

Using Third-Party Supply Chain
  Management Services

Assessing and Improving the Firm's Own Sourcing
  Function

Summary

Supply Chain Management in Action — *Sustainable Sourcing at Bon Appetit*

Bon Appetit provides café and catering services to corporations, universities and specialty venues in 28 states around the U.S. The company is devoted to being a leader in socially responsible food sourcing and business practices. So far, the company has been awarded with numerous distinctions from the Ecological Society of America, the Humane Society of the United States, the Food Alliance Keeper of the Vision Award and many others.

Bon Appetit was founded by leaders firmly committed to giving back to the community and following self-imposed, socially responsible values in every aspect of their business. The company was founded in 1987 and quickly gained a reputation for serving locally grown and organic food that tasted great and was not overly expensive.

How does a company with more than 400 cafés all over the country manage to adhere to policies that call for local sourcing and only working with ethical, socially responsible suppliers on such a large-scale basis? "Bon Appetit has always been decentralized and locally based," says Cary Wheeland, southern California regional vice president for the company.

The Community Alliance with Family Farmers (CAFF) in Davis, California, has partnered with Bon Appetit since the summer of 2006 to bring fresh, local produce to as many Bon Appetit cafés as possible. Anya Fernald, program director of CAFF's Buy Fresh, Buy Local campaign, the Growers Collaborative and the Farm-to-School program, says that Bon Appetit has been a key player in furthering awareness of local farming benefits.

In each café, Bon Appetit chefs are given freedom to create their own menus, and this affords them the opportunity to work with local farmers and meat producers who they meet personally through local farmers' markets or family farm advocacy organizations, such as CAFF, and make their own decisions about what to serve based on seasonal availability. A company-wide initiative dubbed Farm to Fork encourages chefs to buy regional and seasonal products from local farmers within a 150-mile radius.

While many food management companies would charge higher prices for local or organic foods, Bon Appetit officials claim its sustainable purchasing fits into its existing business model. They say that buying directly from farmers and artisans helps keep more money in the producers' pockets, rather than paying a middleman, and still offer reasonable prices. The goal is to keep profits reinvested in the local community rather than with a distant employer.

The company takes its sourcing a step further by actively boycotting purveyors who do not support farm workers' rights, and only purchasing seafood from suppliers that follow the Monterey Bay Aquarium's Seafood Watch guidelines to support sustainable fish populations.

In a July 2007 letter, Bon Appetit urged its 30 chicken and turkey suppliers to move toward a more humane slaughter method called controlled atmosphere killing (CAK) that experts say causes less suffering than traditional slaughter methods.

Source: Cooling, L., "An Appetite for Sustainability," *Inside Supply Management*®, V. 19, No. 2, 2008, pp. 32. Copyright © 2008 by the Institute for Supply Management™. Reprinted by permission.

Introduction

As you have read in Chapters 2 and 3 of this text, purchasing, sourcing or supply management departments are increasingly seen as highly valued, strategic contributors to their organizations because of their ability to impact product design and quality, cost of goods sold, manufacturing cycle time, and hence profitability and competitive position. Another area of concern has slowly been coming into play for purchasing departments over the past five to ten years: the use of ethical and sustainable sourcing practices. Global population growth, increasing environmental awareness, consumers' desires for better corporate responsibility, and declining worldwide levels of natural resources have combined to place unprecedented pressures on the abilities of company personnel to effectively manage firms' supply chains. Additionally, as world economies have floundered recently, firms are squeezing as much cost out of their operations as possible to survive. Thus, as never before, purchasing departments are in a position to have a tremendous impact on their companies' and their supply chains' costs and reputations through use of ethical and sustainable sourcing practices, which include a number of activities discussed in this chapter.

The influence of the purchasing, sourcing, or supply management department both within the organization and outside its boundaries is quite unique, in that it interacts with internal and external customers and suppliers; internal design, production, finance, marketing, and accounting personnel; and also the firm's executive managers. As companies move toward taking a more proactive role in managing their supply chains, purchasing departments are increasingly seen as one of the primary designers and facilitators of important inward- and outward-facing sourcing policies. These policies might include the formation of ethical practices such as in Starbucks' ethical sourcing principles, green sourcing policies as shown in the Supply Chain Management in Action feature, or sustainable natural resource usage policies to reduce deforestation.

The global economic recession of the past few years has indeed hastened many organizations' plans to institute supply chain management strategies to reduce costs, delivery cycle times, and carbon footprints, while improving quality, customer service, and ethical reputations, with the ultimate goals of improving competitiveness, market share, and long-term financial performance. Indeed, the increasing number of global competitors; demands by customers for companies to become more ethically and environmentally focused; the rising costs of fuel and materials; and the desire to deliver more innovative products more frequently and cheaply than competitors have also combined to place added pressures on firms to achieve optimal performance in global supply chain management.

Today, these trends have become the drivers of strategic sourcing and supply chain management initiatives. Taking the notion of sourcing one step further, **strategic sourcing** can be thought of as managing the firm's external resources in ways that support the long-term goals of the firm. This includes the development of ethical and sustainable sourcing initiatives that are also tied to the make-or-buy decision, managing and improving supplier relationships and capabilities, identification and selection of environmentally and socially conscious suppliers, monitoring and rewarding supplier performance, developing and managing second- and third-tier supplier relationships, and use of technology to support these many important sourcing activities. Some of these topics have been introduced in earlier chapters and will only be lightly touched upon here, while others particularly related to ethical and sustainable sourcing will be covered in greater detail in this chapter.

Supply management personnel today must be much more adept at locating, assessing, and developing the *right* suppliers, integrating them into the firm's business processes and strategies and using them to help reduce carbon footprints; developing cost-saving sourcing plans; achieving acceptable supplier delivery performance; and ensuring that purchased materials and products are consistent with internal and external customer requirements. Furthermore, because of recent trends in corporate downsizing and cost reduction, purchasing departments often must do these activities with fewer personnel. These are some tall expectations for purchasing managers. As a matter of fact, in an effort to save money, some firms are even choosing to outsource their entire purchasing function. A report by the British outsourcing advisory body Everest Research Institute, for example, states that this trend is growing at 30 percent per year in the U.K.[3]

Developing socially responsible and environmentally friendly sourcing strategies that also create a competitive advantage is no easy task. However, as proven by Bon Appetit in the opening Supply Chain Management in Action feature, it can be done successfully. Creating and implementing strategies to support ethical and green purchasing can pose benefits for the firms involved but can ultimately fail because of misaligned strategies, lack of commitment, unrealized goals, and loss of trust in buyer–supplier relationships. Purchasing managers proactively managing their firms' supply chains must also come to understand that some sourcing strategies are better suited to some supply chains than to others. Indeed, firms may have dozens of supply chains associated with their most important inbound purchased items and outbound finished products. Some of these supply chains may be driven by a low-cost overall strategy, while others may have the environment, quality, or service as the overriding objective. Even different parts and components used in one product may have diverging supply chain strategies. In this chapter, we discuss the development of successful ethical and sustainable sourcing strategies in the context of a number of other important sourcing strategies.

Ethical and Sustainable Sourcing Defined

Ethical Sourcing

To establish a common ground for further discussion, it is necessary to first define and describe the origins of the terms *ethical* and *sustainable sourcing*. In the most basic sense, **business ethics** is the application of ethical principles to business situations, and has been very widely studied. A library search, for instance, would reveal more than 250 books dedicated solely to the topic of business ethics. Generally speaking, there are two approaches to deciding whether or not an action is ethical. The first approach is known as **utilitarianism**. It maintains that an ethical act creates the greatest good for the greatest number of people. The second approach, known as **rights and duties**, states that some actions are right in themselves without regard for the consequences. This approach maintains that ethical actions recognize the rights of others and the duties those rights impose on the ones performing the actions.

Today, the practice of business ethics may also be referred to as **corporate social responsibility (CSR)**. Much of the discussion to date of CSR assumes that a corporation can act ethically just as an individual can. Whether firms practice CSR because they are forced to do it, feel obliged to do it, or want to do it is a matter for debate, but it is indeed being practiced. Many firms have formal CSR initiatives that include ethical sourcing. U.K.-based Cadbury has been a leader in this respect. They created a CSR committee at the company in 2001 to incorporate corporate responsibility into its primary company goals. This resulted in a number of initiatives including sponsoring an after-school program in Brazil to give job training to mothers while their children played organized soccer matches; sponsoring studies of the ethical sourcing of cocoa, nuts, and sugar; and adopting a policy to reduce water consumption by 20 percent in their business regions where water is scarce.[4]

Ethical sourcing can be defined as "That which attempts to take into account the public consequences of organizational buying or bring about positive social change through organizational buying behavior."[5] Ethical sourcing practices include promoting diversity by intentionally buying from small firms, ethnic minority businesses, and women-owned enterprises; discontinuing purchases from firms that use child labor or other unacceptable labor practices; or sourcing from firms with good labor treatment or environmental protection credentials. Purchasing managers and other corporate executives play a central role in promoting ethical sourcing by creating a supportive organizational culture, developing policies that outline the firm's desire to practice ethical sourcing, communicating these policies to supply chain trading partners, and then developing tactics that specifically describe how ethical sourcing will be implemented. Massachusetts-based athletic footwear retailer Reebok launched its ethical sourcing program in the early 1990s. It emphasizes the roles played by supplier factory managers in maintaining quality workplace conditions. Reebok also tries to collaborate with its competitors in establishing common human rights guidelines, since they all may be buying merchandise from the same factories. In 2002 Reebok unveiled an Internet-based human rights compliance-monitoring software application, generating considerable interest from other firms about buying the application. In response, Reebok established a nonprofit organization built around the technology, and in 2004 launched the Fair Factories Clearinghouse with the backing of the National Retail Federation.[6]

Purchasing goods from suppliers in developing countries can be risky in that if human rights, animal rights, safety or environmental abuses become associated with the firm's suppliers or foreign manufacturing facilities, this could lead to negative publicity for the buyer, along with product boycotts, a tarnished company image, brand degradation, lower employee morale, and ultimately lower sales, profits and stock prices. This very thing happened to running gear manufacturer Nike in the mid-'90s when they contracted with Pakistani factories to make footballs. Ultimately, the work was subcontracted to local villagers, where children as young as ten were drawn into the production processes. Similar problems for Nike also cropped up in Cambodia and Malaysia. In 1998 CEO Phil Knight acknowledged that, "Nike product has become synonymous with slave wages, forced overtime, and arbitrary abuse." Since then, Nike has pledged to reform this image. In Malaysia, for example, they admitted serious breaches in conduct, reimbursed workers, paid to relocate them and then met with representatives of its thirty contract Malaysian factories for a conversation about enforcing labor standards.[7] As companies seek lower sourcing costs, exposure to these types of risk increases. To minimize these risks, ethical sourcing policies should include:

- Determining where all purchased goods come from and how they are made;
- Knowing if suppliers promote basic workplace principles (such as the right to equal opportunity and to earn a decent wage, the prohibition of bonded, prison or child labor, and the right to join a union);
- Use of ethical ratings for suppliers alongside the other standard performance criteria;
- Use of independent verification of vendor compliance;
- Reporting of supplier compliance performance to shareholders;
- Providing detailed ethical sourcing expectations to vendors.[8]

Use of ethical sourcing practices is more difficult than it sounds. Modern supply chains can encompass many countries with varied labor issues, wages and living conditions. Nike's global supply chain, for instance, employs some 800,000 workers in 52 countries. The **Ethical Trading Initiative (ETI)** is an alliance of organizations seeking to take responsibility for improving working conditions and agreeing to implement the ETI Base Code, a standard for ethical practices for the firm and its suppliers. The ETI Base Code is shown in Table 4.1.

Table 4.1	The Ethical Trading Initiative's Base Code
CLAUSES	**ABBREVIATED EXPLANATIONS**
1. Employment is freely chosen	No forced, bonded or involuntary prison labor.Workers are not required to lodge "deposits" with their employer and are free to leave after reasonable notice.
2. Freedom of association and the right to collective bargaining are respected	Workers have the right to join trade unions and to bargain collectively. Employer adopts an open attitude toward the activities of trade unions. Worker representatives are not discriminated against.Where the right to collective bargaining is restricted under law, employer facilitates the development of parallel means for bargaining.
3. Working conditions are safe and hygienic	A safe and hygienic work environment shall be provided. Adequate steps shall be taken to minimize the causes of hazards in the workplace.Workers shall receive regular and recorded health and safety training.Access to clean toilet facilities and sanitary facilities for food storage shall be provided. Accommodations shall be clean, safe and meet the basic needs of workers. The company shall assign responsibility for health and safety to a senior management representative.
4. Child labor shall not be used	There shall be no new recruitment of child labor.Persons under 18 shall not be employed at night or in hazardous conditions.Policies and procedures shall conform to the provisions of the relevant International Labor Organization standards.
5. Living wages are paid	Wages and benefits for a standard work week meet national legal or industry standards, whichever is higher.Wages should be enough to meet basic needs.All workers shall be provided with written and understandable information about their employment conditions before they enter employment and about the particulars of their wages each time that they are paid. Deductions from wages as a disciplinary measure shall not be permitted.
6. Working hours are not excessive	Working hours comply with national laws and benchmark industry standards, whichever affords greater protection.Workers shall not on a regular basis be required to work in excess of 48 hours per week and shall be provided with at least one day off for every 7 day period. Overtime shall be voluntary, shall not exceed 12 hours per week, and shall always be compensated at a premium rate.
7. No discrimination is practiced	There is no discrimination in hiring, compensation, access to training, promotion, termination or retirement based on race, caste, national origin, religion, age, disability, gender, marital status, sexual orientation, union membership or political affiliation.
8. Regular employment is provided	Work performed must be on the basis of recognized employment relationships established through national law and practice.Obligations to employees under labor or social security laws shall not be avoided through the use of labor-only contracting, sub-contracting, or through apprenticeship schemes where there is no intent to impart skills.
9. No harsh or inhumane treatment is allowed	Physical abuse or discipline, the threat of physical abuse, sexual or other harassment or other forms of intimidation shall be prohibited.

Source: Ethical Trading Initiative website: www.ethicaltrade.org

The purchase of **fair trade products** is a recent sourcing activity that is becoming increasingly popular as firms seek to demonstrate a more ethical approach to purchasing. A fair trade product is one manufactured or grown by a disadvantaged producer in a developing country that receives a fair price for their goods. Thus, the term *fair trade* most often refers to farming products such as coffee, cocoa, sugar, tea and cotton that are produced in developing countries and exported to large firms in developed countries. Agencies such as the Fairtrade Foundation, Fairtrade Labelling Organizations International, and the World Fair Trade Organization seek out and certify these types of products as being "fair trade products."[9] In 2006 the rock musician Bono launched the fashion label Red to sell ethically sourced and fair trade certified products. A portion of Red's revenues are used to fight AIDS, tuberculosis and malaria in Africa.[10] Leading retailers offer items for sale that are designated fair trade products. In the U.K., for example, consumers can purchase fair trade rubber gloves with the knowledge that Sri Lankan rubber farmers are benefitting from a fair price, technical support and help in buying equipment. Many consumers are willing to pay more for these items too. Recently, Cadbury pledged to spend £1.5 billion to ensure its Dairy Milk bars sold in the U.K. are certified as fair trade products.[11] Worldwide, fair trade certified product sales amounted to about $4.1 billion in 2008, a 22 percent increase from 2007.[12]

Sustainable Sourcing

While protecting the earth's environment has been a subject of concern for many years, it has more recently become a popular topic of debate as politicians and voters have made global warming an election issue. Former U.S. Vice President and long-time environmentalist Al Gore, for example, recently starred in the award-winning 2006 global warming documentary *An Inconvenient Truth*. Additionally, awards such as the Goldman Environmental Prize have served as a support mechanism for environmental reform, providing global publicity for specific environmental problems. The Goldman Prize began in 1990 and awards $150,000 to each of the prize recipients, with winners announced every April to coincide with Earth Day. Awards so far have been given to 133 people in 75 countries. The 1991 prize winner, Wangari Maathai, won the 2004 Nobel Peace Prize (Al Gore won the Nobel Peace Prize in 2007 for his environmental work).[13] David Bower, longtime director of the Sierra Club; Eileen O'Neill, head of Discovery Channel's Planet Green multimedia initiative; Patrick Moore, Director and co-founder of Greenpeace International; and many others have played major roles in championing the modern environmental movement.[14]

Growing out of this environmental awareness was the idea of **green purchasing**. Green purchasing is a practice aimed at ensuring that purchased products or materials meet environmental objectives of the organization such as waste reduction, hazardous material elimination, recycling, remanufacturing and material reuse. According to the globally recognized Institute for Supply Management, green purchasing is defined as "making environmentally conscious decisions throughout the purchasing process, beginning with product and process design, and through product disposal".[15] Companies like California-based healthcare provider Kaiser Permanente and beer producer Anheuser-Busch have been recognized as corporate trailblazers in green purchasing. In 2001 Kaiser Permanente formed an environmental stewardship council focusing on green buildings, green purchasing and environmentally sustainable operations. Anheuser-Busch, for example, worked with its suppliers to reduce the lid diameter of four types of cans, saving 17.5 million pounds of aluminum as well as reducing the energy needed to produce and transport the cans.[16]

Sustainability, as applied to supply chains, is a broad term that includes green purchasing as well as some aspects of social responsibility and financial performance. It can be defined as "the ability to meet the needs of current supply chain members without hindering the ability to meet the needs of future generations in terms of economic, environmental and social challenges". The idea of sustainability is certainly not new as evidenced by the way early Native Americans thought and lived. And as Gifford Pinchot, the first Chief Forester of the U.S. Forest Service, wrote in an article in 1908:

> Are we going to protect our springs of prosperity, our raw material of industry and commerce and employer of capital and labor combined; or are we going to dissipate them? According as we accept or ignore our responsibility as trustees of the nation's welfare, our children and our children's children for uncounted generations will call us blessed, or will lay their suffering at our doors.[17]

For businesses and their trading partners, sustainability is seen today as doing the right things in ways that make economic sense. The objectives then are not only to sustain the world we live in, but to sustain the organization as well. Like CSR, **social sustainability** concerns involve worker safety, hourly wages, working conditions, child workers, and basic human rights. Indications are that the world is moving from a storehouse of abundant cheap supplies of energy to a place with a finite supply of expensive energy. Customers today are calling for higher-quality goods, greater varieties, reasonable prices, lower lead times, and evidence of environmental stewardship and social responsibility. All of these issues are placing new burdens on supply chain managers, but they also can provide opportunities.

Worldwide leading retailer Wal-Mart, already one of the global leaders in supply chain management, has recently taken a leading role in terms of advocating sustainability. One of Wal-Mart's goals, for example, is to reduce packaging five percent by 2013. This will not only prevent 667 metric tons of carbon dioxide from entering the atmosphere each year, but it will also reduce shipping and fuel costs. Ultimately, Wal-Mart wants to be supplied 100 percent by renewable energy, create zero waste, and sell products that sustain resources and the environment. Wal-Mart expects all these actions to reduce their costs considerably.[18] Matt Kissler, vice president of package and product innovation at Wal-Mart's membership warehouse affiliate Sam's Club, may have gotten to the heart of the matter when he said, "Sustainability is not just about the environment. No matter how good we do things for the environment, if they are not sustainable for our business, sustainability will not work. If what we are doing is not sustainable financially for our business entities, we should not be doing it."[19] As shown in the Global Perspective feature, Wal-Mart is now the primary force behind the formation of a **global sustainability index**, which it hopes will heavily influence how products are both made and purchased in the future.

Sustainable sourcing is one activity then, within the larger umbrella term of sustainability—it includes green purchasing, some form of financial benefit, as well as aspects of ethical sourcing. Very simply, it has been defined as "a process of purchasing goods and services that takes into account the long-term impact on people, profits, and the planet".[20]

Leading companies practicing sustainable sourcing seek to:

- *Grow revenues* by introducing new and differentiated sustainable products and services;

Global Perspective	*Wal-Mart's Global Sustainability Index*

On July 16, 2009, Wal-Mart President and CEO Mike Duke announced the creation of a worldwide sustainability index, and the supply chain management world was immediately talking about the implications—and realities—inherent in this new initiative.

Wal-Mart's intention is to develop the sustainability index over a period of time, in three phases— the final being the implementation of product labels that clearly rate the environmental and sustainable aspects of the product. The overall goal is to take a "research-driven approach" to measure sustainability so consumers can make educated product-buying decisions in the store.

The first step in making this happen is a supplier assessment, using a fifteen-question survey provided to each of Wal-Mart's 100,000 global suppliers. The survey is not mandatory, but is designed to help suppliers evaluate their own sustainability efforts in four areas: energy and climate, natural resources, material efficiency, and people and community.

Wal-Mart is providing initial funding to develop the second phase, which is a sustainability consortium integrating information pulled from the supplier assessment phase. This consortium is a group of universities (Arizona State University and the University of Arkansas are jointly administering the consortium) that will work with retailers, suppliers, nongovernmental organizations (NGOs) and the government to create a global database of information on the life cycle of products. However, the retailer has made it clear that this is not meant to be solely an effort to benefit Wal-Mart. The company intends to work with partners to build a usable, uniform database. "This cannot and should not be a Wal-Mart effort. It can't be a U.S. effort. To succeed, the index has to be global. It has to involve many stakeholders as vital partners," said Duke in the July announcement.

So, the question is: How will this effort actually work out in the real world, and what are the factors that will make the difference between great intentions and great success?

Source: Stokes, S., K. Dooley, and L. Arnseth, "Wal-Mart's Sustainability Index," *Inside Supply Management*®, V. 20, No. 10, 2009, pp. 19–21. Copyright © 2009 by the Institute for Supply Management™. Reprinted by permission.

- *Reduce costs* by increasing resource efficiencies, avoiding use of noncompliant suppliers, and rethinking transportation and distribution designs;
- *Manage risk* by managing brand and reputation, and developing approaches for meeting regulations and for capturing socially and environmentally conscious customers; and
- *Build intangible assets* by further enhancing brand and reputation through social and environmental responsibility.[21]

To accomplish these goals, companies must rely upon close collaborative relationships with their key suppliers and customers to make sustainable sourcing a beneficial reality.

Palm oil, a vegetable oil used in many food and cosmetic products, is one example— consumer goods companies like Kraft, Unilever and Nestle all desire to purchase sustainable palm oil. Consequently, the World Wildlife Fund and Unilever formed the Roundtable for Sustainable Palm Oil to create sustainable practices for palm oil cultivation, to work with the growers and ultimately to certify palm oil producers. Today, certified sustainable palm oil producers get paid higher prices for their palm oil from companies like Kraft and Nestle, which in turn charge higher prices for their sustainable consumer products—prices that many consumers are willing to pay.[22]

The topics of ethical and sustainable sourcing contain some common elements, and can be the source of much confusion in various industries and even within an organization. In a survey of 100 U.K. buyers in both the public and private sectors, only 17 percent said they thought the concepts were fully understood. "The problem is the terms sustainable, green, ethical and fair trade are used interchangeably and in a confusing way," said one survey respondent. "The issue does not just cover what we buy, but how we buy, and this is the area that suffers a lack of understanding," said another.[23]

Governments, cities and leading businesses are now getting involved, to set some clear targets for organizations to achieve. A study of London's carbon footprint, for example, found that Londoners consumed 154,400 gigawatts of energy, acquired 50 million tons of materials and generated 26 million tons of waste annually. In response, the Greater London Authority produced plans to address these unsustainable material flows.[24] In 2005, U.K. Prime Minister Tony Blair set up a business-led group called the Sustainable Procurement Task Force (SPTF) to examine how funds could be spent in a sustainable manner. The aim of the group was to show how sustainable purchases could benefit organizations, help society, boost the economy, and support the natural environment.[25] Masdar City, near Abu Dhabi, is being touted as the world's first carbonneutral city. It incorporates a dense walkable urban pattern that respects the local climate and includes a personal rapid transit system—a network of small public cars that take riders to stops of their choice.[26] Seattle, Washington, has been practicing sustainable purchasing for years. Their Green Purchasing Program promotes use of goods, materials, and services that help to reduce greenhouse gas emissions. Purchasing contracts also mandate 100 percent recycled paper for city work, duplex document production, and toxin-free chemicals in products the city buys.[27]

From the supplier's perspective, there are tools available to help determine what buyers want, in terms of environmentally friendly goods. The EcoMarkets Survey, created by the Canadian environmental marketing agency TerraChoice, for example, surveys up to 6000 business and government buyers annually, to learn how organizations are greening their supply chains. Some of their general findings are that:

- The number of organizations buying green is increasing;
- Energy conservation is the most popular aspect of green sourcing; and
- The market for environmentally friendly products is large and growing rapidly.[28]

Firms, their supply chains, and government agencies alike are coming to realize that every purchase has a global environmental impact, and with careful sourcing, money can be saved. Collection, transport, manufacturing, and scrapping of raw materials and finished products requires the use of fossil fuels; products purchased from distant suppliers require greater amounts of fuel for transportation; products transported via ship or rail use less fuel than trucks or airlines; plant-based products generally have a smaller environmental impact than petroleum-based products; factories powered by solar or wind have a smaller environmental impact than factories powered by oil or coal; and energy-efficient products consume less energy.

Developing Ethical and Sustainable Sourcing Strategies

To achieve the objectives described thus far in this chapter, a number of sourcing strategies must be considered and implemented. Care must be taken, though, when developing these plans. Failure to align sourcing strategies with overall supply chain objectives, for example, may result in considerable resources being expended to design and manage a set of sourcing activities, only to find that the resulting impact on the firm and its supply chains is something much less than ultimately desired.

In one of the more important papers written on this topic, Martin Fisher uses two types of supply chains as examples—those for **functional products** and those for **innovative products**.[29] Functional products are maintenance, repair, and operating (MRO) materials and other commonly purchased items and supplies. These items are characterized by low profit margins, relatively stable demands, and high levels of competition. Thus, companies purchasing functional products most likely concentrate on finding a dependable supplier selling at a low price. Factory maintenance products, for example, might fall into this category. Examples of innovative consumer goods are the Amazon Kindle and GM's Volt; in factory settings, innovative products might be new types of control mechanisms, new software applications, or a new robotics system. Innovative products are characterized by short product life cycles, volatile demand, high profit margins, and relatively less competition. Consequently, the sourcing criteria for these products may be more closely aligned with a supplier's quality reputation, delivery speed and flexibility, and communication capabilities. Many of California-based Apple's purchases, for example, might fall into the innovative product category. Overlaying both of these types of purchases as well is whether or not to invoke an ethical or sustainable sourcing strategy. This adds yet another layer of complexity to the sourcing decision.

Many of the commonly used sourcing strategies of thirty years ago do not work well today. For instance, "squeezing" or hard-bargaining suppliers to generate a lower annual **purchasing spend** (or expense) may ultimately prove harmful to buyer–supplier relationships, eventually leading to deteriorations in quality, ethical reputation, sustainability performance and customer service as suppliers seek ways to cut corners in order to keep their profit margins at desired levels. If long-term sourcing plans are to be successful, they must support the firm's long-term supply chain and business strategies; and suppliers must also see some benefit from the initiatives implemented. The cost-cutting efforts of Chrysler, for example, have included working with existing suppliers to find cost-saving product alternatives instead of resorting to hard-bargaining.[30] A framework for ethical and sustainable sourcing strategy development is shown in Table 4.2.

In Step 1, the firm formalizes its ethical and sustainable sourcing policies. Obviously, these policies will vary based on use of foreign suppliers, types of items purchased, and the firm's experience with this type of sourcing. Ethical sourcing policies should include the importance placed on fair working conditions; use of minority, women-owned, and small businesses; guidelines on human rights and use of child labor, use of subcontracting; and supplier reporting and verification procedures. Sustainable sourcing policies should include supplier compliance in terms of waste reduction/energy conservation, use of renewable energy, hazardous material elimination, recycling, remanufacturing and material reuse.

Table 4.2	Supply Chain Ethical and Sustainable Sourcing Strategy Framework
STEPS	**DESCRIPTION**
1. Establish corporate ethical and sustainable sourcing policies.	Verifies top management support, establishes a vision and direction, enforces the importance of ethical and sustainable sourcing, and reduces confusion.
2. Train purchasing staff; implement policies among users, suppliers.	Ensures that buyers are skilled in environmental and social considerations in sourcing, and that users and suppliers understand why and how purchasing decisions are made.
3. Prioritize items based on ethical and sustainability opportunities and ease of implementation. Get started.	Allows buyers to "pick low hanging fruit" to provide evidence for successful strategy implementation.
4. Develop a performance measurement system.	Measurement provides accountability and a way to improve over time. Should be reviewed periodically.
5. Monitor progress, make improvements. Increase use of certified fair trade and green products and services.	Use performance measures to identify weaknesses. Step up efforts to develop better capabilities in the firm and its supply base.
6. Expand focus to include other departments and customers. Increase brand value.	Use the purchasing department's success and influence to grow awareness in the firm and among customers. Communicate successes and programs to stakeholders.

Source: Based in part on Newman, D., "Steps You Can Take to 'Green' Your Procurement" *Summit* 9(4), 2006: 10; and "Buying a Better World," www.forumforthefuture.org

In Step 2, training and communication of the policies occurs. It is all well and good to develop ethical and sustainable sourcing policies, but the firm must also do an adequate job of implementing these policies. In early 2000, for instance, Canadian retailer Hudson Bay had begun developing proactive sustainable sourcing plans, but in 2002 they were accused of using sweatshops for manufacturing. As it turned out, they had not properly communicated their new vendor codes of conduct to their suppliers. Additionally, the shareholders and general public had no idea of their social compliance programs. This caused a number of actual and perceived problems for Hudson Bay to overcome. Today, their social compliance programs are formalized and widely communicated, and they audit all supplier facilities for compliance to their codes of conduct.[31]

Step 3 is all about just getting started. It is important keep efforts simple early on, find successes quickly, and then build on these successes. As the Wal-Mart executive mentioned earlier, if companies cannot show some financial benefit from ethical and sustainable sourcing policies, then ultimately these efforts will fail. Buyers might consider concentrating on products where the market for fair trade and green products is mature, as with office supplies, cleaning supplies, and some apparel.

Step 4 calls for the design of performance metrics to gauge the success of the firm's efforts in ethical and sustainable sourcing. Measures can be qualitative or quantitative, and in the general areas of cost, quality, time, flexibility, and innovativeness. In managed supply chains, performance indicators should be standardized across trading partners. Metrics for sustainability can be used in the areas of packaging, energy use, hazardous materials, and recycling. Metrics for sustainability could include the number of fair trade certified products purchased, the number of ethical standards adopted by suppliers, the number of suppliers adopting the Ethical Trading Initiative's Base Code, and the number of small and minority suppliers used. As products, suppliers, and markets change, these metrics should be revisited and potentially revised. More on performance measurement can also be found in Chapter 13.

Step 5 is to monitor performance and outcomes and adjust the work plans, priorities, policies, and use of suppliers to more adequately meet the ethical and sustainability goals of the firm. It may be that certain elements in the various programs or conduct codes need to be revised as the firm and its operating environments change. Over time, as the firm and its suppliers adjust to these policies, improvements can be made, more fair trade products and green products will be identified, and further initiatives will be developed.

Finally, Step 6 addresses the impact of ethical and sustainable sourcing on other facets of the organization, its trading partners, and ultimately the firm's brand. As successes are realized, it will become easier for the firm to embrace operating more ethically and sustainably. Eventually, other divisions and trading partners will become interested. Consumers will start expecting it. Increasingly, companies are taking their ethical and sustainable factors and leveraging them for greater brand value. Even during the most recent global recession, consumers prefer organizations that address various ethical and sustainable issues. According to Christopher Satterthwaite, CEO of U.K.-based Chime Communications, "The big message for brands that want to get ahead of the game is that there is a sustainable advantage to be had if they do their homework, find the right sustainability 'fit,' and tell their story in an open and honest way."[32]

As personnel in design, marketing, production, and other departments begin working with purchasing to develop these and other sourcing strategies, a number of initiatives, some of which have already been introduced in earlier chapters, may be used separately or in some combination to support the organization's long-term goals. These proactive sourcing initiatives, when combined with internal operations and customer relationship initiatives, form the foundation for successful supply chain management and, ultimately, competitive advantage for the firm. The remainder of the chapter discusses a number of these strategic sourcing initiatives, many of which are closely associated with ethical and sustainable sourcing.

Supply Base Rationalization Programs

As first mentioned in Chapter 2, firms taking an active role in supply chain management seek to reduce purchases from marginal or poor-performing suppliers while increasing and concentrating purchases among their more desirable, top-performing suppliers. Firms doing this are practicing **supply base rationalization**, also referred to as **supply base reduction** or **supply base optimization**, and this has been a common occurrence since the late 1980s. Indeed, activities aimed at fostering buyer–supplier partnerships and increasing the performance and value of suppliers are simply easier when fewer suppliers are involved. Thus, supply base rationalization programs have the benefits of reduced purchase prices due to quantity discounts, fewer supplier management problems, closer and more frequent collaborations between buyer and supplier, and greater overall levels of quality and delivery reliability, since only the best suppliers remain in the supply base. This topic fits well with ethical and sustainable sourcing efforts—firms may desire to interact more frequently and closely with suppliers exhibiting ethical and sustainable purchasing habits. Firms may wish to use this as a way to screen out suppliers from their supply bases.

At automaker Ford, Paul Wood, manager of global purchasing, describes their sourcing framework: "The framework is designed to develop long-term, closer relationships with significantly fewer suppliers. The theory is that developing closer relationships will result in better quality, lower cost, and improved innovation." The project began with Ford identifying 20 items which accounted for about 50 percent of Ford's annual production spend. "We saw that for each of these items, we might have seven, eight, nine or even more different suppliers. We want to reduce this to three or four suppliers who will supply 100 percent of that commodity." Thus, the remaining suppliers benefit from increased business, and Ford benefits from shared innovation, increased quality and lower cost.[33] Even if the goal in a supply chain is predominantly spend minimization, there are still typically enough competing suppliers such that only the best-performing, highest-quality, lowest-cost suppliers constitute an organization's supply base. Supply base rationalization is a straightforward, simple sourcing strategy, and is often the initial supply chain management effort, usually preceding the formation of long-term buyer–supplier strategic relationships.

Building relationships with suppliers taking a lead in social responsibility can result in many benefits for the firm, including spend reduction, quality improvement, and reputation enhancement. Particularly when economic times are tough, reducing purchasing spend tends to top buyers' agendas, which can lead to sourcing from low-cost countries and can pose significant risks to corporations when suppliers conceal breaches of ethical and quality requirements. To help corporate buyers, the U.K. fair trade organization Tradecraft has produced a number of guidelines, reports, and online tools to show how ethical purchasing can be done in ways to benefit both parties.[34]

Ethical and Sustainable Supplier Certification Programs

Proactively seeking and creating **strategic supplier alliances** have become important objectives of firms looking to manage their supply chains. Strategic alliances are a more formalized type of collaborative relationship, involving commitments to long-term cooperation, shared benefits and costs, joint problem solving, continuous improvement, and information sharing. Because of these relationships, suppliers are able to invest more of their resources toward becoming specialized in areas required by the buyer, to establish production and/or storage facilities close to the buyer's facilities, to purchase compatible communication and information systems, and to invest in better technologies that will ultimately improve supplier performance.

Ethical and sustainable supplier certifications are one way to identify strategic alliance candidates or to further develop existing alliances. In many cases, certification programs are simply based on internationally recognized certifications like the Switzerland-based International Organization for Standardization's ISO 9000 quality certification and ISO 14000 environmental certification.[35] For the organization actively managing its supply chain, these types of certification requirements are useful but may not be specific enough in areas of importance to the firm. In these cases, firms develop their own formal certification programs, which may include ISO 14000 certification as one element of the certification process. Other certification requirements might include, for example, the Forest Stewardship Council (FSC) certification for recycled paper, Energy Star certification for various environmental standards, or Fair Trade certifications for social and ethical performance.

The use of ethical and environmental certifications for suppliers is increasing. The New York-based Rainforest Alliance and California-based Trans-Fair USA certify billions of dollars worth of coffee, bananas and cocoa each year from suppliers in dozens of countries, and in exchange, suppliers work to preserve the environment and improve conditions for farmworkers.[36] Massachusetts-based Integrity Interactive Corp. offers a Web-based service that allows a firm to incorporate a code of ethics into its supply chain members. The website delivers the company's code of ethics to suppliers, collects certifications and reports results back to the initiating company. The certification website allows companies to identify rogue suppliers before they can cause problems or disruptions in the supply chain. Suppliers who fail to certify according to the ethical requirements can then face various consequences. World-class companies like Ryder Systems and H. J. Heinz are busy using the system to certify their suppliers.[37]

Outsourcing Products and Services

Purchasing spend as a percentage of sales has been growing over the years, in part because firms have opted to **outsource** the production of materials, parts, services and assembled components to concentrate more resources and time on the firm's core business activities. Simply put, many organizations are sourcing more while making less these days. In managed supply chains where a higher level of trust permeates buyer–supplier relationships, the use of outsourcing is even greater. In the Arizona-based Center for Advanced Purchasing Studies (CAPS) Cross-Industry Benchmarking Report combining both service and manufacturing firms, the average annual purchase spend as a percentage of sales in the U.S. was approximately 45 percent for 2008, an increase of about five percent from 2006.[38] Firms are outsourcing noncore products and service functions (for example maintenance, janitorial, or other support services) and, in some supply chain situations, more strategic products or services are outsourced that can impact the competitiveness of the firm. Notably, outsourcing gives firms the potential to leverage larger purchase volumes to gain quantity discounts, particularly if purchases are concentrated among fewer suppliers. Additionally, industrial buyers are beginning to make outsourcing decisions based on the supplier's environmental performance, as buyers have become aware of the marketing value of sustainability. In the petrochemical industry, for instance, supply chains are lengthening geographically as basic chemicals and plastics are transported greater distances from plants such as in the Middle East to growing markets in China and India. This is creating a demand for sustainable petrochemical supply chains through network redesign, elimination of waste, full asset utilization and greater volumes. Europe is leading the way in the drive toward sustainable logistics, says Philip Browitt, president of the chemicals business at U.K.-based international logistics company Agility. "There is a huge awareness throughout the European chemical industry of these essential sustainability factors with economic advantage and social pressure driving improved performance," he says.[39]

Aside from allowing firms to concentrate more on core capabilities while potentially reducing their costs, outsourcing can also result in reduced staffing levels or the redeployment of staff, accelerated reengineering efforts, reduced management problems, and gains in manufacturing flexibility. These benefits must be weighed against the risks associated with outsourcing, including loss of control, increased need for supplier management, and an increased reliance on suppliers. When outsourcing strategically important products or services, these risks can be very significant. Consequently, supplier selection can be an extremely important activity when outsourcing.

In cases where firms are actively managing their supply chains, they often outsource products and services to suppliers who are already or are on the verge of becoming strategic partners or key suppliers. These outsourcing arrangements can be used to further solidify a trading relationship, to gain additional negotiating leverage, to reward previous performance, and to minimize the outsourcing risks mentioned in the preceding paragraph. In these cases, outsourcing to highly capable and reliable suppliers can lead to improved product quality and brand reputation in addition to lower prices, particularly when the outsourced product or service is a core product of the supplier. In some trading relationships, outsourcing is done in both directions if the supplier and buyer both have core competencies in product areas desired by the other.

Insourcing

Unfortunately, some firms do not adequately study the decision to outsource, and thus experience problems with product quality, late deliveries, or suppliers otherwise not living up to expectations. In these cases, the outsourcing arrangement is unsuccessful and can result in **insourcing**, also referred to as **backsourcing**. Global market research company Forrester Research reports that 42 percent of buyers were unhappy, for instance, with the level of innovation provided by their outsourcers.[40] Some of the recent outsourcing failures have received significant attention in the press. For example, global financial giant JPMorgan Chase & Co. rescinded its IT outsourcing agreement with IBM after only two years of what was expected to be a seven-year, $5 billion arrangement.[41] Global energy company Chevron also recently arranged to bring back in-house some activities which had been previously outsourced. This created a need in Chevron to develop a careful long-term strategy for evaluating insourcing and outsourcing activities. "When you completely outsource as a 'black box,' you can't rely on a third party to understand how your organization works," says Richard Nitz, telecommunications infrastructure manager at Chevron. Now, Chevron uses their strategic retention model to help them decide what functions to retain at Chevron, and what less strategic functions it makes sense to outsource.[42]

Some companies are turning outsourcing on its head. Jeff Meehan of R. T. London, a furniture manufacturing company headquartered in Michigan, explains, "If we can insource it, we will. Our goal is to shrink the lead time and increase the throughput. The way to do that is by insourcing." R. T. London used to primarily do the final assembly, while outsourcing all their components. Through insourcing and attention to lean manufacturing principles, they have reduced product lead times by 50 percent, increased output, improved customer service, and enabled employees to think more like owners.[43] As a matter of fact, today in the U.S., insourcing has become so popular that overall job losses due to outsourcing is *more than offset* by job gains due to insourcing.[44]

Co-sourcing

In yet another variation of the outsourcing theme, and in many cases the most popular outsourcing arrangement, the use of **co-sourcing**, also referred to as **selective sourcing**, is becoming popular. Co-sourcing refers to the sharing of a process or function between internal staff and an external supplier. In this arrangement, firms will retain the more strategic activities while outsourcing the more resource-intensive, non-value-adding activities. The firm is thus able to retain control over the most vital parts of a product or service. Co-sourcing gives a firm the flexibility to decide what areas to outsource, when, and for how long. This also can be an appealing option for companies that have yet to create long-term supplier relationships, are in transition because of a merger or acquisition, or are facing financial problems.

For some IT services, co-sourcing has been shown to result in the most successful out-sourcing arrangements. One research study found that firms choosing to completely out-source their IT applications experienced lower overall levels of product quality, relationship quality and service quality, as well as higher costs, when compared to firms that co-sourced.[45] For customer contact centers, firms may opt to retain some contact capabilities while outsourcing others. Tom Johnson, managing director at BearingPoint, a global management consulting firm based in Virginia, explains, "Co-sourcing for extended hours, multilingual capabilities, [and] level-two problems or even level one, are certainly ways to drive your cost out … [and] give you expanded capabilities and competencies without taking on the fixed costs." AAA Arizona, for example, uses virtual contact center service provider Arise, based in Florida, to incorporate telecommuting agents to handle their call overflow during busy periods in the morning and late afternoon.[46]

Early Supplier Involvement

As the adoption of concurrent engineering and design for manufacturability techniques becomes more commonplace and relationships with suppliers become more trusted, reliable and long-term, key suppliers often become more heavily involved in the internal operations of their industrial customers, including managing inventories of their products at their customers' points of use, and participating in their customers' new product and process design processes. Key suppliers can become contributors to these efforts by serving in a decision-making capacity for purchase timing and quantities, and on new product and process design teams within the firm. They become involved in managing the buyer firm's inventories and participating in product part and assembly design, new product materials usage, and even the design of the processes to be used in manufacturing new products. Thus, strategic suppliers play a greater role in their customers' decision-making processes as trading relationships mature, which in turn further solidifies the supply chain. California-based semiconductor company Novellus has a long history of getting suppliers involved in the product design process. It has allowed them to reduce production lead times and time to market, while reducing costs and thus producing better profit margins. Previously, Novellus experienced production delays and higher costs as a result of suppliers having problems manufacturing their parts. Now, since the suppliers are part of the design process from the start, these problems don't occur.[47]

While serving on a customer's new product development team, a supplier representative's input can help the firm to reduce material cost, improve new product quality, and reduce product development time. Cost reductions come about through use of more standardized parts, fewer parts, and less-expensive materials. Cost, quality, and delivery timing improvements all come about when suppliers use the information gained through **early supplier involvement** to design parts and processes at their own facilities to match the buyer's specifications. Additionally, since they have been involved early on in the buyer's new product design process, these part and process changes can be timed to be in place and available when first needed by the buyer. Use of these **value engineering** techniques with help from the supplier allows firms to design better quality and cost savings into the products from the time a product first hits the shelves. Over the product's life, this can generate significant savings and revenues while reducing the need for cost-savings initiatives later on.

Early supplier involvement is perhaps one of the most effective supply chain integrative techniques. Buyers and suppliers working together—sharing proprietary design and manufacturing information that their competitors would love to see—establishes a level of trust and cooperation that can result in many future collaborative and potentially successful projects. Discussions of several other early supplier involvement activities follow.

Vendor Managed Inventories

Vendor managed inventory (VMI) services for key customers is perhaps one of the more value-enhancing activities performed by suppliers when their past performance allows customers to develop trust in their ability to manage their inventories, such that inventory carrying costs are minimized and stockouts are avoided. From the customer's perspective, allowing their suppliers to track inventories and determine delivery schedules and order quantities saves time, which may be better spent on more strategic sourcing activities. For the supplier, it means they avoid ill-advised orders from buyers, they get to decide how inventory is set up, when to ship it, how to ship it, where it goes, and they have the opportunity to educate their customers about other products. According to a 2006 *Industry Week* survey, fourteen of the top twenty-five U.S. manufacturing plants between 2002 and 2006 used suppliers to track and replenish inventories. On a dollar volume basis, about fourteen percent of the purchased materials of these firms were vendor managed.[48]

Ideally, these valued suppliers manage their customers' inventories using real-time visibility of inventory movements in their customers' storage areas or at the point of assembly or sale. This can be accomplished with bar code labels and scanners that instantly update computer counts of inventories as the items are used or sold. This data is then made available to trusted suppliers using compatible inventory management systems or a secured website. This allows a supplier to profile demand and determine an accurate forecast, and then ship an order quantity when the inventory levels become low enough—the **reorder point**.

Wal-Mart is generally given credit for popularizing the use of VMI in the mid-1990s when it initiated a relationship with Procter & Gamble to manage its diaper inventories. A similar arrangement with Rubbermaid soon followed.[49] Lake Erie Screw, a fastener and bolt manufacturer located in Indiana, uses a local supplier to manage its inventory of bar code labels. Once a week, bar code inventory data is automatically transmitted to the supplier's inventory tracking system, where it is compared to the reorder point, and established order quantities are shipped when the reorder point is reached.[50]

A somewhat more collaborative form of VMI is termed **co-managed inventories**. In this case, the buyer and supplier reach an agreement regarding the buyer's periodic demand forecasts, how information is shared, the order quantity, when an order is generated and the delivery timing and location. This type of controlled VMI may be preferable for very high-value, strategic item purchases, where the customer desires more input into the day-to-day supply activities, or perhaps when the customer is still assessing a supplier's ability to take full responsibility for the order fulfillment process.

Supplier Co-location

A more advanced and dedicated extension of the vendor managed inventory concept is **supplier co-location**. The concept refers to a situation wherein a supplier's employee is permanently housed in the purchasing department of the buyer's organization, acting as both buyer and supplier representative. This person is given all the rights and duties of an employee for the buyer organization—she forecasts demand, monitors inventory levels and places purchase orders, and has access to all of the files and records of the buyer organization. This special arrangement requires high levels of trust from both organizations and occurs only with long-term buyer–supplier relationships.

By the mid-'90s, many firms had adopted a supplier co-location strategy, including Harley-Davidson, Honeywell, IBM, Intel, DuPont, Ford, Motorola and AT&T. Back then, it was sometimes referred to as JIT II. "One of the real bangs for the buck of JIT II is that suppliers, who have more expertise on the parts they supply than their customers do, can suggest modifications during the design phase that customers would not know about on their own," says Bill Grimes, a former vice president of global supply for Honeywell.[51] When Chrysler planned a $1 billion Jeep plant in Toledo, Ohio, in 2004, they partnered with three suppliers who would manage body, paint and chassis operations. They termed it the most advanced use of supplier co-location yet in North America. "I don't think I'd characterize this as a gamble," said Peter Rosenfeld, executive vice president of procurement for Chrysler Group. "We call it a noble experiment and we think working together with these folks makes a heck of a lot of sense."[52]

Several advantages exist for both partners using supplier co-location. The purchasing organization gets the use of a cost-free employee who understands their particular problems and requirements and who can easily communicate these needs to the supplier. The supplier gets the security of future purchases and the "first mover" advantage of having someone on-site when new items need to be purchased. Communication between both firms also improves with this arrangement. The supplier representative learns very quickly about new products and design changes occurring at the customer's firm that are going to impact the supplier. This person also learns about production problems potentially caused by the supplier's products and customer service performance, and can help to more quickly alleviate these problems. The arrangement thus serves both sides, and creates an even closer working relationship between the two companies. At audio product maker Bose, a team of co-located supplier personnel handling just Bose's transportation function represents a less-than-truckload carrier, a truckload carrier, an import/export brokerage firm, and a major ocean carrier. These representatives are each linked to their respective firm's information system, and work daily with Bose's transportation group and each other to assure parts and products arrive at Bose facilities when they are needed. The system has reduced late shipments by 50 percent, transportation costs by 37 percent, and shipping errors by 87 percent.[53]

Strategic Alliance Development

As the growth of supply chain management continues, firms become more adept at managing their suppliers and more willing to assist them in improving their production and service capabilities. Simply put, **strategic alliance development**, an extension of supplier development (covered in Chapter 3), refers to increasing the firm's *key or strategic suppliers'* capabilities. As supply bases become smaller, more opportunities for creating collaborative relationships with these suppliers also occur. As a whole, then, supply bases become more manageable. The more basic supplier management activities tend to become somewhat less time-consuming as strategic supplier alliances begin to constitute more and more of the supply base; thus, alliance development starts to occupy more of the purchasing function's time and resources.

Business owners and executives are beginning to realize that strategic supplier alliances, if successful, can result in better market penetration, access to new technologies and knowledge, and higher returns on investment than competitors with no such alliances. Massachusetts-based defense contractor Raytheon, for example, uses the formation of strategic supplier alliances as part of its Six Sigma quality initiative.[54] Managing these alliances, though, can result in expensive failures and unrealized goals perhaps as much as 60 to 70 percent of the time, and thus require a significant effort on both sides to assure that these relationships stay beneficial to both parties.[55]

As discussed in Chapter 3, a number of supplier development activities exist, and these become more essential to the firm as outsourcing continues and as the firm comes to depend more on a smaller group of vital suppliers. Alliance development will eventually even extend to a firm's second-tier suppliers, as the firm's key suppliers begin to form their own alliance development activities. Alliance development among the firm and its key suppliers tends to be much more of a collaborative activity, requiring both sides to commit time, people, communication, and monetary resources to achieving goals that will benefit both parties. Instead of simply providing one-time assistance to help solve a particular problem, or presenting a seminar that will soon be forgotten, alliance development results in retained learning because of the commitment of relationship management personnel from both trading partners. The focal firm and its most trusted suppliers jointly decide on improvement activities, resources required, and the means to measure progress. As the improvements and learning take place, suppliers eventually become capable of passing these same capabilities on to their key suppliers, and extending these capabilities up the supply chain.

Strategic alliance development requires companies to improve relationship value systems within their organizations' cultures, learn from their mistakes and from the successes of other alliances within their firms, and make investments to enable collaborative problem solving. Many firms are hiring strategic relationship managers, whose sole job is to build trust, commitment, and mutual value within the alliance. These relationship managers work on negotiating win-win collaborations resulting in mutual benefits, such that alliances become the norm among the various business units in the organization. Strategic supplier alliances, like products, have their own life cycles, requiring ongoing management, development, and negotiating activities to monitor success, manage conflict, evaluate the current fit with partners, revisit the ground rules for working together, and make adjustments through mutual problem solving and information sharing.

Some of the more successful alliance-generating companies like Hewlett-Packard, Oracle, and Eli Lilly & Co. have directors of strategic alliances. They function as the coordinators of the strategic alliance programs and facilitators of other alliance-related activities, such as providing educational programs, developing guidelines for alliance management, finding alliance partners, and creating alliance teams. These alliances also create external visibility for the firm, affect the firm's reputation, and create significant value for the firm. In fact, in their study on strategic alliances, Dyer, Kale, and Singh found that a firm's stock price jumped 1 percent for each announcement of a new alliance.[56] Organizing and managing a successful alliance program is thus very important to the firm's competitiveness. Table 4.3 describes the strategic alliance organization process.

Table 4.3	Maintaining a Successful Strategic Alliance Program
STEPS	**DISCUSSION**
1. Determine the key strategic parameters to organize around.	Can be based on business units, geographic areas, industries, key alliance partners, or combinations of these.
2. Facilitate the dissemination of information.	Alliance generating, management and development information should be centrally controlled and available through internal websites, pamphlets, internal experts, workshops.
3. Elevate the importance of the strategic alliance program.	Assign a director or vice president of alliance programs, reporting to top management. Establish consistent procedures for alliance programs throughout the organization.
4. Provide continuous evaluation of alliance performance, visibility, and support.	Management can increase the value and acceptance of alliance programs when successes are made visible to the firm's lower-level managers and employees. Alliance management requires resources and on-going reevaluation.
5. Reward suppliers as performance merits.	Rewards typically include increased business and other non-monetary awards.

Source: Adapted from Dyer, J., P. Kale, and H. Singh, "How to Make Strategic Alliances Work," *Sloan Management Review* 42(4), 2001: 37–43.

To make strategic alliance programs successful, firms must determine how to organize a program that can cut across functional boundaries; disseminate program information quickly and effectively throughout the organization; acquire the necessary resources; create program acceptance by the line managers and their employees; achieve concrete, measurable success; and reward supplier performance. Some firms have chosen to organize around their key alliance partners by assigning alliance managers to each of these partners. Others have decided to create an alliance board to oversee alliances and coordinate alliance managers in various divisions within the organization or in different geographic regions of the world.

The alliance management function can act as a clearinghouse for information regarding all types of alliance needs, from negotiation strategies to problem-solving assistance to outreach programs and workshops. To give the alliance management function credibility, the program director should report to the organization's top management. This facilitates the use of company resources as well as provides internal visibility to the function. Alliance strategies, goals, policies, and procedures can then be generated and communicated across the entire organization. Finally, since alliance goals change over time, they must be evaluated periodically. Some alliances may no longer be performing adequately, and should be discontinued. Performance evaluation metrics must be established; and, as alliances show signs of success, strategies can be shared across the various alliance boundaries. As briefly mentioned earlier, continued alliance success depends on both the supplier and the buyer getting value from the alliance; the topic of negotiations with strategic alliance relationships follows.

Negotiating Win-Win Strategic Alliance Agreements

When negotiating with strategic alliances, the most advantageous outcome occurs when both parties utilize **collaborative negotiations**. This is sometimes also referred to as **integrative** or **win-win negotiations**. In other words, both sides work together to maximize the joint outcome, or to create a joint optimal result. The belief is that there is more to gain from collaborating, rather than trying to seek an outcome that favors primarily one side's interests (referred to as **distributive negotiations**). For collaborative negotiations to succeed, members from both parties must trust each other, believe in the validity of each other's perspective, and be committed to working together. From the perspective of key supply chain trading partners, these requirements should already be present, so collaborative negotiations may be easier to achieve in actively managed supply chains.

© 2010 Ted Goff www.tedgoff.com

"The way we're doing everything doesn't seem to be working."

Successful collaborative negotiations or bargaining also requires open discussions and a free flow of information between parties, preferably in face-to-face meetings. This is particularly important when the goal is improving CSR or sustainability performance. Global mobile telecommunications company Vodafone, for example, negotiated an arrangement with Ireland's Blood Transfusion Service to supply a way to encourage more blood donations. On the day the mobile clinic is in the phone users' area, a text message is sent to remind them to donate blood. Vodafone gets public relations attention which enhances their reputation, while the blood service gets more donors—a win-win.[57] In contrast, distributive bargaining is adversarial and usually means that some information will be withheld, distorted, delayed, or completely misrepresented. The likelihood that one or the other or some combination of the two methods occurs depends on the nature of the trading relationship, the strategic nature of the item(s) being negotiated, and potentially the balance of power in the relationship. In the automotive sector, particularly at Toyota, collaborative negotiations are described to be part of a *lean thinking* approach to supplier relationships, although automobile manufacturers typically enjoy high levels of buyer dominance, which may tilt the negotiating scales somewhat in the buyer's favor.

To maximize the likelihood of achieving equitable collaborative negotiations, supply chain partners should first develop a collaborative negotiation infrastructure and then facilitate a negotiating approach that supports a win-win outcome. Table 4.4 describes the steps in developing a collaboration infrastructure. Over time, purchasing representatives will get better at collaborative negotiations as they become more familiar with their trading partners' interests, learn from previous negotiations, and determine how best to

Table 4.4	Developing a Collaborative Negotiation Infrastructure
STEPS	**DESCRIPTION**
1. Build a preparation process	Gain an understanding of both parties' interests; brainstorm value-maximizing solutions and terms; identify objective criteria wherein both sides evaluate fairness of an agreement.
2. Develop a negotiation database	Review previous negotiations to catalogue standards, practices, precedents, metrics, creative solutions used, and lessons learned.
3. Design a negotiation launch process	Create an environment allowing parties to first focus on how they will work together to create a shared vocabulary, build working relationships, and map out a shared decision-making process.
4. Institute a feedback mechanism	Create a debriefing process to provide feedback to negotiating teams and capture lessons learned.

Source: Adapted from Kliman, S., "Enabling Win-Win," *Executive Excellence* 17(4), 2000: 9–11.

work with each trading partner. Managers or negotiating team leaders can also aid in this process by maximizing exchanges of information, dealing fairly with negotiating problems, creating an environment of information sharing, and brainstorming options for achieving mutual gains.

Use of E-Procurement Systems

As discussed in Chapter 2, using the Internet in procurement can create enormous benefits for organizations with mostly paper-based procurement systems and a large volume of standard, functional item or maintenance, repair, and operating (MRO) material purchases. The primary strategic benefits of **e-procurement** include significant cost savings and the freeing up of time for purchasing staff to concentrate on more of the firm's core business activities. This comes about because e-procurement systems enable the concentration of a large volume of small purchases with a few suppliers in electronic catalogues, which are made available to the organization's users. The users then select items directly from the catalogues and buy on contracts that allow repeat purchases. The firm's computer system automatically routes transactions for approvals, sends the information along to the accounting system, and routes the purchase order directly to the supplier. The city of Helsinki, Finland, provides a great example of government purchasing benefitting from the use of an e-procurement system. On an annual basis, the city purchases approximately $2.5 billion of items from over 10,000 suppliers. Contracted items are kept in easy-to-use e-catalogs, allowing city buyers to search on items and then purchase. The city also uses the system to promote its values, such as favoring small suppliers or high quality over simply low-cost items. The city also does not own the software—rather, it is available through a Web platform, and the city pays a monthly usage fee.[58]

The use of e-procurement can also aid a firm's sustainability and ethical purchasing efforts. Global bank HSBC, for instance, uses their "Buy Smart" e-procurement system around the world to vastly reduce the use of paper from their ordering and payment process.[59] Firms are using e-procurement software that includes filters for social, environmental, and ethical requirements. Finland-based e-procurement software provider Basware has launched a set of guidelines, for example, to help buyers establish a green supply chain.[60] And finally, South Carolina-based green building materials online directory GreenWizard offers a green-product database that allows companies to post green product descriptions and architects, engineers, and contractors to search for, analyze, and purchase green building materials.[61]

New uses for the Internet appear frequently in purchasing. Several of the most recent uses take advantage of various **social media**, namely, LinkedIn, Twitter, Facebook or other online services. The e-Business Connection feature discusses this use of technology by procurement personnel for networking, knowledge sourcing, and cloud computing.

---

e-Business Connection

Using Social Media in Procurement

Social media, whether it be Twitter, LinkedIn, Yammer or another networking service, is all the rage. Although many uses for social media will likely emerge as it and the profession evolves, there are several ways to capitalize on the medium from a supply chain perspective. Specifically, these are communications repository, advanced networking, knowledge sourcing and SCM cloud computing automation.

Communications repository. Social media messaging systems allow all of the message communications within the system (whether a closed company e-mail system, protected online network [Yammer] or wide open on the Internet to allow "followers" [Twitter]) to be stored and then remain searchable. This allows others to view histories of customer interactions, internal employee interactions or situational/contextual circumstances of value for future use.

Advanced networking. One trend noted among supply management and logistics professionals is their feeling of isolation when they are heads-down and working within their isolated networks. Social media is a great way to always stay connected with both peers and thought-leaders who are relevant to you, your industry or area of specialization right from your desktop or social media-enabled mobile device. And, to be honest, at conferences, networking can be hit-or-miss. Looking at attendee lists or badges doesn't give you the same context as a tweet on Twitter that a certain individual happens to be implementing a similar RFID system to your own and came up with a way of overcoming the same problem you're facing. Social media is truly "networking on steroids" and an easy way for you to network globally in real time and with pinpointed context.

Knowledge sourcing. Once you've expanded your networking reach with the types of people or contacts at relevant companies, you can now turn these social media tools to source knowledge and information on topics of interest or required for projects through keyword searches across social media networks. Social media not only is an excellent method of networking, it is also an incredibly powerful tool for knowledge and idea sourcing—all of which are critical elements when fostering ongoing innovation in your organization and extended supply chain.

SCM cloud computing automation. According to Whatis.com:

> Cloud computing is a general term for anything that involves delivering hosted services over the Internet. These services are broadly divided into three categories: Infrastructure-as-a-Service (IaaS), Platform-as-a-Service (PaaS) and Software-as-a-Service (SaaS). The name cloud computing was inspired by the cloud symbol that's often used to represent the Internet in flow charts and diagrams.

Using social media methods and platforms in conjunction with technologies such as RFID can allow your products to automatically tweet their location, proof of delivery, current status, and even damage or temperature issues in real time.

Source: Ashcroft, J., "Social Media in the Supply Chain," *Inside Supply Management*, V. 20, No. 10, 2009, pp. 12. Copyright © 2009 by the Institute for Supply Management[TM]. Reprinted by permission.

Rewarding Supplier Performance

Rewarding suppliers for improving or maintaining high levels of performance accomplishes several objectives: it provides a continuous incentive to all suppliers to meet and surpass specific performance goals; it provides an incentive for marginal (unrewarded) suppliers to achieve a level of performance that will allow their supplier status to be upgraded, resulting in rewards; and, finally, it gives suppliers an incentive to create and share rewards, in turn, with *their* suppliers. Sharing the benefits of good performance in this way is one of the central foundations of building effective supply chains. As we mentioned at the start of the chapter, suppliers, in addition to buyers, must be able to realize benefits from supply chain relationships. Without this incentive, suppliers may keep any improvements realized within their operations quiet, while keeping the benefits as well. With time, this lack of information and benefit sharing stunts the growth of relationships within the supply chain and results in lower overall supply chain performance.

As many may remember from growing up, performance motivation can come in several forms, including punishment and various reward mechanisms. With suppliers, motivational tools can be used as an integral part of supplier management and supplier development programs. Punishment may take the form of a reduction or elimination of future business with the focal firm, a downgrade of the supplier's status from key to marginal, or a **billback penalty** equal to the incremental cost resulting from a late delivery or poor material quality. On the other hand, when performance meets or exceeds expectations, suppliers can be rewarded in some way.

Many formal strategic supplier agreements allow suppliers to benefit in the following ways:

- A share of the cost reductions resulting from supplier improvements
- A share of the cost savings resulting from a supplier's suggestions made to the focal firm
- More business and/or longer contracts for high performance
- Access to in-house training seminars and other resources
- Company and public recognition in the form of awards.

These benefits tend to stimulate further capital investment among suppliers to improve their operating capabilities, leading to even greater levels of quality, cost, and service performance. The U.S. healthcare industry is a good case in point. Purchasing costs for hospitals tend to be escalating rapidly, so hospital managers are beginning to offer incentives to suppliers to keep costs down. The Nebraska Medical Center (NMC) in Omaha, for example, partnered with Cardinal Health, a health-system consulting firm, in 2003 to explore out-of-the-box options for supply cost reductions. Their agreement with NMC provided an incentive of 30 percent of any savings they generated. They created a just-in-time inventory system that improved control and reduced inventory carrying costs. They also assigned several of their employees to work at the NMC facility (recall from the earlier chapter discussion that this is known as supplier co-location). These and other supply strategies have saved NMC millions of dollars while allowing them to maintain a 99 percent in-stock performance.[62]

Benchmarking Successful Sourcing Practices

Benchmarking, the practice of copying what other businesses do best, is a very effective way to quickly improve sourcing practices and supply chain performance. Without benchmarking, firms must learn through their own experiences the methods and tools that work the best.

Successful benchmarking allows firms to potentially leapfrog the experience-gaining stage by trying things that have worked well for other companies. Meaningful benchmarking data regarding sourcing practices can be obtained in any number of ways, both formal and informal—from using evaluation surveys distributed to a firm's customers and suppliers regarding *their* sourcing and supplier management practices, to discussing sourcing strategies with colleagues at business association meetings or conferences, to collecting published trade information on benchmarking studies.

A large number of resources are available for firms seeking to learn about and implement successful sourcing practices. The Center for Advanced Purchasing Studies (CAPS), an Arizona-based, nonprofit, independent research organization, helps firms achieve competitive advantage by providing leading-edge research information regarding strategic purchasing. For instance, CAPS provides research studies, benchmarking reports, and best practices case studies, along with organizing annual purchasing symposiums and roundtable discussions for purchasing professionals and academics.

Another organization, the Supply-Chain Council headquartered in Washington D.C., helps practitioners reduce their supply chain costs and improve customer service by providing their Supply Chain Operations Reference (SCORE) model as a framework for supply chain improvement. They also provide case studies and bring together practitioners to discuss best practices in periodic business conferences around the world.

The Arizona-based Institute for Supply Management (ISM), established in 1915, provides a wide variety of resources to supply management professionals worldwide, including a monthly publication featuring the latest supply management trends and information and the globally recognized Certified Purchasing Manager (C.P.M.), Certified Professional in Supply Management (CPSM), and Accredited Purchasing Practitioner (A.P.P.) programs. They also publish the globally-recognized *Journal of Supply Chain Management*, organize several annual global supply management conferences, and support many seminars and Web conferences for supply management professionals.

The issue of best purchasing practices has been the subject of a number of research studies over the years, and these findings have proven very beneficial for firms seeking to benchmark best sourcing practices.[63] Some of the research has found a positive relationship between purchasing benchmarking and firm performance. Some of the successful sourcing practices found to be common among the companies studied were:

- use of a central database to access information on parts, suppliers, lead times, and other purchasing information;
- software applications for sharing information with suppliers;
- use of the Internet for supplier searches;
- alliances with key suppliers for specific components;
- supplier certification and the elimination of incoming quality checks for key supplier deliveries;
- involving suppliers in the research and development processes of new products;

- reducing the firm's supply base;
- continuous measurement of supplier performance, and establishing supplier improvement targets; and most recently,
- creating an ethical and sustainable supply chain.

Using Third-Party Supply Chain Management Services

The use of **third-party logistics (3PL)** companies for supply chain management services is a growing trend, as firms seek to gain quick competitive advantage from the deployment of proven, effective supply chain strategies. The term *3PL* today refers to a firm that supplies logistics and possibly other supply chain management services. Much more on this topic can be found in Chapter 9. With the demands for shipping capabilities, delivery speed, and inventory visibility increasing, the trend in outsourcing of supply chain services to 3PLs over the past fifteen years has been increasing at about a ten percent annual rate worldwide. In 2008 almost $500 billion was generated in the global 3PL market.[64] In the U.S., the 3PL sector accounts for about ten percent of total logistics spending, while in Europe, 3PLs account for about 25 percent of total logistics costs.[65] These services assume some or all of a firm's sourcing, materials management, and product distribution responsibilities; charge a fee for their services while saving costs (estimated at 10 to 20 percent of total logistics costs); and ultimately hope to improve service, quality, and profits for the clients.

For firms with limited supply chain management experience, these services can be a worthwhile investment. Even large firms use 3PLs, since supply chain cost savings can amount to tens of millions of dollars annually. As a matter of fact, nearly 80 percent of U.S. Fortune 500 companies are using 3PLs, and the larger it is, the more likely a firm will be to have a 3PL relationship. General Motors, Procter & Gamble, and PepsiCo all use more than thirty 3PLs. L.L. Bean, for example, uses UPS as their primary package and catalog carrier, as well as for product returns.[66]

As supply chain management has grown in strategic importance, some shippers are experimenting with the use of fewer 3PL services, or even one primary 3PL provider and overseer, more commonly referred to as a 4PL or **lead logistics provider (LLP)**. Some shippers argue they need at least two or three 3PLs to guard against service disruptions or coverage problems. "While tactically it is better to consolidate the number of providers, recent capacity shortages have shown that shippers need to ensure they have enough coverage," says Dick Armstrong, CEO of logistics consultant Armstrong & Associates, headquartered in Wisconsin.

Firms can enter new regional and global markets quickly with less capital investment and then leave quickly with smaller losses if sales don't materialize. Some key disadvantages when using 3PL providers include loss of control, loss of communication with customers and suppliers, the potential spread of confidential information to customers and suppliers, and the potential damage to the firm's reputation if mistakes are made by the 3PLs. Companies must realize that these service providers are not internal employees and may not be fully aware of company policies and practices.

Environmental performance may be one of the primary criteria for 3PL selection; in fact, results from the Georgia Institute of Technology's 2008 Third-Party Logistics Study showed that 86 percent of executives polled thought that a green supply chain is some-what or very important. According to Kristin Pierre, an executive with the Green Suppliers Network, five years ago only 12 percent of suppliers were deselected for failing to meet sustainability requirements; today, that number is 32 percent, and five years from now it is projected to be 76 percent. "Green and ethical is no longer an option; it's a necessity," says Pierre.[67] Since the transportation sector is responsible for approximately 15 percent of greenhouse gas emissions, more companies are looking to their logistics providers to reduce their carbon footprints. Ryder Logistics helped New Hampshire-based yogurt maker Stonyfield Farm redesign its delivery network to reduce its carbon footprint by 48 percent.[68]

Finally, as an extension of VMI, some firms today are experimenting with outsourcing most or all of the supply management or purchasing functions to 3PL services. Arguments in favor of this are that overhead costs are reduced, skilled personnel can be utilized, and purchase costs can be lowered since 3PLs gain huge purchase volume leverage by combining demands for the same items from all of their customers, resulting in pricing discounts. The downside, particularly for firms engaged in proactive supply chain management, is that as more of the supply management function is performed by outside services, it ceases to be viewed as a strategic component of the firm. Additionally, the firm risks the loss of important key suppliers. However, firms have successfully outsourced the purchasing of items with less strategic importance, such as MRO items.

Assessing and Improving the Firm's Own Sourcing Function

As has been stated throughout Part II of this textbook, the sourcing function is one of the most value-enhancing functions in any organization. Today, as purchasing staff members are expected more often to generate cost savings and service and quality enhancements for the organization, they must be viewed as strategic internal suppliers of the organization. Bearing this in mind, it may then be preferable to periodically monitor the purchasing or sourcing function's performance against set standards, goals, and/or industry benchmarks. Thus, as the firm strives to continuously improve its products and processes, purchasing can also gauge its success in improving its own value-enhancing contributions to the firm and its varied supply chains.

As was stated earlier in this chapter and in Chapter 3, when discussing supplier assessment, criteria can be utilized to provide feedback to the purchasing staff regarding their contributions to the strategic goals of the firm. Surveys or audits of this nature can be administered as self-assessments among buyers as part of the annual evaluation process, and assessments can also include feedback from internal customers of the supply management or sourcing function, such as engineering and sales, or marketing and finance personnel. Feedback may even be included from supplier representatives. Assessment criteria to evaluate the purchasing department's performance should include some or all of the following:

- participating in and leading multifunctional teams;
- participating in value engineering/value analysis efforts;
- finding and evaluating ethical and sustainable suppliers;

- optimizing the supply base;
- managing and developing local, regional, and global suppliers;
- creating early supplier involvement initiatives;
- the creation of strategic supplier alliances;
- furthering the integration and development of existing key suppliers;
- contributing to new product development efforts;
- utilizing e-procurement systems;
- initiating supplier cost reduction programs;
- contributing to the improvement of purchased product and service quality;
- improving time to market; and
- maintaining and improving internal cooperative relationships.

Since these criteria require both qualitative and quantitative assessments, the performance evaluation tool recommended here would be some form of weighted-factor rating method, as covered in Chapter 3. Because of the tremendous potential value of these many activities, supply management staff members should be continuously auditing their capabilities and successes in these areas.

Thus, the skill set requirements of purchasing professionals have been changing as purchasing, sourcing, or supply management has evolved from the tactical, clerical function it was about thirty years ago to the highly demanding strategic function it is today. To achieve the type of world-class performance suggested by the preceding assessment criteria, sourcing personnel must today exhibit world-class skills. One recent survey of procurement professionals conducted by *Purchasing* magazine found that their top three responsibilities were negotiating contracts, selecting suppliers, and managing supplier relationships. Given the recent economic downturn, controlling costs is also seen as a very important activity of purchasing personnel. Important cost-controlling activities include reducing the supply base, negotiating global agreements with suppliers, and adopting new technologies suited to purchasing activities.[69]

SUMMARY

Achieving supply chain management success often starts with the sourcing activity. We hope we have provided in this chapter, and the previous two, evidence of the strategic role played within the firm by the sourcing function and the impact of sourcing on the management of the supply chain. Firms that fail to recognize this importance will simply not experience the same level of success in the long run. Two relatively new sourcing topics, ethical and sustainable sourcing, are quickly gaining importance with regard to how firms are choosing to operate. Sourcing personnel are playing an important role today in helping the firm to achieve success in these two areas while maintaining cost, quality, and customer service objectives. The sourcing process is thus comprised of a number of related activities that, when taken together, provide competitive advantage for the firm. Firms can maximize this advantage by developing effective supply chain strategies and then assessing and revising these strategies periodically as missions, markets, competitors and technologies change. As we head into the internal operations segment of this text, we hope you will continue to consider the sourcing issues discussed in Part I and how they interact with other processes as materials, services, and information move down the supply chain toward the immediate customers and, eventually, the end users.

KEY TERMS

backsourcing, 114

benchmarking, 124

billback penalty, 123

business ethics, 102

collaborative negotiations, 119

co-managed inventories, 116

corporate social responsibility (CSR), 102

co-sourcing, 114

distributive negotiations, 120

early supplier involvement, 115

e-procurement, 121

ethical sourcing, 103

Ethical Trading Initiative (ETI), 104

fair trade products, 105

functional products, 109

global sustainability index, 106

green purchasing, 105

innovative products, 109

insourcing, 114

integrative or win-win negotiations, 119

lead logistics provider (LLP), 125

outsource, 113

purchasing spend, 109

reorder point, 116

rewarding suppliers, 123

rights and duties, 102

selective sourcing, 114

social media, 122

social sustainability, 106

strategic alliance development, 117

strategic sourcing, 101

strategic supplier alliances, 112

supplier co-location, 117

supply base optimization, 111

supply base rationalization, 111

supply base reduction, 111

sustainability, 106

sustainable sourcing, 106

third-party logistics (3PL), 125

utilitarianism, 102

value engineering, 115

vendor managed inventory (VMI), 116

DISCUSSION QUESTIONS

1. What is the difference between purchasing and strategic sourcing?

2. What is ethical sourcing, and why do firms do it?

3. What are some common practices or activities of ethical sourcing?

4. What are some of the risks of ethical sourcing? What about the potential advantages? Do you think ethical sourcing is a good practice?

5. What is a fair trade product?

6. What is sustainable sourcing, and how does it differ from ethical sourcing? From green purchasing?

7. What are the benefits of sustainable sourcing? Can firms actually make money from sustainable sourcing? Do you think it is a good practice?

8. Can firms buy functional products in an ethical way? A sustainable way? What about innovative products?

9. Where do ethical and sustainable sourcing policies come from in an organization?

10. What is supply base rationalization, and what are its advantages and disadvantages?

11. What are the benefits of obtaining ethical and sustainable certifications? Why would a buyer want its suppliers to have these certifications?

12. What advantages do company-designed supplier certification programs have over industry certifications like ISO 9000?

13. Would a firm ever want to outsource a core product or process? Why or why not?

14. When would firms want to insource a product or process? How is this different from co-sourcing?

15. What is sourcing's role in value engineering, and what benefits does this give to the firm?

16. Why is early supplier involvement a good way to integrate the supply chain?

17. Describe the differences between vendor managed inventories and co-managed inventories, and when it might be advisable to do either of them.

18. Discuss the advantages and risks of supplier co-location.

19. What is the difference between supplier management and alliance development?

20. What makes supplier alliances fail? How can firms reduce the failure rate?

21. Describe the differences between integrative and distributive negotiations, and when each should be used.

22. Why are second- and third-tier suppliers important to the focal firm?

23. What is a common method for developing second-tier suppliers?

24. **Discussion Problem:** If your firm had 500 suppliers and they each had 100 suppliers, how many second-tier suppliers would your firm have? What if your firm reduced its supply base to twenty?

25. When would your firm want to use an e-procurement system?

26. If you work for a company, describe how it rewards and punishes its suppliers. Do you think appropriate methods are used? Why or why not?

27. What are some different ways you could use benchmarking to improve your performance at school?

28. What is a 3PL provider? What advantages could a 3PL provider give to a small firm? A large firm?

29. What is a 4PL? When would you use a 4PL instead of a 3PL?

30. Could your firm use a 3PL to improve its ethical or sustainable purchasing practices?

31. Why would a firm want to monitor its purchasing performance?

32. How would you rate your skill level on the world-class skill set listed at the end of the chapter?

INTERNET QUESTIONS

1. Go to the International Organization for Standardization website (www.iso.org) and write a short description and history of the organization, including the various certifications that can be obtained.

2. Go to the CAPS website (www.capsresearch.org), find the latest cross-industry benchmarking report and determine the overall purchase dollars as a percent of sales in the United States. What benchmarking research is CAPS doing now?

3. Go to the site for the North American Green Purchasing Initiative (www.NAGPI. net), and describe several best practices listed at the site.

4. Go to the Fair Factories Clearinghouse (www.fairfactories.org) and describe some of the events underway at the organization.

5. Go to the Goldman Environmental Prize website, and describe the most recent award winners.

6. What is an ASP? Find some on the Internet that are not listed in the chapter, and describe what they do.

7. Search on the term *sustainability laws* and write a report on recent laws dealing with sustainability.

8. Gather information on business ethics and ethical purchasing, and report on several of the most current news items and controversies.

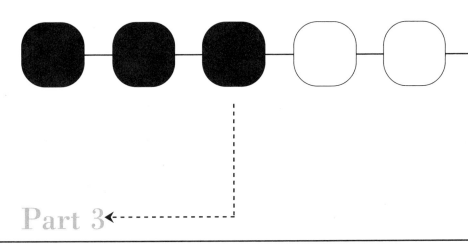

Part 3

Operations Issues in Supply Chain Management

Chapter 5

DEMAND FORECASTING

Forecasting is only one of the three key activities in CPFR [Collaborative Planning, Forecasting and Replenishment]. Planning is the process of working together to organize and to resolve key barriers to rapid and efficient delivery of goods in the supply chain. Replenishment is the activity of accomplishing timely, accurate and complete fulfillment between partners in the supply chain and between distribution centers and selling locations. The middle activity, Forecasting, has to have as its end result a reliable order forecast that the supplier actually uses to drive acquisition and manufacturing to support on time and complete shipping. Many companies have spent a lot of effort on collaborative forecasting, but few are addressing order forecasting. Those partners that are not arriving at an order forecast actually used by the supplier are not getting at the heart of the matter.

Larry Smith, West Marine[1]

Learning Objectives

After completing this chapter, you should be able to

- Explain the role of demand forecasting in a supply chain.
- Identify the components of a forecast.
- Compare and contrast qualitative and quantitative forecasting techniques.
- Assess the accuracy of forecasts.
- Explain collaborative planning, forecasting and replenishment.

Chapter Outline

Introduction

Demand Forecasting

Forecasting Techniques

Qualitative Methods

Quantitative Methods

Components of Time Series

Time Series Forecasting Models

Forecast Accuracy

Useful Forecasting Websites

Collaborative Planning, Forecasting and Replenishment (CPFR)

Software Solutions

Summary

Supply Chain Management in Action   *The ISM Report on Business*

The Institute of Supply Management (ISM), formerly known as the National Association of Purchasing Management (NAPM), surveys more than 300 purchasing and supply executives in the U.S. using a questionnaire seeking information on "changes in production, new orders, new export orders, imports, employment, inventories, prices, leadtimes, and the timeliness of supplier deliveries in their companies comparing the current month to the previous month." The *ISM Report on Business*, available the first business day of each month, is considered to be an accurate indicator of the overall direction of the economy and the health of the manufacturing and non-manufacturing sectors. Three quotes regarding the value of the report follow:[2]

> *I find the surveys conducted by the purchasing and supply managers to be an excellent supplement to the data supplied by various departments and agencies of the government.*
>
> —Alan Greenspan, former Chairman of the Federal Reserve Board

> *The ISM Manufacturing Report on Business has one of the shortest reporting lags of any macro-economic series and gives an important early look at the economy. It also measures some concepts (such as lead times and delivery lags) that can be found nowhere else. It makes an important contribution to the American statistical system and to economic policy.*
>
> —Joseph E. Stiglitz, former Chairman of President Clinton's Council of Economic Advisors

> *The ISM Manufacturing Report on Business is extremely useful. The PMI, the Report's composite index, gives the earliest indication each month of the health of the manufacturing sector. It is an essential component for assessing the state of the economy.*
>
> —Michael J. Boskin, Hoover Institute Senior Fellow

The ISM report provides several indices for the manufacturing sector: Customers' Inventories, New Orders, Production, Manufacturing Employment, Supplier Deliveries, Inventories, Price, Backlog of Orders, New Export Orders, and Imports. The most important index is the Purchasing Managers Index (PMI) developed by Theodore Torda, Senior Economist of the U.S. Department of Commerce, and introduced in 1982. The PMI is a composite of five weighted seasonally adjusted indices (weights are shown in parentheses): New Orders (0.20), Production (0.20), Employment (0.20), Supplier Deliveries (0.20), and Inventories (0.20). A reading below 50 percent represents contraction and a reading over 50 percent indicates expansion in the manufacturing sector of the economy compared to the previous month. The purchasing surveys provide comprehensive information for tracking the economy and developing business forecasts. ISM has reports on both the manufacturing and the non-manufacturing sectors.

Purchasing and supply executives use the report in a variety of ways. For example, the Customers' Inventories Index is a strong indicator of future new orders and production, and is used to measure changes in supply chain activity. Norbert J. Ore, chair of the Institute for Supply Management™ Manufacturing Business Survey Committee, in the May 2010 Manufacturing ISM *Report on Business* noted that "The manufacturing sector grew for the 10th consecutive month during May. The rate of growth as indicated by the PMI is driven by continued strength in new orders and production. Employment continues to grow as manufacturers have added to payrolls for six consecutive months. The recovery continues to broaden as 16 of 18 industries report growth. There are a number of reports, particularly in the tech sector, of shortages of components; this is the result of excessive inventory de-stocking during the downturn."[3] The PMI for May was 59.7 percent. In the same report, Ore also said, "The past relationship between the PMI and the overall economy indicates that the average PMI for January through May (58.9 percent) corresponds to a 5.7 percent increase in real gross domestic product (GDP). In addition, if the PMI for May (59.7 percent) is annualized, it corresponds to a 6 percent increase in real GDP annually."

Introduction

Much has been written about demand-driven supply chains. In today's competitive environment, organizations are moving to a more effective demand-driven supply chain to enable them to respond quickly to shifting demand. Consumers have become more demanding and discriminating. The market has evolved into a "pull" environment with customers dictating to the supplier what products they desire and when they need them delivered. If a retailer cannot get the product it wants at the right quantity, price and time from one supplier, it will look for another company that can meet its demands. Any temporary stockout has a tremendous downside on sales, profitability and customer relationships.

There are several ways to closely match supply and demand. One way is for a supplier to hold plenty of stock available for delivery at any time. While this approach maximizes sales revenues, it is also expensive because of the cost of carrying inventory and the possibility of write-downs at the end of the selling season. Use of flexible pricing is another approach. During heavy demand periods, prices can be raised to reduce peak demand. Price discounts can then be used to increase sales during periods with excess inventory or slow demand. This strategy can still result in lost sales, though, as well as stockouts, and thus cannot be considered an ideal or partnership-friendly approach to satisfying demand. In the short term, companies can also use overtime, subcontracting, or temporary workers to increase capacity to meet demand for their products and services. In the interim, however, firms will lose sales as they train workers, and quality may also tend to suffer.

Managing demand is challenging because of the difficulty in forecasting future consumer requirements accurately. In order for supply chain integration to be successful, suppliers must be able to accurately forecast demand so they can produce and deliver the right quantities demanded by their customers in a timely and cost-effective fashion. Thus, it is imperative that suppliers along the supply chain find ways to better match supply and demand to achieve optimal levels of cost, quality and customer service to enable them to compete with other supply chains. Any problems that adversely affect the timely delivery of products demanded by consumers will have ramifications throughout the entire chain.

Sport Obermeyer, a high-end fashion skiwear design and merchandising company headquartered in Aspen, Colorado, sells its products through department stores and ski shops. Sport Obermeyer's selling season is from September to January, with peak sales in December and January. Since the selling season is short and sales of high-end fashion apparel are more profitable than those of traditional apparel, it is critical that Sport Obermeyer supply the demand for high-end fashion apparel without getting stuck with excessive inventories at the end of the season. With improved forecasting capabilities and implementation of a quick response program that keeps its suppliers notified of forecasts, sales patterns and marketing campaigns, Sport Obermeyer is able to mitigate the supply-demand mismatch problem, thus reducing stockouts during the season and heavy markdowns at the end of the season.[4] Sport Obermeyer thus represents an effective approach to matching supply and demand while minimizing risk and cost.

Demand Forecasting

Forecasting is an important element of demand management. It provides an estimate of future demand and the basis for planning and sound business decisions. Since all organizations deal with an unknown future, some error between a forecast and actual demand is to be expected. Thus, the goal of a good forecasting technique is to minimize the deviation between actual demand and the forecast. Since a forecast is a prediction of the future, factors that influence demand, the impact of these factors, and whether they will continue to influence future demand, must be considered in developing an accurate forecast. In addition, buyers and sellers should share all relevant information to generate a single consensus forecast so that the correct decisions on supply and demand can be made. Improved forecasts benefit not only the focal company but also the trading partners in the supply chain. Having accurate demand forecasts allows the purchasing department to order the right amount of products, the operations department to produce the right amount of products and the logistics department to deliver the right amount of products. Thus, timely and accurate demand information is a critical component of an effective supply chain. Inaccurate forecasts would lead to imbalances in supply and demand. In today's competitive business environment, collaboration (or cooperation and information sharing) between buyers and sellers is the rule rather than the exception. The benefits of better forecasts are lower inventories, reduced stockouts, smoother production plans, reduced costs and improved customer service.

For more than 60 years, the Institute of Supply Management (ISM) has been publishing monthly indices for the manufacturing sector such as Customers' Inventories, New Orders, Production, Manufacturing Employment, Supplier Deliveries, Inventories, Price, Backlog of Orders, New Export Orders and Imports. Many business executives use these indices to forecast the overall direction of the economy and the health of the manufacturing sector. For example, purchasing and supply managers utilize the Customers' Inventories Index to help forecast future new orders and make production decisions and to measure changes in supply chain activity. The *Wall Street Journal* publishes the *ISM Report on Business*, which includes both the manufacturing and nonmanufacturing sectors. The *ISM Report on Business* is profiled in the chapter opening Supply Chain Management in Action feature.

Many have argued that demand forecasting is both an art and a science. Since there are no accurate crystal balls available, it is impossible to expect 100 percent forecast accuracy at all times. The impact of poor communication and inaccurate forecasts resonates all along the supply chain and results in the *bullwhip effect* (described in Chapter 1) causing stockouts, lost sales, high costs of inventory and obsolescence, material shortages, poor responsiveness to market dynamics, and poor profitability. Numerous examples exist showing the problems that companies faced when their sales forecasts did not match customer demands during new product introductions. For instance, Nintendo's Wii, which was introduced at about the same time as Sony's PlayStation 3 (PS3), had exceeded all expectations and outsold Sony by a huge margin. Nintendo consequently struggled to meet the unexpectedly high demand for Wiis. Another example is Apple, which had preorders of 600,000 units for its new iPhone 4 in one day. According to Apple, iPhone 4 preorder sales were ten times higher than the first day of preordering for the iPhone 3G S.[5] Due to the high preorder rate, the system suffered many order and approval malfunctions and delayed the delivery of the phones by at least a month. This indicates the challenge faced by companies in forecasting sales and ramping up production to meet the demand for their products and to defend their market position.

In the airline industry, both Airbus and Boeing are the two major competitors. Competition has been fierce, with each manufacturer trying to get the upper hand. When Airbus unveiled the A380, the largest passenger aircraft ever made with a capacity of more than 500 passengers, it was heralded as the next big invention and would change how the world viewed aviation. To accommodate the A380, airports around the world will have to spend many millions of dollars to upgrade their infrastructures. For example, Los Angeles International airport is expected to spend $53 million on new runways, loading areas and airport improvements.[6] Airbus is also behind schedule in delivering the A380s. Production problems pushed delivery back several times, and cost overruns sent the company into a tailspin. While a total of 202 planes have been ordered, only 29 have been delivered to Air France, Emirates, Lufthansa, Qantas and Singapore Airlines.[7] Boeing took a totally different approach from Airbus, deciding that it was important to have mid-sized planes with high fuel efficiencies. The 787 Dreamliner was developed by Boeing for long-haul flights that could carry between 210 and 330 passengers and could serve both small and large airports. Demand for fuel-efficient airliners such as the 787 Dreamliner is expected to increase as energy prices continue to rise. Thus far, Boeing has received orders totaling 866 planes.[8] The Boeing 787 is one of the fastest-selling airplanes in aviation history. However, design and production problems have delayed the first deliveries. This unexpected outcome could affect future sales of the plane. Thus, we can see that forecasting demand for new products is a difficult proposition.

Forecasting Techniques

Understanding that a forecast is very often inaccurate does not mean that nothing can be done to improve the forecast. Both quantitative and qualitative forecasts can be improved by seeking inputs from trading partners. **Qualitative forecasting methods** are based on opinions and intuition, whereas **quantitative forecasting methods** use mathematical models and relevant historical data to generate forecasts. The quantitative methods can be divided into two groups: time series and associative models.

Qualitative Methods

Qualitative forecasting methods are based on intuition or judgmental evaluation and are generally used when data are limited, unavailable, or not currently relevant. While this approach can be very low cost, its effectiveness depends to a large extent on the skill and experience of the forecaster(s) and the amount of relevant information available.

The qualitative techniques are often used to develop long-range projections when current data is no longer very useful, and for new product introductions when current data does not exist. Discussions of four common qualitative forecasting models follow.

Jury of Executive Opinion

A group of senior management executives who are knowledgeable about the market, their competitors and the business environment collectively develop the forecast. This technique has the advantage of several individuals with considerable experience working together, but if one member's views dominate the discussion, then the value and reliability of the outcome can be diminished. This technique is applicable for long-range planning and new product introductions.

Forecasting high fashion, for instance, is a risky business since there is often no historical basis to generate the forecast. Sport Obermeyer's buying committee estimates its demand based on a general consensus reached by committee members. Because a dominant member of the group might carry more weight in the discussion, the resulting forecast could potentially be biased and inaccurate. Consequently, Sport Obermeyer averages the individual forecast of each committee member to provide an overall demand forecast.[9]

Delphi Method

A group of internal and external experts are surveyed during several rounds in terms of future events and long-term forecasts of demand. Group members do not physically meet and thus avoid the scenario where one or a few experts could dominate a discussion. The answers from the experts are accumulated after each round of the survey and summarized. The summary of responses is then sent out to all the experts in the next round, wherein individual experts can modify their responses based on the group's response summary. This iterative process continues until a consensus is reached. The process can be both time-consuming and very expensive. This approach is applicable for high-risk technology forecasting; large, expensive projects; or major, new product introductions. The quality of the forecast depends largely on the knowledge of the experts.

Sales Force Composite

The sales force represents a good source of market information. This type of forecast is generated based on the sales force's knowledge of the market and estimates of customer needs. Due to the proximity of the sales personnel to the consumers, the forecast tends to be reliable, but individual biases could negatively impact the effectiveness of this approach. For example, if bonuses are paid when actual sales exceed the forecast, there is a tendency for the sales force to under-forecast.

Consumer Survey

A questionnaire is developed that seeks input from customers on important issues such as future buying habits, new product ideas and opinions about existing products. The survey is administered through telephone, mail, Internet, or personal interviews. Data collected from the survey are analyzed using statistical tools and judgment to derive a set of meaningful results. For example, Wyeth-Ayerst, the ninth-largest pharmaceutical company in the world, uses this type of market research to create forecasts for new products.[10] The challenge is to identify a sample of respondents who are representative of the larger population and to get an acceptable response rate.

Quantitative Methods

Quantitative forecasting models use mathematical techniques that are based on historical data and can include causal variables to forecast demand. **Time series forecasting** is based on the assumption that the future is an extension of the past; thus, historical data can be used to predict future demand. **Cause-and-effect forecasting** assumes that one or more factors (independent variables) are related to demand and, therefore, can be used to predict future demand.

Since these forecasts rely solely on past demand data, all quantitative methods become less accurate as the forecast's time horizon increases. Thus, for long-time horizon forecasts, it is generally recommended to utilize a combination of both quantitative and qualitative techniques.

Components of Time Series

A time series typically has four components: trend, cyclical, seasonal and random variations:

Trend Variations

Trends represent either increasing or decreasing movements over many years, and are due to factors such as population growth, population shifts, cultural changes and income shifts. Common trend lines are linear, S-curve, exponential or asymptotic.

Cyclical Variations

Cyclical variations are wavelike movements that are longer than a year and influenced by macroeconomic and political factors. One example is the **business cycle** (recession or expansion). Recent business cycles in the U.S. have been affected by global events such as the 1973 oil embargo, the 1991 Mexican financial crisis, the 1997 Asian economic crisis, the September 11, 2001 terrorist attacks in the U.S., and hurricanes Katrina and Rita in 2005.

Seasonal Variations

Seasonal variations show peaks and valleys that repeat over a consistent interval such as hours, days, weeks, months, years, or seasons. Due to seasonality, many companies do well in certain months and not so well in other months. For example, snow blower sales tend to be higher in the fall and winter, but taper off in the spring and summer. A fast-food restaurant will see higher sales during the day around breakfast, lunch and dinner. U.S. hotels experience large crowds during traditional holidays such as July 4, Labor Day, Thanksgiving, Christmas and New Years.

Random Variations

Random variations are due to unexpected or unpredictable events such as natural disasters (hurricanes, tornadoes, fire), strikes and wars. An example is the recent eruption at Iceland's Eyjafjallajökull volcano, which caused ash clouds to reach mainland Europe. Numerous flights to England and Europe were shut down, which led to the highest air travel disruption since the Second World War.[11] Another natural disaster is the earthquake of magnitude 7.0 that hit Haiti recently. The Haitian government reported that 250,000 residences and 30,000 commercial buildings were badly damaged; 230,000 people died, 300,000 were injured and 1,000,000 made homeless as a result of the earthquake.[12]

Time Series Forecasting Models

As discussed earlier, time series forecasts are dependent on the availability of historical data. Forecasts are estimated by extrapolating the past data into the future. A survey[13] of forecasting models used shows that time series models are the most widely used (72 percent) and judgmental models are the least used (11 percent). The study also finds that within the time series models, the ones most commonly used are the simple models (averages and simple trend) and exponential smoothing. In general, demand forecasts are used in planning for procurement, supply, replenishment and corporate revenue.

Some of the more common time series approaches such as naïve forecast, simple moving average, weighted moving average and exponential smoothing are discussed next.

Naïve Forecast

Using the **naïve forecast**, the estimate for the next period is equal to the actual demand for the immediate past period:

$$F_{t+1} = A_t$$

where F_{t+1} = forecast for period $t+1$;

A_t = actual demand for period t.

For example, if this period's actual demand is 100 units, then next period's forecast is 100 units. This method is inexpensive to understand, develop, store data and operate. However, there is no consideration of causal relationships, and the method may not generate accurate forecasts. Many economic and business series are considered good candidates for using the naïve forecast because the series behave like random walks.

Simple Moving Average Forecast

The **simple moving average forecast** uses historical data to generate a forecast and works well when the demand is fairly stable over time. The formula for the n-period moving average forecast is shown below:

$$F_{t+1} = \frac{\sum_{i=t-n+1}^{t} A_i}{n}$$

where F_{t+1} = forecast for period $t+1$;

n = number of periods used to calculate moving average;

A_i = actual demand in period i.

When n equals 1, the simple moving average forecast is the naïve forecast. The average tends to be more responsive if fewer data points are used to compute the average. However, random events can also impact the average adversely. Thus the decision maker must balance the cost of responding slowly to changes versus the cost of responding to random variations. The advantage of this technique is that it is simple to use and easy to understand. A weakness of the simple moving average method is its inability to respond to trend changes quickly. Example 5.1 illustrates the simple moving average forecast.

Example 5.1   Simple Moving Average Forecasting

PERIOD	DEMAND
1	1600
2	2200
3	2000
4	1600
5	2500
6	3500
7	3300
8	3200
9	3900
10	4700
11	4300
12	4400

Using the data provided, calculate the forecast for period 5 using a four-period simple moving average.

SOLUTION

$$F_5 = \text{forecast for period 5} = \frac{1600 + 2200 + 2000 + 1600}{4} = 1850$$

An Excel spreadsheet solution is shown in Figure 5.1.

Figure 5.1	Simple Moving Average Forecasting Using Excel Spreadsheet

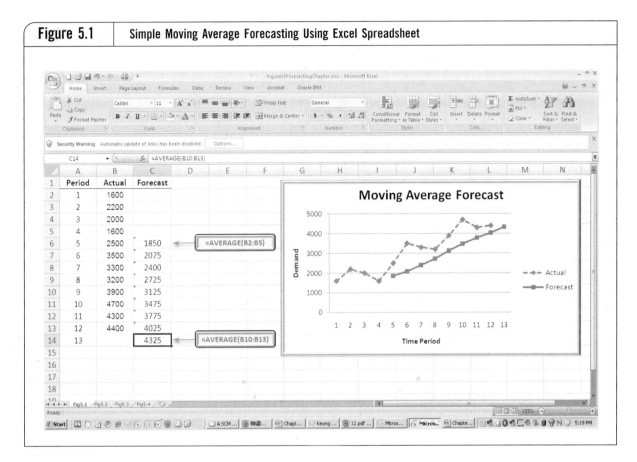

Weighted Moving Average Forecast

The simple moving average forecast places equal weights $(1/n)$ on each of the n-period observations. Under some circumstances, a forecaster may decide that equal weighing is undesirable. An n-period **weighted moving average forecast** is the weighted average of the n-period observations, using unequal weights. The only restriction is that the weights should be nonnegative and sum to one. The formula for the n-period weighted moving average forecast is shown below:

$$F_{t+1} = \sum_{i=t-n+1}^{t} w_i A_i$$

where F_{t+1} = forecast for period $t+1$;

     n = number of periods used in determining the moving average;

     A_i = actual demand in period i;

     w_i = weight assigned to period i; $\Sigma w_i = 1$.

The 3-period weighted moving average forecast with weights (0.5, 0.3, 0.2) is;

$$F_t = 0.5 (A_{t-1} + 0.3 A_{t-2} + 0.2 A_{t-3}).$$

Note that generally a greater emphasis (thus the highest weight) is placed on the most recent observation and, hence, the forecast would react more rapidly than the 3-period simple moving average forecast. However, the forecaster may instead wish to apply the smallest weight to the most recent data such that the forecast would be less affected by abrupt changes in recent data. The weights used thus tend to be based on the experience of the forecaster and this is one of the advantages of this forecasting method. Although the forecast is more responsive to underlying changes in demand, it still lags demand because of the averaging effect. As such, the weighted moving average method does not do a good job of tracking trend changes in the data. Example 5.2 illustrates the weighted moving average forecast.

Example 5.2   Weighted Moving Average Forecasting

Based on data provided in Example 5.1, calculate the forecast for period 5 using a four-period weighted moving average. The weights of 0.4, 0.3, 0.2 and 0.1 are assigned to the most recent, second most recent, third most recent, and fourth most recent periods, respectively.

SOLUTION

$$F_5 = 0.1(1600) + 0.2(2200) + 0.3(2000) + 0.4(1600) = 1840$$

An Excel spreadsheet solution is shown in Figure 5.2.

Exponential Smoothing Forecast

The **exponential smoothing forecast** is a sophisticated weighted moving average forecasting technique in which the forecast for next period's demand is the current period's forecast adjusted by a fraction of the difference between the current period's actual demand and forecast. This approach requires less data than the weighted moving average method because only two data points are needed. Due to its simplicity and minimal data

Figure 5.2   Weighted Moving Average Forecasting Using Excel Spreadsheet

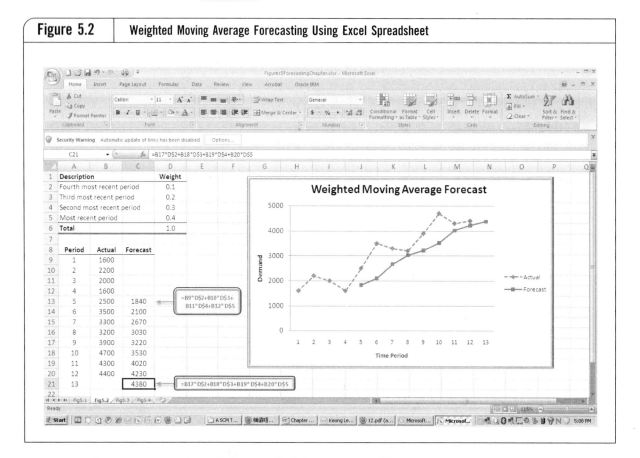

requirement, exponential smoothing is one of the more widely used forecasting techniques. This model, like the other time series models, is suitable for data that show little trend or seasonal patterns. Other higher-order exponential smoothing models (which are not covered here) can be used for data exhibiting trend and seasonality. The exponential smoothing forecasting formula is:

$$F_{t+1} = F_t + \alpha (A_t - F_t)$$

or

$$F_{t+1} = \alpha A_t + (1 - \alpha)F_t$$

where F_{t+1} = forecast for period $t + 1$;

F_t = forecast for period t;

A_t = actual demand for period t;

α = smoothing constant $(0 \leq \alpha \leq 1)$.

The exponential smoothing forecast is equivalent to the naïve forecast when α is equal to 1. With an α value closer to 1, there is a greater emphasis on recent data resulting in a major adjustment of the error in the last period's forecast. Thus with a high α value, the model is more responsive to changes in the recent demand. When α has a low value, more weight is placed on past demand (which is contained in the previous forecast), and the model responds slower to changes in demand. The impact of using a small or large value of α is similar to the effect of using a large or small number of observations in calculating the moving average. In general, the forecast will lag any trend in the actual data because only partial adjustment to the most recent forecast error can be made. The initial forecast can be estimated using the naïve method, that is, the forecast for next period is the actual demand for this period. Example 5.3 illustrates the exponential smoothing forecast.

Example 5.3   Exponential Smoothing Forecasting

Based on data provided in Example 5.1, calculate the forecast for period 3 using the exponential smoothing method. Assume the forecast for period 2 is 1600. Use a smoothing constant (α) of 0.3.

SOLUTION

Given: $F_2 = 1600$, $\alpha = 0.3$

$$F_{t+1} = F_t + \alpha(A_t - F_t)$$
$$F_3 = F_2 + \alpha(A_2 - F_2) = 1600 + 0.3(2200 - 1600) = 1780$$

Thus, the forecast for week 3 is 1780.

An Excel spreadsheet solution is shown in Figure 5.3.

Linear Trend Forecast

A **linear trend forecast** can be estimated using simple linear regression to fit a line to a series of data occurring over time. This model is also referred to as the simple trend model. The trend line is determined using the least squares method, which minimizes the sum of the squared deviations to determine the characteristics of the linear equation. The trend line equation is expressed as:

$$\hat{Y} = b_0 + b_1 x$$

Where $\hat{Y}$ = forecast or dependent variable;

x = time variable;

| Figure 5.3 | Exponential Smoothing Forecasting Using Excel Spreadsheet |

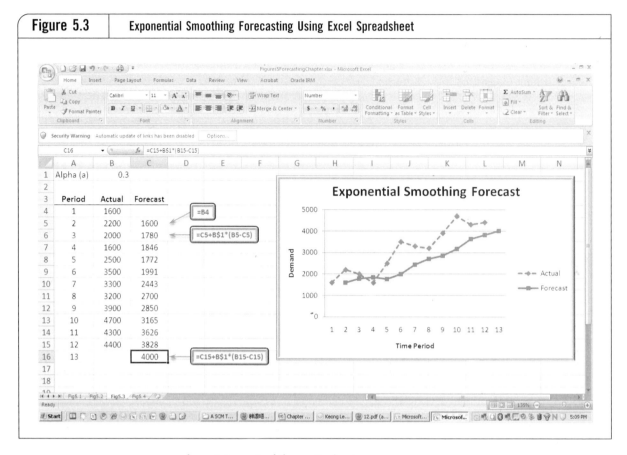

b_0 = intercept of the vertical axis;

b_1 = slope of the trend line.

The coefficients b_0 and b_1 are calculated as follows:

$$b_1 = \frac{n \Sigma (xy) - \Sigma x \Sigma y}{n \Sigma x^2 - (\Sigma x)^2}$$

$$b_0 = \frac{\Sigma y - b_1 \Sigma x}{n}$$

where x = independent variable values;

y = dependent variable values;

n = number of observations.

Example 5.4 illustrates the linear trend forecast.

Cause-and-Effect Models

The cause-and-effect models have a cause (independent variable or variables) and an effect (dependent variable). One of the more common models used is regression analysis. In demand forecasting, the external variables that are related to demand are first identified. Once the relationship between the external variable and demand is determined, it can be used as a forecasting tool. Let's review several cause-and-effect models.

Simple Linear Regression Forecast

When there is only one explanatory variable, we have a **simple regression forecast** equivalent to the linear trend forecast described earlier. The difference is that the

Example 5.4   Linear Trend Forecasting

The demand for toys produced by the Miki Manufacturing Company is shown in the table below.

PERIOD	DEMAND	PERIOD	DEMAND	PERIOD	DEMAND
1	1600	5	2500	9	3900
2	2200	6	3500	10	4700
3	2000	7	3300	11	4300
4	1600	8	3200	12	4400

What is the trend line?

What is the forecast for period 13?

SOLUTION

PERIOD (X)	DEMAND (Y)	X^2	XY
1	1600	1	1600
2	2200	4	4400
3	2000	9	6000
4	1600	16	6400
5	2500	25	12500
6	3500	36	21000
7	3300	49	23100
8	3200	64	25600
9	3900	81	35100
10	4700	100	47000
11	4300	121	47300
12	4400	144	52800
$\Sigma x = 78$	$\Sigma y = 37200$	$\Sigma x^2 = 650$	$\Sigma xy = 282800$

$$b_1 = \frac{n\Sigma(xy) - \Sigma x \Sigma y}{n\Sigma x^2 - (\Sigma x)^2} = \frac{12(282800) - 78(37200)}{12(650) - 78^2} = 286.71$$

$$b_0 = \frac{\Sigma y - b_1 \Sigma x}{n} = \frac{37200 - 286.71(78)}{12} = 1236.4$$

The trend line is $\hat{Y} = 1236.4 + 286.7x$

To forecast the demand for period 13, we substitute $x = 13$ into the trend equation above.

Forecast for period 13 = $1236.4 + 286.7(13) = 4963.5 = 4964$ toys.

An Excel spreadsheet solution is shown in Figure 5.4.

x variable is no longer time but instead an explanatory variable of demand. For example, demand could be dependent on the size of the advertising budget. The regression equation is expressed as:

$$\hat{Y} = b_0 + b_1 x$$

Where $\hat{Y}$ = forecast or dependent variable;

x = explanatory or independent variable;

b_0 = intercept of the vertical axis;

b_1 = slope of the regression line.

Figure 5.4 | Linear Trend Forecasting Using Excel Spreadsheet

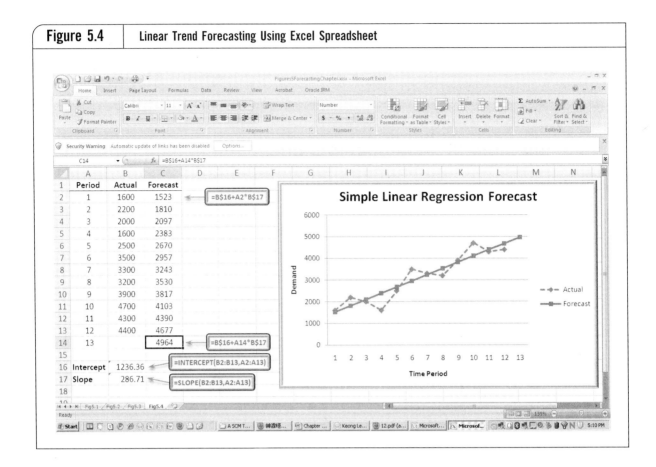

Example 5.5 illustrates the simple linear regression forecast.

Multiple Regression Forecast

When several explanatory variables are used to predict the dependent variable, a **multiple regression forecast** is applicable. Multiple regression analysis works well when the relationships between demand (dependent variable) and several other factors (independent or explanatory variables) impacting demand are strong and stable over time. The multiple regression equation is expressed as:

$$\hat{Y} = b_0 + b_1x_1 + b_2x_2 + \ldots + b_kx_k$$

Where $\hat{Y}$ = forecast or dependent variable;

x_k = k[th] explanatory or independent variable;

b_0 = constant;

b_k = regression coefficient of the independent variable x_k.

Although the mathematics involved in determining the parameters of the equation are complex, numerous software such as Excel, SAS and SPSS statistical packages can be used to solve the equation. Any statistics textbook should provide the formula for calculating the regression coefficient values and discussion of the assumptions and challenges of using multiple regression techniques. Multiple regression forecasting requires

Example 5.5   Simple Linear Regression Forecasting

Data on sales and advertising dollars for the past six months are shown below.

$ SALES (Y)	$ ADVERTISING (X)
100,000	2000
150,000	3000
125,000	2500
50,000	1000
170,000	3500
135,000	2750

Determine the linear relationship between sales and advertising dollars.

SOLUTION

$ SALES (Y)	$ ADVERTISING (X)	X^2	XY
100,000	2000	4,000,000	200,000,000
150,000	3000	9,000,000	450,000,000
125,000	2500	6,250,000	312,500,000
50,000	1000	1,000,000	50,000,000
170,000	3500	12,250,000	595,000,000
135,000	2750	756,2500	371,250,000
$\Sigma y = 730,000$	$\Sigma x = 14,750$	$\Sigma x^2 = 40,062,500$	$\Sigma xy = 1,978,750,000$

$$\hat{Y} = b_0 + b_1 x$$

$$b_1 = n\frac{\Sigma(xy) - \Sigma x \Sigma y}{n\Sigma x^2 - (\Sigma x)^2} = \frac{6(1978750000) - 14750(730000)}{6(40062500) - 14750^2} = 48.438$$

$$b_0 = \frac{\Sigma y - b_1 \Sigma x}{n} = \frac{730000 - 48.43836(14750)}{6} = 2589.041$$

$$\hat{Y} = 2589.04 + 48.44x$$

The linear regression results indicate that a one-dollar increase in advertising will increase sales by $48.44. Further, a planned monthly advertising expenditure of $4000 would yield a sales forecast of $196,349.

much more data than any of the other techniques discussed earlier, and the additional cost must be balanced against possible improvement in the level of forecast accuracy.

Forecast Accuracy

The ultimate goal of any forecasting endeavor is to have an accurate and unbiased forecast. The costs associated with prediction error can be substantial and include the costs of lost sales, safety stock, unsatisfied customers and loss of goodwill. Companies must strive to do a good job of tracking forecast error and taking the necessary steps to improve their forecasting techniques. Typically, forecast error at the disaggregated (stock keeping unit) level is higher than at the aggregated (company as a whole) level. **Forecast error** is the difference between the actual quantity and the forecast. Forecast error can be expressed as:

$$e_t = A_t - F_t$$

where e_t = forecast error for period t;

A_t = actual demand for period t;

F_t = forecast for period t.

Several measures of forecasting accuracy are shown below:

Mean absolute deviation (MAD) $= \dfrac{\sum_{t=1}^{n} |e_t|}{n}$

Mean absolute percentage error (MAPE) $= \dfrac{100}{n} \sum_{t=1}^{n} \left| \dfrac{e_t}{A_t} \right|$

Mean square error (MSE) $= \dfrac{\sum_{t=1}^{n} e_t^2}{n}$

Running sum of forecast errors (RSFE) $= \sum_{t=1}^{n} e_t$

where e_t = forecast error for period t;

A_t = actual demand for period t;

n = number of periods of evaluation.

The RSFE is an indicator of bias in the forecasts. **Forecast bias** measures the tendency of a forecast to be consistently higher or lower than the actual demand. A positive RSFE indicates that the forecasts are generally lower than actual demand which can lead to stockouts. A negative RSFE shows that the forecasts are generally higher than actual demand, which can result in excess inventory carrying costs.

The **tracking signal** is used to determine if the forecast bias is within the acceptable control limits. It is expressed as:

$$\text{Tracking signal} = \frac{RSFE}{MAD}$$

If the tracking signal falls outside preset control limits, there is a bias problem with the forecasting method, and an evaluation of the way forecasts are generated is warranted. A biased forecast will lead to excessive inventories or stockouts. Some inventory experts suggest using ± 4 for high-volume items and ± 8 for lower-volume items, while others prefer a lower limit. For example, GE Silicones started off with a control limit for their tracking signal of ± 4. Over time, the quality of forecasts improved, and the control limits were reduced to ± 3. As tighter limits are instituted, there is a greater probability of finding exceptions that actually require no action, but it also means catching changes in demand earlier. Eventually, with additional improvements in their forecasting system, GE's tracking signal control limits were further reduced to ± 2.2. The greater sensitivity allowed them to quickly identify changing trends and resulted in further improvement in their forecasts.[14] Example 5.6 illustrates the use of these forecast accuracy measures.

In one study, researchers found that bias in the forecast could be intentional, driven by organizational issues such as motivation of staff and satisfaction of customer demands, influencing the generation of forecasts.[15] For example, sales personnel tend to favor under-forecasting so they can meet or exceed sales quotas, and production people tend to over-forecast because having too much inventory presents less of a problem than the alternative. The key to generating accurate forecasts is collaborative forecasting with different partners inside and outside the company working together to eliminate

Example 5.6   Forecast Accuracy Measures

The demand and forecast information for the XYZ Company over a 12-month period is shown in the table below.

PERIOD	DEMAND	FORECAST	PERIOD	DEMAND	FORECAST
1	1600	1523	7	3300	3243
2	2200	1810	8	3200	3530
3	2000	2097	9	3900	3817
4	1600	2383	10	4700	4103
5	2500	2670	11	4300	4390
6	3500	2957	12	4400	4677

Calculate the MAD, MSE, MAPE, RSFE and tracking signal. Assume that the control limit for the tracking signal is ± 3. What can we conclude about the quality of the forecasts?

SOLUTION

PERIOD	DEMAND	FORECAST	ERROR (e)	ABSOLUTE ERROR	e^2	ABSOLUTE % ERROR
1	1600	1523	77	77	5929	4.8
2	2200	1810	390	390	152,100	17.7
3	2000	2097	−97	97	9409	4.9
4	1600	2383	−783	783	613,089	48.9
5	2500	2670	−170	170	28,900	6.8
6	3500	2957	543	543	294,849	15.5
7	3300	3243	57	57	3249	1.7
8	3200	3530	−330	330	108,900	10.3
9	3900	3817	83	83	6889	2.1
10	4700	4103	597	597	356,409	12.7
11	4300	4390	−90	90	8100	2.1
12	4400	4677	−277	277	76,729	6.3
Total			0	3494	1,664,552	133.9
Average				291.17	138,712.7	11.16
			RSFE	MAD	MSE	MAPE

MAD $= 291.2$

MSE $= 138,712.7$

MAPE $= 11.2\%$

RSFE $= 0$

Tracking signal $= \dfrac{RSFE}{MAD} = 0$

The results indicate no bias in the forecasts, and that the tracking signal is well within the control limits of ± 3. However, the forecasts are on average 291 units or 11.2 percent off from actual demand. This situation might require attention to determine the underlying causes of the variation.

forecasting error. A collaborative planning, forecasting and replenishment system, discussed later in the chapter, provides for free exchange of forecasting data, point-of-sale data, promotions and other relevant information between trading partners; this collaborative effort, rather than more sophisticated and expensive forecasting algorithms, can account for significant improvements in forecasting accuracy.

Useful Forecasting Websites

Several forecasting websites that provide a wealth of information on the subject are shown here:

1. Institute for Forecasting Education (www.forecastingeducation.com/)

   The Institute for Forecasting Education (IFE) provides customized workshops for organizations worldwide. IFE also performs business forecasting consulting and can provide assistance with software selection and training. They also maintain a database on forecasting software evaluation.

2. International Institute of Forecasters (www.forecasters.org/)

   The International Institute of Forecasters is the "preeminent organization for scholars and practitioners in the field of forecasting. The IIF is dedicated to stimulating the generation, distribution, and use of knowledge on forecasting in a wide range of fields."

   The International Institute of Forecasters lists the following objectives on their website:

   - *Develop and unify forecasting as a multidisciplinary field of research drawing on management, behavioral sciences, social sciences, engineering, and other fields.*
   - *Contribute to the professional development of analysts, managers, and policy makers with responsibilities for making and using forecasts in business and government.*
   - *Bridge the gap between theory and practice, with practice helping to set the research agenda and research providing useful results.*
   - *Bring together decision makers, forecasters, and researchers from all nations to improve the quality and usefulness of forecasting.*

   The Institute also publishes the *International Journal of Forecasting*, FORESIGHT and *The Oracle*.

3. Forecasting Principles: Evidence-based Forecasting (www.forecastingprinciples.com/)

   The *Forecasting Principles* website provides useful forecasting information and is used by researchers, practitioners, and educators. The site has special interest group discussion areas, forecasting topic exams, forecasting publications, links to forecasting study grants, and a wealth of other information. Their primary source of information is contained in their *Principles of Forecasting*, a comprehensive summary of forecasting knowledge which involved 40 authors and 123 reviewers.

4. Stata (Data Analysis and Statistical Software): Statistical Software Providers (www.stata.com/links/stat_software.html)

   This website provides links to a large number of statistical and forecasting software providers. Additionally, visitors can access information on worldwide forecasting seminars and short courses, user groups, a bookstore, the *Stata Journal* and user manuals.

Collaborative Planning, Forecasting and Replenishment

According to the Voluntary Interindustry Commerce Standards (VICS) Association, **collaborative planning, forecasting and replenishment (CPFR)** is "a set of business processes that entities in a supply chain can use for collaboration on a number of retailer/

manufacturer functions towards overall efficiency in the supply chain."[16] CPFR is a registered trademark of the VICS Association. The Council of Supply Chain Management Professionals (CSCMP) describes CPFR as:

> *A concept that aims to enhance supply chain integration by supporting and assisting joint practices. CPFR seeks cooperative management of inventory through joint visibility and replenishment of products throughout the supply chain. Information shared between suppliers and retailers aids in planning and satisfying customer demands through a supportive system of shared information. This allows for continuous updating of inventory and upcoming requirements, essentially making the end-to-end supply chain process more efficient. Efficiency is also created through the decreased expenditures for merchandising, inventory, logistics, and transportation across all trading partners.*[17]

The objective of CPFR is to optimize the supply chain by improving demand forecast accuracy, delivering the right product at the right time to the right location, reducing inventories across the supply chain, avoiding stockouts and improving customer service. This can be achieved only if the trading partners are working closely together and willing to share information and risk through a common set of processes.

The real value of CPFR comes from an exchange of forecasting information rather than from more sophisticated forecasting algorithms to improve forecasting accuracy. The fact is that forecasts developed solely by the firm tend to be inaccurate. When both the buyer and seller collaborate to develop a single forecast, incorporating knowledge of base sales, promotions, store openings or closings and new product introductions, it is possible to synchronize buyer needs with supplier production plans, thus ensuring efficient replenishment. The jointly managed forecasts can be adjusted in the event that demand or promotions have changed, thus avoiding costly corrections after the fact.

On the surface, when decisions are made with incomplete, one-sided information, it may appear that companies have "optimized" their internal processes when, in reality, inventory has merely shifted along the supply chain. Without supply chain trading partners collaborating and exchanging information, the supply chain will always be suboptimal, resulting in less-than-maximum supply chain profits.

CPFR is an approach that addresses the requirements for good demand management. The benefits of CPFR include the following:

- Strengthens partner relationships
- Provides analysis of sales and order forecasts
- Uses point-of-sale data, seasonal activity, promotions, new product introductions and store openings or closings to improve forecast accuracy
- Manages the demand chain and proactively eliminates problems before they appear
- Allows collaboration on future requirements and plans
- Uses joint planning and promotions management
- Integrates planning, forecasting and logistics activities
- Provides efficient category management and understanding of consumer purchasing patterns
- Provides analysis of key performance metrics (e.g., forecast accuracy, forecast exceptions, product lead times, inventory turnover, percentage stockouts) to reduce supply chain inefficiencies, improve customer service and increase revenues and profitability.

Figure 5.5 | **VICS's CPFR Model with Retailer and Manufacturer Tasks Aligned with Their Corresponding Collaboration Tasks**

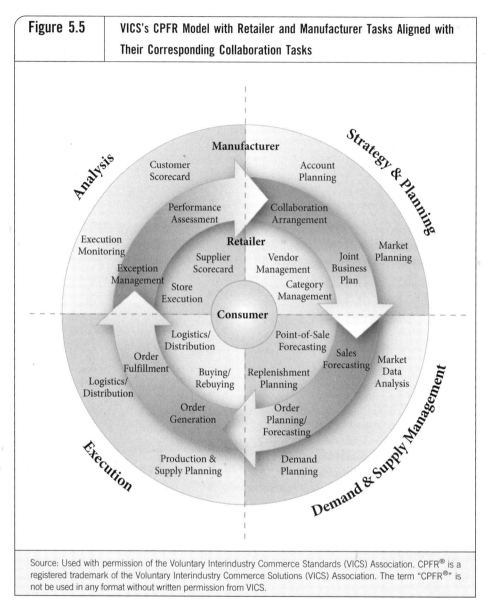

Most companies implement CPFR using some form of the VICS Association CPFR Process Model, as shown in Figure 5.5. The Global Commerce Initiative (GCI) created the GCI Recommended Standard for Globalizing CPFR by combining portions of VICS CPFR publications and their own new materials. GCI is a voluntary body created in 1999 with a mission to "lead global value chain collaboration through the identification of business needs and the implementation of best practices and standards to serve consumers better, faster and at less cost."[18]

The current CPFR model, first introduced by VICS in 2004, involves an iterative cycle of four key activities (see Figure 5.5) where full implementation of every element is not necessary to achieve value. According to VICS, the manufacturer and retailer participate in four collaborative activities to improve performance:[19]

- *Strategy & Planning:* Establish the ground rules for the collaborative relationship. Determine product mix and placement, and develop event plans for the period.

- *Demand & Supply Management:* Forecast the consumer (point-of-sale) demand for the retailer, as well as order and shipment requirements for the manufacturer over the planning horizon.
- *Execution:* Place orders, prepare and deliver shipments, receive and stock products on retail shelves, record sales transactions and make payments
- *Analysis:* Monitor planning and execution activities for exception conditions, aggregate the results and calculate key performance metrics. Share insights and adjust plans for continuously improved results.

In the current VICS CPFR model, the customer is at the center of the collaboration. There are now eight collaboration tasks as follows:[20]

- Task 1: Collaboration Arrangement
- Task 2: Joint Business Plan
- Task 3: Sales Forecasting
- Task 4: Order Planning/Forecasting
- Task 5: Order Generation
- Task 6: Order Fulfillment
- Task 7: Exception Management
- Task 8: Performance Assessment

Figure 5.6 shows a VICS self-assessment template for organizations to evaluate their readiness to implement CPFR programs.

California boating supply retailer West Marine, an early adopter of CPFR, has benefited greatly from its implementation. Within a few years of the start of the CPFR program, West Marine had developed relationships with 200 suppliers, and achieved 85 percent forecast accuracy, 80 percent on-time shipments and 96 percent in-stock deliveries during the peak season. West Marine had to address both business processes and cultural issues. The company worked with its suppliers to match supply and demand. While collaboration with external constituents is critical for CPFR success, it is equally important that effective collaboration within the company is emphasized. For example, logistics, planning and replenishment associates must work closely together. West Marine identified the following ten performance improvement steps in their successful implementation of CPFR:[21]

1. Seek long-term, holistic solutions, not quick or myopic fixes.
2. Reconcile conflicting goals and metrics.
3. Pursue inclusive problem solving; do not depend upon "experts" who don't have accountability for the business.
4. Instill collaborative processes that encourage idea creation, shared problem solving and high adoption rates across organizational boundaries.
5. Use a disciplined and iterative set of methodologies such as CPFR, SCOR, or Six Sigma to help teams define issues, root causes and solutions.
6. Develop a culture of continuous improvement, particularly at the customer-facing associate level, because those employees are most likely to know what's needed.
7. Create clear accountabilities and assign authority with a focus on core business processes rather than on traditional organizational "silos" or loyalties.
8. Commit to technology enablement for execution, communication, exception management and root-cause analysis.

Figure 5.6	CPFR Rollout Readiness Self-Assessment

Place a check mark next to each statement that is true for your business, then sum up the marks to determine your total score.

A. Organizational Readiness
- ☐ The value proposition for collaboration is well understood in the company.
- ☐ There is an agreed company strategy and an adequate budget for collaboration initiatives.
- ☐ Collaboration process owners have been assigned and empowered.
- ☐ Affected organizations have performance goals and incentives aligned with collaboration objectives.

B. Retailer Process Readiness
(Retailers rate themselves and suppliers rate their customers' readiness in this section.)
- ☐ Details of promotions and other retail events are captured and kept up to date so that consumer demand impact can be correlated with them.
- ☐ Consumer demand is forecasted based on historical sales and planned promotional activities.
- ☐ Ordering processes are driven from forecasted consumer demand.
- ☐ Feedback from collaboration can be incorporated in future plans and forecasts.

C. Supplier Readiness
(Suppliers rate themselves and retailers rate their suppliers' readiness in this section.)
- ☐ Supplier sales and service/logistics personnel coordinate their response to customer issues and opportunities.
- ☐ Collaboration (consumer POS) data can be effectively used in the supplier's sales and operations planning (S&OP) process.
- ☐ A unified approach to collaboration allows the supplier's insights to reflect the demands of multiple customers.

D. Technology Readiness
- ☐ Internet data transport (EDIINT AS2) capabilities are production-ready.
- ☐ XML translation capabilities for B2B initiatives are production-ready.
- ☐ Enterprise planning applications have supported interfaces for collaboration data (import and export).
- ☐ A scalable CPFR solution is available.

_____ **Total Score**

Evaluating Your Score

If you scored 11–15
- ☐ Your strategic trading partners should all believe in collaboration.
- ☐ You should be driving CPFR best practices in the industry.

If you scored 6–10
- ☐ You are ready to begin rollouts, starting with demand/supply visibility.
- ☐ Address key gaps to enhance ROI of collaboration.

If you scored 0–5
- ☐ You should act quickly to close gaps, starting with organizational ones.
- ☐ Work to sustain momentum in existing collaboration relationships, to gain experience that can be applied to future efforts.

Figure 5.6	CPFR Rollout Readiness Self-Assessment (continued)

Suggestions for Improving Your Score

Enhancing Organizational Readiness

   ☐ Conduct a collaboration ROI assessment

   ☐ Engage in strategy and program development

Enhancing Retailer Process Readiness

   ☐ Invest in event visibility and demand forecasting technology/processes

   ☐ Enable continuous replenishment processes

Enhancing Supplier Readiness

   ☐ Enhance S&OP practices to leverage customer-specific POS forecast data

   ☐ Implement supplier scorecards

Enhancing Technology Readiness

   ☐ Implement Internet data transport, translation and mapping technologies

   ☐ Establish interoperability among installed enterprise solutions and CPFR programs

Source: Used with permission of the Voluntary Interindustry Commerce Standards (VICS) Association. CPFR® is a registered trademark of the Voluntary Interindustry Commerce Solutions (VICS) Association. The term "CPFR®" is not be used in any format without written permission from VICS.

9. Reduce decision cycle times.

10. Implement rapidly.

West Marine is a classic example of a company that has benefited from implementing CPFR. As part of their CPFR initiative, the company worked closely with suppliers to match supply and demand. The CPFR program has been extended to West Marine's 200 suppliers. ITT's Jabsco division, West Marine's largest customer, also implemented CPFR; and in the process they experienced a reduction in cycle time from 25 days to three days, an increase in total sales of 11 percent and an improvement in on-time deliveries from 74 percent to 94 percent.[22] It must be noted that Jabsco had coupled their existing lean/Six Sigma program with CPFR to achieve these outstanding results.

The success of the relationship can be measured using common performance metrics such as gross margin percent, return on investment and sales growth. Other metrics include in-stock percent at point of sale, inventory turnover, average inventory level, sales forecast accuracy, potential sales lost due to stockouts, manufacturing cycle time, order cycle time, shipping cycle time, problem resolution time, rate of emergency or cancelled orders, and percent shipped or delivered on time.

Using CPFR, companies are working together to develop mutually agreeable plans and are taking responsibility for their actions. The collaborative effort leads to benefits that are greater than if each partner were to go at it independently. According to VICS, the CPFR concept is consumer driven without losing focus on best practices within the supply chain. Setting common goals for organizations pulls individual efforts together into a cohesive plan, supports better execution of the plan and invites improved planning in the next business planning exercise. The improved planning drives sales gains through to the consumer and lowers costs throughout the supply chain.[23] Examples of companies using CPFR include Eastman Kodak, Federated Department Stores, Hewlett-Packard, JC Penney, Kimberly-Clark, Kmart, Nabisco, Procter & Gamble, Target, Wal-Mart and Warner-Lambert. The industries that are most involved with CPFR are consumer products and food & beverage.

Medtronic Sofamor Danek, one of the world's leading medical technology companies, has implemented the i2 Demand Planner software, which is part of the i2 Supply Chain

Management solution. The software "delivers a powerful planning and forecasting tool—enabling enterprises to understand, anticipate and manage customer demand across their value chain. It optimizes collaboration, collection and rationalization of multiple forecasting inputs through a Web-based user friendly interface combined with industry-leading statistical techniques and unlimited causal factors."[24] As a result, Sofamor Danek has reduced forecasting time from weeks to minutes, increased forecast accuracy by 10 to 15 percent for core products and decreased product shortages from 15 percent to 3 percent.[25]

The top three challenges for CPFR implementation are difficulty of making internal changes, cost and trust. As with any major implementation, internal resistance to change must be addressed by top management. Change is always difficult; however, if top management is committed to the project, then the project is much more likely to succeed. Companies will need to educate their employees on the benefits of the process changes and the disadvantages of maintaining the status quo. There is also the question of reducing the scale of CPFR and, therefore, the cost of implementation for smaller trading partners. While cost is an important factor, companies with no plans for adopting CPFR should determine if they are at a competitive disadvantage as more and more companies implement CPFR. Trust, a major cultural issue, is considered a big hurdle to widespread implementation of CPFR because many retailers are reluctant to share the type of proprietary information required by CPFR. While the suppliers of Wal-Mart, for instance, may be willing to share sensitive data with Wal-Mart, they do not want other suppliers to obtain this information. However, other experts do not believe that trust is the stumbling block for mass adoption of CPFR. Jim Uchneat of Benchmarking Partners, Inc., says, "Trust may be a catch-all phrase that covers a host of other problems, but I have never found trust between people to be the issue. CPFR won't shift the power dynamics in a retailer/buyer relationship. If people are hoping that this is the case and refer to this as 'trust,' then they are fooling themselves. Lack of trust is more often related to the unreliable data in systems and the lack of integration internal to retailers and manufacturers."[26]

The real challenge to widespread adoption of CPFR is that it requires a fundamental change in the way buyers and sellers work together. Companies must ensure that their information technology systems, organizational structures, business processes and internal data are conducive to implementing CPFR. For instance, many organizations are hampered by legacy systems that will have to be replaced, lack of executive management support and an unwillingness to share sensitive information.

Software Solutions

A number of forecasting and CPFR software applications and their providers are listed in this section.

Forecasting Software

Forecasts are seldom calculated manually. If a forecaster uses a quantitative method, then a software solution can be used to simplify the process and save the time required to generate a forecast. Several leading forecasting software providers and their products are shown below.

1. *Business Forecast Systems, Inc.* (www.forecastpro.com/)

   "Founded in 1986, Business Forecast Systems, Inc. (BFS), is the maker of Forecast Pro, the leading software solution for business forecasting, and is a premier provider of forecasting education. With more than 35,000 users worldwide, Forecast Pro helps thousands of companies improve planning, cut inventory costs and decrease stockouts by improving the accuracy of their forecasts."

The company offers three editions of Forecast Pro to address the different needs of their customers: Forecast Pro Unlimited, Forecast Pro TRAC and Forecast Pro XE. Several of the forecasting approaches discussed in this chapter such as moving average, trend and exponential smoothing models are included in the software. Washington-based shoe designer Brooks Sports, Inc., is an example of one of the company's customers which has benefited greatly from use of the use of Forecast Pro software. Their use of Forecast Pro is discussed in the e-Business Connection feature.

e-Business Connection	*Collaborative Forecasting Running Smoothly at Brooks Sports*

Brooks Sports designs and develops high-performance running footwear, apparel and accessories which are sold in 80 countries worldwide. In 2001, when the company shifted from a broad product line to focus on high-performance products targeted at serious runners, it was clear that the forecasting process needed to change to support the strategic direction of the company. The existing forecasting process, based entirely on the judgment of the sales team, was limiting the company's ability to grow.

CHALLENGES

The strategy shift created a number of forecasting challenges for Brooks including:

- *Inconsistent style growth*: the new line of products experience growth rates anywhere from 0 to 50 percent annually.
- *Long production planning horizon coupled with short product life*: production and capacity decisions are typically made 18 months before a style is launched, average lead time for a style is 6 months and the product life of Brooks' styles range from 6 to 24 months. This means that planners must sometimes set the entire demand plan for a style prior to ever receiving a customer order, underscoring the importance of accurate forecasts.
- *Increasing "at-once" orders*: "at once" orders, which are placed for immediate shipment, historically accounted for less than 20 percent of total sales. Since 2001, however, "at once" orders have increased to nearly 50 percent of total sales.
- *Evolving size curves*: with its new focus on serious runners, the standard footwear size curve would not adequately reflect distribution of sales by sizes.
- *No exposure to retail sell-through*: the high-performance products are sold primarily through independent specialty stores who don't have the capability to share sales data with vendors.

SOLUTION

With a corporate mandate from senior management emphasizing the importance of creating accurate and timely forecasts, Brooks completely revamped its forecasting process. An independent forecasting group, reporting directly to the COO and CFO, was established to coordinate input from various groups—sales, marketing, product development and production—and to remove bias from the forecasting process.

The forecasting group established a collaborative forecasting process with three primary steps:

Step 1: Produce monthly statistical forecasts at the SKU level to capture level, trend, seasonality and the impact of events based on historical data. Brooks chose Forecast Pro to create these forecasts due to a number of features available in the software:

- Ability to create accurate forecasts
- Flexibility to choose forecast models or let software automatically select models
- Capability to model events (particularly important for predicting spikes in demand with new product launches)
- Support for multiple-level models to produce consistent forecasts at all levels of aggregation
- Powerful override facility to enable collaborative forecasting

"Forecast Pro has been a great solution for Brooks," says Tom Ross, Financial Analyst. "Implementing Forecast Pro's event modeling is very simple, which is an essential feature for us because of our moving product launches. We also use event models to address the challenge of forecasting events that don't occur on a regular basis—such as races—which can have a dramatic impact on the sales of specific products. Another powerful feature of Forecast Pro is the ability to forecast a product hierarchy. This helps us to serve our multiple constituents within Brooks—we review higher-level forecasts with management and easily generate detailed forecasts at the SKU level for demand planning."

Step 2: On a quarterly basis, get sales management and sales reps to forecast sales for a 12-month horizon, focusing on major accounts. This input is gathered via the Web and then aggregated by the forecasting group.

Step 3: Compare the statistical and judgmental forecasts, and make adjustments to create the final monthly forecast. Ninety percent of the final forecasts are the same as the statistical forecasts—changes are most commonly made to the forecasts for new styles where the sales organization has important knowledge to add. These final forecasts are then automatically fed into Brooks' ERP system.

"Forecast Pro allows us to easily apply judgmental overrides, which is critical for us," notes Ross. "We now can systematically track changes, giving us a better understanding of our forecasting performance."

RESULTS

The commitment to forecasting has paid off at Brooks. Forecast accuracy has improved on average by 40 percent, unfulfilled demand has been lowered from approximately 20 percent to less than 5 percent, and closeouts have been reduced by more than 60 percent. The improved forecasting has also helped to smooth out production, resulting in lowered costs and better margins.

Source: www.forecastpro.com/customers/success/brooks.htm.

2. *John Galt* (www.johngalt.com/)

"Founded in 1996, John Galt Solutions has a proven track record of delivering affordable forecasting and inventory management solutions for the consumer-driven supply chain. With the ForecastX Wizard and the Atlas Planning Suite, we provide a wide range of affordable, easy to implement, supply chain planning solutions designed for growing mid-market companies."

The company's basic forecasting software, ForecastX Wizard, is an Excel add-in that can perform statistical forecasting, compute safety stock, develop inventory plans and plan new product introductions. The ForecastX Wizard Premium software provides additional features such as enhanced inventory planning, closed-loop collaboration and streamlined reporting.

"The *Supply & Demand Chain Executive* Magazine selected John Galt Solutions based on its track record for delivering supply chain innovation and excellence. Over 5,000 customers use solutions from John Galt to increase forecast accuracy, optimize inventory levels and maximize supply chain performance."[27]

3. *JustEnough* (www.justenough.com/)

"JustEnough serves more than 500 of the world's leading brands including Replenishment of Levi Strauss's North American stores, Inventory Planning at Nissan, Demand Planning at Carolina Pad, Master Production Scheduling at John West Salmon, Mobile Sales Force Automation at Heineken and Mobile Sales & Trade Marketing at Cadbury. Each year JustEnough calculates over 1.5 billion forecasts and recommends over 826 million orders to more than 8 million suppliers."

4. *SAS* (www.sas.com/)

"SAS Forecast Server generates large quantities of high-quality forecasts quickly and automatically, allowing organizations to plan more effectively for the future. The unsurpassed scalability of SAS Forecast Server enables your business to operate more efficiently at all levels by quickly and automatically producing statistically based forecasts you can trust. SAS Forecast Server bundles the SAS High-Performance Forecasting engine with the SAS Forecast Studio GUI."

SAS's customers include Alcon, Inc. (the world's leading eye-care company), AmBev (Latin America's largest beverage company), America West Airlines (now US Airways), CartaSí (Italy's most commonly used credit card) and Kirin Brewery Company. SAS Forecast Server was awarded the "Trend-Setting Products of the Year" for 2005 by *KMWorld* magazine.

Kirin is an example of a global company that has managed their forecasting function well with SAS Supply Chain Intelligence software (see Global Perspective feature).

Global Perspective — *Kirin Brewery Company Accurately Forecasts and Meets Demand*

Ensuring appropriate inventory is one of the key business goals for any manufacturer, making effective supply chain management (SCM) a priority. Failure to control inventory can have a huge influence on the whole business, including lost sales opportunities caused by short stock and unnecessary costs incurred by excess inventory.

The Kirin spirits and wine business markets approximately 700 product items, including domestic and imported beer, whisky, liqueur, shouchu, and wine. They were determined to carry out a radical renewal of the supply/demand planning system to cope with such inventory issues. The Spirits and Wine SCM System project, which began in April 2003, was based on SAS Supply Chain Intelligence, and brought about dramatic improvements in accuracy of demand forecast and automation of complicated procurement processes. By adjusting inventory levels, the system contributed to cost savings and improved efficiency in operations.

BUILDING A NEW SCM SYSTEM TO IMPROVE EFFICIENCY
The trend of alcoholic beverage consumption in Japan is currently undergoing a shift to low alcohol and light taste. Under these circumstances, Kirin's spirits and wine business endeavors to

further enhance its competitive advantage and improve customer satisfaction by offering a wide variety of such popular products as Chivas Regal, Two Dogs and Franzia, a Californian wine.

"We are not just a beer brewery, but a comprehensive beverage company offering a wide variety of products. We strive to retain consumers' continuous support. To do this, our logistics division, in collaboration with SAS, has developed a new supply chain management system where all current and future distribution can be optimized by demand forecasting. Currently, ordering, shipping, and any changes in inventory for spirits and wine can be consolidated and controlled, based on the methods we have developed for beer and happo-shu (low-malt beer). By fully utilizing the system, we are determined to meet customer demand and improve business productivity," says Keigo Kubota, Manager Spirits & Wine Logistics Section, Logistics Division, Kirin Brewery Company, Limited.

DEMAND FORECASTING FOR MANAGING LEAD TIMES

"The spirits and wine business is largely dependent on imported products. We trade with thirty-four suppliers in fourteen countries. The business requires an extremely long lead time from placing an order to import clearance procedures. Some products can be obtained only by making a reservation more than one year in advance. The lead time also depends on the area, season, and order lot, as well as the tonnage capacity of trucks, which is restricted by law in some nations. These complex factors and conditions are stored in the master database. All decision-making processes, including the timing and volume of placing orders, are automated. In the past, these processes were dependent on individual staff knowledge and experience and carried out with spreadsheets. We succeeded in dramatically improving efficiency for such processes," says Katsutoshi Ishii, Planning Section, Logistics Division.

The Spirits and Wine SCM System has two major strengths. One is that the procurement operation, including order planning and future stock simulation, which has been processed by individual staff, is systemized and automated to generate output. Another strength is that the demand forecast and shipment plan are logically calculated using an appropriate analytical method.

CHOOSING THE MOST RELEVANT OF SEVEN FORECASTING MODELS

The seven-model system specially developed for the spirits and wine business plays the most important role in forecasting demand and preparing the shipping plan. The models are specially designed by arranging dozens of analytical methods, including methods based on past data, methods reflecting the latest performance, and methods for seasonality. Simulations are run using models with different variables and patterns chosen for product characteristics, and then users choose the value of the most accurate forecast among the seven. The new system also solved issues contained in conventional package tools, such as an inability to accumulate forecast data. With this function, transitions of forecast/actual data are grasped and compared on the spot, and sales performance and actual figures are promptly compared on a monthly basis. Furthermore, with the alarm function that notifies the user of deviations from the forecast in the actual figures, we are able to take prompt, appropriate measures against the change.

"Demand forecasting is the key to achieving the objectives of proper inventory. We chose SAS for this solution because of its forecasting accuracy. We asked potential vendors to model actual historical data. We examined and compared the results and found that SAS presented the most accurate forecasting. In addition, SAS offered the best performance in comprehensive cost evaluations in the initial and operational stages, the most experience in system implementation in Japan, and the highest customer support capability and processing speed," said Mr. Ishii.

AIMING TOWARD ACQUISITION OF INTELLIGENCE

The introduction of the new system brought positive results which were immediately noticeable. "I spent most of my time on forecasting the appropriate order volume," says Yuko Hamamoto, Spirits & Wine Logistics Section, Logistics Division. "Now that all such processes are automated,

I am able to focus on verification of forecasted values. I want to make the most of the system by further comprehending the nature and characteristics of the models." Department personnel are now able to control the forecast model themselves and repeat practical simulations. By doing this, they will acquire the capability to identify the value of data and improve their ability to control the forecasts. The Spirits and Wine SCM System also supports improvement of user intelligence in forecast management. "We would like to become more accustomed to the system and will endeavor to improve our understanding of and proficiency in the system," concludes Mr. Kubota. "We are committed to improving the level of forecast management by feeding the issues we've identified back into the secondary development process."

Source: www.sas.com/success/kirin.html.

CPFR Software

A CPFR software solution typically includes a forecasting module and other modules for planning procurement, supply and replenishment among other uses. The supply chain software industry has experienced consolidation over the years with numerous mergers and acquisitions reducing the number of key players in the industry. Examples of two leading suppliers of CPFR solutions are provided below:

1. JDA Software Group, Inc. (www.jda.com/)

   JDA Software Group's clients have previously won the VICS Collaborative Commerce Achievement Award for "CPFR® Implementation Excellence." JDA acquired Manugistics in July 2006, which included the CPFR solution. In January 2010, JDA completed the acquisition of i2 Technologies. i2 Demand Planning Solutions is one of the supply chain software applications provided by i2 and includes:[28]

   - *i2 Demand Manager:* Monitor and adjust demand plans as demand signals across the supply chain evolve.
   - *i2 Profiler:* Identify common selling patterns to create accurate forecasting profiles for short life cycle and seasonal fashion products.
   - *i2 Demand Collaboration:* Resolve demand/supply problems before they adversely affect the customer by gaining better visibility into customer demand.
   - *i2 Planning On Demand:* Optimize the demand and supply planning process for fabless semiconductor companies by using this subscription-based solution.

2. *Oracle* (www.oracle.com/index.html)

   Retek purchased Syncra Systems, a leader in CPFR technology in 2004. Oracle then outbid SAP for Retek in 2005. In addition, Oracle has acquired Demantra, Hyperion and PeopleSoft (which had earlier acquired JD Edwards). Oracle Advanced Supply Chain Planning is an Internet-based planning solution that allows a company to "perform simultaneous material and capacity planning across multiple distribution and manufacturing facilities and time horizons in a single planning run, while at the same time accounting for the latest consensus forecast, sales orders, production status, purchase orders, and inventory policy recommendations."

Cloud computing can also be used to track and forecast demand. Cloud computing is "Internet-based computing, whereby shared resources, software and information are provided to computers and other devices on-demand, like the electricity grid."[29] Many information technology experts have predicted that cloud computing represents the next big trend in how software will be made available on-demand to companies.

SUMMARY

Forecasting is an integral part of demand management since it provides an estimate of future demand and the basis for planning and making sound business decisions. A mismatch in supply and demand could result in excessive inventories and stockouts and loss of profits and goodwill. Proper demand forecasting enables better planning and utilization of resources for businesses to be competitive. Both qualitative and quantitative methods are available to help companies forecast demand better. The qualitative methods are based on judgment and intuition, whereas the quantitative methods use mathematical techniques and historical data to predict future demand. The quantitative forecasting methods can be divided into time series and cause-and-effect models. Since forecasts are seldom completely accurate, management must monitor forecast errors and make the necessary improvements to the forecasting process.

Forecasts made in isolation tend to be inaccurate. Collaborative planning, forecasting and replenishment (CPFR) is an approach in which companies work together to develop mutually agreeable plans while taking responsibility for their actions. The objective of CPFR is to optimize the supply chain by generating a consensus demand forecast, delivering the right product at the right time to the right location, reducing inventories, avoiding stockouts and improving customer service. The Global Commerce Initiative and Voluntary Interindustry Commerce Standards have been instrumental in standardizing and promoting CPFR worldwide. Major corporations such as Wal-Mart, Warner-Lambert, West Marine and Procter & Gamble are early adopters of CPFR.

The computation involved in generating a forecast is seldom done manually. Forecasting software packages such as Forecast Pro, SAS and Microsoft Excel are readily available. Major CPFR solutions providers include JDA Software and Oracle. Recently, cloud computing has made it possible to have forecasting and other supply chain software on-demand on the Internet.

KEY TERMS

business cycle, 139

cause-and-effect forecasting, 138

cloud computing, 161

collaborative planning, forecasting and replenishment (CPFR), 150

exponential smoothing forecast, 142

forecast error, 148

forecast bias, 148

linear trend forecast, 143

multiple regression forecast, 146

mean absolute deviation (MAD), 148

mean absolute percentage error (MAPE), 148

mean square error (MSE), 148

naïve forecast, 140

qualitative forecasting methods, 137

quantitative forecasting methods, 137

running sum of forecast errors (RSFE), 148

simple moving average method, 148

simple regression forecast, 144

time series forecasting, 138

tracking signal, 148

weighted moving average forecast, 141

DISCUSSION QUESTIONS

1. What is demand management?

2. What is demand forecasting?

3. Why is demand forecasting important for effective supply chain management?

4. Explain the impact of a mismatch in supply and demand. What strategies can companies adopt to influence demand?

5. What are qualitative forecasting techniques? When are these methods more suitable?

6. What are the main components of a time series?

7. Explain the difference between a time series model and an associative model. Under what conditions would one model be preferred to the other?

8. What is the impact of the smoothing constant value on the simple exponential smoothing forecast?

9. Compare and contrast the jury of executive opinion and the Delphi techniques.

10. Explain the key differences between the weighted moving average and the simple exponential smoothing forecasting methods.

11. What are three measures of forecasting accuracy?

12. What is a tracking signal? What information does the tracking signal provide that managers can use to improve the quality of forecasts?

13. What are the key features of CPFR? Why would a company consider adopting CPFR?

14. What are the eight tasks associated with the CPFR model? Why is sharing data important in CPFR implementation? What are the benefits of sharing information?

15. West Marine identified the ten performance improvement steps in their successful implementation of CPFR. Is West Marine's approach unique, or can their experience be duplicated at another company? What are the key challenges that other companies will face in implementing CPFR?

16. Why is widespread adoption of CPFR below expectations?

17. What is cloud computing, and how can companies benefit from this technology in solving their supply chain forecasting problems?

SPREADSHEET PROBLEMS

1. Ms. Winnie Lin's company sells computers. Monthly sales for a six-month period are as follows:

MONTH	SALES
Jan	18,000
Feb	22,000
Mar	16,000
Apr	18,000
May	20,000
Jun	24,000

a. Plot the monthly data on a sheet of graph paper.
b. Compute the sales forecast for July using the following approaches: (1) a four-month moving average; (2) a weighted three-month moving average using .50 for June, .30 for May and .20 for April; (3) a linear trend equation (4) exponential smoothing with α (smoothing constant) equal to .40, assuming a February forecast of 18,000
c. Which method do you think is the least appropriate? Why?

2. The owner of the Chocolate Outlet Store wants to forecast chocolate demand. Demand for the preceding four years is shown in the following table:

YEAR	DEMAND (POUNDS)
1	68,800
2	71,000
3	75,500
4	71,200

Forecast demand for Year 5 using the following approaches: (1) a three-year moving average; (2) a three-year weighted moving average using .40 for Year 4, .20 for Year 3 and .40 for Year 2; (3) exponential smoothing with $\alpha = .30$, and assuming the forecast for Period 1 = 68,000.

3. The forecasts generated by two forecasting methods and actual sales are as follows:

MONTH	SALES	FORECAST 1	FORECAST 2
1	269	275	268
2	289	266	287
3	294	290	292
4	278	284	298
5	268	270	274
6	269	268	270
7	260	261	259
8	275	271	275

Compute the MSE, the MAD, the MAPE, the RSFE and the tracking signal for each forecasting method. Which method is better? Why?

Chapter 6

RESOURCE PLANNING SYSTEMS

If you are 'waste conscious,' you already understand that time spent producing parts that will not be shipped out for some time is overproduction, and this wastes resources. Other wastes, such as over-processing parts, also drain resources.[1]

It's not just about profits—although that will always remain the ultimate goal for any enterprise. However, in today's supply chain, there are other factors in play. You might want to temporarily forsake profitability in pursuit of market share. You might want to emphasize different production volumes and different profit margins for strategic reasons. Today, cost-effectiveness and competitiveness are the strategic levers that executives are seeking to run their businesses with maximum flexibility.[2]

Learning Objectives

After completing this chapter, you should be able to

- Understand the chase, level and mixed aggregate production strategies.
- Describe the hierarchical operations planning process in terms of materials planning (APP, MPS, MRP) and capacity planning (RRP, RCCP, CRP).
- Know how to compute available-to-promise quantities, MRP explosion and DRP implosion.
- Understand the limitations of legacy MRP systems, and why organizations are migrating to integrated ERP systems.
- Describe an ERP system, and understand its advantages and disadvantages.
- Understand best-of-breed versus single integrator ERP implementations.

Chapter Outline

Introduction

Operations Planning

The Aggregate Production Plan

Master Production Scheduling

The Bill of Materials

Material Requirements Planning

Capacity Planning

Distribution Requirements Planning

The Legacy Material Requirements Planning Systems

The Development of Enterprise Resource Planning Systems

Implementing Enterprise Resource Planning Systems

Enterprise Resource Planning Software Applications

Enterprise Resource Planning Software Providers

Summary

Supply Chain Management in Action   *Super-Yacht Production Sails with ERP Visual Controls*

Sanlorenzo, the Italian super-yacht manufacturer, says that its Infor ERP Visual implementation, which went live in January, is bringing the complexity of its highly customized products under control.

Ermanno Porro, Sanlorenzo general manager, explains that the specialist yacht builder's move into making 28-35m plastic and fiberglass yachts, 40m aluminum super-yachts and 44m steel mega-yachts meant it required sophisticated resource planning.

It also needed to improve monitoring of production steps on the shop floor, and all the way from order to delivery. And the system had to support a program to optimize and manage custom options in an engineer-to-order environment.

He says Sanlorenzo chose ERP Visual for its ability to manage complex manufacturing environments, as well as to streamline order management and workflow. The company also needed ability to transfer two-way data with Microsoft Project, its preferred live management system.

"Our business is centered on producing highly prestigious yachts that are tailored to the precise requirements of our customers. ERP Visual will help us improve our order management process," says Porro. "We liked Infor because it enables us to extend our ERP solution with other modules and strategic solutions to support future business growth."

Source: Anonymous, "Super-Yacht Production Sails with ERP Visual Controls," *Works Management*, July 2009: 62 (7), 29. Used with permission.

Introduction

Resource planning is the process of determining the production capacity required to meet demand. In the context of resource planning, *capacity* refers to the maximum workload that an organization is capable of completing in a given period of time. A discrepancy between an organization's capacity and demand results in an inefficiency, either in underutilized resources or unfulfilled orders. The goal of resource planning is to minimize this discrepancy.

One of the most critical activities of an organization is to efficiently balance the production plan with capacity; this directly affects how effectively the organization deploys its resource in producing goods and services. Developing feasible operations schedules and capacity plans to meet delivery due dates and minimize waste in manufacturing or service organizations is a complex problem. The need for better operations scheduling continues to challenge operations managers, especially in today's intensely competitive global marketplace. In an environment fostering collaborative buyer–supplier relationships, the challenge of scheduling operations to meet delivery due dates and eliminate waste is becoming more complex. The problem is compounded in an integrated supply chain, where a missed due date or stockout cascades downstream, magnifying the **bullwhip effect** and adversely affecting the entire supply chain.

Operations managers are continuously involved in resource and operations planning to balance capacity and output. Capacity may be stated in terms of labor, materials or equipment. With too much excess capacity, production cost per unit is high due to idle workers and machinery. However, if workers and machinery are stressed, quality levels are likely to deteriorate. Firms generally run their operations at about 85 percent capacity to allow time for scheduled repairs and maintenance and to meet unexpected increases in demand.

This chapter describes the hierarchical operations planning process in terms of materials and capacity planning. A hypothetical industrial example is used to demonstrate the hierarchical planning process. This chapter also discusses the evolution of the manufacturing planning and control system from the material requirements planning to the enterprise resource planning system.

Operations Planning

Operations planning is usually hierarchical and can be divided into three broad categories: (1) **long-range**, (2) **intermediate or medium-range** and (3) **short-range planning horizons**. While the distinctions among the three can be vague, long-range plans usually cover a year or more, tend to be more general, and specify resources and outputs in terms of aggregate hours and units. Medium-range plans normally span six to eighteen months, whereas short-range plans usually cover a few days to a few weeks depending on the type and size of the firm. Long-range plans are established first and are then used to guide the medium-range plans, which are subsequently used to guide the short-range plans. Long-range plans usually involve major, strategic decisions in capacity, such as the construction of new facilities and purchase of capital equipment, whereas medium-range plans involve minor changes in capacity such as changes in employment levels. Short-range plans are the most detailed and specify the exact end items and quantities to make on a weekly, daily or hourly basis.

Figure 6.1 shows the planning horizons and how a business plan cascades into the various hierarchical materials and capacity plans. The **aggregate production plan (APP)** is a long-range materials plan. Since capacity expansion involves the construction of a new facility and major equipment purchases, the aggregate production plan's capacity is usually considered fixed during the planning horizon. The aggregate production plan sets the aggregate output rate, workforce size, utilization and inventory and/or backlog levels for an entire facility. The **master production schedule (MPS)** is a medium-range plan and is more detailed than the aggregate production plan. It shows the quantity and timing of the end items that will be produced. **Material requirements planning (MRP)** is a short-range materials plan. MRP is the detailed planning process for component parts to support the master production schedule. It is a system of converting the end items from the master production schedule into a set of time-phased component part requirements.

Material requirements planning was first developed in the 1960s. As it gained popularity among manufacturers in the 1980s and as computing technologies emerged, MRP grew in scope into manufacturing resource planning (MRP-II). MRP-II combined MRP with master production scheduling, rough-cut capacity planning, capacity requirement planning and other operations planning software modules. Eventually, the MRP-II system evolved into **enterprise resource planning (ERP)** in the 1990s.

Distribution requirements planning (DRP) describes the time-phased net requirements from central supply warehouses and distribution centers. It links production with distribution planning by providing aggregate time-phased net requirements information to the master production schedule.

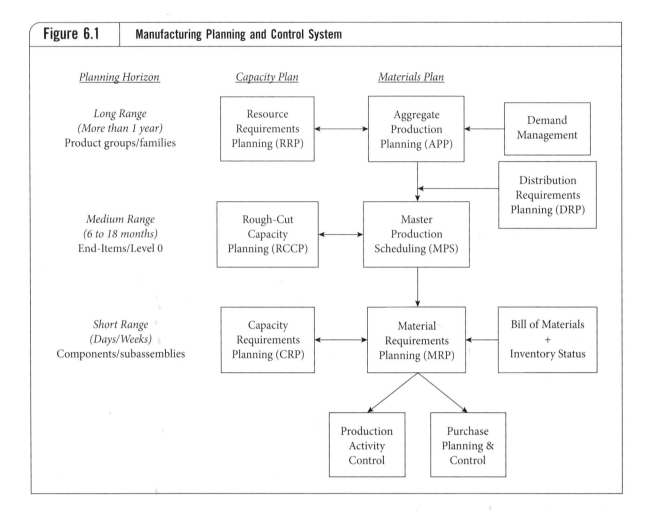

Figure 6.1 | Manufacturing Planning and Control System

The Aggregate Production Plan

Aggregate production planning is a hierarchical planning process that translates annual business plans and demand forecasts into a production plan for all products. As shown in Figure 6.1, *demand management* includes determining the aggregate demand based on forecasts of future demand, customer orders, special promotions and safety stock requirements. This forecast of demand then sets the aggregate utilization, production rate, workforce levels and inventory balances or backlogs. Aggregate production plans are typically stated in terms of product families or groups. A **product family** consists of different products that share similar characteristics, components or manufacturing processes. For example, an all-terrain vehicle (ATV) manufacturer who produces both automatic and manual drive options may group the two different types of ATVs together, since the only difference between them is the drive option. Production processes and material requirements for the two ATVs can be expected to be very similar and, thus, can be grouped into a family.

The planning horizon covered by the APP is normally at least one year and is usually extended or rolled forward by three months every quarter. This allows the firm to see its capacity requirements at least one year ahead on a continuous basis. The APP *disaggregates* the demand forecast information it receives and links the long-range business plan to the medium-range master production schedule. The objective is to provide sufficient finished goods in each period to meet the sales plan while meeting financial and production constraints.

Costs relevant to the aggregate planning decision include inventory cost, setup cost, machine operating cost, hiring cost, firing cost, training cost, overtime cost and costs incurred for hiring part-time and temporary workers to meet peak demand. There are three basic production strategies that firms use for completing the aggregate plan: (1) the *chase strategy*, (2) the *level strategy* and (3) the *mixed strategy*. Example 6.1 provides an illustration of an APP.

The Chase Production Strategy

The pure **chase production strategy** adjusts capacity to match the demand pattern. Using this strategy, the firm will hire and lay off workers to match its production rate to demand. The workforce fluctuates from month to month, but finished goods inventory remains constant. Using Example 6.1, the ATV Corporation will use six workers to make 120 units in January, and then lay off a worker in February to produce 100 units, as shown in Table 6.2. In March, the firm must hire ten additional workers so that it has enough labor to produce 300 units. An additional eight workers must be hired in April. The firm continues its hiring and lay-off policy to ensure its workforce and production capacity matches demand. In December, 180 units will be produced (although the demand is 140) because of the firm's desire to increase its ending inventory by 40 units in December.

The pure chase strategy obviously has a negative motivational impact on the workers, and it assumes that workers can be hired and trained easily to perform the job. In this strategy, the finished goods inventories always remain constant but the workforce fluctuates in response to the demand pattern. Figure 6.2 shows that the chase production curve perfectly overlaps on the demand curve. The inventory level remains constant at 100 units until December, when it increases by 40 units. Hiring, training and termination costs are significant cost components in the chase production strategy.

Example 6.1   An Aggregate Production Plan for the ATV Corporation

The ATV Corporation makes three models of all-terrain vehicles: Model A, Model B and Model C. Model A uses a 0.4-liter engine, Model B uses a 0.5-liter engine and Model C uses a 0.6-liter engine. The aggregate production plan is the twelve-month plan that combines all three models together in total monthly production. The planning horizon is twelve months. The APP determines the size of the workforce, which is the constrained resource. Table 6.1 shows the annual aggregate production plan from January to December, assuming the beginning inventory for January is 100 units (30 units each of Model A and Model B, and 40 units of Model C), and the firm desires to have an ending inventory of 140 units at the end of the year. On average, one unit of ATV requires eight labor hours to produce, and a worker contributes 160 hours (8 hours × 5 days × 4 weeks) per month. Note that the 1,120 labor hours needed in December as shown in Table 6.1 excludes the labor hours (8 hours × 40 units = 320 hours) required to produce the additional 40 units, which is the difference between the January beginning inventory of 100 units and the desired December ending inventory of 140 units.

The final column in Table 6.1 (Planned Capacity) refers to a typical manufacturing workforce situation wherein the firm desires to maintain a minimum core workforce of ten workers while also relying on overtime and subcontracting to handle the forecasted high seasonal demands.

Table 6.1	ATV Corporation's Aggregate Production Plan		
		CAPACITY (LABOR HOURS)	
PERIOD	FORECAST DEMAND	NEEDED	PLANNED
January	120 units	960 hrs	10 workers
February	100 units	800 hrs	10 workers
March	300 units	2,400 hrs	12 workers + overtime
April	460 units	3,680 hrs	18 workers + overtime
May	600 units	4,800 hrs	25 workers + overtime
June	700 units	5,600 hrs	25 workers + overtime + subcontracting
July	760 units	6,080 hrs	25 workers + overtime + subcontracting
August	640 units	5,120 hrs	25 workers + overtime
September	580 units	4,640 hrs	25 workers + overtime
October	400 units	3,200 hrs	20 workers
November	200 units	1,600 hrs	10 workers
December	140 units	1,120 hrs	10 workers
	5,000 units	40,000 hrs	

Table 6.2	An Example of the Chase Production Strategy			
			CAPACITY NEEDED (LABOR)	ENDING
PERIOD	FORECAST DEMAND (UNITS)	PRODUCTION (UNITS)	HOURS	WORKERS	INVENTORY (UNITS)
January	120	120	960	6	100
February	100	100	800	5	100
March	300	300	2,400	15	100
April	460	460	3,680	23	100
May	600	600	4,800	30	100
June	700	700	5,600	35	100
July	760	760	6,080	38	100
August	640	640	5,120	32	100
September	580	580	4,640	29	100
October	400	400	3,200	20	100
November	200	200	1,600	10	100
December	140 + 40	180	1,120 + 320	9	140
	5,040	5,040	40,320	252	

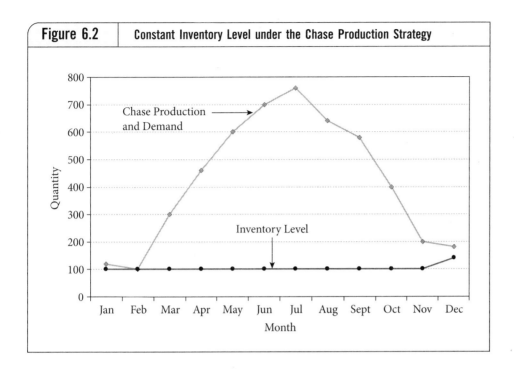

Figure 6.2 | **Constant Inventory Level under the Chase Production Strategy**

This strategy works well for **make-to-order manufacturing firms** since they cannot rely on finished goods inventory to satisfy the fluctuating demand pattern. Make-to-order firms generally produce one-of-a-kind, specialty products based on customer specifications. Make-to-order firms cannot build ahead of orders since they do not know the actual specifications of the finished goods. However, make-to-order products generally require highly skilled labor, capable of producing unique products using general-purpose equipment. Although a chase production strategy works well when unskilled labor is required, the strategy can be problematic when highly skilled workers are needed, especially in a tight labor market.

The Level Production Strategy

A pure **level production strategy** relies on a constant output rate and capacity while varying inventory and backlog levels to handle the fluctuating demand pattern. Using this strategy, the firm keeps its workforce levels constant and relies on fluctuating finished goods inventories and backlogs to meet demand. Since the level production strategy keeps a constant output rate and capacity, it is more suited for firms that require highly skilled labor. The workforce is likely to be more effective and their morale higher when compared to the chase strategy.

Again using the Example 6.1 forecast information, a pure level production strategy calls for a monthly production rate of 420 units ([5,000 units annual demand + 40 units additional ending inventory] ÷ 12 months). Thus, this strategy requires a constant workforce of twenty-one workers, as shown in Table 6.3.

The firm allows finished goods inventories to accrue while cumulative demand remains less than cumulative production, and then relies on a series of backlogs to handle the demand from August through November. Figure 6.3 shows that level production is characterized by the fluctuating inventory/backlog level while the workforce and production

Table 6.3	An Example of Level Production Strategy				
			CAPACITY NEEDED (LABOR)		ENDING INV/ (BACKLOG) (UNITS)
PERIOD	FORECAST DEMAND (UNITS)	PRODUCTION (UNITS)	HOURS	WORKERS	
January	120	420	3,360	21	400
February	100	420	3,360	21	720
March	300	420	3,360	21	840
April	460	420	3,360	21	800
May	600	420	3,360	21	620
June	700	420	3,360	21	340
July	760	420	3,360	21	0
August	640	420	3,360	21	(220)
September	580	420	3,360	21	(380)
October	400	420	3,360	21	(360)
November	200	420	3,360	21	(140)
December	140 + 40	420	3,360	21	140
	5,040	5040	40,320	252	

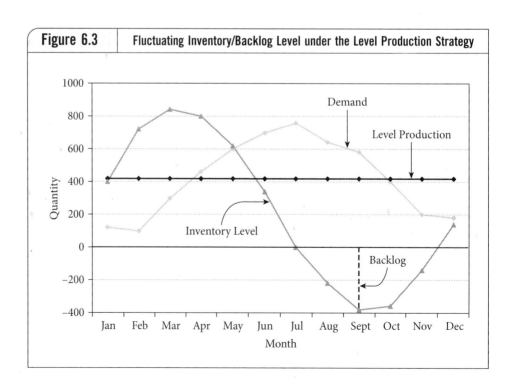

| Figure 6.3 | Fluctuating Inventory/Backlog Level under the Level Production Strategy |

capacity remain constant. Inventory carrying and stockout costs are major cost components in the level production strategy. This strategy works well for **make-to-stock** manufacturing firms, which typically emphasize immediate delivery of off-the-shelf, standard goods at relatively low prices. Firms whose trading partners seek the lowest prices of stock items might select the level production strategy. Besides, this strategy works well in a situation where highly skilled workers are needed in a tight labor market.

The Mixed Production Strategy

Instead of using either the pure chase or level production strategy, many firms use a mixed production strategy that strives to maintain a stable core workforce while using other short-term means such as overtime, an additional shift, subcontracting or the hiring of part-time and temporary workers to manage short-term high demand. Usually, these firms will then schedule preventive maintenance, produce complementary products that require similar resources but different demand cycles, or continue to produce the end items, holding these as finished goods inventory during the off-peak demand periods.

For example, all-terrain-vehicle manufacturers can produce snowmobiles to smooth out the seasonal effect of the two products. Table 6.1 shows the mixed strategy (referred to earlier, using the Planned Capacity column) in which the firm strives to maintain a minimum core workforce of ten workers while avoiding hiring above 25 workers during peak or high demand season. Hiring above 25 workers may strain other capacities, such as machine capacity and the availability of component parts. Instead, the mixed strategy uses overtime and subcontracting to cope with the high demand periods. If labor is the only constrained capacity, it may hire enough workers to run an additional shift to cope with the high demand. We can see here that firms with multiple products and with customers seeking both low-cost and make-to-order items may opt for this type of production strategy to minimize stockouts and cycle time.

Master Production Scheduling

The master production schedule is a time-phased, detailed disaggregation of the aggregate production plan, listing the exact end items to be produced. It is more detailed than the aggregate production plan. The MPS planning horizon is shorter than the aggregate production plan's, but must be longer than the production lead time to ensure the end item can be completed within the planning horizon.

For example, disaggregating ATV Corporation's January and February aggregate production plans may yield the master production schedule shown in Table 6.4. The plan results in time-phased production requirements of the specific model of ATV to produce for every week in January and February. The sum of the weekly MPS matches the quantity of the APP for that same month. For example, the MPS quantities for January and February in Table 6.4 (80, 80 and 60 units for the three models) equal the monthly APP quantities of 120 and 100 units, respectively. The master production schedule provides more detail by breaking down the aggregate production plan into specific weekly demand for Model A, Model B and Model C.

For the service industry, the master production schedule may just be the appointment book or scheduling software, which is created to ensure that capacity in the form of skilled labor matches demand. Master production schedules in the form of appointments are not overbooked to ensure capacity is not strained. The firm continues to revise and

Table 6.4	ATV's Master Production Schedule for January and February			
		MPS QUANTITY		
PERIOD	APP QUANTITY	MODEL A	MODEL B	MODEL C
January—week 1	120 units	10	10	10
January—week 2		10	10	10
January—week 3		20	0	10
January—week 4		0	20	10
February—week 1	100 units	20	0	0
February—week 2		0	20	0
February—week 3		0	0	20
February—week 4		20	20	0
Total	220 units	80	80	60

add appointments to the MPS until it obtains the best possible schedule. An example is to schedule patients' appointments in a hospital by means of a medical appointment scheduling software application.

Master Production Schedule Time Fence

The master production schedule is the production quantity required to meet demand from all sources and is the basis for computing the requirements of all time-phased end items. The material requirements plan uses the MPS to compute component part and subassembly requirements. Frequent changes to the MPS can be costly and may create *system nervousness.*

System nervousness can be defined as a situation wherein a small change in the upper-level production plan causes a major change in the lower-level production plan. For example, in the case of the clinic booking new appointments, it is very difficult for the clinic to book additional appointments for the current period because it is very likely that the appointment book is already fully booked. If a patient insists that she must see the doctor immediately, it is likely that another patient's appointment may have to be delayed or the clinic would need to work overtime to see an additional patient. However, it is much easier for the clinic to book new appointments farther into the future.

System nervousness can create serious problems for manufacturing firms. For example, if the January production plan for the ATV Corporation is suddenly doubled during the second week of January, the firm would be forced to quickly revise purchase orders, component assembly orders, and end-item production orders, causing a ripple effect of change within the firm and up its supply chain to its suppliers. The change would also likely cause missed delivery due dates. The firm needs sufficient lead time to purchase items and manufacture the end items, especially if manufacturing lead times and lot sizes are large.

Many firms use a **time fence system** to deal with this problem. The time fence system separates the planning horizon into two segments: a *firmed* and a *tentative segment.* A firmed segment is also known as a *demand time fence,* and it usually stretches from the current period to a period several weeks into the future. A firmed segment stipulates that the production plan or MPS cannot be altered except with the authorization of senior management. The *tentative segment* is also known as the **planning time fence**, and it typically stretches from the end of the firmed segment to several weeks farther into the future. It usually covers a longer period than the firmed segment, and the master scheduler can change production to meet changing conditions. Beyond the planning time fence, the computer can schedule the MPS quantities automatically, based on existing ordering and scheduling policies.

Available-to-Promise Quantities

In addition to providing time-phased production quantities of specific end items, the MPS also provides vital information on whether additional orders can be accepted for delivery in specific periods. This information is particularly important when customers are relying on the firm to deliver the right quantity of products purchased on the desired delivery date. This information is the **available-to-promise (ATP) quantity**, or the uncommitted portion of the firm's planned production (or scheduled MPS). It is the difference between confirmed customer orders and the quantity the firm planned to produce, based on the MPS. The available-to-promise quantity provides a mechanism to allow the master scheduler or sales personnel to quickly negotiate new orders and delivery due dates with customers or to quickly respond to customers' changing demands. The three basic methods of calculating the available-to-promise quantities are: (1) *discrete available-to-promise*, (2) *cumulative available-to-promise without look ahead* and (3) *cumulative available-to-promise with look ahead*. The discrete available-to-promise (ATP:D) computation is discussed next. Readers who are interested in the other two methods are referred to Fogarty, Blackstone and Hoffmann (1991).[3]

Table 6.5	Discrete ATP Calculation for January and February							
				WEEK				
	1	2	3	4	5	6	7	8
Model A—0.4 liter Engine								
MPS BI = 30	10	10	20	0	20	0	0	20
Committed Customer Orders	10	0	28	0	0	20	0	10
ATP:D	30	2	0	0	0	0	0	10
Model B—0.5 liter Engine								
MPS BI = 30	10	10	0	20	0	20	0	20
Committed Customer Orders	20	10	7	0	0	20	18	0
ATP:D	13	0	0	2	0	0	0	20
Model C—0.6 Liter Engine								
MPS BI = 40	10	10	10	10	0	0	20	0
Committed Customer Orders	20	10	0	0	0	10	0	15
ATP:D	30	0	10	0	0	0	5	0

The ATV Corporation's January and February master production schedule for Model A, Model B and Model C is used in Table 6.5 to demonstrate the ATP:D method for computing the ATP quantities. Let us assume that there are four weeks each in January and February, which are shown in the first row and are labeled Week 1 to Week 8. The MPS row indicates the time-phased production quantities derived from the master production schedule in Table 6.4. These are the quantities to be produced by manufacturing as planned. The number labeled "BI" is the beginning inventory heading in to the first week of January. Committed customer orders are orders that have already been booked for specific customers. Finally, the ATP:D quantities are the remaining unbooked or unpromised units.

Calculating Discrete Available-to-Promise Quantities

The discrete available-to-promise (ATP:D) is computed as follows:

1. The ATP for the first period is the sum of the beginning inventory and the MPS, minus the sum of all the committed customer orders (CCOs) from period 1 up to but not including the period of the next scheduled MPS.
2. For all subsequent periods, there are two possibilities:
   a. If no MPS has been scheduled for the period, the ATP is zero.
   b. If an MPS has been scheduled for the period, the ATP is the MPS quantity minus the sum of all CCOs from that period up to but not including the period of the next scheduled MPS.
3. If an ATP for any period is negative, the deficit must be subtracted from the most recent positive ATP, and the quantities must be revised to reflect these changes.

As a check, the sum of the BI and MPS quantities for all periods must equal the sum of all CCOs and ATPs. Using these guidelines, the ATP:D quantities in Table 6.5 are computed as follows:

Model A

1. $ATP_1 = BI + MPS_1 - CCO_1 = 30 + 10 - 10 = 30$
2. $ATP_2 = MPS_2 - CCO_2 = 10 - 0 = 10$
3. $ATP_3 = MPS_3 - CCO_3 - CCO_4 = 20 - 28 - 0 = -8$ (use 8 units from ATP_2)
   Revising: $ATP_2 = 10 - 8 = 2$ and $ATP_3 = -8 + 8 = 0$
4. $ATP_4 = 0$ (no scheduled MPS)
5. $ATP_5 = MPS_5 - CCO_5 - CCO_6 - CCO_7 = 20 - 0 - 20 - 0 = 0$
6. $ATP_6 = 0$ (no scheduled MPS)
7. $ATP_7 = 0$ (no scheduled MPS)
8. $ATP_8 = MPS_8 - CCO_8 = 20 - 10 = 10$

Checking the calculations, the sum of the BI and MPS quantities for the eight periods equals 110 units, which is also the sum of the CCOs and the ATPs for the same periods. Further, the calculation shows that 30 units of the Model A ATV can be promised for delivery in the first week of January or later, two units can be promised in the second week or later, and another ten units can be promised for delivery in the eighth week or later. The eight-period total ATP of 42 units is the difference between the sum of the beginning inventory and MPS (110 units), and the sum of the committed customer orders (68 units) for the eight weeks. Also note that although no MPS has been scheduled for the sixth week, the committed customer orders of twenty units are still possible, since the units can come from the uncommitted MPS of the previous weeks.

Model B

1. $ATP_1 = BI + MPS_1 - CCO_1 = 30 + 10 - 20 = 20$
2. $ATP_2 = MPS_2 - CCO_2 - CCO_3 = 10 - 10 - 7 = -7$ (use 7 units from ATP_1)
   Revising: $ATP_1 = 20 - 7 = 13$ and $ATP_2 = -7 + 7 = 0$
3. $ATP_3 = 0$ (no scheduled MPS)
4. $ATP_4 = MPS_4 - CCO_4 - CCO_5 = 20 - 0 - 0 = 20$
5. $ATP_5 = 0$ (no scheduled MPS)
6. $ATP_6 = MPS_6 - CCO_6 - CCO_7 = 20 - 20 - 18 = -18$ (use 18 units from ATP_4
   since $ATP_5 = 0$)
   Revising: $ATP_4 = 20 - 18 = 2$ and $ATP_6 = -18 + 18 = 0$
7. $ATP_7 = 0$ (no scheduled MPS)
8. $ATP_8 = MPS_8 - CCO_8 = 20 - 0 = 20$

Checking, the BI plus the eight MPS weekly quantities equals 110 units and the CCOs plus the ATPs for the eight periods also equals 110 units. The calculation shows that thirteen units of the Model B ATV can be promised for delivery in the first week or later, two units can be promised for delivery in the fourth week or later, and another twenty units can be promised for delivery in the eighth week or later. The eight-period total ATP of 35 units is the difference between the sum of the beginning inventory and MPS (110 units), and the sum of the committed customer orders (75 unit) for the eight-week period. Note that although no MPS has been scheduled for the seventh week, the CCO of eighteen units came from the uncommitted MPS quantities of the previous weeks.

Model C

1. $ATP_1 = BI + MPS_1 - CCO_1 = 40 + 10 - 20 = 30$
2. $ATP_2 = MPS_2 - CCO_2 = 10 - 10 = 0$
3. $ATP_3 = MPS_3 - CCO_3 = 10 - 0 = 10$
4. $ATP_4 = MPS_4 - CCO_4 - CCO_5 - CCO_6 = 10 - 0 - 0 - 10 = 0$
5. $ATP_5 = 0$ (no scheduled MPS)
6. $ATP_6 = 0$ (no scheduled MPS)
7. $ATP_7 = MPS_7 - CCO_7 - CCO_8 = 20 - 0 - 15 = 5$
8. $ATP_8 = 0$ (no scheduled MPS)

Checking, the total BI and eight-period MPS is 100 units and the total CCOs and ATPs for the eight periods is also 100 units. The calculation shows that 30 units of Model C ATV can be promised for delivery in the first week of January or later, ten units can be promised in the third week or later, and another five units can be promised for delivery in the seventh week or later. The eight-period total ATP of 45 units is the difference between the sum of the BI and MPS (100 units) and the sum of the committed customer orders (55 units) for the eight-week period.

Note that while the total uncommitted production quantity can easily be computed by subtracting all CCOs from the scheduled MPS, it lacks time-phased information. For this reason, the ATP quantities must be determined as shown. This enables the master scheduler or salesperson to quickly book or confirm new sales to be delivered on specific due dates. Reacting quickly to demand changes and delivering orders on time are necessities in high-performing supply chains, and the tools discussed here enable firms to effectively meet customer needs. In supply chain relationships, using the MPS and ATP information effectively is essential to maintaining speed and flexibility (which impacts customer service) throughout the supply chain as products make their way to end users.

The Bill of Materials

The **bill of materials (BOM)** is an engineering document that shows an inclusive listing of all component parts and subassemblies making up the end item. Figure 6.4 is an example of a *multilevel bill of materials* for the ATV Corporation's all-terrain vehicles. It shows the parent-component relationships and the exact quantity of each component, known as the **planning factor**, required for making a higher-level part or assembly. For example, "engine assembly" is the immediate *parent* of "engine block," and conversely "engine block" is an immediate *component* of "engine assembly." The "24-inch solid steel bar" is a *common component part*, because it is a component of the "6-inch steel bar" and the "12-inch steel bar." The *planning factor* of "connecting rods" shows that four connecting rods are needed to make one "piston assembly." Note that twelve "piston rings" (3 × 4) are needed to assemble one ATV since there are three "piston rings" in each "piston subassembly," and there are four "piston subassemblies" in each "piston assembly."

Figure 6.4	**Bill of Materials for the ATV**

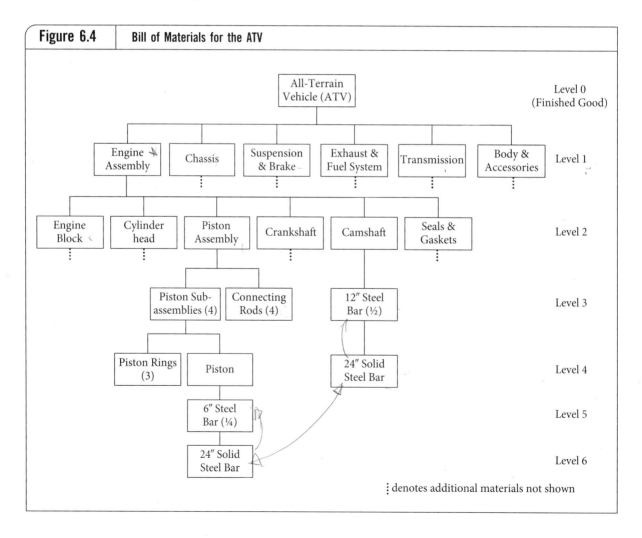

: denotes additional materials not shown

The BOM is shown in various levels, starting from Level 0. The level numbers increase as one moves down on the BOM. Level 0 is the final product, which is the **independent demand** item. In this case, it is the ATV. It has a demand pattern that is subject to trends and seasonal variations, and to general market conditions. Gross requirements of Level 0 items come from the master production schedule (i.e., Table 6.4 in the ATV Corporation example). The next level in the BOM is Level 1, which consists of all components and subassemblies required for the final assembly of one unit of an ATV. The gross requirements of Level 1 components and subassemblies are computed based on the demand for ATVs as specified in Level 0. Therefore, the requirements for all the items in Level 1 and below are called **dependent demand** items. For example, the engine assembly, chassis, suspension and brake, and transmission used to assemble the ATV are dependent demand items. However, if the components or subassemblies are sold as *service parts* to customers for repairing their ATVs, then they are independent demand items.

Correspondingly, the multilevel bill of materials can also be presented as an **indented bill of materials** as shown in Table 6.6. At each level of indentation, the level

Table 6.6	Indented Bill of Materials—All-Terrain Vehicles	
PART DESCRIPTION	**LEVEL**	**PLANNING FACTOR**
Engine Assembly	1	1
Engine Block (components not shown)	2	1
Cylinder Head (components not shown)	2	1
Piston Assembly	2	1
Piston Subassembly	3	4
Piston Rings	4	3
Pistons	4	1
6" Steel Bar	5	¼
24" Solid Steel Bar	6	1
Connecting Rods	3	4
Crankshaft (components not shown)	2	1
Camshaft	2	1
12" Steel Bar	3	½
24" Solid Steel Bar	4	1
Seals & Gaskets (components not shown)	2	1
Chassis (components not shown)	1	1
Suspension & Brake (components not shown)	1	1
Exhaust & Fuel System (components not shown)	1	1
Transmission (components not shown)	1	1
Body & Accessories (components not shown)	1	1

number increases by one. The indented bill of materials in Table 6.6 can be seen as an illustration of the multilevel bill of materials (Figure 6.4) rotated 90 degrees counterclockwise.

Another type of bill of materials is the **super bill of materials**, which is useful for planning purposes. It is also referred to as a *planning bill of materials, pseudo bill of materials, phantom bill of materials* or *family bill of materials*. Using the ATV Corporation's BOM in Figure 6.4 as an example, a simplified product structure diagram can be created for the family of ATVs that consists of different engine sizes (i.e., models) and transmission options. Instead of stating the planning factor, the percentage of each option is used. Figure 6.5 shows that 33⅓ percent of the ATVs are Model A, Model B and Model C, respectively. Similarly, 75 percent of the ATVs use automatic transmissions and the remaining 25 percent use manual transmissions. Therefore, the ATV Corporation's January planned production (120 units) consists of 40 units each of Model A, Model B and Model C (see Table 6.4). Similarly, 90 (75 percent × 120) units of the ATVs will be manufactured with automatic transmissions, and the remaining 30 (25 percent × 120) units will be manufactured with manual transmissions.

The super bill of materials enables the firm to forecast the total demand of ATVs and then break down the forecast into different models and transmission options using the correct percentage, instead of forecasting the demand for each option individually. It provides quick information on the quantity of components for each option needed for the scheduled production. In addition, it also reduces the number of master production schedules. For the ATV Corporation example, the number of master production schedules was reduced from six (3 models × 2 transmission options) to one.

When the exact proportion of each option is uncertain, the percentage can be increased slightly to cover the uncertainty. For example, the ATV Corporation may increase its automatic transmission option to 78 percent and manual option to 27 percent, for a total of 105 percent. The firm raises its total planned production by 5 percent to cover uncertainty. This is known as **option overplanning**.

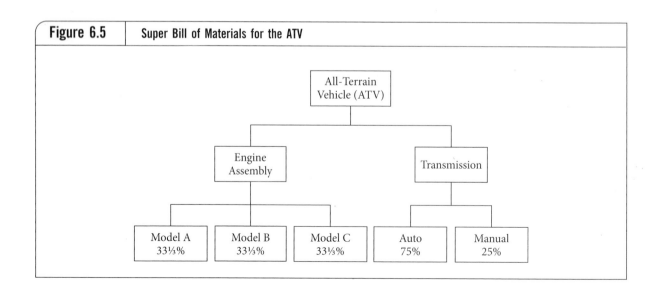

Figure 6.5 | **Super Bill of Materials for the ATV**

Material Requirements Planning

As illustrated in the ATV bill of materials in Figure 6.4, dependent demand is a term used to describe the internal demand for parts based on the independent demand of the final product in which the parts are used. Subassemblies, components and raw materials are examples of dependent demand items. Dependent demand may have a pattern of abrupt and dramatic changes because of its dependency on the demand of the final product, especially if the final product is produced in large lot sizes. Once the independent demand of the final product is known or forecasted, the dependent demand item requirements can be exactly calculated using material requirements planning (MRP) software, along with when the items should be assembled or purchased.

For example, the ATV Corporation's MPS (Table 6.4) shows that 120 ATVs will be produced in January. The firm thus knows that 120 handlebars and 480 wheel rims will be needed. The demand for handlebars, wheel rims and all of the other dependent demand items can be calculated using the MRP, based on the bill of materials (BOM) and the demand of the final product as stated on the MPS.

Material requirements planning is a software-based production planning and inventory control system that has been used widely by manufacturing firms for computing dependent demand and timing requirements. With the advent of computer and information technologies, the span of MRP evolved to include aggregate production planning, master production scheduling and capacity requirements planning to become **closed-loop MRP**. It further evolved into manufacturing resource planning (MRP-II) by including other aspects of materials and resource planning. A complete MRP-II system consists of many modules that enable the firm to book orders, schedule production, control inventory, manage distribution and perform accounting and financial analyses.

While there are hundreds of suppliers still selling and supporting their original MRP systems, some suppliers have expanded their systems to enable the users to perform more sophisticated analyses and integrate organization-wide activities, including operations and facilities that are located in different countries from the head office. This new generation of MRP system is known as the enterprise resource planning (ERP) system.

Material requirements planning is used to calculate the exact quantities, need dates and planned order releases for components and subassemblies needed to manufacture the final products listed on the MPS. MRP begins the computation process by first obtaining the requirements of the final product (the Level 0 item on the BOM) from the MPS to calculate the requirements of Level 1 components and then working its way down to the lowest level components, taking into account existing inventories and the time required for each processing step. While these manufacturing and delivery lead times are disregarded in the MPS, they are considered in the MRP computation process. For example, if a parent item requires an immediate component with a three-week lead time, the component must be ordered three weeks ahead of the need date.

For MRP, a dependent demand management system, to work effectively, it requires: (1) the independent demand information (the demand for the final product or service part) from the MPS; (2) parent-component relationships from the bill of materials, including the planning factor and lead-time information; and (3) the inventory status of the final product and all of the components. MRP takes this information to compute the *net requirements* of the final product and components, and then offsets the net requirements with appropriate lead times to ensure orders are released on time for fabricating the higher level components or purchasing the lower level components. This information, called **planned order releases**, is the most important output of the MRP. For items manufactured in-house, planned order releases are transmitted to the shop floor, but for purchased items, planned order releases are transmitted to suppliers directly or via the purchasing department.

A key benefit of MRP is that production information—such as scheduled receipts, on-hand inventories, net requirements and planned order releases—is available for the entire planning horizon; thus, it provides *visibility* for schedulers to plan ahead. However, the need for offsetting net requirements by the lead time to obtain planned order releases causes a *loss of visibility* in the planning horizon of components. This problem is especially acute for products with a deep bill of materials. Another drawback of the MRP is that it ignores capacity and shop floor conditions.

Terms used in Material Requirements Planning

Prior to examining how the MRP logic works, let us look at some terms as they apply to the MRP:

- *Parent*: The item generating the demand for lower level components. Level 0 is the final product. It is the parent of all Level 1 components. Similarly, each Level 1 item becomes the parent of the Level 2 components used to make that item. For example, Figure 6.4 shows that "piston assembly" is a parent of "piston subassemblies" and "connecting rods."

- *Components*: The parts demanded by a parent. For example, Figure 6.4 shows that "piston assembly" is a component of "engine assembly."

- *Gross requirement*: A time-phased requirement prior to considering on-hand inventory and lead time to obtain the item. The gross requirement is satisfied from inventory and production.

- *Net requirement*: The unsatisfied item requirement for a specific time period. It equals the gross requirement for that period minus the current on-hand inventory and any scheduled receipts.

- *Scheduled receipt*: A committed order awaiting delivery for a specific period. It is an order released in a past period and due to be received in a specific later period. This information is updated automatically by the MRP software logic system once an order has been placed. For example, an item with a two-week lead time ordered on the first week of the month becomes a scheduled receipt on the third week.

- *Projected on-hand inventory*: The projected inventory at the end of the period. It equals the beginning inventory minus the gross requirement, plus the scheduled receipt and any planned receipt from an earlier planned order release.

- *Planned order release*: A specific order to be released to the shop (if the component is made in-house) or to the supplier (if the component is purchased) to ensure that it is available on the need date. A key consideration here is that the *planned order releases of the parent translate into gross requirements of the components*.

- *Time bucket*: The time period used on the MRP. It is usually expressed in days or weeks. The current period is the *action time bucket*.

- *Explosion*: The common term used to describe the process of converting a parent item's planned order releases into component gross requirements.

- *Planning factor*: The number of components needed to produce one unit of the parent item. For example, Figure 6.4 shows that three "piston rings" are needed to produce one "piston subassembly" (this is also a very important consideration).

- *Firmed planned order*: A planned order that the MRP software logic system cannot automatically change when conditions change. The primary purpose of a firmed planned order is to prevent *system nervousness*, similar to the time fence system explained earlier in the master production schedule discussion.

- *Pegging*: Relates gross requirements for a component to the planned order releases that created the requirements.

- *Low-level coding*: Assigns the lowest level on the bill of materials to all common components to avoid duplicate MRP computations. For example, Figure 6.4 shows that "24-inch solid steel bar" is a common component that appears in Level 4 and Level 6. Instead of computing its planned order releases at Level 4 and Level 6 separately, a low-level code of 6 is assigned to the item. Its net requirements at Level 4 are added to those at Level 6, and the MRP explosion logic is performed at Level 6 only.

- *Lot size*: The order size for MRP logic. Lot size may be determined by various lot-sizing techniques, such as EOQ (a fixed order quantity) or lot-for-lot (order whatever amount is needed each period). A lot size of 50 calls for orders to be placed in multiples of 50. With a net requirement of 85 units, using lot-for-lot (LFL) order sizing will result in an order of 85 units; however, an order of 100 units would be placed when using a fixed order quantity of 50.

- *Safety stock*: Protects against uncertainties in demand, supply, quality and lead time. Its implication in MRP logic is that the minimum projected on-hand inventory should not fall below the safety stock level.

An MRP example is provided in Example 6.2.

Level 0 MRP Computation—Model A ATV

The first row is the planning horizon for the eight weeks in January and February. The gross requirements are derived directly from the MPS. The scheduled receipt of ten units in Week 2 is due to an order placed last week, or earlier but scheduled to be delivered on Week 2. The order size for the Model A ATV is in multiples of ten units, the lead time is two weeks, and the desired safety stock is fifteen units. The projected on-hand inventory of twenty units for the first week is computed by taking the beginning inventory of 30 units and subtracting the gross requirement of ten units in that week. The projected on-hand inventory of twenty units in Week 2 is computed by taking the previous balance of twenty units, adding the scheduled receipt of ten units, and subtracting the gross requirement of ten units.

During the third week, additional Model A ATVs must be received to ensure the on-hand balance is above the safety stock level of fifteen units. Since the opening inventory of twenty units is consumed to meet the gross requirement, the net requirement here is fifteen units. Given that orders must be in multiples of ten, twenty units must be ordered in the first week to satisfy both the lead time and the safety stock requirements. Simply stated, if twenty units are needed in the third week, the two-week lead time requires the order to be placed two weeks earlier, which explains why there is a planned order release of twenty units in the first week. The on-hand inventory balance of twenty units at the

Example 6.2   An MRP Example at the ATV Corporation

Model A's production schedule for the ATV Corporation is used to illustrate the MRP logic. Its gross requirements are first obtained from the master production schedule in Table 6.4, and the inventory status shows that 30 units of Model A are available at the start of the year. The parent-component relationships and planning factors are available from the BOM in Figure 6.4. Assuming the following lot sizes (Q), lead times (LT) and safety stocks (SS) are used, the MRP computations of the Model A ATV and some of its components are as follows:

MODEL A ATV—LEVEL 0		1	2	3	4	5	6	7	8
Gross Requirements		10	10	20	0	20	0	0	20
Scheduled Receipts			10						
Projected On-hand Inventory	30	20	20	20	20	20	20	20	20
Planned Order Releases		20		20			20		

Q = 10; LT = 2; SS = 15

×1 ×1 ×1

Engine Assembly—Level 1		1	2	3	4	5	6	7	8
Gross Requirements		20		20			20		
Scheduled Receipts		20							
Projected On-hand Inventory	2	2	2	0	0	0	0	0	0
Planned Order Releases		18			20				

Q = LFL; LT = 2; SS = 0

×1 ×1

Piston Assembly—Level 2		1	2	3	4	5	6	7	8
Gross Requirements		18			20				
Scheduled Receipts		20							
Projected On-hand Inventory	10	12	12	12	22	22	22	22	22
Planned Order Releases				30					

Q = 30; LT = 1; SS = 10

×4

Connecting Rods—Level 3		1	2	3	4	5	6	7	8
Gross Requirements				120					
Scheduled Receipts									
Projected On-hand Inventory	22	22	22	52	52	52	52	52	52
Planned Order Releases			150						

Q = 50; LT = 1; SS = 20

end of the third week is computed by taking the previous balance of twenty units, adding the planned order receipt of twenty units (due to the planned order release in the first week), and subtracting the gross requirement of twenty units.

Similarly, the gross requirements of twenty units each in the fifth and eighth week consumed the beginning of period inventory, triggering a net requirement of fifteen units for those periods and a planned order release of twenty units each during the third and sixth week, respectively.

Level 1 MRP Computation—Engine Assembly

The BOM in Figure 6.4 indicates that the gross requirements for the engine assembly are derived from the planned order releases of the Model A ATV. Since the planning factor is one unit, the Model A ATV's planned order releases translate directly into gross requirements for engine assembly in the first, third and sixth week. The scheduled receipt of twenty units in the first week is due to a committed order placed previously. The gross requirements of twenty units each for the third and sixth week triggered net requirements of eighteen and twenty units, which turn into planned order releases for the first and fourth week, respectively (note here that no safety stock is required and the lot size is LFL, thus order sizes vary according to whatever quantities are needed to have end-of-period inventories of zero).

Level 2 MRP Computation—Piston Assembly

The gross requirements for the piston assembly are derived directly from the planned order releases of engine assembly (recall that based on the BOM in Figure 6.4, the engine assembly is the immediate parent of the piston assembly and the planning factor is one). Therefore, the gross requirements of piston assembly are eighteen and twenty units, respectively, for the first and fourth weeks. Computations of its projected on-hand balances and planned order releases are similar to earlier examples (note here that inventories must not drop below the safety stock requirement of ten and order quantities must be made in multiples of 30).

Level 3 MRP Computation—Connecting Rods

The BOM in Figure 6.4 indicates that four connecting rods are required for each piston assembly. Thus, the gross requirement for connecting rods in the third week is obtained by multiplying the planned order releases for piston assemblies by four. Due to the requirement to offset the lead times in each MRP computation, the planned order release for connecting rods can be determined only up to the second period, although the gross requirements of the Model A ATV are known for the first eight weeks. This is known as *loss of visibility*, as discussed earlier.

Since there are no lower-level components shown for the connecting rods, we can assume that the ATV Corporation purchases this component. Thus, the planned order releases would be used by the purchasing department (as shown by the purchase planning and control function in Figure 6.1) to communicate order quantities and delivery requirements to its connecting rod supplier. Production activity control involves all aspects of shop floor scheduling, dispatching, routing and other control activities. In supply chain settings, manufacturing firms share their planned order release information with their strategic suppliers through **electronic data interchange (EDI)**, their ERP system or other forms of communication. Since the firm manufactures its own piston assemblies, the planned order release information for this part is communicated to shop floor operators and used to trigger production in that week. We can see, then, that planned order releases for purchased items eventually become the independent demand gross requirements for the firm's suppliers. Communicating this information accurately and quickly to strategic suppliers is a necessary element in an effective supply chain information system.

Capacity Planning

The material plans (the aggregate production plan, the master production schedule, and the material requirements plan) discussed so far have focused exclusively on production and materials management, but organizations must also address capacity constraints.

Excess capacity wastes valuable resources such as idle equipment and facilities, while insufficient capacity adversely affects quality levels and customer service. Thus, a set of capacity plans is used in conjunction with the materials plan to ensure capacity is not over- or underutilized.

In the context of capacity planning, **capacity** refers to a firm's labor and machine resources. It is the maximum amount of output that an organization is capable of completing in a given period of time. Capacity planning follows the basic hierarchy of the materials planning system as shown in Figure 6.1. At the aggregate level, **resource requirements planning (RRP)**, a long-range capacity planning module, is used to check whether aggregate resources are capable of satisfying the aggregate production plan. Typical resources considered at this stage include gross labor hours and machine hours. Generally, capacity expansion decisions at this level involve a long-range commitment, such as new machines or facilities. If existing resources are unable to meet the aggregate production plan, then the plan must be revised. The revised APP is reevaluated using the resource requirements plan until a feasible production plan is obtained.

Once the aggregate production plan is determined to be feasible, the aggregate production information is disaggregated into a more detailed medium-range production plan, the master production schedule. Although RRP has already determined that aggregate capacity is sufficient to satisfy the APP, medium-range capacity may not be able to satisfy the MPS. For example, the master production schedule may call for normal production quantities when much of the workforce typically takes vacation. Therefore, the medium-range capacity plan, or **rough-cut capacity plan (RCCP)**, is used to check the feasibility of the master production schedule.

The RCCP takes the master production schedule and converts it from production to capacity required, then compares it to capacity available during each production period. If the medium-range capacity and production schedule are feasible, the master production schedule is firmed up. Otherwise, it is revised, or the capacity is adjusted accordingly. Options for increasing medium-range capacity include overtime, subcontracting, adding resources, and an alternate routing of the production sequence.

Capacity requirements planning (CRP) is a short-range capacity planning technique that is used to check the feasibility of the material requirements plan. The time-phased material requirements plan is used to compute the detailed capacity requirements for each workstation during specific periods to manufacture the items specified in the MRP. Although the RCCP may show that sufficient capacity exists to execute the master production schedule, the CRP may indicate that production capacity is inadequate during specific periods.

Capacity Strategy

Capacity expansion or contraction is an integral part of an organization's manufacturing strategy. Effectively balancing capacity with demand is an intricate management decision as it directly affects a firm's competitiveness. Short- to medium-term capacity can be increased through the use of overtime, additional shifts, and subcontracting, whereas long-term capacity can be increased by introducing new manufacturing techniques, hiring additional workers and adding new machines and facilities. Conversely, capacity contraction can be attained by reducing the workforce, and disposing idle machines and facilities.

The three commonly recognized capacity strategies are lead, lag and match capacity strategies. A **lead capacity strategy** is a proactive approach that adds or subtracts capacity in anticipation of future market conditions and demand, whereas a **lag capacity strategy** is a reactive approach that adjusts its capacity in response to demand. In favorable market conditions, the lag strategy generally does not add capacity until the firm is operating at full capacity. The lag capacity strategy is a conservative approach that may result in lost opportunity when demand increases rapidly, whereas the lead strategy is more aggressive and can often result in excess inventory and idle capacity. Leaders in the electronics industry usually favor the lead capacity strategy because of the short product life cycles. A **match or tracking capacity strategy** is a moderate strategy that adjusts capacity in small amounts in response to demand and changing market conditions.

Distribution Requirements Planning

Distribution requirements planning (DRP) is a time-phased finished-goods inventory replenishment plan in a distribution network. Distribution requirements planning is a logical extension of the MRP system, and its logic is analogous to MRP. Distribution requirements planning ties the physical distribution system to the manufacturing planning and control system by determining the aggregate time-phased net requirements of the finished goods, and provides demand information for adjusting the MPS. A major difference between MRP and DRP is that while MRP is driven by the production schedule specified in the MPS to compute the time-phased requirements of components, DRP is driven by customer demand of the finished goods. Hence, MRP operates in a dependent demand situation, whereas DRP operates in an independent demand setting. The result of MRP execution is the production of finished-goods inventory at the manufacturing site, whereas DRP time-phases the movements of finished goods inventory from the manufacturing site to the central supply warehouse and distribution centers.

An obvious advantage of the DRP system is that it extends manufacturing planning and control visibility into the distribution system, thus allowing the firm to adjust its production plans and to avoid stocking excessive finished goods inventory. By now it should be clear that excessive inventory is a major cause of the bullwhip effect. Distribution requirements planning provides time-phased demand information needed for the manufacturing and distribution systems to effectively allocate finished goods inventory and production capacity to improve customer service and inventory investment. A distribution requirements planning example is provided in Example 6.3.

The Legacy Material Requirements Planning Systems

For over four decades, an MRP system was the first choice among manufacturing firms in the U.S. for planning and managing their purchasing, production and inventories. To improve the efficiency and effectiveness of the manufacturing planning and control system, many manufacturers have utilized electronic data interchange (EDI) to relay

Example 6.3   A DRP Example at the ATV Corporation

ATV Corporation's January and February distribution schedule for its Model A ATV is used to illustrate the DRP replenishment schedules from the firm's central supply warehouse to its two distribution centers. The time buckets used in the DRP are the same weekly time buckets used in the MRP system. DRP uses the order quantity, delivery lead time, on-hand balance and safety stock information to determine the planned order releases necessary to meet anticipated market demand.

Gross requirements from the two distribution centers in Las Vegas and East Lansing are first obtained from the demand management system. The same MRP logic is used to compute the planned order releases of the two distribution centers. The gross requirements of the central supply warehouse reflect the cascading demand of Las Vegas and East Lansing distribution centers. The gross requirements of fourteen units in the first week for the central supply warehouse are the sum of the planned order releases of the two distribution centers. The planned order releases of the central supply warehouse are passed on to the manufacturing facility, where they are absorbed into the MPS. This process is commonly referred to as **implosion**, where demand information is gathered from a number of field distribution centers and aggregated in the central warehouse, and eventually passed onto the manufacturing facility. While both the processes are similar, the *implosion* DRP logic is different from the *explosion* notion in MRP, where a Level 0 finished good is broken into its component requirements.

Scheduled Receipts and Projected On-hand Inventory

Las Vegas Distribution Center (Q = 2; LT = 2; SS = 0)

Model A ATV		1	2	3	4	5	6	7	8
Gross Requirements		0	1	1	0	1	0	6	0
Scheduled Receipts									
Projected On-hand	1	1	0	1	1	0	0	0	0
Planned Order Releases		2	0	0	0	6	0	0	0

East Lansing Distribution Center (Q = 2; LT = 1; SS = 0)

Model A ATV		1	2	3	4	5	6	7	8
Gross Requirements		3	11	0	1	0	2	0	15
Scheduled Receipts									
Projected On-hand	3	1	1	1	0	0	0	0	1
Planned Order Releases		12	0	0	0	2	0	16	0

2 + 12 = 14

6 + 2 = 8

Central Supply Warehouse		1	2	3	4	5	6	7	8
Gross Requirements		▼14	0	0	0	▼8	▼16	0	0
Scheduled Receipts									
Projected On-hand Inventory	16	2	2	2	2	4	3	3	3
Planned Order Releases		0	0	10	15	0	0	0	0

Q = 5; LT = 2; SS = 2

planned order releases to their suppliers. This information system has worked well for coordinating internal production, as well as purchasing.

By the end of the twentieth century, however, the global business environment was rapidly changing. Many savvy manufacturers and service providers were building multiplant international sites, either to take advantage of cheaper raw materials and labor or to expand their market. Business executives found themselves spending more time dealing with international subcontractors using different currencies and languages among varying political environments. The need to access real-time information on customers' requirements, production levels and available capacities, company-wide inventory levels and plants capable of meeting current order requirements increased. The existing MRP systems simply could not handle these added tasks.

To fully coordinate the information requirements for purchasing, planning, scheduling and distribution of an organization operating in a complex global environment, an enterprise-wide information system was needed. Thus, ERP systems that operated from a single, centralized database were engineered to replace the older legacy MRP systems.

The term **legacy MRP system** is a broad label used to describe an older information system that usually works at an operational level to schedule production within an organization. Many legacy systems were implemented in the 1960s, 1970s and 1980s and subjected to extensive modifications as requirements changed over the years. Today, these systems have lasted beyond their originally intended life span. The continuous modifications of these systems made them complex and cumbersome to work with, especially when considering they were not designed to be user-friendly in the first place. Legacy systems were designed to perform a very specific operational function and were programmed as independent entities with little regard for meeting requirements or coordinating with other functional areas. Communication between legacy systems is often limited, and visibility across functional areas is severely restricted. Legacy systems were implemented to gather data for transactional purposes and, thus, lacked any of the analytical capabilities required for today's complex global environment.

Manufacturing Resource Planning

The development of the legacy system can be traced back to the evolution of the MRP system, the closed-loop MRP system, and the **manufacturing resource planning (MRP-II)** system. The development of closed-loop MRP was a natural extension of the MRP system. It was an attempt to further develop the MRP into a formal and explicit manufacturing planning and control system by adding capacity requirements planning and feedback to describe the progress of orders being manufactured. The originally developed MRP is a part of the closed-loop MRP system.

Manufacturing resource planning was an outgrowth of the closed-loop MRP system. Business and sales plans were incorporated, and a financial function was added to link financial management to operations, marketing and other functional areas. The concept of manufacturing resource planning was that the information system should link internal operations to the financial function to provide management with current data, including sales, purchasing, production, inventory and cash flow. It should also be able to perform "what-if" analyses as internal and external conditions change. For example, MRP-II enables the firm to determine the impact on profit and cash flow if the firm is only able to fill 85 percent of its orders due to late deliveries of raw materials. MRP-II is an explicit and formal manufacturing information system that integrates the internal functions of an organization, enabling it to coordinate manufacturing plans with sales, while providing management with essential accounting and financial information.

Today, manufacturing resource planning has further evolved to include other functional areas of the organization. Although it synchronizes an organization's information systems and provides insight into the implications of aggregate production plans, master production schedules, capacities, materials plans and sales, it primarily focuses on one unit's internal operations. It lacks the capability to link the many operations of an organization's foreign branches with its headquarters. It also lacks the capability to directly interface with external supply chain members. For this reason, enterprise-wide information systems began to be developed.

The Development of Enterprise Resource Planning Systems

While traditional or legacy MRP systems continue to be used and modified to include other functional areas of an organization, the emergence and growth of supply chain management, e-commerce and global operations have created the need to exchange information directly with suppliers, customers and foreign branches of organizations. The concept of the manufacturing information system thus evolved to directly connect all functional areas and operations of an organization and, in some cases, its suppliers and customers via a common software infrastructure and database. This type of manufacturing information system is referred to as an enterprise resource planning (ERP) system.

The typical ERP system is an umbrella system that ties together a variety of specialized systems, such as production and inventory planning, purchasing, logistics and warehousing, finance and accounting, human resource management, customer relationship management and supplier relationship management using a common, shared, centralized database. However, exactly what is tied together varies on a case-by-case basis, based on the ERP system capabilities and the needs of the organization. Figure 6.6 illustrates a

| Figure 6.6 | A Generic ERP System |

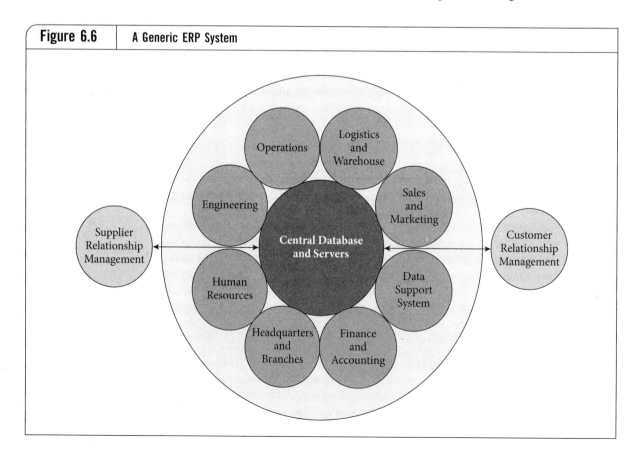

generic ERP system, where a centralized database and software application infrastructure are used to drive a firm's information systems and to link the operations of its branches, key suppliers and key customers with the firm's headquarters.

Enterprise resource planning is a broadly used industrial term to describe the multi-module application software for managing an enterprise's functional activities, suppliers and customers. Initially, ERP software focused on integrating the internal business activities of a multifacility organization, or enterprise, to ensure that it was operating under the same information system. With the onset of supply chain management, ERP vendors today are designing their products to include modules for managing suppliers and customers. For example, ERP enables an organization to deal directly with key suppliers to assess the availability of their resources, as if they are an extended member of the firm. Similarly, ERP also allows key customers to directly access the firm's inventory information and manufacturing and delivery schedules.

ERP utilizes the idea of a centralized and shared database system to tie the entire organization together, as opposed to the traditional legacy MRP system that uses multiple databases and interfaces that frequently result in duplicate and inconsistent information across different branches or even departments within an organization. With ERP, information is entered once at the source and made available to all users. It eliminates the inconsistency and incompatibility created when different functional areas use different systems with overlapping data.

The legacy MRP system typically utilizes multiple software packages and databases for different functional areas. Usually, each functional area implements its own information system based on its unique needs, with very little input or coordination from the other functional areas. The different packages within an organization often are incompatible with each other and prevent transactions from taking place directly between systems. The multiple databases also cause the same information to be stored in multiple locations; thus, multiple entries of the same data are required. This need to enter the same data repeatedly is a major cause of inconsistency in database management. For example, a customer, ATV Inc., may be entered as ATV Inc. in one database and ATV Incorporated in another database. From an information system's perspective, ATV Inc. and ATV Incorporated are two distinct customers.

With a shared, centralized database system, ERP is capable of automating business processes rapidly and accurately. For example, when taking a sales order, a sales agent has all the necessary information of the customer (for example, the credit history, rating and limit from the finance and accounting module), the company's production and inventory levels (from the operations module), and the delivery schedule (from the sales and marketing module) to complete the sale. After the sale is confirmed and entered into the centralized database, other supply chain partners affected by the transaction can directly utilize the same information system to take appropriate proactive actions. For example, suppliers can find out the production schedules planned by upstream supply chain members so that raw materials and components can be produced accordingly to support sales. Similarly, downstream companies can also utilize the same information system and database to access delivery schedules of raw materials and components ordered from their upstream supply chain members.

Thus, ERP integrates the internal operations of an enterprise with a common software platform and centralized database system. It also ties together supply chain member processes using the same information system. ERP provides the mechanism for supply chain members to share information so that scarce resources can be fully utilized to meet

Example 6.4   A Hypothetical ERP Transaction

The following example demonstrates a hypothetical ERP transaction for the ATV Corporation. The ATV Corporation makes three models of all-terrain vehicles: Model A, Model B and Model C. The corporation is headquartered in the U.S. with manufacturing facilities in the U.S. and Mexico. ATV sells its products in the U.S., Canada and Mexico. Its sales representatives make quarterly visits to customers to take sales orders and provide necessary customer services. The following steps describe a sales transaction by a sales representative during a typical visit to a retail customer in Canada.

We assume here that a dealer ordered 100 units of Model A and 150 units of Model B, to be delivered within 30 days.

1. *Ordering:* The field sales representative takes the order of 100 units of Model A and 150 units of Model B. Using the Internet, the sales rep accesses the sales and marketing module of the ERP system at the ATV Corporation headquarters in the U.S. to check the price and other related information, such as quantity discounts, guarantees and rebates. The sales rep also accesses the customer's credit history and rating from the finance and accounting module.

2. *Availability:* Simultaneously, the ERP system checks the inventory status and the available-to-promise quantities of its manufacturing facilities in the U.S. and Mexico and notifies the sales rep whether or not the order can be filled on time. The sales rep finds that the Mexico factory has sufficient inventory to fill the Model A order immediately, while the Model B order can be manufactured in ten days from the U.S. factory. Logistics information shows that shipping from Mexico to Canada takes two weeks, and delivery time from the U.S. factory takes one week. Thus, the entire order is accepted, and the factory in Mexico receives instructions to ship 100 units of Model A to Canada immediately. The inventory status is updated accordingly. An invoice in English will be printed, and the finance and accounting module will be updated to reflect the partial delivery upon shipment of the goods from Mexico.

3. *Manufacturing:* The operations module immediately schedules the production of 150 units of Model B at the U.S. factory. All dependent demand items and labor necessary to produce 150 units of Model B are scheduled to meet the due date. For components manufactured in-house, planned order releases are transmitted to the shop floor. For purchased items, the information is sent to the suppliers.

    The human resource module checks to ensure that there are sufficient workers in the U.S. factory to complete the order. If not, the personnel manager will be notified and additional workers may be employed.

4. *Order Tracking:* An advance shipping notice (ASN) that provides delivery information to the dealer's receiving operations is transmitted. The customer relationship management module allows the customer to track the status of its order.

demand, while minimizing the bullwhip effect and supply chain inventories. Production changes and other modifications can also be executed quickly and efficiently to minimize delivery lead times. Example 6.4 illustrates a typical ERP transaction.

The Rapid Growth of Enterprise Resource Planning Systems

The use of ERP systems has gradually spread from manufacturing to the service sector and has become commonly used in many university classrooms. Many universities in the

U.S., for instance, have cooperated with major ERP software providers to integrate ERP training into their business curricula. There are many reasons, some of which are discussed in the following paragraph, for the rapid growth of ERP since the early 1990s.

At the turn of the 21st century, many firms were uncertain as to how the Year 2000 Millennium Bug or Y2K bug (conversion of the year from 1999 to 2000) would affect their information systems. Most information systems installed were programmed to use the last two digits of the year (e.g., the year 1998 would be shown as 98). Using the same logic, the year 2000 would be recorded as 00, which might also be interpreted as the year 1900, or 98 years prior to 1998. This could adversely affect time-sensitive programming logic (e.g., interest calculations). In addition, the legacy MRP systems had been modified so extensively over the years that the many layers of program codes made it too complex and redundant to correctly assess the true impact of Y2K. The extensive modifications to the legacy systems had also made them too expensive to maintain. Thus, many savvy business managers took a proactive approach to set aside sufficient budgetary funds to replace their legacy MRP systems with the more efficient ERP systems to reduce costs and deal with the Y2K problem as well.

The rapid development of computer and information technology over the last two decades has also contributed positively to the growth of ERP. Tasks that were previously limited to mainframe computers are today easily implemented on servers and desktop computers that cost only a fraction of the capital investment previously needed. Information systems that were previously off-limits are now accessible to many smaller organizations. ERP is expected to remain the key building block of global business management information systems. As the global business environment continues to change, ERP is expected to evolve to become more flexible to adapt to mergers and acquisitions and to provide more real-time monitoring and response.

Implementing Enterprise Resource Planning Systems

ERP systems have continued to evolve, and integration of e-commerce, customer relationship management (CRM) and supplier relationship management (SRM) applications are now considered ERP requirements by most organizations. While many firms believe a well-designed and implemented ERP system can translate into a substantial competitive advantage, research analysts and industrial practitioners are still debating the usefulness of ERP, and the advantages and disadvantages of using a **best-of-breed solution** versus a **single integrator solution**. It is important to understand that ERP is not a panacea for poor business decisions, but a valuable tool that can be used to enhance competitiveness.

The *best-of-breed* solution picks the best application or module for each individual function in the supply chain (thus, best of breed). The resulting system includes several different applications that must be integrated to work as a single coordinated system to achieve the global scope required of the ERP. A major criticism of the best-of-breed solution is that multiple software infrastructures and databases may have to be used to link the multiple applications obtained from different vendors. This may severely affect the ability of the system to update the databases rapidly and efficiently—a similar problem of the legacy MRP systems.

The *single integrator* approach picks all the desired applications from a single vendor for the ERP system. The obvious advantages are that all of the applications should work well together, and getting the system up and running should be easier. As companies become more global, and as firms desire to expand their systems with other compatible modules later on, the notion of using a single integrator solution becomes more attractive. On the other hand, as information technology continues to evolve and as competition increases in the ERP software market, ERP vendors are designing their products to be more compatible with each other. Therefore, implementing an ERP system using the best-of-breed solution approach is becoming easier. Best-of-breed vendors will continue to fill a void in the ERP market with specialized applications that mainstream ERP vendors cannot provide.

Choosing whether to utilize a single integrator ERP solution or to combine niche software is a challenge facing many companies today. If the firm's IT department has its way, the company will choose a single integrator solution for their ERP implementation; if people overseeing other business processes have their way, a company is more likely to choose the best-of-breed solution.[4]

The emergence of the single integrator ERP solution over the last ten years does not signal the extinction of best-of-breed software vendors. While it is rare now, to find major companies using best-of-breed ERP packages, best-of-breed vendors will continue to fill the niches left by the large ERP vendors. Some businesses require unique best-of-breed software to do advanced analytical decision making. Businesses are often interested in tasks that extend beyond core ERP functions, into areas like sales and operations planning or analyses using ERP data. Many best-of-breed ERP vendors have thrived by creating early software innovations around the "edges of ERP," exploiting gaps left by ERP product suites. Many of these surviving vendors for example, are in inventory management systems.[5] Finally, businesses often turn to best-of-breed system vendors when the cost savings expected from their ERP implementations fail to materialize. In general, best-of-breeds are better suited to more intricate workplaces, while single integrator ERP solutions fit the less complex business environments.[6]

Implementing an ERP system has proven to be a real challenge for many companies. Most ERP systems are written based on the best practices of selected firms. Thus, a condition required for implementation of the system is that the user's business processes must conform to the approaches used in the software logic. These processes can be significantly different from those currently used within the company. Having to adapt a company's business processes to conform to a software program is a radical departure from the conventional business practice of requiring the software to be designed around the business processes.

Two primary requirements of successful implementation of ERP are computer support and accurate, realistic inputs. Instead of implementing the entire system at once, some organizations choose to implement only those applications or modules that are absolutely critical to operations at that time. New modules are then added in later phases. This ensures that the system can be implemented as quickly as possible while minimizing interruption of the existing system. However, many implementations have failed due to a variety of reasons, as follows:

- *Lack of top management commitment*: While management may be willing to set aside sufficient funds to implement a new ERP system, it may not take an active role in the implementation process. Often, this leads users to revert to the old processes or systems because of their lack of knowledge of or interest in learning the capabilities of the new ERP system.

- *Lack of adequate resources*: Implementing a new ERP system is a long-term commitment requiring substantial capital investment. Although the cost has become more affordable due to the rapid advent of computer technology, full implementation may still be out of reach for many small organizations. In addition, small firms may not have the necessary workforce and expertise to implement the complex system.

- *Lack of proper training*: Many employees may already be familiar with their legacy MRP systems. Thus, when a new ERP system is implemented, top management may assume that users are already adequately prepared and underestimate the training required to get the new system up and running. Lack of financial resources can also reduce the amount of training available for its workforce.

- *Lack of communication*: Lack of communication within an organization, or between the firm and its ERP software provider can also be a major hindrance for successful implementation. Lack of communication usually results in the wrong specifications and requirements being implemented.

- *Incompatible system environment*: In certain cases, the firm's environment does not give ERP a distinct advantage over other systems. For example, there is no advantage for a small, family-owned used-car dealer in a small town to implement an expensive new ERP system.

Advantages and Disadvantages of Enterprise Resource Planning Systems

When properly installed and operating, an ERP system can provide a firm and its supply chain partners with a significant competitive advantage, which can fully justify the investments of time and money in ERP. A fully functional ERP system is capable of enhancing the firm's capability to fully utilize capacity, accurately schedule production, reduce inventory, meet delivery due dates and enhance the efficiency and effectiveness of the supply chain. Let us look at some specific advantages and disadvantages.

Enterprise Resource Planning System Advantages

As mentioned earlier, the primary advantage of ERP over the legacy MRP systems is that ERP uses a single database and a common software infrastructure to provide a broader scope and up-to-date information, enabling management to make better decisions that can benefit the entire supply chain. ERP is also fairly robust in providing real-time information and, thus, is able to communicate information about operational changes to supply chain members with little delay. ERP systems are also designed to take advantage of Internet technology. Thus, users are able to access the system via the Internet.

ERP helps organizations reduce supply chain inventories due to the added visibility throughout the entire supply chain. It enables the supply, manufacturing and logistics processes to flow smoothly by providing visibility of the order fulfillment process throughout the supply chain. Supply chain visibility leads to reductions of the bullwhip effect and helps supply chain members to better plan production and end-product deliveries to customers.

ERP systems also help organizations to standardize manufacturing processes. Manufacturing firms often find that multiple business units across the company make the same product using different processes and information systems. ERP systems enable the firm to automate some of the steps of a manufacturing process. Process standardization eliminates redundant resources and increases productivity.

ERP enables an organization, especially a multi-business-unit enterprise, to efficiently track employees' time and performance and to communicate with them via a standardized method. Performance can be monitored across the entire organization using the same measurements and standards. The use of a single software platform and database also allows the ERP system to integrate financial, production, supply and customer order information. By having this information in one software system rather than scattered among many different systems that cannot communicate with one another, companies can keep track of materials, orders and financial status efficiently and coordinate manufacturing, inventory and shipping among many different locations and business units at the same time.

Today, small to medium size enterprises are frequently turning to the use of subscription-based ERP systems owned by a third party and provided over the Internet. These types of Internet services are termed **cloud computing** or **software-as-a-service (SaaS) models**. The e-Business Connection feature describes use of a cloud computing ERP system.

e-Business Connection	*Cloud Computing Takes On ERP*

The software-as-a-service (SaaS) model is well established in some enterprise software markets. Under the SaaS model, users pay a subscription, either monthly or yearly, to access applications hosted in the vendor's data center. Because users are accessing remote applications, this model is also referred to as "cloud computing."

All SaaS vendors concede that their ultimate success in the market depends on their ability to overcome some critical challenges, such as making it easier for their applications to integrate with all the applications companies currently rely to run their businesses; and delivering solutions that can be easily configured to support any company's unique business processes.

For California-based Orthera, a maker of custom orthotics and one of SaaS vendor Amitive's first customers, flexibility was just as important as avoiding the IT hassles that typically come with purchasing and installing a solution on the user company's premises.

Orthera custom configures its products for each customer, based on a scan of the customer's feet taken at Orthera's retail partner locations. Orthera is a recent start-up, and Thomas Pichler, CEO, says the SaaS model has made it easier for the company to land new customers. For instance, Pichler says, "We were closing a deal with a very large, warehouse-style retailer, and needed a Web-based solution to avoid having the retailer install and maintain the software at each individual store. Moreover, as a small company, we recognized the efficiency and cost savings of having an end-to-end solution that would span all business processes, including: order creation directly at retail locations; order validation at Orthera headquarters; creating manufacturing work orders; tracking orders through production; and managing shipments. We couldn't do all that with an on-premise solution."

Amar Singh, president and CEO of Amitive, says Amitive's solution is a highly configurable, SaaS-based application platform rather than a narrow SaaS application. While SaaS experts talk about "multi-tenant" architectures that allow the vendor to centrally store configurations unique to each user company while maintaining one single version of the software, Singh says Amitive's architecture takes this concept further. It does this, he says, by eschewing predefined data structures, instead using rules and workflow settings to adapt the software. Singh contends this allows Amitive's platform to be molded rapidly to many scenarios.

For Orthera, Amitive needed to support a unique business model: selling via retail locations where foot scans would be conducted and orders placed via Web kiosks, with manufacturing and fulfillment handled in a matter of days by Orthera and its partners. Pichler says Amitive's platform didn't force any changes on the envisioned business process. "Because this kind of business model was unheard of just a few years ago, taking any off-the-shelf software product with a pre-defined data structure meant that we would have compromised the very nature of how we run our business and what we promise the customer," says Pinchler. "Retrofitting an existing solution -if it could be done at all- would have resulted in not only higher cost to us, but more importantly, compromising the consumer experience."

Source: Michel, R. "Cloud Computing Moves Toward the Factory." *Manufacturing Business Technology,* V. 27, No. 5 (2009): 10. Used with permission.

Enterprise Resource Planning System Disadvantages

While the benefits of ERP systems can be impressive, ERP is not without shortcomings. For example, a substantial capital investment is needed to purchase and implement the system. Considerable time and money must be set aside to evaluate ERP software applications, to purchase the necessary hardware and software, and then to train employees to operate the new system. Total cost of ERP ownership includes hardware, software, professional services, training and other internal staff costs. ERP systems are very complex and have proven difficult to implement, particularly in large multi-business unit organizations.

However, the primary criticism of ERP is that the software is designed around a specific business model based on specific business processes. Although business processes are usually adopted based on best practices in the industry, the adopting firm must change its business model and associated processes to fit the built-in business model designed into the ERP system. Thus as mentioned earlier, the adopting firm must restructure its processes to be compatible with the new ERP system. This has resulted in a very unusual situation where a software system determines the business practices and processes a firm should implement, instead of designing the software to support existing business practices and processes.

Despite the widespread adoption of costly ERP systems by large firms since the Y2K scramble, many implementation challenges remain unsolved, and scores of ERP systems today are grossly underutilized.[7] Intricate business process reengineering challenges arise when business processes are adapted to the software. Consequently, firms struggle to justify their investment and find ways to better utilize their ERP systems. This raises the question of whether large firms can effectively manage their operations and supply chain activities without sophisticated information technology. The Global Perspective feature describes Kennametal's problems with their ERP system.

Enterprise Resource Planning Software Applications

ERP systems typically consist of many modules that are linked together to access and share a common database. Each module performs different functions within the organization and is designed so that it can be installed on its own or with a combination of

Global Perspective

ERP Problems at Kennametal

Kennametal, a global $2 billion maker of construction tools, has spent $10 million on ERP maintenance contracts during the past 13 years and not once could the company take advantage of upgrades, says CIO Steve Hanna. The company's implementation was too customized: the time and effort needed to tweak and test the upgrade outweighed any benefits. But Hanna kept trying. Late last year, he priced the cost of consultants to help with an ERP re-implementation and was shocked by estimates ranging from $15 million up to $54 million.

The major ERP suites are "old and not as flexible as some newer stuff, and they can't build flexibility in," Hanna says. "Modifying it takes our time and money and training." His ears practically steam from frustration. "You tell me: What am I missing here?"

Buying and installing ERP was never a cakewalk. In the 1990s, in courthouses across the country, lawyers told tales of intractable disputes between vendors and customers, of how ERP actually ruined some companies. No doubt ERP projects forced the CIOs of many others onto blood-pressure meds. But as the years rolled by, ERP vendors and CIOs worked out their problems and companies began to install these multimillion-dollar systems to make sense of their complicated operations. In doing so, they were able to run better and faster than the competition—at least until the competition caught up.

The fact that it can take an army of developers to build new features into ERP suites slows the vendors down. But it's also an obstacle for customers. The 6,446 customizations—Hanna counted them—that Kennametal made to its ERP software over the years prevented the company from taking advantage of new technology its vendor did build in. "We couldn't implement one single enhancement pack ever," he says. He declines to name the vendor.

So even if he could pay up to $54 million for integrators and consultants to help Kennametal move to the latest version of the ERP suite, he doesn't want to. Instead, he plans to turn Kennametal's old ERP management strategy on its head by putting in as vanilla a version of SAP as possible. He and CEO Carlos Cardoso are willing to change Kennametal's internal business processes to match the way SAP works, Hanna says, rather than the other way around.

Kennametal will also take on the implementation itself. He hired IBM to consult about requirements definitions and to identify business processes that must be revamped to conform to SAP's procedures. Meanwhile, Kennametal staff will do the legwork. The project is so important to Kennametal that it must succeed in order for the company's leaders, including Hanna and Cardoso, to achieve their performance goals for the year. "I'm going to make it work," says Hanna.

Source: Nash, K. "Reviving ERP: Enterprise Resource Planning has Become a Legacy System," *CIO* V. 23, No. 7 (2010): 1. Used with permission.

other modules. Most ERP software providers design their products to be compatible with their competitors' products, so that modules from different providers can be combined. Integration of customer relationship management, supplier relationship management and e-procurement modules into the ERP system is now becoming relatively commonplace. Although each ERP software provider configures its products differently from its competitors, some common modules of ERP systems are described here:

- *Accounting and finance*: This module assists an organization in maintaining financial control and accountability. It tracks accounting and financial information such as revenues, costs, assets, liabilities and other accounting and financial information of the company. It is also capable of generating routine and advanced accounting and financial reports, product costing, budgeting and analyses.

- *Customer relationship management*: This module provides the capability to manage customers. It enables collaboration between the organization and its customers by providing relevant, personalized, and up-to-date information. It also enables customers to track sales orders. The customer relationship management module allows the user to communicate effectively with existing customers and acquire new customers through sales automation and partner relationship management. Finally, it allows the firm to segment customers and track their purchase activities, and then design customized promotions appealing to each customer segment.

- *Human resource management*: It helps an organization plan, develop, manage and control its human resources. It allows the firm to deploy the right people to support its overall strategic goals and to plan the optimal workforce levels based on production levels.

- *Manufacturing*: It schedules materials and tracks production, capacity and the flow of goods through the manufacturing process. It may even include the capability for quality planning, inspection and certifications.

- *Supplier relationship management*: This module allows the firm to manage its suppliers. It automates processes and enables the firm to more effectively collaborate with all its suppliers corporate-wide. It also monitors supplier performance and tracks deliveries of goods purchased. It enables the user to effectively manage business processes through real-time collaboration during design, production and distribution planning with suppliers.

- *Supply chain management*: This module handles the planning, execution and control of activities involved in a supply chain. It assists the firm in strengthening its supply chain networks to improve delivery performance. It may also cover various logistics functions, including transportation, warehousing and inventory management. The supply chain management module creates value by allowing the user to optimize its internal and external supply chains.

ERP systems have continued to evolve in the twenty-first century. One of the latest developments is the integration of e-business capabilities to use the Internet to conduct business transactions, such as sales, purchasing, inventory management and customer service. Customers and suppliers are demanding access to certain information, such as order status, inventory levels and invoice reconciliation through the ERP system. As information technology continues to become more sophisticated, ERP software providers continue to add new functions and capabilities to their systems.

Enterprise Resource Planning Software Providers

There are hundreds of ERP software providers, each targeting a specific market segment and industry type. Thus, choosing an appropriate ERP software package can be very challenging. SAP, Oracle, PeopleSoft, JD Edwards and Baan have been among the most popular ERP providers. However, there was a series of mergers and acquisitions in the maturing ERP industry in early 2000s. In 2003, JD Edwards was acquired by PeopleSoft, which was subsequently purchased by the database giant Oracle in 2005. Baan was sold to Invensys in 2000, but was later acquired by SSA Global Technologies in 2003. In 2006, Infor Global Solutions bought SSA Global Technologies. While Microsoft Corporation is the world's largest software company, SAP is the largest ERP provider, followed by Oracle in terms of market share.

While Oracle has focused on aggressively acquiring other ERP vendors to broaden its product line, the German-based SAP has adopted an internal software development strategy to expand the functionality of its products. Microsoft has also gained a foothold in the ERP market with its purchase of Great Plains in 2001 and Navision in 2002. In addition to the mainstream ERP software systems, there are also many specialized companies in the business of producing add-on software to provide specific functions or interact with preexisting legacy systems.

SUMMARY

While both manufacturing and service organizations rely on effective production and capacity planning to balance demand and capacity, manufacturers have the added advantage of being able to build up inventory as stored capacity. Service firms are unable to inventory their services, so they rely upon backlogs or reservations, cross-training or queues to match supply with demand. However, excess capacity results in underutilized equipment and workforce and eventually leads to unnecessary cost, adversely impacting all firms along the supply chain.

This chapter covers materials planning, capacity planning and enterprise resource planning, which are all widely used for balancing demand with supply. An example was used to demonstrate how the aggregate production plan, master production schedule, material requirements plan and distribution requirements plan are related to each other. This chapter also briefly discusses how the various materials plans are related to the capacity plans. A central piece of the materials plan is the material requirements plan, which takes information from the master production schedule, the bill of materials and inventory status to compute planned order releases. For items that are produced in-house, planned order releases are released to the shop floor to trigger production. For purchased items, planned order releases are released to suppliers.

Finally, this chapter discusses the enterprise resource planning system, including its relationships with the traditional MRP and MRP-II systems, its advantages and disadvantages, implementation issues, ERP modules and major ERP software providers. The goal of ERP development was to build a single software application that runs off a common shared database to serve the needs of an entire organization, regardless of its units' geographical locations and the currency used. Despite its complexity and considerable costs, ERP provides a way to integrate different business functions of different businesses, on different continents. The integrated approach can have a tremendous payback if companies select the right applications and implement the software correctly. Unfortunately, many companies that have installed these systems have failed to realize all of the benefits expected.

Implementing ERP should be viewed as a long-term, ongoing project. No matter what resources a firm has initially committed to replacing legacy systems, selecting and implementing ERP applications and training users, ERP requires ongoing management commitment and resources. As needs and technologies change and new applications are designed, new functionality and business processes will need to be continuously revisited and improved.

KEY TERMS

aggregate production plan (APP), 167

available-to-promise (ATP) quantity, 175

best-of-breed solution, 193

bill of materials (BOM), 178

bullwhip effect, 166

capacity, 186

capacity requirements planning (CRP), 186

chase production strategy, 169

closed-loop MRP, 181

cloud computing, 197

dependent demand, 179

distribution requirements planning (DRP), 187

electronic data interchange (EDI), 185

enterprise resource planning (ERP), 167

implosion, 188

indented bill of materials, 179

independent demand, 179

intermediate or medium-range planning horizon, 167

lag capacity strategy, 187

lead capacity strategy, 187

legacy MRP system, 189

level production strategy, 171

long-range, 167

make-to-order manufacturing firms, 171

DISCUSSION QUESTIONS

1. Why is it important to balance production capacity with market demand?

2. Describe long-range, medium-range and short-range planning in the context of materials plan and capacity plan. How are they related?

3. Describe aggregate production planning, master production planning, material requirements planning and distribution requirements planning. How are these plans related?

4. Describe how MRP evolved into closed-loop MRP, MRP-II and eventually into ERP.

5. Compare and contrast chase versus level production strategies. Which is more appropriate for an industry where highly skilled laborers are needed? Why?

6. Is a level production strategy suitable for a pure service industry, such as professional accounting and tax services or law firms? Can these firms inventory their outputs?

7. What is the purpose of low-level coding?

8. What is the purpose of available-to-promise quantity, and how is it different from on-hand inventory?

9. What is system nervousness? Discuss how it can be minimized or avoided.

10. What are the crucial inputs for material requirements planning?

11. What is a BOM, and how is it different from the super BOM?

12. Are manufacturing or purchasing lead times considered in the MPS and the MRP?

13. What is the difference between scheduled receipts and planned order releases?

14. What is the difference between an MRP explosion and a DRP implosion?

15. Briefly describe resource requirements planning, rough-cut capacity planning and capacity requirements planning. How are these plans related?

16. How are the various capacity plans (ERP, RCCP, CRP) related to the material plans (APP, MPS, MRP)?

17. Why are production planning and capacity planning important to SCM?

18. Why have so many firms rushed to implement ERP systems over the past ten years?

19. Describe the limitations of a legacy MRP system.

20. Why is it important to learn the fundamentals of the traditional MRP system, even if it is considered an outdated, legacy system?

21. What are the advantages of an ERP system over the legacy MRP system?

22. Explain best-of-breed and single integrator ERP implementations. What are the advantages and disadvantages of the best-of-breed implementation?

23. Explain why many ERP implementations have failed to yield the expected benefits over the last ten years.

INTERNET QUESTIONS

1. Visit the websites of SAP, Oracle and Microsoft, and use the information to write a brief report of each company and its ERP software. Do their products offer the same configuration or functionality?

2. Use the Internet to search for relevant information to prepare a brief report on how SAP and Oracle expanded their product lines. Which of the two firms is known for its aggressive strategy of acquiring smaller best-of-breed providers?

3. Use the Internet to search for information to write a report on whether the trend is toward single integrator or best-of-breed ERP implementation.

4. Use resources available on the Internet to prepare a report on the current and projected ERP market total revenue and the rate of growth over the next five years.

5. Use resources available on the Internet to prepare a story about a firm that has successfully implemented an ERP system.

6. Use resources available on the Internet to prepare a report that describes a failed ERP implementation. What can be learned from this company?

7. Explore the websites of SAP and Oracle, and use the information to write a report to discuss their (a) supply chain management, (b) supplier relationship management, and (c) customer relationship management software applications.

8. Use resources on the Internet to write a report describing Microsoft's strategy and competitive position in the ERP market.

9. Use resources on the Internet to write a report on the current stage of ERP implementation in the U.S., Europe and China.

SPREADSHEET PROBLEMS

1. Given the following production plan, use a (a) chase production strategy and (b) level production strategy to compute the monthly production, ending inventory/(backlog) and workforce levels. A worker is capable of producing 100 units per month. Assume the beginning inventory as of January is zero, and the firm desires to have zero inventory at the end of June.

MONTH	JAN	FEB	MAR	APR	MAY	JUN
Demand	2000	3000	5000	6000	6000	2000
Production						
Ending Inventory						
Workforce						

2. Given the following production plan, use a (a) chase production strategy and (b) level production strategy to compute the monthly production, ending inventory/(backlog) and workforce levels. A worker can produce 50 units per month. Assume that the beginning inventory in January is 500 units, and the firm desires to have 200 of inventory at the end of June.

MONTH	JAN	FEB	MAR	APR	MAY	JUN
Demand	2000	3000	5000	6000	6000	2000
Production						
Ending Inventory						
Workforce						

3. Given the following production schedule, compute the available-to-promise quantities.

WEEK		1	2	3	4	5	6	7	8
Model A									
MPS	BI = 60	20	30	20	20	20	50	0	20
Committed Customer Orders		50	10	30	10	20	20	10	0
ATP:D									

4. Given the following production schedule, compute the available-to-promise quantities.

WEEK		1	2	3	4	5	6	7	8
Model B									
MPS	BI = 20	20	0	20	20	0	20	20	20
Committed Customer Orders		10	10	10	10	10	0	0	10
ATP:D									

5. The bills of materials for two finished products (D and E), inventory status, and other relevant information are given below. Compute the planned order releases and projected on-hand balances for parts D, E and F.

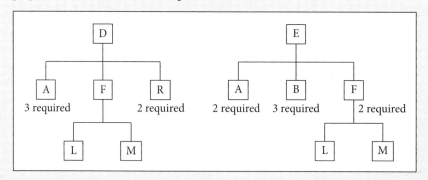

PART D		1	2	3	4	5	6
Gross Requirements		7	11	9	5	8	6
Scheduled Receipts							
Projected On-hand Inventory	10						
Planned Order Releases							

Q = 30; LT = 1; SS = 0

PART E		1	2	3	4	5	6
Gross Requirements		10	12	15	11	6	8
Scheduled Receipts			11				
Projected On-hand Inventory	15						
Planned Order Releases							

Q = LFL; LT = 2; SS = 3

PART F		1	2	3	4	5	6
Gross Requirements							
Scheduled Receipts		60					
Projected On-hand Inventory	20						
Planned Order Releases							

Q = 60; LT = 1; SS = 0

6. The bill of materials for a finished product E, inventory status and other relevant information are given below. Compute the planned order releases and projected on-hand balances for parts E, F and M.

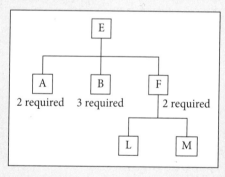

PART E		1	2	3	4	5	6
Gross Requirements		20	0	0	20	0	40
Scheduled Receipts							
Projected On-hand Inventory	20						
Planned Order Releases							

Q = 50; LT = 2; SS = 0

PART F		1	2	3	4	5	6
Gross Requirements							
Scheduled Receipts				50			
Projected On-hand Inventory	120						
Planned Order Releases							

Q = 50; LT = 2; SS = 20

PART M		1	2	3	4	5	6
Gross Requirements							
Scheduled Receipts		60					
Projected On-hand Inventory	10						
Planned Order Releases							

Q = 60; LT = 1; SS = 30

7. Crop-Quick Inc. replenishes its three distribution centers in Boston, Denver and Houston from its Las Vegas central supply warehouse. The distribution schedule for one of its products for the next six weeks is shown below. Use proper distribution requirements planning logic to complete the replenishment schedules of the three distribution centers and the central supply warehouse.

BOSTON DISTRIBUTION CENTER		1	2	3	4	5	6
Gross Requirements		0	20	0	55	0	0
Scheduled Receipts							
Projected On-hand Inventory	10						
Planned Order Releases							

Q = 30; LT = 1; SS = 5

DENVER DISTRIBUTION CENTER		1	2	3	4	5	6
Gross Requirements		0	20	10	0	0	20
Scheduled Receipts			11				
Projected On-hand Inventory	15						
Planned Order Releases							

Q = LFL; LT = 2; SS = 2

HOUSTON DISTRIBUTION CENTER		1	2	3	4	5	6
Gross Requirements		50	0	0	45	0	0
Scheduled Receipts							
Projected On-hand Inventory	20						
Planned Order Releases							

Q = 60; LT = 1; SS = 0

LAS VEGAS CENTRAL WAREHOUSE		1	2	3	4	5	6
Gross Requirements							
Scheduled Receipts							
Projected On-hand Inventory	50						
Planned Order Releases							

Q = 20; LT = 1; SS = 0

Chapter 7

INVENTORY MANAGEMENT

The most expensive, sophisticated software package will not automatically result in an optimal level of inventory for an electrical wholesaler. 'Optimal' means a high level of customer service and inventory turns, but with low inventory investment. To achieve and maintain an optimal level, employees educated in the principles of effective inventory management must understand how to set certain parameters; then set them and keep them set right.[1]

Learning Objectives

After completing this chapter, you should be able to

- Distinguish dependent from independent demand inventories.
- Describe the four basic types of inventories and their functions.
- Understand the costs of inventory and inventory turnovers.
- Understand ABC classification, ABC inventory matrix and cycle counting.
- Know RFID and how it can be used in inventory management.
- Understand the EOQ model and its underlying assumptions.
- Understand the Quantity Discount and the EMQ Models and their relationships with the basic EOQ model.
- Understand and be able to distinguish among the various statistical ROP models.
- Understand the continuous review and periodic review systems.

Chapter Outline

Supply Chain Management in Action	*Bobcat's Five Steps to Improved Inventory Management*

Most companies are trying to minimize their raw material inventories in an effort to reduce costs and improve cash flow. But at the same time, they need to balance their ability to respond to customer trends, so there is a need to have the right inventory on hand at the right time. One company that has achieved impressive results in this area is Bobcat North America. The company designs, manufactures and distributes compact equipment, including skid loaders, mini-excavators and utility vehicles. Bobcat utilizes a number of strategies to ensure it has just the right amount of inventory on-hand.

Product customization. "We want to be flexible and agile, so that we don't have a lot of excess inventory sitting around," says Jim Adkins, vice president of sourcing and supply chain. Bobcat doesn't offer a standard machine but focuses on customizing products. The company will build a standard machine up to a certain point, and then customize it on the last 30 or 40 feet of the production line.

Inventory management automation. Bobcat allows its Oracle ERP system to run automatically. Until a few years ago, everything was being run manually on a legacy MRP system. Now, the company uses the tools available on Oracle to allow things to run on a more automated basis. Also, the company uses lead time, sales and other pertinent information to set appropriate inventory levels for each part. Bobcat also uses vendor managed inventory.

Kitting. Kitting is a process in which related parts are grouped and supplied together as one unit. In the past, Bobcat had a "supermarket" approach to parts. Under this approach, parts were available as needed on the factory floor. But more recently Bobcat began to adopt kitting and pull all of the parts back into a parts control area. This provides visual lines of sight on all of the parts. Bobcat has also replaced cycle-counting with spot-checking.

Review global sourcing. Bobcat revised its global supply strategy and used cost-benefit analysis to evaluate the trade-off between its freight and custom costs. The company must achieve at least a twenty to thirty percent cost savings before it will consider global sourcing. The total delivery lead time, shipping accuracy and the risks associated with global sourcing are important criteria in outsourcing.

Supply chain communication. Last but not least, Bobcat has increased its emphasis on communication, not just between internal departments, but throughout its entire supply chain.

As a result of its multi-strategy approach, Bobcat was able to reduce its inventory from roughly $100 million to $20 million without running out of parts.

Source: Atkinson, W., March 2010, "Bobcat's five steps to improved inventory management," *Purchasing* 139(3), March 2010: 10–11. Used with permission.

Introduction

Inventory can be one of the most expensive assets of an organization. It may account for more than ten percent of total revenue or total assets for some organizations. Although companies in the manufacturing sector usually carry more inventory than service firms, effective inventory management is nonetheless important to both manufacturers and service organizations. Table 7.1 shows the amount of inventory, and the ratio of inventory to total revenue and total assets, of a few large globally recognized manufacturing and service firms. While the inventory to total assets ratio for service organizations such as casino hotels (such as the first two companies shown in Table 7.1) is relatively low compared to most manufacturers, inventory management for service firms poses a different challenge. Casino hotels for example carry a wide range of perishable food items to stock the diverse restaurants operating within their properties. Managing perishable inventory presents a unique challenge to operations managers.

Inventory management policy affects how efficiently a firm deploys its assets in producing goods and services. Developing effective inventory control systems to reduce waste and stockouts in manufacturing or service organizations is a complex problem. The right amount of inventory supports manufacturing, logistics and other functions, but excessive inventory is a sign of poor inventory management that creates unnecessary waste of scarce resources. In addition, excessive inventory adversely affects financial performance. The need for better inventory management systems continues to challenge operations managers.

This chapter first explains the difference between dependent demand and independent demand items. Then it focuses on the independent demand items to describe the basic concepts and tools of inventory management, including the ABC inventory control system, inventory costs and radio frequency identification. The chapter also discusses the three fundamental deterministic inventory models and the two major types of stochastic inventory models.

Table 7.1	Inventory Investment Compared to Total Revenue and Total Assets					
COMPANY	FINANCIAL YEAR END	TOTAL REVENUE ($)	TOTAL ASSETS ($)	YEAR END INVENTORY ($)	INVENTORY/ TOTAL REVENUE (%)	INVENTORY/ TOTAL ASSETS (%)
Las Vegas Sands Corp.	Dec 31, 09	4,563	20,572	27	0.59	0.13
MGM Mirage	Dec 31, 09	5,979	22,518	102	1.71	0.45
Microsoft Corp.	Jun 30, 09	58,437	77,888	717	1.23	0.92
Ford Motor Co.	Dec 31, 09	111,308	194,850	5,450	4.90	2.80
Toyota Motor Corp.	Mar 31, 09	208,995	295,857	14,857	7.11	5.02
Honda Motor Co.	Mar 31, 09	103,116	121,735	12,813	12.43	10.53
Wal-Mart Stores, Inc.	Jan 31, 10	408,214	170,706	33,160	8.12	19.43
Target Corp.	Feb 3, 09	65,357	44,533	7,179	10.98	16.12
Pfizer, Inc.	Dec 31, 09	50,009	212,949	12,403	24.80	5.82
Intel Corp.	Dec 26, 09	35,127	53,095	2,935	8.36	5.53
Advanced Micro Devices, Inc.	Dec 26, 09	5,403	9,078	567	10.49	6.25

Note: All numbers in millions, except ratios
Source: Annual Reports on Form 10-K

Dependent Demand and Independent Demand

Inventory management models are generally separated by the nature and types of the inventory being considered and can be classified as *dependent demand* and *independent demand models*.

Dependent demand is the internal demand for parts based on the demand of the final product in which the parts are used. Subassemblies, components and raw materials are examples of dependent demand items. Dependent demand may have a pattern of abrupt and dramatic changes because of its dependency on the demand of the final product, particularly if the final product is produced in large lot sizes. Dependent demand can be calculated once the demand of the final product is known. Hence, material requirements planning (MRP) software is often used to compute exact material requirements.

The dependent demand inventory system was discussed in Chapter 6. For example, the ATV Corporation's master production schedule discussed in Table 6.4 in Chapter 6 shows that 120 all-terrain vehicles will be produced in January. The firm thus knows that 120 handlebars and 480 wheel rims will be needed. The demand for handlebars, wheel rims and other dependent demand items can be calculated based on the bill of materials and the demand of the final product as stated on the master production schedule.

Independent demand is the demand for a firm's end products and has a demand pattern affected by trends, seasonal patterns and general market conditions. For example, the demand for an all-terrain vehicle is independent demand. Batteries, headlights, seals and gaskets originally used in assembling the all-terrain vehicles are dependent demands; however, the replacement batteries, headlights, seals and gaskets sold as *service parts* to the repair shops or end users are independent demand items. Similarly, the original battery used in assembling your new car is a dependent demand item for the automobile manufacturer, but the new battery that you bought to replace the original battery is an independent demand item. Independent demand items cannot be derived using the material requirements planning logic from the demand for other items and, thus, must be forecasted based on market conditions.

Concepts and Tools of Inventory Management

Savvy operations managers are concerned with controlling inventories not only within their organizations, but also throughout their entire supply chains. An effective independent demand inventory system ensures smooth operations and allows manufacturing firms to store up production capacity in the form of work-in-process and finished goods inventories. While some service firms are unable to inventory their output, such organizations may rely on appointment backlogs, labor scheduling and cross-training to balance supply and demand.

All manufacturing and service organizations are concerned with effective inventory planning and control. Inventory requires capital investment, handling and storage space, and it is also subject to deterioration and shrinkage. Although a firm's operating costs and financial performance can be improved by reducing inventory, the risk of stockouts can be devastating to customer service. Therefore, companies must strike a delicate balance between inventory investment and customer service. This section discusses some important concepts and tools of inventory management. Vendor-managed inventory and co-managed inventory, discussed in Chapter 4, will not be explored here.

The Functions and Basic Types of Inventory

Inventory includes all the materials and goods that are purchased, partially completed materials and component parts and the finished goods produced. The primary functions of inventory are to *buffer* uncertainty in the marketplace and to *decouple*, or break the dependencies between stages in the supply chain. For example, an appropriate amount of inventory, known as *safety stock* or *buffer stock*, can be used to cushion uncertainties due to fluctuation in supply, demand and/or delivery lead time. Similarly, the right amount of inventory enables a work center to operate without interruption when other work centers in the same production process are off-line for maintenance or repair. Keeping the correct amount of inventory at each work center also allows a faster work center to operate smoothly when it is constrained by slower upstream work centers.

In this increasingly global environment, it is not unusual that organizations use the concept of *geographical specialization* to manufacture their products in the developing countries. In this scenario, the developing countries specialize in cheap labor and abundant raw materials, whereas the manufacturing firms provide the technology and capital to produce the goods. The ability to geographically separate the consumption of the finished goods from production is a key function of inventory. For manufacturers, inventory also acts as *stored capacity*. For instance, snowmobile manufacturers can build up inventory by producing snowmobiles year-round in anticipation of peak demand during the busy winter season.

There are four broad categories of inventories: raw materials; work-in-process; finished goods; and maintenance, repair and operating (MRO) supplies.

- *Raw materials* are unprocessed purchased inputs or materials for manufacturing the finished goods. Raw materials become part of finished goods after the manufacturing process is completed. There are many reasons for keeping raw material inventories, including volume purchases to create transportation economies or take advantage of quantity discounts; stockpiling in anticipation of future price increases or to avoid a potential short supply; or keeping safety stock to guard against supplier delivery or quality problems.

- *Work-in-process* (WIP) describes materials that are partially processed but not yet ready for sales. One reason to keep WIP inventories is to decouple processing stages or to break the dependencies between work centers.

- *Finished goods* are completed products ready for shipment. Finished goods inventories are often kept to buffer against unexpected demand changes and in anticipation of production process downtime; to ensure production economies when the setup cost is very high; or to stabilize production rates, especially for seasonal products.

- *Maintenance, repair and operating* (MRO) supplies are materials and supplies used when producing the products but are not parts of the products. Solvents, cutting tools and lubricants for machines are examples of MRO supplies. The two main reasons for storing MRO supplies are to gain purchase economies and to avoid material shortages that may shut down production.

Inventory Costs

The bottom line of effective inventory management is to control inventory costs and minimize stockouts. Inventory costs can be categorized in many ways: as direct and indirect costs; fixed and variable costs; and order (or setup) and holding (or carrying) costs.

Direct costs are those that are directly traceable to the unit produced, such as the amount of materials and labor used to produce a unit of the finished good. **Indirect costs** are those that cannot be traced directly to the unit produced and they are synonymous with manufacturing overhead. Maintenance, repair and operating supplies; heating; lighting; buildings; equipment; and plant security are examples of indirect costs. **Fixed costs** are independent of the output quantity, but **variable costs** change as a function of the output level. Buildings, equipment, plant security, heating and lighting are examples of fixed costs, whereas direct materials and labor costs are variable costs. A key focus of inventory management is to control variable costs since fixed costs are generally considered *sunk costs*. Sunk costs are costs that have already been incurred and cannot be recovered or reversed.

Order costs are the direct variable costs associated with placing an order with the supplier, whereas **holding** or **carrying costs** are the costs incurred for holding inventory in storage. Order costs include managerial and clerical costs for preparing the purchase, as well as other incidental expenses that can be traced directly to the purchase. Examples of holding costs include handling charges, warehousing expenses, insurance, pilferage, shrinkage, taxes and the cost of capital. In a manufacturing context, **setup costs** are used in place of order costs to describe the costs associated with setting up machines and equipment to produce a batch of product. However, in inventory management discussions, *order costs* and *setup costs* are often used interchangeably.

Inventory Investment

Inventory serves many important functions for manufacturing and service firms; however, excessive inventory is detrimental to a firm's financial health and competitive edge. Whether inventory is an asset that contributes to organizational objectives or a liability depends on its management. The chapter opening Supply Chain Management in Action feature for example, describes Bobcat North America's inventory management strategies to ensure that it has just the right amount of inventory on-hand.

Inventory is expensive and it ties up a firm's working capital. Moreover, inventory requires storage space and incurs other carrying costs. Some products such as perishable food items and hazardous materials require special handling and storage that add to the cost of holding inventory. Inventory can also deteriorate quickly while it is in storage. In addition, inventory can become obsolete very quickly as new materials and technologies are introduced. Most importantly, large piles of inventory delay a firm's ability to respond swiftly to production problems and changes in technologies and market conditions.

Inventory investment can be measured in various ways. The typical annual physical stock counts to determine the total dollars invested in inventory provides an absolute measure of inventory investment. The inventory value is then reported in a firm's balance sheet. This value can be used to compare to the budget and past inventory investment. However, the absolute dollars invested in inventory does not provide sufficient evidence about whether the company is using its inventory wisely. A widely used measure to determine how efficiently a firm is using its inventory to generate revenue is the **inventory turnover ratio** or **inventory turnovers**. This ratio shows how many times a company turns over its inventory in an accounting period. Faster turnovers are generally viewed as a positive trend because it indicates the company is able to generate more revenue per dollar in inventory investment. Moreover, faster turnovers allow the company to increase cash flow and reduce warehousing and carrying costs. Conversely, a low inventory turnover may point to overstocking or deficiencies in the product line or marketing effort.

The formula for the inventory turnover ratio can be stated as:

$$\text{Inventory turnover ratio} = \frac{\text{Cost of Revenue}}{\text{Average Inventory}}.$$

Inventory turnover ratio can be computed for any accounting period—monthly, quarterly or annually. Cost of revenue is also the cost of goods sold, which is readily available from a firm's income statement. Average inventory is the mean of the beginning and ending inventory. However, a firm's inventory may fluctuate widely in a financial year; thus, the average of the beginning and ending inventory may be a poor indicator of the firm's average inventory for the year. In this case, the average of the twelve monthly ending inventories can be used as the average inventory when computing the annual inventory turnover ratio. Table 7.2 shows the annual inventory turnovers for the organizations in Table 7.1. Since the average of the monthly inventories was not available in the *annual reports*, the financial year-end closing inventory was used to compute the ratio. In 2009, Las Vegas Sands Corp. (LVS) for example, turned over its inventory a staggering 107 times. However, the nature of LVS's business suggests that a major portion of its revenue came from hotel room and gaming sales, but the inventory may consist of mostly goods for the restaurants. Therefore, the revenue generated by hotel room and gaming sales could be excluded from the calculation of the ratio.

The ABC Inventory Control System

A common problem with many inventory management systems is the challenge to maintain accurate inventory records. Many organizations use **cycle counting** to reconcile discrepancies between their physical inventory and inventory record on a monthly or quarterly basis. Cycle counting, or physically counting inventory on a periodic basis, also helps to identify obsolete stocks and inventory problems so that remedial action can be taken in a reasonable amount of time. However, cycle counting can be costly and time-consuming and can disrupt operations.

The **ABC inventory control system** is a useful technique for determining which inventories should be counted more frequently and managed more closely and which others should not. ABC analysis is often combined with the **80/20 rule** or **Pareto analysis**. The 80/20 rule suggests that 80 percent of the objective can be achieved by doing 20 percent of the tasks, but the remaining 20 percent of the objective will take up 80 percent of the tasks. The Pareto analysis recommends that tasks falling into the first category be assigned the highest priority and managed closely.

The ABC inventory control system prioritizes inventory items into Groups A, B and C. However, it is not uncommon that some firms choose to use more than three categories. The *A items* are given the highest priority, while *C items* have the lowest priority and are typically the most numerous (the *B items* fall somewhere in between). Greater attention, safety stocks and resources are devoted to the high-priority or *A items*. The priority is most often determined by annual dollar usage. However, priority may also be determined by product shelf life, sales volume, whether the materials are critical components, or other criteria.

When prioritizing inventories by annual dollar usage, the ABC system suggests that approximately 20 percent of the items make up about 80 percent of the total annual dollar usage, and these items are classified as the *A items*. The *B items* make up roughly 40 percent of the items and account for about 15 percent of the total annual dollar usage, while the *C items* are the remaining 40 percent of the items, making up about 5 percent

Table 7.2	Inventory Turnover Ratios				
COMPANY	FINANCIAL YEAR END	TOTAL REVENUE ($)	COST OF REVENUE ($)	YEAR END INVENTORY ($)	INVENTORY TURNOVER RATIO
Las Vegas Sands Corp.	Dec 31, 09	4,563	2,907	27	107.67
MGM Mirage	Dec 31, 09	5,979	3,539	102	34.70
Microsoft Corp.	Jun 30, 10	62,484	12,395	740	16.75
Ford Motor Co.	Dec 31, 09	118,308	100,016	5,450	18.35
Toyota Motor Corp.	Mar 31, 10	202,814	178,551	15,220	11.73
Honda Motor Co.	Mar 31, 10	91,815	68,651	10,010	6.86
Wal-Mart Stores, Inc.	Jan 31, 10	408,214	304,657	33,160	9.19
Target Corp.	Jan 30, 10	65,357	45,583	7,180	6.14
Pfizer, Inc.	Dec 31, 09	50,009	8,888	12,403	0.72
Intel Corp.	Dec 26, 09	35,127	15,566	2,935	5.30
Advanced Micro Devices, Inc.	Dec 26, 09	5,403	3,131	567	5.52

Note: All numbers in millions, except ratios.

Source: publicly available annual report information

of the total annual dollar usage of inventory. A summary of the classification is provided in Table 7.3. Since the *A items* are the highest annual dollar usage items, they should be monitored more frequently and may have higher safety stock levels to guard against stockouts, particularly if these items are used in products sold to supply chain trading partners. The *C items* would then be counted less frequently, and stockouts may be allowed to save inventory space and carrying costs.

ABC inventory classification can be done monthly, quarterly, annually or any fixed period. For the fast-moving consumer market, an *A item* may become a *C item* within months or even weeks. Thus, ABC inventory classification based on annual dollar usage would not be very useful to management. An illustration of an ABC inventory classification using annual dollar usage is shown in Example 7.1.

The ABC Inventory Matrix

The ABC Inventory analysis can be expanded to assist in identifying obsolete stocks and to analyze whether a company is stocking the correct inventory by comparing two ABC analyses. First, an ABC analysis is completed based on annual inventory dollar usage (as shown in Example 7.1) to classify inventories into A, B and C groups. Next, a second ABC analysis is performed based on current or on-hand inventory dollar value (as shown in Example 7.2) to classify inventories again into A, B and C groups. Finally, the two ABC analyses are combined to form an **ABC inventory matrix** as shown in Figure 7.1. The *A items* based on current inventory value should match the *A items* based on annual inventory dollar usage, falling within the unshaded diagonal region of the figure. Similarly, the B and C items should match when comparing the two ABC analyses. Otherwise, the company is stocking the wrong items. The ABC inventory matrix also suggests that some overlaps are expected between two

Table 7.3	ABC Inventory Classification	
CLASSIFICATIONS	PERCENT OF TOTAL ANNUAL DOLLAR USAGE	PERCENT OF TOTAL INVENTORY ITEMS
A Items	80	20
B Items	15	40
C Items	5	40

Example 7.1   ABC Inventory Classification Based on Annual Dollar Usage

Note that in this example, the *A items* only account for about 67 percent of the total annual dollar volume, while the *B items* account for about 28 percent. This illustrates that judgment must also be applied when using the ABC classification method, and the 80/20 rule should only be used as a general guideline.

INVENTORY ITEM NUMBER	ITEM COST ($)	ANNUAL USAGE (UNITS)	ANNUAL USAGE ($)	PERCENT OF TOTAL ANNUAL DOLLAR USAGE	CLASSIFICATION BY ANNUAL DOLLAR USAGE
A246	1.00	22,000	22,000	35.2	A
N376	0.50	40,000	20,000	32.0	A
C024	4.25	1,468	6,239	10.0	B
R221	12.00	410	4,920	7.8	B
P112	2.25	1,600	3,600	5.8	B
R116	0.12	25,000	3,000	4.8	B
T049	8.50	124	1,054	1.7	C
B615	0.25	3,500	875	1.4	C
L227	1.25	440	550	0.9	C
T519	26.00	10	260	0.4	C
Total Annual Dollar Usage:			$62,498	100%	

Example 7.2   ABC Inventory Classification Based on Current Inventory Value

INVENTORY ITEM NUMBER	ITEM COST ($)	CURRENT INVENTORY (UNITS)	CURRENT INVENTORY VALUE ($)	% OF TOTAL INVENTORY VALUE ($)	CLASSIFICATION BY TOTAL INVENTORY VALUE	ANNUAL DOLLAR USAGE
T519	26.00	300	7,800	40.5	A	C
A246	1.00	5,600	5,600	29.1	A	A
L227	1.25	1,200	1,500	7.8	B	C
C024	4.25	348	1,479	7.7	B	B
R221	12.00	80	960	5.0	B	B
P112	2.25	352	792	4.1	B	B
T049	8.50	50	425	2.2	C	C
N376	0.50	800	400	2.1	C	A
R116	0.12	2,100	252	1.3	C	B
B615	0.25	120	30	0.2	C	C
Total Physical Inventory (dollars):			$19,238	100%		

borderline classifications (as indicated by the wide diagonal region). For instance, some marginal *B items* based on annual inventory dollar usage might appear as *C items* based on the current inventory value classification and vice versa.

Referring to Figure 7.1, plots in the upper-left shaded triangle of the ABC inventory matrix indicate that some *A items* based on annual inventory dollar usage are showing up as *B* or *C items* based on the current inventory value classification and that some *B items* have similarly been classified as *C items*. This suggests that the company has current inventories for its *A* and *B items* that are too low, and is risking stockouts of their higher dollar usage items. Conversely, plots in the lower-right shaded triangle show that some *C items* based on annual inventory dollar usage are showing up as *A* and *B items* based on current inventory value, and some *B items* are similarly showing up as *A items*; thus indicating that the company has current inventories for its *B* and *C items* that are too high, and is incurring excess inventory carrying costs. This may also point to the presence of excessive *obsolete stock* if the inventory turnover ratios are very low. Obsolete stocks should be disposed of so that valuable inventory investment and warehouse space can be used for productive inventory. When used in conjunction with inventory turnovers, the ABC inventory matrix is a powerful tool for managing inventory investment. Example 7.2 shows the classifications based on current inventory value for the same ten items shown in Example 7.1, and it also shows the annual dollar usage classifications.

The two ABC analyses from Examples 7.1 and 7.2 are combined and plotted on the ABC inventory matrix shown in Figure 7.2. Each inventory item is plotted on the matrix using the "percent of total current inventory" on the horizontal axis and the "percent of total annual dollar usage" on the vertical axis. For instance, the coordinate of the item "T519" would be (40.5, 0.4). The vertical axis ranges from 0.4 percent to 35.2 percent, and the horizontal axis ranges from 0.2 percent to 40.5 percent, thus "T519" falls on

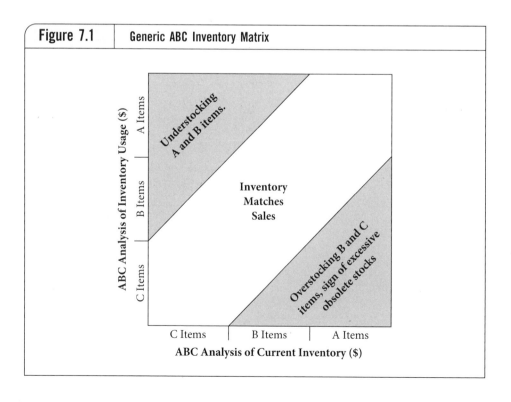

| **Figure 7.1** | **Generic ABC Inventory Matrix** |

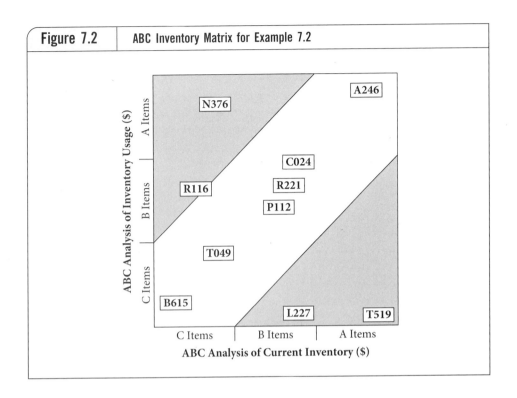

Figure 7.2 | **ABC Inventory Matrix for Example 7.2**

the extreme lower-right corner of the matrix. The plots in Figure 7.2 show that six of the inventory items fell along the diagonal, suggesting the appropriate stocking levels. The company has probably overstocked items "T519" and "L227" and understocked "N376" and possibly "R116". It is important however, that the inventory turnover ratios for each item be used in conjunction with the ABC inventory matrix to get a sense of how fast or slow inventories are turning over.

Radio Frequency Identification

The barcode has been used to identify the manufacturer and content of a carton for decades. However, it cannot store enough information to differentiate goods at the item level. Direct line of sight is required to read a barcode, and the information stored on it is static and not updatable. **Radio frequency identification (RFID)** has been used as an eventual successor to the barcode for tracking an individual unit of goods. RFID does not require direct line of sight to read a tag, and information on the tag is updatable. RFID technology is also used in libraries, passport identification, animal tracking, medical discipline, toll payments and in many other fields. The e-Business Connection feature provides an overview of the challenge and status of current RFID implementation in North America, Europe and China.

There are two major RFID standards: the **electronic product code (EPC)** standard managed by the EPCglobal, Inc.,[2] a subsidiary of GS1 that created the UPC barcode; and the 18000 standard of the International Standards Organization (ISO). Wal-Mart Stores, Inc. and the Department of Defense are the two largest adopters of RFID. By 2005, both organizations had issued mandates for their top suppliers to use RFID technology to identify their products.[3] Wal-Mart Stores adopted the EPC standard, whereas the Department of Defense chose the EPC standard for general purpose applications and

e-Business Connection

Status Report and Challenges of Current RFID Implementations[5]

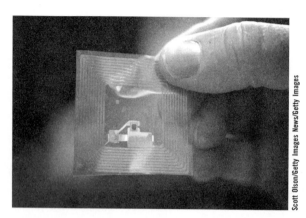

An RFID Tag

Scott Olson/Getty Images News/Getty Images

Radio frequency identification (RFID) is one of the latest developments in inventory management. RFID technology has also been adopted by major retailers worldwide, including Marks & Spencer and Tesco in the U.K. and Metro Group in Germany. In the U.S., a couple of years after Wal-Mart issued its RFID mandate, more than 100 top suppliers began to ship RFID-tagged pallets and cases to the giant retailer by early 2005. The company then expanded its mandate to another 500 large suppliers, and then again to include its top 1,000 suppliers by the end of 2007. Similarly, the U.S. Department of Defense also required that pallets delivered to its warehouse from its largest suppliers be tagged with RFID.

Tagging strategies differ considerably by region. In the U.S., the focus is on case- or pallet-level tagging, whereas European retailers focus on item level tagging. U.S. retailers focus on case- and pallet-level tagging for inventory management to help reduce inventory and stockouts while simultaneously improving customer service. Consumer-privacy issues and high implementation costs for hardware and tags deter American retailers from moving into item-level tagging. In Europe, the cultural climate has made it easier to deploy RFID, and retailers are using the technology at the item level for category management and garment sorting, and are looking at RFID for smart shelves such as automatic replenishment. While most retailers in Asia expect to gain from integrating RFID technology across the supply chain, China is skeptical about sharing potentially confidential information with foreign businesses and lags behind other nations in RFID technology. In Japan, the RFID market focuses on government applications, logistics usage and asset tagging.

However, rapid industry adoption has proved more challenging than initially believed and, as in the case of Wal-Mart, has had mixed success. Tag and RFID system costs are among the major impediments to a faster adoption of the technology. RFID tags can cost ten to twenty times more than simple barcodes. Globally, the RFID industry still does not have its own ultra-high-frequency (UHF) spectrum allocation. Differences between radio frequencies in different parts of the world are another major hurdle to broader adoption. While the U.S. favors the 915 MHz UHF, the Europeans prefer the 868 MHz UHF. The Chinese use frequencies from 840.25–844.75 MHz to 920.25–924.75MHz; while in Japan, 125–134 kHz, 13.56 MHz, 2.4–2.5 GHz and 5.8 GHz are used, with the 950–956 MHz UHF allocated for unlicensed, low-power use. Finally, with limited benefit information from a few RFID pilot projects, it is difficult for a company to calculate returns.

While considerable progress has been made on code standardization over the last few years, much work remains to be done. The U.S. and Europe have jointly worked on a common standard based on the modified EPCglobal UHF Gen-2 standard, but China and Japan have decided to develop their own. China supports its own EPC classification system for domestic product labeling, whereas Japan uses its Ubiquitous ID standard. Using competing RFID standards is likely to eventually lead to the need for costly multiprotocol readers that can handle tags that comply with the different standards. Despite all the challenges, RFID is ultimately likely to replace barcode technology in inventory management.

Source: Wen Hui Tan

the ISO standard for air interface communications between the readers and the tags. The EPC standard is more widely adopted, especially in the commercial sector.

Similar to barcode technology, a reader is used to read the information stored in RFID tags. However, the reader does not have to be placed directly in line of sight of the tag to read the radio signal—a significant advantage of RFID over barcode. The EPC standards call for six classes of tags as shown in Table 7.4. Class 0 tags are read only, but class 1 tags can be programmed once to update the information stored on the tags. Similar to a rewritable CD, class 2 tags can be rewritten multiple times. Classes 0, 1 and 2 are passive tags that do not store power on the tags and classes 3 and 4 are active tags that contain a power source to boost their range. Class 5 tags can communicate with other class 5 tags and other devices. The current EPC standard is the 96-bit UHF Class 1, General 2 write once read many (WORM) tag. This generation of tags is expected to pave the way to the Class 2 high memory full read/write tags. A 256-bit version of the tag is being created at this writing, but full details are not yet available.

The current 96-bit EPC is a number made up of a header and three sets of data as shown in Figure 7.3. The 8-bit *header* identifies the version of the EPC being used; the 28-bit *EPC manager* identifies the manufacturer (and even plant) of the product; the 24-bit *object class* identifies the unique product family; and the 36-bit *serial number* uniquely identifies the individual physical item being read. The 8-bit header can identify 256 (2^8) versions of EPC; the 28-bit EPC manager can classify 268,435,456 (2^{28})

Table 7.4	EPCglobal's Tag Classes	
EPC CLASS TYPE	**FEATURES**	**TAG TYPE**
Class 0	Read only	Passive (64 bits only)
Class 1	Write once, read many	Passive (minimum 96 bits)
Class 2	Read/write	Passive (minimum 96 bits)
Class 3	Read/write with battery power to enhance range	Semi-active
Class 4	Read/write active transmitter	Active
Class 5	Read/write active transmitter	Active tag that can communicate with other class 5 tags

Figure 7.3	Structure of the Electronic Product Code

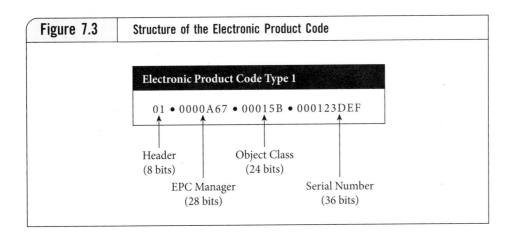

companies; the 24-bit object class can identify 16,777,216 (2^{24}) product families per company; and the 36-bit serial number can differentiate 68,719,476,736 (2^{36}) specific items per product family. Using this mammoth combination that is unmatched by the barcode, it is not difficult to envisage that RFID can revolutionize inventory management in the supply chain.

Components of a Radio Frequency Identification System

An RFID solution consists of four parts: the tag, reader, communication network and RFID software. The tag consists of a computer chip and an antenna for wireless communication with the handheld or fixed-position RFID reader, and the communication network connects the readers to transmit inventory information to the enterprise information system. The RFID software manages the collection, synchronization and communication of the data with warehouse management, ERP and supply chain planning systems and stores the information in a database. Figure 7.4 shows a generic RFID system.

Though RFID was designed for use at the item level to identify individual items, current implementation focuses at the aggregate level where tags are placed on cases, crates, pallets or containers due to the high cost of the tags. An RFID tag costs approximately 10 cents today compared to $2 in 1999,[4] but it is still not financially feasible to tag individual low-ticket items. Thus, the existing focus is at the aggregate level focusing on cases or pallets of items, although some retailers have started to place RFID tags on individual high-ticket items like cameras and electronic products to prevent theft and closely manage the expensive inventory.

How Radio Frequency Identification Automates the Supply Chain

RFID is a valuable technology for tracking inventory in the supply chain. It can synchronize information and physical flow of goods across the supply chain from manufacturers to retail outlets and to the consumers at the right place at the right time. Likewise, RFID can track returned goods through the supply chain and prevent counterfeit. It also helps to reduce out-of-stock items. There is no doubt that RFID is an invaluable tool for improving inventory management and supply chain efficiencies. The steps by which the RFID can automate the supply chain follow.

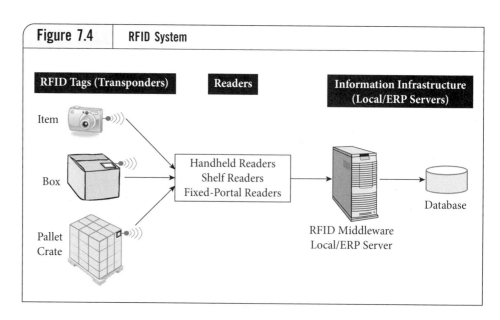

Figure 7.4   RFID System

RFID Tags (Transponders)   Readers   Information Infrastructure (Local/ERP Servers)

Item

Box

Pallet Crate

Handheld Readers
Shelf Readers
Fixed-Portal Readers

RFID Middleware
Local/ERP Server

Database

1. *Materials Management*: As a supply vehicle enters the warehouse, the fixed-portal RFID reader positioned at the entrance reads the tags on the pallets or individual items to provide handling, routing and storage information of the incoming goods. Inventory status can be updated automatically.

2. *Manufacturing*: An RFID tag can be placed on the unit being produced so that specific customer configurations can be incorporated automatically during the production process. This is invaluable in a make-to-order environment.

3. *Distribution Center*: As the logistics vehicle arrives at the loading dock, the fixed-portal RFID reader communicates with the tag on the vehicle to confirm that it is approved to pick up goods. When the loaded vehicle leaves the dock and crosses the portal, the reader picks up the signals from the tags to alert the RFID software and ERP system to update the inventory automatically and initiate an advance shipping notice (ASN), proof of pickup and invoices.

4. *Retail Store*: As the delivery vehicle enters the unloading dock, the fixed-portal reader picks up the signals from the tags and the RFID software application processes the signals to provide specific handling instructions and initiate automatic routing of the goods. The RFID reader can also be placed on the store shelf to trigger automatic replenishments when an item reaches its reorder point. Moreover, inventory status can be updated in real time automatically at any stage of the supply chain, and handheld readers can be used to assist in cycle counting. Item-level tagging can be used to recommend complementary products. For instance, a computer screen and a reader can be placed in the changing room, so when a consumer tests a tagged suit in the changing room, the reader picks up the signal to suggest matching shirts and shoes on an LCD screen. When RFID is fully implemented at the item level, it is not difficult to envisage that instead of waiting for a cashier, a consumer should be able to simply walk out the door of a store with the purchase. A reader built into the door should be able to recognize the items in the cart and charge the customer accordingly. The customer does not even have to stop to pay for the purchase if a prearranged credit facility or account has been established with the store.

The Global Perspective feature provides a look at some global organizations and their use of RFID in their supply chains.

Global Perspective	*RFID is Helping to Revolutionize Supply Chains*

Today, RFID technology is revolutionizing the supply chain. Lower prices, new tags and the convergence of RFID technology with GPS, WiFi, satellite and sensor technology that monitor more than just the location of goods are driving up adoption rates. Here are two examples of how RFID is solving problems beyond tracking pallets and cartons.

In the intermodal shipping business, the goal is to have just the right number of containers to maximize the turn time. Without visibility into the location of containers and how they're moving through the supply chain, however, shippers can spend a lot of money to have enough assets to meet its needs. That's why Horizon Lines, the largest domestic ocean carrier with 21 vessels servicing trade lanes in Alaska, Hawaii, Guam and Puerto Rico, invested in RFID technology to tag and track its fleet of more than 6,000 intermodal containers across the supply chain. The system uses long-range active RFID tags that can be read on a truck traveling at 70 miles per hour from as far away as 1,500 feet. The first route is in Alaska where there is just one north/south highway and the state department of transportation allowed Horizon to install RFID readers along that highway.

Horizon begins tracking its assets in Tacoma and Seattle, Washington, where cargo containers bound for Alaska are loaded. Each container has an active RFID tag with a unique identification number. The empty container is read at the DC gate, when the container is loaded, and finally when the container is loaded on a ship. As it travels to Fairbanks or Seward, readers installed in key locations along the highway read the long-range RFID tags and alert Horizon's customers that the container is in route. Meanwhile, Horizon's customers are able to prepare their DC staffs to unload the trailer soon after it arrives and get it back on the road. Horizon reads the container on its return trip back so that it can quickly be put back into service when it arrives in Anchorage.

A commercial aircraft is one of the most complicated and sophisticated machines ever built. Getting the right part to the right place, at the right time and even on the right side of the aircraft is imperative. That's why Airbus is developing solutions that will use RFID to error-proof its operations. On the final assembly line for the A380 aircraft in Hamburg, Germany, RFID tags are placed on the containers that deliver items required to finish the cabin of the aircraft as they travel from the warehouse to the assembly line. In this application, parts are placed inside an RFID-enabled container that can be delivered to one of six docks. Each dock has two elevators and four floors. RFID readers are located at each entrance and exit on each floor. If the materials handler is going to the correct area, he gets a green light confirmation. If he tries to get on the wrong elevator or get off on the wrong floor, he gets a red light. With as many as 750 parts containers per airplane, this helps avoid a disruption later on. Airbus is also using RFID to track the transportation of subassemblies, such as fuselage sections, wings and tailpieces, from a subassembly site to production facilities. The subassemblies are tagged and read by readers installed on special cargo-loading devices that load jigs onto cargo planes. As with the containers on the elevators, a materials handler will be notified by lights if he tries to load the wrong jig onto a cargo plane.

Source: Trebilcock, B., "RFID: Against the Grain," *Modern Materials Handling*, V. 64, No. 11 (2009): 23. Used with permission.

Inventory Models

A variety of inventory models for independent demand items are reviewed in this section by classifying the models into two broad categories. First, the deterministic inventory models are discussed that assume demand, delivery lead time and other parameters are deterministic. These models use fixed parameters to derive the optimum *order quantity* to minimize *total inventory costs*. Thus, these models are also known as the **fixed order quantity models**. The economic order quantity, quantity discount and economic manufacturing quantity models are the three most widely used fixed order quantity models. Following this, the statistical reorder point is discussed, where demand and/or lead time are not constant but can be estimated by means of a normal distribution. Finally, the continuous review and periodic review systems are briefly discussed.

The Economic Order Quantity Model

The **economic order quantity (EOQ) model** is a classic independent demand inventory system that provides many useful ordering decisions. The basic order decision is to determine the optimal order size that minimizes total annual inventory costs—that is, the sum of the annual order cost and the annual inventory holding cost. The issue revolves around the trade-off between annual inventory holding cost and annual order cost. When the order size for an item is small, orders have to be placed on a frequent basis, causing high annual order costs. However, the firm then has a low average inventory level for this item, result-ing in low annual inventory holding costs. When the order size for an item is large, orders are placed less frequently, causing lower annual order costs. Unfortunately, this also causes the average inventory level for this item to be high, resulting in higher annual expenses to hold the inventory. The EOQ model thus seeks to find an optimal order size that mini-mizes the sum of the two annual costs. In EOQ computations, the term *carrying cost* is often used in place of holding cost and *setup cost* is used in place of order cost.

Assumptions of the Economic Order Quantity Model

Users must carefully consider the following assumptions when determining the eco-nomic order quantity:

1. *The demand is known and constant.* For example, if there are 365 days per year and the annual demand is known to be 730 units, then daily usage must be exactly two units throughout the entire year.

2. *Order lead time is known and constant.* For example, if the delivery lead time is known to be ten days, every delivery will arrive exactly ten days after the order is placed.

3. *Replenishment is instantaneous.* The entire order is delivered at one time and partial shipments are not allowed.

4. *Price is constant.* Quantity or price discounts are not allowed.

5. *The holding cost is known and constant.* The cost or rate to hold inventory must be known and constant.

6. *Order cost is known and constant.* The cost of placing an order must be known and remains constant for all orders.

7. *Stockouts are not allowed.* Inventory must be available at all times.

Deriving the Economic Order Quantity

The economic order quantity can be derived easily from the total annual inventory cost formula using basic calculus. The total annual inventory cost is the sum of the annual purchase cost, the annual holding cost and the annual order cost. The formula can be shown as:

$$TAIC = \text{Annual purchase cost} + \text{Annual holding cost} + \text{Annual order cost}$$

$$TAIC = APC + AHC + AOC = (R \times C) + (Q/2) \times (k \times C) + (R/Q) \times S$$

where

$TAIC$ = total annual inventory cost

APC = annual purchase cost

AHC = annual holding cost

AOC = annual order cost

R = annual requirement or demand

C = purchase cost per unit

S = cost of placing one order

k = holding rate, where annual holding cost per unit = $k \times C$

Q = order quantity

Since R, C, k and S are deterministic (i.e., assumed to be constant terms), Q is the only unknown variable in the $TAIC$ equation. The optimum Q (the EOQ) can be obtained by taking the first derivative of $TAIC$ with respect to Q and then setting it equal to zero. A second derivative of $TAIC$ can also be taken with respect to Q to prove that the $TAIC$ is a concave function, and thus $\frac{dTAIC}{dQ} = 0$ is at the lowest point (i.e., minimum) of the total annual inventory cost curve. Thus:

$$\frac{dTAIC}{dQ} = 0 + (½ \times k \times C) + (-1 \times R \times S \times 1/Q^2)$$
$$= \frac{kC}{2} - \frac{RS}{Q^2}.$$

Then setting $\frac{dTAIC}{dQ}$ equal to zero,

$$\frac{kC}{2} - \frac{RS}{Q^2} = 0$$
$$\Rightarrow \frac{kC}{2} = \frac{RS}{Q^2}$$
$$\Rightarrow Q^2 = \frac{2RS}{kC}$$
$$\Rightarrow EOQ = \sqrt{\frac{2RS}{kC}}.$$

The second derivative of $TAIC$ is

$$\frac{d^2 TAIC}{dQ^2} = 0 - \left(-2 \times \frac{RS}{Q^3}\right) = \left(\frac{2RS}{Q^3}\right) \geq 0,$$

implying that the $TAIC$ is at its minimum when $\frac{dTAIC}{dQ} = 0$.

The annual purchase cost drops off after the first derivative is taken. The managerial implication here is that purchase cost does not affect the order decision if there is no quantity discount (the annual purchase cost remains constant regardless of the order size, as long as the same annual quantity is purchased). Thus, the annual purchase cost is ignored in the classic EOQ model. Example 7.3 provides an illustration of calculating the EOQ. It should be noted that all demand must be converted to the annual requirement, and holding cost is the product of holding rate and unit cost of the item. For example, if the annual holding rate (k) is 12 percent and the item cost (C) is $10 per unit, the holding cost (kC) is $1.20 per unit per year.

Figure 7.5 shows the relationships between annual holding cost, annual order cost and total annual holding plus order cost. Using the data in Example 7.3, at the EOQ (600 units), annual holding cost ($1,200) equals annual order cost ($1,200). At or close to the EOQ, the annual total cost curve is rather flat, indicating that it is not very sensitive to small variations in the economic order quantity. Therefore, the classic EOQ model is said to be very *robust* to minor errors in estimating cost parameters, such as holding rate, order cost or annual usage. Table 7.5 for example, compares the annual total cost at an EOQ of 600 units and at 10 percent below and above the EOQ. The analysis shows that the cost variations range from only 0.01 percent to 0.56 percent above the minimum total cost.

Figure 7.5 and Table 7.5 show that if the order size is smaller than the EOQ, the annual holding cost is slightly lower, whereas the annual order cost is slightly higher. The net effect is a slightly higher annual total cost. Similarly, if the order quantity is slightly larger than the EOQ, the annual holding cost is slightly higher, whereas the annual order cost is slightly lower. The net effect is a slightly higher annual total cost.

Example 7.3   Calculating the EOQ at the Las Vegas Corporation

The Las Vegas Corporation purchases a critical component from one of its key suppliers. The operations manager wants to determine the economic order quantity, along with when to reorder, to ensure the annual inventory cost is minimized. The following information was obtained from historical data.

$$
\begin{aligned}
\text{Annual requirements } (R) &= 7{,}200 \text{ units} \\
\text{Setup cost } (S) &= \$100 \text{ per order} \\
\text{Holding rate } (k) &= 20\% \text{ per year} \\
\text{Unit cost } (C) &= \$20 \text{ per unit} \\
\text{Order lead time } (LT) &= 6 \text{ days} \\
\text{Number of days per year} &= 360
\end{aligned}
$$

Thus,

$$
EOQ = \sqrt{\frac{2RS}{kC}} = \sqrt{\frac{2 \times 7{,}200 \text{ units} \times \$100}{0.20 \times \$20}} = 600 \text{ units}
$$

1. The annual purchase cost = $R \times C$ = 7,200 units × $20 = $144,000.
2. The annual holding cost = $(Q/2) \times k \times C$ = (600/2) × 0.20 × $20 = $1,200.
3. The annual order cost = $(R/Q) \times S$ = (7,200/600) × $100 = $1,200.
   (Note that when using the EOQ, the annual holding cost equals the annual order cost.)
4. The total annual inventory cost = $144,000 + $1,200 + $1,200 = $146,400.
5. For an order lead time of six days, the reorder point (ROP) would be:
   ROP = (7,200/360) × 6 = 120 units
   Thus, the purchasing manager should reorder the component from the supplier whenever the physical or on-hand stock is down to 120 units, and 600 units should be ordered each time. The order cycle can also be computed as follows:
6. Number of orders placed per year = 7,200/600 = 12 orders.
7. Time between orders = 360/12 = 30 days.

Figure 7.5   The Economic Order Quantity and Total Costs

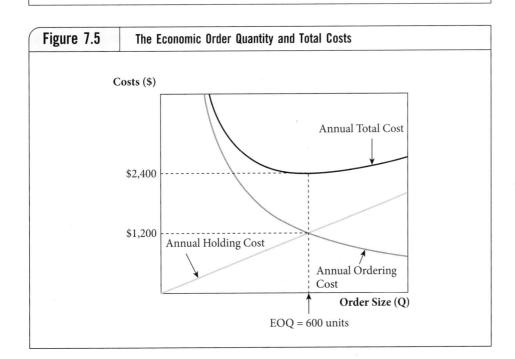

Table 7.5	Percent Variation in Total Annual Cost			
Q (units)	AHC ($)	AOC ($)	ATC ($)	Variation (%)
540	1080.00	1333.33	2413.33	0.56
550	1100.00	1309.09	2409.09	0.38
560	1120.00	1285.71	2405.71	0.24
570	1140.00	1263.16	2403.16	0.13
580	1160.00	1241.38	2401.38	0.06
590	1180.00	1220.34	2400.34	0.01
EOQ=600	1200.00	1200.00	2400.00*	0.00
610	1220.00	1180.33	2400.33	0.01
620	1240.00	1161.29	2401.29	0.05
630	1260.00	1142.86	2402.86	0.12
640	1280.00	1125.00	2405.00	0.21
650	1300.00	1107.69	2407.69	0.32
660	1320.00	1090.91	2410.91	0.45
* indicates minimum total cost at the EOQ				

Figure 7.6 shows the movement of physical inventory and the relationships of EOQ, average inventory, lead time, reorder point and the order cycle. Continuing with the use of the data in Example 7.3, at Time 0, the firm is assumed to start with a complete order of 600 units. The inventory is consumed at a steady rate of 20 units

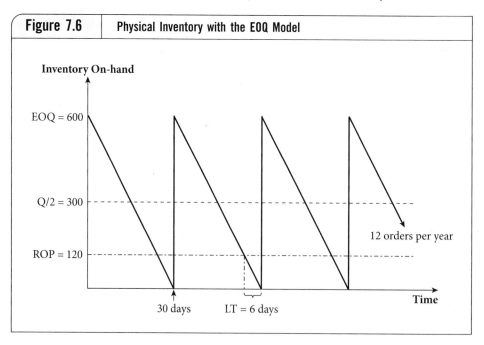

Figure 7.6   Physical Inventory with the EOQ Model

per day. On the 24th day, the ROP of 120 is reached and the firm places its first order of 600 units. It arrives six days later (on the thirtieth day). The 120 units of inventory are will be totally consumed immediately prior to the arrival of the first order. The vertical line on the thirtieth day shows that all 600 units are received (this is the instantaneous replenishment assumption of the EOQ model). A total of twelve orders (including the initial 600 units) will be placed during the year to satisfy the annual requirement of 7,200 units.

The Quantity Discount Model

The **quantity discount model** or **price-break model** is one variation of the classic EOQ model. It relaxes the constant price assumption by allowing purchase quantity discounts. In this case, the unit price of an item is allowed to vary with the order size. For example, a supplier may offer a price of $5 per unit for orders up to 200 units, $4.50 per unit for orders between 201 and 500, and $4 per unit for orders of more than 500 units. This creates an incentive for the buyer to purchase in larger quantities to take advantage of the quantity discount, provided the savings is greater than the extra cost of holding larger inventory levels. Unlike the EOQ model, the annual purchase cost now becomes an important factor in determining the optimal order size and the corresponding total annual inventory cost. The quantity discount model must consider the trade-off between purchasing in larger quantities to take advantage of the price discount (while also reducing the number of orders required per year) and the higher costs of holding inventory. With the quantity discount model, there are thus two variables in the *TAIC* equation (the purchase price C and the order quantity Q). Hence a new approach is needed to find the optimal order quantity.

The purchase price per unit, C, is no longer fixed, as assumed in the classical EOQ model derivations. Consequently, the total annual inventory cost must now include the annual purchase cost, which varies depending on the order quantity. The new total annual inventory cost formula can now be stated as:

$$\text{Total Annual Inventory Cost} = \text{Annual purchase cost} + \text{Annual holding cost} + \text{Annual order cost,}$$

or

$$TAIC = APC + AHC + AOC = (R \times C) + (Q/2) \times (k \times C) + (R/Q) \times S$$

The quantity discount model yields a total annual inventory cost curve for each price level; hence, no single curve is relevant to all purchase quantities. The relevant total annual inventory cost curve is a combination of the cost curves for each price level, starting with the top curve where the price is the highest, and dropping down curve by curve at the price break point. A **price break point** is the minimum quantity required to get a price discount. There is an EOQ associated with each price level, however the EOQ may not be *feasible* at that particular price level because the order quantity may not lie in the given quantity range for that unit price. Due to the stepwise shape of the total inventory cost curve, the optimal order quantity lies at either a *feasible EOQ* or at a *price break point*.

A fairly straightforward two-step procedure can be used to solve the quantity discount problem. Briefly, the two steps can be stated as follows:

1. Starting with the lowest purchase price, compute the EOQ for each price level until a feasible EOQ is found. If the feasible EOQ found is for the lowest

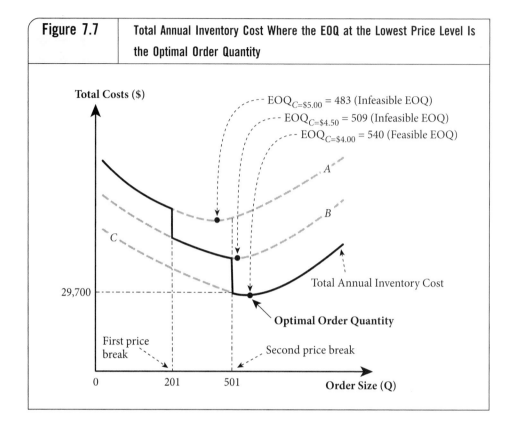

Figure 7.7 | Total Annual Inventory Cost Where the EOQ at the Lowest Price Level Is the Optimal Order Quantity

purchase price, this is the optimal order quantity. The reason is that the EOQ for the lowest price level is the lowest point on the total annual inventory cost curve (see Figure 7.7). If the feasible EOQ is not associated with the lowest price level, proceed to step 2.

2. Compute the total annual inventory cost for the feasible EOQ found in step 1, and for all the price break points at each *lower* price level. Price break points *above* the feasible EOQ will result in higher total annual inventory cost, thus need not be evaluated. The order quantity that yields the lowest total annual inventory cost is the optimal order quantity.

Examples 7.4 and 7.5 illustrate the quantity discount model.

The Economic Manufacturing Quantity Model

The **Economic Manufacturing Quantity (EMQ)** or **Production Order Quantity (POQ) model** is another variation of the classic EOQ model. It relaxes the *instantaneous replenishment* assumption by allowing usage or partial delivery during production. The EMQ model is especially appropriate for a manufacturing environment where items are being manufactured and consumed simultaneously; hence the name economic manufacturing quantity. Inventory builds up gradually during the production period rather than at once as in the EOQ model.

For instance, let us assume that the production lot size for a manufactured product is 600 units, the manufacturer's production rate is 100 units per day, and its demand is

> ### Example 7.4   Finding the Optimal Order Quantity with Quantity Discounts at the Kuantan Corporation
>
> The Kuantan Corporation purchases a component from a supplier who offers quantity discounts to encourage larger order quantities. The supply chain manager of the company wants to determine the optimal order quantity to ensure the total annual inventory cost is minimized. The company's annual demand forecast for the item is 7,290 units, the order cost is $20 per order and the annual holding rate is 25 percent. The price schedule for the item is:
>
> | ORDER QUANTITY | PRICE PER UNIT |
> |----------------|----------------|
> | 1–200 | $5.00 |
> | 201–500 | $4.50 |
> | 501 and above | $4.00 |
>
> The two questions of interest here are: 1) what is the optimal order quantity that will minimize the total annual inventory cost for this component? And 2) what is the total annual inventory cost?
>
> **SOLUTION:**
>
> **Step 1:** Find the first feasible EOQ starting with the lowest price level:
>
> $$EOQ_{C\,=\,\$4.00} = \sqrt{\frac{2 \times 7{,}290 \text{ units} \times \$20}{0.25 \times \$4}} = 540 \text{ units}$$
>
> This is a *feasible* EOQ because order size of 540 units falls within the order quantity range for the price level of $4.00 per unit. Thus, 540 units is the optimal order quantity. In this case, the optimal order size falls on a feasible EOQ. The minimum total annual inventory cost is then:
>
> $$\begin{aligned} TAIC &= APC + AHC + AOC = (R \times C) + (Q/2) \times (k \times C) + (R/Q) \times S \\ &= (7{,}290 \times \$4) + (540/2 \times 0.25 \times \$4) + (7{,}290/540 \times \$20) \\ &= \$29{,}160 + \$270 + \$270 = \$29{,}700 \end{aligned}$$
>
> The annual holding cost equals the annual order cost because the optimal order quantity falls is an EOQ.
>
> Cost curves A, B and C in Figure 7.7 are the annual inventory costs at price levels of $5, $4.50 and $4 respectively. Since each cost curve is only applicable for its price range, the relevant total annual inventory cost is the combination of these three cost curves where the total cost drops vertically at each price break point, curve by curve, to the next lower cost curve. Figure 7.7 shows that the feasible EOQ for the lowest price level is the lowest point on the total annual inventory cost curve; thus, it is the optimal order quantity. The two infeasible EOQs for the price levels of $4.50 and $5 are also shown in Figure 7.7 to reiterate that if an EOQ falls outside of its price range, it is irrelevant to the total annual inventory cost.

40 units per day. The manufacturer thus needs six days (600/100) to produce a batch of 600 units. While being produced, the items are also consumed simultaneously; hence inventory builds up at the rate of 60 units (100 − 40) per day for six days. The maximum inventory is 360 units (60 × 6 days), which is less than the lot size of 600 units as would have been in the case of the classic EOQ model. The lower inventory level implies that the holding cost of the EMQ model is less than the EOQ model given the same cost parameters. It is also clear that the production rate must be greater than the demand rate; otherwise, there would not be any inventory buildups. On the seventh day, the production of the first batch stops and the inventory starts to deplete at the

Example 7.5   Finding the Optimal Order Quantity with Quantity Discounts at the Soon Corporation

The Soon Corporation is a multinational company that purchases one of its crucial components from a supplier who offers quantity discounts to encourage larger order quantities. The supply chain manager of the company wants to determine the optimal order quantity to minimize the total annual inventory cost. The company's annual demand forecast for the item is 1,000 units, its order cost is $20 per order, and its annual holding rate is 25 percent. The price schedule is:

ORDER QUANTITY	PRICE PER UNIT
1–200	$5.00
201–500	$4.50
501 and above	$4.00

The first price break point is 201 units and the second is 501 units. What is the optimal order quantity that will minimize the total annual inventory cost for this component and what is the total annual inventory cost?

SOLUTION:

Step 1: Find the first feasible EOQ starting with the lowest price level:

A. $EOQ_{c=\$4.00} = \sqrt{\dfrac{2 \times 1,000 \text{ units} \times \$20}{0.25 \times \$4}} = 200$ units

This quantity is *infeasible* because an order quantity of 200 units does not fall within the required order quantity range to qualify for the $4 price level (the unit price for an order quantity of 200 units is $5). Next, we evaluate the EOQ at the next higher price level of $4.50:

B. $EOQ_{c=\$4.50} = \sqrt{\dfrac{2 \times 1,000 \text{ units} \times \$20}{0.25 \times \$4.50}} = 189$ units

This quantity is also *infeasible* because it fails to qualify for the $4.50 price level. Moving on to the next higher price level of $5:

C. $EOQ_{c=\$5.00} = \sqrt{\dfrac{2 \times 1,000 \text{ units} \times \$20}{0.25 \times \$5}} = 179$ units

This order quantity is the *first feasible EOQ* because a 179-unit order quantity corresponds to the correct price level of $5 per unit.

Step 2: Find the total annual inventory costs for the first feasible EOQ found in step 1 and for the price break points at each lower price level (201 units at $4.50 and 501 units at $4).

$$TAIC = APC + AHC + AOC = (R \times C) + (Q/2) \times (k \times C) + (R/Q) \times S$$

A) $TAIC_{EOQ=179,\ C=\$5}$ $= (1,000 \times \$5) + (179/2 \times 0.25 \times \$5) + (1,000/179 \times \$20)$
$= \$5,000 + \$111.88 + \$111.73 = \$5,223.61$

B) $TAIC_{Q=201,\ C=\$4.50}$ $= (1,000 \times \$4.50) + (201/2 \times 0.25 \times \$4.50) + (1,000/201 \times \$20)$
$= \$4,500 + \$113.06 + \$99.50 = \$4,712.56$

C) $TAIC_{Q=501,\ C=\$4}$ $= (1,000 \times \$4) + (501/2 \times 0.25 \times \$4) + (1,000/501 \times \$20)$
$= \$4,000 + \$250.50 + \$39.92 = \$4,290.42$

Comparing the total annual inventory costs in A, B and C, the optimal order quantity is 501 units, which qualifies for the deepest discount. In this case, the optimal order size falls

> ### Example 7.5   Finding the Optimal Order Quantity with Quantity Discounts at the Soon Corporation (continued)
>
> on a *price break point*; hence, the annual holding cost ($250.50) does not equal the annual order cost ($39.92). When the quantity discount is large compared to the holding cost, it makes sense to purchase in large quantities and hold more inventory. However, this ignores the fact that excessive inventory hides production problems and can become obsolete very quickly. In the attempt to find the optimal order quantity to minimize inventory cost, a manager should also consider the impact of excessive inventory on firm performance. Figure 7.8 demonstrates the characteristics of the cost curves for this example. Cost curves A, B and C are the annual inventory costs at price levels of $5, $4.50 and $4 respectively. The relevant total annual inventory cost is derived from these three cost curves by joining the relevant portion of each cost curve vertically at the price break points.

Figure 7.8	Total Annual Inventory Cost Where the Optimal Order Quantity Is at the Price Break Point

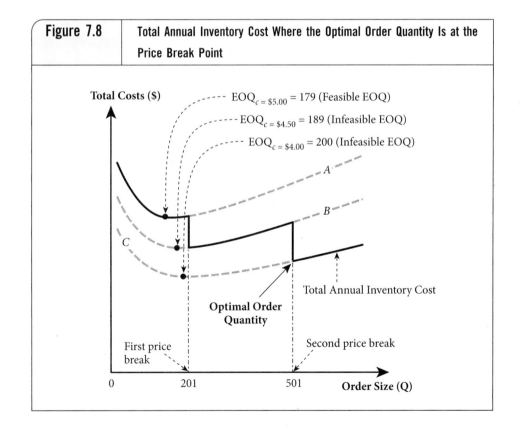

demand rate of 40 units for the next 9 days (360/40). The first production lot and the subsequent usage of the inventory take 15 days (6 + 9) to complete, and then the second cycle repeats.

Figure 7.9 depicts the inventory versus time for the EMQ model. The item is produced in lot size of Q, at the production rate of P and consumed at the demand rate of D. Hence, inventory builds up at the rate of $(P - D)$ during the production period,

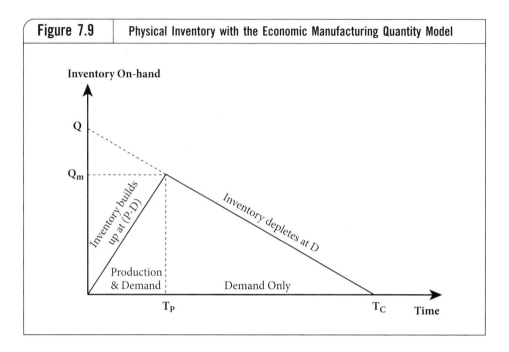

Figure 7.9 | **Physical Inventory with the Economic Manufacturing Quantity Model**

T_P. At the end of the production period (T_P), inventory begins to deplete at the demand rate of D until it is exhausted at the end of the inventory cycle, T_C.

The production rate, P, which can be expressed as Q/T_P, is the production lot size divided by the time required to produce the lot. The maximum inventory, Q_M, can be obtained by multiplying the inventory build-up rate with the production period, and can be expressed as $(P - D) \times T_p$. These relationships can be stated as:

$$P = \frac{Q}{T_P} \text{ and } Q_M = (P - D) \times T_P.$$

Therefore, $T_P = \frac{Q}{P}$ and substituting $\frac{Q}{P}$ for T_P in Q_M gives,

$$Q_M = (P - D) \times \frac{Q}{P}$$
$$= \frac{PQ}{P} - \frac{DQ}{P}$$
$$= Q\left(1 - \frac{D}{P}\right)$$

Hence, the average inventory, $\frac{Q_M}{2} = \frac{Q}{2}\left(1 - \frac{D}{P}\right)$.

The total annual inventory cost can be stated as:

Total Annual Inventory Cost = Annual product cost + Annual holding cost
+ Annual setup cost,

or

$$TAIC = APC + AHC + ASC = (R \times C) + \left[\frac{Q}{2}\left(1 - \frac{D}{P}\right) \times k \times C\right] + [(R/Q) \times S]$$

where

$TAIC$ = total annual inventory cost
APC = annual product cost
AHC = annual holding cost
ASC = annual setup cost
R = annual requirement or demand
C = total cost of one unit of the finished product
S = cost of setting up the equipment to process one batch of the product
k = holding rate, where annual holding cost per unit = k $\times$ C
Q = order quantity

Like the EOQ model where Q is the only unknown variable in the $TAIC$ equation, the optimum manufacturing quantity, Q (the EMQ) can be obtained by taking the first derivative of $TAIC$ with respect to Q and then setting it equal to zero. A second derivative of $TAIC$ can also be taken with respect to Q to prove that the $TAIC$ is a concave function, and thus $\frac{dTAIC}{dQ} = 0$ is at the lowest point of the cost curve. Thus:

$$\frac{dTAIC}{dQ} = 0 + \left[\frac{1}{2} \left(1 - \frac{D}{P} \right) \times k \times C \right] + \left[-1 \times R \times S \times 1/Q^2 \right]$$
$$= \left[\frac{kC}{2} \left(1 - \frac{D}{P} \right) \right] - \frac{RS}{Q^2}.$$

Then setting $\frac{dTAIC}{dQ}$ equal to zero and solving for the EMQ,

$$\left[\frac{kC}{2} \left(1 - \frac{D}{P} \right) \right] - \frac{RS}{Q^2} = 0$$

$$\Rightarrow \left[\frac{kC}{2} \left(1 - \frac{D}{P} \right) \right] = \frac{RS}{Q^2}$$

$$\Rightarrow Q_2 = \frac{2RS}{kC \left(1 - \frac{D}{P} \right)} = \frac{2RS}{kC \left(\frac{P - D}{P} \right)} = \frac{2RS}{kC} \left(\frac{P}{P - D} \right)$$

And the

$$EMQ = \sqrt{ \left(\frac{2RS}{kC} \right) \left(\frac{P}{P - D} \right) }$$

The second derivative of the $TAIC$ is:

$$\frac{d^2 TAIC}{dQ^2} = 0 - \left(-2 \times \frac{RS}{Q^3} \right) = \left(\frac{2RS}{Q^3} \right) \geq 0,$$

implying that the $TAIC$ is at its minimum when $\frac{dTAIC}{dQ} = 0$.

Similar to the EOQ model, the annual product cost drops off after the first derivative is taken, indicating that product cost does not affect the order decision if the unit cost of each product produced is constant; thus, the annual product cost is also ignored in the EMQ model. Example 7.6 provides an illustration of calculating the EMQ for a manufacturing company.

Example 7.6   Calculating the EMQ at the Lone Wild Boar Corporation

The Lone Wild Boar Corporation manufactures a crucial component internally using the most advanced technology. The supply chain manager wants to determine the economic manufacturing quantity to ensure that the total annual inventory cost is minimized. The daily production rate (P) for the component is 200 units, annual demand (R) is 18,000 units, setup cost (S) is $100 per setup and the annual holding rate (k) is 25 percent. The manager estimates that the total cost (C) of a finished component is $120. It is assumed that the plant operates year-round and there are 360 days per year.

SOLUTION:

1. The daily demand rate, $D = 18,000/360 = 50$ units per day.

2. $EMQ = \sqrt{\left(\frac{2RS}{kC}\right)\left(\frac{P}{P-D}\right)} = \sqrt{\left(\frac{2 \times 18,000 \times 100}{0.25 \times 120}\right)\left(\frac{200}{200-50}\right)} = 400$ units.

3. The highest inventory level, $Q_M = Q\left(1 - \frac{D}{P}\right) = 400\left(1 - \frac{50}{200}\right) = 300$ units.

4. The annual product cost $= R \times C = 18,000$ units $\times \$120 = \$2,160,000$.

5. The annual holding cost $= \frac{Q_M}{2} \times k \times C = \frac{300}{2} \times 0.25 \times \$120 = \$4,500$.

6. The annual setup cost $= R/Q \times S = (18,000/400) \times \$100 = \$4,500$.

   (Note that at the EMQ, the annual holding cost equals the annual setup cost.)

7. The $TAIC = \$2,160,000 + \$4,500 + \$4,500 = \$2,169,000$.

8. The length of a production period, $T_P = \frac{EMQ}{P} = 400/200 = 2$ days.

9. The length of each inventory cycle, $T_C = \frac{EMQ}{D} = 400/50 = 8$ days.

10. The rate of inventory buildup during production, $(P - D) = 200 - 50 = 150$ units per day.

11. The number of inventory cycles per year $= 360$ days/8 days $= 45$ cycles.

Figure 7.10 illustrates the EMQ model for the Lone Wild Boar Corporation. A unique observation regarding the classic EOQ, quantity discount and the EMQ models is that when ordering at the EOQ or EMQ, the annual order or setup cost equals the annual holding cost, except in the quantity discount model when the optimal order quantity falls on a price break point.

The Statistical Reorder Point

The two major inventory management decisions are to determine 1) the right order quantity or lot size and 2) when to release an order. Three basic independent demand lot-sizing techniques have been discussed, but as of yet, the question of when to order has not been fully discussed. The **reorder point (ROP)** is the lowest inventory level at which a new order must be placed to avoid a stockout. In a deterministic setting where both the demand and delivery lead time are known and constant, Example 7.3 showed that the reorder point was equal to the demand during the order's delivery lead time. In reality, the demand and delivery lead time tends to vary. Uncertain demand or lead time raises the possibility of stockouts, thus requiring *safety stock* to be held to safeguard against variations in demand or lead time. Next, we discuss how the probabilistic demand pattern and lead time affect the ROP.

The Statistical Reorder Point with Probabilistic Demand and Constant Lead Time

This model assumes the lead time of a product is constant while the demand during the delivery lead time is unknown but can be specified using a normal

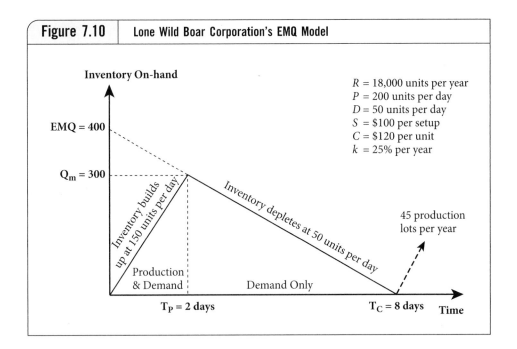

Figure 7.10 | **Lone Wild Boar Corporation's EMQ Model**

Inventory On-hand

R = 18,000 units per year
P = 200 units per day
D = 50 units per day
S = $100 per setup
C = $120 per unit
k = 25% per year

EMQ = 400

Q_m = 300

Inventory builds up at 150 units per day

Inventory depletes at 50 units per day

45 production lots per year

Production & Demand

Demand Only

T_P = 2 days

T_C = 8 days   Time

distribution. Since the statistical reorder point is to determine the lowest inventory level at which a new order should be placed, demand prior to a purchase order does not directly affect the ROP. Figure 7.11 illustrates the relationship between safety stock and the probability of a stockout. If the average demand during the lead time is represented by μ, and the ROP is represented by x, then the safety stock is $(x - \mu)$, which can be derived from the standard deviation formula $(Z = \frac{x-\mu}{\sigma})$. Then, if the probability of stockout is represented by α, the probability that inventory is sufficient to cover demand or the *in-stock probability* is $(1 - \alpha)$. The in-stock probability is commonly referred to as the **service level** (actually, the calculation of the true service level requires use of a loss function for a stockout, which is beyond the scope of this text). Next, the Z-value can be determined from the standardized normal curve and a desire to achieve a specific service level (see the Z-Table in the Appendix). For example, a 97.5 percent service level (α = 2.5 percent) corresponds to the Z-value of 1.96. Note that at the middle of the normal curve, where the reorder point equals the average demand, the required safety stock is zero and the probability of stockout would be 50 percent.

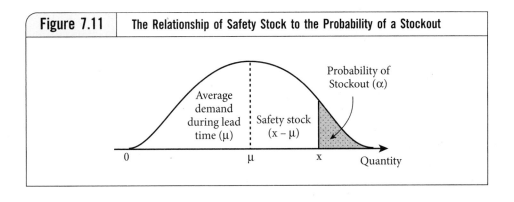

Figure 7.11 | **The Relationship of Safety Stock to the Probability of a Stockout**

Probability of Stockout (α)

Average demand during lead time (μ)

Safety stock $(x - \mu)$

0   μ x   Quantity

The statistical reorder point (x) can be calculated as the average demand during the order's delivery lead time plus the desired safety stock, or:

$$\text{ROP} = \bar{d}_{LT} + Z\sigma_{dLT}$$

The safety stock $Z\sigma_{dLT}$ or $(x - \mu)$ can be derived from the standard deviation formula of the normal curve as shown earlier, and σ_{dLT} is the standard deviation of demand during the delivery lead time. Example 7.7 illustrates the calculation of the ROP with probabilistic demand and constant delivery lead time.

The safety stock computation as shown in Example 7.7 needs to be modified if the standard deviation is available for daily demand and not lead time demand. In this situation, if the delivery lead time is greater than one day, the standard deviation of daily demand (σ_d) must be converted to the standard deviation of lead time demand (σ_{dLT}). If the daily demand is identically distributed, we can use the statistical premise that the variance of a series of independent occurrences is equal to the sum of the variances. That is, the variance of demand during the lead time equals the sum of the variances of all the identical daily demand that covers the lead time period. This can be expressed as:

$$\sigma_{dLT}^2 = \sigma_d^2 + \sigma_d^2 + \sigma_d^2 + \ldots = \sigma_d^2\,(LT),$$

Where

σ_{dLT}^2 = variance of demand during the lead time
σ_d^2 = variance of the identically and independently distributed daily demand
LT = lead time in days

Thus, the standard deviation of demand during the lead time is $\sigma_{dLT} = \sigma_d\sqrt{LT}$. Hence the safety stock and the statistical reorder point can also be stated as:

Example 7.7   Calculating the Statistical Reorder Point Using Probabilistic Demand and Constant Delivery Lead Times at London, Inc.

London, Inc. stocks a crucial part that has a normally distributed demand pattern during the reorder period. Past demand shows that the average demand during lead time (μ) for the part is 550 units, and the standard deviation of demand during lead time (σ_{dLT}) is 40 units. The supply chain manager wants to determine the safety stock and statistical reorder point that result in 5 percent stockouts or a service level of 95 percent. Alternately, the manager wants to know the additional safety stock required to attain a 99 percent service level.

SOLUTION
The normal distribution Z-table in the Appendix shows that a 95 percent service level (5 percent stockouts allowed) corresponds to a Z-value of 1.65 standard deviations above the mean.

The required safety stock is

$$(x - \mu) = Z\sigma_{dLT} = 1.65 \times 40 = 66 \text{ units}.$$

The ROP $= \bar{d}_{LT} + Z\sigma_{dLT} = 550 + 66 \text{ units} = 616 \text{ units}$. This means the manager must reorder the part from their supplier when their current stock level reaches 616 units.

Alternately, the required safety stock at a 99 percent service level $= Z\sigma_{dLT} = 2.33 \times 40 = 93 \text{ units}$. The additional safety stock compared to the 95 percent service level is 27 units.

Example 7.8   Calculating the Statistical Reorder Point at Brussels, Inc. Using the Standard Deviation of Daily Demand and Constant Delivery Lead Times

Brussels, Inc., is a local liquor retailer specializing in selling beer at big discounts. Historical data shows that the demand for beer has a normal distribution. The average daily demand for beer at Brussels is 150 cases, and its standard deviation for daily demand is 30 cases. Brussels' supplier maintains a very reliable and constant lead time of six days. The manager desires to determine the standard deviation of demand during lead time, the safety stock and statistical reorder point that results in a 97.5 percent service level and the safety stock reduction if the manager decides to attain a 90 percent service level.

SOLUTION

Average daily demand, $\bar{d} = 150$ cases

Standard deviation of daily demand, $d = 30$ cases

Lead time, $LT = 6$ days

$$\text{The standard deviation of demand during lead time, } \sigma_{dLT} = \sigma_d\sqrt{LT}$$
$$= 30\sqrt{6} = 73.5 \text{ cases}$$

The Z-Table shows that a 97.5 percent service level (2.5 percent stockouts allowed) corresponds to the Z-value of 1.96 standard deviations above the mean.

The corresponding safety stock, $Z\sigma_d\sqrt{LT} = 1.96 \times 30\sqrt{6} = 144$ cases.

The ROP $= \bar{d}_{LT} + Z\sigma_d\sqrt{LT} = (150 \times 6) + 144 = 1{,}044$ cases. Thus ordering more beer when they have a current inventory of 1,044 cases will result in a 97.5 percent service level.

For the lower service level of 90 percent, safety stock $= Z\sigma_d\sqrt{LT} = 1.28 \times 30\sqrt{6} = 94$ cases.

The safety stock reduction would be 50 cases.

$$\text{Safety stock} = Z\sigma_d\sqrt{LT}$$

and

$$\text{ROP} = \bar{d}_{LT} + Z\sigma_d\sqrt{LT}.$$

Example 7.8 illustrates this calculation.

The Statistical Reorder Point with Constant Demand and Probabilistic Lead Time

When the demand of a product is constant and the lead time is unknown but can be specified by means of a normal distribution, the safety stock is used to buffer against variations in the lead time instead of demand. The safety stock is then (daily demand $\times$ $Z\sigma_{LT}$), and the reorder point is:

ROP = (daily demand $\times$ average lead time in days) + (daily demand $\times$ $Z\sigma_{LT}$),

where

σ_{LT} is the standard deviation of lead time in days.

The calculation is demonstrated in Example 7.9.

The Statistical Reorder Point with Probabilistic Demand and Lead Time

When both the demand and lead time of a product are unknown but can be specified by means of a normal distribution, safety stock must be held to cover the

Example 7.9   Calculating the Statistical Reorder Point at the Harpert Store Using Constant Demand and Probabilistic Lead Time

The Harpert Store has an exclusive contract with Brussums Electronics to sell their most popular mp3 player. The demand of this mp3 player is very stable at 120 units per day. However, the delivery lead times vary and can be specified by a normal distribution with a mean lead time of eight days and a standard deviation of two days. The supply chain manager at Brussums desires to calculate the safety stock and reorder point for a 95 percent service level (in-stock probability).

SOLUTION

Daily demand (d) = 120 units.

Mean lead time ($\overline{LT}$) = 8 days.

Standard deviation of lead time (σ_{LT}) = 2 days

A service level of 95 percent yields a Z = 1.65 from the Z-Table.

$$\text{Required safety stock} = (d \times Z\sigma_{LT}) = 120 \text{ units} \times 1.65 \times 2 = 396 \text{ units.}$$
$$\text{ROP} = (d \times \overline{LT}) + (d \times Z\sigma_{LT}) = (120 \times 8) + 396 = 1,356 \text{ units.}$$

Brussums must order more mp3 players from Harpert when their current inventory reaches 1,356 units.

---

variations in both demand and lead time, resulting in higher safety stocks when compared to variations in the demand or lead time only. The reorder point can be computed as follows:[6]

$$\text{ROP} = (\overline{d} \times \overline{LT}) + Z\sigma_{dLT}$$

Where

$$\sigma_{dLT} = \text{Standard deviation of demand during the lead time}$$
$$= \sqrt{\sigma_{LT}^2 (\overline{d})^2 + \sigma_d^2 (\overline{LT})}$$

And where

σ_{LT} = Standard deviation of lead time days, and

σ_d = Standard deviation of daily demand.

Note that this standard deviation formula (σ_{dLT}) can be applied to all the previous reorder point examples by observing the following fact: "constant" or "no variation" means zero standard deviation. Therefore:

1. When the lead time and demand are constant, then σ_{LT} and σ_d are zero, and the average daily demand and average lead time would be the deterministic demand and lead time. Thus, the reorder point is the demand during lead time period.

2. When the daily demand is probabilistic and lead time is constant, then σ_{LT} is zero and the average lead time would be the deterministic lead time. Using this guideline, the reorder point in Example 7.8 can also be computed as:

$$\text{ROP} = (150 \times 6) + 1.96\sqrt{0^2(150)^2 + 30^2(6)} = 900 + 1.96 \times 30\sqrt{6} = 1,044 \text{ cases.}$$

3. When the daily demand is constant and the lead time is probabilistic, then σ_d is zero and the average daily demand would be the deterministic daily

Example 7.10 **Calculating the Statistical Reorder Point at the Dosseldorf Store Using Probabilistic Demand and Delivery Lead Time**

The Dosseldorf Store is the sole distributor of a popular cell phone. The demand of this cell phone is normally distributed with an average daily demand of 120 units and a standard deviation of 18 units per day. The cell phones are ordered and shipped directly from the manufacturer. Past delivery records for the manufacturer show that delivery lead times are normally distributed with an average of 8 days and a standard deviation of two days. The supply chain manager at Dosseldorf desires to determine the safety stock required and the reorder point for a 95 percent service level.

SOLUTION

Average daily demand, $\bar{d}$ = 120 units.

Standard deviation of daily demand, σ_d = 18 units.

Average lead time, $\overline{LT}$ = 8 days.

Standard deviation of lead time, σ_{LT} = 2 days.

A desired service level of 95 percent yields Z = 1.65 from the Z-Table.

$$
\begin{aligned}
\text{The required safety stock} \quad &= \quad Z\sigma_{dLT} \\
&= \quad 1.65 \times \sqrt{\sigma_{LT}^2\,(\bar{d})^2 + \sigma_d^2\,(\overline{LT})} \\
&= \quad 1.65 \times \sqrt{2^2\,(120)^2 + 18^2\,(8)} = 1.65 \times 245.34 = 405 \text{ units.} \\
\text{The ROP} &= (\bar{d} \times \overline{LT}) + Z\sigma_{dLT} = (120 \times 8) + 405 = 1,365 \text{ units.}
\end{aligned}
$$

Dosseldorf must order more cell phones from their supplier when their current stock reaches 1,365 units to achieve a 95 percent service level.

demand. Using this guideline, the reorder point in Example 7.9 can also be computed as:

$$
\text{ROP} = (120 \times 8) + 1.65\sqrt{2^2(120)^2 + 0^2(8)} = 960 + 1.65 \times 2 \times 120 = 1,356 \text{ units.}
$$

Example 7.10 demonstrates the safety stock and reorder point computation when both the daily demand and lead time are probabilistic.

The Continuous Review and the Periodic Review Inventory Systems

The order quantity and reorder point inventory models discussed thus far assume that the physical inventory levels are precisely known at every point in time. This implies that stock movements must be updated in real time, and that there are no discrepancies between physical inventory and the stock record. In other words, a *continuous review* of the physical inventory is required to make sure that orders are initiated when physical inventories reach their reorder points. In practice, a **continuous review system** can be difficult to achiev and very expensive to implement. Inventory review costs can be lowered by using a **periodic review system** instead, where physical inventory is reviewed at regular intervals, such as weekly or monthly. However, more safety stock would be required for the periodic review system to buffer the added variation due to the longer review period.

When analyzing the continuous review and the periodic review systems, the following symbols are used:

s = order point

S = maximum inventory level

Q = order quantity

R = periodic review

n = 1, 2, 3...

The Continuous Review System

The continuous review system implies that physical inventory is known at all times, so it is more expensive to administer. However, the only uncertainty is the magnitude of demand during the delivery lead time; thus, the only safety stock required is for potential stockouts during this time period. There are two continuous review systems, described below.

1. (s, Q) *continuous review policy*: This policy orders the same quantity Q when physical inventory reaches the reorder point s. The quantity Q can be determined by one of the fixed order quantity methods (such as the EOQ). This policy works properly only if the quantity demanded is one unit at a time. Otherwise, the inventory level may fall below the reorder point s.

2. (s, S) *continuous review policy*: When current inventory reaches or falls below the reorder point s, sufficient units are ordered to bring the inventory up to a pre-determined level S. If the quantity demanded size is one unit at a time, this system is similar to the (s, Q) policy. However, if the demand size is larger than one unit and when physical inventory falls below the reorder point, then the order size is larger than Q. For instance, suppose s = 10, S = 120, and current inventory is 11 units. If the next demand is 3 units, then on-hand inventory will be reduced to 8 units. Consequently an order size of 112 units would be released.

The Periodic Review System

The periodic review system reviews physical inventory at specific intervals of time. Although this system is cheaper to administer, a higher level of safety stock is needed to buffer against uncertainty in demand over a longer planning horizon. There are three periodic review systems, described below.

1. (nQ, s, R) *periodic review policy*: If at the time of inventory review, the physical inventory is equal to or less than the reorder point s, the quantity nQ is ordered to bring the inventory up to the level between s and (s + Q). Recall that n = 1, 2, 3, ..., and the order size is then some multiple of Q. No order is placed if the current inventory is higher than the reorder point. For example, let s = 100 and Q = 50. If the current inventory is 20 units at the time of the review, then 2Q quantities (2 × 50 = 100) are ordered to bring the inventory level up to 120 units.

2. (S, R) *periodic review policy*: At each review time, a sufficient quantity is ordered to bring the inventory up to a pre-determined maximum inventory level S. This policy places a variable sized order as long as the physical inventory is less than the maximum inventory level S. If order cost is high, this is obviously not a

preferred system. However, it may work well if a large variety of items are ordered from the same supplier.

3. (*s, S, R*) *policy*: If at the time of inventory review, the physical inventory is equal to or less than the reorder point *s*, a sufficient quantity is ordered to bring the inventory level up to the maximum inventory level *S*. However, if the physical inventory is higher than the reorder point *s*, no order is placed. This policy addresses the major deficiency of the (*S, R*) policy.

SUMMARY

Organizations rely on inventory to balance supply and demand, and to buffer uncertainties in the supply chain. However, inventory can be one of the most expensive assets of an organization; hence it must be managed closely. The right amount of inventory supports business operations, but too little of it can adversely affect customer service. Conversely, excess inventory not only leads to unnecessary inventory carrying cost but hides production problems and other flaws in a company.

This chapter covers the crucial roles of inventory and various inventory management techniques that are widely used for balancing demand with supply. The classic ABC inventory classification was discussed along with the ABC inventory matrix as a means to monitor if a firm is stocking the right inventories. Ample examples were used to demonstrate the order size and order period inventory models. This chapter also covered one of the latest developments in inventory management—RFID. Radio frequency identification certainly has the potential to drastically change the way inventories are managed in the future.

KEY TERMS

ABC inventory control system, 213

ABC inventory matrix, 214

continuous review system, 239

cycle counting, 213

dependent demand, 210

direct costs, 212

economic manufacturing quantity (EMQ), 228

economic order quantity (EOQ) model, 222

electronic product code (EPC), 217

fixed costs, 212

fixed order quantity models, 222

holding or carrying costs, 212

independent demand, 210

indirect costs, 212

inventory turnovers, 212

inventory turnover ratio, 212

order costs, 212

Pareto analysis, 213

periodic review system, 239

price-break model, 227

price break point, 227

production order quantity (POQ) model, 228

quantity discount model, 227

radio frequency identification (RFID), 217

reorder point (ROP), 234

service level, 235

setup costs, 212

variable costs, 212

80/20 rule, 213

DISCUSSION QUESTIONS

1. Describe and provide examples of dependent and independent demand.

2. Describe the four basic types of inventory.

3. What is the ABC inventory system, and how is it used to manage inventory?

4. What is the ABC inventory matrix, and how is it used to manage inventory?

5. Describe inventory turnover and how it can be used to manage inventory.

6. Why is it important to conduct cycle counting?

7. What is the electronic product code (EPC)?

8. Briefly describe how RFID can be used to manage inventory.

9. Explain why item-level tagging is more expensive than case-level tagging in RFID.

10. What is the purpose of the EOQ and the ROP? How can they be used together?

11. What are the assumptions of the EOQ model?

12. What are the two major costs considered in the EOQ model? Why is the total purchase price not a factor affecting the order quantity?

13. How is the quantity discount model related to the EOQ model?

14. How is the EMQ model related to the EOQ model?

15. Discuss whether the EOQ model is still useful if a small error was made while estimating one of the cost parameters used in the EOQ computation.

16. Assume that you used the EOQ model to compute the order quantity for an item, and the answer was twenty units. Unfortunately, the minimum lot size for the item is twenty-four units. Discuss how this is going to impact your annual holding cost, annual order cost and annual total inventory cost.

17. Explain whether the continuous review or periodic review inventory system is likely to result in higher safety stock. Which is likely to require more time and effort to administer? Why?

18. Use the inventory turnover ratios in Table 7.2 to comment on which firm is the most efficient in deploying its inventory to generate sales.

19. What is the order quantity when the annual order or setup cost equals the annual holding cost in the (a) EOQ model, (b) quantity discount model, and (c) EMQ model?

20. Why is inventory management important to SCM?

INTERNET QUESTIONS

1. Visit the website of EPCglobal, Inc., and use the information to write a brief report on RFID technology and the state of RFID implementation.

2. Use the Internet to search for relevant information to prepare a brief report on the state of RFID implementation in North America, Europe and Asia.

3. Use resources available on the Internet to prepare a report on the RFID implementation at Wal-Mart Stores, Inc.

4. Use resources available on the Internet (e.g., http://finance.yahoo.com/) to access the annual reports (financial statements and balance sheets) of three of your favorite listed companies to (a) extract their latest total revenue, cost of revenue, total assets and year-end or average inventory, and use these numbers to (b) prepare their inventory/total revenue ratio, inventory/total assets ratio and the inventory turnover ratio. Comment on how they performed based on these ratios. (Hint: See Tables 7.1 and 7.2.)

PROBLEMS

1. The revenue for a firm is $2,500,000. Its cost of revenue is $850,000, and its average inventory for the year is $62,000. What is their inventory turnover?

2. Given the following information, what is the annual inventory turnover ratio?

Revenue	$2,2000,000
Cost of Revenue	$1,250,000
Quarter 1 Ending Inventory	$85,000
Quarter 2 Ending Inventory	$98,000
Quarter 3 Ending Inventory	$125,000
Quarter 4 Ending Inventory	$68,000

3. Given the following information, compute the economic order quantity, annual holding cost, annual order cost and annual total inventory cost.

Annual requirements (R)	=	50,000 units
Order cost (S)	=	$150 per order
Holding rate (k)	=	15%
Unit cost (C)	=	$100 per unit

4. The annual requirement of a part is 360,000 units. The order cost is $120 per order, the holding rate is 12 percent and the part cost is $2,500 per unit. What are the (a) EOQ, (b) annual holding cost, (c) annual order cost, and (d) annual total inventory cost?

5. The weekly requirement of a part is 950 units. The order cost is $85 per order, the holding cost is $5 per unit per year and the part cost is $250 per unit. The firm operates fifty-two weeks per year. Compute the (a) EOQ, (b) annual holding cost, (c) annual order cost, and (d) annual total inventory cost.

6. The monthly demand for a part is 1,500 units. The order cost is $285 per order, the holding cost is $56 per unit per year and the part cost is $850 per unit. The firm operates twelve months per year. Compute the (a) EOQ, (b) annual holding cost, (c) annual order cost, and (d) annual total inventory cost.

7. Icy Snowmobile, Inc., has an annual demand for 1,200 snowmobiles. Their purchase cost for each snowmobile is $2,500. It costs about $250 to place an order, and the holding rate is 35 percent of the unit cost. Compute the (a) EOQ, (b) annual holding cost, (c) annual order cost, and (d) total annual inventory cost.

8. Steamy Speedboats has an annual demand for 1,500 speedboats. Its supplier offers quantity discounts to promote larger order quantities. The cost to place an order is $300, and the holding rate is 32 percent of the purchase cost. The purchase cost for each speedboat is based on the price schedule given below. Compute the (a) optimal order quantity, (b) annual purchase cost, (c) annual holding cost, (d) annual order cost, and (e) total annual inventory cost.

ORDER QUANTITY	PRICE PER UNIT
1–50	$18,500
51–100	$18,000
101–150	$17,400
151 and above	$16,800

9. Using the Steamy Speedboats problem above, assume that the order cost has dropped from $300 to $50. What are the (a) optimal order quantity, (b) annual purchase cost, (c) annual holding cost, (d) annual order cost, and (e) total annual inventory cost?

10. Using the Steamy Speedboats problem above, assume that the holding rate has dropped from 32 percent to 15 percent. What are the (a) optimal order quantity, (b) annual purchase cost, (c) annual holding cost, (d) annual order cost, and (e) total annual inventory cost?

11. Frankfurt Electronics produces a component internally using a state-of-the-art technology. The operations manager wants to determine the optimal lot size to ensure that the total annual inventory cost is minimized. The daily production rate for the component is 500 units, annual demand is 36,000 units, setup cost is $150 per setup, and the annual holding rate is 30 percent. The manager estimates that the total cost of a finished component is $80. If we assume that the plant operates year-round, and there are 360 days per year, what are the (a) daily demand, (b) optimal lot size, (c) highest inventory, (d) annual product cost, (e) annual holding cost, (f) annual setup cost, (g) total annual inventory cost, (h) length of a production period, (i) length of each inventory cycle, (j) rate of inventory buildup during the production cycle, and (k) the number of inventory cycles per year? Plot the movement of the inventory during one production cycle using time on the horizontal axis and on-hand inventory on the vertical axis (see Figure 7.10).

12. Paris Store stocks a part that has a normal distribution demand pattern during the reorder period. Its average demand during lead time is 650 units, and the standard deviation of demand during lead time is 60 units. What are the safety stock and statistical reorder point that result in a 97.5 percent service level?

13. Lindner Congress Bookstore sells a unique calculator to college students. The demand for this calculator has a normal distribution with an average daily demand of fifteen units and a standard deviation of four units per day. The lead time for this calculator is very stable at five days. Compute the standard deviation of demand during lead time, and determine the safety stock and statistical reorder point that result in 5 percent stockouts.

14. The daily demand of a product is very stable at 250 units per day. However, its delivery lead time varies and can be specified by a normal distribution with a mean lead time of twelve days and standard deviation of three days. What are the safety stock and reorder point for a 97.5 percent service level?

15. The daily demand of a product can be specified by a normal distribution. Its average daily demand is 250 units with a standard deviation of 40 units. The delivery lead time of this product is also normally distributed with an average of ten days and a standard deviation of three days. What are the safety stock and reorder point for a 95 percent service level?

SPREADSHEET PROBLEMS

1. Given the following inventory information, perform an ABC analysis.

ITEM NUMBER	UNIT COST ($)	ANNUAL USAGE (UNITS)
B8867	6.00	100
J1252	5.25	6,500
K9667	0.25	4,000
L2425	1.00	1,500
M4554	5.50	2,000
T6334	70.00	500
W9856	0.75	800

X2215	1.50	8,000
Y3214	32.00	1,000
Y6339	4.00	3,500

2. Given the following inventory information, construct an (a) ABC analysis by annual dollar usage, (b) ABC analysis by current inventory value, and (c) an ABC inventory matrix. Is the firm stocking the correct inventories?

ITEM NUMBER	UNIT COST ($)	ANNUAL USAGE (UNITS)	CURRENT INVENTORY (UNITS)
B8867	6.00	100	8,000
J1252	5.25	6,500	120
K9667	0.25	4,000	1,000
L2425	1.00	1,500	375
M4554	5.50	2,000	500
T6334	70.00	500	800
W9856	0.75	800	20,000
X2215	1.50	8,000	2,000
Y3214	32.00	1,000	500
Y6339	4.00	3,500	125

3. Given the following inventory information, construct an (a) ABC analysis by annual dollar usage, (b) ABC analysis by current inventory value, and (c) an ABC inventory matrix. Is the firm stocking the correct inventories?

ITEM NUMBER	UNIT COST ($)	ANNUAL USAGE (UNITS)	CURRENT INVENTORY (UNITS)
A967	32.00	1	4,500
B886	6.00	100	8,000
C314	5.25	32	115
D879	12.50	54	254
E536	0.05	125	120
F876	0.07	423	500
G112	0.12	500	1008
H098	1.22	235	750
J125	5.25	6,500	120
K966	0.25	4,000	1,000
L242	1.00	1,500	375
M455	5.50	2,000	500
N007	7.21	54	525
P231	5.25	32	300
Q954	3.25	25	240
T633	70.00	500	800
W985	0.75	800	20,000
X221	1.50	8,000	2,000
Y321	32.00	1,000	500
Z633	4.00	3,500	125

4. Given the following information for an important purchased part, compute the (a) EOQ, (b) total purchase cost, (c) annual holding cost, (d) annual order cost, (e) annual total cost, (f) reorder point, (g) number of orders placed per year and (h) time between orders. Use Microsoft Excel to plot the cost curves (annual holding cost, annual order cost and annual total cost) on the vertical axis, and the order quantity on the horizontal axis.

```
Annual requirements (R)    =   5,000 units
Order cost (S)             =   $100 per order
Holding rate (k)           =   20%
Unit cost (C)              =   $20 per unit
Lead time (LT)             =   6 days
Number of days per year    =   360 days
```

5. Given the following information for an important purchased part, compute the
(a) EOQ, (b) total purchase cost, (c) annual holding cost, (d) annual order cost,
(e) annual total cost, (f) reorder point, (g) number of orders placed per year and
(h) time between orders. Use Microsoft Excel to plot the cost curves (annual holding
cost, annual order cost and annual total cost) on the vertical axis, and the order
quantity on the horizontal axis.

```
Monthly demand         =   3,500 units
Order cost (S)         =   $250 per order
Holding cost (kC)      =   $8.65 per unit per year
Unit cost (C)          =   $85 per unit
Lead time (LT)         =   12 days
Number of days per year =  365 days
```

Chapter 8

PROCESS MANAGEMENT—LEAN AND SIX SIGMA IN THE SUPPLY CHAIN

For most manufacturers, energy is a cost of doing business and in an era of lean manufacturing, it makes perfect sense to treat overuse of energy as a waste and ruthlessly reduce it.[1]

I apologize for causing trouble and worries for many customers over the quality and safety of Toyota. We sincerely acknowledge safety concerns from our customers.[2]

Learning Objectives

After completing this chapter, you should be able to

- Discuss and compare the major elements of lean and Six Sigma.
- Describe why lean and Six Sigma are integral parts of SCM.
- Discuss the Toyota Production System and its association with lean production.
- Discuss the linkage between lean programs and environmental protection.
- Describe the historical developments of lean and Six Sigma.
- Describe and use the various tools of Six Sigma.
- Understand the importance of statistical process control for improving quality.

Chapter Outline

Introduction

Lean Production and the Toyota Production System

Lean Thinking and Supply Chain Management

The Elements of Lean

Lean Systems and the Environment

The Origins of Six Sigma Quality

Comparing Six Sigma and Lean

Six Sigma and Supply Chain Management

The Elements of Six Sigma

The Statistical Tools of Six Sigma

Summary

<table><tr><td>**Supply Chain Management in Action**</td><td>*Lean Manufacturing and the Kaizen Philosophy at Mars*</td></tr></table>

When Frank Mars realized he needed to expand his operations in the early 1920s, he opted to relocate from Minneapolis to Chicago, purchasing 26 acres of a former golf course. Completed in 1929, the factory opened its doors at the very time the country was grappling with the beginnings of the Great Depression. The "showplace of the candy world" not only impressed visitors with its outer beauty but eventually showcased Mars' ongoing drive to improve efficiency through automation.

The front lawn also remains scrupulously attended to, tempting would-be duffers to practice their putting. No such doing, asserts Bill Tumpane, plant director of the facility. Tradition matters. So does Frank Mars' vision. He cites the phenomenal improvements made during the past two years: a 40% boost in output—a result of Kaizen-directed suggestions from employees—as well as various investments in infrastructure improvements, everything from processing equipment investments to parking lot repaving.

What operators and managers want these days at the Chicago facility are more efficient, problem-free product runs. And thanks to Mars Snackfood's lean manufacturing and Kaizen-centered philosophy, it's happening. Kaizen focuses on small but continual improvements by involving everyone from plant managers to production workers. Typically, the plant will have five Kaizen events during the course of the year, all conducted during off-peak production cycles, explains Jim McDermott, operations manager. "Just recently, we held a Kaizen event for our line 3 wrapping room," he says. "The associates get together for a week and literally attack the line 3 wrappers, looking for issues such as where downtime happens, where waste happens. They then come up with ideas to eliminate those problems. After implementing the suggestions, we saw a 20% improvement in efficiencies." Multiply those events several times across the production floor and the numbers add up. As McDermott points out, output per shift improved from 48 tons to 60 tons on one line over the course of three years.

Such involvement partly stems from the empowerment employees have regarding both quality and output. "Every associate has the authority to stop a line if they see a serious safety or quality issue," Tumpane says. "There's an escalation protocol we use, but if it's an issue, we shut it down." Such involvement also applies to quality control.

"Operators own it," says shift manager Dave Spehek. "The expectations are for the operator to conduct a variety of tests during production." Those tests, which occur hourly, range from weight checks to package inspections. In general, quality control inspections take up 25% of an operator's time. The company's quality control department then takes the data and analyzes it, compiling a track record of each line's performance on quality.

Source: Pacyniak, B., "Packing Plenty of Punch at 80," *Candy Industry* 174(10), 2009: 12–17. Used with permission.

Introduction

As already discussed in earlier chapters, supply chain management is all about achieving low cost along with high levels of quality and responsiveness throughout the supply chain. Customers today expect these things, making it necessary for firms to adopt strategic initiatives emphasizing speed, innovation, cooperation, quality and efficiencies.

Lean thinking and Six Sigma quality, two important operating philosophies that are central to the success of supply chain management, seek to achieve these strategic initiatives, while at the same time resolving the trade-offs that can exist when simultaneously pursuing the goals of high quality, fast response and low cost.

In the 1990s, supply chain management emerged as the paradigm that combined several strategies already in use, including **quick response (QR)**, **efficient consumer response (ECR)**, just-in-time (JIT) and Japanese **keiretsu relationships**. The first two are concerned with speed and flexibility, while *keiretsu* involves partnership arrangements. The QR program was developed by the U.S. textile industry in the mid-1980s as an offshoot of JIT and was based on merchandisers and suppliers working together to respond more quickly to consumer needs by sharing information, resulting in better customer service and less inventory and waste. In the early 1990s, ECR was developed by a U.S. grocery industry task force charged with making grocery supply chains more competitive. In this case, point-of-purchase transactions at grocery stores were forwarded via computer to distributors and manufacturers, allowing the stores to keep stocks replenished while minimizing the need for safety stock inventories. *Keiretsu networks* are cooperative coalitions between Japanese manufacturing firms and their suppliers. In many cases, *keiretsus* are formed as the result of financial support given to suppliers by a manufacturing firm.

Supply chain management is thus closely associated with JIT. While many may argue that Henry Ford and his company essentially invented JIT practices, the term **just-in-time** was originally associated with Toyota managers like Mr. Taiichi Ohno along with his *kanban system*, encompassing continuous problem solving in order to eliminate waste. Use of the term *lean* has begun to replace use of the term JIT, and is associated with the Toyota Production System. Lean thinking is broader, although closely related to JIT, and describes a philosophy incorporating tools that seek to economically optimize time, human resources, assets and productivity while improving product and service quality. In the early 1980s, these practices started making their way to the Western world, first as JIT and then today as **lean production**, **lean manufacturing**, or simply **lean thinking**. Lean thinking has evolved into a way of doing business for many organizations.

Quality assessment and improvement is a necessary element of lean production. First, as the process of waste elimination begins to shrink inventories, problems with human resource requirements, queues, lead times, quality and timing are typically uncovered both in production and with inbound and outbound materials. Eventually, these problems are remedied, resulting in higher levels of quality and customer service. Second, as the drive to continuously reduce throughput times continues, the need for a continuing emphasis on improving quality throughout the productive system results in the need for an overall quality improvement or Six Sigma program. **Six Sigma** stresses a commitment by the firm's top management to help the firm identify customer expectations and excel in meeting and exceeding those expectations. Since environmental changes (such as the most recent global recession) along with changes in technology and competition cause customer expectations to change, firms must then commit to a program of continual reassessment and improvement; this, too, is an integral part of Six Sigma. Thus, to achieve the primary objectives of low cost, high quality and fast response, supply chain management requires the use of lean and Six Sigma thinking throughout the supply chain.

Lean Production and the Toyota Production System

The term lean production essentially refers to the **Toyota Production System** in its entirety, a system that was created by several of Toyota's key executives over a number of decades. In 2010, Toyota came under fire for a number of recalls involving over eight million vehicles worldwide for several quality and safety problems. While these problems were indeed serious as evidenced by the apology by Toyota president Akido Toyoda shown in the chapter opening quotes, they should not diminish the value of lean production or the Toyota Production System. In fact, Toyota has promised a return to their "customer first" principles.[3] More about Toyota's recent recall problems can be seen in the Global Perspectives feature. Several of the important events in the creation of the Toyota Production System are described next.

Global Perspective   *Even the Best Can Stumble*

What began in the factories of Toyota Motor Corp. as just-in-time (JIT) manufacturing and was copied by many factories around the world, came full circle for Toyota in 2009 and 2010 when millions of automobiles were recalled, due to unresolved quality and safety problems dating as far back as 2004. Toyota's long-standing reputation for quality and their drive to cut costs while attempting to become the world's leading auto manufacturer caused complacency in all-important safeguards such as frequently checking quality and safety metrics. These safeguards are necessary, for instance, when a single supplier is used so that economies of scale can help cut procurement costs. If the supplier's product is faulty, however, a large number of end products can be affected. Adding to this potential problem is the fact that most cars today are highly computerized, providing another layer of manufacturing complexity and requiring even more stringent checks for quality and safety.

These factors all combined to create what eventually would become a very costly, embarrassing and even tragic situation for Toyota starting in 2004 and lasting at least into 2010. Several of the events leading up to Toyota's recall crisis are listed below:

- 2000—Toyota launches a program to cut the costs of key auto parts by 30 percent. The program saves Toyota almost $10 billion by 2005.
- 2004—Problems with unintended acceleration of some vehicles are noticed by the U.S. National Highway Traffic Safety Administration (NHTSA).
- 2006—A surge in recalls for "quality glitches" causes delays in some new model introductions. Toyota has more U.S. recalls in 2006 than any other manufacturer.
- 2007—Toyota surpasses GM in global auto sales.
- 2007—Toyota recalls 55,000 U.S. vehicles for floormats entrapping gas pedals after a NTSA investigation.
- 2007—State Farm Insurance Co. tells NHTSA of a significant increase in accidents among policyholders involving Toyotas.
- 2007—Toyota attorney resigns, claiming he found numerous cases where Toyota withheld evidence from U.S. courts and government. Toyota disputes the claims.
- 2007—U.S. quality watchdog *Consumer Reports* magazine drops three Toyota models from its recommended list.
- Nov. 2009—Toyota recalls 4.2 million U.S. vehicles for floormats entrapping gas pedals.
- Jan. 21, 2010—Toyota recalls 2.3 million U.S. vehicles for "sticky" gas pedals.
- Jan. 26, 2010—Toyota halts U.S. sales of eight models involved in Jan. 21 recall.
- Jan. 27, 2010—Toyota recalls additional 1.1 million U.S. vehicles for floormats entrapping gas pedals.
- Jan. 29, 2010—NHTSA begins investigating Indiana-based CTS Corp. for making the sticky gas pedals used in Toyotas. CTS denies their gas pedals are at fault.

Global Perspective

Even the Best Can Stumble (continued)

- Feb. 2, 2010—Toyota falls to number three position in U.S. auto sales behind GM and Ford.
- Feb. 9, 2010—Toyota recalls 437,000 Prius and other hybrid autos worldwide for braking problems caused by faulty software. Toyota president publicly apologizes for quality and safety problems.

The very public apologies by president Akido Toyoda in early February 2010 began the long road to market share and reputation recovery for Toyota. They designed, tested and began installing a repair for the gas pedal/acceleration problem at about the same time, although by some measures it was too late in coming—complaints gathered by the U.S. government attributed as many as 34 traffic deaths over the decade to the sudden acceleration problem. In a second apology, and reading from an English-language statement, president Toyoda said, "We will do everything in our power to regain the confidence of our customers." Thus, while Toyota is credited for perfecting JIT and lean manufacturing, they apparently forgot what it was all about. It will be interesting to look back and see how Toyota has fared since the writing of this profile.[4]

Mr. Sakichi Toyoda invented the power loom in 1902 and in 1926 founded the Toyoda Automatic Loom Works. In 1937, he sold his loom patents to finance an automobile manufacturing plant to compete with Ford and General Motors; the new plant accounted for over 90 percent of the vehicles manufactured in Japan at the time. Sakichi's son Kiichiro Toyoda was named managing director of the new facility.[5]

Kiichiro spent a year in Detroit studying Ford's manufacturing system and others, and then returned to Japan, where he adapted what he learned to the production of small quantities of automobiles, using smaller, more frequently delivered batches of materials. This later was referred to as the just-in-time system within Toyota. Ford's system was designed such that parts were fabricated, delivered directly to the assembly line and then assembled onto a vehicle within just a few minutes. Henry Ford had called this *flow production*, the precursor to JIT.[6]

Mr. Eiji Toyoda, nephew of Sakichi, began working at Toyoda in 1936 and was named managing director of the renamed and reorganized Toyoda Automotive Works in 1950. Eiji, too, traveled to Detroit to study Ford's automobile manufacturing system and was particularly impressed with their quality improvement activities, most notably their employee suggestion system. He was also impressed with Ford's daily automobile output of 7,000 cars, compared to Toyota's cumulative thirteen-year output of just 2,700 cars. Back in Japan, he implemented the concepts he had seen in the U.S., and this became the foundation of what was later referred to as the Toyota Production System.

In 1957, the company was again renamed and became the Toyota Company. They introduced their first U.S. car that year—the Toyopet Crown. While popular in Japan, the car's quality, speed and styling problems resulted in sales of only 288 units in fourteen months in the U.S. Consequently, Toyota withdrew from the U.S. market, to better analyze U.S. consumers and their demands for reliability. "No detail was unimportant, and they paid very close attention to customers," says Dave Cole, chairman of the Michigan-based Centre for Automotive Research. In 1965, the Corona was introduced in the U.S., and by

1972, U.S. sales had reached 1 million units.[7] In 1982, Eiji established Toyota Motor Sales USA, and finally, in 1983, Eiji renamed the firm the Toyota Motor Corporation.

Taiichi Ohno began his career at the Toyoda Automatic Loom Works in 1932. He eventually expanded on the concepts established by Kiichiro and Eiji, developing and refining methods to produce items only as they were needed for assembly. He visited Detroit several times to observe auto manufacturing techniques. After World War II, the Toyoda production facilities were rebuilt, with Taiichi playing a major role in establishing the low-batch production principles he developed earlier. These principles proved very valuable at the time, since postwar Japan was experiencing severe materials shortages. What Taiichi and Eiji had both realized during their trips to the U.S. was the tremendous waste everywhere (referred to as **muda** in Japan). These wastes of labor, inventories, space, time and processing were certainly things Toyoda could not afford. From this realization came the idea that parts should be produced only as needed by the next step in an entire production process. When a type of signal or card (called a **kanban**) was used, the system became much more effective. This began to be called the *kanban system* or JIT system within Toyoda.

Refinements to the JIT concepts continued under Taiichi's tutelage, and he later attributed the system to two things—Henry Ford's autobiography, wherein he explained the Ford manufacturing system (now considered the forerunner of modern lean systems); and U.S. supermarket operations characterized by daily supply deliveries, which Ohno observed during a visit to the U.S. in 1956. The final two notable people in the development of the Toyota Production System were Shigeo Shingo, a quality consultant hired by Toyota, and W. Edwards Deming, who happened to be in Japan after the war helping to conduct the census and who had begun attending professional meetings to discuss statistical quality control techniques. In the 1950s in Japan, Deming created and discussed his fourteen-point quality management guidelines, as well as his ideas for continuous improvement, with many Japanese manufacturing engineers and managers.

Shingo developed the concept of **poka-yoke** in 1961, when he was employed at Toyota. Poka-yoke means error- or mistake-proofing. The idea is to design processes such that mistakes or defects are prevented from occurring in the first place, and if they do occur, further errors are also prevented. These fail-safe mechanisms can be electrical, mechanical, visual, procedural or any other method that prevents problems, errors or defects, and they can be implemented anywhere in the organization. Poka-yoke thus leads to higher levels of quality and customer service.[8]

By 1959, Toyota was making 100,000 cars per year. In the latter part of the 1950s, however, as mentioned earlier, they were experiencing quality problems that were impacting potential sales in the U.S. To remedy this, Toyota implemented what they referred to as total quality control (TQC) in concert with their JIT system. This then became the final piece of the Toyota Production System, and was later refined and renamed total quality management (TQM). Interestingly, in the first quarter of 2007, Toyota sold more vehicles worldwide than General Motors, ending GM's 76-year reign as the world's largest automaker.[9]

Actually, the term *lean production* did not originate at Toyota. It was first used in a benchmarking study conducted by the International Motor Vehicle Program (IMVP) at the Massachusetts Institute of Technology. The IMVP conducted a global automobile quality and productivity benchmarking study that culminated in the book *The Machine that Changed the World* in 1990, which presented the elements of lean production and the benchmarking results.[10] The word *lean* was suggested because the Japanese plants in the benchmarking study, when compared to their U.S. counterparts, used half the manufacturing labor, half the space and half the engineering hours to produce a new automobile model in half the time. They also used much less than half the average inventory levels to produce the same number of vehicles, and had far fewer defects.

The use of lean thinking has spread rapidly over the years among many manufacturers in numerous industries. Pennsylvania-based Industrial Scientific Corp., a gas detection instrument manufacturer, has been working with lean for about five years—today there are one-third fewer people on the manufacturing floor while output is up by 30 percent and order lead times have gone from two weeks to less than three days. Texas-based Photo Etch, an aerospace manufacturer, implemented lean and reduced their manufacturing lead times by half, while defects plummeted. They also now use 30 percent less floor space, which is allowing them to explore other business opportunities; "… the normal aerospace business has less than two turns of inventory," explains CEO Randy Fry. "We're at 7.5 and want to go to 15. That frees up a lot of cash."[11]

Finally, it should be emphasized that the lean thinking approach is suited for services, small businesses and nonprofits as well as manufacturing facilities. Implementing lean can start with something as simple as a watch. "Your first tool, if you're going to explore lean, probably should be a stopwatch so that you can just watch someone do what it is you need to do," explains lean practitioner Kevin Gingerich of Illinois-based Bosch Rexroth Linear Motion and Assembly Technologies. "You just time each piece of a manufacturing process or an assembly process, and you start to understand the wasted time involved."[12]

Many hospitals have implemented lean programs to improve employee productivity, improve patient flow (and thus reduce patient time at the hospital), and reduce materials costs. The Flinders Medical Centre in Australia used lean thinking to map patient flow in their emergency care area and was able to reduce emergency room congestion and decrease by 50 percent the number of people leaving without completing their care.[13] Small businesses, too, can benefit—Mike Shanahan, co-owner of Connecticut-based small manufacturer Cadco, Ltd., used lean thinking to speed up the production of warming trays and revise the layout of their facility. According to Mr. Shanahan, "The concept of lean is nothing like we thought it would be. It doesn't have to be complicated, unruly or expensive. In my eyes, it's all about finding the simplest way to accomplish a task or an operation. And its success can be measured in either small increments, astounding results or something in between. Either way, it can be applied to almost any operation or any size."[14] And finally, the U.S. Navy used lean thinking to analyze their ordnance requisition and shipping process. They mapped the requisition process while measuring the touches and the process time for each step. As a result of several changes, they reduced their requisition cycle time by about 50 percent, and their backlog of orders decreased.[15]

Lean Thinking and Supply Chain Management

Simply put, the objective of supply chain management is to balance the flow of materials with customer requirements throughout the supply chain, such that costs, quality and customer service are at optimal levels. Lean production emphasizes reduction of waste, continuous improvement, and the synchronization of material flows from within the organization and eventually including the organization's first-tier suppliers and customers. In many respects, then, supply chain management seeks to incorporate lean thinking across the entire supply chain. Supply chain management encourages cross-training, satisfying internal customer demand, moving products through the production system quickly, and communicating end-customer demand forecasts and production schedules up the supply chain. In addition, it seeks to optimize inventory levels across the entire supply chain.

Further, when implemented within the focal firm and among its supply chain trading partners, the realized benefits of lean are much more significant.

Recently, more and more firms have begun implementing lean strategies along their supply chains. When *Logistics Management* magazine conducted lean surveys among hundreds of their manufacturing subscribers in 2005 and 2008, they saw significant growth in the percentages of firms adopting most of the lean supply chain attributes in the surveys, such as the adoption of data standards and process standardization among supply chain partners.[16]

A number of good examples of using lean across the supply chain exist. For example, the $20 billion global personal care product company Kimberly-Clark used lean thinking to reduce their North American network of 70 distribution centers to nine regional mega-centers. From 2006 to 2008, this leaner network resulted in 24 million fewer miles traveled between Kimberly-Clark distribution centers and client locations, saving millions of gallons of diesel fuel. Additionally, it actually reduced the average transit times to many of their customers.[17] Recently, Pennsylvania-based thermoform manufacturer McClarin Plastics presented lean certification sessions to its employees, suppliers and customers to lean out their supply chains. The goals were to reduce waste, supplier turnover and manufacturing space and time. "This will bring everyone involved in a related supply chain together to learn how their performance affects others. The positive bottom line impact from the resulting relationships and understanding could be huge," explains Roger Kirk, vice president of marketing and engineering at McClarin.[18]

Many firms do not implement all of the lean activities but rather, select elements based on resources, product characteristics, customer needs and supplier capabilities. Coffeehouse giant Starbucks has a V.P. of lean thinking who travels from region to region with his lean team, looking for ways to reduce the wasted movements of its baristas. This in turn gives baristas more time to interact with customers and improve the Starbucks experience. The results are streamlined operations, happier customers and a better bottom line.[19]

Organizations that are successfully managing their supply chains evolve through four stages, as shown in Table 8.1. In Stage 1, the firm is internally focused, organizational functions are managed separately, and performance is monitored based on achieving departmental goals. This **silo effect** causes the firm to be reactive and short-term-goal oriented. At this stage, no internal functional integration is occurring.

In Stage 2, the firm has begun integrating efforts and resources among internal functions. In this stage, the focus of the firm has started to shift toward an emphasis on the flow of goods and information through the firm to achieve production efficiencies and reduce throughput times.

In Stage 3, internal integration of goods and information has been achieved, and the focus begins to shift toward linking suppliers and customers to the firm's processes. Thus, at this stage, there is an emphasis on using logistics capabilities to manage the movement and storage of goods from inbound material deliveries to internal part movements, to outbound product distribution. Lean production activities can begin to be used as the firm realizes the impact of reduced throughput times on customer service and inventory cost. As inventory levels are reduced, the need for improved quality and response times from suppliers is magnified, and firms begin to take a more proactive approach to managing and developing their suppliers' lean capabilities. Since successful use of lean production activities also impacts the firm's customers in terms of better quality products more flexibility and faster delivery times, firms realize the need to proactively manage their customers' lean capabilities as well.

Table 8.1	Supply Chain Management Evolution		
Stage 1: **Internally Focused**	**Stage 2:** **Functional Integration**	**Stage 3:** **Internal Integration**	**Stage 4:** **External integration**
• Functional silos • Top-down management • Internal measures used to monitor performance • Reactive, short-term planning • No internal integration	• Focus on internal flow of goods • Emphasis on cost reduction • Realization of efficiencies gained by internal integration	• Realization of integration of goods flow throughout firm • Focus on logistics and lean production activities to manage flow of goods and information • Measurement of supplier performance and customer service performance	• Extending integration efforts to suppliers and customers • Realization of need to control goods and information to 2nd- and 3rd-tier suppliers, customers • Emphasis on alliance development and communication capabilities

Source: Adapted from Stevens, G. C., "Integrating the Supply Chain," *International Journal of Physical Distribution and Logistics Management* 19(8), 1989: 3–8.

Stage 4 is characterized by efforts to broaden the firm's supply chain influence beyond immediate or first-tier suppliers and customers, as well as strengthening relationships with existing key suppliers and customers. Firms have become comfortable with lean processes and are seeking ways to further improve the flow of information, as well as waste reduction, quality, flexibility and processing efficiencies. They begin to work with their most important suppliers and customers to aid in their respective lean implementation efforts. Supply chain management and external integration have become legitimate concerns at this stage.

Thus, throughout Stages 3 and 4, we see an emphasis on lean activities to integrate the firm's processes with its trading partners. The following section is a discussion of the lean elements.

The Elements of Lean

Table 8.2 presents the major lean elements that are discussed in this section of the chapter, along with a short description of each element. Readers should note that lean programs can vary significantly, based on a company's resource capabilities, product and process orientation, and past failures or successes with other improvement projects. Firms with a mature lean program will most likely be practicing a significant number of these elements.

Waste Reduction

One of the primary and long-term goals of all lean endeavors is waste reduction. The desired outcome of waste reduction is value enhancement. Firms can thus reduce costs and add value to their products and services by eliminating waste from their productive systems. Robert Martichenko, president of LeanCor LLC, a lean logistics consultancy based in Kentucky, points out that the best way to reduce waste is to "lower the water level" or slowly reduce inventories, until only what is crucial to a smooth production flow is left. Anything else is not necessary, and is therefore a waste that can be eliminated.[20]

Table 8.2	The Elements of Lean
ELEMENTS	**DESCRIPTION**
Waste reduction	Eliminating waste is the primary concern of the lean philosophy. Includes reducing excess inventories, material movements, production steps, scrap losses, rejects and rework.
Lean supply chain relationships	Firms work with buyers and customers with the mutual goal of eliminating waste, improving speed and improving quality. Key suppliers are considered partners, and close customer relationships are sought.
Lean layouts	WIP inventories are positioned close to each process, and layouts are designed where possible to reduce movements of people and materials. Processes are positioned to allow smooth flow of work through the facility.
Inventory and setup time reduction	Inventories are reduced by reducing production batch sizes, setup times and safety stocks. Tends to create or uncover processing problems, which are then managed and controlled.
Small batch scheduling	Firms produce frequent small batches of product, with frequent product changes to enable a level production schedule. Smaller, more frequent purchase orders are communicated to suppliers, and more frequent deliveries are offered to customers. *Kanbans* are used to pull WIP through the system.
Continuous improvement	As queues and lead times are reduced, problems surface more quickly, causing the need for continual attention to problem solving and process improvement. With lower safety stocks, quality levels must be high to avoid process shutdowns. Attention to supplier quality levels is high.
Workforce empowerment	Employees are cross-trained to add processing flexibility and to increase the workforce's ability to solve problems. Employees are trained to provide quality inspections as parts enter a process area. Employee roles are expanded, and employees are given top management support and resources to identify and fix problems.

Waste is a catch-all term encompassing things such as excess wait times, inventories, material and people movements, processing steps, variabilities and *any other non-value-adding activity.* Taiichi Ohno of Toyota described what he called the **seven wastes**, which have since been applied across many industries around the world, to identify and reduce waste. The seven wastes are shown and described in Table 8.3. The common term across the seven wastes is *excess*. Obviously, firms require some level of inventories, material and worker movements and processing time, but the idea is to determine the *right* levels of these things and then decide how best to achieve them.

Waste reduction is also a key objective in almost any green or sustainability program. The U.S. Government Printing Office (GPO), for example, focuses on decreasing waste through use of recycling programs. These efforts diverted over 64 percent of their total waste stream to recycling streams in 2008, which reduced greenhouse gas emissions by an estimated 15 billion tons.[21] The next section discusses this topic in greater detail.

Unfortunately, many companies view many forms of waste as simply a cost of doing business. To identify and eliminate waste, workers and managers must be continually assessing processes, methods and materials for their value contributions to the firm's salable products and services. This is accomplished through worker–management interactions and commitment to the continued elimination of waste, as well as frequent solicitation of feedback from customers. Significant waste reduction results in a number of positive outcomes including lower costs, shorter lead times, better quality and greater

Table 8.3	The Seven Wastes
WASTES	**DESCRIPTION**
Overproducing	Production of unnecessary items to maintain high utilizations.
Waiting	Excess idle machine and operator time; materials experiencing excess wait time for processing.
Transportation	Excess movement of materials between processing steps; transporting items long distances using multiple handling steps.
Overprocessing	Non-value-adding manufacturing, handling, packaging or inspection activities.
Excess inventory	Storage of excess raw materials, work-in-process and finished goods.
Excess movement	Unnecessary movements of employees to complete a task.
Scrap and rework	Scrap materials and product rework activities due to poor-quality materials or processing.

Source: Based in part on Avni, T., "Simulation Modeling Primer," *IIE Solutions* 31(9), 1999: 38–41.

competitiveness. With the recent economic downturn, eliminating waste can enable firms to stay profitable while sales levels have declined. Implementing lean programs has thus seen an increase in popularity over the past few years.

Using the Five-Ss to Reduce Waste

Another method used for waste reduction has been termed the **Five-Ss**. The original Five-Ss came from Toyota and were Japanese words relating to industrial housekeeping. The idea is that by implementing the Five-Ss, the workplace will be cleaner, more organized and safer, thereby reducing processing waste and improving productivity. California-based APL Logistics has been practicing lean and uses the Five-Ss to improve safety and productivity in their warehouses. "The Five-Ss tell everyone that everything has a place. We have every kind of visual indicator of what you do for safety in our facility. When things are in order, it is easier for employees to find product. It is a more disciplined environment, which gives employees more pride in their job," says general manger Doug Tatum.[22] Table 8.4 lists and describes each of these terms, and presents the equivalent S-terms used in the English version of the Five-S system.

Table 8.4	The Five-Ss		
JAPANESE S-TERM	**ENGLISH TRANSLATION**	**ENGLISH S-TERM IN USE**	
1. Seiri	Organization	Sort	
2. Seiton	Tidiness	Set in order	
3. Seiso	Purity	Sweep	
4. Seiketsu	Cleanliness	Standardize	
5. Shitsuke	Discipline	Self-discipline	

Source: Becker, J., "Implementing 5S: To Promote Safety & Housekeeping," *Professional Safety* 46(8), 2001: 29–31.

The goals of the first two (*seiri*/sorting and *seiton*/simplifying) are to eliminate searching for parts and tools, avoid unnecessary movements and avoid using the wrong tools or parts. Work area tools and materials are evaluated for their appropriateness, and approved items are arranged and stored near their place of use. *Seiso*/sweep refers to proper workplace cleaning and maintenance, while *seiketsu*/standardize seeks to reduce processing variabilities by eliminating nonstandard activities and resources. *Shitsuke*/self-discipline deals with forming and refining effective work habits.

The Five-S system can be employed in any service or manufacturing environment. Many lean efforts begin with implementation of the Five-Ss. Firms conduct a "waste hunt" using the Five-Ss and then follow up with a "red-tag event" to remove or further evaluate all inessential, red-tagged items. Some companies have also added a sixth-S, for safety, to assess the safety of work conditions and reduce the risk profile of the work area.[23]

Lean Supply Chain Relationships

Quite commonly, firms must hold safety stocks of purchased products because their suppliers' delivery times are inconsistent or the quality of the purchased goods do not always meet specifications. Internally, extra work-in-process inventories are stored as a way to deal with temperamental processing equipment or other variabilities causing processing problems. On the distribution side, firms hold stocks of finished goods in warehouses prior to shipment to customers, in some cases for months at a time, to avoid stockouts and maintain customer service levels. Holding these inbound, internal and outbound inventories costs the firm money while not adding much, if any value to the products or the firm; thus, they are considered wastes.

When the focal firm, its suppliers and its customers begin to work together to identify customer requirements, remove wastes, reduce costs and improve quality and customer service, it marks the beginning of lean supply chain relationships. Kentucky-based homebuilder Jagoe Homes began implementing a lean program a few years ago with their employees and subcontractors, and is now seeing significant benefits in several areas, despite a weak housing market. "That led us to our philosophy that we want a small number of extremely capable trades (subcontractors) with low turnover. Lean gives both the builder and the trade partners the tools to eliminate waste, reduce cost and remain competitive, by working together," says co-owner Brad Jagoe. "Another big thing with lean is that, although we have tremendously reduced waste, the specs in our houses have actually increased. A lot of our competitors have just cheapened the house. But by eliminating waste, wasted trips and non-value-added items, we've been able to increase the features that customers value," he adds.[24]

Using lean thinking with suppliers includes having them deliver smaller quantities, more frequently, to the point of use at the focal firm. This serves to reduce average inventory levels. More frequent deliveries, though, mean higher inbound transportation costs; to reduce these costs, suppliers often distribute products from warehouses or production facilities located near the buyer. To entice suppliers to make these investments in warehouses, buyers in many cases must use fewer suppliers so they can give suppliers a greater share of their purchasing needs.

Making small, frequent purchases from just a few suppliers puts the focal firm in a position of greater dependence on these suppliers. It is therefore extremely important that deliveries always be on time, delivered to the right location, in the right quantities and be of high quality, since existing inventories will be lower. To encourage closer

relationships and better collaboration with its best suppliers, consumer products company Procter & Gamble holds an annual "Goldmine Day," for instance, where suppliers
can meet with each other and with Procter & Gamble to share ideas and information.
"I like that P&G was telling us of its plans and that the company would not be able to
get where it wants to go without the collective ideas of its partners," said one participant.
"The event probably got a lot of the strategic partners talking to one another more than
they were prior to the event," he added.[25]

Firms can also use lean thinking with their key customers. As these relationships
develop, the focal firm begins to reserve greater levels of capacity for a smaller number
of large, steady customers. They locate production or warehousing facilities close to
these customers and make frequent small deliveries of finished products to their points
of use within the customers' facilities, thus reducing transportation times and average
inventory levels. Lean thinking with customers means determining how to give them
exactly what they want when they want it, while minimizing waste as much as possible.
At MeadWestvaco's paper mill in Alabama, they use customer feedback to influence
plant investments that ultimately result in better product quality and acceptability.
"Without question, customers are driving our business model," says Jack Goldfrank,
coated board division president. The company conducts a customer survey every
eighteen months to assess product, service, reputation, practices, price and value. The
surveys allow them to determine where customers want improvements, and if any
trends exist.[26]

It can be seen, then, that mutual dependencies and mutual benefits occur among all of
these **lean supply chain relationships**, resulting in increased product value and competitiveness for all of the partners.

Lean Layouts

The primary design objective with **lean layouts** is to reduce wasted movements of
workers, customers and/or work-in-process (WIP), and achieve smooth product flow
through the facility. Moving parts and people around the production floor does not add
value. Lean layouts allow people and materials to move only when and where they are
needed, as quickly as possible. Thus, whenever possible, processing centers, offices or
departments that frequently transfer parts, customers or workers between them should
be located close together, to minimize this movement or time waste.

Lean layouts are very visual, meaning that lines of visibility are unobstructed, making
it easy for operators at one processing center to monitor work occurring at other centers.
In manufacturing facilities, all purchased and WIP inventories are located on the production floor at their points of use, and the good visibility makes it easy to spot inventory buildups when bottlenecks occur. When these and other production problems
occur, they are spotted and rectified quickly. The relative closeness of the processing centers facilitates teamwork and joint problem solving and requires less floor space than
conventional production layouts.

Lean layouts allow problems to be tracked to their source more quickly as well. As
material and parts flow from one processing center to the next, a quality problem,
when found, can generally be traced to the previous work center, provided inspections
are performed at each processing stage. In the U.K., the British Aerospace Military
Aircraft facility at Yorkshire was redesigned using lean concepts. One of the goals was to
eliminate the non-value-added days where components sat between processing stages.

After rearranging the layout, some parts that had traveled 3 kilometers during processing, moved only one-tenth of that distance. In addition, it was projected that productivity would increase by 20 percent and inventory levels would fall by 55 percent.[27]

Manufacturing Cells

Manufacturing cells or **work cells** are designed to process any parts, components or jobs requiring the same or similar processing steps, saving duplication of equipment and labor. These similarly processed parts are termed **part families**. In many cases these manufacturing cells are U-shaped to facilitate easier operator and material movements within the cell. In assembly line facilities, manufacturing cells are positioned close to the line, feeding finished components directly to the line instead of delivering them to a stock area where they would be brought back out when needed. Manufacturing cells are themselves actually small assembly lines and are designed to be flexible, allowing machine configurations to change as processing requirements dictate.

Inventory and Setup Time Reduction

In lean parlance, excess inventories are considered a waste, since they tend to hide a number of purchasing, production and quality problems within the organization. Just as water hides boat-damaging rocks beneath its surface, so excess inventory hides value-damaging problems along the supply chain. And, just as reducing water levels causes rocks to become detectable, so too the reduction of inventory levels causes problems to surface in the organization and among its trading partners. Once these problems are detected, they can be solved, improving product value and allowing the system to run more effectively with lower inventory investment. For example, reducing safety stocks of purchased materials will cause stockouts and potential manufacturing disruptions when late deliveries occur. Firms must then either find a way to resolve the delivery problem with the supplier or find a more reliable supplier. Either way, the end result is a smoother-running supply chain with less inventory investment. The same story can be applied to production machinery. Properly maintained equipment breaks down less often, so less safety stock is needed to keep downstream processing areas fed with parts to be further processed.

Another way to reduce inventory levels is to reduce purchase order quantities and production lot sizes. Figure 8.1 illustrates this point. When order quantities and lot sizes are cut in half, average inventories are also cut in half, assuming usage remains constant. Unfortunately, this means that the firm must make more purchase orders (potentially increasing annual order costs). Thus, ordering costs must be reduced, which can be accomplished by automating or simplifying the purchasing process as discussed in Chapter 2.

Since reducing manufacturing lot sizes means increasing the number of **setups**, and since setting up production equipment for the next production run takes valuable time, increasing the number of setups means the firm must find ways to reduce setup times. Setup times can be reduced in a number of ways including doing setup preparation work while the previous production lot is still being processed, moving machine tools closer to the machines, improving tooling or die couplings, standardizing setup procedures, practicing various methods to reduce setup times, and purchasing machines that require less setup time.

Finally, once inventories have been reduced and the flow problems uncovered and solved, the firm can reduce inventories still further, uncovering yet another set of problems to be solved. With each inventory reduction iteration, the firm runs leaner, cheaper, faster and with higher levels of product quality.

Figure 8.1	Relationship between Order Quantity, Lot Size and Average Inventory

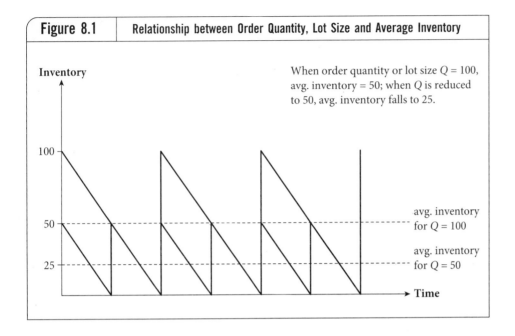

When order quantity or lot size $Q = 100$, avg. inventory = 50; when Q is reduced to 50, avg. inventory falls to 25.

Small Batch Scheduling

Saying that a manufacturer should purchase small quantities, more frequently, from good suppliers, and should produce items using small lot sizes with more setups is one thing, but actually accomplishing this feat is something else. Many firms have tried and failed, eventually returning to carrying higher levels of inventory and producing with large lot sizes, rather than dealing with the many problems accompanying lean production. Use of level schedules of small batches, however, communicated throughout the production process and to outside suppliers, is what is needed to accomplish lean production.

Small batch scheduling drives down costs by reducing purchased, WIP and finished-goods inventories, and it also makes the firm more flexible to meet varying customer demand. Figure 8.2 illustrates this point: In the same period of time, the firm with small lot sizes and short setup times can change products nine times, while the firm with large lot sizes and long setup times can only change products three times (and has yet to produce any units of product D). Maintaining a set, level, small batch production schedule will allow suppliers to anticipate and schedule deliveries also, resulting in fewer late deliveries.

Texas-based National Coupling Co. has been using lean manufacturing since 2002 and today can produce about 1,500 coupling assemblies per week, with setups involving 60 to 80 product families. This equates to about six assemblies every ten minutes on their assembly line. "With setups reduced to less than five minutes, we can maintain a high-velocity, high variability production line," says Ken Oberholz, vice president of operations. This flexibility allows them to always make the right assemblies at the right time, with everything driven by customer requirements. "In an emergency we can drop a coupling order in the front of the line and 90 minutes later they're in assembly, and that's without interrupting production," adds Oberholz.[28]

Moving small production batches through a lean production facility is often accomplished with the use of **kanbans**. The Japanese word *kanban* has several meanings in

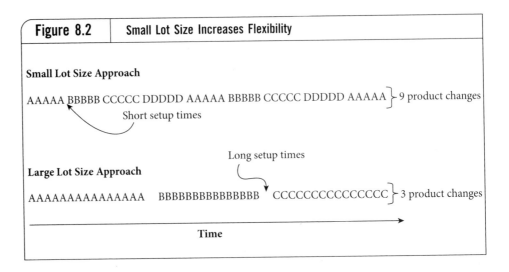

Figure 8.2 | **Small Lot Size Increases Flexibility**

Japan—it can refer to a shop sign or billboard, as in "The Donut Shoppe," or more historically, to a uniform worn by servants of the samurai to indicate they acted on the authority of their clan or lord. Mr. Chihiro Nakao, a former Toyota manager who worked directly with Taiichi Ohno, recalls a story about the origins of the word *kanban* at Toyota—Mr. Ohno supposedly caught a worker trying to pull materials early from an upstream workcenter to create some safety stock and he yelled, "Who are you and where did you come from?! What makes you think you have any right to this material?! Show me your kanban!"[29] This became the origin of the more modern "permission slip" or "authority" definition of the word kanban. In lean facilities it has come to simply refer to a signal. When manufacturing cells need parts or materials, they use a kanban to signal their need for items from the upstream manufacturing cell, processing unit, or external supplier providing the needed material. In this way, nothing is provided until a downstream demand occurs. That is why a lean system is also known as a **pull system**. Ideally, parts are placed in standardized containers, and kanbans exist for each container. Figure 8.3 illustrates how a kanban pull system works. When finished components are moved from Work Cell B to the final assembly line, the following things occur:

1. The container holding finished parts in Work Cell B's output area is emptied and a **production kanban** (a light, flag or sign) is used to tell Work Cell B to begin processing more components to restock the empty container in its output area.

2. During this stage, when parts are moved from Work Cell B's input area to its processing area, the container holding these parts is emptied and a **withdrawal kanban** (a light, flag or sign) is used to indicate to Work Cell A that more parts are needed. This authorizes a full container of parts to move from Work Cell A's output area to Work Cell B's input area, and the empty container is moved to Work Cell A's output area.

3. As this movement occurs, a production kanban is used to authorize Work Cell A to begin processing parts to restock its empty container in the output area.

4. Finally, as full containers of parts are emptied and used in Work Cell A's processing area, the emptied containers in Work Cell A's input area create a withdrawal kanban seen by the external supplier, who then restocks Work Cell A's empty containers in the input area.

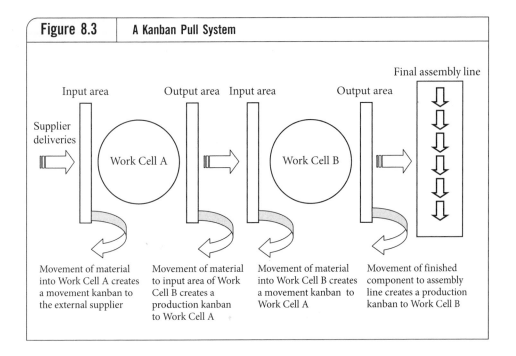

Figure 8.3   A Kanban Pull System

Final assembly line

Input area   Output area   Input area   Output area

Supplier deliveries

Work Cell A

Work Cell B

Movement of material into Work Cell A creates a movement kanban to the external supplier

Movement of material to input area of Work Cell B creates a production kanban to Work Cell A

Movement of material into Work Cell B creates a movement kanban to Work Cell A

Movement of finished component to assembly line creates a production kanban to Work Cell B

Thus, it can be seen that kanbans are used to control the flow of inventory through the facility. Inventories are not allowed to accumulate beyond the size of each container and the number of containers in the system. When containers are full, production stops until another production kanban is encountered. The U.K.-based cutting tool manufacturer Dormer Tools, for example, implemented lean production to better compete with Chinese manufacturers. Machines were prioritized using kanban cards, which helped to reduce WIP inventories by 25 percent and reduce lead times from twelve weeks to four.[30]

A simple relationship can be used to determine the number of containers or kanban card sets for a lean production system:

$$\text{No. of containers} = \frac{DT(1 + S)}{C},$$

where

D = the demand rate of the assembly line;

T = the time for a container to make an entire circuit through the system, from being filled, moved, being emptied, and returned to be filled again;

C = the container size, in number of parts; and

S = the safety stock factor, from 0 to 100 percent.

For example, suppose the assembly line demand is twenty of Part 1 per hour for Work Cell B, and the standard container used for this part holds five Part 1's. If it takes two hours for a container to make a circuit from Work Cell B to the assembly line and back again, and if it is desired to carry 10 percent excess of Part 1 in the system, then the number of containers needed in the system is 8.8 or 9, when rounding up. The maximum inventory for this system would then be the total number of containers times the container size, or 45 units. Finally, reducing inventory in the system (one of the objectives of lean production) occurs by reducing the number of containers. Consequently, when the number of containers is reduced, the circuit time for each container would also have to be reduced to enable the demand to be met. This can be done by reducing setup time, processing time, wait time, move time or some combination of these.

Continuous Improvement

As alluded to already, lean systems are never-ending works in progress. Compact layouts are designed to allow work to flow sequentially and quickly through the facility. Inventory is moved from supplier delivery vehicles to the shop floor and placed in containers in designated work cell storage areas.

Purchase orders and production batches are small. In this system, problems often will surface, at least initially, as suppliers struggle to deliver frequently and on time, and as workers strive to maintain output levels while spending more time during the day, setting up machines for small production runs. To make the lean system work better, employees continuously seek ways to reduce supplier delivery and quality problems, and in the production area they solve movement problems, visibility problems, machine breakdown problems, machine setup problems and internal quality problems. In Japanese manufacturing facilities, this is known as **kaizen**.

Once the problems created by the small batch sizes are solved, removal of an inventory container from one of the work cells starts the problem-solving cycle all over again—thus the need for continuous improvement in all lean systems. Until things are always where they need to be, at the expected time and in the right quality and quantity, improvements must be sought.

Quality improvement is certainly part of the ongoing continuous improvement efforts in lean systems. For example, receiving a batch of goods from an external supplier or an internal work cell that does not satisfy design requirements is like not getting a shipment at all. Because of low safety stock levels, processing areas needing these supplies will very quickly be out of stock and unable to work. High-quality levels are then necessary throughout the production system to meet demand. Further discussion of quality and continuous improvement can be found in the next section of this chapter.

Workforce Commitment

Since lean systems depend so much on waste reduction and continuous improvement for their success, dedicated employees must play a significant role in this process. Managers must show strong support for lean production efforts by providing subordinates with the skills, tools, time and other necessary resources to identify process problems and implement solutions. Managers must create a culture in which workers are encouraged to speak out when problems exist. At the Scania engine plant in Sweden, the facility is idled every Wednesday at 8 a.m. for 26 minutes so every work team can hold an improvement meeting based on ideas on a whiteboard. Workers check the progress of each open idea, remove those that have been completed, and discuss new ones that were posted during the week. If additional resources or approvals are required, ideas move up to the whiteboard of the next level of management. All boards are public. Top management's whiteboard is placed in the middle of the plant where everyone can see what is being worked on.[31]

In lean manufacturing systems, employees are cross-trained in many of the various production processes to enable capacities to be adjusted at different work cells as needed when machines break down or workers are absent. Employees are given time during their day to work on reducing machine setup times as well as solve other production problems as they occur. They are also expected to perform a number of quality checks on processed items coming into the work cell. When quality problems are found, workers are empowered to shut down the production process until the source of the problem can be found and corrected. Most employees who work for lean companies enjoy their jobs; they are given a number of responsibilities and are considered one of the most important parts of a successful lean organization.

Lean Systems and the Environment

In Chapter 4, the topics of ethical and sustainable procurement were introduced, and their importance to supply chain management was discussed. Since lean systems are ultimately concerned with waste reduction throughout the firm and its supply chains, the linkage between lean and environmental sustainability should be clear.

Many organizations have realized the positive impact lean systems can have on the environment—adopting lean practices reduces waste, the cost of environmental management, and also leads to improved environmental performance. Further, lean systems increase the possibility that firms will adopt more advanced environmental management systems, leading to yet further performance improvements. Professors King and Lennox analyzed thousands of companies in the early 1990s and found ample evidence of this linkage between the concept of lean and environmental sustainability. They found that firms minimizing inventories and adopting quality standards were more likely to practice pollution prevention and also had lower toxic chemical emissions.[32]

Other examples abound. Illinois-based Hospira, maker of pharmaceutical products, is not only dedicated to eliminating waste in all areas of production, but is also making headway on reducing the 2.4 billion pounds of waste that hospitals produce every year in the U.S.. As an example, Hospira developed and launched a new IV (intravenous) bag that produces 40–70 percent less waste than other flexible IV bags.[33] At New Jersey-based printing company Pictorial Offset Corp., managements' desire to reduce waste led them to remove 300 chemical products from the plant and begin recycling corrugated and steel strapping waste. The firm has achieved a number of industry environmental firsts, including obtaining the ISO 9000 and ISO 14000 certifications simultaneously. They are also recognized as being **carbon-neutral** in part by planting 5,000 trees in New Jersey to offset the carbon footprint of its operations. These practices have also helped Pictorial Offset's sales—they have gained a number of new clients who sought out the printing firm because of their environmental reputation.[34] In an effort to reduce waste and save money, automaker GM announced that by the end of 2010, half of its manufacturing facilities would become landfill-free. Recycled aluminum is used in making engine components, waste oil is reconditioned for reuse, and its recycled metal scrap sales alone bring in over $1 billion per year. And finally, Kansas-based print cartridge remanufacturer InkCycle has used lean thinking to modify their manufacturing process to reuse original components a greater number of times, and they are converting their automotive fleet to hybrid vehicles.[35]

As we have shown in this first portion of the chapter, creating lean processes is a necessary element in successful supply chain management. A second, equally necessary element is the practice of continuous quality improvement. And one of the best examples of this is Six Sigma quality. A discussion of Six Sigma quality and its relationship to supply chain management follows.

The Origins of Six Sigma Quality

Six Sigma quality, often referred to simply as Six Sigma, was pioneered by global communications leader Motorola in 1987. It is a statistics-based decision-making framework designed to make significant quality improvements in value-adding processes. Six Sigma (with capital Ss) is a registered trademark of Motorola. In the 1980s, a senior staff engineer at Motorola named Mikel Harry formed a team of engineers to experiment with problem solving using statistical analyses, and this became the foundation for Six Sigma. Richard Schroeder, the company's vice president of customer service, heard about Harry's work and applied the methodology to his own work at Motorola. Soon, both groups were announcing large reductions in errors and related costs. Ultimately, both men left Motorola and formed the Six Sigma Academy. Today, the firm has been renamed SSA & Company and is based in New York City.[36]

Quality perfection is represented by the term Six Sigma, which refers to the statistical likelihood that 99.99966 percent of the time, a process sample average will fall inside a control limit placed 4.5 standard deviations (or sigmas) above the true process mean, assuming the process is in control. This represents the goal of having a defect occur in a process only 0.00034 percent of the time, or 3.4 times out of every million measurement opportunities—very close to perfection. This description makes it sound like the methodology should be called 4½ sigma. The 1½ sigma difference is the subject of much debate, and refers to a somewhat confusing term called **sigma drift**.[37] Sigma drift posits that process variations will grow over time as process measurements drift off target. In truth, any process exhibiting a change in process variation of 1.5 standard deviations would be detected using quality control charts, instigating an improvement effort to get the process back on target. Table 8.5 shows the **defects per million opportunities (DPMO)** to be expected for various sigmas, using the Six Sigma methodology.

Table 8.5	Six Sigma DPMO Metrics	
NO. STANDARD DEVIATIONS ABOVE THE MEAN	**PERCENT OF DEFECT-FREE OUTPUT**	**DEFECTS PER MILLION OPPORTUNITIES (DPMO)**
2	69.15	308,537
2.5	84.13	158,686
3	93.32	66,807
3.5	97.73	22,750
4	99.38	6,210
4.5	99.865	1,350
5	99.977	233
5.5	99.9968	32
6	99.99966	3.4

Note: Standard deviations include 1.5 sigma "drift."

The Six Sigma concept, however, is not just concerned with statistics. It is a broad improvement strategy that includes the concepts and tools of total quality management (TQM), a focus on the customer, performance measurement and formal training in quality control methods. Six Sigma embodies more of an organizational culture wherein everyone from CEO to production worker to frontline service employee is involved in quality assessment and improvement. Six Sigma is proactive in nature and seeks to permanently fix the root causes of problems, instead of repeatedly spending time and money tinkering with and patching up processes as problems occur in the business. In Six Sigma, sources of process variation are sought out and remedied prior to the time these variations can cause production and customer satisfaction problems.

Today, many organizations practice Six Sigma, including early adopters Honeywell, General Electric and Dow Chemical. In 1999, Ford Motor Company became the first U.S. automaker to adopt the Six Sigma strategy. Automobile manufacturing provides a great example of the need for Six Sigma thinking. Since automobiles have roughly 20,000 **opportunities for a defect to occur (OFD)**, and assuming an automobile company operates at an impressive 5½ sigma level (32 DPMO), this would equate to about one defect for every two cars produced. Improving to the Six Sigma level would mean about one defect for every 15 automobiles produced. Calculating the DPMO can be accomplished using the following formula:

$$DPMO = \frac{\text{number of defects}}{(\text{OFD per unit})(\text{number of units})} \times 1,000,000$$

Example 8.1 illustrates the calculation of DPMO and the use of the Six Sigma DPMO metrics shown in Table 8.5.

Increasingly, companies are using Six Sigma programs to generate cost savings or increased sales through process improvements. In fact, Motorola at one time stated that their savings from the use of Six Sigma had exceeded $17 billion.[38] This type of outcome is possible as firms identify customer requirements, uncover all of the opportunities for errors or defects to occur, review performance against Six Sigma performance standards, and then take the actions necessary to achieve those standards. The most successful projects meet strategic business objectives, reduce product and service variations to optimal levels, and produce a product or service that satisfies the customer.

Example 8.1   Calculating DPMO for Blakester's Speedy Pizza

Blake, owner of Blakester's Speedy Pizza, a home delivery pizza operation, keeps track of customer complaints. For each pizza delivery, there are three possible causes of complaints: a late delivery, a cold pizza or an incorrect pizza. Each week, Blake calculates the rate of delivery "defects" per total pizza deliveries, and then uses this information to determine his company's Six Sigma quality level. During the past week, his company delivered 620 pizzas. His drivers received sixteen late delivery complaints, nineteen cold pizza complaints and five incorrect pizza complaints.

Blake's defects per million opportunities is:

$$DPMO = \frac{\text{number of defects}}{(\text{OFD per unit})(\text{number of units})} \times 1,000,000$$

$$= \frac{40}{(3)(620)} \times 1,000,000 = 21,505 \text{ defective pizza deliveries per million.}$$

From Table 8.5, it can be concluded that Blakester's is operating at slightly better than 3.5 Sigma.

"This is where we pick up each unit
and shake out the quality defects."

Source: © 1999 Ted Goff www.tedgoff.com

Like all improvement programs, however, Six Sigma cannot guarantee continued or even initial business success. Poor management decisions and investments, and a company culture not conducive to change, can undermine even the best Six Sigma program. Ironically, Six Sigma originator Motorola has struggled financially for a number of years and has laid off tens of thousands of workers since 2000.[39] Camera and film maker Polaroid, another early user of Six Sigma, filed for Chapter 11 bankruptcy protection in 2001, and the following year they sold their name and all assets to a subsidiary of Illinois-based Bank One Corp.[40]

Comparing Six Sigma and Lean

Six Sigma and lean thinking actually have many similarities. For lean practices to be successful, purchased parts and assemblies, work-in-process and finished goods must all meet or exceed quality requirements. Also, recall that one of the elements of lean is continuous improvement, and these are the areas where the practice of Six Sigma can be put to good use in a lean system. Evidence suggests that firms are now pursuing both of these initiatives simultaneously. The Avery Point Group, an executive search firm headquartered in Connecticut, did a sampling of Internet job board postings and found that about half of the companies seeking candidates with one of the two skill sets wanted the other skill set as well. Tim Noble, managing principal of Avery Point Group explains, "Core to both methodologies is the idea that challenges need to be approached with an open mind, because solutions can sometimes come from the most unlikely of sources. True Six Sigma and lean practitioners will view this marriage with an open mind and realize that these are truly complementary tool sets, not competing philosophies."[41]

Successful companies over the long term must ultimately offer high-quality goods at reasonable prices while providing a high level of customer service. Rearranging factory floor layouts and reducing batch sizes and setup times will reduce manufacturing lead times and inventory levels, providing better delivery performance and lower cost. These are lean production activities. Use of statistical quality control charts to monitor processes, creating long-term relationships with high-quality suppliers and reducing delivery problems fall under the purview of Six Sigma. This short explanation describes how the two concepts can work together to achieve better overall firm performance. Lean production is all about reducing waste, while Six Sigma is all about improving quality.

Lean Six

A term is now being used to describe the melding of lean production and Six Sigma quality practices—**Lean Six Sigma**, or simply **Lean Six**. In 2009, for example, the U.S. Navy commissioned the nuclear aircraft carrier U.S.S. George H. W. Bush, built by global security company Northrop Grumman using lean manufacturing and Six Sigma extensively to improve quality, reduce costs and shorten cycle time. Since 2007, the U.S. Defense Department's Lean Six Sigma office has completed more than 330 projects and trained more than 1,000 officials on the techniques of Lean Six, allowing them to take on new projects themselves. Further, more than 30,000 department employees have been trained in Lean Six. After posting financial losses in 2008, Swiss chemical company Clariant replaced their CEO, who began a multiyear restructuring program to generate cash and reduce spending. Lean Six is being used to supplement these efforts.[42] Texas-based oilfield services company Halliburton used Lean Six as a way to improve their suppliers' performance and to improve customer service in the face of increased oilfield demand. Their experiences are highlighted in the e-Business Connection feature.

And finally, after the dot-com bust of 2001, many companies began considering implementing some form of lean, Six Sigma, or combination approach. Four companies in particular that had implemented Lean Six after 2001 were studied by *Electronic Business* magazine in 2006: Canada-based Celestica; ON Semiconductor headquartered in Arizona; California-based Solectron; and Xerox, headquartered in Connecticut. All four firms were healthier in 2006 than in 2001, and three claimed their business turnaround was a direct result of Lean Six. At last look, Celestica, ON Semiconductor and Xerox had challenging years in 2008 and 2009 but were viable, growing and profitable companies during a tough world economy. Solectron was acquired in 2007 by Singapore-based Flextronics, which is also a profitable company.[43]

Six Sigma and Supply Chain Management

By now, the supply chain management objectives of better customer service, lower costs and higher quality should be starting to sound familiar. To sustain and improve competitiveness, firms must perform better in these areas than their competitors. Through better process integration and communication, trading partners along the supply chain realize how poor-quality products and services can cause negative chain reactions to occur, such as greater levels of safety stock throughout the supply chain; lost time and productivity due to product and component repairs; the increased costs of customer returns and warranty repairs; and, finally, loss of customers and damage to reputations.

The impact of poor quality on the supply chain and potential damage to a firm's reputation can be illustrated by the problems toy-maker Mattel had to deal with regarding the Chinese-made toys it was selling in many of its global markets. In August 2007,

e-Business Connection

Lean Six Sigma at Halliburton

A lot of companies begin looking at Lean Six Sigma and other efficiency improvement strategies when business tightens as a way to reduce excess costs. But Halliburton took the opposite approach and implemented Lean Six Sigma as a way to improve its customer service in the face of growing demand.

When Texas-based Halliburton began to implement Lean Six Sigma in 2004, it was experiencing extraordinary growth in the oil and gas sector, essentially doubling the size of its business. "As a result, one of the things we wanted to focus on was speed of delivery, especially cycle time reduction," explains Len Cooper, senior vice president of supply chain at Halliburton.

As a first step, Halliburton's supply chain team began to conduct value stream mapping (a Lean tool) and evaluating productive time vs. non-productive time, and examining where it could reduce non-productive time. That, in turn, would shorten the overall delivery cycle of its products and services. Almost immediately the company's manufacturing cycle times were reduced, which drove higher asset utilization out of their equipment. In fact, between 2004 and 2008, Halliburton was able to triple the output from its manufacturing plants without any meaningful increase in the total capital footprint for those plants. "If we had not gone through the Lean process, we would have had to make substantial investments to support that type of output growth," states Cooper. "The Lean process alleviated the need for that incremental capital investment."

Halliburton began engaging its suppliers in Lean Six Sigma strategies in 2006. "We actually began to offer them our assistance and expertise, and invest resources, to catalyze them to adopt the same approaches we use internally," says Cooper.

As Cooper explains, the rationale for pushing the Lean principles to the suppliers was simple: "We would rather have our best suppliers grow with us, especially in these times, rather than go out and find more suppliers in order to gain access to additional capacity."

In some cases, there was initial reluctance among suppliers to the idea of having a customer (Halliburton) provide strategies. "Some suppliers' perception was that a customer was trying to come in and tell them how to run the businesses," says Cooper. To build cooperation for the initiatives with these suppliers, as well as to encourage other suppliers to cooperate, Halliburton utilized a number of strategies. "First, we explained what we wanted to do, why we wanted to do it, what the objectives were, and what the benefits would be for us and them," Cooper states. Secondly, Halliburton focused mostly on Lean strategies with suppliers and less so on Six Sigma because, as Cooper explains, "Lean focuses on speed and throughput, which is easier for suppliers to apply and is in fact a goal for our suppliers." Six Sigma, he notes, is a more technical, data-driven, analytical approach.

The third strategy for bringing suppliers along was showing them some of the data related to Halliburton's own experience with Lean Six Sigma. This made many of them more receptive, because they could see how it could reduce their own capital investment footprint. And finally, Halliburton sent some of its own people out to its key supplier plants to guide them in starting their own Lean Six Sigma programs. As a result of the company's initiatives, the success rate for supplier involvement was high. "We now have some suppliers with very robust Lean Six Sigma programs that are equally successful to ours," he reports.

Source: Atkinson, W., "Halliburton Pushes Lean Six Sigma to Its Supply Base," *Purchasing* 138(3), 2009: 18. Used with permission.

Mattel announced it was pulling 9 million Chinese-made Barbies, Polly Pockets and other toys off store shelves, only two weeks after it had already pulled 1.5 million Fisher-Price infant toys off shelves. The quality problems included use of lead paint and tiny magnets that could be swallowed. Some magnets were in fact swallowed, causing physical harm to the children involved. Obviously, the cost to Mattel and its suppliers, the toy retailers, and the children who played with these toys was very high.[44] Thus, the impacts of poor quality and, conversely, high quality as well can be felt throughout the supply chain and ultimately by end customers.

Six Sigma is an enterprise-wide philosophy, encompassing suppliers, employees and customers. It emphasizes a commitment by the organization to strive toward excellence in the production of goods and services that customers want. Firms implementing a Six Sigma program have made a decision to understand, meet, and then strive to exceed customer expectations; and this is the overriding objective in all Six Sigma programs.

Since Six Sigma is all about pleasing the customer, a very straightforward customer-oriented definition of quality can be employed here—*the ability to satisfy customer expectations*. This definition is echoed by the American Society for Quality when it states: "Quality is defined by the customer through his/her satisfaction." In this sense, both a fast-food hamburger and a steakhouse chopped sirloin sandwich can be considered to possess equally high quality, if they meet or exceed the expectations of their customers.

In a supply chain setting, quality is exemplified by a machine tool manufacturer identifying its industrial customers, determining their tooling needs and requirements, and then setting out to design, modify or improve their processes to meet those requirements and make the sale. With worldwide competition expanding along with the drive to cut costs, find new customers and improve profits, the growing desire to practice Six Sigma or some other form of quality improvement can be seen in all industries and all sizes of organizations.

In countries such as China and India, where competitive advantage has largely been due to a low cost of labor, many Chinese and Indian companies are now looking to quality management as a way to help them compete in global markets. The Automotive Industry Action Group (a group of U.S. automaker representatives who meet to discuss business problems) offers training and other assistance to firms in these and other Pacific Rim countries as a way to more quickly assimilate suppliers into the global automotive supply chain.[45]

Good supply chain trading partners use Six Sigma methods to assure that their suppliers are performing well and that their customers' needs are being met. Ultimately, this translates into end consumers getting what they want, when they want it, for a price they are willing to pay. While Six Sigma programs tend to vary somewhat in the details from one organization to another, all tend to employ a mix of qualitative and quantitative elements aimed at achieving customer satisfaction. The most common elements addressed in most Six Sigma programs are discussed in the following section.

The Elements of Six Sigma

The philosophy and tools of Six Sigma are borrowed from a number of resources including quality professionals such as W. Edwards Deming, Philip Crosby and Joseph Juran; the Malcolm Baldrige National Quality Award and the International Organization for Standardization's ISO 9000 and 14000 families of standards; the Motorola and General

Electric practices relating to Six Sigma; and statistical process control techniques originally developed by Walter Shewhart. From these resources, a number of commonly used elements emerge that are collectively known today as Six Sigma quality. A few of the quality resources are discussed next, followed by a brief look at the qualitative and quantitative elements of Six Sigma.

Deming's Contributions

W. Edwards Deming's Theory of Management as explained in his book *Out of the Crisis* essentially states that since managers are responsible for creating the systems that make organizations work, they (not the workers) must also be held responsible for the organization's problems. Thus, only management can fix problems, through application of the right tools, resources, encouragement, commitment and cultural change. Deming's Theory of Management was the centerpiece of his teachings around the world (Deming died in 1993) and includes his Fourteen Points for Management, shown in Table 8.6.[46]

Deming's Fourteen Points are all related to Six Sigma principles, covering the qualitative as well as quantitative aspects of quality management. He was convinced that high quality was the outcome of an all-encompassing philosophy geared toward personal and organizational growth. He argued that growth occurred through top management vision, support and value placed on all employees and suppliers. Value is demonstrated through investments in training, equipment, continuing education, support for finding and fixing problems and teamwork both within the firm and with suppliers. Use of statistical methods, elimination of inspected-in quality, and elimination of solely cost-based decisions are also required to improve quality. Today, Deming's work lives on through the Deming Institute, a nonprofit organization he founded to foster a greater understanding of his principles and vision. The institute provides conferences, seminars and training materials to managers seeking to make use of the Deming operating philosophy.[47]

Crosby's Contributions

Philip Crosby, a former vice president of quality at the New York-based manufacturer ITT Corporation, was a highly sought-after quality consultant during the latter part of his life and wrote several books concerning quality and striving for zero defects, most notably *Quality Is Free* and *Quality Without Tears* (he died in 2001).[48] His findings about quality improvement programs as discussed in *Quality Is Free* were that these programs invariably more than paid for themselves. In *Quality Without Tears*, Crosby discussed his four Absolutes of Quality, shown in Table 8.7. Industrial giants such as IBM and General Motors have benefited greatly from implementing Crosby's ideas. Crosby emphasized a commitment to quality improvement by top management, development of a prevention system, employee education and training, and continuous assessment—all very similar to the teachings of Deming.

Juran's Contributions

Joseph Juran, founder of the Juran Institute, helped to write and develop the *Quality Control Handbook* in 1951 (now in its fifth edition[49]) and wrote a number of other books on quality as well. Born in 1904, Juran remained an active lecturer until his death in 2008 at the age of 103. He also remained active by writing and by overseeing his Juran Foundation in New York. "My job of contributing to the welfare of my fellow man," Juran wrote, "is the great unfinished business."[50]

Table 8.6	Deming's Fourteen Points for Management
1. Create constancy of purpose for improvement of product and service.	Define values, mission and vision to provide long-term direction for management and employees. Invest in innovation, training and research.
2. Adopt the new philosophy.	Adversarial management–worker relationships and quota work systems no longer work in today's work environment. Management must work toward cooperative relationships aimed at increasing quality and customer satisfaction.
3. Cease dependence on mass inspection.	Inspecting products does not create value or prevent poor quality. Workers must use statistical process control to improve quality.
4. End the practice of awarding business on the basis of price tag alone.	Purchases should not be based on low cost; buyers should develop long-term relationships with a few good suppliers.
5. Constantly improve the production and service system.	Significant quality improvement comes from continual incremental improvements that reduce variation and eliminate common causes.
6. Institute training.	Managers need to learn how the company works. Employees should receive adequate job training and statistical process control training.
7. Adopt and institute leadership.	Managers are leaders, not supervisors. They help, coach, encourage and provide guidance to employees.
8. Drive out fear.	A supportive organization will drive out fear of reprisal, failure, change, the unknown and loss of control. Fear causes short-term thinking.
9. Break down barriers between departments.	Cross-functional teams focus workers, break down departmental barriers and allow workers to see the big picture.
10. Eliminate slogans, exhortations and targets for the workforce.	Slogans and motivational programs are aimed at the wrong people. They don't help workers do a better job. These cause worker frustration and resentment.
11. Eliminate numerical quotas for workers and managers.	Quotas are short-term thinking and cause fear. Numerical goals have no value unless methods are in place that will allow them to be achieved.
12. Remove barriers that rob people of pride of workmanship.	Barriers are performance and merit ratings. Workers have become a commodity. Workers are given boring tasks with no proper tools, and performance is appraised by supervisors who know nothing about the job. Managers won't act on worker suggestions. This must change.
13. Encourage education and self-improvement for everyone.	All employees should be encouraged to further broaden their skills and improve through continuing education.
14. Take action to accomplish the transformation.	Management must have the courage to break with tradition and explain to a critical mass of people that the changes will involve everyone. Management must speak with one voice.

Like Deming, Juran helped to engineer the Japanese quality revolution starting in the 1950s. Juran, similar to both Crosby and Deming, strived to introduce new types of thinking about quality to business managers and employees, but Juran's recommendations did vary somewhat from those of Crosby and Deming. He is recognized as the person who brought the human element to the practice of quality improvement. Juran did not seek cultural change but sought to work within the system to instigate change. He felt that to get managers to listen, one's message had to be spoken in dollars. To get

Table 8.7	Crosby's Four Absolutes of Quality
1. The definition of quality is conformance to requirements.	Adopt a do-it-right-the-first-time attitude. Never sell a faulty product to a customer.
2. The system of quality is prevention.	Use SPC as part of the prevention system. Make corrective changes when problems occur. Take preventative action.
3. The performance standard is zero defects.	Insist on zero defects from suppliers and workers. Education, training and commitment will eliminate defects.
4. The measure of quality is the price of nonconformance.	The price of nonconformance is the cost of poor quality. Implementing a prevention program will eliminate this.

workers to listen, one had to speak about specific things. So he advocated the determination of the costs of poor quality to get the attention of managers, and the use of statistical control methods for workers.

Juran's recommendations were focused on his Quality Trilogy, shown in Table 8.8. He found in his dealings with companies that most had given priority to quality control but paid little attention to quality planning and improvement. Thus, while both Japan and the U.S. were using quality control techniques since the 1950s, Japan's overall quality levels grew faster than those of the U.S. because Japan's quality planning and improvement efforts were much greater.

Many characteristics of the Deming, Crosby and Juran philosophies are quite similar. All three focus on top management commitment, the need for continuous improvement efforts, training and the use of statistical methods for quality control purposes.

The Malcolm Baldrige National Quality Award

The **U.S. Baldrige Quality Award** was signed into law on August 20, 1987, and is named in honor of then U.S. President Reagan's Secretary of Commerce, who helped draft an early version of the award, and who was tragically killed in a rodeo accident shortly before the award was enacted. The objectives of the award, which is given only to U.S. firms, are to stimulate U.S. firms to improve quality and productivity, to recognize firms for their quality achievements, to establish criteria and guidelines so that organizations

Table 8.8	Juran's Quality Trilogy
1. Quality planning	The process of preparing to meet quality goals. Identify internal and external customers, determine their needs and develop products that satisfy those needs. Managers set short- and long-term goals, establish priorities and compare results to previous plans.
2. Quality control	The process of meeting quality goals during operations. Determine what to control, establish measurements and standards of performance, measure performance, interpret the difference between the actual measure and the standard and take action if necessary.
3. Quality improvement	The process of breaking through to unprecedented levels of performance. Show the need for improvement, identify projects for improvement, organize support for the projects, diagnose causes, implement remedies for the causes and provide control to maintain improvements.

Table 8.9	Malcolm Baldrige National Quality Award Recipients					
YEAR	SMALL BUSINESS	MANUFACTURING	SERVICE	EDUCATION	HEALTH CARE	NONPROFIT
1988	Globe Metallurgical	Motorola Westinghouse Commercial Nuclear Fuel Div.				
1989		Xerox Bus. Products and Systems Milliken & Co.				
1990	Wallace Co.	Cadillac Motor Car Co. IBM Rochester	FedEx Corp.			
1991	Marlow Industries	Solectron Corp. Zytec Corp.				
1992	Granite Rock Co.	AT&T Network Sys. Group Texas Instruments Defense Sys. & Electronics Grp.	AT&T Universal Card Svcs. The Ritz-Carlton Hotel Co.			
1993	Ames Rubber Corp.	Eastman Chemical Co.				
1994	Wainwright Indus.		AT&T Consumer Comm. Svcs. GTE Directories			
1995		Armstrong World Ind. Bldg. Prod. Ops. Corning Telecomm. Prod. Div.				
1996	Custom Research Trident Precision Mfg.	ADAC Laboratories	Dana Comm. Credit			
1997		3M Dental Prod. Div. Solectron	Merrill Lynch Credit Xerox Business Svcs.			
1998	Texas Nameplate	Boeing Airlift and Tanker Programs Solar Turbines				
1999	Sunny Fresh Foods	ST Microelectronics Region Americas	BI The Ritz-Carlton Hotel Co.			
2000	Los Alamos Nat'l. Bank	Dana Corp. Spicer Driveshaft Div. KARLEE Co.	Operations Mgt. Int'l.			
2001	Pal's Sudden Svc.	Clarke American Checks		Chugach Sch. Dist. Pearl River Sch. Dist. Univ. of Wisc.-Stout		

can independently evaluate their quality improvement efforts, and to provide examples and guidance to those companies wanting to learn how to manage and improve quality and productivity.

The Baldrige Award is administered by the National Institute of Standards and Technology (NIST) and is presented by the President of the U.S. each year to small businesses; service and manufacturing firms; and educational, healthcare and nonprofit organizations that are judged to be outstanding in seven areas: leadership; strategic planning; customer and market focus; measurement, analysis and knowledge management; human resource focus; process management; and results. Up to three awards can be given annually in each of the categories. Table 8.9 shows the Baldrige Award winners from 1988 through 2009.[51]

All Malcolm Baldrige Award applications are reviewed by quality professional volunteers and scored in the seven categorical areas listed above. Finalists are visited to reassess performance and tabulate final scores, with the winners selected from this group. Organizations are encouraged by NIST to obtain a copy of the Baldrige Award criteria and perform self-assessments using the form and its point scoring guidelines. Completing a self-assessment using the Baldrige Award criteria identifies the firm's

Table 8.9   Malcolm Baldrige National Quality Award Recipients (continued)

YEAR	SMALL BUSINESS	MANUFACTURING	SERVICE	EDUCATION	HEALTH CARE	NONPROFIT
2002	Branch-Smith Printing Div.	Motorola Commercial, Gov't., and Indus. Sol. Sector			SSM Health Care	
2003	Stoner	Medrad	Boeing Aerospace Support Caterpillar Financial Svcs. Corp.	Community Consol. Sch. Dist. 15	Baptist Hosp. St. Luke's Hosp. of Kan. City	
2004	Texas Nameplate	The Bama Companies		K. W. Monfort Coll. of Bus.	R. W. Johnson Univ. Hosp.	
2005	Park Place Lexus	Sunny Fresh Foods	DynMcDermott Petroleum Opns.	Jenks Public Schools Richland College	Bronson Meth. Hosp.	
2006	MESA Products		Premier		N. Mississippi Medical Center	
2007	PRO-TEC Coating				Mercy Health Sys. Sharp HealthCare	City of Coral Springs US Army ARDEC
2008		Cargill Corn Milling		Iredell-Statesville Schools	Poudre Valley Health System	
2009	MidwayUSA	Honeywell Federal Mfg. & Technologies			Heartland Health	VA Cooperative Studies Program

strengths and weaknesses and can aid in implementing various quality and productivity improvement initiatives. Reviewing the Baldrige Award criteria reveals a number of areas consistent with the Six Sigma philosophy, and, to date, thousands of firms have requested copies of the official application.

The ISO 9000 and 14000 Families of Management Standards

In 1946, delegates from 25 countries met in London and decided to create a new international organization, with the objective "to facilitate the international coordination and unification of industrial standards." The new organization, called the International Organization for Standardization, or ISO, officially began operations on February 23, 1947. Now located in Geneva, Switzerland, the ISO today has 159 member countries.[52]

ISO standards are voluntary, are developed in response to market demand, and are based on consensus among the member countries. This ensures widespread applicability of the standards. ISO considers evolving technology and member interests by requiring a review of its standards at least every five years to decide whether they should be maintained, updated or withdrawn. In this way, ISO standards retain their position as state of the art.

ISO standards are technical agreements that provide the framework for compatible technology worldwide. Developing consensus on this international scale is a major operation. In all, there are some 3,000 ISO technical groups with approximately 50,000 experts participating annually to develop ISO standards. To date, ISO has published over 16,000 international standards. Examples include standards for agriculture and construction, mechanical engineering, medical devices and information technology developments, such as the digital coding of audio-visual signals for multimedia applications.

In 1987, ISO adopted the ISO 9000 series of five international quality standards, revised them in 1994, and again in 2000. The standards have been adopted in the U.S. by the American National Standards Institute (ANSI) and the American Society for Quality (ASQ). The standards apply to all types of businesses. In many cases worldwide, companies will not buy from suppliers who do not possess an ISO 9000 certification.

After the rapid acceptance of ISO 9000, and the increase of environmental standards around the world, ISO assessed the need for international environmental management standards. They formed an advisory group on the environment in 1991, which eventually led to the adoption of the ISO 14000 family of international environmental management standards in 1997. The standards were revised in 2004. The most recently adopted 14000 standards are the ISO 14064 standard for greenhouse gas accounting and verification and the ISO 14065 standard, which provides the requirements for the accreditation of bodies that carry out these activities. These standards will help organizations address climate change and support emissions trading schemes.

Together, the ISO 9000 and 14000 families of certifications are the most widely used standards of ISO, with more than 1 million organizations in 175 countries holding one or both types of certifications. The standards that have earned the ISO 9000 and ISO 14000 families a worldwide reputation are known as "generic management system standards," meaning that the same standards can be applied to any type of organization. Generic also means that no matter what the organization's scope of activity, if it wants to establish a quality management system or an environmental management system, then relevant standards of the ISO 9000 or ISO 14000 families provide the requirements.

The DMAIC Improvement Cycle

Figure 8.4 shows the five-step DMAIC improvement cycle, an important element of Six Sigma, listing the sequence of steps necessary to drive process improvement. The cycle can be applied to any process or project, both in services and manufacturing firms. The improvement cycle begins with customer requirements and then seeks to analyze and modify processes or projects so they meet those requirements. Each of the steps is described here:

1. *Define*: Identify customers and their service or product requirements critical to achieving customer satisfaction, also known as **critical-to-quality (CTQ) characteristics**. Identify any gaps between the CTQ characteristics and process outputs. Where gaps exist, create Six Sigma projects to alleviate the gaps.

2. *Measure*: Prepare a data-collection plan to quantify process performance. Determine what to measure for each process gap and how to measure it. Use check sheets to organize measurements.

3. *Analyze*: Perform a process analysis using the performance data collected. Use Pareto charts and fishbone diagrams to identify the root causes of the process variations or defects.

4. *Improve*: Design an improvement plan; then remove the causes of process variation by implementing the improvement plan. This will require modifying, redesigning, or reengineering the process. Document the improvement and confirm that process gaps have been significantly reduced or eliminated.

5. *Control*: Monitor the process to assure that performance levels are maintained. Design and use statistical process control charts to continuously monitor and control the process. When performance gaps are once again identified, repeat Steps 1–5.

Using the DMAIC improvement cycle allows the firm to continuously monitor and improve processes that are keys to customer satisfaction. By concentrating on these key processes and the CTQ characteristics, firms can make large and radical improvements in processes, products and customer satisfaction.

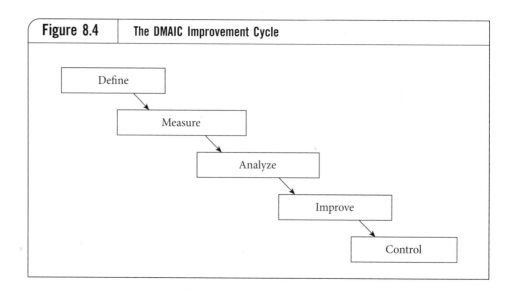

| **Figure 8.4** | **The DMAIC Improvement Cycle** |

Six Sigma Training Levels

In order to develop and successfully complete Six Sigma improvement projects, specific training in quality improvement methods is required. A number of organizations offer various training courses and certifications in Six Sigma methods, and the somewhat standardized training levels are summarized in Table 8.10. Global manufacturing giant GE began using Six Sigma in the 1980s, and today, all GE employees are receiving training in the strategy, statistical tools and techniques of Six Sigma. Eventually, all employees earn their Six Sigma Green Belt designations. Training courses are offered at various levels including basic Six Sigma awareness seminars, team training, Master Black Belt, Black Belt and Green Belt training.[53] Several of the statistical tools of Six Sigma are discussed next.

The Statistical Tools of Six Sigma

Flow Diagrams

Also called **process diagrams** or **process maps**, this tool is the necessary first step to evaluating any manufacturing or service process. **Flow diagrams** use annotated boxes representing process action elements and ovals representing wait periods, connected by arrows to show the flow of products or customers through the process. Once a process or series of processes is mapped out, potential problem areas can be identified and further evaluated for excess inventories, wait times, or capacity problems. An example of a customer flow diagram for a restaurant is shown in Figure 8.5. Using the diagram,

Table 8.10	A General Description of Six Sigma Training Levels[54]
TRAINING LEVELS	**DESCRIPTION**
Yellow Belt	Basic understanding of the Six Sigma Methodology and the tools within the DMAIC problem-solving process, including process mapping, cause-and-effect tools, simple data analysis and process improvement and control methods. Role is to be an effective team member on process improvement project teams.
Green Belt	A specially trained team member allowed to work on small, carefully defined Six Sigma projects, requiring less than a Black Belt's full-time commitment. Has enhanced problem-solving skills, and can gather data and execute experiments in support of a Black Belt project. They spend approximately 25 percent of their time on Six Sigma projects of their own or in support of Black Belt projects.
Black Belt	Has a thorough knowledge of Six Sigma philosophies and principles. Exhibits team leadership, understands team dynamics and assigns team members with roles and responsibilities. Has a complete understanding of the DMAIC model in accordance with the Six Sigma principles, a basic knowledge of lean concepts and can quickly identify "non-value-added" activities. Knowledge and use of advanced statistics, coaches successful project teams and provides group assessments. Identifies projects and selects project team members, acts as an internal consultant, mentors Green Belts and project teams, provides feedback to management.
Master Black Belt	A proven mastery of process variability reduction, waste reduction, and growth principles, and can effectively present training at all levels. Challenges conventional wisdom through the demonstration of the application of the Six Sigma methodology, and provides guidance and knowledge to lead and change organizations. Directs Black and Green Belts on the performance of their Six Sigma projects and also provides guidance and direction to management teams regarding the technical proficiency of Black Belt candidates, the selection of projects and the overall health of a Six Sigma program.

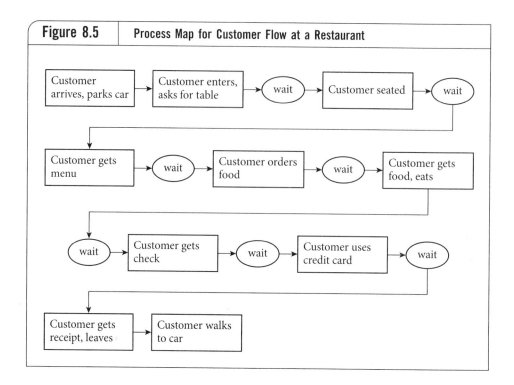

Figure 8.5 | **Process Map for Customer Flow at a Restaurant**

restaurant managers could then observe each process activity and wait period element, looking for potential problems requiring further analysis.

Check Sheets

Check sheets allow users to determine frequencies for specific problems. For the restaurant example shown in Figure 8.5, managers could make a list of potential problem areas based on experience and observation, and then direct employees to keep counts of each problem occurrence on check sheets for a given period of time (long enough to allow for true problem level determinations). At the end of the data-collection period, problem areas can be reviewed and compared. Figure 8.6 shows a typical check sheet that might be used in a restaurant.

Pareto Charts

Pareto charts, useful for many applications, are based on the work of Vilfredo Pareto, a nineteenth-century economist. For our purposes here, the charts are useful for presenting data in an organized fashion, indicating process problems from most to least severe. It only makes sense when utilizing a firm's resources to work on solving the most severe problems first (Pareto theory applied here suggests that most of a firm's problem "events" are accounted for by just a few of the problems). As shown in Figure 8.6, the top two problems account for about 40 percent of the instances where problems were observed. Figure 8.7 shows two Pareto charts for the problems counted in Figure 8.6. Note that we could look at the total problem events either from a problem-type or day-of-the-week perspective and see that *long wait* and *bad server* are the two troublesome problems, while Saturdays and Fridays are the days when most of the problem events occur. Finding and implementing solutions for these two problems would significantly decrease the number of problem events at the restaurant.

Figure 8.6		Problem Check Sheet for a Restaurant

Problem	Mon.	Tues.	Wed.	Thurs.	Fri.	Sat.	Sun.	Totals	% of Total
long wait	//////	/////	////////	//////	//////////	///////////	////	48	26.5
cold food		//	/	/	///	//		9	5.0
bad food	//	/	///		/	////		11	6.1
wrong food	/////	//	/	//	/////	///	/	19	10.5
bad server	//////	///	/////	/	//////	//	/	24	13.3
bad table		/	//		/	///	/	8	4.4
room temp.			//	///	/////	/////		15	8.3
too expensive	/	//	/	/	///	///		11	6.1
no parking			//		/////	////////		14	7.7
wrong change	///////	/	////		////	///		18	9.9
other		/	//			/		4	2.2
Totals	26	18	31	14	42	43	7	181	100

Figure 8.7		Pareto Charts for Restaurant Problems

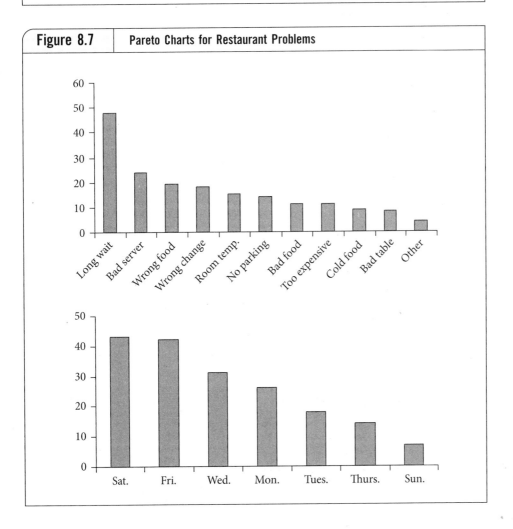

Cause-and-Effect Diagrams

Once a problem has been identified, **cause-and-effect diagrams** (also called **fishbone diagrams** or **Ishikawa diagrams**) can be used to aid in brainstorming and isolating the causes of a problem. Figure 8.8 illustrates a cause-and-effect diagram for the most troublesome *long wait* problem of Figure 8.7. The problem is shown at the front end of the diagram. Each of the four diagonals of the diagram represents potential groups of causes. The four groups of causes shown—Material, Machine, Methods and Manpower, or the 4 Ms—are the standard classifications of problem causes and represent a very thorough list for problem–cause analyses. In almost all cases, problem causes will be in one or more of these four areas.

Typically, Six Sigma team members will gather and brainstorm the potential causes for a problem in these four areas. Each branch on the four diagonals represents one potential cause. Subcauses are also part of the brainstorming process and are shown as smaller branches attached to each of the primary causes. Breaking a problem down like this into its causes and subcauses allows workers to then go back to the process and determine the relative significance of each cause and subcause using more specific

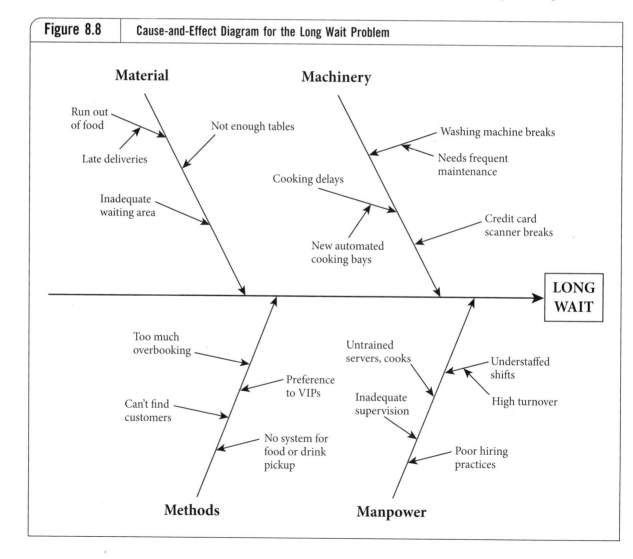

Figure 8.8 | **Cause-and-Effect Diagram for the Long Wait Problem**

checklists and Pareto charts once again. Eventually, the firm begins working to eliminate the causes of the problem, starting with the most significant causes and subcauses, until most of the problem's impact disappears.

A properly thought-out cause-and-effect diagram can be a very powerful tool for use in Six Sigma efforts. Without its use, workers and management risk trying to eliminate causes that have little to do with the problem at hand, or working on problems that are quite minor compared to other, more significant problems. Once most of a problem's causes are identified and eliminated, the associated process should be back under control and meeting customer requirements. At this point, firms can design and begin using statistical process control charts, discussed next.

Statistical Process Control

A necessary part of any quality improvement effort, **statistical process control (SPC)** allows firms to visually monitor process performance, compare the performance to desired levels or standards, and take corrective steps quickly before process variabilities get out of control and damage products, services and customer relationships. Once a process is working correctly, firms gather process performance data, create **control charts** to monitor process variabilities, and then collect and plot sample measurements of the process over time. The means of these sample measures are plotted on the control charts. If the sample means fall within the acceptable control limits and appear *normally distributed* around the desired measurement, the process is said to be in *statistical control* and it is permitted to continue; sample measurements and control chart plots also continue. When a sample plot falls out of the acceptable limits, or when the plots no longer appear normally distributed around the desired measurement, the process is deemed to be *out of control*. The process is then stopped, problems and their causes are identified and the causes are eliminated as described earlier. Control chart plots can then resume.

Control charts are graphic representations of process performance over time, showing the desired measurement (the center line of the control chart) and the process's upper and lower control limits. This visual aid makes it very easy for operators or other workers to plot data and compare performance over time.

Variations

Variations in process measurements can be either **natural variations** or **assignable variations**. All processes are affected by these variations, and environmental noise or natural variations are to be expected. When only natural variations are present, the process is in statistical control. Assignable variations are those that can be traced to a specific cause (such as the causes shown in Figure 8.8). These assignable variations are created by causes that can be identified and eliminated and thus become the objective of statistical process control efforts.

Samples

Because of the presence of variations in process measures, samples of data are collected and the sample means are then plotted onto control charts. Sample measures can be either **variable data** or **attribute data**, and each requires a different type of control chart. Variable data are continuous, such as weight, time and length (as in the weight of a box of cereal, the time to serve a customer, or the length of a steel rod). Attribute data indicate the presence of some attribute such as color, satisfaction, workability or beauty (for instance, determining whether or not a car was painted the right color if a customer liked the meal, if the light bulb worked, or if the dress was pretty).

Variable data samples are shown as the mean of the sample's measures (for instance, an average of 12.04 ounces in five boxes of cereal), whereas attribute data are shown as the percent defectives within a sample (for instance, 10 percent or 0.10 of the light bulb sample that did not work). Let us look at the two types of control charts next.

Variable Data Control Charts

When measuring and plotting variable process data, two types of control charts are needed: the $\bar{x}$-chart and the R-chart. The $\bar{x}$-chart is used to track the central tendency of the sample means, while the R-chart is used to track sample ranges, or the variation of the measurements within each sample. A perfect process would have sample means equal to the desired measure and sample ranges equal to zero. It is necessary to view *both of these charts* in unison, since a sample's mean might look fine, even though several of the measures might be far from the desirable measure, making the sample range very high. Also, the sample's range might look fine (all measures are quite close to one another), even though all of the measures are far from the desired measure, making the sample's mean unacceptable. For variable data then, both the $\bar{x}$-chart and the R-chart must show that the samples are in control before the process itself is considered in control.

Constructing the $\bar{x}$-chart and the R-chart

The first step in constructing any control chart is to gather data (provided the process is already in control and working well). Typically about twenty-five or thirty samples of size five to ten are collected, spaced out over a period of time. Then for each sample, the mean ($\bar{x}$) and the range (R) are calculated. Next, the *overall mean* ($\bar{\bar{x}}$) and the *average range, * ($\bar{R}$) of all the samples are calculated. The $\bar{\bar{x}}$ and $\bar{R}$ measures become the center lines (the desired measures) of their respective control charts. Example 8.2 provides the data used to illustrate the calculation of the center lines of the $\bar{x}$-chart and the R-chart. The formulas used to calculate the center lines $\bar{\bar{x}}$ and $\bar{R}$ are:

$$\bar{\bar{x}} = \frac{\sum_{i=1}^{k}\bar{x}_i}{k} \quad \text{and} \quad \bar{R} = \frac{\sum_{i=1}^{k}R_i}{k},$$

where k indicates the number of samples and i indicates the specific sample.

For the data shown in Example 8.2 for the Hayley Girl Soup Co., we see that $\bar{\bar{x}} = 11.96$ and $\bar{R} = 0.39$. If these measures are seen as acceptable by the Hayley Girl Soup Co., then they can use these to construct their control charts. These means are also used to calculate the upper and lower control limits for the two control charts. The formulas are:

$$\text{UCL}_{\bar{x}} = \bar{\bar{x}} + A_2\bar{R} \quad \text{and} \quad \text{LCL}_{\bar{x}} = \bar{\bar{x}} - A_2\bar{R}$$
$$\text{UCL}_R = D_4\bar{R} \quad \text{and} \quad \text{LCL}_R = D_3\bar{R},$$

where A_2, D_3, and D_4 are constants based on the size of each sample, and are shown in Table 8.11 (the constants used are based on an assumption that the sampling distribution is normal, and that the control limits are ± 3.0 standard deviations from the population mean, which contains 99.73 percent of the sampling distribution). The constants for various sample sizes are shown in Table 8.11.

Using the data in Example 8.2 and Table 8.11 for a sample size of four, the upper and lower control limits can be determined for both the $\bar{x}$-chart and the R-chart for the Hayley Girl Soup Co. variable data:

$$\text{UCL}_{\bar{x}} = \bar{\bar{x}} + A_2\bar{R} = 11.96 + 0.729\,(\,0.39\,) = 12.24$$
$$\text{LCL}_{\bar{x}} = \bar{\bar{x}} - A_2\bar{R} = 11.96 - 0.729\,(\,0.39\,) = 11.68$$

Example 8.2   Variable Control Chart Data for Soup Cans at Hayley Girl Soup Co.

The Hayley Girl Soup Co., a soup manufacturer, has collected process data in order to construct control charts to use in their canning facility. They collected 24 samples of four cans each hour over a 24-hour period, and the data is shown below for each sample:

HOUR	1	2	3	4	$\bar{x}$	R
1	12	12.2	11.7	11.6	11.88	0.6
2	11.5	11.7	11.6	12.3	11.78	0.8
3	11.9	12.2	12.1	12	12.05	0.3
4	12.1	11.8	12.1	11.7	11.93	0.4
5	12.2	12.3	11.7	11.9	12.03	0.6
6	12.1	11.9	12.3	12.2	12.13	0.4
7	12	11.7	11.6	12.1	11.85	0.5
8	12	12.1	12.2	12.3	12.15	0.3
9	11.8	11.9	12	12	11.93	0.2
10	12.1	11.9	11.8	11.7	11.88	0.3
11	12.1	12	12.1	11.9	12.03	0.2
12	11.9	11.9	11.7	11.8	11.83	0.2
13	12	12	11.8	12.1	11.98	0.3
14	12.1	11.9	12	11.7	11.93	0.4
15	12	12	11.7	11.2	11.73	0.8
16	12.1	12	12	11.9	12.00	0.2
17	12.1	12.2	12	11.9	12.05	0.3
18	12.2	12	11.7	11.8	11.93	0.5
19	12	12.1	12.3	12	12.10	0.3
20	12	12.2	11.9	12	12.03	0.3
21	11.9	11.8	12.1	12	11.95	0.3
22	12.1	11.8	11.9	12	11.95	0.3
23	12.1	12	11.9	11.9	11.98	0.2
24	12	12.3	11.7	12	12.00	0.6
MEANS					**11.96**	**0.39**

Table 8.11	Constants for Computing Control Chart Limits $(\pm 3\sigma)$[55]		
Sample Size, n	Mean Factor, A_2	UCL, D_4	LCL, D_3
2	1.88	3.268	0
3	1.023	2.574	0
4	0.729	2.282	0
5	0.577	2.115	0
6	0.483	2.004	0
7	0.419	1.924	0.076
8	0.373	1.864	0.136
9	0.337	1.816	0.184
10	0.308	1.777	0.223

and

$$UCL_R = D_4\overline{R} = 2.282\,(0.39) = 0.89$$
$$LCL_R = D_3\overline{R} = 0\,(0.39) = 0$$

Next, we can use the means and control limits to construct our two control charts. In Figure 8.9, the original data sample means and ranges have been plotted onto the two variable data control charts, showing the center lines and the control limits. From these plots, it appears that the process is indeed in statistical control, and the Hayley Girl Soup Co. can begin using these charts to monitor the canning process. If the process appears out of control on either chart, the control charts would not be useful and should be discarded until problems are identified and eliminated and the process is once again in statistical control.

Once a good set of control charts have been created and samples from the process are being statistically monitored, the following steps should be followed:

1. Collect samples of size 4–5 periodically (depending on the type of process and ease of data collection).

2. Plot the sample means on both control charts, monitoring whether or not the process is in control.

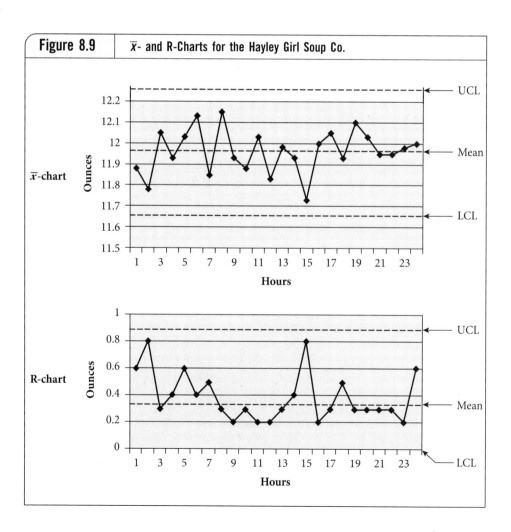

Figure 8.9 | **x̄- and R-Charts for the Hayley Girl Soup Co.**

3. When the process appears out of control, use check sheets, Pareto charts and fishbone diagrams to investigate causes and eliminate process variations.

4. Repeat steps 1–3.

Attribute Data Control Charts

When collecting attribute data regarding whether or not a process is producing good or bad (nondefective or defective) output, use of $\bar{x}$- and R-charts no longer applies. In these cases, either **P-charts**, which monitor the *percent defective* in each sample, or **C-charts**, which count the *number of defects* per unit of output are used. Each of these are discussed next.

Using and Constructing P-Charts

This is the most commonly used attribute control chart. If we use large sample sizes when collecting data samples, we can assume they are normally distributed and use the following formulas to calculate the center line ($\bar{P}$) and the upper and lower control limits for the P-chart:

$$\bar{P} = \frac{\sum_{i=1}^{k} P_i}{k},$$

where $\bar{P}$ is the mean fraction defective for all samples collected, k represents the number of samples, P is the fraction defective in one sample, and i represents the specific sample; and

$$UCL_P = \bar{P} + z\sigma_P$$
$$LCL_P = \bar{P} - z\sigma_P,$$

where z is the number of standard deviations from the mean (recall when $z = 3$, the control limits will contain 99.73 percent of all the sample data plots), and σ_P is the standard deviation of the sampling distribution. The sample standard deviation is calculated using

$$\sigma_P = \sqrt{\frac{(\bar{P})(1-\bar{P})}{n}},$$

where n is the size of each sample. Example 8.3 provides the data used to determine $\bar{P}$, σ_P, and the control limits for the P-chart.

As shown in Example 8.3, $\bar{P} = 0.014$. Calculating σ_P, yields

$$\sigma_P = \sqrt{\frac{(0.014)(0.986)}{100}} = 0.012.$$

Now the control limits can be calculated (assuming limits containing 99.73 percent of the data points are desired, or $z = 3$):

$$UCL_P = 0.014 + 3(0.012) = 0.05,$$

and

$$LCL_P = 0.014 - 3(0.012) = 0.$$

Note that the lower control limit is truncated at zero, as is the case in most P-charts. Figure 8.10 shows the P-chart for the CeeJay Lightbulb Co. with the fraction defectives from Example 8.3. Viewing the chart it is seen that the process appears to be in control, since the data points are randomly dispersed around the centerline, and about half the data points are on each side of the centerline. Thus, the CeeJay Lightbulb Co. can begin using this control chart to monitor their lightbulb quality.

Example 8.3   Attribute Control Chart Data for the CeeJay Lightbulb Co.

The CeeJay Lightbulb Co. makes 100-watt light bulbs, and they have decided to begin monitoring their quality using a P-chart. So, over the past 30 days, they have collected and tested 100 bulbs each day. The chart below shows the fraction defectives for each sample and the overall average fraction defective, or $\overline{P}$.

DAY	FRACTION DEFECTIVE	DAY	FRACTION DEFECTIVE
1	0.01	16	0.04
2	0.02	17	0
3	0	18	0
4	0.03	19	0.01
5	0	20	0.03
6	0.01	21	0.02
7	0.04	22	0
8	0	23	0.01
9	0	24	0.02
10	0.02	25	0.01
11	0.02	26	0.03
12	0.03	27	0
13	0	28	0.02
14	0.04	29	0.01
15	0.01	30	0

$$\overline{P} = 0.014$$

Figure 8.10   P-Chart for the CeeJay Lightbulb Co.

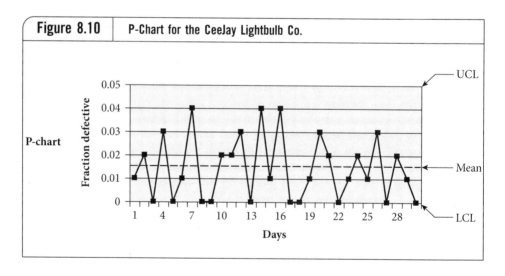

Using C-Charts

When multiple errors can occur in a process resulting in a defective unit, then we can use C-charts to control the *number* of defects per unit of output. C-charts are useful when a number of mistakes or errors can occur per unit of output, but they occur infrequently. Examples can include a hotel stay, a printed textbook or a construction project. The control limits for C-charts are based on the assumption of a Poisson probability distribution of the item of interest (commonly used when defects are infrequent). In this case, the distribution variance is equal to its mean. For C-charts, then,

> ## Example 8.4   Monitoring Editorial Defects at Casey Publishing, Inc.
>
> Eight editorial assistants are monitored for defects in the firm's printed work on a monthly basis. Over the past 30 days, a total number of 872 editorial mistakes were found. Computing the centerline and control limits, we find:
>
> $$\bar{c} = \frac{872}{30} = 29.1 \text{ mistakes per day, and the}$$
> $$\text{UCL}_c = 29.1 + 3\sqrt{29.1} = 45.3 \text{ and LCL}_c = 29.1 - 3\sqrt{29.1} = 12.9.$$

$\bar{c}$ = mean errors per unit of measure (and also the sample variance),
$\sqrt{\bar{c}}$ = sample standard deviation, and
$\bar{c} \pm 3\sqrt{\bar{c}}$ = control limits.

Example 8.4 can be used to illustrate the calculation of the C-chart's control limits. In the example, the units of measure are days; thus, the average daily defects are 29.1 (the centerline and also the variance). The upper and lower control limits are 45.3 and 12.9, respectively. The Casey Publishing Co. can now use the C-chart centerline and control limits based on the 30-day error data to monitor their daily editorial error rate.

Acceptance Sampling

When shipments of a product are received from suppliers, or before they are shipped to customers, samples can be taken from the batch of units and measured against some quality acceptance standard. The quality of the sample is then assumed to represent the quality of the entire shipment (particularly when shipments contain many units of product, sampling is far less time-consuming than testing every unit to determine the overall quality of an incoming or outgoing shipment). Ideally, if strategic alliance members within a supply chain are using Six Sigma quality improvement tools to build quality into the products they provide, acceptance sampling can be eliminated and used only when new or nonalliance suppliers furnish products or materials to the firm. In these situations, **acceptance sampling** can be used to determine whether or not a shipment will be accepted, returned to the supplier, or used for billback purposes when defects are fixed or units are eliminated by the buyer.

One question that arises is how big to make the test sample. One way to assure that the quality of the sample represents the quality of the entire shipment is to make the sample size equal to the size of the shipment (in other words, examine every unit). Since this is usually impractical, firms must assume the risk of incorrectly judging the quality of the shipment based on the size of the sample: the smaller the sample size, the greater the risk of incorrectly judging the shipment's quality.

There is a cost to both the supplier and buyer when incorrect quality assessments are made. When a buyer rejects a shipment of high-quality units because the sample quality level *did not* meet the acceptance standard, this is termed **producer's risk**. When this happens, it is called a **type-I error**. Conversely, when a buyer accepts a shipment of low-quality units because the sample *did* meet the acceptance standard, this is termed **consumer's risk** and is the result of a **type-II error**. Obviously, trading partners wish to avoid or minimize the occurrence of both of these outcomes. To minimize type-I and type-II errors, buyers and sellers must derive an acceptable sampling plan by agreeing on unacceptable defect levels and a sample size big enough to result in minimal numbers of type-I and type-II errors.

Statistical Process Control and Supply Chain Management

Ideally, long-standing strategic supply chain partners would not need to monitor their inbound and outbound product quality—quality would already be extremely high, and employees could spend their time in more productive pursuits. However, most processes and suppliers are not yet perfect, and the level of competition is so fierce in most industries that firms find they must continually be assessing and reassessing process and product quality levels. Managers should identify processes that are critical to achieving the firm's objectives, decide how to monitor process performance, gather data and create the appropriate control charts and create policies for collecting process samples and monitoring process and product quality over time. Managers must also work to create a culture where quality improvements are encouraged and employees are empowered to make the changes that will result in improved product and service quality.

SUMMARY

Supply chain management, lean systems and Six Sigma quality management make up a hierarchy for breakthrough competitive advantage. In order for supply chain management to reach its full potential and provide benefits to its members, trading partners must adopt a lean operating philosophy. Similarly, the primary ingredient in the success of a lean program is the use of Six Sigma thinking and improvement tools. There are a number of practices mentioned within each of these topics that overlap or are very similar such as top management support, workforce involvement and continuous improvement. This is not surprising given the close ties between supply chain management, lean and Six Sigma. Considerable time has been spent here covering lean and Six Sigma because of their critical importance in achieving successful supply chain management, and it is hoped that you have gained an appreciation for the topics presented here.

KEY TERMS

acceptance sampling, 291

assignable variations, 285

attribute data, 285

carbon-neutral, 267

cause-and-effect diagrams, 284

C-chart, 289

check sheets, 282

consumer's risk, 291

control charts, 285

critical-to-quality (CTQ) characteristics, 280

defects per million opportunities (DPMO), 268

efficient consumer response (ECR), 251

fishbone diagrams, 284

Five-Ss, 259

flow diagrams, 281

Ishikawa diagrams, 284

just-in-time, 251

kaizen, 266

kanban, 254

keiretsu relationships, 251

lean layouts, 261

lean manufacturing, 251

lean production, 251

lean six, 271

lean Six Sigma, 271

lean supply chain relationships, 261

lean thinking, 251

manufacturing cells, 262

muda, 254

natural variations, 285

opportunities for a defect to occur (OFD), 269

Pareto charts, 282

part families, 262

P-chart, 289

poka-yoke, 254

production kanban, 264

process diagrams, 281

process maps, 281

producer's risk, 291

pull system, 264

quick response (QR), 251

silo effect, 256

Six Sigma, 251

R-chart, 286

setups, 262

seven wastes, 258

sigma drift, 268

statistical process control (SPC), 285

Toyota Production System, 251

type-I error, 291

type-II error, 291

U.S. Baldrige Quality Award, 276

variable data, 285

work cells, 262

withdrawal kanban, 264

$\bar{x}$-chart, 286

DISCUSSION QUESTIONS

1. Explain why lean production and Six Sigma are so important to successful supply chain management.

2. Briefly explain the primary concerns and objectives of lean production.

3. How is lean production associated with JIT?

4. What does the Toyota Production System have to do with JIT and lean production?

5. What person or people at Toyota is (are) most responsible for the development of the JIT concept?

6. Looking at Table 8.1, which stage of supply chain management would you say Wal-Mart is in? How about a locally owned sandwich shop and the university you are attending?

7. How is lean thinking associated with supply chain management?

8. Use an example to show how you could use lean thinking with a supplier and a customer.

9. What are the seven wastes? Can you discuss them in terms of a business you are familiar with?

10. Apply the Five-Ss to improve how you could complete your daily homework or study assignments.

11. What are the advantages and disadvantages of making small, frequent purchases from just a few suppliers? How do we overcome the disadvantages?

12. Why should lean layouts be "visual"?

13. What are manufacturing cells, and why are they important in lean production?

14. Reducing lot sizes and increasing setups are common practices in most lean production settings. Why?

15. What are *kanbans* and why are they used in lean systems?

16. What is *kaizen*, and why is it so important for successful lean production?

17. Discuss the linkage between lean systems and environmental sustainability.

18. Describe Six Sigma's origins and the main parties involved. Why do you think the concept is called "Six Sigma"?

19. Describe the lean Six Sigma approach.

20. Describe three ways your university could improve quality.

21. Describe Deming's Theory of Management, and how it can be used to improve quality.

22. In looking at the list of Baldrige Award winners (Table 8.9), do you think these firms have high-quality products? How successful are they now?

23. In viewing the Baldrige Award's seven performance categories, how would your firm stack up in these areas (use the university or your most recent job if you are not currently employed).

24. What are the two most widely used ISO standards, and why are they so popular?

25. What are critical-to-quality characteristics, and how are they used in Six Sigma?

26. Construct a flow diagram of the registration process at your university. What areas would you investigate further to identify problems?

27. Construct a cause-and-effect diagram for the following problem: The university course registration process is too long. Brainstorm some potential causes.

28. What are the two types of process variation, and which one does statistical process control seek to eliminate? What can be done with the other one?

29. Describe "variable data" and explain why two control charts are needed to assure that these types of processes are under control.

30. Can a process exhibit sample measurements that are all inside the control limits and still be considered out of control? Explain.

31. What are some variable data and attribute data that could be collected to track the quality of education at your university?

32. How could P-charts be used in a manufacturing facility?

33. Can a process be considered in control but *incapable* of meeting design requirements? Explain.

34. If one goal of a supplier partnership is to eliminate acceptance sampling, then who does it?

INTERNET QUESTIONS

1. Go to the Baldrige Award website (www.quality.nist.gov), and find out what organizations have won the award since this book was published. Report on any new developments with respect to the Baldrige Award and its recipients—have any declared bankruptcy?

2. Why isn't the International Organization for Standardization called the IOS? (Hint: There is a discussion of this topic at the ISO website, www.iso.ch.)

3. Write a report on Toyota and its recent quality and recall problems since 2009.

4. Search the Internet and article databases at your university for the terms *sustainability* and *supply chain management,* and write a report on the importance of sustainability in the practice of supply chain management, using company examples.

5. Search the Internet and article databases at your university for the term *Lean Six,* and write a report on the latest uses of this method using company examples.

PROBLEMS

1. Mejza Compressors uses a lean production assembly line to make its compressors. In one assembly area, the demand is 100 parts per eight-hour day. It uses a container that holds eight parts. It typically takes about six hours to round-trip a container from one work center to the next and back again. Mejza also desires to hold 15 percent safety stock of this part in the system. How many containers should Mejza Compressors be using?

2. Eakins Enterprises makes model boats, and it is switching to a lean manufacturing process. At one assembly area, Eakins is using one part container that holds 250 parts, and it wants the output to be approximately 100 finished parts per hour; they also desire a 10 percent safety stock for this part. How fast will the container have to make it through the system to accomplish this?

3. Jim Corner, owner of Corner Bike Rentals, wants to start analyzing his company's quality. For each bike rental, there are four types of customer complaints: (a) bike not working properly, (b) bike wrong size, (c) bike uncomfortable, and (d) bike broken during operation. During the past week, his company rented 280 bikes. He received 26 total complaints.

a. What is his company's DPMO for the past week?
b. What is their Six Sigma operating level?

4. The following sample information was obtained by taking four doughnuts per hour for twelve hours from Fawcett Bakery's doughnut process and weighing them:

HOUR	WEIGHT (GRAMS)	HOUR	WEIGHT (GRAMS)
1	110, 105, 98, 100	7	89, 102, 101, 99
2	79, 102, 100, 104	8	100, 101, 98, 96
3	100, 102, 100, 96	9	98, 95, 101, 100
4	94, 98, 99, 101	10	99, 100, 97, 102
5	98, 104, 97, 100	11	102, 97, 100, 101
6	104, 97, 99, 100	12	98, 100, 100, 97

For the data shown above,

a. Find the $\bar{x}$ and R for each sample.
b. Find the $\bar{\bar{x}}$ and $\bar{R}$ for the twelve samples.
c. Find the 3-sigma UCL and LCL for the mean and range charts.
d. Does the process look to be in statistical control. Why or why not?

5. Through process measuring a number of pizza delivery times, Mary Jane's Pizzeria finds the mean of all samples to be 27.4 minutes, with an average sample range of 5.2 minutes. They tracked four deliveries per hour for 18 hours to obtain their samples.

a. Is this an example of variable or attribute sampling data?
b. Find the UCL and LCL for both the $\bar{x}$- and R-charts.

6. Ten customers per hour were asked by the cashier at Stanley's Deli if they liked their meal, and the fraction that said "no" are shown below, for a twelve-hour period.

HOUR	FRACTION DEFECTIVE	HOUR	FRACTION DEFECTIVE
1	0	7	0.1
2	0.2	8	0
3	0.4	9	0
4	0.1	10	0.2
5	0.1	11	0
6	0.2	12	0.1

For the data shown above, find

a. $\bar{P}$.
b. σ_P.
c. The 3-sigma UCL and LCL.
d. Does customer satisfaction at Stanley's appear to be in statistical control? How could we improve the analysis?

7. Roberto's Steakhouse tracks customer complaints every day and then follows up with their customers to resolve problems. For the past 30 days, they received a total of 22 complaints from unhappy customers. Using this information, calculate

a. $\bar{c}$.
b. The 3-sigma control limits.

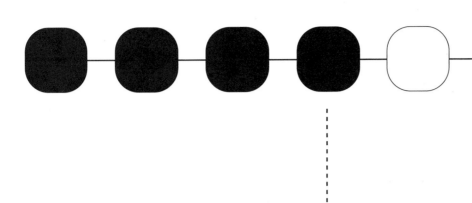

Part 4

Distribution Issues in Supply Chain Management

Chapter 9

DOMESTIC U.S. AND GLOBAL LOGISTICS

In the United States, more than 20 billion tons of goods are moved annually, goods moved are valued at more than $13 trillion and 365 pounds of freight are moved daily for each resident.[1]

In 2008, total transportation was responsible for 69 percent of oil consumption ... Perhaps more illustrative, the transportation sector as a whole is today 95 percent reliant on petroleum products for delivered energy—with no substitutes available at scale. This extraordinary reliance on a single fuel to power an indispensable sector of our economy has exposed the United States to a significant vulnerability, both for our economy and for our national security.[2]

Learning Objectives

After completing this chapter, you should be able to

- Understand the strategic importance of logistics.
- Identify the various modes of transportation.
- Understand how U.S. regulation and deregulation have impacted transportation.
- Discuss the global aspects of logistics.
- Describe how logistics affects supply chain management.
- Examine and understand the interrelatedness of transportation, warehousing and material handling.
- Identify a number of third-party logistics service providers.
- Describe the various reverse logistics activities.
- Discuss some of the e-commerce issues in logistics management.

Chapter Outline

Supply Chain Management in Action   *Distribution Evolution at PDS*

Third-party logistics and wholesale food and grocery distribution share one thing in common: both industries operate on razor thin margins. That puts a premium on squeezing as much cost as possible out of warehousing, distribution and transportation operations.

Prime Distribution Services (PDS) understands that idea better than most companies. A third-party logistics provider headquartered near Indianapolis in Plainfield, Indiana, PDS was founded 20 years ago to offer distribution services to vendors of the club store services supply chain. And, since most of PDS's customers are food vendors, they are more likely than most to pay attention to logistics costs.

During the last 20 years, PDS has built a business out of reducing those costs by providing food vendors with a single point of distribution that incorporates warehousing, crossdocking, packaging and multi-vendor freight consolidation into their supply chain.

As the retail distribution chain has evolved, so has PDS. PDS combined an estimated one million square feet of conventional warehouse space spread across several locations in Indianapolis into a single 1.2 million square foot facility. And where the old operations were paper-driven, the new facility includes automated systems to facilitate greater control over inventory, more responsive order management and two case-pick modules to facilitate the efficient building of mixed SKU pallets. Automated materials and information handling systems include a state of the art warehouse management system (WMS) to manage inventory and direct picking operations; scan tunnels to automatically scan barcode labels and verify and automatically route cartons after picking; and a conveyor and sortation system to divert orders to packing and verification stations.

The system went live in 2009 and PDS is seeing improvements in productivity and accuracy, according to Scott Zurawski, director of warehouse operations and logistics. More importantly, he describes the system as the first step of several phases to improve operations across the company and better serve its customers. "Our leadership and our organization are geared toward a lean warehousing operation," says Zurawski. "We're trying to build sustainability and quality into every process."

Today, in addition to the Plainfield distribution center, PDS also operates a 260,000 square-foot facility in Mesquite, Texas and a 311,000 square-foot facility in Stockton, California. "Our primary focus was and is LTL consolidation for retail vendors, especially food vendors," says Zurawski. "They ship their inventory to us and we'll pick and ship consolidated truck load orders to their retail customers while maintaining 99 percent on time delivery." Those vendors save money by shipping one full truckload of their product to PDS instead of paying extra to ship multiple LTL shipments to their customers; they also benefit because PDS has the systems and expertise to meet retailers' labeling and shipping requirements. Vendors benefit by having a single point of distribution for their retail outlets, lowering their inventory requirements.

The new solution may just have been installed in 2009, but according to Zurawski, he and his team at PDS are already looking to the future. "We are very comfortable with what we've accomplished, but the concept of continual improvement is challenging us to reinvent ourselves and make more improvements. We're striving to become a world-class logistics company," he says. "We're ready to focus on lean and green initiatives."

Source: Trebilcock, B., "Distribution Evolution at PDS," *Modern Materials Handling* 65, no. 2 (2010): 14. Used with permission.

Introduction

Logistics is necessary for moving purchased materials from suppliers to buyers, moving work-in-process materials within a firm, moving finished goods to customers, returning or recycling goods and also for storing these items along the way in supply chains. Effective logistics systems are needed for commerce to exist in any industrialized society. Products have little value to customers until they are moved to customers' usage areas, at a point in time when they are needed. Logistics thus provides what are termed **time utility** and **place utility**. Time utility is created when customers get products delivered at precisely the right time, not earlier and not later. The logistics function creates time utility by determining how deliveries can be made in a timely manner and where items should be held prior to delivery. Place utility is created when customers get things delivered to their desired locations.

The official definition of **logistics** from the globally recognized Council of Supply Chain Management Professionals is: "that part of supply chain management that plans, implements and controls the efficient, effective forward and reverse flow and storage of goods, services and related information between the point of origin and the point of consumption in order to meet customers' requirements."[3]

So it can be seen that transportation, warehousing, information systems and customer service play very significant roles in the logistics function. For supply chains in particular, logistics is what creates the flow of goods between supply chain partners, such that costs, service requirements, competitive advantage and finally profits can be optimized.

When moving around within a city, between cities or between countries, it is impossible to ignore the business of logistics, whether it be large trucks ambling along the roadways, trains pulling boxcars, cattle cars and tankers next to highways, warehouses storing goods in cities' industrial sections, airplanes taking off at airports, container ships unloading cargo or barges floating slowly down rivers. In the U.S. and other highly industrialized nations, the movement of goods is ever-pervasive. Without it, we as consumers would never have opportunities to find what we want, when we want it, at the many retail outlets we routinely visit each day.

Using the latest available information from the U.S. Bureau of Transportation Statistics, at the end of 2007 the total annual U.S. for-hire logistics services contribution to the U.S. gross domestic product (GDP) was approximately 2.9 percent, or $407 billion. Table 9.1 shows the growth of for-hire logistics expenditures in the U.S., which has almost quadrupled in 27 years. Notice that for the past twenty years or so, for-hire logistics expenditures have stayed close to 3 percent of GDP. Also note that aside from warehousing and "other," everything has remained fairly steady for the past twenty years. This may be due in part to the need for faster and more flexible warehousing services and from the increased security placed on transportation services entering the U.S. since 2001.

In this chapter, the many logistics activities are discussed, along with logistics nomenclature and related events affecting businesses each day. Included are discussions of the modes of transportation, transportation regulation and deregulation, warehousing and distribution, a number of logistics decisions firms must make, the impact of logistics on supply chain management, the global issues affecting logistics, the impact of e-commerce on logistics activities and management of product returns, also called reverse logistics. Some of the transportation basics are reviewed next.

Table 9.1	Total U.S. For-Hire Logistics Services Contribution to GDP (Current $ billions)							
	1980	**1985**	**1990**	**1995**	**2000**	**2005**	**2006**	**2007**
Total U.S. GDP	2790	4220	5803	7398	9817	12422	13178	13808
For-Hire Logistics Services GDP (% U.S. GDP)	102.3 (3.7)	136.3 (3.2)	169.4 (2.9)	226.3 (3.1)	301.6 (3.1)	364.7 (2.9)	387.4 (2.9)	407.2 (2.9)
Truck GDP (% For-Hire GDP)	28.1 (27.5)	39.0 (28.6)	52.6 (31.1)	70.1 (31.0)	92.8 (30.8)	118.4 (32.5)	122.5 (31.6)	127.6 (31.3)
Rail GDP (% For-Hire GDP)	22.4 (21.9)	23.1 (16.9)	20.6 (12.2)	25.0 (11.0)	25.5 (8.5)	33.5 (9.2)	39.0 (10.1)	40.5 (9.9)
Water GDP (% For-Hire GDP)	3.3 (3.2)	3.7 (2.7)	4.6 (2.7)	5.8 (2.6)	7.2 (2.4)	10.0 (2.7)	10.8 (3.0)	10.7 (2.6)
Air GDP (% For-Hire GDP)	12.8 (12.5)	19.0 (13.9)	26.8 (15.8)	41.0 (18.1)	57.7 (19.1)	48.3 (13.2)	50.3 (13.8)	55.2 (15.1)
Pipeline GDP (% For-Hire GDP)	6.1 (6.0)	8.7 (6.4)	7.2 (4.3)	8.1 (3.6)	8.7 (2.9)	9.5 (2.6)	11.4 (3.1)	12.0 (3.3)
Warehouse GDP (% For-Hire GDP)	5.6 (5.5)	8.4 (6.2)	11.8 (7.0)	16.8 (7.4)	25.0 (8.3)	35.6 (9.8)	37.3 (10.2)	40.3 (11.1)
Other GDP[a] (% For-Hire GDP)	24.1 (23.6)	34.3 (25.2)	45.7 (27.0)	59.5 (26.3)	84.7 (28.1)	109.5 (30.0)	116.1 (31.8)	120.8 (33.1)

Source: U.S. Dept. of Commerce, Bureau of Transportation Statistics, www.bts.gov/publications.
[a]Includes transit, ground passenger and other transportation and support activities.

The Fundamentals of Transportation

This section reviews a number of important transportation elements within the logistics function, including the objective of transportation, legal forms of transportation, the modes of transportation, intermodal transportation, transportation pricing, transportation security and transportation regulation and deregulation in the U.S. This provides a good foundation for discussion of the remaining topics in the chapter, as well as an appreciation for the complex nature of transportation issues in logistics.

The Objective of Transportation

Although you may think the overriding objective of transportation is obvious—that is, moving people and things from one place to another—for-hire transportation services can go broke doing this inefficiently. For example, over the past twenty years a number of U.S. passenger airlines have sought bankruptcy protection and asked for concessions from labor unions to keep operating. Some of these airlines include United Airlines, Continental Airlines, America West, US Airways, Delta Air Lines, Northwest Airlines, Hawaiian Airlines and Aloha Airlines. The steep economic downturn from 2008 to 2010, combined with high fuel prices, only made things more troublesome for transportation companies. The airline industry lost almost $30 billion in 2008 and 2009. During this same period, over 4,000 U.S. trucking companies went bankrupt, representing about 160,000 trucks.[4]

Logistics managers seek to maximize value for their employers by correctly communicating the firm's service needs to transportation providers while negotiating services and prices such that the transportation provider's delivery costs are covered and allowing an acceptable profit contribution and then making sure the desired services are performed as effectively as possible. In the transportation industry, competitive prices may not be high enough to cover firms' fixed and variable costs and this has created a tremendous problem for a number of airlines and trucking companies as mentioned above. In the most general terms, transportation objectives should then be to *satisfy customer requirements while minimizing costs and making a reasonable profit*. For logistics or perhaps supply chain managers, this also means deciding which forms of transportation, material handling and storage, along with the most appropriate vehicle scheduling and routing to use.

Legal Forms of Transportation

For-hire transportation service companies are classified legally as common, contract, exempt or private carriers. The distinguishing characteristics of each of these classifications are discussed below.

Common Carriers

Common carriers offer transportation services to all shippers at published rates, between designated locations. Common carriers must offer their transportation services to the general public without discrimination, meaning they must charge the same rates for the same service to all customers. In the U.S., a common carrier is legally bound to carry all passengers or freight as long as there is enough space, the fee is paid and no reasonable grounds to refuse exist. A common carrier refusing to carry a person or cargo may be sued for damages. Because common carriers are given the authority to serve the general public, they are the most heavily regulated of all carrier classifications. Some U.S. examples of common carriers are Southwest Air, Amtrak, Greyhound and Carnival Cruise Lines.

Contract Carriers

Contract carriers might also be common carriers; however, as such, they are not bound to serve the general public. Instead, contract carriers serve specific customers under contractual agreements. Typical contracts are for movement of a specified cargo for a negotiated and agreed-upon price. Some contract carriers have specific capabilities that allow them to offer lower prices than common carriers might charge for the same service. For instance, Southwest Air might enter into a contractual agreement with the Dallas Cowboys football team to provide transportation for the team's out-of-town games. Shippers and carriers are free to negotiate contractual agreements for price, the commodity carried, liability, delivery timing and types of service. Turkish Airlines, for example, recently signed a two-year contract to provide transportation for the FC Barcelona and Manchester United European football teams.[5]

Exempt Carriers

Exempt carriers are also for-hire carriers, but they are exempt from regulation of services and rates. Carriers are classified as exempt if they transport certain exempt products such as produce, livestock, coal or newspapers. School buses, taxis and ambulances are also examples of exempt carriers. The exempt status was originally established to allow farmers to transport agricultural products on public roads, but today the status has been broadened to include a number of commodities. Rail carriers hauling coal between specific locations are exempt from economic regulation, for instance. All carriers can also act as exempt carriers for these specific commodities and routes.

Private Carrier

A **private carrier** is not subject to economic regulation and typically transports goods for the company owning the carrier. Firms transporting their own products typically own and operate fleets large enough to make the cost of transportation less than what it would be if the firm hired a transportation provider. Flexibility and control of product movements also play major roles in the ownership of a private carrier. Wal-Mart, for instance, with its private fleet of trucks, was able to respond even quicker than U.S. government relief workers after Hurricane Katrina struck the Louisiana Gulf Coast in the summer of 2005. Immediately after the disaster, Wal-Mart began hauling food, water and other relief supplies with their private fleet of trucks to community members and other organizations helping in the affected areas. In three weeks, they hauled 2,500 truckloads of supplies to these areas; additionally, they were able to reopen their stores quickly in the hardest hit areas. Shortly after the hurricane, New Orleans Sheriff Harry Lee was quoted as saying, "If [the] American government would have responded like Wal-Mart has responded, we wouldn't be in this crisis."[6]

The Modes of Transportation

There are five modes of transportation: motor, rail, air, water and pipeline carriers. These modes and the amount of freight they hauled each year between 1980 and 2007 in the U.S. were shown in Table 9.1. Each of these modes offers distinct advantages to customers and their selection depends on a number of factors including the goods to be transported, how quickly the goods are needed, the price shippers are willing to pay and the locations of shippers and customers. Discussions of each of the modes follows.

Motor Carriers

Motor carriers (or trucks) are the most flexible mode of transportation and, as shown on Table 9.1, account for almost one-third of all U.S. for-hire transportation expenditures. Motor carriage offers door-to-door service, local pickup and delivery and small as well as large shipment hauling. It has very low fixed and variable costs and can compete favorably with rail and air carriers for short to medium hauls (distances shorter than 1,000 miles) and is still competitive with other forms of transportation for long cross-country shipments, particularly if there are multiple delivery destinations. Motor carriers can also offer a variety of specialized services from refrigerated, to livestock, to automobile hauling.

The primary disadvantages for motor carriers are weather and traffic problems. The tragic collapse of the eight-lane Minneapolis, Minnesota, I-35 West bridge over the Mississippi River in August 2007 killed thirteen people and provided a painful reminder of the importance of a nation's transportation infrastructure. Per day, more than 140,000 vehicles, including approximately 5,700 commercial vehicles, used Minnesota's busiest bridge. In 2005, the bridge was inspected and received a low rating, indicating that it should have been either repaired or replaced.[7]

Motor carriers are most often classified as **less-than-truckload (LTL) carriers** or **truckload (TL) carriers**. LTL carriers move small packages or shipments that take up less than one truckload and the shipping fees are higher per hundred weight (cwt) than TL fees, since the carrier must consolidate many small shipments into one truckload, and then break the truckload back down into individual shipments at the destination for individual deliveries. However, for limited item shippers, using LTL carriers is still a much less expensive alternative than using a TL carrier. The LTL industry in the U.S. is made up of a small number of national LTL carriers such as YRC Worldwide, FedEx Freight,

Con-Way Freight and UPS Freight and a larger number of regional LTL carriers (specializing in shipments of fewer than 500 miles). Most of the regional carriers are small, privately owned companies that specialize in overnight and second-day deliveries. Recently, freight movements have been down due to the recession (recall the chapter's opening quote) and the LTL industry is consolidating. In 2009, the top seven U.S. LTL carriers accounted for over 63 percent of all LTL carrier revenues.[8]

Motor carriers can also be classified based on the types of goods they haul. **General freight carriers** carry the majority of goods shipped in the U.S. and include common carriers, whereas **specialized carriers** transport liquid petroleum, household goods, agricultural commodities, building materials and other specialized items. In Australia, extra-long truck and trailer combinations (referred to as **road trains**) transport goods between geographically dispersed communities not served by rail (see the Global Perspective feature for more discussions of this and other unique transportation services).

Global Perspective   *Biggest, Longest and Fastest*

In transportation, bigger, longer and faster in many cases means better. Since economies of scale in transporting goods and people can mean fewer trips, less fuel consumed, better equipment utilization and lower labor costs, logistics providers have occasionally utilized transportation equipment with enormous capacities to gain the benefits of transportation scale economies. And with the continuing demand for shipping speed, some companies are designing ever-faster systems to satisfy demand. Several examples of this are provided here.

MOTOR CARRIERS

In Australia and several other countries, large tractor units pull three, four and even more self-tracking trailers along long stretches of open road between cities in unpopulated areas with no rail service. These long tractor/trailer combinations are also known as road trains. In Australia, road trains can legally be up to 180 ft. in length (although in some areas of the Australian Outback they are even longer), barreling along at speeds of up to 65 mph. In 2006, the record was set in Clifton, Queensland, Australia, for road train length when a Mack Titan tractor pulled 112 semi-trailers measuring 4836 feet, weighing 2,900,000 pounds, for 328 feet. Pictures of road trains can be seen at www.roadtrains.com and a number of great videos exist on YouTube.com.[9]

RAIL CARRIERS

If you want high-speed, on-time train service, the Japanese Shinkansen bullet train is the only way to go. Started in 1964, the bullet train was an instant success, traveling 125 mph from Tokyo to Osaka and carrying one billion passengers by 1976. Shinkansen trains now can travel up to 200 mph between a number of Japanese cities and are kept extremely close to published arrival times—in 2003, the Shinkansen's average arrival time for 160,000 trips was within six seconds of scheduled arrival time! Now that's customer service! The Shinkansen trains are only used for passenger service and run on tracks parallel to the freight train tracks. The high speeds are extremely tough on rail tracks, however, which gobble up about one-third of all maintenance costs. Pictures of these bullet trains can be found at www.railway-technology.com/projects/shinkansen.[10]

AIR CARRIERS

The new Airbus A380 jetliner and the old Spruce Goose may be big, but they are nowhere near the biggest—that title belongs to the Antonov An-225 commercial jet freighter. It was built in 1988 for the Soviet space program to airlift rocket boosters and their space shuttle. When the

Soviet Union collapsed in 1990 and put the space program on hold, the aircraft was temporarily mothballed, then eventually put into commercial cargo service. It was refurbished and put back into service in 2001 for Antonov Airlines. It has allowed the transporting of things once thought impossible by air, such as locomotives and 150-ton generators. It also has allowed vast quantities of relief supplies to be quickly transported to disaster areas, such as quake-stricken Haiti in February 2010. For those thinking the Hughes H4 Hercules, or *Spruce Goose*, is the biggest aircraft, it actually has a greater wingspan but is significantly shorter and lighter. The An-225 can carry up to 550,000 pounds, cruise at 500 mph and travel up to 9,500 miles. Pictures of the An-225 can be seen at www.antonov.com.[11]

WATER CARRIERS

The largest supertanker ever built was the *Seawise Giant*, built by Sumitomo Heavy Industries in 1979. The ship was 1,504 feet long, had 46 tanks, 340,000 square feet of deck, and was too big to pass through the English Channel, the Suez Canal or the Panama Canal. Fully loaded, the ship weighed 646,000 tons and standing on end, it would be taller than the Empire State Building. The ship was by far the largest ship ever built and had a number of owners and names over the years, but is now beached in an Indian scrapyard (a picture of the ship can be seen at www.bluepulz.com/?Id=2245). By comparison, the largest containership ever built was the *Emma Maersk*, built in 2006 by the Moller-Maersk Group. It can carry up to 15,000 standard 20-foot containers, is 1,300 feet long and can cruise at about 29 mph.[12]

PIPELINE CARRIERS

The world's longest pipeline is claimed by several sources. In the North Sea, the world's longest underwater pipeline, finished in 2007 by Norsk Hydro ASA, delivers natural gas from Norway's offshore gas fields to processing plants 746 miles away in the U.K. The sections of pipe were assembled and welded together using the world's largest pipeline-laying ships and then laid continuously on the seafloor, in depths up to 3,000 feet. The world's longest on-land pipeline is the 3,000-mile East Siberia-Pacific Ocean oil pipeline, finished in 2009 and built by the Russian company Transneft. The current capacity of the 48-inch pipeline is about 600,000 barrels per day, but is expected to go much higher. It was the largest development project in Russian history and will be used to supply oil to markets in Japan, Korea and the U.S.[13]

Rail Carriers

Rail carriers compete most favorably when the distance is long and the shipments are heavy or bulky. At one time in the U.S., rail carriers transported the majority of goods shipped; however, since World War II, their share of the transportation market has steadily fallen. Today, U.S. railroads account for only approximately 10 percent of total for-hire transportation expenditures, as shown on Table 9.1.

Rail service is relatively slow and inflexible; however, rail carriers are less expensive than air and motor carriers and can compete fairly well on long hauls. To better compete, railroads have begun purchasing motor carrier companies and can thus offer point-to-point pickup and delivery service using motor carriers and flatcars that carry truck trailers (known as *trailer-on-flatcar service* or *TOFC* service). Railroads are also at somewhat of a disadvantage compared with motor carriers with respect to shipment damage, equipment availability and service frequency.

Since rail companies use each other's rail cars, keeping track of rail cars and getting them where they are needed can be problematic. However, with advances in railroad routing and scheduling software and rail car identification systems, this has become less of a problem for rail carriers. **Real-time location systems (RTLS)** on rail cars use active, WiFi-enabled radio frequency identification (RFID) tags to allow tracking of rail cars (and their assets) in real time. The tag is programmed to broadcast a signal identifying its location at regular time intervals. Sensors can also be added to the RTLS tags to monitor the temperature inside refrigerated cars, for example, and transmit a signal if the temperature goes out of a preset range.[14] In the U.S., railroad infrastructure and aging equipment have also been problems for the railroads; however, there has been a spending resurgence since the mid-1980s to replace worn track segments and rail cars, to upgrade terminals and to consolidate through mergers and acquisitions.

One of the trends in rail transportation is the use of **high-speed trains**. Today, they are operated in the U.S. by Amtrak along the northeast corridor (Boston–New York–Washington D.C.). Bombardier Inc., a Montreal-based transportation and aerospace company, designed and manufactured Amtrak's Acela Express, an electric high-speed train. These trains can make the Washington D.C. to Boston trip in about 6.5 hours, averaging approximately 70 miles per hour, although top speeds can reach 120 miles per hour (other, slower trains and lack of straight-line track have tended to reduce the average speeds).[15]

While the Acela Express is the only high-speed railroad operating in the U.S., other states such as California, Illinois and Florida are considering use of high-speed trains. In fact, $8 billion in federal stimulus money has been earmarked for high-speed passenger train service in the U.S. Florida is perhaps the most likely recipient and has applied for some of this money to build a line connecting Tampa and Orlando, potentially using the Japanese platypus-nosed, Shinkansen bullet-train (see the Global Perspective feature for more on the Shinkansen train). The train could make the 85-mile trip in about 45 minutes with top speeds approaching 200 miles per hour. China has also announced that it is investing $2 billion in high-speed rail service.[16]

Countries such as France and Japan already have extensive high-speed rail lines operating. The inaugural high-speed French rail service between Paris and Lyon was in 1981 and has since expanded to connect cities across France and in neighboring countries. France holds the record for the fastest wheeled train (357 miles per hour on April 3, 2007) and also for the world's highest average speed for regular passenger service. The Japanese shinkansen high-speed rail began operations in 1964 between Tokyo and Osaka. Today, the shinkansen rail network has expanded to many cities in Japan, with average speeds in the 170 miles per hour range. A number of other European countries also use high-speed rail. High-speed rail can provide an attractive alternative to air and other forms of ground transportation, depending on the cost and location of terminals.[17]

Air Carriers

Transporting goods by air is very expensive relative to other modes, but also very fast, particularly for long distances. Looking again at Table 9.1, it can be seen that **air carriers** account for approximately 15 percent of the total annual U.S. for-hire transportation expenditures. The amount of freight hauled, however, is quite small, since airlines cannot carry extremely heavy or bulky cargo (an exception is the world's largest commercial cargo airliner, the Ukrainian-built Antonov An-225, which can carry a payload more than twice the weight of what a Boeing 747 freighter can carry; see the Global Perspective feature for further discussion of the An-225[18]). For light, high-value goods that need to travel long distances quickly, air transportation is the best of the modal alternatives. For movements over water, the only other modal alternative is water carriage, where the transportation decision is based on timing, cost and shipment weight. Though the incidence of shipment damage is quite low and schedule frequency is good, air transportation is limited in terms of geographic coverage. Most small cities in the U.S., for example, do not have airports or regularly scheduled air service; therefore, air transportation service must be combined with motor carrier service for these locations.

Today, about half of the goods transported by air are carried by freight-only airlines like FedEx, the world's largest air cargo airline. This represents a significant change since the late 1960s when most air cargo was hauled by passenger airlines. Today, most passenger air carriers are opting to use smaller, more fuel-efficient aircraft, which has reduced their ability to haul cargo. Growth in markets such as China fueled large increases in international air cargo in the 1980s and 1990s; today, though, the world air cargo market has declined significantly due to increasing fuel prices and the recent economic recession. Between 2000 and 2009, for example, airlines lost a combined $49 billion.[19]

Water Carriers

Shipping goods by **water carrier** is very inexpensive but also very slow and inflexible. There are several types of water transportation including inland waterway, lake, coastal and intercoastal ocean and global deep-sea carriers. Most of the inland waterway transportation is used to haul heavy, bulky, low-value materials such as coal, grain and sand, and competes primarily with rail and pipeline carriers. Inland water transport is obviously limited to areas accessible by water and hence growth in this area of transportation is also limited. Based on information from Table 9.1, water transportation as a percent of total for-hire logistics services has remained fairly steady at about 3 percent for the past 30 years. Like rail and air transportation, water carriers are typically paired with motor carriers to enable door-to-door pick-up and delivery service.

In the U.K., efforts are underway to increase inland waterway carrier usage, as this has less environmental impact when compared to motor freight carriers. British Waterways, the organization responsible for managing U.K. waterways, is investing heavily to reduce highway congestion and pollution by increasing trade along their inland waterways. For example, a single river barge can carry the equivalent of 24 truckloads of freight. Freight on inland waterways also produces lower emissions, less noise and is visually unobtrusive. At present, 3.5 million tons of non-time-sensitive freight per year are moved via 2,000 miles of U.K. inland waterways.[20] On the Mississippi River, barges with up to 30 floating containers as long as a quarter of a mile can be seen moving corn, soybeans and other goods from port to port.

There have also been developments in **deep-sea transportation** that have made water transportation cheaper and more desirable, even with the slow transportation times. The development and use of supertankers and containerships has added a new dimension to water transportation. Many of today's oil supertankers are more than 1,200 feet long (that's four U.S. football fields) and carry over 2 million barrels of oil. The largest oil supertanker was the *Seawise Giant*, measuring 1,500 feet in length and able to carry more than 560,000 tons or 4 million barrels of oil (see the Global Perspective feature for more discussion of the *Seawise Giant*).[21] Oil-producing nations can now cheaply ship large quantities of oil anywhere around the globe where demand exists, and even small shippers can ship items overseas cheaply, because of the ability to consolidate small shipments in containers that are placed on board containerships.

Shipping containers allow almost any packaged product to be shipped overseas and they add an element of protection to the cargo. Containerships carry the majority of the world's water-transported manufactured goods, and they can carry more than 10,000 standard twenty-foot containers (these are normally twenty feet in length, 8.5 feet in height and eight feet wide but can vary), holding up to 52,000 pounds each, with a total containership value sometimes as high as $300 million. At any given time, there are approximately five to six million containers being shipped between countries using containerships.[22]

Pipeline Carriers

Pipeline carriers are very specialized with respect to the products they can carry; however, once the initial investment of the pipeline is recovered, there is very little additional maintenance cost, so long-term pipeline transportation tends to be very inexpensive. Pipelines can haul materials that are only in a liquid or gaseous state and so the growth potential for pipelines is quite limited. One of the items pipelines haul is coal, and they do this by first pulverizing coal into small particles and then suspending it in water to form **coal slurry**. When the coal slurry reaches its destination, the coal and water are separated. Other items transported include water, oil, gasoline and natural gas. The continuous nature of pipeline flow is what makes it unique. Once the product reaches its destination, it is continuously available. Pipelines are today being constructed to haul large quantities of natural gas and oil from desolate areas to existing processing facilities hundreds and even thousands of miles away (see the Global Perspective feature for more discussion of oil and gas pipelines). So long as the world remains dependent on energy products such as coal, oil and natural gas, there will be a need for pipeline transportation.

Intermodal Transportation

Intermodal transportation, or the use of combinations of the various transportation modes, is becoming an extremely popular transportation arrangement and makes the movement of goods much more convenient and efficient. Most large intermodal transportation companies today such as U.S. companies J.B. Hunt, Hub Group and FedEx offer one-stop, door-to-door shipping capabilities—they transport shippers' goods for a price, then determine the best intermodal transportation and warehousing arrangements to meet customer requirements as cheaply as possible.

Here is a shipping example using a number of intermodal combinations:

> *A manufacturing company packs a standard eight-foot container for shipment to an overseas customer. The container is sealed and connected to a motor carrier trailer for transport to a nearby rail terminal. The container is then loaded onto a flatcar and double-stacked with another container, where it is then transported to a seaport on the U.S. West Coast. Upon arrival, the container is placed aboard a container ship and transported to Japan. In Japan, the container is off-loaded and moves through customs, where it is then loaded onto another motor carrier trailer for transport to its final destination, where it finally is unpacked. In this example, goods were only packed and unpacked one time. The container was used in three modes of transportation and remained sealed until the final destination when customs authorities unsealed, examined and accepted the goods.*

The above example highlights a number of intermodal transportation combinations. The most common are truck **trailer-on-flatcar (TOFC)** and **container-on-flatcar (COFC)**, also called **piggyback service**. The same containers can be placed on board containerships and freight airliners. These combinations attempt to combine the flexibility of motor carriers with the economy of rail and/or water carriers. The BNSF Railway, headquartered in

Texas, operates one of the largest railroad networks in North America, with over 30,000 track miles covering 28 states and two Canadian provinces. BNSF moves more intermodal traffic than any other rail system in the world today, and intermodal combinations account for about half of the number of units transported by BNSF. In 2010, BNSF had 38,000 employees, 5,000 locomotives and approximately 190,000 freight cars.[23]

Another example of intermodal transportation are **ROROs,** or roll-on-roll-off, containerships. These allow truck trailers, automobiles, heavy equipment and specialty cargo to be directly driven on and off the ship, into secured below-deck garages without use of cranes. The New Jersey-based Atlantic Container Line operates the largest and most versatile RORO containerships in the world, capable of carrying a wide variety of oversized cargo. Their RORO vessels are some of the most flexible ships operating today; their G-3 vessels can carry 1,000 automobiles and 1,850 standard twenty-foot containers.[24]

Transportation Pricing

The two basic pricing strategies used by logistics service providers are **cost-of-service pricing** and **value-of-service pricing**. Further, when the shipments are large enough, carriers and shippers enter into **negotiated pricing**. Obviously, shippers want low prices and carriers want high profits, and these desires are often at odds with one another. Not too many years ago, carriers like UPS simply distributed their costs evenly and charged a uniform rate to all customers. As computer pricing models improved, logistics companies were able to more closely identify their costs for various types of customers and differential pricing became more the norm, with residential customers and infrequent users seeing significant price increases. More recently, as economic conditions worsened, causing excess capacity due to lower shipping demand, pricing has once again been varied to stay competitive and shippers have been able to negotiate better terms.[25] These and other pricing topics are discussed below.

Cost-of-Service Pricing

Cost-of-service pricing is used when carriers establish prices based on their fixed and variable costs of transportation. To accomplish this, carriers must be able to identify the relevant costs and then accurately allocate these to each shipment. Cost-of-service pricing varies based on volume and distance. As shipping volume increases, the portion of fixed costs that are allocated to each shipment goes down, allowing the carrier to reduce prices. Large-volume shipments also allow carriers to charge carload or truckload rates instead of less-than-carload or less-than-truckload rates. As the shipping distance increases, prices will tend to rise, but not proportionally with distance, because fixed costs are essentially constant regardless of distance. Cost-of-service pricing represents the base, or lowest, shipping price for carriers; and in a highly competitive market, carriers will price just above or near these levels to maintain some level of profitability. As we have seen in this most recent worldwide recession, many carriers were unable to maintain prices at even these lowest levels, resulting in a number of bankruptcies. Some notable examples are Arrow Trucking, Japan Airlines and a French ocean carrier now on the brink, CMA CGM.[26]

Value-of-Service Pricing

In this case, carriers price their services at the highest levels the market will bear. Prices are thus based on the level of competition and the current volume of demand for each service. This is a profit-maximizing pricing approach. If a carrier has a service that is in high demand with little competition, prices will tend to be quite high. As other carriers notice the high profit potential of this service, competition will eventually increase and prices will fall. As the level of competition increases, carriers will seek ways to reduce their costs to maintain profitability.

In the highly competitive passenger airline industry, which was hit hard through 2009 by lower demand for travel, Southwest Airlines has been able to keep their costs low by using only one type of airplane, flying relatively short distances between stops, keeping their planes in the air and using fuel price hedging strategies, which have enabled them to remain profitable through 2009, their 37th consecutive annual profit.[27] Online booking capabilities for airlines, combined with revenue management software to control prices as demand fluctuates, have allowed airlines to use value-of-service pricing to maximize revenues.

Negotiated Pricing

Since the deregulation of transportation in the U.S., negotiating transportation prices has become much more common among business shippers and logistics providers. In addition, shippers today are inclined to develop alliances with logistics companies because of the key role they play in allowing firms and their supply chains to be more responsive to changing demand. This has also tended to increase the use of negotiated prices. Shippers want carriers to use cost-of-service pricing, while carriers want to use value-of-service pricing. To maintain an equitable partnership, prices are negotiated such that they fall somewhere between these two levels, allowing carriers to cover their fixed and variable costs and make a reasonable profit, and allowing shippers to get the logistics services they want at a reasonable price.

Terms of Sale

In many cases, suppliers' terms of sale affect transportation costs. When products are purchased from a supplier, they may quote a price that includes transportation to the buyer's location. This is known as **FOB destination pricing**, or free-on-board to the shipment's destination. This also means that the supplier will be the legal owner of the product until it safely reaches its destination. For high-value shipments, small shipments, or when the buyer has little transportation expertise, FOB destination is typically preferred. Otherwise, the buyer may decide to purchase goods and supply its own transportation to the shipping destination; in this case, the supplier quotes the lower **FOB origination pricing**. The goods then become the legal responsibility of the buyer at the shipment pickup location.

Rate Categories

Carrier prices or rates can be classified in a number of different ways. **Line haul rates** are the charges for moving goods to a nonlocal destination (e.g., between cities), and these can be further classified as *class rates*, *exception rates*, *commodity rates* and *miscellaneous rates*. In the U.S., **class rates** are published annually by the National Motor Freight Traffic Association (NMFTA), a nonprofit group comprised of approximately 1,000 motor carrier companies. The class rate standards, called the National Motor Freight Classification (NMFC), are based on the value of the type of freight, its ease of handling, its weight and dimensions. There are eighteen classes numbered from 50 to 500—the higher the class rating, the higher the price.[28] **Exception rates** are rates that are lower than the NMFC class rates for specific origin-destination locations or volumes and generally are established on an account-by-account basis. **Commodity rates** apply to minimum quantities of products that are shipped between two specified locations. **Miscellaneous rates** apply to contract rates that are negotiated between two parties and to shipments containing a variety of products (in this case, the rate is based on the overall weight of the shipment). Today, many of the rates carriers charge are classified as miscellaneous, since negotiated rates tend to be used primarily for large shipments.

Transportation Security

Transportation security in the U.S., particularly **airline security**, has become a very important issue since September 11, 2001. Congress passed the Aviation and Transportation Security Act on Nov. 19, 2001, creating a large organization (the Transportation Security Administration, or TSA) to oversee transportation security, while giving high hopes to the many government security contractors. Today, the TSA oversees more than 400 U.S. airports. In addition, the Department of Homeland Security (DHS) was created in 2003 with a first-year budget of more than $41 billion to provide overall U.S. security leadership.

A number of problems and actions have resulted from this heightened emphasis on security in the U.S. The TSA has had numerous agency chiefs since 9/11 and has spent more than $12 billion to improve security on airplanes and in airports. The latest DHS initiative is the outfitting of advanced imaging technology (AIT) units in hundreds of U.S. airports in 2010. Travelers will be required to go through these full-body scanners, which can identify any harmful devices hidden beneath clothing. The AITs use harmless millimeter wave technology to generate images reflected from the bodies being scanned.[29] Air cargo transported on passenger aircraft is also subjected to high levels of security checks in the U.S. By 2010, 100 percent of it must be prescreened, according to the Improving America's Security Act of 2007. "It can wreck a huge part of the supply chain if they don't implement it correctly," claims Ken Dunlap, the North America Director of Security for the International Air Transport Association.[30]

Other forms of U.S. transportation have taken a backseat to the airlines when it comes to security concerns and funding. In fact, the TSA's proposed 2011 budget allocates 68 percent of its resources to aviation security and only 2 percent to all other transportation modes.[31] Presently, the DHS scans 98 percent of imported cargo for radiation and U.S. Customs and Border Protection screens U.S.-bound containers at 58 ports around the world. Additionally, the U.S. Congress passed a law calling for 100 percent scanning of *all* U.S.-bound cargo by 2012.[32]

With respect to the other modes of transportation, the TSA has been working with railroads to reduce the number of hours that toxic chemicals can spend in transit, resulting in a 54 percent reduction since 2006 in the overall risk of a rail tanker exploding and exposing people to toxic gases. The TSA also has a Pipeline Security Division, which essentially mandates all pipeline operators to implement a pipeline security program. For many truckers and other transportation workers such as U.S. deepwater port workers, one of the latest transportation security initiatives is the use of the **Transportation Worker Identification Credential (TWIC)**, which was mandated by the Maritime Transportation Security Act of 2002 and the Safe Port Act of 2006. The TWIC became mandatory for port workers in 2009 and the TSA is currently trying to upgrade the technology to allow use of a device that would read a card's biometrics without it being swiped, greatly reducing the card reader time and reducing congestion at port entry locations.[33] Another type of smart card system is the use of PrePass, which allows prequalified U.S. motor carriers to bypass state inspection and weigh stations, saving many thousands of lost work hours and gallons of fuel for truckers. This system is described in the e-Business Connection feature.

e-Business Connection

U.S. Motor Carriers Use PrePass to Bypass Inspection Facilities

In the mid-80s, Heavy Vehicle Electronic License Plate (HELP) launched an ambitious intelligent vehicle-highway system initiative. The result of their efforts is known today as PrePass—a system that uses sophisticated technology allowing qualified carriers in the U.S. to comply electronically with participating states' safety, credentials and weight requirements at state highway weigh stations, commercial vehicle inspection facilities and ports of entry. Cleared vehicles bypass enforcement facilities while traveling at highway speed, eliminating the need to stop.

HELP still exists as a non-profit public/private partnership that provides PrePass equipment to states without the use of public funds. Fleets fund the system with monthly service charges. Carrier participation is strictly voluntary and eligibility is subject to strict safety qualifications.

Vehicles participating in the program are pre-certified. Customers' safety records and credentials are routinely verified with state and federal agencies to ensure adherence to the safety and bypass criteria established by PrePass and member states. "PrePass will improve highway safety by decreasing the number of commercial vehicles exiting and entering the interstate highways from our scale facilities. The opportunity for crashes therefore decreases," said Sam Nolen, director, Illinois State Police.

If an approaching PrePass-equipped vehicle's weight and credentials are satisfactory, a green light and audible signal from a windshield-mounted transponder advises the driver to bypass the weigh station. Otherwise, a red light and audible signal advises the driver to pull into the weigh station for regular processing.

Bypassing inspection facilities saves drivers and their companies time on the road, thereby reducing fuel and operating costs, while increasing productivity. Dan Frieden, president of Air Ride Express' truck division, says, "The trucking industry is as competitive as ever these days, everyone is looking for an advantage. PrePass gives us that advantage by saving us time, fuel and money."

Since the program's inception, over 350 million inspections have been avoided, resulting in a savings of almost 30 million hours, based on an estimated five minutes per screening, and almost 140 million gallons of fuel, based on an estimated 0.4 gallons per pull-in. PrePass has also made a contribution to cleaner air since it cuts emissions by reducing fuel consumption and the idling inherent to waiting in inspection lines. Based on EPA estimates, since its inception the program has reduced emissions by more than 300,000 metric tons.

PrePass also benefits member states because the system enables enforcement officials to electronically ensure motor carrier compliance with state weight, safety and credential requirements before vehicles reach state inspection facilities. The system essentially rewards carriers with good safety records, thereby giving carriers an incentive to conform to safety regulations and credential requirements. Not all motor carriers are eligible to participate in the program. Only those with a history of safe operations can take advantage of the benefits the program offers. PrePass has worked with member states to develop bypass eligibility criteria that are used to determine bypass frequencies and random pull-in rates for qualified vehicles.

Source: Gelinas, T., "Save Time and Fuel with PrePass," *Fleet Equipment* 35, no. 8 (2009): 4. Used with permission.

Transportation Regulation and Deregulation in the U.S.

The transportation industry in the U.S. has gone through periods of both government regulation and deregulation. On the one hand, **transportation regulation** is argued by many to be good in that it tends to assure adequate transportation service throughout the country while protecting consumers in terms of monopoly pricing, safety and liability. On the other hand, **transportation deregulation** is also argued to be good because it encourages competition and allows prices to adjust as supply, demand and negotiations dictate. In addition, antitrust laws already in place tend to protect transportation consumers. This debate was the subject of a study in 1994 to determine the impact deregulation had on the U.S. motor carrier industry. The study concluded that transportation deregulation has resulted in greater use of cost-of-service pricing, rising freight rates for LTL shipments and more safety problems as operators have tended to let fleets age and to reduce maintenance levels.[34] Today, the U.S. transportation industry remains essentially deregulated; however, a number of regulations (primarily safety and security regulations) carriers must adhere to, still exist. Some of the history of transportation regulation and deregulation in the U.S. is reviewed next.

Transportation Regulation

Table 9.2 summarizes the major transportation regulations in the U.S., starting with the **Granger Laws** of the 1870s, which led to the Interstate Commerce Act of 1887. Before this time, the railroads in the U.S. were charging high rates and discriminating against small shippers. So a number of Midwestern states passed laws to broadly regulate the railroads to establish maximum rates, prohibit local discrimination, forbid rail mergers (to encourage competition) and prohibit free passes to public officials. Though the U.S. Supreme Court later struck down these laws, the Granger movement made Congress realize the impacts of railroad monopolies. This led to the passage of the Interstate Commerce Act of 1887.

The 1887 act created the Interstate Commerce Commission (ICC), which required rail carriers to charge reasonable rates; to publish rates, file them with the ICC and make them available to the public; and prohibited discriminatory practices (charging some shippers less than others for the same service). The act also prohibited agreements between railroads to pool traffic or revenues. Between 1887 and 1910, a number of amendments made to the 1887 act increased the ICC's control and enforcement power. These amendments restricted railroads from providing rates and services that were not in the public's best interest, created penalties for failure to follow published rates or for offering and accepting rebates, set maximum rates and prevented railroads from owning pipelines or water carriers, unless approved by the ICC.

By 1917, increased competition combined with the rate restrictions had created a rail system unable to offer the efficient service the U.S. government needed in its war efforts, and thus the federal government seized the railroads. Railroad companies were guaranteed a profit while the government poured large sums of money into upgrading the rail system. By the end of World War I, Congress had come to realize that all of the negative controls placed on railroads were unhealthy for the industry. They wanted to return the railroads to private ownership. This brought about the first of a number of regulations aimed at positive control, namely the **Transportation Act of 1920**.

The 1920 act instructed the ICC to ensure that rates were high enough to provide a fair return for the railroads each year (Congress initially set this at six percent return per year). When companies made more than the prescribed six percent, half of the excess

Table 9.2		U.S. Transportation Regulations
Date	**Regulation**	**Summary**
1870s	Granger Laws	Midwestern states passed laws to establish maximum rates, prohibit discrimination and forbid mergers for railroads.
1887	Interstate Commerce Act	States cannot regulate transportation; established Interstate Commerce Commission; regulated and published rates, outlawed discriminatory pricing, prohibited pooling agreements, to encourage competition.
1920	Transportation Act	Instructed the ICC to establish rates that allowed RRs to earn a fair return; established minimum rates; gave control to ICC to set intrastate rates; allowed pooling agreements if they were in the public's best interest.
1935	Motor Carrier Act	Extended the ICA of 1887 to include motor carriers and brought them under ICC control; established five classes of operators: common, contract, private, exempt and broker; mergers must be OK'd by ICC.
1938	Civil Aeronautics Act	Established the Civil Aeronautics Board to regulate air carriers; new entrants had to get CAB approval; CAB controlled rates; Civil Aeronautics Administration controlled air safety.
1940	Transportation Act	Extended the ICA of 1887 to include ICC control over domestic water transportation; ICC controlled entry, rates and services.
1942	Freight Forwarders Act	Extended the ICA of 1887 to include ICC control over freight forwarders; ICC controlled entry, rates and services.
1948	Reed-Bulwinkle Act	Amendment to the ICA of 1887 legalizing rate bureaus or conferences.
1958	Transportation Act	Amended the rule of rate making by stating that rates couldn't be held up to protect the traffic of any other mode.
1958	Federal Aviation Act	Created the Federal Aviation Agency to assume the mission of the CAA; FAA empowered to manage and develop U.S. airspace and plan the U.S. airport system.
1966	Dept. of Transportation Act	Assumed mission of FAA and a number of other agencies for research, promotion, safety and administration of transportation; organized into nine operating and six administrative divisions; also established the National Transportation Safety Board.
1970	Railway Passenger Service Act	Created the National Railroad Passenger Corp. to preserve and upgrade intercity rail passenger service; resulted in the creation of Amtrak.

was taken and used to fund low-interest loans to the weaker operators for updating their systems and increasing efficiency. The act also allowed the ICC to set minimum rates, allowed joint use of terminal facilities, allowed railroads to enter into pooling agreements and allowed rail company acquisitions and consolidations. Finally, to keep the railroads from becoming overcapitalized, the act prohibited railroads from issuing securities without ICC approval. The rail system thus became a regulated monopoly.

From 1935 to 1942, regulations were passed that applied to other modes of transportation and these were similar in nature to the 1920 act. A great deal of money was spent during the 1920s and during the Depression building the U.S. highway system. The time became ripe, then, for the emergence of for-hire motor carriers. The number of small trucking companies grew tremendously during this period, creating competition for the railroads, as shippers opted to use the cheaper for-hire motor carriers. The **Motor Carrier Act of 1935** brought motor carriers under ICC control, thus controlling entry into the market, establishing motor carrier classes of operation, setting reasonable rates, mandating ICC approval for any mergers or acquisitions and controlling the issuance of securities.

In 1938, the federal government enacted another extension of the Interstate Commerce Act by including regulation of air carriers in the **Civil Aeronautics Act of 1938**. This act promoted the development of the air transportation system and the air safety and airline efficiency by establishing the Civil Aeronautics Board to oversee market entry, establish routes with appropriate levels of competition, develop regional feeder airlines and set reasonable rates. The Civil Aeronautics Administration was also established to regulate air safety.

The **Transportation Act of 1940** further extended the Interstate Commerce Act of 1887 by establishing ICC control over domestic water transportation. The provisions for domestic water carriers were similar to those imposed on rail and motor carriers. In 1942, the 1887 act was once again extended to cover freight forwarders, with the usual entry, rate and service controls of the ICC. Freight forwarders were also prohibited from owning any carriers.

A number of other congressional enactments occurred up through 1970, further strengthening and refining the control of the transportation market. In 1948, the **Reed-Bulwinkle Act** gave groups of carriers the ability to form rate bureaus or conferences wherein they could propose rate changes to the ICC. The **Transportation Act of 1958** established temporary loan guarantees to railroads, liberalized control over intrastate rail rates, amended the rule of rate-making to ensure more intermodal competition and clarified the differences between private and for-hire motor carriers. The **Federal Aviation Act of 1958** replaced the Civil Aeronautics Administration with the Federal Aviation Administration (FAA) and gave the FAA authority to prescribe air traffic rules, make safety regulations and plan the national airport system. In 1966, the **Department of Transportation Act** created the Department of Transportation (DOT) to coordinate the executive functions of all government entities dealing with transportation-related matters. It was hoped that centralized coordination of all the transportation agencies would lead to more effective transportation promotion and planning. Finally, to preserve and improve the rail system's ability to service passengers, the **Railway Passenger Service Act** was passed in 1970, thus creating Amtrak.

Transportation Deregulation

Commencing in 1976, Congress enacted a number of laws to reduce and eliminate transportation regulations. These are summarized in Table 9.3. This began the movement toward less regulation by allowing market forces to determine prices, entry and services. At this point in U.S. transportation history, consumers and politicians had the opinion that transportation regulation was administered more for the benefit of the carriers than the public. In addition, with the bankruptcy filings of a number of railroads in the mid-1970s combined with the Arab oil embargo of the same time period, regulation was receiving much of the blame for an inefficient transportation system.

The **Railroad Revitalization and Regulatory Reform Act**, commonly known as the 4-R Act, was passed in 1976 and made several regulatory changes to help the railroads. First, railroads were allowed to change rates without ICC approval, limited by *threshold costs* on one end and *market dominance* on the other. Threshold costs were defined as the firm's variable costs and the ICC determined whether the firm was in a market dominant position (absence of market competition). A number of ICC procedures were also sped up to aid transportation manager decision making. These same ideas appeared again in later deregulation efforts.

Table 9.3	U.S. Transportation Deregulation	
Date	Deregulation	Summary
1976	Railroad Revitalization and Regulatory Reform Act	The "4-R Act." Railroads were allowed to change rates without ICC approval, within limits; ICC procedures were sped up.
1977	Air Cargo Deregulation Act	Freed all air cargo carriers from CAB regulations
1978	Air Passenger Deregulation Act	Airlines freed to expand routes, change fares within limits; small community routes were subsidized; CAB ceases to exist in 1985.
1980	Motor Carrier Act	Fewer restrictions on entry, routes, rates and private carriers.
1980	Staggers Rail Act	Freed railroads to establish rates within limits; legalized contract rates; shortened ICC procedure turnaround.
1982	Bus Regulatory Reform Act	Amended the 1980 MCA to include buses.
1984	Shipping Act	Partial deregulation of ocean transportation
1994	Trucking Industry Regulatory Reform Act	Motor carriers freed from filing rates with the ICC.
1994	FAA Authorization Act	Freed intermodal air carriers from economic regulation by the states.
1995	ICC Termination Act	Eliminated the ICC and moved regulatory duties to Dept. of Transportation.
1998	Ocean Shipping Reform Act	Deregulated ocean liner shipping; allowed contract shipping; rate filing not required.

Air freight was deregulated in 1977. No longer were there any barriers to entry provided the firms were deemed fit by the Civil Aeronautics Board. Size restrictions were also lifted and carriers were free to charge any rate provided there was no discrimination. Finally, carriers did not have to file freight rates with the CAB. This was followed soon after by deregulation of air passenger service in 1978. The targeted beneficiary of passenger airline deregulation was the traveler. In introducing the bill to the Senate floor, Senator Ted Kennedy, one of the bill's principal sponsors, proclaimed, "This bill, while preserving the government's authority to regulate health and safety, frees airlines to do what business is supposed to do—serve consumers better for less." This was a phased-in approach, wherein carriers could slowly add routes to their systems while protecting other routes from competition. Fares could be adjusted within limits without CAB approval. To protect small communities from losing service, all cities with service in 1977 were guaranteed service for ten additional years. In 1981, all route restrictions were to be released, allowing any carrier to operate any route. Airline rates and mergers were to be released from regulation in 1983. Finally, the CAB was to shut down in 1985.

The impacts of deregulation on the U.S. airline industry were enormous—there were 34 air passenger carriers in 1977 and by 1982 the number had increased to 90. Some fares dropped substantially, while other fares went up, and routes to low-demand areas decreased substantially. By 1981, among the major U.S. airlines, only American, Delta and TWA were making a profit. A number of notable airline failures also occurred in the years following deregulation. Braniff, for instance, after deregulation, expanded rapidly in the U.S. and abroad, purchased a large number of planes, loaded up on debt and then declared bankruptcy in 1982. They emerged from bankruptcy as a smaller airline;

then seven years later declared bankruptcy again, after failing to obtain financing. A short time later, Braniff ceased operations completely. People Express, a new low-fare, no-frills airline that began right after deregulation, followed the Braniff large-expansion-high-debt model, and similarly had trouble operating in 1986, eventually selling out to rival Texas Air, which filed for bankruptcy as well in 1990. In all, some 150 airlines came and went during this period.[35]

Motor carriers were deregulated in 1980. The objectives of this act were to promote competitive as well as safe and efficient motor transportation. Entry regulations were relaxed to make it easier to enter the market—firms had only to show a "useful public purpose" would be served. Route restrictions were removed and restrictions deemed to be wasteful of fuel, inefficient or contrary to public interest were also removed. As with the 4-R Act, a **zone of rate freedom** was also used. And, as with air passenger deregulation, a large number of new motor carriers began service. By 1981, more than 2,400 new motor carriers had started up in the U.S.

Railroads were further deregulated with the **Staggers Rail Act of 1980**. The financial condition of railroads was worsening and this act was aimed at improving finances for the rail industry. With this act, rail carriers were free to change rates within a zone of rate freedom, but the ceiling or market dominance rate was established more definitively as 160 percent of variable costs and varied up to 180 percent depending on ICC cost formulas. After 1984, rate increases were to be tied to the rate of inflation. Contract rates were also allowed between railroads and shippers.

The **Shipping Act of 1984** marked the end of the initial push by Congress to deregulate the entire U.S. transportation industry. This act allowed ocean carriers to pool or share shipments, assign ports, publish rates and enter into contracts with shippers. More recently, with the passage of the **ICC Termination Act of 1995** and the **Ocean Shipping Reform Act of 1998**, the Interstate Commerce Commission was eliminated and the requirement for ocean carriers to file rates with the Federal Maritime Commission also came to an end.

Thus, a number of changes in the U.S. transportation industry over the past century have occurred. Economic regulation of transportation occurred for several reasons. Initial transportation regulations were instituted to *establish the ground rules* as new forms of transportation developed and to *control prices, services and routes* when monopoly power existed in the industry. Later, regulations were eased to *encourage competition* and *increase efficiency and safety*. In the future, as economic conditions change and as technology, political and social changes occur, transportation regulations will also continue to change, as we have seen since 2001 with transportation security regulations.

Warehousing and Distribution

Warehousing provides a very strategic supply chain service, in that it enables firms to store their purchases, work-in-progress and finished goods, as well as perform breakbulk and assembly activities, while allowing faster and more frequent deliveries of finished products to customers, which in turn results in better customer service when the system is designed and managed correctly. Right now, readers may be questioning the need for warehouses, particularly as this textbook has been singing the praises of lean or low inventories, efficient supply chains and the like. But just the opposite is true today. As disposable income in the U.S. increases, consumers buy more goods that must move through various distribution systems. Even though U.S. freight distribution systems move goods from manufacturers to end users in an increasingly efficient manner, the growth in demand for warehouse space has overcome this improved efficiency. Not only is the number of warehouses growing, but they're getting larger too. Five years ago in the U.S., average warehouse size was approximately 250,000 square feet. Today, 400,000-square-foot warehouses are becoming more prevalent (that's almost five soccer fields). Denver-based ProLogis, a real estate developer, estimates that the available square footage of commercial warehouses in the U.S. (excluding privately owned warehouses) is greater than 5 billion square feet.[36]

In many cases today, warehouses aren't used to store things, but rather to receive bulk shipments, break them down, repackage various items into outgoing orders and then distribute these orders to a manufacturing location or retail center. These activities are collectively referred to as **crossdocking**. In this case, the warehouse is more accurately described as a **distribution center**. In other cases, firms are moving warehouses closer to suppliers, closer to customers, or to more centralized locations, depending on the storage objectives and customer service requirements. So, warehouses are still very much in use—some just to store things and others to provide efficient throughput of goods. This section discusses a number of warehousing issues including their importance and the types of warehouses, risk pooling and warehouse location, and lean warehousing.

The Importance and Types of Warehouses

Firms hold inventories for a number of reasons as explained in Chapter 6, wherein warehouses are used to support purchasing, production and distribution activities. Firms order raw materials, parts and assemblies, which are typically shipped to a warehouse location close to or inside the buyer's location, and then eventually transferred to the buyer's various operations as needed. In a retail setting, the warehouse might be regionally located, with the retailer receiving bulk orders from many suppliers, breaking these down and reassembling outgoing orders for delivery to each retail location, and then using a private fleet of trucks or for-hire transportation providers to move orders to the retail locations. Similar distribution centers are used when manufacturers deliver bulk shipments to regional market areas and then break these down and ship LTL order quantities to customers.

Conversely, firms may operate **consolidation warehouses** to collect large numbers of LTL shipments from nearby regional sources of supply, where these are then consolidated and transported in TL or CL quantities to a manufacturing or user facility located at some distance from the consolidation center. The use of consolidation warehouses and distribution centers allows firms to realize both purchase economies and transportation economies. Firms can buy goods in bulk at lower unit costs and then ship these goods at TL or CL rates either to a distribution center or directly to a manufacturing center. They can also purchase and move small quantity purchases at LTL rates to nearby consolidation warehouses.

Private Warehouses

Just as with the private forms of transportation, **private warehouses** refer to warehouses that are owned by the firm storing the goods. For firms with large volumes of goods to store or transfer, private warehouses represent an opportunity to reduce the costs of warehousing. Currently, United Parcel Service, Wal-Mart and Sears Holding Corp. are the three largest private warehouse operators in North America.[37] Besides the long-term cost benefit private warehouses can provide, another consideration is the level of control provided by private warehouses. Firms can decide what to store, what to process, what types of security to provide and the types of equipment to use, among other operational aspects of warehouses. Private warehousing can also enable the firm to better utilize its workforce and expertise in terms of transportation, warehousing and distribution center activities. Also, as supply chains become more global to take advantage of cheaper sources of supply or labor, the use of private warehouses tends to increase. Finally, private warehouses can generate income and tax advantages through leasing of excess capacity and/or asset depreciation. For these reasons, private warehousing accounts for the vast majority of overall warehouse space in the U.S.[38]

Owning warehouses, though, can also represent a significant financial risk and loss of flexibility to the firm. The costs to build, equip and then operate a warehouse can be very high and most small to moderate-sized firms simply cannot afford private warehouses. Private warehouses also bind firms to locations that may not prove optimal as time passes. Warehouse size or capacity is also somewhat inflexible, at least in the short term. Another problem can be insurance. Insurance companies, in many cases, do not like insuring goods in private warehouses, simply because security levels can be meager or nonexistent, creating a significant concern regarding fires or thefts of goods. Storing fine art in private warehouses is one such example. "We have all this exposure at the private warehouses, where we might have half a billion or $800 million of art, but we know nothing about how they're operated and how they're secured," says Thomas Burns, vice president at fine art insurer Fortress Corp.[39]

Public Warehouses

As the name implies, **public warehouses** are for-profit organizations that contract or lease a wide range of light manufacturing, warehousing and distribution services to other companies. Public warehouses provide a number of specialized services that firms can use to create customized services for various shipments and goods. These services include the following:

- *Breakbulk*—large-quantity shipments are broken down so that items can be combined into specific customer orders and then shipped out.
- *Repackaging*—after **breakbulk**, items are repackaged for specific customer orders. Warehouses can also do individual product packaging and labeling.
- *Assembly*—some public warehouses provide final assembly operations to satisfy customer requests and to create customized final products.
- *Quality inspections*—warehouse personnel can perform incoming and outgoing quality inspections.
- *Material handling, equipment maintenance and documentation services.*
- *Short- and long-term storage.*

Besides the services shown here, public warehouses provide the short-term flexibility and investment cost savings that private warehouses cannot offer. If demand changes or products change, the short-term commitments required at public warehouses allow firms to quickly change warehouse locations. Public warehouses allow firms to test market areas and withdraw quickly if demand does not materialize as expected. The cost for firms to use a public warehouse can also be very small if the capacity requirements are minimal. Nabisco, for instance, spends several million dollars per year to outsource to ten major public warehouse providers and about 200 carriers for its warehousing and delivery business, which delivers to large food chains, mass merchants, drugstores, retailers and grocery wholesalers.[40]

One of the main disadvantages associated with public warehouses is the lack of control provided to the goods owners. Other problems include communication problems with warehouse personnel, lack of specialized services or capacity at the desired locations and the lack of care and security that might be given to products.

Firms might find it advantageous to use public warehouses in some locations and private warehouses in others. For large, established markets and relatively mature products, large firms may decide that owning and operating a warehouse makes the most sense, whereas the same firm may lease space and pay for services at public warehouses in developing markets and low-demand areas.

Today, public warehouses are finding new ways to add value for their clients, including the offering of specialized services such as refrigerated warehouses, customs clearance, reverse logistics, freight consolidation, claims processing, real-time information control and direct-store deliveries. During the most recent economic downturn, use of public warehousing and other transportation management services grew tremendously as shippers sought to reduce supply chain costs. New Jersey-based Ultra Logistics grew significantly during the recession for precisely this reason. It now handles more than 40,000 JIT truckloads per year for clients such as Kraft Foods, Con-Agra, Anheuser-Busch and L'Oreal.[41]

Risk Pooling and Warehouse Location

One of the more important decisions regarding private warehouses is where to locate them. This decision will affect the number of warehouses needed, required capacities, system inventory levels, customer service levels and warehousing system costs. For a given market area, as the number of warehouses used increases, the system becomes more *decentralized*. In a decentralized warehousing system, responsiveness and delivery service levels will increase since goods can be delivered more quickly to customers; however, warehousing system operating and inventory costs will also increase. Other costs that come into play here are outgoing transportation costs to customers and the transportation costs associated with the incoming deliveries of goods to each warehouse. Thus, the trade-off between costs and customer service must be carefully considered as the firm makes its warehouse location decisions. This brings up the very important topic of **risk pooling**, which is discussed below.

Risk Pooling

Risk pooling describes the relationship between the number of warehouses, system inventories and customer service, and it can be explained as follows:

> When market demand is random, it is very likely that higher-than-average demand from some customers will be offset by lower-than-average demand from other customers. As the number of customers served by a single warehouse increases, these demand variabilities will tend to offset each other more often, thus reducing overall demand variance and the likelihood of stockouts. Consequently, the amount of safety stock in a warehouse system required to guard against stockouts decreases. Thus, the more centralized *a warehousing system is, the* lower the safety stock *required to achieve a given system-wide customer service level (recall that in inventory parlance the customer service level is inversely proportional to the number of stockouts per period).*

As mentioned above, risk pooling assumes that demand at the markets served by a warehouse system is negatively correlated (higher-than-average demand in one market area tends to be offset by lower-than-average demand in another market area). In smaller market areas served by warehouses, this may not hold true, and warehouses would then require higher levels of safety stock. This is why a smaller number of centralized warehouses serving large market areas require lower overall system inventories, compared to a larger number of decentralized warehouses serving the same markets.

A good illustration of this principle occurred in Europe after the formation of the European Union in 1993. Prior to that time, European logistics systems were formed along national lines. In other words, each country's distribution systems operated independently of the others, with warehouses located in each country. With the arrival of a single European market in 1993, these distribution systems no longer made economic sense. For instance, Becton Dickinson, an American manufacturer of diagnostics equipment, was burdened in Europe in the early 1990s with a very inefficient and costly distribution system. Their inventory carrying costs and stock write-offs were high, while their stockouts were numerous. After the formation of the European Union, the company closed their distribution centers in Sweden, France, Germany and Belgium and shifted all of their distribution operations to a single automated center in Belgium. In less than a year, average stock levels were down 45 percent, write-offs fell by 65 percent and stockouts were reduced by 75 percent. Other companies in Europe had similar results.[42]

The effect of risk pooling can be estimated numerically by the **square root rule**, which suggests that the system average inventory (as impacted by changing the number of warehouses in the system) is equal to the original system inventory times the ratio of the square root of the new number of warehouses to the square root of the original number of warehouses.[43] A simple illustration of risk pooling is shown in Example 9.1. In the example, reducing the number of warehouses from two to one causes a reduction in average inventory of approximately 29 percent.

The differences between centralized and decentralized warehousing systems can be summarized as follows:

- *Safety stock and average system inventory*—as the firm moves toward fewer warehouses and a more centralized warehousing system, safety stocks and thus

---

Example 9.1   Risk Pooling

Perkins Western Boot Emporium currently owns two warehouses in Houston and Seattle to store its boots before shipping them out to various retail customers across the western U.S. Greg Perkins, the owner, is considering a change to one centralized warehouse in Denver to service all of their retail customers and is curious to know the impact this will have on their system inventory requirements. Their current average inventory level is approximately 6,000 boots at each warehouse. He has found that this level of stock will result in warehouse stockouts approximately one percent of the time. Using the square root rule, he calculates the new average inventory level needed at the central Denver warehouse to maintain the same low level of stockouts:

$$S_2 = \frac{\sqrt{N_2}}{\sqrt{N_1}}(S_1) = \frac{1.0}{1.41}(12,000) = 8,511 \text{ boots},$$

where

S_1 = total system stock of boots for the N1 warehouses;

S_2 = total system stock of boots for the N2 warehouses;

N_1 = number of warehouses in the original system; and

N_2 = number of warehouses in the proposed system

average inventory levels across the system are decreased. The magnitude of the reduction depends on the demand correlations in the various market areas.

- *Responsiveness*—as warehouse centralization increases, delivery lead times increase, increasing the risk of late deliveries to customers and reducing the ability of the organization to respond quickly to changes in demand. Customer service levels may thus decrease, because of issues such as traffic problems and weather delays.

- *Customer service to the warehouse*—as centralization increases, customer service levels provided by the warehouses' suppliers is likely to increase, reducing the likelihood of stockouts for a given level of average system warehouse inventory.

- *Transportation costs*—as centralization increases, outbound transportation costs increase, as LTL shipments must travel farther to reach customers. Inbound transportation costs decrease, since manufacturers and other suppliers are able to ship larger quantities at TL rates to fewer warehouse locations. The overall impact on transportation costs thus depends on the specific warehouse locations, the goods stored, the locations of suppliers and the modes of transportation used.

- *Warehouse system capital and operating costs*—as centralization increases, warehouse capital and operating costs decrease because there are fewer warehouses, fewer employees, less equipment and less maintenance costs.

Warehouse Location

A number of location models and theories have been proposed over the years to optimally locate factories, services and warehouses. In Chapter 11, a number of location analysis tools are discussed, and these can certainly be useful for locating warehouses. Early in the development of modern transportation and warehousing networks, several well-known economists posited theories regarding warehouse locations that are discussed in this section.

German economist Johann Heinrich von Thünen, who is often regarded as the "father of location theory," argued in the 1820s that transportation costs alone should be minimized when considering facility locations.[44] His model assumed that market prices and manufacturing costs would be identical regardless of the location of the warehouse, so the optimum location would be the one that resulted in the minimum transportation costs. Another German economist a century later, Alfred Weber, proposed an industrial location theory very similar to von Thünen's; he argued that the optimum location would be found when the sum of the inbound and outbound transportation costs was minimized.[45]

In the 1940s, Edgar Hoover recommended three types of location strategies: the market positioned, product positioned and intermediately positioned strategies.[46] The **market positioned strategy** locates warehouses close to customers, to maximize customer service levels. This strategy is recommended when high levels of distribution flexibility and customer service. The **product positioned strategy** locates warehouses close to the sources of supply to enable the firm to collect various goods while minimizing inbound transportation costs. This strategy works well when there are large numbers of goods purchased from many sources of supply and assortments of goods ordered by customers. The **intermediately positioned strategy** places warehouses midway between the sources of supply and the customers. This strategy is recommended when distribution service requirements are relatively high and customers order product assortments purchased from many suppliers.

In the 1950s, Melvin Greenhut's location theory was based on profit instead of transportation costs.[47] He argued that the optimum location would be the one that maximized profits, which may not coincide with the minimum cost location, because demand and prices can potentially vary based on location.

Several location heuristics have been developed based on transportation costs, one of which is the center-of-gravity approach, discussed in Chapter 11. The weakness of this approach, as well as some of those discussed here, is that they fail to consider a number of other factors such as labor availability, labor rates, land cost, building codes, tax structure, construction costs, utility costs and the local environment. Additionally, if a firm is using a public warehouse, the location selection criteria would need to include warehouse services, lease costs, communication capabilities, reporting frequency and the operator's reputation. These factors may best be addressed using a weighted factor location analysis, also discussed in Chapter 11.

Lean Warehousing

As firms develop their supply chain management capabilities, items will be moving more quickly through inbound and outbound warehouses and distribution centers. These warehouses and distribution centers will thus have to develop leaner capabilities. Some examples of these capabilities include the following:

- *Greater emphasis on crossdocking*—warehouse employees must receive shipments and mix these quickly into outgoing shipments. Far fewer goods will be stored for any appreciable time and average warehouse inventory levels will decrease, while the number of stockkeeping units will increase.

- *Reduced lot sizes and shipping quantities*—inbound and/or outbound shipping quantities are likely to be smaller and more frequent, containing mixed quantities of goods, and thus requiring more handling.

- *A commitment to customers and service quality*—warehouse employees must perform warehouse activities so as to meet the requirements of their inbound and outbound suppliers and customers.

- *Increased automation*—to improve handling speed and reliability, more warehouse activities will become automated, from scanner/barcode computer tracking systems, to warehouse management software applications, to automated storage and retrieval systems.

- *Increased assembly operations*—as more firms implement lean systems and mass customization, warehouses will be called upon to perform final assembly operations to meet specific customer requirements. This will change the skill requirements of warehouse employees, along with equipment requirements.

Most distribution centers have adopted many **lean warehousing** concepts. Indiana-based Prime Distribution Services (PDS) offers distribution services to suppliers in club-store grocery supply chains. They offer warehousing, crossdocking, packaging and freight consolidation to suppliers who are looking to increase speed and reduce costs as much as possible to compete in the extremely low-profit-margin grocery industry. Consequently, PDS distribution capabilities have had to evolve to survive. They recently combined several distribution centers into a single 1.2 million-square-foot heavily automated facility that provides greater control over inventory, more responsive order management and easier building of mixed SKU pallets. They have a state-of-the-art warehouse management system to manage picking operations, and automated barcode scanning, sorting and routing capabilities to divert orders to packing stations. They have seen improvements in productivity and order accuracy since moving to the new facility. "Our leadership and our organization are geared toward a lean warehousing operation," says Scott Zurawski, director of PDS warehouse operations. "We're trying to build sustainability and quality into every process."[48]

The Impacts of Logistics on Supply Chain Management

As mentioned in this chapter's introduction, logistics refers to the movement and storage of products from point of origin to point of consumption within the firm and throughout the supply chain and is thus responsible for creating time utility and place utility. In a managed supply chain setting, these logistics elements are extremely important in that products must be routinely delivered to each supply chain customer on time, to the correct location, at the desired level of quality and at a reasonable cost. As mistakes occur in deliveries along the supply chain, more safety stocks must be held, impacting both customer service levels and costs. To make up for lost time, overnight deliveries might also have be used, adding yet more costs to the transportation bill.

For global supply chains, the logistics function is even more critical. Providing adequate transportation and storage, getting items through customs, delivering to foreign locations in a timely fashion, and logistics pricing can all impact the ability of a supply chain to serve a foreign market competitively. In many cases, firms are forced to use outside agents or **third-party logistics services (3PLs)** to move items into foreign locations effectively.

Purchases from foreign suppliers are also similarly affected by logistics considerations. When firms begin evaluating and using foreign suppliers, logistics costs and timing become critical factors in the sourcing decision. For instance, Chinese suppliers delivering goods to buyers along the U.S. East Coast are in many cases favoring an all-water route through the Panama Canal, rather than dealing with port and traffic congestion on the U.S. West Coast and then trucking and rail transportation within the U.S. Buyers get cheaper freight rates and can plan on shipments arriving at a specific time when using an all-water route, whereas the chances of domestic U.S. shipments being held up because of port and traffic congestion and missed rail connections can be significant. All-water shipments have risen about 65 percent since the early 1990s.[49] Containerized cargo numbers are up in every Eastern U.S. port. Primarily, the growth has been the result of increased growth in global trade in general and an increase specifically in Asia Pacific trade. The Port of Virginia, for example, has over 50 distribution centers and has seen its business increase as retailers ship to the port and then feed goods to their nearby East Coast distribution centers.[50] In many cases, buyers with limited foreign purchasing experience must use a knowledgeable 3PL service to purchase from foreign suppliers and make logistics decisions effectively and efficiently.

Thus, the value created for supply chains by logistics can easily be seen. It is what effectively links each supply chain partner. Poor logistics management can literally bring a supply chain to its knees, regardless of the production cost or quality of the products. Alternatively, good logistics management can be one of the elements creating a competitive advantage for supply chains. A number of these topics are explored further in this section.

Third-Party Logistics (3PL) Services

Most logistics service companies offer both transportation and warehousing services, allowing firms to make better use of distribution alternatives such as transportation mode, storage location and customs clearance. Some 3PLs even provide complete end-to-end supply chain management services, including network optimization, light manufacturing and other value-added services. Tennessee-based 3PL company OHL has experienced an increase in e-commerce business in recent years. "We've been very active in the e-fulfillment space. That business continues to grow for us, especially as companies that may not have had a direct-to-consumer presence add that to their services. In some instances, we also provide gift wrapping and personalization services," says Bob Spieth, President of Contract Logistics for OHL.[51] For small firms with no internal logistics expertise and large firms with many sizeable and varied logistics needs, outsourcing logistics requirements to these 3PLs can help firms get the services they require at reasonable prices. Many firms outsource some or all of their logistics needs to allow more attention to be placed on core competencies. In tough economic times, firms look to 3PLs to help reduce costs while maintaining customer service levels. In 2009, 80 percent of U.S. companies used a 3PL for at least one area of their supply chains. In Europe, about 66 percent of every logistics euro spent was on outsourcing.[52] Whatever the reason, demand for 3PL services is growing rapidly.

Studies performed by the Georgia Institute of Technology indicate a clear advantage gained by outsourcing logistics functions to 3PLs. One of their studies found that companies using 3PLs realized a 13 percent logistics cost savings. Supply chain management professor C. John Langley at the Georgia Institute of Technology argues that firms should increase the number of services outsourced to 3PLs. "Shippers want to outsource activities that are more routine and repetitive rather than customer-focused. As long as this continues, shippers are not exploiting the full range of services they can benefit from," he says. Ohio-based ODW Logistics, for example, offers pick-and-pack fulfillment, labeling, point-of-sale displays, assembly/kitting, product inspections/quality assurance, bundling, international import/export services, special product handling, packaging and crossdocking from five shared logistics centers and four contract logistics locations in the U.S.[53]

Outsourcing End-to-End Supply Chain Management Activities

In some cases, firms may opt to partner with a 3PL for the provision of most or all supply chain management activities. For small firms, it may be a question of lack of expertise. The sheer scale of supply chain activities and cost may also attract very large firms that prefer to free up valuable resources for other activities. For example, global automaker General Motors formed a joint venture with CNF, Inc. (now renamed Con-way Inc. and based in California) to manage the automaker's entire supply chain, specifically all of GM's existing third-party logistics providers for both inbound and outbound movements over a three-year transition period. The joint venture company, Vector SCM, termed a **lead logistics provider** or **fourth-party logistics provider (4PL)**, managed all of GM's worldwide 3PL providers.[54] Vector also assumed responsibility for managing some 180 million pounds of materials from GM's 12,000 worldwide suppliers every day.[55]

3PL Supply Base Reduction

As discussed in the *Supply Management* section of this text, reducing the supply base can provide a number of advantages for the organization. With 3PL suppliers, the discussion is very similar—using fewer 3PLs enables the firm to select and use only the best-performing 3PLs as well as to give these 3PLs a bigger share of the firm's logistics needs. This in turn results in better levels of service and potentially cheaper prices. The larger share of business given to each 3PL can be used as leverage when negotiating prices, shipping schedules and services. By the end of 2005, for instance, Hewlett-Packard had halved the number of 3PLs it was using and continued to reduce this number even further. Other companies are similarly seeking to achieve an "irreducible minimum" number of 3PL suppliers.[56] Thus, 3PL supply base reduction should become an integral part of an effective logistics management strategy particularly in markets characterized by numerous 3PL choices.

Mode and 3PL Selection

When attempting to minimize logistics costs and/or improve customer service along the supply chain, firms must identify the most desirable transportation modes and 3PL services available for the various markets they serve as well as for their inbound purchased materials. Also, other costs will be affected by this decision, including inventory-in-transit carrying costs, packaging costs, warehousing costs and shipment damage costs. Part II of this text discussed the topic of evaluating and selecting suppliers, and again, the topic here is very similar. Firms use a mix of quantitative and qualitative factors to evaluate and select 3PLs and there are a number of comparative methods available to aid in the decision process, the most common of which is the weighted factor analysis. In a number of surveys conducted, important selection factors were found to be transit-time reliability, transportation rates, total transit time, willingness to negotiate rates and services, damage-free delivery frequency, financial stability, use of electronic data interchange and willingness to expedite deliveries.[57]

Creating Strategic Logistics Alliances

Building an effective supply chain very often includes the creation of strategic alliances with providers of logistics services. In fact, in several surveys of various businesses and industries, transportation and warehousing companies were included as supply chain partners in more than 50 percent of the survey respondents who were actively managing their supply chains.[58] In today's business climate, partnering with a 3PL makes even more sense. "Now, more and more companies are moving from their costly and older processes to outsource their logistics in favor of focusing on their core competencies," says Tony Zasimovich, vice president of logistics services at California-based APL Logistics.[59] These partnerships underscore the importance and role played by logistics in supply chain management. A few examples are given here.

Automobile supply chains are getting longer and more complex as companies search for lower-cost and higher-quality suppliers. This has made collaborations with 3PLs even more important. Not too long ago, U.S. automakers focused on squeezing logistics suppliers for cost reductions. "They considered logistics a commodity," says Gregory Hines, president of National Logistics Management, a Michigan-based 3PL. "The right cost is not necessarily the lowest cost. One company can't do everything and partnership alliances are a key," he adds.[60] Partnerships between railroads and automakers in the U.S. mean that seven out of every ten vehicles produced are moved by rail to dealerships, along with a large percentage of the vehicle parts moving to assembly plants. Railroads have invested billions of dollars fabricating special boxcars designed to the automakers' specifications, autorack rail cars with premium cushioning, auto-carrier trucks, a network of vehicle distribution centers and information systems that allow railroad companies to function as an integral part of automakers' organizations.[61]

Ohio-based bowling supplies distributor Ace Mitchell Bowlers Mart partnered with 3PL provider C.H. Robinson Worldwide in 2007 to see if they could find improvements in their $1 million annual LTL transportation costs. "We thought we had a pretty good handle on things," says Todd Williams, Ace's vice president. In reality, C.H. Robinson found out that Ace's regional LTL carriers were shipping Ace Mitchell products on their own schedules with little coordination, creating many small load trips. Worst of all, they found that workers were stacking skids of bowling balls on top of each other and actually puncturing boxes, resulting in product being delivered in damaged condition. The Robinson team designed a coordinated delivery system to combine LTL shipments into the more efficient TL moves, and provide some direct-to-customer intermodal moves as well, resulting in a 20 percent reduction in annual transportation costs and much less product damage.[62]

Other Transportation Intermediaries

In some cases, companies utilize **transportation intermediaries**, which may not own any significant logistics capital assets, to find the most appropriate transportation mode or 3PL service. For many small companies, where logistics expertise may be limited, and in some cases for large companies, where the scale of logistics needs are great, use of these transportation services can make good economic sense. A few of these intermediaries are discussed next.

Freight Forwarders

Freight forwarders consolidate large numbers of small shipments to fill entire truck trailers or rail cars to achieve truckload or carload transportation rates. They can also provide air transportation consolidation services. These companies pass some of the savings on to the small shippers and then keep the rest as fees. Thus, freight forwarders provide valuable services to both the shipper (lower shipping prices) and the carrier (extra business and higher equipment utilization). Freight forwarders can specialize in either domestic or global shipments, as well as air or ground shipments. These companies also provide documentation services, special freight handling and customs clearance.

Several changes in the freight forwarding arena have recently been occurring, primarily due to the abundance of capacity and cheap shipping options as a result of the poor world economy, and as border security has tightened particularly in the U.S. The freight forwarding business actually has been booming recently as shippers look for ways to further reduce costs. FedEx Trade Networks, the air freight forwarder subsidiary of FedEx, opened over twenty additional freight forwarding offices around the world in 2009 and 2010 to take advantage of the growing demand for this service.[63] Use of Web-based regulatory compliance software by freight forwarders shifted into high gear as the Importer Security Filing mandate of the U.S. Customs and Border Protection Program went into effect early in 2010. Importers and carriers must file 12 data elements before a U.S.-bound container can be loaded aboard a ship at a foreign port. This is the first all-electronic trade program of U.S. Customs and points the way toward their paperless future. Trade compliance has thus become the latest expertise area for freight forwarders.[64]

Transportation Brokers

Also referred to as **load brokers**, **transportation brokers** bring shippers and transportation companies (mainly truckers) together. The transportation broker is legally authorized to act on the shipper's or carrier's behalf, and typically these companies are hired because of their extensive knowledge of the many transportation alternatives available or simply due to the many shippers needing transportation. Minnesota-based transportation broker C.H. Robinson Worldwide provides a good example of the way these middlemen can be profitable even in the depressed transportation industry. They buy cheap transport capacity on trucks, rail cars and cargo ships on the spot markets and then resell it to shippers at higher contract rates. The company "does well in a world where there is more [transport] supply than there is demand for products to ship," says Jon Fisher, a portfolio manager at Fifth Third Asset Management, Inc.[65]

Typical arrangements might find small businesses using a transportation broker to handle many of their shipping needs, or trucking companies using brokers to find a back-haul job after a delivery is completed. A number of transportation broker directories exist, enabling shippers and carriers to find one meeting their needs. For instance, the Red Book Transportation Broker Ratings online directory of transportation brokers assists carriers in locating transportation brokers in the U.S. and Canada. The website provides user ratings of the various transportation brokers as well as information about each of the brokers and their services. Many others are online transportation brokers who assist shippers in locating freight haulers, such as FreightQuote.com and Direct Freight Services, that offer services such as matching up empty cargo space with shipper needs for a monthly service.[66]

Shippers' Associations

The American Institute for Shippers' Associations (AISA) defines **shippers' associations** as "non-profit membership cooperatives which make domestic or international arrangements for the movement of members' cargo." Thus, their job is to consolidate only their members' shipments into full carloads, truckloads or container loads to achieve volume discounts for the members, and to negotiate for improved terms of service. These associations also benefit the transportation companies, in that they help to better utilize their equipment. Because shippers' associations do not identify themselves as 3PLs, brokers or transportation providers, they are not required to publish or adhere to a number of U.S. transportation regulations and can keep service contracts confidential. Some of the disadvantages of membership include required minimum shipment volumes to receive the benefits of reduced rates and some ocean carriers' refusal to do business with shippers' associations. A number of these cooperatives exist for different industries. For example, the Midwest Shippers' Association specializes in the shipping of specialty grains, and has about 100 members such as grain processors, traders, seed and equipment suppliers, and includes 19 shipping and logistics providers.[67]

Intermodal Marketing Companies

Intermodal marketing companies (IMCs) are companies that act as intermediaries between intermodal railroad companies and shippers. They typically purchase large blocks of flatcars for piggyback service and then find shippers to fill containers, or motor carriers with truckloads, to load the flatcars. Essentially these are transportation brokers for the rail industry. They get volume discounts from the railroads and pass some of this on to the shippers. These companies facilitate intermodal shipping and have become an important service to railroads. Many IMCs utilize Internet, cell phone and satellite transmissions to allow real-time communications among themselves, the carriers and the shippers. For example Illinois-based Hub Group is the largest IMC in North America and their automated online network allows electronic order entries and continuous shipment visibility. During the economic slowdown, they were able to improve market share by converting all-truck moves to intermodal, while providing shippers lower costs combined with better service.[68]

Environmental Sustainability in Logistics

Today, firms are facing growing pressure to improve environmental performance from customers as well as local, state and federal governing bodies. Further, as shown in one of the chapter's opening quotes, an enormous portion of the world's oil reserves are consumed to move goods around the globe. Today, companies have realized the impact of transportation on carbon footprints, total costs and overall oil consumption and are doing something about it. Governments are also taking note of voter sentiment and beginning to enact more stringent environmental protection laws regarding transportation. Some examples are provided here.

In logistics, one of the big energy wastes comes from trucks returning from their deliveries empty. Empty Miles, an Internet subscriber service offered by VICS (the Voluntary Interindustry Commerce Solutions Association), seeks to eliminate much of this problem. Members post regularly available truck backhaul capacities on their delivery routes, while shippers post their goods in need of regular shipment. Empty Miles finds matches of these capacities and goods. Shippers pay lower than normal transportation rates, while carriers obtain revenues for an otherwise empty backhaul. Retailer Macy's, for example, has seen its delivery costs decline significantly from use of the Empty Miles portal, while logistics provider Schneider National has seen its backhaul revenue jump by 25 percent. The potential environmental and economic benefits are huge—the National Private Truck Council estimates that 28 percent of the trucks on U.S. highways are currently running empty. Empty Miles is also good for supply chain relationships: "It allows partnerships to evolve that would not naturally evolve," says Bill Connell executive vice president of logistics at Macy's.[69]

Actually, a number of nonprofit organizations have been formed to help firms in their sustainability efforts. In the U.S., the Environmental Protection Agency launched SmartWay, a certification that represents a more fuel efficient transportation option. The SmartWay brand signifies a product or service that reduces transportation-related emissions. The SmartWay website allows users to locate alternative fuel station locations, identify greener vehicles to purchase and select certified SmartWay transportation companies.[70] The Coalition for Responsible Transportation (CRT) includes importers, exporters and motor and water carriers who are taking leadership roles in their industries to develop environmental transportation initiatives. Since its inception in 2007, members like Target, Gap, Best Buy, Home Depot, Nike and Wal-Mart have been instrumental in developing sustainable solutions to reduce truck pollution at U.S. deepwater ports without disrupting the flow of commerce.[71]

Europe's 3PLs and ports have been leading the way toward sustainability by introducing a number of green management initiatives. The logistics arm of Denmark's AP Moller-Maersk Group has launched a graphical representation system called Supply Chain Carbon Dashboard that allows customers to track their supply chain carbon footprint. "It immediately allows you to identify carbon hotspots in your supply chain," says Erling Nielsen, head of Maersk's supply chain development team. Global freight management company Geodis Wilson of the Netherlands has a tool that measures the environmental impact of its customers' transport solutions. It might find, for example, that a shipment to the U.S. from Gothenburg, Sweden, could reduce carbon emissions by 16 percent compared to one originating in Rotterdam. German logistics company DB Schenker's EcoTransIT Internet application allows customers to compare the energy consumption, CO_2 and pollutant emissions of all modes of transportation available in Europe, given the origination, destination, shipment volume and freight being transported. Shippers can then select the best route and obtain all the emissions and energy data. Finally, the EcoPorts Foundation, a nonprofit association founded by a group of eight European ports, acts as a network platform to create effective collaborations addressing sustainability issues in European ports and supply chains. More than 150 European ports are linked in the network.[72]

Over the past few years, the global fast-food giant Subway has staked their claim of being the world's greenest fast-food restaurant, and a green logistics strategy has played a key role in this effort. Over a three-year span, Subway has reduced their oil consumption by 277,000 barrels per year while growing their North American store locations by 12 percent. For example, they purchase fresh produce locally, have convinced many of their suppliers to add distribution centers closer to clusters of Subway restaurants, and have optimized their warehouse network with several large redistribution centers to allow truckload purchases of meats with outbound shipments to their regional distribution centers.[73]

Logistics Management Software Applications

As mentioned briefly in Chapter 6, logistics management software applications can be added to ERP software suites of applications, as the firm's needs and the users' level of experience dictates. Some of the more popular logistics management applications include **transportation management systems**, **warehouse management systems** and **global trade management systems**. Companies typically find significant benefits with these logistics execution systems. Until recently, purchases in this area were growing rapidly, but have slowed somewhat due to the global recession. Many shippers have been opting to use fee-based Internet logistics management portals instead of outright purchases of logistics software to further manage cost outlays. Still, use of some form of logistics software remains quite high. According to an industry survey conducted early in 2010, 88 percent of the respondents were currently using logistics management software and 75 percent indicated they planned to buy additional logistics applications or upgrade during the year. Further, these respondents expected paybacks in one to two years.[74] These systems are briefly discussed next.

Transportation Management Systems

Transportation costs are a significant portion of total logistics costs for many organizations. To help reduce these costs while optimizing service levels, transportation management system (TMS) applications allow firms to find carriers, select the best mix of transportation services and pricing to determine the best use of containers or truck trailers, better manage transportation contracts, rank transportation options, clear customs, track fuel usage and product movements, and track carrier performance. Additionally, regulatory bodies, shippers and customers want to know the locations of goods in-transit; thus, real-time information about a shipment's location while it is being transported to a final destination is required. Consequently, information may need to be provided by the manufacturer, 3PLs, agents, freight forwarders and others as products move through global supply chains. Technologies employed to provide this visibility include barcode scanners, RFID tags, the Internet and GPS devices.

Assisting in the management of all this transportation-related information is the job of a TMS. Missouri-based manufacturer American Railcar Industries, for example, was having difficulty tracking its inbound shipments from suppliers. "We had visibility when the product was ready at suppliers, but then it went into a black hole once it left our vendors' docks until it arrived at our location," says American Railcar purchasing agent Brent Roever. In 2009, they incorporated a Web-based TMS solution into their purchasing and logistics processes. Now, all of their purchase orders flow from their ERP system into the TMS, where a preselected list of suppliers can view the orders. Suppliers respond to the orders and indicate how and when the order will be shipped. The system then notifies the purchasing team at American Railcar when the shipment was picked up and when it is expected at the specified location based on established delivery times.[75]

The desire to secure national borders against unwanted shipments has increased recently due to terrorist concerns, causing a number of countries to more closely regulate the flow of goods across their borders. This has potentially added transportation delay problems to shipments as companies deal with an added layer of bureaucracy and reporting at various border entry sites. To help mitigate delay problems, many TMS software applications now have capabilities for customs declaration, calculation and payment of tariffs, duties and duty drawbacks, and advanced filing of shipment manifests.

Warehouse Management Systems

Many firms are purchasing ERP systems that include a TMS coupled with a warehouse management system (WMS) to further enhance their supply chain management effectiveness. For example, a company might use their TMS to forecast shipping volumes based on data provided by their WMS and then recommend the most efficient modes of shipping. The WMS could then pick and schedule warehouse usage based on TMS shipping information. Warehouse management systems track and control the flow of goods from the receiving dock of a warehouse or distribution center until the item is loaded for outbound shipment to the customer. RFID tags placed on products and pallets within the distribution center are used to control the flow of goods. The goals of a WMS include reducing distribution center labor costs, streamlining the flow of goods, reducing the time products spend in the distribution center, managing distribution center capacity, reducing paperwork and managing the crossdocking process. A WMS can improve warehouse productivity by repositioning product to reduce the distance that product and pickers must travel. Reducing these travel times can improve productivity by 10 to 20 percent.

Nebraska-based retailer Cabela's recently installed a WMS in its three distribution centers, two return centers and twenty retail stores. They use the system to track inventories in their retail locations, replenish stock as sales occur and monitor receiving and returns. The system helps Cabela's handle 300,000 SKUs from 5,000 vendors at all of their facilities. They have realized improvements in operating costs, customer service, information visibility and the ability to make configuration changes for their multichannel network. "In the past, configuration changes took days or weeks to complete," says Baloo Eledath, director of enterprise solutions at Cabela's. "We now handle them within an hour with our WMS."[76]

Use of TMSs and WMSs has increased the use of RFID tags and technologies. EastPack, for instance, New Zealand's largest Kiwi fruit pack house, must meet strict food traceability regulations. The company uses RFID tags on all pallets of food shipped out and tracks the locations of each pallet throughout its operations in real time, reporting the whereabouts to its WMS. Within two months of going live with the system, EastPack was able to move 30 percent more fruit trays per day with fewer lift trucks.[77]

Global Trade Management Systems

As global supply chains become more common, the need to comply with foreign and domestic security regulations also increases. This, combined with the continued search for cheaper supplies and reduced logistics expenditures, has brought about the need for global trade management (GTM) systems. "The more borders you cross, the more documents you have to file," says William McNeill, research analyst with business research firm AMR Research. "No one wants to make mistakes because once you get caught up in customs you lose money while your competitors' products sail through the supply chain," he adds.

For many firms, the new U.S. Customs and Border Protection (CBP) security filing requirement (shippers and carriers must submit cargo information to the CBP 24 hours prior to ocean freight being loaded onto a vessel bound for the U.S.) has only added to the import documentation headaches. Illinois-based fastener importer XL Screw Corp., with 100 to 300 import filings per month, decided it needed an in-house GTM system. The system proved to be a simple answer to CBP requirements. The biggest benefit for XL Screw is the ability to enter data for a specific shipment, store it in the system and then use it to complete forms for other shipments.[78] Paper and plastic packaging supplier Bunzl Distribution USA adopted a GTM platform in 2009 to make their import supply chain more compliant and transparent. Used in over 50 branch offices in the U.S. and Canada, the GTM solution improves visibility of their inbound shipments, monitors carrier and supplier performance, and automates customs entry, which improves customer service and reduces brokerage fees while improving compliance with international trade regulations. "In today's market, it is critically important for companies to support their low-cost country sourcing strategies with systems that can integrate across a supply network to reduce cycle time and improve cash-to-cash cycles," says John Preuninger, president of GTM solution provider Management Dynamics.[79]

Global Logistics

For global goods movements, logistics managers must be aware of a number of issues not impacting domestic movements such as 3PL services and costs, regulatory requirements, import/export limitations, port and warehousing issues and the modes of transportation available. In the U.S., freight movement to Europe or Asia involves either air or water transportation and then most likely motor and/or rail transportation to the final destination. Between most contiguous countries, rail and motor carrier shipments tend to be the most common modes of transportation. There are also many logistics problems and infrastructure differences found as goods are moved from one country to another. In Europe, rail transportation tends to be much more prevalent and reliable than rail transportation in the U.S., because European tracks, facilities and equipment are newer and better maintained. This is partly because most transportation modes in Europe are government owned and maintained. Water carriers may be the dominant mode of transportation in countries with a great deal of coastline and developed inland waterways. In under- and undeveloped countries, ports may be very poorly maintained and equipped and the highway system may be almost nonexistent. A number of these and other global logistics topics are discussed next.

Global Freight Security

While a number of logistics security topics have already been discussed, one issue needing further discussion is motor freight security at U.S. border crossings. In the past few years, the trucking industry has worked with U.S. Customs to develop the **Customs-Trade Partnership Against Terrorism program (C-TPAT)** and its security program called the **Free and Secure Trade program (FAST)**. The overall goal is to ensure the security of global supply chains in general and international trucking in particular. To participate in FAST, motor carriers must become C-TPAT certified, and their commercial drivers must complete an application and undergo a background check. FAST participants receive expedited cargo clearance provided their customers are also C-TPAT certified and they receive access to a dedicated FAST lane at border crossings.[80]

These and other customs clearance requirements are causing a high level of congestion at both U.S. borders (Canada and Mexico). "Free trade is being threatened by a thickening of the border," says Gerry Fedchun, president of the Canadian Automotive Parts Manufacturers' Association.[81] More than 80 percent of all Canadian export trade goes to the U.S. and 70 percent of what flows to the U.S. from Canada goes by way of trucks crossing the border. On many days, trucks are lined up for hours crossing into the U.S. from Canada. In fact, a Canadian trucking industry found that the cost of border processing and waiting was four percent of the entire industry's annual revenues. And at the Mexican border, things are much worse—it takes an average of three days, for instance, for a truck to cross from Laredo, Texas, into Mexico; a load must be touched seven times by various agencies before it can clear the Mexican border. Mexican truckers are simply no longer allowed into the U.S. beyond an imposed 20-mile commercial zone; a pilot program allowing them further into the U.S. was abandoned in March of 2009, as the U.S. Congress argued that it created safety, security and U.S. trucking industry employment problems. This action in turn caused Mexico to impose billions of dollars in retaliatory tariffs on 90 U.S. export products. These issues remain troublesome for motor carriers and their U.S. border crossings.[82]

Global Logistics Intermediaries

Global logistics intermediaries provide global shipping, consolidation and import/export services for firms and offer expertise that can prove very useful for most organizations involved in global commerce. A number of these intermediaries that have not already been discussed are briefly discussed here.

Customs Brokers

Customs brokers move global shipments through customs for companies as well as handle the necessary documentation required to accompany the shipments. These specialists are often used by companies requiring expertise in exporting goods to foreign countries; their knowledge of the many import requirements of various countries can significantly reduce the time required to move goods internationally and clear them through customs.

International or Foreign Freight Forwarders

These services move goods for companies from domestic production facilities to foreign destinations (or vice versa) using surface and air transportation and warehousing. They consolidate small shipments into larger TL, CL or container shipments, decide what transportation modes and methods to use, handle all of the documentation requirements and then disperse the shipments at their destination. They also determine the best routing to use; oversee storage, breakbulk and repackaging requirements; and provide for any other logistics requirements of the seller. Use of **foreign freight forwarders** can reduce logistics costs, increase customer service and allow shippers to focus resources on other activities. Many companies exporting or importing goods use the services of foreign freight forwarders because of their expertise and presence in foreign markets.

Until recently, many shippers were importing and shipping high-quality, low-cost goods from "far-shore" operations (e.g., U.S. buyers purchasing goods from Chinese manufacturers). Today, some buyers are utilizing a strategy called **right-shoring**. Right-shoring combines near-shore, far-shore and domestic opportunities into a single, flexible and cost-driven approach to purchasing and logistics. As crude oil prices fluctuate, labor costs rise and the value of the U.S. dollar declines, global shippers find they must be much more flexible regarding where products are purchased. This has created an even greater need for globally connected freight forwarders.[83]

Trading Companies

Trading companies put buyers and sellers from different countries together and handle all of the export/import arrangements, documentation and transportation for both goods and services. Most trading companies are involved in exporting and they usually take title to the goods until sold to foreign buyers. They enjoy economies of scale when exporting goods as they ship large quantities of consolidated shipments, using established transportation and warehousing services. In the U.S., the Export Trading Company Act was signed into law in 1982 to promote U.S. exports and to help U.S. exporters improve their competitiveness. Within the U.S. Department of Commerce, the Export Trading Company Affairs (ETCA) office helps promote the development of joint ventures between U.S. and foreign companies and the use of export trade intermediaries. The ETCA office was created by the Export Trading Company Act of 1982.[84]

Non-Vessel Operating Common Carriers

Also referred to as NVOCCs or simply NVOs, **non-vessel operating common carriers** operate very similarly to international freight forwarders, but normally use only scheduled ocean liners. They consolidate small international shipments from a number of shippers into full container loads and then handle all of the documentation and transportation arrangements from the shippers' dock area. NVOCCs assume responsibility for cargo from point of origin to final destination; however, they do not own any vessels. They enter into contracts with ocean liners, which may then subcontract with rail or motor carriers for land travel.

Foreign-Trade Zones

Foreign-trade zones (FTZs) are secure sites within the U.S. under the supervision of the U.S. Customs Service. These sites are authorized by the Foreign-Trade Zones Board, chaired by the U.S. Secretary of Commerce, and are comparable to the so-called *free trade zones* that exist in many other countries today. FTZs are considered to be outside U.S. Customs territory, where foreign or domestic merchandise can enter without formal customs entry or payment of duties or excise taxes. Companies operating in FTZs bring goods and materials into the site and might use storage, assembly, testing, packaging, repairing and export services. No retail activities are allowed, however. If the final product is exported out of the U.S., no domestic duties or excise taxes are levied. If the final product is imported into the U.S. from the FTZ, duties and taxes are paid only at the time the goods leave the FTZ.

Congress established the Foreign-Trade Zones Board in 1934 to encourage U.S. firms to participate in global trade. As of 2009, there were over 230 active FTZs in the U.S., used by about 3,200 companies, directly supporting over 350,000 U.S. workers with more than $500 billion in merchandise moving through these areas each year. Petroleum, pharmaceutical, automotive and electronics companies are the largest users of U.S. FTZs.[85]

The North American Free Trade Agreement

The **North American Free Trade Agreement (NAFTA)** was initially agreed upon in December 1992, with the U.S. Congress passing it in November 1993, and put into effect on January 1, 1994. It will eventually remove most barriers to trade and investment among the U.S., Canada and Mexico.[86] Many **tariffs** (published import fees) and quotas were eliminated immediately and most others were to be eliminated by 2008. NAFTA forms the world's second-largest open market with a combined economy of more than $14 trillion and a population exceeding 435 million people—somewhat smaller in size than the European Union. The objectives of NAFTA are to facilitate cross-border trade among the three countries, increase investment opportunities and promote fair trade.

NAFTA has not been without its detractors. U.S. labor groups have argued that jobs are being lost as companies move to Mexico to take advantage of cheap foreign labor, undermining labor union negotiating power. As described earlier, free access to U.S. highways by Mexican truckers (one NAFTA provision) is not currently allowed by the U.S. Environmental groups have been concerned that pollution and food safety laws have become more difficult to enforce. Others argue that because of subsidized agricultural exports to Mexico, the small Mexican farmer is being run out of business. Some in the U.S. saw NAFTA as a way to grow the Mexican economy and curb illegal immigration into the U.S. However, migration into the U.S., both legal and illegal, has increased since NAFTA began, mainly due to the Mexican peso crisis, enduring poverty in southern Mexico and the impact of Chinese competition on Mexican industries. In response to these and other concerns, supplementary agreements continue to be added to NAFTA.

Each of the three countries is also seeking and entering into trade agreements with other countries, and the recent recession has reduced cross-border trade as demand has decreased and protectionist policies have come back into play. Mexico has signed free trade agreements with Japan, other Latin American countries and even the EU. The U.S. has signed on to the Trans-Pacific Partnership agreement which includes Australia, New Zealand, Singapore and Vietnam. Canada is in negotiations to enter a trade agreement with the EU. And as the countries hunker down while the global economy suffers, there are examples of buying more from domestic suppliers. "In the U.S., there is the Buy American Act and in Canada there are, for example, certain provisions in the Green Energy Act in Ontario that require that any wind or solar powered equipment used in a power project meets certain Ontario content requirements," says Gary Graham, partner at law firm Gowling Lafleur Henderson.[87]

Reverse Logistics

Reverse logistics (also known as **returns management**) refers to the backward flow of goods *from* customers in the supply chain occurring when goods are returned, either by the end-product consumer or by a business customer within the supply chain. In other words, reverse logistics refers to the movement, storage and processing of returned goods. Returns are increasing in part today because of the growth of online shopping, direct-to-store shipments and direct-to-home shipments. Recently, the use of cheap and untested foreign suppliers has also caused a relatively high number of product recalls in the U.S. On August 1, 2007, California-based Mattel, the world's biggest toymaker, recalled almost 1 million Chinese-made toys because they were covered with paint containing lead. The very next week, Mattel again was forced to announce a large recall for toys containing small magnets that posed a choking hazard. In fact, eight of Mattel's nine toy recalls from 2004 to 2007 were for Chinese-made products.[88]

Retail customer returns account for approximately 6 percent of sales and can sometimes be as high as 40 percent. And the logistical costs to process these returns can also be very high—now running approximately $100 billion each year in the U.S. for transportation, handling, refurbishment, repackaging, remarketing, disposal and lost sales. Besides the significant impact on costs, returns also can have a direct negative impact on the environment, customer service, the firm's reputation and profitability if not managed properly. "Reverse logistics is all about damage control and making the process as customer-friendly as possible," says Lou Cerny, vice president of Sedlak Management Consultants. "You've already disappointed the customer once, now you have to close the loop as soon as possible."[89]

Many firms hire a 3PL company specializing in reverse logistics to ensure these items are managed correctly. Texas-based computer maker Dell, Inc., known for its supply chain management capabilities, has set its sights on creating the same sort of reputation for its reverse supply chain. They have contracted with GENCO Supply Chain Solutions to manage Dell's testing, repairing, remanufacturing services. Texas-based InteliSol will provide parts-harvesting and other recovery services for Dell within the same returns management facility. As a matter of fact, in its inaugural corporate sustainability index, New Hampshire-based Technology Business Research, Inc., announced Dell received top honors for 2009 particularly for its recycling and renewable energy use.[90]

The Impact of Reverse Logistics on the Supply Chain

Returns can represent significant challenges to a supply chain. In many cases, reverse logistics is viewed as an unwanted activity of supply chain management. In these cases, reverse logistics is seen simply as a cost of doing business or a regulatory compliance issue. Problems include the inability of information systems to handle returns or monitor reverse product flow, lack of worker training in reverse logistics procedures, little or no identification on returned packages, the need for adequate inspection and testing of returns, and the placing of potentially damaged returned products into sales stocks. A poor reverse logistics system can affect the entire supply chain financially and can have a large impact on how a consumer views a product brand, potentially impacting future sales. A recent report by global business consulting company Accenture found that reverse logistics costs four to five times more than forward logistics and on average requires twelve times as many processing steps. Their findings though, also suggest that reverse logistics represents a huge source of untapped value.[91]

From a marketing perspective, an effective returns process can create goodwill and enhance customers' perceptions of product quality and purchase risk. From a quality perspective, product failure and returns information can be used by quality personnel in root cause analyses and by design personnel to reduce future design errors (the number-one reason for a product return is a defective or damaged item). From a logistics perspective, returned products can still create value as original products, refurbished products or repair parts. This also tends to reduce disposal costs. Thus, while 46 percent of companies report losing money on product returns, about eight percent actually report making money. Online shoe merchant Zappos has a very high return rate (about 35 percent) but views this as a competitive advantage—they provide free returns no questions asked, but also boast very high repurchase rates.[92] Finally, retail giant Wal-Mart recently stated in a meeting with 1,000 suppliers and government officials in Beijing that they intend to do away entirely with defective product returns by 2012 using on-site audits, enforcement of environmental and social standards and the threat of lost future business.[93]

Reverse Logistics and the Environment

Reverse logistics can have a positive impact on the environment through activities such as recycling, reusing materials and products, or refurbishing used products. **Green reverse logistics programs** include reducing the environmental impact of certain modes of transportation used for returns, reducing the amount of disposed packaging and product materials by redesigning products and processes, and making use of reusable totes and pallets. "Sustainability is playing an important role in reverse logistics," says Paul Vassallo, marketing director for UPS. "More and more companies are looking to reduce their impact on the environment and search for carbon-neutral ways to dispose of product."[94]

Traditionally, organizations have used landfills for routine product and material disposal, but today, landfills have become much more expensive to use. Local, state and federal governments are also imposing stricter rules and higher costs regarding the use of landfills. These changes have led to innovative ways of dealing with used products or product waste. The Campbell Soup Company now uses a system that tears soup cans into small strips and then washes and separates the metal. It also crushes and washes glass containers. The remaining vegetable matter is dried and sold as feed to local farmers.[95] Advanced Micro Devices, based in Texas, works with its suppliers to find ways to decrease packaging waste and handling activities. In one instance, the company had traditionally used 55-gallon drums to store some of their bulk chemicals, but changed to 300-gallon totes and eventually to bulk tankers to reduce packaging waste that would eventually be delivered to a landfill.[96]

SUMMARY

This chapter has discussed the important role logistics plays in general and to supply chains in particular. Though this is a very broad topic, we have attempted to review the elements within U.S. domestic and global logistics to give the reader an adequate understanding of the entire field of logistics and its relationship with supply chain management. These elements include the basics of transportation, third-party transportation providers, warehousing, sustainability in logistics, global logistics and reverse logistics. It is hoped that readers have gained an understanding of the many elements within the broad topic of logistics and why these are so important to the successful management of supply chains.

KEY TERMS

air carriers, 307

airline security, 312

breakbulk, 320

Civil Aeronautics Act of 1938, 316

class rates, 311

coal slurry, 309

commodity rates, 311

common carriers, 303

consolidation warehouses, 319

container-on-flatcar (COFC), 311

contract carriers, 303

cost-of-service pricing, 310

crossdocking, 319

customs brokers, 334

Customs-Trade Partnership Against Terrorism program (C-TPAT), 333

deep-sea transportation, 308

Department of Transportation Act, 316

distribution center, 319

exception rates, 311

exempt carriers, 303

Federal Aviation Act of 1958, 316

FOB destination pricing, 311

FOB origination pricing, 311

foreign freight forwarders, 334

foreign-trade zones, 335

fourth-party logistics provider (4PL), 326

Free and Secure Trade program (FAST), 333

freight forwarders, 330

general freight carriers, 305

global trade management systems, 331

Granger Laws, 314

green reverse logistics programs, 338

high-speed trains, 307

ICC Termination Act of 1995, 318

intermediately positioned strategy, 323

intermodal marketing companies, 329

intermodal transportation, 309

lead logistics provider, 326

lean warehousing, 324

less-than-truckload (LTL) carriers, 304

line haul rates, 311

load brokers, 328

logistics, 301

market positioned strategy, 323

Miscellaneous rates, 311

Motor Carrier Act of 1935, 315

motor carriers, 304

negotiated pricing, 310

non-vessel operating common carriers, 335

North American Free Trade Agreement (NAFTA), 335

Ocean Shipping Reform Act of 1998, 318

piggyback service, 309

pipeline carriers, 309

place utility, 301

private carrier, 304

private warehouses, 319

product positioned strategy, 323

public warehouses, 320

rail carriers, 306

Railroad Revitalization and Regulatory Reform Act, 316

Railway Passenger Service Act, 316

real-time location systems (RTLS), 307

Reed-Bulwinkle Act, 316

returns management, 336

reverse logistics, 336

right-shoring, 334

risk pooling, 321

road trains, 305

ROROs, 310

DISCUSSION QUESTIONS

1. Why are logistics issues important to business success?

2. What are the important activities or elements in logistics?

3. List the legal forms and modes of transportation. Which mode is the least expensive? Which mode carries the most freight? Which mode is growing the fastest? Shrinking the fastest?

4. What are some intermodal transportation alternatives?

5. What does "piggyback service" refer to?

6. Why is it that the fastest trains are found outside the U.S.? Is this a problem for the U.S?

7. When would you want to use value-of-service pricing instead of cost-of-service pricing?

8. What is FOB destination pricing and when would you want to use it?

9. What does transportation security refer to, and which mode of transportation is most affected by security concerns?

10. Is government regulation of transportation good or bad? Why?

11. Is transportation in the U.S. regulated today or deregulated? Why?

12. Describe three different types of warehouses and the advantages of each.

13. If storing goods in a warehouse is bad, since it increases inventory carrying costs, why are the number and size of warehouses increasing in the U.S.?

14. What is the difference between a distribution center and a warehouse?

15. Define risk pooling and the advantages and disadvantages of centralized warehousing. What assumption does risk pooling make?

16. *Chapter Problem:* For the following warehouse system information, determine the average inventory levels for three warehouses and then one warehouse, using the square root rule:

Current warehouse system—six warehouses with 3,000 units at each warehouse.

17. What are the advantages and disadvantages of centralized and decentralized warehousing systems? Which type do you think Wal-Mart should have?

18. What is a lean warehouse? When are they used?

19. Why is logistics so important for successful supply chain management?

20. What are 3PLs and why are they used? Why is their use growing so rapidly? What are 4PLs and why are they used?

21. Can 3PLs be effective supply chain partners? Why?

22. Are transportation intermediaries also a form of 3PL? Explain.

23. What are the impacts of logistics on environmental sustainability? How can these impacts be minimized?

24. What are the most common logistics management software applications and why are they beneficial to users?

25. What do you think the most pressing global logistics problem is? Why?

26. Describe several global logistics intermediaries. Could they also be considered 3PLs?

27. What are foreign trade zones? What benefits do they provide?

28. How has NAFTA affected trade among the U.S., Canada and Mexico? Is NAFTA good for domestic U.S. and Mexican producers?

29. What is reverse logistics? How does it impact supply chain management?

30. How can reverse logistics have a positive impact on the environment? On profits? On customer service? On repeat purchases?

INTERNET QUESTIONS

1. Go to the BNSF website (www.bnsf.com) and describe the types of intermodal services offered.

2. Go to the NTE website (www.nte.com) and find two highly rated carriers and two poorly rated carriers.

3. Search on the term "green logistics" and write a report on logistics strategies that are used to reduce carbon emissions.

4. Search on the term "logistics management software" and describe how these software applications help to assure port security and global cargo security.

Chapter 10

CUSTOMER RELATIONSHIP MANAGEMENT

Today, it's all about predicting what the customer wants before they even know they want it and then making them think it was their decision in the first place.[1]

Good CRM, especially the social kind, is like being able to speak your cat's—or your customer's—language. That may not sound like a goal worth striving for, but trust me, it's huge. Think about that the next time your cat deposits its "customer feedback" in your shoe.[2]

Learning Objectives

After completing this chapter, you should be able to

- Discuss the strategic importance of CRM.
- Describe the components of a CRM initiative.
- Calculate customer lifetime value.
- Discuss the implementation procedures used for CRM programs.
- Describe how information is used to create customer satisfaction and greater profits for the firm.
- Discuss the importance of data security in CRM.
- Describe how social media and cloud computing have impacted CRM.

Chapter Outline

Customer Relationship Management Defined

CRM's Role in Supply Chain Management

Key Tools and Components of CRM

Designing and Implementing a Successful CRM Program

Recent Trends in CRM

Summary

Supply Chain Management in Action
CEO Richard Braddock Discusses Online Grocer FreshDirect's Customer Focus

At FreshDirect, we went through our own learning experience building and then rebuilding our business to be much more customer-focused. We created best practices that have earned us healthy sales growth during a time when most companies are suffering. That said, the key to our intense customer focus is data—collecting it, analyzing it and using it to create the ultimate customer experience.

Working with intensive customer focus begins with a daily meeting among our senior managers. We use a daily operations report to review our business yesterday, today and tomorrow against a series of metrics that extend from the market through the various aspects of our fulfillment (plant, transportation, service and marketing) and assign individual accountabilities. We use this to take immediate action where we have problems, and also to identify areas for longer-term program improvement.

To grow and keep our database fresh, FreshDirect surveys customers in great depth both weekly and monthly, using a research tool called Linescale. The weekly surveys focus on key metrics for success, broader aspects of loyalty, a few key product categories, and relevant "issues of the day," such as the economy. The monthly survey concentrates on product and service components tracked monthly among both total and core customers, and also asks questions about some of our intended product improvements, as well as price and value selection. The responses are helpful in digging deeper into likes/dislikes on an individual basis.

PUTTING KNOWLEDGE INTO ACTION

With the information gathered and our internal analysis, FreshDirect has been able to develop initiatives that answer customers' wants and needs. We also demonstrate that we listen to their concerns and are dedicated to making their experience with FreshDirect a happy one. As we put it, "Our food is fresh. Our customers are spoiled."

For example, our data analysis process helped us realize that customers were concerned that they were unable to personally inspect produce and seafood products purchased on our site. To resolve this issue, FreshDirect repurposed our production process and hired produce and seafood experts to rate these products daily. More than 60 percent of our customers tell us they now use this rating system when they buy from us.

Additionally, we keep a detailed record of every customer's historic relationship with us and are able to leverage that data in real time to enhance the customer experience. For example, FreshDirect reminds customers of their five most frequently purchased items so they can easily add these products to their cart. Using this same principle, FreshDirect has improved our cross-sell feature. When a customer orders a steak, for instance, our site has always recommended cross-sells. More recently, we added the ability to remind customers exactly what they ordered in the past when they ordered that steak (or what customers like them ordered). This feature immediately doubled usage of our cross-sell feature. These two items together have increased our revenue by 10 percent, because we're using our superior data, in real time, to give our customers a better experience. As importantly, no one who walks into a store today can receive a similar experience.

These efforts and other programs designed to improve our loyal customers' experience have improved the share of our business conducted by those customers from 25 percent to 60 percent in the past year. This loyal base has allowed us to continue to grow on a monthly basis as we have pushed through the recession, and to make money doing it.

THE BOTTOM LINE

Approaching your operations with an intense customer focus will not only help you keep existing customers coming back, but it will also turn new customers into loyal fans. Almost everyone today says they know they should be close to their customers, but few are using these new tools to manage the customers' experience with day-by-day intensity.

With that in mind, rather than approach the economic recovery as simply a chance to get back to business as usual, look to accelerate. Find new and interesting ways to acquaint yourself with your customers, because the better you understand their needs, the more value you can provide. And, most important, pick up the pace of your marketing—no more leisurely annual marketing plans: make a commitment to changing and improving every day, based on the more-demanding customers you have to serve. You will not only set yourself apart from the competition, but better position your business to withstand the next downturn.

Source: Braddock, R., "FreshDirect's Secret Ingredient: Customer Focus," *Customer Relationship Management* 13(2), 2009: 24–25. Used with permission.

Introduction

Customer relationship management becomes necessary as soon as a company finds a market and some customers for its products and services. To keep customers satisfied, coming back and telling others, firms must continually develop new products and services while discovering ways to add more value to existing products and services. This is particularly true in today's tough economic climate, which has made customers smarter and more willing to switch company allegiances. The often-told story that "finding a new customer costs five times as much as keeping an old customer" is one of the motivations behind customer relationship management. Over time, value continues to be demonstrated to customers through reliable on-time delivery, high-quality products and services, competitive pricing, innovative new products and services, attention to various customer needs and the flexibility to respond to those needs adequately. Managing customer relationships starts with building core competencies that focus on customer requirements, and then continues with delivering products and services in a manner resulting in high levels of customer satisfaction.

Today, customer relationship management, or CRM, has come to be associated with automated transaction and communication applications—a suite of software modules or a portion of the larger enterprise resource planning system as described in Chapter 7. The market for CRM applications is growing rapidly—estimated to be $11 billion for 2010, a 30 percent increase from 2008.[3] Most large firms have made very sizeable investments in CRM applications along with company websites that capture data in an effort to automate the customer relationship process, and in some respects these have provided significant benefits to the companies and their customers. Additionally, as the speed and capabilities of computers and software increase, the ability to capture and analyze customer data will also increase, further cementing this relationship between customer relationship management and automated processes.

Interestingly, a recent survey by *Marketing Week* magazine showed that 77 percent of the responding companies used a CRM software application, but only half thought their CRM applications were effective. Another interesting finding was that while most firms were investing in CRM software, 71 percent of the respondents said their companies' investments in user training were either limited or nonexistent.[4] As this finding suggests, CRM applications can create problems if adopting companies seek to replace automation for dealing directly with customers, if users don't know how to make full use of the software, or if company objectives exceed the capabilities of the software. Treating customers right must therefore go beyond the purchase and use of CRM software.

Customers today like the convenience of communicating or transacting over the Internet; however, individualized contact between a company and its customers is also needed to ultimately keep customers satisfied and coming back. Two of the most recent trends in CRM are use of social networks and cloud computing, and both of these will be discussed in this chapter. Companies are using both as a means to build better customer relationships. Some applications allow a company, for instance, to extract information automatically about people from a social network like LinkedIn and load it directly into one of its CRM systems. Other applications include the use of a service provider's eMarketing cloud to send e-mail "blasts" to thousands of customers.

Businesses today are rediscovering the need to provide personalized services to their customers. Many have come full circle, starting with Internet Business to Business (B2B) and Business to Customer (B2C) transactions. Today, we see that a firm's Internet presence, though desirable for many types of information or product transactions, is not sufficient to satisfy most customers in a wide range of industries. Touching products and talking face-to-face with company representatives remain integral parts of the supplier–customer interface. Thus, CRM must still include talking to customers, understanding their behavior and their requirements, and then building a system to satisfy those requirements.

With technological changes occurring as rapidly as they are today, many new and exciting ways to obtain and utilize customer information have been developed, and many of these will be highlighted throughout this chapter. As supplier–customer interactions become more automated and more e-services are created, organizations will still find they must continue to identify and develop new ways to add value to customer relationships in order to maintain a competitive advantage. Cultivating the human element in customer relationships will always remain a necessary factor in creating that value. Ultimately, CRM, if used effectively, allows both sides to win—customers get what they want from businesses, while businesses continue to find new customers and satisfy old ones.

Customer Relationship Management Defined

Simply put, customer relationship management refers to *building and maintaining profitable long-term customer relationships*. The elements comprising CRM vary based on the industry, the size of the company and familiarity with CRM software applications. In the final analysis, though, all forms of CRM seek to keep the firm's customers satisfied, which creates profits or other benefits for the firm. A few specific definitions of CRM are provided here:

- "The infrastructure that enables the delineation of and increase in customer value, and the correct means by which to motivate valuable customers to remain loyal—indeed to buy again."[5]
- "Managing the relationships among people within an organization and between customers and the company's customer service representatives in order to improve the bottom line."[6]

- "A Core business strategy for managing and optimizing all customer interactions across an organization's traditional and electronic interfaces."[7]

Because of the intense competitive environment in most markets today, CRM has become one of the leading business strategies—and potentially one of the most costly. Most executives who haven't already implemented CRM applications are planning on investing in them soon. And while investments in CRM are in the billions of dollars each year as previously stated, it appears that much of this investment is not fundamentally improving customer relationships, making customers more loyal, or resulting in positive returns for many of the companies implementing CRM. As a matter of fact, in a recent U.S. retail industry survey, 85 percent of retail consumers who considered themselves "loyal" would be willing to shop elsewhere if properly enticed.[8] In one industry survey, only 25 percent of the respondents reported significant improvements in performance after implementing CRM. In another survey, while many CRM projects made money for the firms and met expectations, 70 percent of the projects either resulted in business losses or created no bottom-line improvements.[9]

So why are many CRM programs failing? Perhaps it is because some company managers simply don't understand or care about what their customers want or what their CRM users need. In one example, a researcher talked to hundreds of employees of a large global technology organization that had branded their CRM efforts a failure after three years and a $300 million investment. He found that only 24 percent had even heard of the program, only 15 percent of those involved with the implementation had been asked to provide any input, and the key system users had not received any training.[10] Given these findings, is the program's failure surprising? Though corporations may collect customers' purchase, credit and personal information, place it on a database, use it to initiate some type of direct marketing opportunity, and possibly even sell the database information to other companies, no substantive efforts are put forth to engender a customer's trust and loyalty—*to build customer relationships.* If building and maintaining relationships were truly what companies were seeking, they would, for instance, return phone messages, make it easy to return or service products, and make it easy for customers to get accurate information and contact the right people inside the organization. Consider this—how often in your dealings with organizations have you been made to feel valued?

Too often, companies today have delegated customer relationship management, certainly one of the most important activities of the firm, to third-party CRM services, software developers and internal IT departments whose goal is to design databases and use models, for instance, to predict consumer buying patterns. Though it is a potentially valuable support element in CRM programs, data mining alone does not build the customer relationship. A number of years ago, Jessica Keyes, a well-known information system author and consultant, stated in an interview in the magazine *Infotrends,* "Technology does not beget a competitive advantage, any more than paint and canvas beget a Van Gogh."[11] These kinds of activities should be used in tandem with individual attention to build genuine long-term value for customers. Successful CRM programs require cultural change, effective CRM project management and employee engagement, leading to strategies that are focused on cultivating long-term relationships with customers, aided by the software capabilities found in CRM applications.

Simply put, companies need to *treat their customers right.* This means providing not only the products and services customers want at competitive prices, but also support services and other offerings that add value and create real satisfaction for customers. Because customers are not all the same, firms must identify and segment their customers, and then provide different sets of desired products and services to each segment.

As noted CRM consultant Barton Goldenberg has been telling clients for 25 years—a successful CRM initiative is 50 percent people, 30 percent process and 20 percent technology.[12] Thus, a successful CRM program is both simple and complex. It is simple in that it involves training users and treating customers right, to make them feel valued. It is complex in that it also means finding affordable ways to identify (potentially millions of) customers and their needs, and then designing customer contact strategies geared toward creating customer satisfaction and loyalty among your segments of customers. Doing these things right will produce bottom line results.

The services of e-tailer Amazon.com for example, are very simple for the consumer, though actually some very complicated CRM tasks take place behind the scenes. "I think what ensured that Amazon was a dotcom winner was being dedicated to the initial principle of focusing on the customer," says Ms. Rakhi Parekh, group product manager at Amazon.co.uk. "We started off by passing-on the cost advantage of the model to consumers, with low prices, then extended that to clever use of their data so that we could work out what else they might enjoy."[13]

CRM's Role in Supply Chain Management

In Chapters 2, 3 and 4, the importance of building and maintaining strong relationships with good suppliers was discussed, in order to enhance value along the supply chain and create profits for supply chain participants. In those chapters, the focal firm was the customer, which received benefits when high-quality suppliers were found that were willing to design services and products around their customers' needs. The focal firm had purchase requirements that needed to be met. The distribution side of the firm's supply chain, though, is equally important. In this chapter, our focal firm is now the supplier, seeking to be a key, value-enhancing supplier to its customers. To be successful, the firm must find ways to meet its customers' needs; otherwise, just as any firm would react with a nonperforming supplier, the customer goes elsewhere and takes years of future purchases with them. Regardless of a firm's place in the supply chain—retailer, wholesaler, distributor, manufacturer or logistics provider—the importance of meeting and exceeding the needs and expectations of customers cannot be understated.

In an integrated supply chain setting, the need to be a good supplier—to adequately meet the needs of supply chain customers—is paramount to the success of supply chains. As products make their way along the supply chain to the end user, close, trusting and high-performance relationships must be created among all of the key supplier–customer pairs along the way. Thus, just as firms must create methods for finding and developing good suppliers, they must also create methods for becoming and staying good suppliers.

Because many firms do not sell directly to the end-product consumer, CRM in supply chain settings should also include first-tier customer training and education to ensure proper use of purchased products and, consequently, maximum end-customer benefit. In these situations, business customers have a significant influence on the brand and reputation of the focal firm's products. Just as with suppliers, it may be necessary for a firm to certify its business customers' abilities to adequately represent the firm's products. Automakers, for example, go to great lengths to encourage strong consumer-focused relationships at their dealerships to make sure their products are represented adequately. General Motors (GM) Canada is building CRM capabilities across all of their marketing channels including direct mail, telemarketing, the Internet, e-mail and its hundreds of dealers across Canada. Harry Kuntz, director of corporate marketing for GM, says

"As important as a marketing program is, ongoing communication is extremely important because what we're trying to do in the end is to be able to identify different customers, their different needs, and be able to talk to them differently."[14]

Key Tools and Components of CRM

A number of elements are required for the development of effective CRM initiatives, and these include segmenting customers, predicting customer behaviors, determining customer value, personalizing customer communications, automating the sales force and managing customer service capabilities. Each of these elements is discussed in detail below.

Segmenting Customers

One of the most basic activities in CRM is to **segment customers**. Companies group customers in varieties of ways so that customized communications and marketing efforts can be directed to specific customer groups. Efforts to up-sell and cross-sell can be directed to some groups, while efforts to discourage further purchases might be made to others. The recent global recession may also have changed some customer preferences, which is in turn changing how firms are segmenting and marketing to these segments. European retailer Tesco is now offering hundreds of cheaper branded products from kids' clothing to skincare products to appeal to consumers trying to economize on their weekly shopping expenditures.[15]

Customer segmentation can occur based on sales territory or region, preferred sales channel, profitability, products purchased, sales history, demographic information, desired product features and service preferences, just to name a few. Analyzing customer information can tell companies something about customer preferences and the likelihood of their responding to various types of **target marketing** efforts. By targeting specific customer segments, firms can save money by avoiding marketing efforts aimed at the wrong customers. Additionally, firms can avoid becoming a nuisance to some customers, which may drive them to competitors. Tesco, which sends out millions of mailers each month to its customers with promotional offers, uses 150,000 variants of the mailer to appeal to the varied lifestyles of its many demographic segments.[16] The global insurance and financial services company Hartford Financial Services Group, for example, has provided auto and homeowner insurance to people above the age of 60 for more than twenty years. Their call center's automated voice answering system features a low-pitched male voice to allow words to be heard very clearly; speech recognition has been incorporated into their touch-tone system; and the company has nine gerontologists on staff to advise the firm on everything from service to product design to marketing.[17]

Permission Marketing

An extension of target marketing is **relationship marketing** or **permission marketing**. The idea here is to let customers select the type and time of communication with organizations. These days, consumers are bombarded with thousands of commercial messages each day in every form of communication imaginable. The general consensus is that there are simply far too many ads, consumers ignore most of them, and no one is really trying to do anything to reduce it. On the contrary, the advertising industry seems forever on the lookout for new ways to introduce commercial messages. One of the latest is **mobile marketing**, or placing advertising messages on mobile phones. Users opt-in to get all of their services on cell phones, including advertising. "Mobile phones are the one thing that people carry with them all of the time and it's the most intimate of devices because advertisers can target consumers individually and offer them coupons and come-ons to buy products or services literally when they're around the corner from a store," says Bill Jones, president of Air2Web, a mobile advertising firm.[18] The newest form of mobile marketing is the use of quick response codes, or **QR codes**. It involves using the camera function on a smart phone, such as an iPhone or BlackBerry, and installing a QR code reader on the phone. Suppose you're on your way to the airport and want an update on your flight. You could simply point your phone camera at a QR code on your boarding pass and instantly receive a flight update on your phone. Even better, you could take a photo of the flight's QR code on your computer screen and have the e-boarding pass sent directly to your phone. In the U.S., airlines are already rolling out this feature.[19]

Thus in permission marketing, customers choose to be placed on (opt-in) and then taken off (opt-out) of e-mail or traditional mailing lists for information about goods and services. It is becoming possible on websites for consumers to specify exactly what they are interested in, when they want information, what type of information they want and how they want it communicated. This kind of customer self-segmenting requires sophisticated software capabilities to track individual customers and their interaction preferences as well as the capability to update these preferences over time. With this capability, firms can better design multiple, parallel marketing campaigns around small, specific segments of their customer base, automate portions of the marketing process and simultaneously free up time previously spent manually managing the marketing process.

On MySpace.com, for example, companies can create their own customized pages that potential consumers choose to visit. Because visitors to these pages are self-selecting, this essentially amounts to permission marketing. This enables companies to identify interested consumers, engage them in dialogues, and market goods and services to them. As of 2010, the Toyota Yaris MySpace site, for example, had more than 45,000 "friends."[20] Other social websites, such as Facebook, Twitter and YouTube, offer similar arrangements. The Toyota Yaris Facebook page, for example had over 16,000 "fans" as of 2010. Boston's Rialto Restaurant and Bar sends e-mail newsletters each month to their growing list of 6,600 subscribers. It contains a message from the chef, a recipe, seasonal menu previews and event announcements. Each message is linked to the restaurant's website for more information. About 30 percent of the e-mails are opened, with hundreds clicking on links or picking up the phone. Chef Jody Adams says their goal is "more to engage our customers than to sell to them." And their investment is minimal: about five hours to design the newsletter each month and a monthly fee of $84 to e-mail marketing firm Constant Contact.[21]

Cross-Selling

Cross-selling occurs when customers are sold additional products as the result of an initial purchase. The specific purchase allows the seller to segment the customer. E-mails to customers from Amazon.com describing other books bought by people who purchased the same book the customer just bought is an attempt at cross-selling. If the additional products or services purchased are even more profitable than the original purchase, this can provide significant additional profits. In addition, if firms are successful at cross-selling the right products at the right time to the right customers, then customers perceive this as individualized attention, and it results in more satisfied and loyal customers.

When Bank of America acquired Merrill Lynch in 2009 for $50 billion, a number of cross-selling opportunities arose, since its wealth management employees could view each customer's savings and checking accounts along with their investment portfolios. One year later, these cross-selling opportunities were bearing fruit—global wealth management business had increased, and profit margins were in excess of 20 percent, which was significantly higher than industry averages.[22] Cross-selling to a bank's customers as a growth strategy makes sense too, particularly in the current economic recession. A 2009 survey by market research company Forrester found that 60 percent of consumers said they were less likely to switch their banking provider, making new customer acquisitions even more expensive for banks. "It costs a lot less to mail to 10 percent of your best customers than it does to mail to 100,000 prospects," says Grover Pagano, vice president for analytics at Texas-based Harland Clarke, a direct marketing service.[23]

Predicting Customer Behaviors

By understanding customers' current purchasing behaviors, future behaviors can be predicted. Using data-mining software and customer behavior analytics allows firms to predict which products customers are likely to purchase next and how much they would be willing to pay. In this way, companies can revise pricing policies, offer discounts and design promotions to specific customer segments. Sheldon Gilbert, the creator of Proclivity, a behavior-predicting software used by New York-based Proclivity Systems, knows all about you—your favorite color, how many times you added that flat screen TV to your online shopping cart without buying it and what you like to do in your spare time. Sheldon explains, "Every time you click a link, it's a request for information you're making to a server. We can then mine the data stored on the servers to create a profile of a person's likes and dislikes or proclivities." Using this information to advise which offers should be presented to which customers, Gilbert's company has increased online sales by as much as 30 percent for clients like upscale department store Barney's New York.[24] Hilton Hotels' CRM software analyzes demographic information from its Hilton Honors program, and behavioral patterns are used to help create direct-mail campaigns and to help hotel managers plan for upcoming seasonal activity by business travelers.[25] One of the more desirable CRM attributes falling under this category is **customer defection analysis**.

Customer Defection Analysis

Reducing customer defections, or **customer churn**, is a necessary component of managing long-term profitable customer relationships. And it pays handsomely as well. According to Harvard Business School research, a 5 percent improvement in customer retention can result in a 75 percent increase in profits.[26] Today, competition in almost every product category is very high, and along with it, customer savvy. "The average consumer has more information at his fingertips with which to make informed decisions about a relationship with companies than he has had in the past," says Jonathan Trichel, principal of customer and market strategy at Deloitte Consulting. Knowing which customers have quit purchasing and why can be very valuable information for organizations. Recent research has found that the top four reasons for defection are rude employees/poor attitudes, overall poor service, employees socializing and not paying attention to customers, and slow service.[27] Not only can these customers be approached to encourage additional purchases, but the knowledge gained can be used to reduce future defections. "If I've got an 80 percent satisfaction rate, the focus needs to be on the 20 percent of dissatisfied customers," says Bob Furniss, president of CRM consultancy Touchpoint

Associates of Tennessee. "If I can understand what's occurring in the 20 percent, then my impact is much more profound than being satisfied with the satisfaction rate."[28]

Offers of money or free minutes from telephone service companies are examples of efforts to regain customers who have defected to another phone service. In some cases, though, organizations may actually want some customers (unprofitable ones) to defect. By determining the value or profitability of each of the defecting customers, firms can design appropriate policies for retaining or regaining some customers as well as other policies to discourage additional purchases from some customer (or essentially *fire customers*). In some department stores, for instance, customers who repeatedly return merchandise are at some point given only store credit instead of cash. By monitoring purchase histories, these firms can see if this type of discouragement makes customers quit returning merchandise.

Customer Value Determination

Until recently, determining **customer value** or **customer profitability** was difficult for most CRM systems. Today, though, by integrating with ERP systems, capturing customer profitability information is possible for many businesses. However, use of this information can potentially cause poor decisions to be made regarding some customers. For instance, some customers that are unprofitable now may become profitable later. A health club, for instance, may have some unmarried members who rarely make other purchases at the club but frequently visit and use the facility. Though such members may be seen as unprofitable, it is likely that if they are satisfied with the club, they will tell others; and at some point they may marry and upgrade to a family membership. Thus, it is necessary to determine **customer lifetime value (CLV)** or profitability such that appropriate benefits, communications, services or policies can be directed toward (or withheld from) customers or customer segments.

Unless a firm has knowledge of customer profitability, they may be directing sizeable resources catering to customers who are actually unprofitable. For instance, in a study published by consultant and database marketing author Arthur Middleton Hughes, he described how Boston-based Fleet Bank's marketing staff was working hard trying to retain customers who were actually unprofitable. In fact, half of Fleet's customers were deemed unprofitable, with the bottom 28 percent gobbling up 22 percent of the bank's total annual profits.[29] Calculating CLV is based on a projection of a customer's lifetime purchases, the average profit margin on the items they purchase and the net present value of the customer's projected profits. Example 10.1 illustrates this calculation.

Determining the focal firm's share of their customers' total purchases can also help to focus resources on managing the right customers. Consider two business customers, for example, one whose purchases from the focal firm are worth $2 million per year and the other whose purchases amount to $1 million per year. At first glance, the first customer might seem more valuable; however, if that customer's total purchases from all suppliers for similar products is $3 million, whereas the second firm's total purchases of similar products is $20 million, then the second firm suddenly has much more potential for additional sales and should be managed more carefully.

Personalizing Customer Communications

Knowledge of customers, their behaviors and their preferences allows firms to customize communications aimed at specific groups of customers. Referring to customers

Example 10.1   Calculating Customer Lifetime Value

The Kentucky Bluegrass Seed Company sells grass seed and other Kentucky-area plant seeds to area plant nurseries. They have decided to begin calculating the expected lifetime profitability of each of their nursery customers in order to design differential grass and plant seed promotions. Their top two customers have the following characteristics:

	AVG. ANNUAL SALES	AVG. PROFIT MARGIN	EXPECTED LIFETIME
Nursery A:	$22,000	20%	5 years
Nursery B:	$16,000	15%	15 years

Using a discount rate of 8 percent, and treating the average sales figures as annuities, the present value of the two nursery lifetime values is:

$$NPV_A = a \left[\frac{(1+i)^n - 1}{i(1+i)^n} \right] = \$22,000\,(.2) \left[\frac{(1+.08)^5 - 1}{.08(1+.08)^5} \right] = \$4,400 \left[\frac{0.469}{0.118} \right] = \$17,488$$

$$NPV_B = a \left[\frac{(1+i)^n - 1}{i(1+i)^n} \right] = \$16,000\,(.15) \left[\frac{(1+.08)^{15} - 1}{.08(1+.08)^{15}} \right] = \$2,400 \left[\frac{2.172}{0.254} \right] = \$20,522$$

where

a = average annual profit, or the (annual sales) × (profit margin)
i = annual discount rate
n = expected lifetime in years.

Based on these calculations, Nursery B is the more important customer because of the higher expected lifetime value.

by their first name, or suggesting services used in the past communicates value to the customer and is likely to result in greater levels of sales. The Ritz-Carlton Hotel, for instance, profiles its customers in order to provide the accommodations each person prefers on subsequent visits. Websites of online retailers can remember a customer's credit card number, name, clickstreams and items purchased in order to personalize future site visits by offering products, ads and shipping preferences that fit each customer's profile.

CRM software that can analyze a customer's **clickstream**, or how they navigate a website, can tailor a website's images, ads or discounts based on past usage of the site. Website businesses may also send personalized e-mails, for instance, with incentives to lure customers back, if it has been a while since their last purchase. A quick-change oil and lube shop might send a postcard to a customer's address every 90 days, reminding them it's time for an oil change while offering a discount on the next visit. On the same card, they may also offer discounts on other services that the customer has used in the past, such as a radiator flush, a tune-up or a tire rotation. With time, this customization capability improves, as the firm learns of additional services, products and purchasing behaviors exhibited by various customers.

Event-Based Marketing

Another form of personalized communication comes with the ability to offer individual promotions tied to specific events. Banks, for example, may try to market automated mortgage payment services to all of their customers who have recently applied for and received a home mortgage loan. The same bank might offer home improvement loans to customers once their mortgages reach an age of five years. The idea with **event-based marketing** is to offer the right products and services to customers at the right time. When entertainment venues ask for the birth dates of their customers as they buy season passes or day passes, for instance, they can direct future discounts to occur on days they are likely to be celebrating. With large volumes of customers, event-based promotion strategies are impossible without computer automation, so event-based marketing capabilities tend to be popular among firms seeking to purchase CRM systems.

Automated Sales Force Tools

Sales force automation (SFA) products are used for documenting field activities, communicating with the home office, and retrieval of sales history and other company-specific documents in the field. Today, sales personnel need better ways to manage their accounts, their business opportunities and communications while away from the office. To supply these capabilities, firms have been using CRM tools since the early 1990s to help management and its sales force keep up with the ever more complicated layers of information that are required as customers and prospects increase. When field sales personnel have ready access to the latest forecasts, sales, inventory, marketing plans and account information, it allows more accurate and timely decisions to be made in the field, ultimately increasing sales force productivity and improving customer service capabilities.

North Carolina-based Coca-Cola Bottling Co. Consolidated recently reorganized to improve the execution of its sales force. They split the team, with one part specializing in distribution while the other focused on improving sales. With this change, Consolidated had to address a communication gap between the two groups as well as enable its sales force to handle more products, new product information, marketing materials and in-store execution capabilities. To handle these needs, the company rolled out new mobile devices featuring a custom-built sales force automation solution. Orders are taken on the new handheld devices, wirelessly transmitted to Consolidated's network and then prepared for delivery. Account managers can take orders, conduct surveys and use collaboration tools. "The biggest efficiency the technology has brought is more time spent out in the field doing core selling," says Consolidated's president Bill Elmore. "Our account managers trust that the hardware and software will do what they need it to do, so there is more time spent selling on the front end than on the backend trying to figure out how to key information in."[30] Some of the desired CRM capabilities in the area of sales force automation are discussed next.

Sales Activity Management

These tools are customized to each firm's sales policies and procedures and offer sales personnel a sequence of sales activities that guides them through the sales process with customers. These standardized sales process steps assure that the proper sales activities are performed and also put forth a uniform sales process across the entire organization. The use of a **sales activity management system** reduces errors, improves sales force productivity and boosts customer satisfaction. Along with the prescribed sales steps, field sales representatives can be reminded of key customer activities as they are needed, generate mailings for inactive customers, be assigned tasks by management and generate to-do lists. Pharmaceutical distributor AmerisourceBergen, headquartered in Pennsylvania, needed an easy way to reach customers with a consistent message. With the help of a consultant and an automated message management software application, they created an interactive portal on their internal network for their sales reps. This allowed sales personnel to customize presentation slides, brochures, proposals, e-mail, follow-up letters and other forms of client communication. "It's true situational selling," says Scan Markey, VP of business operations at AmerisourceBergen. "And it's cool how it saves time, not having to mill through a myriad of collateral or making your own sales pieces."[31]

Sales Territory Management

Sales territory management systems allow sales managers to obtain current information and reporting capabilities regarding each salesperson's activities on each customer's account, total sales in general for each sales representative, their sales territories and any ongoing sales initiatives. Using these tools, sales managers can create sales teams specifically suited to a customer's needs, generate profiles of sales personnel, track performance and keep up with new leads generated in the field.

Lead Management

Using a **lead management system** allows sales representatives to follow prescribed sales tactics when dealing with sales prospects or opportunities to aid in closing the deal with a client. These products can generate additional steps as needed to help refine the deal closing and negotiation process. During this process, sales representatives can generate product configurations and price quotes directly, using laptops or handheld devices remotely linked to the firm's server. In addition, leads can be assigned to field sales personnel as they are generated, based on the requirements of the prospect and the skill sets of the sales representatives. Thus, lead management capabilities should result in higher deal-closing success rates in less time. Another common characteristic allows managers to track the closing success of sales personnel and the future orders generated by each lead.

Knowledge Management

Sales personnel require access to a variety of information before, during and after a sale including information on contracts, client and competitor profiles, client sales histories, corporate policies, expense reimbursement forms, regulatory issues and laws, sales presentations, promotional materials and previous client correspondence. Easy access to this information enables quick decision making, better customer service, and a better-equipped and more productive sales staff. When sales and other skilled personnel leave an organization, years of accumulated knowledge walk out the door with them, unless a system is in place to capture this information for others to use. A **knowledge management system** gives the organization this capability. Iowa-based Dupaco Community Credit Union recently installed several CRM tools including a knowledge management system. "We've seen a clear improvement in consistency of message and we understand situations better thanks to our CRM tools. Members don't have to repeat themselves when talking with different staff about service delivery or issue resolution because all employees have the notes from previous conversations at their fingertips," says senior VP of information services Steve Ervolino.[32]

Managing Customer Service Capabilities

The key element of any successful CRM initiative is the ability to provide good **customer service**. In fact, with any process that deals with the customer, one of the primary objectives is always to provide adequate levels of customer service. But what does customer service actually mean? In Chapter 7, customer service was discussed in terms of safety stock and managing inventory. In Chapter 9, customer service was tied to delivering goods on time. And as mentioned earlier in this chapter, customer service can also mean answering customers' questions and having disputes or product and service problems fixed appropriately and quickly. Thus, many definitions of customer service can be found. As a matter of fact, numerous customer service rankings exist and are published each year. Unfortunately, complaints about shoddy customer service abound in many organizations today, and this represents one area where organizations can create real competitive advantage if customer service processes are designed and operated correctly. The next section defines customer service and discusses several elements of customer service.

Customer Service Defined

One customer service definition that covers most of the elements mentioned above is the "**Seven Rs Rule**."[33] The seven Rs stand for having the *right* product, in the *right* quantity, in the *right* condition, at the *right* place, at the *right* time, for the *right* customer, at the *right* cost. In logistics parlance, for instance, a **perfect order** occurs when all seven Rs are satisfied. This customer service definition can be applied to any service provider or manufacturer, and for any customer. A misstep in any of the seven areas results in lower levels of customer service. Consequently, competitive advantage can be engendered by creating an organization that routinely satisfies the seven Rs.

Organizational performance measures are often designed around satisfying some of the seven Rs. For example, reducing stockouts to one percent means that customers get the product or service they want 99 percent of the time; and having an on-time delivery performance of 97 percent means that customers get their orders at the right time 97 percent of the time. Other customer service measures are typically designed to measure *flexibility* (responding to changes in customer orders), *information system response* (responding to requests for information), *recovery* (the ability to solve customer problems) and *post-sales support* (providing operating information, parts, equipment and repairs). In the airline industry, customer service is measured using frequencies of lost or damaged baggage, bumped passengers, canceled flights, on-time flights and customer complaints. In the U.S., Alaska Airlines and JetBlue were the top-rated air carriers in terms of overall customer service in 2009, while United, Frontier and AirTran were rated the worst according to a survey by J.D. Power and Associates.[34] Other customer service winners and losers are shown in the Global Perspective feature.

Global Perspective
The Best of the Best and the Worst of the Worst

The following is a partial listing of companies in several industries (shown alphabetically) that have been recognized for providing the best (and the worst) customer service. Also included are short descriptions of what made these companies so good (or so bad). While some of the company names might not be recognizable, what makes them stand out is certainly worth noting.

THE VERY BEST

Air New Zealand (Auckland, NZ)—named airline of the year for 2010 by *Air Transport World* magazine. At a time when most airlines are losing huge amounts of money, Air New Zealand makes profits by offering customers the warmth and caring of the Kiwi culture from the moment they contact the airline. In 2009, over 80 percent of flights arrived within 15 minutes of scheduled arrival times; it reduced mishandled bags by 19 percent (which was already 60 percent lower than average); and it received only 12,000 complaints from over 2.3 million passengers carried.[35]

Amazon.com (Washington)—ranked best in 2010 for customer service by MSN Money–Zogby International survey. Amazon is like your own personal shopper and a free, organized and polite one too. Amazon says its offerings are always driven by the customer. Upgrades like an expanded product line and package tracking were based on customer requests. It also provides free shipping to good customers, which costs the company about $500 million per year.[36]

L.L. Bean (Maine)—named best in customer service for 2010 by *Business Week* magazine and J.D. Powers and Associates. L.L. Bean won by providing a high level of product quality, good catalog product descriptions, ordering ease and customer-friendly return policies. Their business-as-usual strategy in a tough market includes new store openings, their annual Northern Lights Christmas celebration in Freeport, Maine, free valet parking and free gift wrapping.[37]

Cox Communications (Georgia)—winner of 2009 J.D. Powers and Associates residential telephone customer satisfaction study. "Our customer service representatives, field service technicians and neighborhood Cox employees are the ones who make the Cox experience an award-recognized one," says David Pugliese, Cox senior vice president of product marketing. Cox ranked very high in performance and reliability, customer service, billing, cost of service and overall satisfaction.[38]

UnitedHealth Group (Minnesota)—named 2009 Best Health Plan Provider by Business *Insurance* magazine Readers Choice Awards. They developed mobile medical units using teleconferencing technology to serve remote communities; introduced a diabetes preventive healthcare plan to help employers address rising diabetes costs; and launched a health literacy program to fund schools' obesity initiatives.[39]

THE VERY WORST

AOL (New York)—ranked worst in customer service for 2010 by MSN Money–Zogby International survey. AOL provides online services such as MapQuest, AIM and Moviefone. AOL has won this distinction for three years in a row, and to quote one respondent, "Is it your business model to get your customers to hate you?" AOL representatives declined to comment.[40]

AT&T (Texas)—ranked lowest in customer satisfaction from *Consumer Reports* magazine survey of readers in 26 major U.S. cities. Complaints were dropped call frequency, low service availability, low circuit capacity and poor voice service. As suggested by the magazine, if readers are ready to buy the Apple iPhone, they should prepare to be disappointed with the service but expect to love the phone anyway.[41]

Bank of America (North Carolina)—ranked number two behind AOL for worst customer service in 2010 by MSN Money–Zogby International survey. Bank of America spokesperson blamed the rating on the current economic conditions, although Bank of America has ranked in the bottom ten since the first survey was conducted in 2007. A major source of problems according to respondents was debit card overdraft fees.[42]

Charter Cable (Missouri)—given the lowest ratings for 2008, 2009 and 2010 by *Consumer Reports* magazine for bundled television, Internet and phone service. The main problem areas were customer support, billing, added fees and price after the introductory offer. Charter re-emerged from bankruptcy in November 2009.[43]

Comcast (Pennsylvania)—While improving, Comcast (cable provider) remained for a second year on the worst customer service list for 2010 conducted by MSN Money–Zogby International survey. Also named Worst Company in America 2010 by consumer advocate website Consumerist.com readers poll. "We know that customer service has been an issue for us," says spokesperson Jenni Moyer. Their biggest problems were field technicians showing up late and not fixing the problem on the first visit.[44]

Providing great customer service keeps customers returning; however, this also comes at a cost. Firms must consider the costs of providing good customer service (such as faster transport, greater safety stock levels, more service provider training and better communication systems) as well as the benefits (keeping customers' future profit streams). In organized supply chain relationships, firms often work together in determining (and paying for) adequate customer service, because the costs of poor customer service can be substantial.

© 2008 Ted Goff

"We're having a special on old-fashioned customer service, the kind you used to get before you had to pay extra for it."

Customer service elements can be classified as **pretransaction, transaction** and **posttransaction elements**. Each of these is briefly discussed next.

- *Pretransaction elements:* These customer service elements precede the actual product or service purchase; examples are customer service policies, the mission statement, organizational structure and system flexibility.
- *Transaction elements:* These elements occur during the sale of the product or service and include the order lead time, the order processing capabilities and the distribution system accuracy.
- *Posttransaction elements:* These elements refer to the after-sale services and include warranty repair capabilities, complaint resolution, product returns and operating information.

To provide high levels of service and value to customers, firms seek to continually satisfy the seven Rs while also developing adequate customer service capabilities before, during and after the sale. Call centers have been used in many organizations to improve customer service and supply chain performance, and this topic is discussed next.

Call Centers

Call centers or **customer contact centers** have existed for many years, and some organizations have used these effectively to satisfy and keep customers loyal, although others have seen them as a necessary cost of doing business and a drain on profits. As call centers became automated, customer service representatives were able to quickly see how similar questions were answered in the past and resolve problems more quickly, resulting in greater call center effectiveness. Call center systems can categorize calls, determine average resolution time and forecast future call volume. These automated systems can reduce call center labor costs and training time, and improve the overall productivity of the staff, while improving customer service levels. Lately, call centers have implemented virtual queuing systems as well, as callers see this as a very convenient call center characteristic. The virtual queue allows callers to request a callback from an agent without losing their place in the phone queue, which frees up callers' time, reduces caller frustration and also reduces call center toll charges for keeping callers on hold. Atmos Energy, a natural gas distributor in the U.S., implemented a virtual queuing system and found that most callers actually preferred the virtual queue, average call time was reduced by 10 percent and caller complaints decreased.[45]

Unfortunately, the call center process can get bogged down when agents are not hired or trained effectively. Critics and many consumers have also argued that automated answering programs and hard-to-understand call center agents in outsourced foreign call centers are acting to reduce customer satisfaction. In a study of 1,000 North American consumers conducted in 2007 by Massachusetts-based Aspect Software, automated call center systems were given an overall grade of "D" for efficiency, ease of use, speed, quality, wait time, transfers and caller empathy. The report also found, however, that a consumer who is satisfied with an automated experience is 2.5 times *more likely* to conduct business with the firm in the future.[46] "The good news is that there are more people open to trying automation," says Paul Stockford, chief analyst at Arizona-based contact center research firm Saddletree Research. "The bad news is the automation is still not delivering the way it should."

Contrary to popular belief, most call center work today is done in-house. In the U.K., for example, 80 percent of all call centers are housed within the firm. Much of the emphasis in call center management is on product training and information software usage. "There's nothing worse than phoning your service provider and finding you know more than the person on the other end of the line," says Neil Armstrong, marketing director at U.K. broadband service provider PlusNet.[47] As firms seek to cut costs, though, the lower labor costs of foreign call centers can make outsourcing an attractive option for some companies. However, additional risks such as loss of corporate culture, lack of control, image or brand problems associated with use of foreign workers and loss of "personal touch" with customers can mitigate any gains from call center outsourcing. In the U.S., nearshore locations such as the Dominican Republic, Jamaica and Nicaragua can offer lower labor costs, good English- and Spanish-speaking capabilities, and proximity such that management has better control over training and tools used by offshore call centers. Additionally, companies are experimenting with use of domestic call centers and even home-based agents, which can also provide lower costs while avoiding the image problem. Market intelligence provider IDC estimates that about 25 percent of all U.S. call center jobs are outsourced. According to Robert Creviston, vice president of human resources at California-based Waste Management, "You can save labor dollars, but if sales dollars walk out the door after, then outsourcing is not beneficial. We haven't gotten to a point where we're standardized enough in our process to consider outsourcing."[48]

Today, organizations are realizing how important call centers can be in managing customer relationships. In many firms, call centers have a dedicated, well-trained staff providing 24/7 call support. And they have implemented technologies to better customize the help and information customers receive. For example, calls can be routed to various call center geographic locations based on the time of day, specialization required or the current wait time at each of the call center locations. NICE Systems Ltd. of Israel, for example, sells an automated system that digitally records customer-agent conversations and scans for words such as "cancel"; these conversations are flagged and then managers are sent reports with the customers' names so they can potentially resolve customer problems.[49]

Website Self-Service

Websites act as support mechanisms for call centers by making commonly requested information available to visitors of the site. Customers can, among other things, access their account information, and get flight schedules, operating hours, contact information, locations, directions and product information or return policies. On most sites, organizations provide space for e-mailing questions or complaints; some sites even offer online chat capabilities with company personnel or with other customers who are currently visiting the site. Well-designed **website self-service** capabilities can further reduce the need for call center staffers, while adequately handling most customer queries. It is estimated that answering a customer query on a phone costs about $7, while dealing with a customer using an automated online system costs about $0.10. California-based Blue Coat, an application delivery network provider, gives customers a knowledgebase application for finding answers on their website. Additionally, the website guides customers in updating their knowledgebase applications as well as provides customer feedback to in-house new product developers.[50]

Measuring Customer Satisfaction

Measuring customer satisfaction remains somewhat of a tricky proposition. Customers are frequently given opportunities to provide feedback about a product, service or organization through customer feedback cards placed at cash registers or on tables and customer surveys provided with purchased products or shown on firm websites. In most cases, the only time these forms are filled out is when customers are experiencing a problem. Given this, companies still can find valuable uses for the information. Responses can be analyzed and used to solve the most commonly occurring problems. In CRM programs, customer satisfaction surveys can be personalized to fit specific customer segments, and responses can be matched to the respondent's profile to provide the company direction on how to improve its communication and service capabilities for various groups of customers.

The design of the surveys themselves can be a particular problem for companies. In many cases, surveys don't ask the questions customers want to answer. On many website surveys, customers are more often asked about the design of the website instead of how the firm is performing or what the customer may be happy or unhappy about. In a study of both brick-and-mortar and Internet banks, for instance, less than half of all the banks studied even used customer comment cards or surveys, and only two banks in the study (both were Internet banks) offered service quality surveys.[51]

On the other hand, actually talking with and listening to customers, and then taking action based on what customers are saying, lets customers know the firm is completely engaged. Domino's Pizza, for example, completely redesigned its product after listening to unflattering customer satisfaction comments. According to new product development expert and author Don Adams, many companies are starting with a new product, validating it by testing it with some customers and then measuring their success by watching sales. Instead, companies should start with customers and end up with the product. "There's no substitute for respectful dialogue with customers," says Adams. "People inside companies tend to get defensive about their products and processes," he adds. "It's only human. But when you can cut through that defensiveness and show them 'Hey, this really isn't working for our customers,' well that's where true service and value finally begin."[52]

In this section of the chapter, the common elements necessary for successful CRM programs were reviewed. Many of these involve the use of technology and software. But having numerous software applications does not necessarily guarantee CRM success. A number of other factors come into play before, during and after programs are implemented that must be adhered to, in order to give the firm and its CRM program a good chance of finding and keeping profitable customers. The next section will discuss this very important aspect of CRM.

Designing and Implementing a Successful CRM Program

Designing and then implementing a CRM program can be a real challenge, because it requires an understanding of and commitment to the firm's customers, adherence to CRM goals, knowledge of the tools available to aid in CRM, support from the firm's top executives and the various departments that will be using the CRM tools, and a continuous awareness of customers' changing requirements. Poor planning is typically the cause for most unsuccessful CRM initiatives, because of the temptation to start working on a solution or to hire a CRM application provider before understanding the problem. The firm must first answer this question: *What are the problems a CRM program is going to solve?* This must involve employees from all functional groupings across the firm, as well as input from the firm's key customers. Putting together a sound CRM plan will force the organization to think about CRM needs, technology alternatives and the providers that sell them. Selecting the right tools and providers is an important step, but should not occur until a CRM plan is completed.

Aside from creating a CRM plan and getting the firm's employees to buy into the idea and uses of CRM, managers must also consider any existing CRM initiatives implemented in piecemeal fashion across the firm. Integrating new and existing applications into one enterprise-wide initiative should be one of the primary objectives of the CRM implementation process. Additionally, the firm must decide on specific performance outcomes and assessments for the program and provide adequate training to the CRM application users.

Creating the CRM Plan

Putting together a solid plan for a CRM project is crucial both as an aid to purchasing and implementing CRM applications, and to obtain executive management approval and funding for the project. The plan should include the objectives of the CRM program, its fit with corporate strategy, new applications to be purchased or used, the integration or replacement of existing methods or legacy CRM systems, the requirements for personnel, training, policies, upgrades and maintenance, and the costs and time frame for implementation. Once this document is completed, the firm will have a roadmap for guiding the purchase and implementation process, as well as the organizational performance measures to be used once the program is in place.

New York-based Travel Dynamics International, for instance, a luxury small-ship charter cruise operator, had multiple software systems to handle customer-oriented processes, and they realized some customers were not being served adequately. "Clients were slipping through the cracks. We were not efficient, and there were process gaps," says Nikos Papagapitos, manager of technology and special projects at Travel Dynamics. They ended up merging a Microsoft CRM application with their legacy application in December 2008. "It was a complete 180 from before, instead of looking in four or five places, we had one integrated database for everything. Now if a person calls in, we can see their history with us, and can record what made them choose us in the first place," Papagapitos explains.[53]

The objectives of any CRM initiative should be customer focused. Examples might include increasing sales per customer, improving overall customer satisfaction, more closely integrating the firm's key customers with internal processes or increasing supply chain responsiveness. These will vary somewhat based on the overall strategic focus of the firm. Once these objectives are in place, tactical goals and plans can be instituted at the functional level, consistent with the CRM objectives. Finally, tactical performance measures can be used to track the ongoing performance of the CRM program. This performance will serve to justify the initial and ongoing costs of the program.

Involving CRM Users from the Outset

In order to get acceptance of a new CRM initiative, employee involvement and support is required. This comes about by enlisting the help of everyone affected by the initiative from the very beginning. Employees need to understand how the CRM initiative will affect their jobs before they will buy into the program. Creating a project team with members from sales, customer service, marketing, finance and production, for instance, will tremendously aid in the selection, training, use and acceptance of the CRM system. The team can contact CRM application providers and collect information regarding capabilities and costs, and they can also collect baseline customer service, sales, complaint and other meaningful performance information. The team should also be heavily involved in evaluating and selecting the applications, and then implementing and integrating the applications in each department. As the implementation, or "burn-in," continues, closely monitoring system performance will keep users convinced of the value of the initiative, and keep everyone committed to its success.

Quite a lot of research has been conducted to study CRM implementations, and most have found a direct relationship between program success and employee involvement. Recently, for example, several researchers in New Zealand talked with managers at three banks which had implemented CRM programs several years earlier. Two of the banks had failed to focus on employee buy-in, while the third bank introduced a new sales culture to complement their CRM project, to win employee support. Eventually, the third bank's CRM system proved to be much more successful. In another example, Beene Garter, a Michigan area accounting firm, designed an internal contest to "sell" CRM to its employees. "Teams were assigned 'homework' on client records and the software tracked who entered updates," says Den Ouden of Beene Garter. "The contest mirrored components of the Olympics and was called 'Go for the Gold' to tie into the software name, GoldMine. At the closing ceremony, the best-performing teams received 'gold' medals and gift cards," she adds. Their success was remarkable. Users' attitudes about the CRM project changed from anxiety associated with entering all the data to familiarity, which created easy adoption and continuous use.[54]

Selecting the Right Application and Provider

Once the organization has completed its plan for CRM, they should have a fairly good idea of what they are going to do, and which activities will require automation or technology. The job then becomes one of finding an appropriate application and deciding how much customization will be required to get the job done.

Finding the best application and supplier can be accomplished a number of ways, including:

- visiting a CRM-oriented tradeshow
- using a CRM consulting firm
- searching CRM or business publications such as *Call Center Magazine, Call Center News*, and *Inside Supply Management*[55]
- using the knowledge of internal IT personnel, who already know the market, and
- searching the many CRM supplier directories and websites

Firms should seek help from a number of these alternatives, and internal IT personnel should be viewed as internal consultants in the application and supplier identification and selection process. Firms must analyze and compare the various products available. In her CRM handbook, Dyché recommends comparing the following software characteristics:[56]

- integration and connection requirements (the hardware, software and networking capabilities)
- processing and performance requirements (the volume of data and number of users it can support)
- security requirements
- reporting requirements (preformatted and customized reporting capabilities)
- usability requirements (ability for users to customize the software, display graphics and print information)
- function-enabling features (workflow management, e-mail response engine, predictive modeling capabilities)
- performance capabilities (response times for various queries), and
- system availability (ability to accommodate various time zones)

Comparing these CRM capabilities should narrow the list of qualified vendors substantially. When finally selecting a supplier for the application, one of the primary criteria for firms to consider is the support available from the application provider. Vendors offering implementation and after-sale user support that meets the needs of the firm (for instance,

24/7 phone support) should be valued more highly than other vendors. Suppliers offering free trial usage to verify the product's capabilities is another element that needs to be considered. Finally, cost and contract negotiations should be carefully considered.

Integrating Existing CRM Applications

In most firms, CRM systems are not one single product, but rather a suite of various applications that have been implemented over time. One of the biggest mistakes made is that departments across the firm implement various CRM applications without communicating these actions to other departments. Eventually, these systems will interfere with each other as they communicate with the same customer, sending confusing and irritating signals that can chase customers away quickly.

Customer contact mechanisms need to be coordinated so that every CRM application user in the firm knows about all the activity associated with each customer. Today, this lack of integration is leading to real problems as call centers and sales offices seek to please and retain customers by adopting customer loyalty programs, customer tracking mechanisms and various customer satisfaction programs without making this information widely known and available within the firm. Additionally, multiple stand-alone CRM applications throughout the company result in duplication of effort, incompatible formats, wasted money and disgruntled customers. Compatible CRM modules are needed that are linked to one centralized database or **data warehouse** containing all customer information. Thus, from one database, users in the organization can retrieve information on a customer's profile, purchase history, promotion responses, payment history, Web visitations, merchandise returns, warranty repairs and call center contacts.

By integrating CRM information obtained throughout the firm, decision makers in the firm can analyze the information and make much more customer-focused decisions. Using predictive models and statistical analyses, firms can identify customers most likely to purchase certain products, respond to a new promotion, or churn. This ability to track a 360-degree view of each customer at the enterprise level allows firms to truly personalize and focus their efforts and products where they will do the most good, resulting in maximum benefit for the firm *and* its customers.

With interest income shrinking and loan demand weakening at banks, bankers today are rethinking how they can broaden customer relationships. According to Alabama-based consulting firm Bancography, a bank customer with one product will stay with that bank for about eighteen months, but when adding two more products, the expected customer lifetime jumps to about 6.8 years. MidSouth Bank in Louisiana recently converted to a new Oracle CRM system that gathers all customer information into a central database, allowing product innovations aligned with customer needs. "It's the 360-degree view of the customer you hear about," says the bank's marketing officer Alex Calicchia. "It's about giving the frontline in particular, the ability to look at a given moment, what's in the customer's wallet today and what's missing from that wallet."[57]

Establishing Performance Measures

Performance measures linked to CRM system objectives (and customers) allow users and managers to witness the progression of the system in meeting its original objectives. It also serves to keep everyone excited and informed about the benefits of a well-designed program, and will identify any implementation or usage problems as they occur, allowing causes to be found and solutions to be implemented quickly.

At the organizational level, performance measures should concentrate on areas deemed strategically important, such as CRM productivity, new customers added or sales generated from the CRM program. Some examples of these measures are listed in Table 10.1. Note that the performance measures are spread between the customers, the CRM system itself and the users. Additionally, all of the metrics should be transparent and easy to measure. At the user level, other more tactical performance measures should be developed and tracked, supporting the firm-wide strategic measures. Linking performance measures in this way will give the firm the best chance of a successful program implementation and continued revision and use of the program into the future.

Training for CRM Users

Another important step in the implementation process is to provide and require training for all of the initial system users, and then provide training on an ongoing basis as applications are added or as other personnel begin to see the benefits of the CRM system. Training can also help convince key users such as sales, call center and marketing personnel of the benefits and uses of CRM applications. Training is one area crucial to CRM program success. Unfortunately, in a recent survey conducted by *Customer Relationship Management* magazine, 43 percent of the respondents said their end-user training "needed improvement."[58] Unless the users are shown the personal gains they'll receive for taking time to learn the software and its capabilities, the CRM applications will most likely go unused or underused.

Training managers and users in the key customer contact areas can also help the firm decide what customizations to the CRM applications are required before the system is put into use. This is particularly important for larger firms where supply chains and the

Table 10.1	CRM Performance Measures		
PERFORMANCE MEASUREMENT TYPE	**DEPARTMENT OR USER-LEVEL PERFORMANCE MEASURES**		
	FIELD SALES	**CALL CENTER**	**MARKETING**
Customer Loyalty	1. % customer repurchases 2. avg. # repurchases 3. # customer referrals	1. # customer product information requests 2. # customer praises	1. % customers responding to solicitations or promotions 2. avg. # of campaign responses
Customer Satisfaction	1. # customer visits to resolve problems 2. # field service visits per customer	1. # logged complaints per customer 2. customer satisfaction survey results	1. % customers who have responded more than once to promotions
Average Sales Revenue per Customer	1. # sales quotas met 2. % repeat visits resulting in sales	1. # customer calls for catalogs 2. # customer phone orders	1. # website visits per customer 2. website purchases per customer
CRM Productivity	1. % sales quotas met among FS reps. 2. # new leads generated 3. % new leads closed	1. avg. caller time 2. # complaints successfully resolved 3. sales generated from customer calls	1. # segment catalogs produced 2. # promotional e-mails sent 3. # marketing campaigns
CRM User Satisfaction	1. annual internal user satisfaction survey	1. annual internal user satisfaction survey	1. annual internal user satisfaction survey
CRM User Training	1. hrs. training per year per rep. 2. # CRM applications trained per rep.	1. hrs. training per year per agent 2. # CRM applications trained per agent	1. hrs. training per year per user 2. # CRM applications trained per user

sales and marketing processes are complex. In many cases, CRM system implementation means that other systems already in place will be phased out or merged with the new system. Training can help personnel decide how best to phase out old systems and phase in the new ones. CRM consultant Barton Goldenberg suggests that firms should create a training profile for each of its CRM system users to provide training before, during and after the implementation process in one or more of these areas: computer literacy training, business process training, CRM application training, remedial training and new user training.[59]

Recent Trends in CRM

Three topics have significantly impacted the practice of CRM within the past few years and these are customer data privacy, cloud computing and social media. These topics are discussed next.

Customer Data Privacy

A number of trends are affecting the way CRM programs are designed today, and these trends will likely continue to influence CRM programs, application providers, the companies that use them and finally the customers themselves. One of these is **data privacy**. As the use of the Internet increases, there is growing concern about customers' personal information becoming compromised or being shared with other companies in order to generate income. New privacy regulations are springing up as consumer protection groups continue to push for stronger Internet regulatory measures. As consumer fears mount, companies must take a proactive stand at reassuring customers that their information will be protected, as well as convincing them to allow information to be used in the first place.

Unfortunately, customer data is sometimes compromised, and this news frequently hits the popular media outlets. For example, international banking company HSBC Holdings PLC announced that an employee stole 24,000 Swiss account records in 2007 and tried selling the information to foreign governments interested in finding tax dodgers. French authorities finally captured the culprit and retrieved the data in 2008 and returned it to HSBC. Later, the bank pledged to spend $100 million to upgrade security. Data breaches in the U.S. are a huge concern—according to the California-based consumer advocacy group Privacy Rights Clearinghouse, 200 million instances of data breaches occurred from 2005 through 2008. Additionally, the Federal Trade Commission estimates that 9 million people have their identities stolen each year. And these breaches are expensive—the average cost to manage and repair a data breach is about $6.3 million.[60]

Safeguarding customer information is a legal and ethical responsibility for any company collecting, processing and transmitting sensitive customer data. Data privacy laws such as the Data Protection Act in the U.K., the Internet Privacy Law in the E.U., and the U.S. Patriot Act, just to name a few, provide laws for protecting customer information and require compliance by all firms engaged in handling customer information. Some of the independent measures firms can take to improve information security are to develop a privacy policy and post it on the company website as well as on other information-gathering forms; allow customers to opt-in and out of mailing lists and promotional campaigns; allow customers to access their accounts online so they can view the information collected about them; require customers to state their privacy preferences, build this into their profiles and use these preferences when developing one-to-one promotions; make someone in the firm responsible for enforcing privacy policies and communicating these to employees and customers; and continuously monitor employee desktop applications, website activity, e-mails, instant messages and phone calls.

Social Media

Not too many years ago, employees were banned from visiting **social media** sites deemed unsuitable for conducting business such as Facebook and Twitter. Today, companies are beginning to see potential value in these and other social media applications. A 2009 survey sought to identify the B2B sales potential of these social sites, and found that most of the sales potential had yet to be realized. At the time, the site with the most potential for B2B sales was found to be LinkedIn.[61] A recent poll by New York-based customer polling agency Harris Interactive found that people are increasingly using social media sites to share good and bad business experiences. In fact, use of these sites grew by 100 percent from 2008 to 2009. Consumers are actually moving away from contacting companies directly with their concerns, preferring instead to talk about their experiences using blogs and social networking sites. And this is precisely how firms can save money with the use of social media. Firms can use social media sites to create user forums where technical support and other customer questions are answered by other customers. In many cases, companies are finding this to be an improvement over answers given by the firms' own help desks. Companies like Intel and Linksys have found that the investment to create these social communities can be recouped in less than a year, given the zero labor cost of the social media sites.[62] Dell Computers has been using several online communities to engage customers and receive customer feedback since 2006. A discussion of their social community is shown in the e-Business Connection feature.

---

e-Business Connection   *Dell Online's Social Community*

After first creating online support forums where experts engaged with customers who had questions or issues about Dell products, in 2006 Dell started getting engaged with outreach. The company was listening to customer conversations spanning the Web and was able to build a small team to reach out directly to those customers to connect, engage and converse with them. In doing so, Dell was able to attract participation on its site, where a community took root—in fact, several communities. There's one for general consumers, for small businesses, for customers in the education market and for its largest enterprise customers. Dell claims to have made 3.5 million connections across the Web so far.

In 2007, Dell launched the Salesforce.com-powered IdeaStorm as "a way to talk directly with our customers," according to the website. The community was created to give customers a place to conduct online brainstorming sessions, to share ideas and to collaborate with Dell. The company says its goal through IdeaStorm is "to hear what new products or services you'd like to see Dell develop. We hope this site fosters a candid and robust conversation about your ideas."

On IdeaStorm, members are allowed to view and post suggestions to Dell. They are also allowed to vote up or vote down what they like or dislike. In its three years, IdeaStorm has had more than 10,000 ideas posted and has, more impressively, implemented nearly 400 ideas. One example? "There was feedback from the Linux community for us to have an offering in that space," says Manish Mehta, Dell Online's vice president of global online. "We made changes in keyboard design and layout as well."

In addition to IdeaStorm, Dell introduced Storm Sessions in December 2009. Unlike IdeaStorm, which allows users to comment on anything and everything, Storm Sessions is more targeted. Dell

posts a topic and asks customers for feedback. If Dell has a particular area it's interested in getting suggestions about it will send out a Storm Session to a particular segment of the community
—the segment to which that Session is most likely to be relevant. Mehta calls the new feature a
"really nice way to marry what the community wants to tell us with what we want to know."

Dell claims its community outclasses many others because customers feel no restrictions on their
input. But any successful community also offers a sense of belonging. Mehta recalls a meeting
Dell had with some of its community VIPs. "We flew in people who've been on our online community forums for more than a decade," he says. "There were some people there who have helped
35,000 customers, and you can only imagine how many they've impacted by their solutions. We
asked them why they do this. Now, some of them are still Dell customers, some have moved on
[to other products], but [what we've found is that] they're still helping because there's still this
underlying culture that sits within communities that's all about helpfulness and sharing."

Source: Martinez, J., "Marketing to a Community," *Customer Relationship Management* 14(6), 2010:
30–35. Used with permission.

Others think the financial impact of social media is not so easy to determine. For
instance, according to Esteban Kolsky, a CRM consultant and industry expert, making
financial use of social media is going to be very difficult for many organizations.
"We've tried enterprise feedback management, surveys, speech, service, and nothing has
worked. Now here's a shiny new object called social media and people think that we're
going to get it right. Unfortunately, they don't realize the social media part is ten times
more complicated than other attempts because of the move from structured to unstruc-
tured [data]."[63]

Some business examples of social networking success and failure already exist.
Intercontinental Hotels Group, owner of the Crowne Plaza and Holiday Inn chains, is
using California-based Jive Social Business Software to create an online community
where loyalty program members can get information and share experiences. The Jive
analytics also allow Intercontinental management to track customer keywords and customer sentiment on a topic along a spectrum from positive to negative. Additionally, Jive
can export information to business intelligence applications and a video portal.[64]

In March 2010, one of food product manufacturing giant Nestle's Facebook friends
used a negatively modified Nestle logo as her Facebook photo and others soon did likewise, as a way to criticize Nestle's use of palm oil in some of its products. Nestle's
response was to delete these comments from their Facebook fan page, while adding a
warning to those who might be breaking trademark laws. Environmental activist group
Greenpeace soon joined the Facebook discussion about Nestle's use of palm oil, along
with many other activists, arguing that the company was contributing to the destruction
of Indonesian rainforests when purchasing palm oil. The fan page quickly got out of
control as large numbers of negative comments took over the site. Eventually, Nestle
apologized and announced it had partnered with The Forest Trust to assure that its
palm oil products were 100 percent sustainable by 2015. Since that time, Nestle's
Facebook page has been much more fan-friendly.[65]

Really talking to customers and listening to what they are saying is the value of social
media. The concept of owning customers is fading as companies realize that customers'
jobs, families and friends are much more important than the brands they buy.
Companies wanting to succeed with social media need to use it to listen. "Listening is
the infrastructure that enables you to collect all this information and process it and

analyze it," says Suresh Vittal, an analyst at Forrester Research.[66] General Motors, for instance, is talking and listening. After enduring a Chapter 11 bankruptcy, a government bailout and several miserable sales years, GM began using Facebook and Twitter to raise brand awareness and rebuild some goodwill. "The way we look at it is, Twitter is almost the beginning of the conversation. It's a cocktail party. You walk in, and you're pretty much talking to anyone who's there. Facebook is the dinner party, where it's people you know a little bit, who have opted in to become part of your brand. Twitter conversations are a lot more open and a free-for-all, but there's value in both," says Chris Barger, director of global social media for GM.[67]

Cloud Computing

Another current CRM trend is the use of **on-demand computing**. Mark Benioff and Salesforce.com first introduced the concept of on-demand computing back in 1999 in a San Francisco garage. To this company, "no software" was not just a slogan but a mantra. Within two years, Salesforce.com had 3,500 customers, 53,000 subscribers and was named the fastest-growing online CRM company by Morgan Stanley. By the end of 2008, they had about 52,000 customers, 1.1 million subscribers and 3,300 full-time employees. In a world dominated by expensive CRM software, high implementation costs and questionable success rates, Benioff's model was simple—online basic CRM applications, low costs, quick implementation and good results.[68]

Today, there are a large number of these **application service providers**, or ASPs, providing on-demand applications (not just for CRM, as we have shown in previous chapters), also referred to as the **software-as-a-service model**, or **SaaS model**. Perhaps as many as 50 percent of all CRM programs are now designed and maintained for clients by ASPs. In many cases, firms do not have the resources, time, knowledge or infrastructure to buy and build an effective CRM system, so they use Internet-based on-demand CRM services. For small companies with limited resources needing some basic CRM functions, the SaaS model has been a real boon. For larger companies with thousands of users seeking a wider range of functionality and customization, purchased CRM applications are still the desired platform and may even be cheaper in the long run, since user subscription fees for on-demand services are continuous and can become quite costly over time.

These days, on-demand computing and the SaaS model are more often referred to as **cloud computing**, since users are able to access business applications online with only a browser. The software and user data are stored on the ASP's computer (as in "somewhere up in the clouds"). Similarly, Facebook and MySpace users are in the clouds when they store pictures and other information on the ASP's computers. The demand for cloud computing has been high recently, as firms have sought ways to cut costs without losing customers. Worldwide, cloud computing revenues were $7.5 billion in 2009 and are expected to exceed $14 billion by 2013.[69]

As more and more customers seek cloud computing applications, full-service business application providers like Cisco, SAP, IBM, Oracle and Microsoft are scrambling to acquire and develop cloud computing products. These full-service providers hope to be one-stop shops where customers can purchase software, hardware and networking capabilities to build and manage **private clouds** (where the data centers are owned by the corporate users and managed in-house) or just subscribe to various cloud computing applications as needed. "With a private cloud, I can control some of the aspects that bother me about a public cloud, such as security or the system going down," says Gary Matuszak, global chairman for KPMG's information, communications and entertainment practices.[70]

Domino's Pizza, for instance, is right now considering switching from a private cloud to Microsoft's Azure cloud computing system. Domino's currently operates Pizza Tracker and several other applications on their private cloud. "Resiliency is huge," says Jim Vitek, Domino's director of e-commerce. "If the stores go down, the customers go to the competition. Downtime is lost sales." Moving to the Azure cloud could help Domino's deal with demand spikes, such as during the Super Bowl. Global wireless technology provider Qualcomm has already discontinued its traditional CRM applications in favor of Salesforce.com's CRM cloud services. "We replaced them all," says Mark Silber, Qualcomm's IT architect. The move allowed Qualcomm to reduce its CRM costs by 60 percent.[71]

SUMMARY

In this chapter, we introduced and discussed the elements of CRM, its place within the field of supply chain management, the requirements for successful CRM program implementation and the current trends in CRM. As we learned, customer relationship management is really all about treating customers right, and for as long as there have been businesses, some firms have been very successful at keeping customers satisfied and coming back, while others have not. For the past ten or fifteen years, though, both the level of competition in the marketplace as well as available computer technology and software capabilities have been increasing quite dramatically. Thus, we have seen a shift in CRM toward use of technology, software and the Internet to better analyze, segment and serve customers with the objective of maximizing long-term customer profitability.

Firms today are learning how to combine many channels of customer contact to better serve customers, resulting in better customer satisfaction and more sales. Though many traditional CRM applications are expensive, firms can use a structured approach to design an appropriate plan, and then analyze and select the right applications and vendors to implement a successful CRM program.

KEY TERMS

application service providers, 369

call centers, 359

clickstream, 353

cloud computing, 369

cross-selling, 350

customer churn, 351

customer contact centers, 359

customer defection analysis, 351

customer lifetime value (CLV), 352

customer profitability, 352

customer service, 355

customer value, 352

data privacy, 366

data warehouse, 364

event-based marketing, 354

knowledge management system, 355

lead management system, 355

mobile marketing, 349

on-demand computing, 369

perfect order, 356

permission marketing, 349

posttransaction, 358

pretransaction, 358

private clouds, 369

QR codes, 350

relationship marketing, 349

sales activity management system, 354

sales force automation (SFA), 354

sales territory management systems, 355

segment customers, 349

Seven Rs Rule, 356

social media, 367

software-as-a-service (SaaS) model, 369

target marketing, 349

transaction, 358

website self-service, 360

DISCUSSION QUESTIONS

1. Define the term "customer relationship management". What has caused this definition to change over the past twenty years?

2. How does the actual practice of CRM differ from the use of CRM software?

3. Why have so many CRM efforts failed? Can you cite a personal example of a CRM effort?

4. Describe why CRM is so important in managing supply chains. Use an example in your discussion.

5. What is segmenting customers, and why is it perhaps the most important activity in CRM?

6. Define these terms: permission marketing, cross-selling and churn reduction.

7. How would an analysis of customer defections help the firm become more competitive?

8. Why is the determination of customer lifetime value important?

9. *Chapter Problem:* From the information given, rank the customers in terms of their lifetime value.

	AVG. ANNUAL SALES	AVG. PROFIT MARGIN	EXPECTED LIFETIME
Customer A:	$2,500	17 %	8 years
Customer B:	$4,000	12 %	6 years
Customer C:	$1,200	30 %	12 years

Use a discount rate of 6 percent and treat the average annual sales figures as annuities. Should any of these customers be fired?

10. How can CRM applications increase the effectiveness and productivity of a firm's sales force?

11. How does *your definition* of customer service compare to the Seven Rs Rule?

12. Describe the types of customer service that come before, during and after the sale. Why are they important to CRM?

13. Are call centers good for CRM? Explain.

14. Do you think call center outsourcing negatively affects customer service? Explain.

15. Could self-service websites be used in place of call centers?

16. How should customer satisfaction be measured at a bank? A restaurant? A manufacturing firm? A retailer?

17. Do you think CRM applications unnecessarily invade customers' privacy? Explain.

18. Describe the steps necessary for designing and implementing a successful CRM program.

19. What is the most common mistake made when designing and implementing a CRM program?

20. How do you think CRM performance should be measured? Suggest several performance measures.

21. What sort of problems generally occur with a firm's existing CRM applications?

22. How can firms help to assure the privacy and security of their customers' information and data?

23. How do various social media impact an organization's CRM methods? Should firms use social media for attracting new customers?

24. What is cloud computing and what are its advantages for CRM?

25. What is the difference between on-demand computing, the software-as-a-service model and cloud computing?

INTERNET QUESTIONS

1. Go to the website www.callcentermagazine.com, and look at several new issues of the magazine. Describe a new development in call center usage or technology.

2. Identify an on-demand Internet CRM provider, and see if you can determine what is "free" and what is not.

3. Search on the term "call center technology," and describe a few of the latest uses of technology in call centers.

4. What are some of the latest developments in Internet privacy laws?

5. Identify some of this year's best and worst customer service providers. Have any companies remained on the list provided in the Global Perspective feature?

Chapter 11

GLOBAL LOCATION DECISIONS

Within IBM, we see the need for locations and particularly cities, to become "Smarter Cities." This concept captures the need for locations in general and cities in particular to leverage new technology and new intelligence to optimize their natural, physical, human and cultural resources to ensure sustainable prosperity for their citizens. Recent events in the world economy have shown that the imperative to become smarter is now greater than ever.[1]

"No two countries that both had McDonald's had fought a war against each other since each got its McDonald's".

—Thomas Friedman in The Lexus and the Olive Tree

Learning Objectives

After completing this chapter, you should be able to

- Explain the impact of global location decisions on a supply chain.
- Identify the factors influencing location decisions.
- Understand the impact of the regional trade agreements on location decisions.
- Use several location evaluation models.
- Understand the advantages of business clusters.
- Explain the importance of sustainable development.

Chapter Outline

When IBM needed a location for a new 750,000 SF semiconductor plant, they turned to New Jersey-based WDG Consulting to recommend the best location for their new facility. Initially, IBM identified three potential greenfield (vacant) locations and WDG Consulting instituted a U.S. search to identify a number of other suitable location candidates. To accomplish this, they assessed a list of potential locations using location criteria such as land availability, air quality, water and sewer capacity, electric power availability, taxes, workforce availability, estimated payroll costs and land costs.

Working with the IBM team, WDG finalized a list of three greenfield locations and three other sites with structures to analyze using more comprehensive research. The additional analysis included use of factors with greatest importance to a semiconductor manufacturer, a review of maps and satellite images to assess potential sites, interviews with other high-tech company personnel, university professors and utility, airport and environmental officials and finally, on-site inspections of sites and existing structures.

Ultimately, WDG Consulting assessed their research findings using criteria that IBM deemed most important to the success of their proposed $1.2 billion semiconductor facility. Among the most important criteria in determining the final location were the existing infrastructure (water availability, water and sewer treatment capacities, electricity and telecommunications access), highway access, environmental considerations, local and state tax rates, skilled workforce availability, operating costs, permit time and cost, availability of university resources, quality of life considerations and the estimated time to startup operations. Upon completion of the data collection and analysis, WDG Consulting recommended a location in Manassas, Virginia for IBM's semiconductor operations. One of the more influential factors was the presence of a vacant site which would reduce capital costs and expedite time to market.

Today, IBM enjoys a successful operating experience in Manassas. Some of the reasons for this success include the following:

- Total operating costs 10 percent below original projections;
- Utility capacities that meet requirements with minimal downtime;
- Readily available technical, assembly and engineering workers;
- Low employee turnover;
- Reasonable tax treatment;
- An impressive local and regional supplier base;
- The willingness of universities to customize training for IBM; and
- Supportive state and local governments.

Source: www.wdgconsulting.com/WDGC_Project_case_studies_IBM.htm.

Introduction

Locating a facility is an important decision affecting the efficiency and effectiveness of managing the supply chain, level of service provided to customers and the firm's overall competitive advantage. A supply chain is a network of facilities and the location of production facilities, offices, distribution centers and retail sites determines the efficient flow of goods to and from these facilities. Once a decision on locating a facility is made, it is costly to move or shut down the facility. Thus, facility location has a long-term impact on the supply chain and must be an integral part of the firm's supply chain strategy. With increased globalization and investments in technology infrastructure, faster transportation, improved communications and open markets, companies can locate anywhere in the world—previously thought to be impossible.

It would appear that easy access to global markets and corporate networks makes the role of location less important as a source of competitive advantage. However, successful business clusters such as Silicon Valley, Wall Street, the California wine region and the Italian leather fashion cluster show that location still matters. The existence of business clusters in many industries provides clear evidence that innovation and successful competition are concentrated geographically. Dr. Michael Porter suggests that the immediate business environment is just as important as those issues that impact companies internally in affecting location decisions.[2] Business clusters are discussed in detail later in this chapter.

Global location decisions involve determining the location of the facility, defining its strategic role and identifying markets to be served by the facility. For example, Honda's global location strategy of building cost-effective manufacturing facilities in areas that best meet the requirements of local customers has served the company well. Honda's "Small Born" manufacturing strategy is to start small and expand production as local demand increases. This approach allows the company to be efficient and profitable, even when production volumes are low. Honda's first auto plant in the U.S. was built in Marysville, Ohio. Then the company added a second factory in East Liberty, Ohio. As demand for Honda automobiles continued to increase, Honda opened a facility to assemble the Odyssey mini-vans in Alabama and an auto plant producing Civic GX Natural Gas Vehicles in Indiana. Honda's Ridgeline trucks, which were built previously in Canada, are today produced in the Alabama plant. Toyota, Nissan, Mercedes, BMW and Hyundai have also built assembly plants in the U.S. to cater to the local automobile markets.[3]

Global Location Strategies

Global location decisions are made to optimize the performance of the supply chain and be consistent with the firm's competitive strategy. According to Frank Kern, Senior Vice President, IBM Global Business Services, "Corporations today are faced with unprecedented pressures to adapt and reinvent themselves to survive and prosper in a new economic environment. This comes with profound implications for how they approach their physical infrastructures and global operations. An emphasis on gaining access to new and growing markets is being replaced in their current location strategies by consolidation and cost reduction. In their search for lower costs, companies have reduced their overall level of investment, but have also widened the scope of their search to encompass new and more cost efficient locations. For example, some African countries have seen their share of global investment grow, as they are increasingly seen as locations that offer attractive operating environments and costs."[4] A firm competing on cost is more likely to select a location that provides a cost advantage. For instance, Amazon.com, as profiled in the e-Business Connection feature, locates warehouses in areas that will minimize logistics and inventory costs. Many toy manufacturers have

e-Business Connection	*Amazon.com's Facility Network*

Jeff Bezos founded Amazon.com in 1995. Amazon's corporate mission is "to be Earth's most customer-centric company for three primary customer sets: consumer customers, seller customers and developer customers."[5] The company's global operations are in Canada, China, France, Germany, Japan and United Kingdom. Its internationally focused websites include www.amazon.com, www.amazon.ca, www.amazon.de, www.amazon.fr, www.amazon.co.jp, www.amazon.co.uk and www.amazon.cn. In 2009, Amazon served more than 1.5 million customers with nearly 50 percent of sales from the international segment.[6]

The early belief in electronic commerce was that millions of customers could be served without requiring the type of infrastructure of a Sears or a Wal-Mart. However, online retailers are finding out that without their own warehouses and shipping capabilities, customer service could suffer. In the late 1990s, Amazon.com went on a warehouse-building spree, adding new facilities in Nevada, Kentucky and Kansas to its existing distribution system. The objective was to improve logistics and cut shipping times to customers. Amazon now offers "Guaranteed Accelerated Delivery" dates on selected items with one- or two-day express shipping.

While recognizing that distribution systems will help the company manage the delivery process better and improve customer service, there is still a need to turn a profit. With the heavy investments in distribution centers in the U.S. and worldwide, companies are finding that the flow of goods through the distribution system must be improved to reduce distribution costs.

Amazon.com used the NetWorks Strategy module from its Manugistics e-Business suite to organize the movement of products through its transportation and facility network in the U.S. and Europe. The NetWorks Strategy module determines which of Amazon.com's distribution centers to retain or expand and the quantity of each product to keep in stock. In addition, the software plans shipments, decides what to put in each shipping container, schedules transportation, tracks and expedites shipments and computes the shipping cost. The company currently has fulfillment centers in nine U.S. states: Arizona, Delaware, Indiana, Kansas, Kentucky, Nevada, Pennsylvania, Texas and Virginia. Fulfillment centers in Europe are located in the United Kingdom, France and Germany. In Asia, the fulfillment centers are found in China and Japan. By strategically locating its distribution centers and improving operations, Amazon.com is able to enhance its supply chain by reducing its inventory, minimizing logistics cost and improving the speed and reliability of delivery of orders to its customers.

also moved their factories to Vietnam, Thailand or China because of cost advantages provided by these countries.

A firm that competes on speed of delivery such as the FedEx Corporation uses the hub and spoke approach to location determination. FedEx's first and largest hub in the U.S. is in Memphis, Tennessee. This site has a five-mile perimeter with parking for 175 aircraft and 300 miles of conveyor belts. The Memphis Hub employs over 4,000 employees during the day and 8,000 at night. Supporting the largest air cargo fleet in the world, the facility handles about 3.3 million packages per day and is the heart of the company's sorting operations. FedEx has instituted procedures to ensure that packages are moved as efficiently as possible. FedEx has smaller U.S. hubs in Anchorage, Chicago, Fort Worth, Indianapolis, Los Angeles, Newark and Oakland and foreign hubs in Germany, France,

Japan, Philippines, China, the United Arab Emirates and the U.K. Each of the hubs has been picked for its central location and easy access to customers.[7]

To get the most out of foreign-based facilities, managers must treat these plants as a source of competitive advantage. These foreign facilities have a strategic role to perform. Professor Kasra Ferdows of Georgetown University suggests a framework consisting of six strategic roles depending on the strategic reason for the facility's location and the scope of its activities:[8]

- *Offshore factory:* An **offshore factory** manufactures products at low cost with minimum investment in technical and managerial resources. These products tend to be exported. An offshore factory imports or locally acquires parts and then exports all of the finished products. The primary objective is simply to take advantage of low labor costs. For example, in the early 1970s, Intel built a labor-intensive offshore factory to produce simple, low-cost components in Penang, Malaysia.

- *Source factory:* A **source factory** has a broader strategic role than an offshore factory with plant management heavily involved in supplier selection and production planning. The source factory's location is dictated by low production cost, fairly developed infrastructure and availability of skilled workers. Hewlett-Packard's plant in Singapore started as an offshore plant in 1970 but with significant investments over a ten-year period was able to become a source factory for calculators and keyboards.[9]

- *Server factory:* A **server factory** is set up primarily to take advantage of government incentives, minimize exchange risk, avoid tariff barriers and reduce taxes and logistics costs to supply the regional market where the factory is located. An example would be Coca-Cola's international bottling plants, each serving a small geographic region.

- *Contributor factory:* The **contributor factory** plays a greater strategic role than a server factory by getting involved in product development and engineering, production planning, making critical procurement decisions and developing suppliers. In 1973, Sony built a new server factory in Bridgend, Wales. By 1988, the factory was involved in the design and development of many of the products it produced and now serves as a contributor factory in Sony's global manufacturing network.[10]

- *Outpost factory:* The **outpost factory** is set up in a location with an abundance of advanced suppliers, competitors, research facilities and knowledge centers to get access to the most current information on materials, components, technologies and products. Since the facility normally produces something, its secondary role can be that of a server or an offshore factory. For example, Lego still produces molds and toys in Denmark, Germany, Switzerland and the U.S. in spite of the higher manufacturing cost.[11] Lego's factories serve as outpost facilities with access to research facilities, institutions of higher learning and sophisticated suppliers of plastic materials.

- *Lead factory:* A **lead factory** is a source of product and process innovation and competitive advantage for the entire organization. It translates its knowledge of the market, competitors and customers into new products. In the early 1970s, both Intel and Hewlett-Packard established offshore factories in Southeast Asia. Over time, the strategic roles of these factories were upgraded to that of lead factories.

Critical Location Factors

One of the most challenging tasks as a company grows, relocates or starts up is where to position assets strategically to create a long-term competitive advantage. Some of the questions and concerns that need to be addressed for each potential location follow:

- What will be the reaction of shareholders, customers, competitors and employees?
- Will the location provide a sustainable competitive advantage?
- What will be the impact on product or service quality?
- Can the right people be hired?
- What will be the effect on the supply chain?
- What is the projected cost?
- What will be the impact on delivery performance?
- How will the market react?
- Is the transfer of people necessary and, if so, are employees willing to move?

There are basically three levels of location decisions: the global market or country selection, the sub-region or state selection and the community and site selection. The process starts with an analysis of the market region of the world that bears a strategic interest to the organization; and, eventually, a country is targeted. Once the country is selected, the focus shifts to finding a subregion or state within the country that best meets the company's location requirements. Finally, the community and site for the facility are selected. The weighted-factor rating model, which is discussed later in this chapter, can be used to make a location decision at each of the levels we have mentioned. Table 11.1 lists a number of factors affecting each of the three levels of location decisions and a discussion of these factors follows.

Regional Trade Agreements and the World Trade Organization

An understanding of regional trade agreements and the **World Trade Organization (WTO)** is critical to the facility location decision process because of their impact on tariffs, costs and the free flow of goods and services. The WTO is the successor to the General Agreement on Tariffs and Trade (GATT), which was responsible for setting up the multilateral trading system after the Second World War. Today, the WTO is the "only global international organization dealing with the rules of trade between nations"[12] and has 153 members. Its functions include administering the WTO agreements, providing a forum for trade negotiations, handling trade disputes, monitoring national trade policies, providing technical assistance and training programs for developing countries and cooperating with other international organizations.

There are 462 regional trade agreements under GATT and the WTO in force today.[13] Examples of the better-known regional trade agreements are the **European Union (EU)**, the **North American Free Trade Agreement (NAFTA)**, the **Southern Common Market (MERCOSUR)**, the **Association of Southeast Asian Nations (ASEAN)** and the **Common Market for Eastern and Southern Africa (COMESA)**. Several of these are discussed here:

- *The European Union (EU):* Set up after the Second World War, the European Union was officially launched on May 9, 1950, with France's proposal to create a European federation consisting of six countries: Belgium, Germany, France,

Table 11.1	Important Factors in the Location Decision Process		
LOCATION FACTOR	**COUNTRY**	**REGION/STATE**	**COMMUNITY**
Regional trade agreements—trade barriers, tariff and import duties	X		
Competitiveness of nations—economic performance, government efficiency, business efficiency and infrastructure	X		
Government taxes and incentives	X		
Currency stability	X		
Environmental issues	X	X	X
Access and proximity to markets	X	X	X
Labor issues	X	X	X
Access to suppliers	X	X	X
Transportation issues	X	X	X
Utility availability and cost	X	X	X
Quality-of-life issues	X	X	X
State taxes and incentives		X	X
Right-to-work laws		X	X
Local taxes and incentives			X
Land availability and cost			X

Italy, Luxembourg and the Netherlands. A series of accessions in 1973 (Denmark, Ireland and the U.K.), 1981 (Greece), 1986 (Spain and Portugal), 1995 (Austria, Finland and Sweden), 2004 (Czech Republic, Estonia, Cyprus, Latvia, Lithuania, Hungary, Malta, Poland, Slovenia and Slovakia) and 2007 (Bulgaria and Romania) has resulted in a total of 27 member states. Currently, the EU has three additional candidate countries of Croatia, Republic of Macedonia and Turkey.[14] Two highlights of the EU are the establishment of the single market in 1993 and the introduction of the euro notes and coins on January 1, 2002. The EU has a population of half a billion people, third largest after China and India and with a GDP more than that of the U.S.

- *The North American Free Trade Agreement (NAFTA):* This trade agreement among the U.S., Canada and Mexico was implemented on January 1, 1994. NAFTA created the world's largest free trade area, currently with over 440 million people and producing more than US$17 trillion of goods and services annually. Many tariffs were eliminated with an immediate effect, while others were phased out over periods ranging from five to fifteen years. U.S. trade with

Canada and Mexico totaled $735 billion in 2009; with exports totaling $334 billion and imports totaling $401 billion.[15]

- *The Southern Common Market (MERCOSUR):* This agreement among Argentina, Brazil, Paraguay and Uruguay was formed in March 1991 with the signing of the Treaty of Asuncion. The agreement was created with the goal of forming a common market/customs union between the participating countries and was based on economic cooperation between Argentina and Brazil that had been in place since 1986. Associate members include Bolivia, Chile, Colombia, Ecuador and Peru. Venezuela signed a membership agreement on June 17, 2006, but its full membership entry must be ratified by the Paraguayan parliament. The total population of the four member states is currently over 240 million.[16]

- *The Association of Southeast Asian Nations (ASEAN):* This association was created in 1967 and is comprised of the ten countries in the Southeast Asian region: Brunei, Cambodia, Indonesia, Laos, Malaysia, Myanmar, Philippines, Singapore, Thailand and Vietnam. The primary objective of ASEAN is "to accelerate the economic growth, social progress and cultural development in the region through joint endeavors in the spirit of equality and partnership in order to strengthen the foundation for a prosperous and peaceful community of Southeast Asian Nations."[17]

- *Common Market for Eastern and Southern Africa (COMESA):* COMESA's vision is to "be a fully integrated, internationally competitive regional economic community with high standards of living for all its people, ready to merge into an African Economic Community."[18] COMESA has nineteen member states, with a current total population exceeding 430 million, annual imports of US$152 billion and exports in excess of US$157 billion. The member countries are Burundi, Comoros, D.R. Congo, Djibouti, Egypt, Eritrea, Ethiopia, Kenya, Libya, Madagascar, Malawi, Mauritius, Rwanda, Seychelles, Sudan, Swaziland, Uganda, Zambia and Zimbabwe.[19]

Competitiveness of Nations

A nation's competitiveness is defined by the Organization of Economic Cooperation and Development (OECD) as "the degree to which a country can, under free and fair market conditions, produce goods and services which meet the rest of international markets, while simultaneously maintaining and expanding the real incomes of its people over the long term."[20] There are two competing sources for national competitiveness rankings. One is the *World Competitiveness Yearbook* published annually by the Swiss business school IMD and the other is *The Global Competitiveness Report,* prepared by the World Economic Forum. Since the two organizations use different criteria for their rankings, the lists vary somewhat. The rankings from both publications are shown in Table 11.2.[21]

IMD's World Competitiveness Yearbook features 58 industrialized and emerging economies and provides businesses with the basic information on location decisions. There are 327 criteria, which are broadly grouped into four competitiveness factors:[22]

- *Economic Performance* (76 criteria): "Macro-economic evaluation of the domestic economy: Domestic Economy, International Trade, International Investment, Employment and Prices."

- *Government Efficiency* (71 criteria): "Extent to which government policies are conducive to competitiveness: Public Finance, Fiscal Policy, Institutional Framework, Business Legislation and Societal Framework."

Table 11.2	International Competitiveness Rankings	
RANKING	2009-10 GLOBAL COMPETITIVENESS REPORT (WORLD ECONOMIC FORUM)	2010 WORLD COMPETITIVENESS YEARBOOK (IMD)
1	Switzerland	Singapore
2	United States	Hong Kong
3	Singapore	United States
4	Sweden	Switzerland
5	Denmark	Australia
6	Finland	Sweden
7	Germany	Canada
8	Japan	Taiwan
9	Canada	Norway
10	Netherlands	Malaysia
11	Hong Kong	Luxembourg
12	Taiwan	Netherlands
13	United Kingdom	Denmark
14	Norway	Austria
15	Australia	Qatar
16	France	Germany
17	Austria	Israel
18	Belgium	China
19	Korea, Rep.	Finland
20	New Zealand	New Zealand

Source: www.weforum.org/pdf/GCR09/GCR20092010fullrankings.pdf; and www.imd.ch/research/publications/wcy/upload/scoreboard.pdf.

- *Business Efficiency* (67 criteria): "Extent to which the national environment encourages enterprises to perform in an innovative, profitable and responsible manner: Productivity and Efficiency, Labor Market, Finance, Management Practices and Attitudes and Values."
- *Infrastructure* (113 criteria): "Extent to which basic, technological, scientific and human resources meet the needs of business: Basic Infrastructure, Technological Infrastructure, Scientific Infrastructure, Health and Environment and Education."

The yearbook provides an analysis of the data collected and ranks nations according to their abilities to create and maintain an organization's competitiveness. Data from the report can be used to compare countries globally, to see five-year trends, to understand strengths and weaknesses and to examine factors and sub-factors. In addition, businesses can use the yearbook to determine investment plans and assess locations for new operations. The top three countries for 2010 are Singapore, Hong Kong and the U.S.

The World Economic Forum defines competitiveness as "the set of institutions, policies and factors that determine the level of productivity of a country."[23] Their Global Competitiveness Report examined 139 economies in the current issue and used what the Forum describes as their "12 Pillars of Competitiveness" to determine the rankings. These are briefly described below.

The World Economic Forum's 12 Pillars of Competitiveness

1. Institutions—the legal and administrative framework.
2. Infrastructure—the transportation, telecommunications and power networks.
3. Macroeconomic stability—the level of debt and interest rates on debt.
4. Health and primary education—investment in health services and quantity and quality of basic education.
5. Higher education and training—amount of secondary, tertiary, vocational and on-the-job training in the workforce.
6. Goods market efficiency—overall environment for exchange of goods.
7. Labor market efficiency—the environment for male and female workers.
8. Financial market sophistication—how resources are channeled to businesses.
9. Technological readiness—how readily the economy adapts to new technologies.
10. Market size—the availability of domestic and international markets for firms.
11. Business sophistication—the quality of the overall business networks and quality of individual firms' operations and strategies.
12. Innovation—overall support for innovative activities.

The top three countries according to the Global Competitiveness Report for 2009/10 are Switzerland, the U.S. and Singapore. The criteria covered in the World Competitiveness Report represent issues that organizations would like to know about before making a country location decision. All things equal, a country that has a higher competitiveness ranking would provide a better business climate for locating a facility than another country that is listed as less competitive.

In yet another competitiveness ranking, the global audit and tax service KPMG's *Competitive Alternatives* study examines business competitiveness in 112 major cities in ten countries: Australia, Canada, France, Germany, Italy, Japan, Mexico, the Netherlands, the U.K. and the U.S. The study, described in the Global Perspective feature, analyzes 26 major cost factors such as labor, taxes, real estate and utilities over a ten-year planning horizon and presents an independent assessment of international business location costs. While the study is limited to ten countries, it nonetheless provides a useful guide for organizations considering locating in these countries.

Government Taxes and Incentives

Government incentives, business attitude, economic stability and taxes are important location factors. Several levels of government must be considered when evaluating

Global Perspective

Mexico and Canada Rank the Best in Affordable Business Climates

Mexico and Canada retained their top rankings as affordable jurisdictions to conduct business, according to KPMG's *Competitive Alternatives 2010* study, which compares business costs in 10 countries in North America, Europe and Asia Pacific. Changes in exchange rates, energy costs, transportation costs and taxes are the main factors influencing international competitiveness over the last two years.

Competitive Alternatives examines business competitiveness in 112 cities in Australia, Canada, France, Germany, Italy, Japan, Mexico, the Netherlands, the U.K. and the U.S. The study measures 26 significant cost components that are most likely to vary by location including: labor, taxes, real estate and utilities, as they apply to 17 business operations over a 10-year planning horizon. The rankings for the ten countries for 2008 and 2010 are shown here:

COUNTRY	2010 RANK	2008 RANK
Mexico	1	1
Canada	2	2
Netherlands	3	7
Australia	4	4
United Kingdom	5	6
France	6	5
Italy	7	8
United States	8	3
Germany	9	10
Japan	10	9

"The global recession has not been the only factor impacting international business over the last two years," said Simon Harding, Associate Partner in KPMG's Advisory Services practice. "Divergent trends in exchange rates, utility and transportation costs, taxes and incentives have all helped to shape the international competitiveness environment in 2010. The degree of variation in business costs between major cities in some countries is also quite remarkable. All of these factors highlight the importance of having access to up-to-date intelligence on international business competitiveness issues for both businesses and governments."

Source: Press Release KPMG; available from www.competitivealternatives.com/media/pressrel_international_03302010.pdf. Used with permission.

potential locations. At the federal level, a *tariff* is a tax imposed by the government on imported goods to protect local industries, support the country's balance of payments or raise revenue. Thus, countries with high tariffs would discourage companies from importing goods into the country. At the same time, high tariffs encourage multinational corporations to set up factories to produce locally. However, membership in the WTO requires countries to open up their markets and to reduce the tariffs imposed on imported goods. Regional trade agreements such as NAFTA, MERCOSUR and EU also serve to reduce tariffs among member nations to promote free movement of goods. Many countries have set up *foreign trade zones (FTZs)* where materials can be imported duty-free as long as the imports are used as inputs to production of goods that are eventually exported. If the goods are sold domestically, no duty is paid until they leave the free trade zones.

In the U.S., 43 states have a personal income tax and 46 states have a corporate income tax. For example, Nevada is a business-friendly state that does not have a corporate income tax, state personal income tax, corporate franchise tax or inventory tax. Companies such as Amazon.com have taken advantage of this by setting up warehouses in Nevada. The other states that do not have an individual income tax are Alaska, Florida, South Dakota, Texas, Washington and Wyoming.[24] Location incentives at the state and local government levels are also important.

Currency Stability

One factor that impacts business costs and consequently location decisions is any instability in currency exchange rates. Any organization involved with international business will be subjected to the risk of currency fluctuation. For example, Amazon.com is exposed to foreign exchange rate fluctuations and risks associated with their international operations as reported in their annual report:[25]

> The results of operations of and certain of our intercompany balances associated with, our international websites are exposed to foreign exchange rate fluctuations. Upon translation, operating results may differ materially from expectations and we may record significant gains or losses on the remeasurement of intercompany balances. As we have expanded our international operations, our exposure to exchange rate fluctuations has increased. We also hold cash equivalents and/or marketable securities primarily in Euros, British Pounds and Japanese Yen. If the U.S. Dollar strengthens compared to these currencies, cash equivalents and marketable securities balances, when translated, may be materially less than expected and vice versa.

Environmental Issues

How the environment is managed has a significant impact on human health. The inability to dispose of solid and hazardous waste, plus the presence of illegal waste, contributes to high incidences of diseases such as hepatitis A and amebiasis. Global warming, air pollution and acid rain are issues that are increasingly being debated as the price to pay for industrialization. Millions of people live in cities with unsafe air and with asthma cases at an all-time high. In response to rising environmental concerns, the Clinton Administration negotiated the North American Agreement on Environmental Cooperation (NAAEC) as a supplementary environmental agreement to NAFTA. The key objectives of the agreement are to "foster the protection and improvement of the environment in the territories of the Parties for the well-being of present and future generations and promote sustainable development based on cooperation and mutually supportive environmental and economic policies."[26] The agreement provides a framework for the three NAFTA countries to conserve, protect and enhance the North American environment and to effectively enforce the environmental laws.

With trade liberalization, there is a need for environmental cooperation. The WTO understands the need for sound national and international environmental policies. An earlier WTO report on trade and the environment addressed three key questions: (1) Is economic integration through trade and investment a threat to the environment? (2) Does trade undermine the regulatory efforts of governments to control pollution and resource degradation? and (3) Will economic growth driven by trade help the move toward sustainable use of the world's environmental resources?[27] Several environmental trends were identified in the report:

- The increasing use of global energy resources has raised the level of greenhouse gas emissions.
- Consumption of ozone depletion substances (contributing to global warming) has gone down, but it will take another 50 years to get back to normal levels.
- Sulphur dioxide emissions (a cause of acid rain) continue to increase in developing countries.
- Excessive generation of nitrogen continues from fertilizers, human sewage and burning of fossil fuels.
- Continued deforestation occurs in developing countries.

The increasing global water consumption will result in water shortages in many countries without serious water conservation efforts.

The report finds that neither trade nor economic growth is the real issue. The challenge is "to strengthen the mechanisms and institutions for multilateral environmental cooperation, just like countries fifty years ago decided that it was to their benefit to cooperate on trade matters."[28] These are still the same issues we are concerned with today.

Consumers and nongovernment agencies are now pressuring multinationals to be more environmentally conscious. Global organizations are assessing their total environmental footprints by focusing on carbon and life-cycle analysis. The life-cycle approach looks beyond just the carbon footprint since it focuses on a cradle-to-grave analysis of how products and services affect the environment.[29] Wal-Mart had recently initiated a program to assist suppliers in managing their energy and materials usage and carbon emissions and now companies such as Procter & Gamble, IBM and Pacific Gas & Electric have adopted this approach.

Access and Proximity to Markets

A recent survey on manufacturing competitiveness in China found that a large portion of businesses indicated that their main reason for being in China was to have access to the local markets rather than for export reasons.[30] The study also shows that an increasing number of companies are also considering moving their manufacturing to lower cost locations in central or western parts of China. As we can see here, many companies are now expanding into China not only to take advantage of the lower cost but also to reach out to the local markets. Likewise, Honda is a global company that aims to build plants in locations that best satisfy the needs of local customers. Honda has assembly plants in the U.S., Japan, Malaysia, China and Indonesia, to name a few markets where Honda sells its vehicles.

In the service industry, proximity to customers is even more critical. Few customers will frequent a remotely located gas station or a supermarket if another more accessible alternative is available. Similarly, fast-food restaurants are well situated next to busy highway intersections to take advantage of heavy traffic areas. Wal-Mart's early super-centers were located in predominantly rural markets to avoid direct competition with major discount stores in large metropolitan areas. Many regional chains, such as Jamesway, Bradlees, Caldor, Venture, Hills and McCrory's went out of business because they were not competitive with larger and more efficient chains such as Wal-Mart and Target.[31] More recently, Wal-Mart has changed its location strategy to include urban locations in the west and northeast regions of the U.S. In China, Wal-Mart's location strategy has also focused more on downtown areas, where most of the customers are located.

Labor Issues

Issues such as labor availability, productivity and skill; unemployment and underemployment rates; wage rates; turnover rates; labor force competitors; and employment trends are key labor factors in making facility location decisions. Mexico has long competed on cheap labor but cannot continue to depend on this source of competitive advantage because of the emergence of lower labor cost countries like China. While China's labor cost is low compared to many countries, inflation and high economic growth has contributed to a sharp increase in wages there. Consequently, the apparel industry, which depends heavily on cheap labor, is beginning to see a shift in production from the "textile hub" in Southern China to Vietnam because of the comparatively cheaper labor cost there.

Although it is true that low labor cost is an important factor in making location decisions, sustainable competitive advantage depends on productive use of inputs and continual product and process innovations. Singapore is an example of a country that first relied on cheap labor to attract foreign direct investments. Over time, Singaporeans were able to increase the level of worker skills and develop human resource capabilities. The country moved from a producer of low-cost goods to one making high-value-added products.

Access to Suppliers

Many firms prefer locations close to suppliers because of material availability and transportation cost reasons. The proximity of suppliers has an impact on the delivery of materials and, consequently, the effectiveness of the supply chain. For example, Royal Philips Electronics moved its computer monitor plant in Mexico to an existing plant in China because of a more competitive supplier base.[32] Japanese electronics makers are also finding that China is a better place to set up manufacturing facilities even though it means that the cost to transport finished products to the U.S. market is higher. The reason is that a high proportion of components needed to make finished electronic products are made in China.

Utility Availability and Cost

The availability and cost of electricity, water and gas are also important location considerations. In economically emerging countries, it is not unusual that the supply of electricity has not kept pace with the high speed of development, resulting in work stoppages from electrical outages. Even developed countries such as the U.S. are not immune from energy problems, although for different reasons. For example, California experienced rolling blackouts in the early 2000s, causing an electrical crisis.

In heavy industries such as steel and aluminum mills, the availability and cost of energy are critical considerations. The concern for companies is to have the power available when needed and at an affordable price. Consequently, areas such as upstate New York, the Tennessee Valley and parts of Canada, which provide low-cost power, are gaining in location popularity because of their plentiful energy supply. With the explosive growth in energy-intensive industries such as machinery, auto and steel, demand for electricity has outpaced the generation capacity in China and the country has experienced power shortages in the past. However, the power generated by the completed Three Gorges Dam Project, the world's largest hydropower complex, will help meet China's rapidly growing energy needs. With an increasing number of manufacturing facilities being added in China, the country must continue to invest in clean power generating plants.

Quality-of-Life Issues

Quality of life can be defined as "a feeling of well-being, fulfillment or satisfaction resulting from factors in the external environments."[33] So what exactly are the issues affecting quality of life? While there is no definitive agreement on a set of **quality-of-life factors**, the Chamber of Commerce in Jacksonville, Florida, has annually prepared a report on the quality of life in the metropolitan area based on a comprehensive set of factors, which include the following:[34]

- *Achieving Educational Excellence:* Performance in terms of high-school graduation rates, college entrance test scores, teacher salaries, student-teacher ratios and number of degrees awarded at universities and higher-education institutions provides an indicator of the quality of the education system.

- *Growing a Vibrant Economy:* Performance indicators such as net employment growth, new housing starts and the unemployment rate show the economic health of the community. The economy must also be sufficiently diverse to allow for long-term careers for both spouses.

- *Preserving the Natural Environment:* Performance indicators include air-quality index, average daily water use and the amount of recycled waste diverted from landfills. A viable recycling program and clean air indicate a community's commitment to a green environment and the future health of the community.

- *Promoting Social Well-being and Harmony:* Performance indicators include whether racism is a problem, number of births to single mothers, volunteerism rate and homeless survey count. A community where people and organizations contribute time and money to helping others in need shows a happy, affluent and caring environment.

- *Enjoying Arts, Culture and Recreation:* Performance measures include the public and private support for the arts, number of public performances and events and library circulation. A community that offers choice in terms of cultural, entertainment, recreational and sporting activities is a more attractive location than one that offers fewer of these options.

- *Sustaining a Healthy Community:* Performance indicators include the infant mortality rate, number of people without health insurance, cancer death rate, suicide rate and new HIV cases. Recently, the U.S. medical profession has been facing a dramatic increase in malpractice insurance premiums in many states, with the result that many medical doctors are moving to areas with lower insurance costs. The ability to access good, affordable medical care provides residents with peace of mind and determines whether the community is a desirable place to live.

- *Maintaining Responsive Government:* Performance measures in this category include voter turnout, satisfaction rate with city services, number of neighborhood organizations and diverse and representative government. In the current economic situation, many state and local governments in the U.S. have been struggling to balance their budgets due to a weak economy and are considering cutting services and increasing taxes. This in turn, will tend to negatively impact the quality of life.

- *Moving Around Efficiently and Safely:* This factor can be measured by indicators such as the average commute time to work, bus ridership, number of airport passengers and the motor vehicle accident rate. If the roads are constantly jammed with traffic, this causes huge losses of productive time. In the warehousing and distribution industry, the quality of the highways, railways, waterways and airways has a significant impact on the performance of the supply chain in such areas as transportation cost, speed of delivery and customer satisfaction. The ability to travel easily within the area and to other locations affects the quality of life of the residents.

- *Keeping the Community Safe:* Performance indicators here include violent crime rate, percentage of people who feel safe in their neighborhood, people reporting being victims of crime and the murder rate. In the U.S., there has been a trend toward suburban living because of the perception of safer neighborhoods and, therefore, a better place to live. In Mexico, especially in towns close to the U.S. border, many foreign businesses are concerned about the crime rate and the safety of expatriates working in *maquiladora* industries. Mexican drug cartels and organized crime gangs have contributed to the increased violence and deaths of thousands of innocent people along the border. Thus, the presence of crime could frighten off firms considering locating in that area.

Right-to-Work Laws

In the U.S. today, there are 22 states with **right-to-work laws**: Alabama, Arizona, Arkansas, Florida, Georgia, Idaho, Iowa, Kansas, Louisiana, Mississippi, Nebraska, Nevada, North Carolina, North Dakota, Oklahoma, South Carolina, South Dakota, Tennessee, Texas, Utah, Virginia and Wyoming. A right-to-work law "secures the right of employees to decide for themselves whether or not to join or financially support a union."[35] In the last two decades, there has been a shift in the U.S. auto industry to the South, with assembly plants built in Tennessee, South Carolina and Alabama, all of which are right-to-work states. Dubbed the *Southern Auto Corridor*, this cluster represents a new era in U.S. auto manufacturing. The trend to locate in the sunny, incentive-friendly, non-unionized South will continue to grow.

Land Availability and Cost

As land and construction costs in big cities continue to escalate, the trend is to locate in the suburbs and rural areas. Suburban locations can be attractive because of the cost and wide choice of land, available workforce and developed transportation network. As mentioned earlier, when Honda first decided to set up a factory in the U.S., they located in Marysville, a small town about 40 miles from Columbus, Ohio. Affordable land near the highway was readily available and Honda could draw its workforce from several communities around Marysville. Similarly, when Honda built its assembly plant in Alabama to meet the increased demand for its Odyssey minivans and sport utility vehicles, the site was located in Lincoln, 40 miles east of Birmingham. When Honeywell decided to move its manufacturing facility in Phoenix, Arizona, to China, the decision was to go to Suzhou, a city about 30 miles from Shanghai. Although the Pudong industrial zone in Shanghai was an attractive site, Suzhou had lower land and labor costs, which were deemed important decision factors.

Facility Location Techniques

Two techniques that are commonly used by organizations to assist in making global location decisions are described here: the weighted-factor rating model and the break-even model. The two techniques are discussed below.

The Weighted-Factor Rating Model

The **weighted-factor rating model** is a method commonly used to compare the attractiveness of several locations along a number of quantitative and qualitative dimensions. Selecting a facility location using this approach involves the following steps:

1. Identify the factors that are considered important to the facility location decision.
2. Assign weights to each factor in terms of their relative importance. Typically, the weights sum to 1.
3. Determine a relative performance score for each factor considered. Typically, the score varies from 1 to 100, although other scoring schemes can be used.
4. Multiply the factor score by the weight associated with each factor and sum the weighted scores across all factors.
5. The location with the highest total weighted score is the recommended location.

Since the factors, the individual weights and the scores are subject to interpretation and bias by the analyst, it is highly recommended that a team approach be used when performing this type of analysis. Ideally, the team should include representatives from marketing, purchasing, production, finance and transportation and possibly a key supplier and customer impacted by the location.

Determining the scores for each factor can include several intermediate steps. Comparing a labor cost score, for instance, would include determining the acceptable wage scale, along with insurance, taxes and training costs and any other associated labor costs for each potential location. Then the total labor costs can be compared and translated into the final labor cost scores for each location by assigning the lowest-cost location the maximum score and then assigning the other locations a score based on their respective labor costs. Example 11.1 illustrates the use of the weighted-factor rating model.

The Break-Even Model

The **break-even model** is a useful location analysis technique when fixed and variable costs can be determined for each potential location. This method involves the following steps:

1. Identify the locations to be considered.
2. Determine the fixed cost for each facility. The components of fixed cost are the costs of land, property taxes, insurance, equipment and buildings.
3. Determine the unit variable cost for each facility. The components of variable cost are the costs of labor, materials, utilities and transportation.
4. Construct the total cost lines for each location on a graph.

Example 11.1   Using the Weighted-Factor Rating Model

The following factors have been identified as critical to making a location decision among the three countries of China, Singapore and Indonesia. A group of functional managers has determined the factors, weights and scores to be used in the analysis.

IMPORTANT LOCATION FACTORS	FACTOR WEIGHTS (SUM TO 1)	CHINA SCORES (1 – 100)	SINGAPORE SCORES (1 – 100)	INDONESIA SCORES (1 – 100)
Labor cost	0.2	100	40	90
Proximity to market	0.15	100	60	80
Supply chain compatibility	0.25	80	80	60
Quality of life	0.3	70	90	60
Stability of government	0.1	80	100	50

In which country should the new facility be located?

SOLUTION

The weighted scores for the three countries are calculated as follows:

$$
\begin{aligned}
\text{China} \quad &= \quad 0.20\,(\,100\,) + 0.15\,(\,100\,) + 0.25\,(\,80\,) + 0.30\,(\,70\,) + 0.10\,(\,80\,) \\
&= \quad 20 + 15 + 20 + 21 + 8 = 84. \\
\text{Singapore} \quad &= \quad 0.20\,(\,40\,) + 0.15\,(\,60\,) + 0.25\,(\,80\,) + 0.30\,(\,90\,) + 0.10\,(\,100\,) \\
&= \quad 8 + 9 + 20 + 27 + 10 = 74. \\
\text{Indonesia} \quad &= \quad 0.20\,(\,90\,) + 0.15\,(\,80\,) + 0.25\,(\,60\,) + 0.30\,(\,60\,) + (\,50\,) \\
&= \quad 18 + 12 + 15 + 18 + 5 = 68.
\end{aligned}
$$

Based on the total weighted score, China would be the recommended country in which to locate the new facility.

5. Determine the break-even points on the graph. Alternatively, the break-even points can be solved algebraically.

6. Identify the range over which each location has the lowest cost.

Example 11.2 illustrates the use of the break-even model.

Helpful On-Line Information for Location Analysis

Two websites are available that provide useful information for location analysis:

1. *Development Alliance, The Site Selectors' Portal for Community Information*— found at www.developmentalliance.com: The Development Alliance website is developed by Conway Data, Inc., publishers of *Site Selection* magazine. The Development Alliance website is a portal for community information on finding the best global business location and includes community demographics, U.S. metropolitan statistical data, U.S. state contact information, World Bank's tool for evaluating 175 countries, government contact information, a free trade zone directory, listings of properties for sale and a service providers directory.

Example 11.2 Using the Break-Even Model

Three locations have been identified as suitable candidates for building a new factory. The fixed and unit variable costs for each of three potential locations have been estimated and are shown in the following table.

LOCATION	ANNUAL FIXED COST	UNIT VARIABLE COST
A	$500	$300
B	$750	$200
C	$900	$100

The forecasted demand is 3,000 units per year. What is the best location?

SOLUTION

First, plot the three total cost curves, represented by

$$TC_A = 500{,}000 + 300Q$$
$$TC_B = 750{,}000 + 200Q$$
$$TC_C = 900{,}000 + 100Q$$

The three curves are shown in Figure 11.1.

Determine the break-even points between Location A and Location B as follows:

$$TC_A = TC_B$$
$$500{,}000 + 300Q = 750{,}000 + 200Q$$
$$100Q = 250{,}000 \text{ and then } Q = 2{,}500 \text{ units.}$$

This indicates that producing less than 2,500 units per year would be cheaper at Location A (when the lower fixed cost predominates), while producing more than 2,500 units per year would be cheaper at Location B (when the lower variable cost predominates).

Next, determine the break-even points between Location B and Location C as follows:

$$TC_B = TC_C$$
$$750{,}000 + 200Q = 900{,}000 + 100Q$$
$$100Q = 150{,}000 \text{ and then } Q = 1{,}500 \text{ units.}$$

This indicates that producing less than 1,500 units per year would be cheaper at Location B, while producing more than 1,500 units per year would be cheaper at Location C.

Finally, determine the break-even points between Location A and Location C as follows:

$$TC_A = TC_C$$
$$500{,}000 + 300Q = 900{,}000 + 100Q$$
$$200Q = 400{,}000 \text{ and then } Q = 2{,}000 \text{ units.}$$

This indicates that producing less than 2,000 units per year would be cheaper at Location A, while producing more than 2,000 units per year would be cheaper at Location C.

Based on the cost curves shown in Figure 11.1, Location C has the lowest total cost when producing the forecasted quantity of 3,000 units per year. If, however, the annual demand forecast were 1,000 units, then Location A would be preferred. From Figure 11.1, it can be seen that Location B would never be the preferred location when comparing the costs of all three sites simultaneously.

| Figure 11.1 | Break-Even Graph |

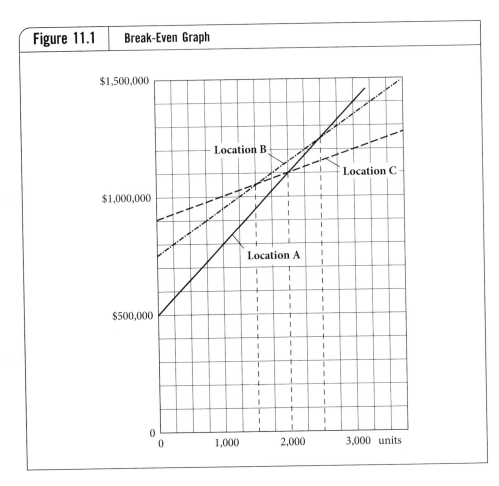

2. *Mapping Analytics*—found at www.mappinganalytics.com/site-selection/site-selection. html. The focus of Mapping Analytics is "business management, including sales, marketing, real estate, strategic planning and GIS consulting."[36] Their clients are from a wide variety of businesses including manufacturing/distribution, banking/ finance, retail, real estate, restaurants, marketing/media/advertising, insurance and healthcare. The key site selection services provided by the company are customer profiling, location mapping, competitive analysis, trade area mapping, demographic, census and market data analysis, market potential analysis and site impact analysis.[37]

Business Clusters

Over the last decade, a number of trends have dramatically impacted the facility location process. Markets are increasingly globalized due to the liberalization of trade, technological advances and increased demand from many regions of the world. Countries compete against one another for foreign direct investment. Having the necessary information to compare countries across a multitude of factors will help managers make better location decisions. Today, more **business clusters** are being created globally. Research parks and special economic/industrial zones serve as magnets for business clusters.

The concept of business clusters represents a new way of thinking about location decisions, challenges conventional logic on how companies should be configured and provides a different approach to organizing a supply chain. So what exactly are these *business clusters?* According to Michael Porter, "clusters are geographic concentrations of interconnected companies and institutions in a particular field. Clusters encompass an array of linked industries and other entities important to competition."[38] Locating research and development, component manufacturing, assembly operations, marketing and other associated businesses in one area can improve the supply chain, technology sharing and information sharing.

Silicon Valley and Hollywood in California are probably the two most well-known and successful business clusters. Another high-tech cluster fashioned after Silicon Valley is Massachusetts' Route 128. A competitiveness study conducted by the U.K. government found that "business development is often strongest when firms cluster together, creating a critical mass of growth, collaboration and competition and opportunities for investment and knowledge sharing."[39]

Governments today recognize the need to develop existing clusters of similar businesses into world-class units. Although clusters are more prevalent in advanced economies such as in the U.S. and Europe, countries such as Mexico, Singapore, India and Taiwan have also created high-tech clusters with the participation of foreign companies.[40] A discussion of each of these follows:

- *Mexico:* Mexico has long been a hotbed for electronic manufacturers, with many located in cities such as Tijuana, Mexicali, Tecate, Chihuahua, Saltillo, Reynosa and Guadalajara. Examples of major global companies operating in Mexico are IBM, Motorola, Hewlett-Packard, Siemens, Ericsson, Samsung, LG Electronics, Sony and Panasonic. With NAFTA, goods can be exported duty-free to North America, allowing Mexico to become an electronics manufacturing center for the Americas. Mexico produces nearly one-quarter of the world's television receivers.

- *Singapore:* Singapore has replaced Japan as the most attractive country for U.S. high-tech manufacturing investment in the Asia Pacific region. Singapore has the greatest technology penetration rates in Asia, the highest per capita GDP in Asia and a highly skilled workforce. Approximately half of the world's computer disk drives are produced in Singapore.

- *Taiwan:* Taiwan, dubbed the "Silicon Island" by *Forbes,* is a leading manufacturer of computer hardware and has the largest global market share for motherboards, modems and scanners. Intel and Compaq are two major investors in Taiwan, due partly to the large pool of engineers possessing technical degrees.

- *India:* India is a major player in the software industry and country of choice for customized software development. India has the world's third-largest pool of scientific and technical personnel. India provides a significant cost advantage due to the low labor cost. Companies such as IBM, Microsoft, Oracle and Motorola have built facilities in India's silicon valleys: Bangalore, Hyderabad and Mumbai (formerly Bombay).

There are several reasons why clusters are successful. One is the close cooperation, coordination and trust among clustered companies in related industries. Another reason is the fierce competition for customers among rival companies located in the cluster.

Companies are more productive in their operations because of access to the local supplier base, information and technology. Companies are able to recruit from the local pool of skilled and experienced workers, thus reducing hiring costs. Due to the intensity of competition within the business cluster, peer pressure and constant comparison among rivals, companies tend to respond quicker to customer needs and trends. Clusters thus provide the competitive environment that promotes increasing innovation and profitability.

Not all clusters are successful. For example, Michigan suffered through plant closings and employee layoffs in the auto industry due to the industry's over-reliance on gas-guzzling auto designs and the oil shock in the 1970s. The groupthink mentality among the cluster participants of General Motors, Ford and Chrysler in Detroit made it more difficult for individual companies to try new ideas and see the need for radical innovation in fuel economy automobile designs.

Sustainable Development

The World Commission on Environment and Development (the Brundtland Commission) defines **sustainable development** as "development that meets the needs of the present without compromising the ability of future generations to meet their own needs."[41] Sustainable development is important because what we do today will affect future generations. The critical issues in sustainable development are energy consumption/production, air pollution and climate change. These issues are strongly related to one another and need to be considered in an integrated manner and linked to economic, social and environmental policies. Luis Alberto Ferraté Felice, Minister of the Environment and Natural Resources of Guatemala and the United Nations Commission on Sustainable Development Chair, said that "Sustainable development requires a transformation of values and principles that directly influence development strategies and lifestyles."[42]

The increased global consumption of fossil fuels has increased global warming. In addition, prices of crude oil have continued to rise as demand has increased. More expensive oil translates to increased cost of production of goods and delivery of services. Ultimately this will affect supply chain costs. This calls for the development of cleaner, more fuel efficient and affordable energy technologies as well as renewable energy technologies.

It is clear that industrial development is the engine for economic growth and eradicating poverty in emerging countries. However, resource efficiency and technology innovation are opportunities for reducing cost and increasing competitiveness and employment, issues that are central to managing an effective supply chain. Air pollution has serious impacts on human health, environment and the economy. A related issue is climate change and preserving the world's ecosystem. Due to the importance of climate change, most countries joined an international treaty, the United Nations Framework Convention on Climate Change (UNFCCC) "to begin to consider what can be done to reduce global warming and to cope with whatever temperature increases are inevitable."[43] A number of nations also approved an addition to the treaty: the Kyoto Protocol, which includes more powerful and legally binding measures. The Kyoto Protocol "sets binding targets for 37 industrialized countries and the European community for reducing greenhouse gas (GHG) emissions. These amount to an average of five percent against 1990 levels over the five-year period 2008–2012."[44]

A similar term, **green development**, has been used to describe environmentally friendly development. The difference between green development and sustainable development is that green development "prioritizes what its proponents consider to be environmental sustainability over economic and cultural considerations."[45] An example would be the installation of a state-of-the-art waste treatment plant with very high maintenance cost in a poor country. Due to the high maintenance cost, the ideal plant from an environmental standpoint may not be sustainable and likely will be shut down. From a sustainable development perspective, it would be acceptable to have a less effective environmental technology but one that can be maintained by the users of the equipment. When decision makers consider both economic and social issues in addition to environmental concerns, then sustainable development is more logical.

SUMMARY

Facility location decisions can provide organizations with a competitive advantage and, therefore, must be an integral part of their overall strategic plans. The effectiveness of a supply chain is influenced greatly by where facilities are located. Increased globalization and improved technologies have resulted in a variety of options for companies to locate their facilities. Today, companies must consider a number of factors when analyzing potential locations; several comparison methods are available when considering the country, region and community for a facility location. Business clusters often provide for strong business development, collaboration, growth opportunities and improved supply chain management. The existence of successful clusters suggests that innovation and competition are concentrated geographically. China today represents an attractive location for many of the world's top companies due to its inexpensive labor and huge market. There has been much discussion about sustainable development and the greening of the supply chain.

KEY TERMS

Association of Southeast Asian Nations (ASEAN), 380

break-even model, 391

business clusters, 394

Common Market for Eastern and Southern Africa (COMESA), 380

contributor factory, 379

European Union (EU), 380

green development, 397

lead factory, 379

North American Free Trade Agreement (NAFTA), 380

offshore factory, 379

outpost factory, 379

quality of life, 389

quality-of-life factors, 389

right-to-work law, 390

server factory, 379

source factory, 379

Southern Common Market (MERCOSUR), 380

sustainable development, 396

weighted-factor rating model, 391

World Trade Organization (WTO), 380

DISCUSSION QUESTIONS

1. What is the impact of facility decisions on a supply chain?
2. Why is demand management important for effective supply chain management?
3. What are business clusters? Provide several examples of business clusters in a variety of countries. What are the advantages of clustering?
4. What are the factors influencing facility location?
5. Discuss the major regional trade agreements in Asia, Africa, Europe, Latin America and North America.
6. What is the World Trade Organization and what is its role in world trade?
7. What are the critical factors in making community and site decisions?
8. Discuss Wal-Mart's location strategy.
9. Define *quality of life*. Why is quality of life an important factor in facility location? Is the set of quality-of-life factors used by the Chamber of Commerce in Jacksonville, Florida, a good one? Please explain.

10. What is a right-to-work state? What are the advantages or disadvantages of doing business in a right-to-work state?

11. Why is China an attractive location for many businesses?

12. What are the challenges of doing business in China?

13. Discuss the six strategic roles of a foreign facility.

14. What is sustainable development and why is this policy important to a country and the world at large?

15. What is the difference between green development and sustainable development?

INTERNET QUESTIONS

1. What are the key factors used in the World Competitiveness Ranking? Go to the website of IMD—World Competitiveness Yearbook at www02.imd.ch/wcy. Select any three countries in the Asia Pacific region. Prepare a report discussing the pros and cons for each of these countries to locate a business there.

2. What are the factors used in the Global Competitiveness Report? Go to the World Economic Forum website at www.weforum.org/en/initiatives/gcp/Global% 20Competitivenss%20Report/index.htm. Select any three countries in South America. Prepare a report discussing the pros and cons for each of these countries to locate a business there.

3. Go to the website of the World Trade Organization at www.wto.org. Outline the development that led to China's entry into the WTO. What is the impact of China's accession into the WTO on U.S. companies?

4. Go to the website of STAT-US/Internet (a service of the U.S. Department of Commerce) at www.stat-usa.org. First, select a country and an industry you wish to study. Then, based on the country report, prepare an assessment of the suitability of the country for doing business in the particular industry you selected earlier.

SPREADSHEET PROBLEMS

1. The Soft Toys Company has collected information on fixed and variable costs for four potential plant locations.

LOCATION	ANNUAL FIXED COST	UNIT VARIABLE COST
A	$200,000	$50
B	$300,000	$45
C	$400,000	$25
D	$600,000	$20

a. Plot the total cost curves for the four plant locations on a single graph.

b. Compute the range of demand for which each location has a cost advantage.

c. Which plant location is best if demand is 30,000 units?

2. The Bruhaha Brewery is planning to expand internationally. The company has identified six critical location factors and their relative weights. The scores for each of the three potential sites are shown in the following table. Which site should be selected?

CRITICAL LOCATION FACTORS	FACTOR WEIGHT (SUM TO 1)	COLUMBUS SCORES (1—100)	LAS VEGAS SCORES (1—100)	SPOKANE SCORES (1—100)
Labor cost	0.15	70	90	50
Proximity to market	0.25	100	90	80
Supplier base	0.2	80	100	70
Quality of life	0.3	90	60	60
Taxes	0.1	60	80	90

Chapter 12

SERVICE RESPONSE LOGISTICS

Where are all the good middle-class jobs in manufacturing that used to pay so well? Some are gone, because American manufacturing has become so much more productive. But there are more good jobs than ever. Look for them in the service sector.[1]

Is your facility too big? How can you rearrange the space to create fewer processes for getting the food product to the customer? How can you rearrange the equipment to enable your staff to prepare foods faster and with fewer people?[2]

Learning Objectives

After completing this chapter, you should be able to

- Understand how supply chain management in services differs from supply chain management in manufacturing.
- Define service response logistics and describe all of its elements.
- Understand the importance of service layouts and perform a layout analysis using several techniques.
- Describe the strategies for managing capacity, wait times, distribution and quality in services.
- Understand queuing system design issues and calculate queue characteristics.
- Use various techniques for managing customers' perceived waiting times.
- Understand the different distribution channels available for services.
- Define service quality and describe how to measure it and improve it.

Chapter Outline

Introduction

An Overview of Service Operations

Supply Chain Management in Services

The Primary Concerns of Service Response Logistics

Summary

Supply Chain Management in Action   *A Place for Mom Improves Website Productivity*

Founded in 2000, A Place for Mom is the largest service for elder-care referrals in the U.S. "We help families find all sorts of elderly-care solutions for their loved ones - nursing homes, assisted living, home care," says Ben Villa, the service's senior product manager. "We advertise all over the Web, on search, email and basically we need to generate leads by means of people filling out our online form."

That online form would appear via a rather generic landing page, which is what A Place for Mom would serve up to those who clicked on any of its ads and search results - regardless of whether those potential customers had searched for "assisted living" or "nursing home." "It was a one-size-fits-all form," says Villa. "There was no customization to it." Visitors would sometimes fail to become leads because the site was insufficiently specific to their needs.

Eager for both a new site layout and a better mechanism for bringing leads to its portal, A Place for Mom turned to SiteSpect, a provider of Web optimization solutions, in November 2008. Using SiteSpect's ability to gauge the essential nature of individual page links, A Place for Mom found that a number of leads were getting lost in the clicking process. So the company streamlined its site, reoriented link positions and simplified form fields. Testing proved, for example, that 98 percent of users ignored one of the form fields on the landing page and simply doing away with this field increased conversion rates.

The SiteSpect implementation has improved lead generation through new keyword searches. "We've tested probably a few hundred variations of our form," Villa says. "At any given moment we'll [be testing] maybe six variation families. Users will see maybe 20 versions of a page."

When people search "Kansas City retirement homes," for instance, they're now taken to a landing page that includes a form about retirement communities above a display of various retirement facilities. Once a visitor has input several pieces of information - name, email, phone and how she heard about the company - A Place for Mom will then connect the lead with an elder-care advisor, who helps identify an appropriate community.

In just the first three months after optimizing its keyword searches, Villa says, A Place for Mom saw a 30 percent boost in conversions, on the way to an overall 70 percent improvement. It's the subtleties that make the difference, he says. A Place for Mom used to pay to show up on searches for phrases such as "I'm looking for elder care near...," but has since expanded to "find assisted living near..." or "find nursing homes near...." The small variations have delivered a big payoff, according to Villa.

The SiteSpect platform provides visibility into statistics such as how many visitors came to a certain page, how many converted and from which variations. Villa says he consistently runs new variations to see what sticks - often two or three a week. Some succeed and some don't - to varying degrees - but Villa says A Place for Mom is quick to adopt the changes that help the company better serve its customers.

Source: McKay, L., "The New-Age Home," *Customer Relationship Management*, V. 14, No. 2 (2010): 43–44. Used with permission.

Introduction

While most of the concepts of supply chain management discussed up to this point in the text can be applied to service organizations, this chapter specifically introduces and discusses supply chain concepts suited particularly to services and the service activities of manufacturers. Service firms differ from manufacturers in a number of ways including the tangibility of the end product, the involvement of the customer in the production process, the assessment of product quality, the labor content contained in the end products and facility location considerations. Many services are considered **pure services**, offering little or no tangible products to customers. Examples are consultants, lawyers, entertainers and stockbrokers. Other services may offer end products containing a tangible component such as restaurants, repair facilities, transportation providers and public warehouses. Most manufacturers, on the other hand, have tangible products with a relatively small service component that might include maintenance, warranty repair and delivery services, along with customer call centers.

In most services, customers are either directly or indirectly involved in the production of the service itself. In this sense, services are said to provide **state utility**, meaning that services do something to things that are owned by the customer (such as transport and store their supplies, repair their machines, cut their hair and provide their healthcare). Managing the interactions between service firms and their customers while the service is being performed is the topic of this chapter and is of paramount importance to the ultimate success of service organizations.

To generate initial and repeat customer visits, service firms must be located nearby (or transported to) their customers, they must know what their customers want and they must be able to satisfy these needs quickly and in a cost-effective manner. This requires service firms to adequately hire, train and schedule service representatives; to acquire technologies and equipment to aid in the provision of services; and to provide the right facility network and procedures to continually satisfy customers. Problems or mistakes that occur during the delivery of services most likely mean an increase in service delivery time, a reduction in customer satisfaction, lower perceived service quality and maybe even lost current and future sales.

The important role services play in the global economy is becoming more evident today as developed countries become increasingly service oriented, as the Internet creates global "e-preneurs" whose businesses exist solely on the Internet, as productivity gains in manufacturing mean fewer laborers are needed to make the same numbers of products and as global spending on research and development continues to expand. Web-based elder-care referral business A Place for Mom, featured in the Supply Chain Management in Action feature, is one such example. In the U.S., for instance, services accounted for about 79 percent of the nation's gross domestic product (GDP) in 2009 and about 77 percent of private non-farm employment (which is up from 70 percent in 1990). In the U.K., services provide about 80 percent of the jobs; in France, 72 percent; in Japan, 68 percent; and in each case, the percentage of service employment is rising.[3] And, as stated in one of the opening chapter quotes, these new service jobs are mainly in professions that pay as much as or more than the manufacturing sector.

Firms today are attempting to identify the customer-desired service elements in their product offerings and provide better value through attention to these elements. These efforts are at the heart of service operations and the topic of service response logistics. Let's first review service operations in general and then move on to discuss service response logistics in particular.

An Overview of Service Operations

Services are by far the largest sector of any post-industrialized nation and include organizations such as retailers, wholesalers, transportation and storage companies, healthcare providers, financial institutions, schools, real estate companies, government agencies, hotels and consulting companies. Since the 1950s, the ratio of services to manufacturing and agriculture in terms of its percentage of the U.S. workforce has been increasing quite dramatically and it is extremely likely that new entrants to the job market will be employed in some service role. In the U.S. and other developed economies, as the population as a whole became wealthier, people began demanding more services. In 1950, Americans spent two-thirds of their personal consumption income on manufactured goods. Today, Americans spend only 40 percent on goods.[4]

India's economic rise in the past fifteen years, similar to many other emerging economies, has been the result of a shift away from an agrarian economy toward a more service-oriented economy, which has improved the standard of living in India and boosted domestic consumption. This has helped to bolster overall productivity and competitiveness of India's firms, creating higher-value jobs. Services now account for 63 percent of India's GDP.[5]

Some of the differences between goods and services are listed below:

- Services *cannot be inventoried*. Typically, services are produced and consumed simultaneously—once the airline has landed, surgical operations are performed and advice is given, customers have "consumed" the service. For this reason, services often struggle to find ways to utilize their employees during slow periods and, conversely, manage demand or increase the ability to serve customers during busy periods.

- Services are often *unique*. High-quality service providers with well-trained and motivated employees have the capability of customizing services to satisfy each customer—insurance policies, legal services and even fast-food services can be uniquely designed and then delivered to customers. Thus, hiring and training become important issues for satisfying individual customer needs.

- Services have *high customer-server interactions*. Service uniqueness demands more server attention, whether it means delivering purchased products to a specific location on the manufacturing shop floor, analyzing data, answering customer questions, resolving complaints or repairing machinery. Many services today are finding ways to automate or standardize services or utilize customers to provide some of their own service, to reduce costs and improve productivity. For instance, the past few years have seen a rapid growth in automated, self-serve services such as purchasing books, banking online and completing one's tax forms.

- Services are *decentralized*. Service facilities must be decentralized because of their inability to inventory their services. Therefore, finding good, high customer-traffic locations is extremely important (even Internet-based services must locate their signs or advertisements where they will be easily seen by people using search engines).

Thus, services, whether they are stand-alone organizations or departments in goods-producing firms, must be managed in ways that will take into account these various service characteristics. A number of service elements are discussed next.

Service Productivity

The basic measure of productivity is shown by the following formula:

$$\text{Productivity} = \frac{\text{Outputs produced}}{\text{Inputs used}},$$

where service outputs produced might be customers served, the number of services performed or simply sales dollars; and inputs might be shown as labor hours or labor dollars (for a **single-factor productivity** measure). Alternately, inputs can be represented by the sum of labor, material, energy and capital costs (for a **multiple-factor productivity** measure). The productivity measures used in an organization might be based on manager preferences or industry standards and firms tend to measure productivity to provide a way to gauge successes in employee training, equipment or technology investments and cost reduction efforts.

Productivity and its growth over time are commonly used indicators of a firm's (and a country's) economic success. For most services, automation can be a troublesome issue and the labor content per unit of output can be quite high relative to manufactured goods. These two things can lead to a declining productivity growth rate as a nation's economy becomes less manufacturing oriented and more service oriented (as discussed above in reference to the U.S. and other economies). This productivity growth problem has been termed **Baumol's disease**, named after noted U.S. economist William Baumol in the 1960s when he and his colleague, William Bowen, argued that productivity growth tends to be low in service-oriented economies. And, in fact, this effect was realized in the U.S. from the mid-1970s through the mid-1990s as productivity growth averaged a relatively low 1.5 percent per year. Since the mid-1990s, however, productivity growth in the U.S. has been up and down, leading to other theories such as the **Wal-Mart effect**, which postulates that the booming growth in information technology has allowed many big-box retailers such as Wal-Mart to realize large productivity growth rates. Today, some economists are even saying that Baumol's disease has been cured.[6]

In services with high labor costs, there is often a desire to reduce labor costs to improve productivity (since labor cost is considered a productivity input). This can lead companies to relocate to lower labor cost countries, outsource jobs to lower labor cost areas or to simply lay off workers. These can be risky strategies, since relocating to foreign countries can create cultural and training problems, outsourcing reduces managerial control and reducing the workforce can adversely affect service quality and service availability.

Other strategies for increasing service productivity attack the numerator of the productivity equation. One example is the use of technology. In another example, Adam Fein, president of Pennsylvania-based Pembroke Consulting, states, "In the warehouse, the productivity improvements from wireless networks come from substituting technology for potentially error-prone human activities such as order processing, inventory control or picking."[7]

Productivity improvements can also be realized through better education and training. Hallmark Consumer Services, a U.K. logistics company, purchased a warehouse management software application and then provided their warehouse employees with the necessary training to operate the system. "The training cost us £7500 and the productivity gains alone were £7000 our first year," says Chris Hall, managing director of Hallmark. "The WMS software was an investment of £20,000 and will have paid for itself in less than three years on labor savings alone."[8]

Improving service productivity can be quite challenging because of the desire in many cases for customized, labor-intensive services and because of the difficulty of assessing service quality (for instance, was the car fixed properly? Was the client properly defended? Was the hired comedian funny?). A complete discussion of service quality appears later in the chapter.

Global Service Issues

The growth and exportation of services are occurring everywhere as world economies improve and the demand for services increases. Even during the recent trying periods of general business slowdowns, a number of services are finding ways to stay competitive and expand. Just a few examples of recent global service growth include DineEquity, owner of the newly revitalized IHOP restaurant brand and Applebee's restaurants, which has grown to over 3,400 global locations to become the world's largest full-service restaurant company; retailer Uniqlo, which is the largest clothing retailer in Japan and is doubling its overseas operations each year; and Capco, the Belgium-based financial services consultancy, which has quickly been adding consulting offices in North America to position itself for increased opportunities in the post-financial crisis world.[9]

Successfully managing services as they expand into foreign markets involves a number of issues including:

- *Labor, facilities and infrastructure support.* Cultural differences, education and expertise levels can prove to be problematic for firms unfamiliar with local human resources. Firms must also become adept at locating the most appropriate support facilities, suppliers, transportation providers, communication systems and housing.

- *Legal and political issues.* Local laws may restrict foreign competitors, limit use of certain resources, attach tariffs to prices or otherwise impose barriers to global service expansion. Some countries require foreign companies to form joint ventures with local business partners.

- *Domestic competitors and the economic climate.* Managers must be aware of the local competitors, the services they offer, their pricing structures and the current state of the local economy. Firms can devise competitive strategies by modifying their services to gain competitive advantage.

- *Identifying global customers.* Perhaps most importantly, firms must find out where their potential global customers are, through use of the Internet, foreign government agencies, trading partners or foreign trade intermediaries. Once potential customers are identified, services can begin to decide how their service products can be modified to meet the needs of these customers.

More on global service expansion can be found later in the chapter.

Service Strategy Development

Manufacturing and service organizations use three generic competitive strategies: cost leadership, differentiation and focus.[10] Each of these is briefly discussed below in relation to services.

Cost Leadership Strategy

Using a **cost leadership strategy** requires a large capital investment in automated, state-of-the-art equipment and significant efforts in the areas of controlling and reducing costs, doing things right the first time, standardizing services and aiming marketing efforts at cost-conscious consumers. A case in point is the recent huge growth in demand for cheap air travel in India. Two of the airlines currently fighting for customers in India are Delhi-based IndiGo and SpiceJet. In both cases, there are efforts to offer routine, no-frills services at low prices while keeping seats filled. Marketing efforts are geared toward attracting cost-conscious customers with little or no service customization needs. There are also continued and committed efforts to keep costs low. Both airlines posted profits in 2009, while the larger Indian airlines such as Air India lost money in the same period.[11]

Differentiation Strategy

Implementing a **differentiation strategy** is based on creating a service that is considered unique. The uniqueness can take many forms including customer service excellence (Ritz-Carlton hotels), brand image (the Google logo and variations for holidays), variety (Wal-Mart's merchandise) and use of technology (Southwest Airlines' website "ding" notification). Differentiation strategies are often created as the result of companies listening to their customers. Retailers are beginning to engage customers more effectively through various touch-points such as the phone, store locations, catalogs, online stores and chat sites. Jo-Ann Stores, a U.S. decorating and sewing products retailer, created a website with more than 50,000 products that enables customers to easily find, preview and buy products, along with presenting customers offers paralleling their interests. As a result, more than 90 percent of online visitors purchase something.[12] Differentiation does not necessarily mean higher costs; it merely refers to the ability of the service to offer unique elements in their services. In many cases, though, it may mean the customer is willing to pay more for the service. Advertisements, logos, awards and company reputations all play a part in creating the perception of uniqueness among a service's potential customers. The Global Perspective feature provides a view of Canada-based breakfast restaurant Tim Hortons' differentiation strategy for growth in the U.S.

Global Perspective

Tim Hortons' Differentiation Strategy for Growth

Just how important is it to be first? Ask Ontario-based Tim Hortons, the self-described McDonald's of Canada, which is struggling for a foothold in the U.S. market. Hortons has built a massive following in Canada and developed a small cult in the U.S., based on high-quality coffee, indulgent doughnuts and what's described as consistently good service. When it comes to the U.S., Darren Tristano, exec VP of Technomic, a Chicago-based restaurant-industry consultancy, said Tim Hortons might be paying the price for being second. "When you look at the Canadian marketplace, they were first to market and that's a big deal," he said. "The opposite is true here. Dunkin' Donuts is approaching 6,000 locations, and they're coming into Dunkin's backyard and trying to compete on quality."

Hortons has about 500 U.S. locations, concentrated in Western New York, Ohio and Michigan. The chain has about 3,500 locations in Canada. Dunkin' is based in Canton, Massachusetts, with a loyal following in the Northeast. Still, it doesn't seem to take much Hortons exposure to make a fan. Anthony Claudia, a Colorado-based film executive, tried the coffee while working on a project in Ontario. "It's kind of like the Canadian version of Dunkin' Donuts, but a lot better," he said.

In the U.S., Mr. Tristano said Hortons is "definitely catching up, but it's going to take some time to establish the brand." Then again, the chain is not exactly a new arrival. Hortons opened its first U.S. location in Buffalo, N.Y, in the mid-1980s. But its concerted push began about ten years later, Hortons' Chief Operating Officer David Clanachan said in an interview. The company merged with Wendy's in 1995 and became a stand-alone public company in 2006. "We consider ourselves to be a strong regional brand with aspirations to grow our business throughout the full landscape," Mr. Clanachan said. He added that Canadians and Americans aren't so different; they're all looking to save money. "We believe price-value never goes out of style," he said. But that might be part of the problem.

RBC Capital Markets analyst Irene Nattel wrote that Hortons has the value-as-brand attribute sealed up in Canada, but not in the U.S. "American consumers less familiar with the brand need to be educated on that positioning, particularly in the current economic environment." She said the chain is tweaking offerings in 2009 to create more value combos.

Even though awareness is low, the chain has $200 million in U.S. sales and spends about five percent of that on advertising, a percentage higher than what is spent by McDonald's. In addition to a brand-awareness deficit, Harry Balzer of New York-based market research company NPD Group said differentiation is a hurdle. The chain competes with McDonald's, Dunkin' and Starbucks, which make up about 45 percent of restaurant-coffee consumption. "New is a powerful thing, but you have to be more than just new," he said.

Source: York, E., "Hortons Struggles for Growth in U.S.," *Advertising Age,* 80(10), 2009: 6. Used with permission.

Focus Strategy

A **focus strategy** incorporates the idea that a service can serve a narrow target market or niche better than other firms that are trying to serve a broader market. Companies that specialize in these market niches can provide customized services and expertise to suit the needs of these customers. For instance, a neighborhood hobby shop is more likely to serve the needs of hobby enthusiasts than a big-box retailer like Carrefour, even though they might sell some of the same merchandise. Within each focused market niche, firms can then exhibit characteristics of differentiation or cost leadership. Illinois-based Dawson Logistics, for example, has found success providing specialty reverse logistics services to pharmaceutical distributors and assembly and delivery services to escalator and elevator companies.[13]

The Service Delivery System

Customers actually purchase a bundle of attributes when purchasing services, including the *explicit service* itself (storage and use of your money at a bank) along with the *supporting facility* (the bank building, drive-up tellers and website); *facilitating goods* (the deposit forms, monthly statements and coffee in the lobby); and *implicit services* (the security provided, friendly atmosphere in the bank, privacy and convenience). Successful services deliver this bundle of attributes in the most efficient way, while still satisfying customer requirements. Services must therefore define this **service bundle** and then design an effective delivery system with it in mind.

Service delivery systems fall along a continuum with mass-produced, low-customer-contact systems at one extreme (such as ATMs) and highly customized, high-customer-contact systems at the other (such as an expensive beauty salon). Many delivery system designs seek to physically separate high-contact (front-of-the-house) operations from low-contact (back-of-the-house) operations to allow use of various management techniques to maximize the performance of each area (such as in a restaurant). Back-of-the-house operations tend to be managed as a manufacturing center, where the emphasis is on maximizing quality outputs while achieving economies of scale. Technical people are hired for specific well-defined tasks and technology is employed to increase productivity. On the other hand, **front-of-the-house operations** are characterized by hiring front-line service providers with good pubic relations skills, taking care of customers and giving employees the power and resources to solve customers' problems quickly and effectively.

Hospitals provide a good example of a business characterized by a clear separation of services requiring customer contact and services not requiring customer contact. Administrative offices, labs, drug storage, laundry and food preparation, for instance, are **back-of-the-house operations** typically never seen by patients in a hospital, although managing these elements of the hospital service bundle can make a tremendous difference in its profitability. No customer contact exists, so the emphasis is on materials, storage, office and other technical skills. However, nursing and physician patient care, prescription services and emergency room front-of-the-house services directly involve patients in the delivery of services. In these cases, the customer-server interaction must be managed so that customers get what they came for in a quick and effective way.

Auditing the Service Delivery System

The service bundle delivery system should be audited periodically to assess the system's ability to meet the firm's and the customers' expectations in a cost-effective way. Monitoring customer complaints, talking to and observing customers and tracking customer feedback using customer comment cards and website comment forms (as well as looking at the bottom line) are ways to continually monitor the system. **Walk-through service audits** should also be performed by management, covering service system attributes from the time customers initially encounter the service until they leave. Several tools have been developed and used for this purpose including service system surveys to be completed by managers, employees and/or customers and service process maps (as discussed in Chapter 8). The objective of the service audit is to identify service system problems or areas in need of improvement.

Service Location and Layout Strategies

Good location strategies provide barriers to entry and competitive positioning for services as well as generate additional demand. Once a location has been secured, firms can begin to consider layout strategies to maximize customer service, server productivity and overall efficiency. Since location strategies and analysis models were discussed in Chapter 11, only a brief discussion of location considerations is included here, followed by the design of service layouts.

Location Strategies

Location decisions are extremely important for most services because they have a significant impact on customer visits and, consequently, the long-term profits of the company (how likely is it that customers would visit a clothing store, for instance, in an otherwise abandoned shopping center?). Location decisions are viewed as long-term decisions because of the typical high cost of construction, remodeling and relocation. (Note: Here, it is assumed that service locations are permanent structures, although

© 2010 Ted Goff www.tedgoff.com

"Wow! You're the very first customer
who's ever found us!"

some services actually are not bound by this assumption, as with a small legal office rent-ing space in an office building or a music teacher who visits customers.)

Global market opportunities, global competitors and technological and demographic changes contribute to the importance of a good location. In all location evaluations, it is desirable to consider a number of relevant factors to reduce the reliance on intuition. Although intuition can certainly be a valuable location analysis tool, many disastrous location decisions have been made on the basis of intuition and not much more. Las Vegas gambler, entrepreneur and self-proclaimed "Polish maverick" Bob Stupak built the 1,149-foot Stratosphere Hotel and Casino, which opened in a rundown neighborhood on the fringes of the famous Las Vegas Boulevard or "Strip" in 1996. Within just a few months, the hotel was in financial trouble, partly because of the lack of foot traffic in the area. Stupak defaulted on payments to the bondholders who had put up the con-struction funds and corporate raider Carl Icahn subsequently bought the bonds for pen-nies on the dollar. He assumed control of the hotel in 1998.[14]

A number of location analysis models can be used as an aid in the location decision and these include the weighted factor location model, the location break-even model and the center of gravity model (refer to Chapter 11 for use of these models).

Layout Strategies

Service layout strategies work in combination with location decisions to further sup-port the overall business strategies of differentiation, low cost or market focus. Office lay-outs tend to be departmentalized to allow specialists to share resources; many retailers like Tesco also tend to be departmentalized to assist customers in finding items to purchase, whereas others may have centers throughout the store to entice customers to try things out and buy on impulse; commercial airliner layouts segment customers, reduce the time to restock and service the galleys and lavatories and allow for fast passenger boarding and exit (at least in theory!); casino layouts are designed to get customers in quickly and then keep them there by spacing out the attractions; and self-serve buffet restaurant layouts are designed to process customers quickly. These are just a few examples and many service layouts use multiple layout strategies. As customer preferences, products, technologies and service strategies change, layouts also tend to change. Several specific service layout design tools are illustrated below.

Departmental Layouts That Reduce Distance Traveled

Service layouts can be designed to reduce the travel times of customers or service workers when moving from one area to another. An example of a layout where this might be a primary consideration would be a health clinic. The waiting area is located in front where customers enter and the examination rooms are located nearby. The doctors' offices might be centrally located, whereas the lab, storage and x-ray rooms might be located farther to the back of the clinic away from most of the patients. A primary consideration is how far nurses, doctors and patients have to walk to reach the various areas within the clinic. The objective would be to place high-volume traffic departments close to each other to minimize the total distance traveled per day. Example 12.1 illustrates a design tool useful for this type of layout.

Departmental Layouts That Maximize Closeness Desirability

Designing service layouts to place certain desirable pairs of departments closer to one another is another useful type of layout analysis tool and is often used for retail or office layouts. Here, the importance is placed on the relationship between various departments. In a convenience store, for instance, it would be extremely important to have the cashier close to the entrance and the cold food items in the back, close to the cold storage areas and the rear loading doors of the store. In an office setting, it might be desirable to have the receptionist close to the office entrance and the file room, with the managers close to the conference room. For each department pair, then, a **closeness desirability rating** must be determined, with the objective being to design a layout that maximizes an overall desirability rating for the entire office. Example 12.2 illustrates this concept. It should also be noted that it might be advisable to use both of the analysis techniques illustrated in Examples 12.1 and 12.2 for a given layout problem; in this way, the evaluation team could consider the best layout from both a distance traveled and closeness desirability perspective.

Supply Chain Management in Services

In many respects, service-producing organizations are like goods-producing organizations: both types make purchases and therefore deal with suppliers, incur order costs and inventory carrying costs; and in both cases the purchased inventories must be transported, counted, assessed for quality and stored somewhere. For some services, purchased items are part of the service provided and are extremely important sources of competitive advantage (e.g., at a retailer or restaurant), whereas for others, this may be a very minor concern (e.g., law offices and barber shops). In many cases, service firms

Example 12.1   Layout of Valley Health Clinic

The Bryson Health Clinic wants to see whether there is a better layout that will reduce the time doctors and nurses spend walking throughout the clinic. The existing layout is shown below, along with the number of trips and the distances between each department.

Existing Layout

| Storage (F) | Doctor's offices (C) | Exam rooms (B) | | Lobby & waiting area (A) |
| Nurses (E) | Lab & x-ray (D) | | | |

Interdepartmental Doctors' and Nurses' Trips/Day

	B	C	D	E	F
A	55	0	0	50	0
B		40	15	40	0
C			15	60	10
D				30	0
E					18

Distances between Departments (meters)

	B	C	D	E	F
A	20	40	40	60	60
B		20	20	40	40
C			10	20	20
D				20	20
E					10

To analyze the existing layout, the distance traveled must be calculated as follows:

Total distance traveled $= \sum_{i=1}^{n} \sum_{j=1}^{n} T_{ij} D_{ij}$

Where n = number of departments

i,j = individual departments

T_{ij} = number of trips between departments i and j

D_{ij} = distance from department i to department j

The objective is to find the layout resulting in the lowest total distance traveled per day. For the layout of the Bryson Health Clinic above, we find:

$$\text{Total distance traveled per day} = 55\,(20) + 50\,(60) + 40\,(20) + 15\,(20) + 40\,(40)$$
$$+\ 15\,(10) + 60\,(20) + 10\,(20)$$
$$+\ 30\,(20) + 18\,(10) = 9{,}130 \text{ meters}$$

From the layout and distances shown, it can be seen that the nursing station needs to be closer to the lobby and waiting area, closer to the exam rooms and closer to the doctors' offices. This can be accomplished by switching departments E and D (nurses and lab/x-ray). This also creates a trade-off, since now departments C, B and A will all be farther from department D. To calculate the new total distance traveled per day, the distance table must be modified as shown below. The asterisks denote changes made to the table.

Distances between Departments

	B	C	D	E	F
A	20	40	60*	40*	60
B		20	40*	20*	40
C			20*	10*	20
D				20	10*
E					20*

The new total distance can then be calculated as follows:

$$\text{Total distance traveled per day} = 55\,(20) + 50\,(40) + 40\,(20) + 15\,(40) + 40\,(20) + 15\,(20)$$
$$+\ 60\,(10) + 10\,(20) + 30\,(20) + 18\,(20) = 7{,}360 \text{ meters}$$

This is a better layout (not necessarily the best) and only one of a large number of potential layouts. Typically a number of layouts are evaluated as shown here, until either the lowest-total-distance layout or some reasonable alternative layout is found.

also purchase **facilitating products** such as computers, furniture and office supplies that are not part of the services sold but rather consumed inside the firm and these materials must also be managed. Table 12.1 shows some typical transportation, warehousing and inventory activities at several different types of services.

In other respects, though, service firms are unlike goods-producing organizations, in that services typically deal with the end customers in their supply chains, whereas most goods-producing firms deal with wholesalers, distributors, other manufacturers or retailers. In other words, service products are typically not passed on to customers further down a distribution channel. Thus, any goods that are delivered as part of the service are typically consumed or used by immediate customers.

Service firms deal very closely with their customers and the services performed in many cases contain higher labor content than manufactured products. Customers probably have no idea what resources or facilitating goods were used to deliver the services they purchase; rather, customers' primary concerns are with the service itself and the way it is delivered. For this reason, the distribution elements of interest to services revolve around customers and how they are being served. A good example of this can

Example 12.2 Closeness Desirability Rating for an Office Layout

Existing Office Layout

File room (F)	Engineering offices (C)	Marketing offices (B)	Secretary & waiting area (A)
Purchasing (E)	President's office (D)	Conference room (H)	Copy room (G)

Desirability Ratings

	B	C	D	E	F	G	H
A	2	0	−1	2	2	3	−1
B		0	2	1	1	0	3
C			2	2	0	0	1
D				1	−1	−1	3
E					3	1	2
F						3	1
G							0

The desirability ratings are based on a (−1 to 3) scale, where −1 = undesirable, 0 = unimportant, 1 = slightly important, 2 = moderately important and 3 = very important. To calculate the score for the above layout, we count the closeness desirability score only when departments are adjacent to each other. For this layout:

$$\text{Closeness desirability score} = (A/B:2) + (A/H:-1) + (A/G:3) + (B/C:0) + (B/H:3)$$
$$+ (C/F:0) + (C/D:2) + (D/E:1) + (D/H:3)$$
$$+ (E/F:3) + (G/H:0) = 16 \text{ points}$$

Note that department pairs are not counted twice and are also not counted if only the corners are touching. To find a better layout, we could place the department pairs with a rating of 3 adjacent to each other and place adjacent pairs with a rating of −1 such that they are not adjacent. For instance, the file room (F) could be moved adjacent to the copy room (G) and the conference room (H) could be moved farther away from the secretary and waiting area (A). The new layout might look like this:

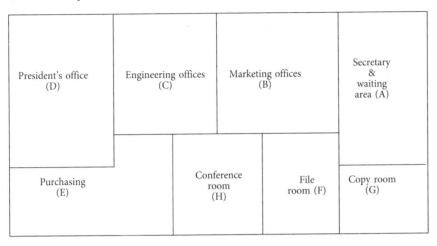

New Office Layout

The closeness desirability score for the new layout shown above would then be

Closeness desirability score = (A/B:2) + (A/F:2) + (A/G:3) + (B/C:0) + (B/H:3)
                              + (B/F:1) + (C/D:2) + (C/E:2) + (C/H:1) + (D/E:1)
                              + (E/H:2) + (H/F:1) + (F/G:3) = 23 points

On the basis of this analysis, it can be concluded that the second layout is better; like the previous example, though, there are many potential layouts, so a number of those should be evaluated prior to selecting the most appropriate one.

be found in the transportation industry. When shippers want things moved, they want the move performed at a specific time, delivered to a specific place, delivered on time and performed as economically as possible. Most large transportation companies today have sophisticated information systems to allow customers to track deliveries as well as determine the best combination of warehousing, transportation method, port-of-entry, routing, pricing and consolidation. Fiat Group Brazil, for instance, honored Ryder System, Inc., with their 2007 Qualitas Award for their reliable and flexible logistics services, inventory tracking and transportation management capabilities. Toyota recognized Ryder System for the same thing in 2006.[15]

Service Quality and Customers

The satisfaction or perceived level of quality a customer experiences with regard to the service is of paramount concern to most services. The concept of **service quality** includes many elements and these can change over time—recently, for example, customers of many businesses include sustainability as an element in their definitions of service quality. "We are in a commodity world and 'green' allows you to emerge from the pack," says Andrew Winston, author of *Green Recovery*. "It is a tie-breaker and it can even be a deal-breaker," he adds. In 2009, 18 percent of fine-dining restaurants, 27 percent of quick service restaurants and 43 percent of family-oriented restaurants said they planned to devote more of their resources toward going green.[16]

Table 12.1	Transportation and Warehousing Activities in Services	
SERVICES	**TRANSPORTATION ACTIVITIES**	**WAREHOUSING & INVENTORY ACTIVITIES**
Banks	• Movements of checks, coins/cash among branches and operations centers • Movement of checks to cities with Federal Reserve processing centers	• Office supplies and coins/cash • Furniture and computers • Records
Hospitals	• Movement of medical supplies to stockrooms • Transfers of patients • Movement of medical records, test results and films among units	• Surgical/medical supplies • Pharmaceutical supplies • Office furniture • Medical equipment
Telephone Cos.	• Inbound transportation of switches, parts and equipment to warehouses • Transportation of construction equipment and supplies to job sites • Routing of consumer products to retail outlets	• Parts, equipment, consumer products • Repair truck parts and equipment • Construction supplies

Source: Adapted from Drazen, E. L., R. E. Moll and M. F. Roetter. *Logistics in Service Industries*. Oak Brook, IL: Council of Logistics Management, 1991: 24–26.

Service quality assessments vary based on both the tangible and intangible elements of the services supplied and the satisfaction of the customers receiving the services. Call centers fail to satisfy a lot of customers for example, providing room for significant improvement in service quality. The "gold standard" of call center service quality is the *first call resolution score* or the percent of callers whose problem is solved on their first call. Companies like Canada-based Service Quality Measurement Group survey call center customers and then identify what call centers with the highest first call resolution score are doing right. These best practices are then communicated to their call center clients.[17]

All the elements of supply chain management including supplier selection, transportation, warehousing, process management, quality assessment, distribution and customer service hold strategic importance for the long-term success of service organizations. While the previous chapters and sections above have presented and discussed many of these elements, the remainder of this chapter is devoted to the portion of supply chain management of greatest concern to service organizations and the service arms of goods-producing companies—namely, the activities associated with the production and delivery of the actual service.

The Primary Concerns of Service Response Logistics

Service response logistics is the management and coordination of the organization's activities that occur while the service is being performed.[18] Managing these activities often means the difference between a successful service experience and a failure. The four primary activities of concern in service response logistics are the management of service capacity, waiting times, distribution channels and service quality. Since a service cannot be inventoried, managing service capacity enables the firm to meet variable demand—perhaps the most important concern of all services. When demand variability cannot be adequately met, the firm must resort to managing queues or waiting times to keep customers satisfied. Demand management tactics also play a role in the service firm's ability to satisfy varying levels of demand. Customer waiting times are closely related to the customer's view of service quality and, ultimately, customer satisfaction. Since services usually must be decentralized to attract customers and provide adequate service delivery times, use of various distribution channels also becomes important to the delivery of service products. Each of these service elements is discussed in detail in the following sections.

Managing Service Capacity

Service capacity is most often defined as the number of customers per day the firm's service delivery systems *are designed to serve*, although it could also be some other period of time such as customers per hour or customers per shift. Capacity measures can be stated somewhat differently too, depending on the service industry standard—for instance, airline companies define capacity in terms of available seat miles per day. Most services desire to operate at some optimal capacity level (less than maximum capacity) to reduce the likelihood of having queues and long waiting times develop. For service employees dealing directly with customers, service capacity is largely dependent on the number of employees providing the services and the equipment they use in providing the services.

Since service outputs can't be inventoried, firms are forced to either turn away customers when demand exceeds capacity, make them wait in line or hire additional personnel. Since hiring, training, supervising and equipping service personnel are quite costly (in many cases 75 percent of total operating costs), the decision of how many service personnel to hire greatly affects costs, productivity and ultimately sales and profits. Ideally, firms want enough service capacity (or service personnel) to satisfy demand, without having significant excess (and costly) capacity. This can be a tricky proposition if demand varies throughout the day, week or month, as is typical in a great many services. So an important part of a service manager's job is to forecast demand for various segments of time and customer service processes and then provide (or withhold) capacity to meet the forecasted demand.

When things work out right, a service operates at an optimal **capacity utilization**. Capacity utilization is defined as:

$$\text{Capacity utilization} = \frac{\text{Actual customers served per period}}{\text{Capacity}}.$$

As utilization approaches (and sometimes even exceeds) 1.0, services become more congested, service times increase, wait times increase and the perceived quality of service deteriorates. With utilization close to 1.0, even a slightly greater than average service time for several customers can cause queues to become very long (some readers may recall, for instance, waiting one or two hours beyond an appointment time to see a busy doctor). Thus, an optimal utilization would leave some level of capacity unutilized (perhaps 15 to 25 percent depending on the volatility of demand), so that variations in service times and customer demand won't severely affect waiting times.

The two most basic strategies for managing capacity are to use a **level demand strategy** (when the firm utilizes a constant amount of capacity regardless of demand variations) or a **chase demand strategy** (when the amount of capacity varies with demand). When a level demand strategy is used, the firm is required to use demand management or **queue management** tactics to deal with excess customers. When a chase demand strategy is used, effective plans must be in place to utilize, transfer or reduce service capacity when there is excess available and to develop or borrow capacity quickly when demand exceeds capacity. Capacity management techniques that are useful when demand exceeds available service capacity are discussed next, followed by a discussion of capacity management when service capacity exceeds demand.

Capacity Management When Demand Exceeds the Available Service Capacity

An initial observation might be to simply let customers wait or hire workers when demand exceeds existing capacity and then lay them off when capacity exceeds demand. Most likely, though, firms would like to avoid these options because of the expenses of finding, hiring, training and supervising new workers; the loss of current and future business when people wait too long in queues; as well as the expense and damage to the firm's reputation when laying-off workers. Instead, a number of efficient methods can be employed to minimize the costs of hiring workers and then letting them go and the cost of letting customers wait in line. These include cross-training and sharing employees, using part-time employees, using customers, using technology, using employee scheduling strategies and, finally, using demand management techniques to smooth or shift demand. Each of these methods is discussed next.

Cross-Training and Sharing Employees

Have you ever been waiting in line to pay for items at a retail store and thought to yourself, "Why don't they use some of these other workers that are just standing around to ring up customers' purchases?" Many service firms, though, do make wide use of this employee-sharing strategy. Quite often in many service firms, some processes are temporarily overutilized while other processes remain under- or unutilized. Rather than hiring someone to add capacity to the overutilized processes, progressive firms have adequately hired and cross-trained workers to be proficient in a number of different process functions. Thus, when demand temporarily exceeds service capacity in one area, creating a customer queue, idle workers can quickly move to that process to help serve customers and reduce the time customers spend waiting in a queue.

By sharing employees among a number of processes, firms create the capability to quickly expand capacity as demand dictates while simultaneously minimizing the costs of having customers wait or hiring and laying off workers. This type of resource sharing arrangement can occur in almost any type of organization, from retailers to banks, hospitals or universities.

Using Part-Time Employees

Use of part-time employees is also seen as a low-cost way to vary capacity. The hourly wages and costs of fringe benefits are typically lower than those of full-time employees. Firms use full-time employees to serve that stable portion of daily demand, while scheduling part-timers for those historically busy periods (such as lunch and dinner times, holidays, weekends or busy seasons). Part-time employees can also be used to fill in during the vacation periods, off days and sick days of full-time employees. Laying-off part-time employees during slower periods is also viewed as more acceptable to the permanent full-time workforce and is somewhat expected by the part-time employees.

Using Customers

As the need to contain costs and improve productivity and competitiveness continues, firms are finding that customers themselves can be used to provide certain services, as long as it is seen by customers as value enhancing. The benefits of self-service include faster service, more customized service and lower prices, since firms need fewer employees. The benefits for the companies include lower labor costs and additional service capacity. In this sense, customers are "hidden employees," allowing the firm to hire fewer workers and to vary capacity to some extent as needed. The trade-off for customers is that they expect to pay less for the service, since they are doing some of the work. This might include pumping gas, filling soda cups, filing taxes or filing legal forms.

In other cases, though, customers might actually pay the same or more for the service as when using self-checkout at hotels or using 24-hour automated teller machines, if customers perceive the work they perform as saving time or providing some other benefit. Thus, if firms can identify service process jobs that customers can perform, if they can provide process directions that are easy to understand and learn and if they can adequately satisfy customers who are being asked to perform the work, then using customers as employees can provide yet another method for managing capacity. St. Louis-based pharmacy Express Scripts is installing self-service kiosks that allow customers to receive real-time, customized information on their medications, such as options for saving money with generic substitutes and mail-order prescriptions.[19]

Using Technology

Providing technological assistance in the form of computers or other equipment to service company personnel can improve the ability of servers to process customers, resulting in more service capacity, faster service completion times, better service quality and the need for fewer employees. Voice-activated telephone response systems, online banking, purchasing, selling and comment systems and field sales software applications are just a few examples of technology helping the provision of services. Some forms of technology may completely replace the need for sales or other types of customer service personnel as in the case of Amazon.com and other online retailers. Advances in software capabilities and cloud computing have also allowed services to share use of expensive software systems like reservation systems and property management systems, which greatly improve productivity while reducing labor and software development costs. The e-Business Connection feature profiles a number of organizations sharing these software systems.

---

e-Business Connection   *Sharing IT Service Capacity*

Board members for Hotel Technology Next Generation (HTNG)—a global trade association of hoteliers and technology companies that includes Starwood Hotels & Resorts Worldwide, Marriott International, Hyatt and InterContinental Hotels Group—have been actively discussing possible areas for shared services among participants, including shared property management systems, reservation systems and networks. "It's a preliminary discussion right now," says Tom Conophy, CIO for global IT at InterContinental Hotels Group in Atlanta. "But there is a desire to explore where you can share infrastructure or applications, like financial apps, that are less competitive from a guest point of view."

The idea of IT services shared among industry rivals isn't new, but attempts to establish them have a spotty track record. Previous initiatives, such as an effort in the early 1990s to form a shared travel reservation network called Confirm, were started but never materialized, though it was backed by Sabre Holdings, American Airlines and a few other travel industry players.

Meanwhile, the technological world has been transformed by the global expansion of broadband networks, open source and the emergence of cloud computing, which make any discussion about sharing systems considerably more practical. "With the advent of cloud computing, I think that's going to open up the doors to this type of collaboration," says Conophy.

Getting the benefits of shared IT services, however, requires a lot of negotiation and hand holding. These partnerships are fraught with challenges ranging from contractual issues to security and liability concerns. CIOs who consider hosting IT services for one or more organizations would face the uphill battle of gaining buy-in from others in senior management, particularly if the service "isn't core to the rest of your organization's business and if it would take cycles away from the normal job of a CIO," says Beach Clark, CIO at the Georgia Aquarium in Atlanta. Clark notes that an industry consortium is building software for keeping animal records. "It's years behind schedule, so there's some skepticism" among his senior executive peers. "I think we will follow the lead of some of our peers in the industry on adopting [it]."

With respect to sharing a hotel reservation system, participants are discussing how much they would have to modify the functionality to suit the individual company's needs, says Conophy. "What you need is freedom in a framework," he adds, meaning that any agreement to share software would include provisions entitling participants to customize portions of the application.

Also, the service being delivered has to be as good, if not better, than what IT organizations are currently providing in-house, says Gary Curtis, global managing director for Accenture Technology Consulting. Curtis has worked with multinational companies to restructure IT operations, including incorporating shared services within some of them. He notes that whether a shared services provider is an independent company that's established by member firms or a member hosting an IT service, it "has to pass the same test" as an outsourcer, such as an audit to demonstrate it has the proper controls and governance in place for operating the service.

Finally, to address privacy and security concerns, it's important for shared services participants to be clear up-front about the types of data that need to be kept private and the information that can be shared freely among members, says Ed Grainger-Happ, U.S. and U.K. CIO with non-profit organization Save the Children. Confidentiality arrangements should be written tightly to prevent one or more participants from taking proprietary information or processes away from any of the other members, advises Rob Scott, managing partner at Scott & Scott, a Dallas-based law firm that specializes in software licensing.

In the end, CIOs have to decide which, if any, IT activities could be shared or operated by another business in order to drive down operating costs and free up precious resources for more ground-breaking endeavors. "Do we want 100 people working on developing and maintaining a hotel reservation system?" asks Todd Thompson, CIO at Starwood Hotels. "Or do we want 100 people focused on building innovative solutions for our company?"

Source: Hoffman, T. "Common Ground: Sharing IT Services with Other Companies in Your Industry is Back in Vogue, Thanks to Cloud Computing, the Economy and New Ways to Collaborate." CIO 22(17), 2009: 1–5. Used with permission.

Technology can also enable service standardization—providing the service exactly the same way every time, as with automated teller machines or ticketing machines. In many cases, service standardization is viewed as a high-quality characteristic by customers seeking specific, periodic services. Standardization allows services to be accessed anywhere at anytime without the need for relearning the service process.

Using Employee Scheduling Policies

By properly scheduling workers during the day, service capacity can be varied to accommodate varying demand. Businesses must first forecast demand in half-hour or one-hour increments during the day and then convert the demand to staffing requirements for each period, given the average service capabilities for workers. The problem of assigning workers to shifts is complicated by the number of hours each day and the number of days each week the business is open, the timing of days off and consecutive days off and employee shift preferences. The objective of worker scheduling is to service demand with the minimum number of employees, while also assigning equitable work shifts to employees. Employee scheduling software is available to provide managers with multiple scheduling solutions to this problem.

Use of part-time workers, as stated earlier, makes scheduling easier and is illustrated in Example 12.3. In the example, the manager finds a need for two full-time workers, one 3-day worker, one 2-day worker and two 1-day workers.

Using Demand Management Techniques

Even when accurate forecasting and good capacity management techniques are used, there are many occasions when demand exceeds available capacity. As stated earlier, forcing customers to wait in line for a long period of time may result in lost current and future business and damage to the firm's reputation. Organizations can try to reduce demand during busy periods using several short-term **demand management** techniques. These include raising prices during busy periods to reduce demand and shift it to less

Example 12.3   Use of Part-Time Counter-Help at Laurie's Plumbing Supply

The manager of Laurie's Plumbing Supply has determined her counter-help requirements as shown below for the five-day workweek. Given these requirements, she sees that she needs two full-time employees working all five days, resulting in the part-time requirements as shown (found by subtracting two from each workday requirement). To satisfy these requirements with the fewest number of part-time employees, she begins by assigning Part-timer No. 1 to the maximum number of workdays (Monday, Thursday and Friday). Part-timer No. 2 is assigned to the maximum number of workdays remaining (Monday and Friday). Then Part-timers 3 and 4 are assigned to the remaining workday (Friday).

	MONDAY	TUESDAY	WEDNESDAY	THURSDAY	FRIDAY
Workers Required	4	2	2	3	6
Full-time Workers	2	2	2	2	2
Part-time Workers	2	0	0	1	4
Part-timer No. 1	1			1	1
Part-timer No. 2	1				1
Part-timer No. 3					1
Part-timer No. 4					1

busy periods, taking reservations or appointments to schedule demand for less busy periods, discouraging undesirable demand through use of screening procedures and marketing ads and segmenting demand to facilitate better service (examples include use of first-class and economy-class seating and use of express and regular checkout stations). These tactics are combined with the capacity management techniques discussed earlier to provide the firm with the ability to better serve customers. The next section describes capacity management techniques for periods when service capacity exceeds demand.

Capacity Management When Available Service Capacity Exceeds Demand

When capacity exceeds demand, the firm is faced with the problem of how to utilize excess capacity. Too much excess capacity means higher fixed costs, resulting in higher prices for the service provided and may also affect customers' perceptions of quality (readers may recall their own quality perceptions when walking into a deserted restaurant at peak dinner hours). Besides the obvious long-term solution of laying workers off and selling facilities, firms may be able to find other uses for service capacity and use demand management techniques to stimulate demand.

Finding Other Uses for Service Capacity

One way to utilize excess capacity is to develop additional service products. Periodic lack of demand might be particularly troublesome for services with seasonal demand such as hotels, airlines and ski resorts. For these services, management may try to develop service products that the firm can provide during their characteristically slow periods. This might include airlines partnering with resorts to provide vacation packages during off-peak seasonal periods, hotels booking business conferences during slow periods or ski resorts designing mountain bike trails or building cement luge runs for summer use. Firms can also make use of cross-training to shift or transfer employees to other areas needing more capacity. For instance, swimming pool builders might train and then use their construction workers to build pool enclosures during the winter months. In an interesting use of excess electricity capacity, Canada is gearing up for handling the electricity demand for electric cars, estimated to be 500,000 units by 2018. Currently, Canada's hydro, coal, natural gas and nuclear power sources go largely unused during nighttime hours and this power simply can't all be turned off; rather, it becomes wasted power. Consequently, Canada is developing smart electricity meters to charge users drastically cheaper rates for power usage during off-peak hours, which will allow electric cars to be recharged at night for perhaps 42 cents. "We have the resources and the electricity," says Al Cormier, executive director of the not-for-profit organization Electric Mobility Canada. "We should take advantage of this opportunity." Ontario is on track to install smart meters in all homes and businesses by the end of 2010.[20]

Using Demand Management Techniques

When capacity exceeds demand, demand management techniques are used to stimulate additional demand. These include lowering prices during off-peak periods, as in early-bird dinner specials or mid-week hotel rates, as well as designing aggressive marketing campaigns for use during slow business periods.

Managing capacity in services thus involves techniques to adjust capacity and either stimulate or shift demand to match capacity to demand. When an oversupply or undersupply of capacity exists, service times, waiting times, cost and service quality all suffer, all of which ultimately impact the competitiveness of the firm. The second concern in service response logistics is discussed next—managing queue times.

Managing Queue Times

Queue times are frequently encountered every day including waiting at traffic lights, waiting for a table at a restaurant and waiting on hold on the telephone. Ideally, service managers would like to design **queuing systems** such that customers never have to wait in a queue; however, the cost of maintaining enough service capacity to handle peak demand and unexpectedly high levels of demand is simply too expensive. Thus, managers use information they have about their customers as well as their service employees to design adequate queuing systems and then couple this with the management of customers' perceived waiting times to minimize the negative impact of waiting in line. Thus, good queue management consists of the management of *actual waiting time* and *perceived waiting time*. To accomplish this, managers must consider a number of issues:

- What is the average arrival rate of the customers?
- In what order will customers be serviced?
- What is the average service rate of the service providers?
- What is the average service time requirement of each customer?
- How are customer arrival and service times distributed?
- How long will customers actually wait in the queue before they either leave or lower their perceptions of service quality?
- How can customers be kept in line even longer without lowering their perceptions of service quality?

Answers to these questions will allow the firm to adequately design a queuing system that will provide acceptable service to most customers while minimizing the service system cost and the cost of lost and disgruntled customers. Properly thought-out and designed queuing systems decrease waiting times and subsequently the need for further managing waiting times; however, occasionally, waiting time management tactics must be utilized to decrease perceived waiting times. The design of queuing systems is discussed first, followed by a discussion of managing perceived waiting times.

Queuing System Design

The four types of queuing system configurations are shown in Figure 12.1. The most appropriate queuing system depends on the volume of customers to be served, the willingness of customers to wait in the queue, the physical constraints imposed by the service structure and the number and sequence of services to be performed. The outputs from various queuing systems that managers need to compare are the average number of customers in line and in the system, the average waiting time in line and in the system and the average server utilization. As alluded to earlier, the primary elements of all queuing systems are the *input process*, the *queue characteristics* and the *service characteristics*. These elements are discussed next, along with several applications.

The Input Process

The customer arrivals are referred to here as the **demand source**. The size of the demand source can be considered either infinite or finite. Many situations (along with the examples covered later) assume an unlimited or infinite demand source such as customers arriving at a retail outlet, whereas other situations have a finite-sized demand source, such as ticketed customers showing up for a concert at an arena.

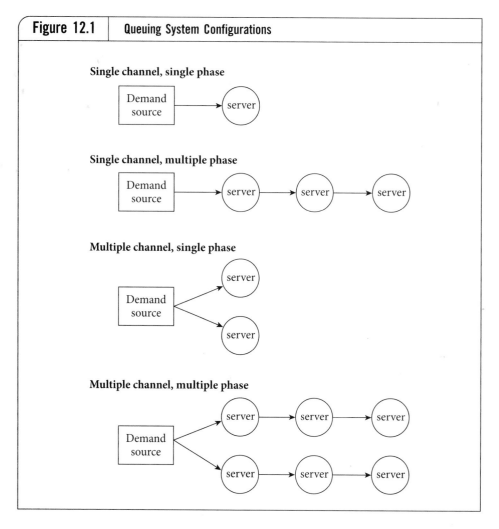

Figure 12.1 | **Queuing System Configurations**

Single channel, single phase

Single channel, multiple phase

Multiple channel, single phase

Multiple channel, multiple phase

Customers also arrive at a service according to some **arrival pattern**. When students show up for a scheduled class, this is an example of a known or deterministic interarrival time. In many cases as in a retail establishment, customers show up in a random pattern and the *Poisson distribution* is commonly used to describe these customer arrivals. Using the Poisson distribution, the probability of x customers arriving within some time period T is expressed as:

$$P_{x(T)} = \frac{e^{-\lambda T} (\lambda T)^x}{x!}$$

where λ = average customer arrivals in time period T

e = 2.71828 (natural log base) and

$x!$ = x factorial = $x(x - 1)(x - 2)...(1)$.

Example 12.4 illustrates the use of this formula.

If we assume the number of arrivals per time period is Poisson distributed with a mean arrival rate of λ, then the interarrival time (time between arrivals) is described by the *negative exponential distribution*, with a mean interarrival time of $1/\lambda$ (so if the mean

Example 12.4 Arrivals per Hour at Jay's Quick Lube Shop

Jay's Quick Lube Shop can service an average of four cars per hour with a partial crew of three employees and the owner Jay is interested in calculating the probability they can handle all the customers on Saturdays with the partial crew, instead of his usual full crew of five. Given an average arrival rate of three customers per hour on Saturdays, he uses the Poisson distribution to calculate the probabilities of various customer arrivals per hour, shown below.

NUMBER OF ARRIVALS, x	$P_x(\text{for } T = 1 \text{ hour}) = \dfrac{e^{-3}3^x}{x!}$	CUMULATIVE PROBABILITY
0	0.0498	0.0498
1	0.1494	0.1992
2	0.2240	0.4232
3	0.2240	0.6472
4	0.1680	0.8152

By summing the probabilities for each of the arrival levels, Jay figures that he can handle the demand per hour approximately 82 percent of the time. Conversely, he figures that approximately 18 percent of the time, demand per hour will be greater than four customers, causing queues to develop.

arrival rate is 10 per hour, then the mean interarrival time is 60 minutes/10 arrivals or 6 minutes/arrival).

Most queuing models assume that customers stay in the queue once they join it. In other words, customers do not exhibit **balking** (refusing to join the queue once they see how long it is) or **reneging** (leaving the queue before completing the service). Though most people have done this at one time or another, queuing analysis becomes much more complex when these arrival characteristics are allowed.

The Queue Characteristics

Queuing models generally assume the length of a queue can grow to an infinite length, although for some situations this is not appropriate (e.g., people with tickets waiting to enter a concert). Queuing configurations can contain single or multiple queues (e.g., the single winding queue at Wendy's versus the multiple queues at most McDonald's). Another queue characteristic is the **queue discipline**. The discipline describes the order in which customers are served. The most common queue discipline is first-come-first-served, although other examples include most-needy-first-served (in emergency rooms) and most-important-first-served (a VIP queue at a nightclub).

Virtual Queues

Technology is impacting queuing systems such that **virtual queues** are becoming more commonplace. Customers' places in the queue are tracked by a computerized system that allows them to roam the premises until their place is called. This reduces balking and reneging while allowing customers to make better use of their time. For instance, the Lavi Industries' Qtrac system registers customers via a touch-screen kiosk (in shopping malls), which prints a ticket that includes expected waiting time. Customers are then free to shop until their name appears on an LCD monitor. In ten hospitals in Shanghai, waiting patients can input their cell phone numbers into a computer system that sends them a text message when they become fifth in line, allowing them to leave without fear they will miss an appointment.[21]

The Service Characteristics

The service can be provided either by a single server or by multiple servers that act in series or in parallel. Multiple servers acting in parallel is referred to as a **multiple-channel queuing system**. Multiple servers acting in series is referred to as a **multiple-phase queuing system**. Figure 12.1 shows these queuing configurations.

The *single-channel, single-phase* configuration is the most basic. For standard distribution patterns of customer arrival and service times, the formulas to evaluate this type of system are very straightforward. An example is the one-person retail shop. The *single-channel, multiple-phase* queuing system is the next configuration shown. For this system, customers all contact the same servers, but receive more than one service and encounter a queue at each service. An example of this type of service is a dentist's office where customers are checked-in by a receptionist, get their teeth cleaned by a dental hygienist, get their teeth x-rayed by a dental assistant and then get a dental exam by a dentist. For each service, longer-than-average service times by the preceding customer can mean waiting line buildups within the system. The third configuration shown is the *multiple-channel, single-phase* system. Customers enter the system, receive one service from any one of a number of servers and then exit. Examples of this are retailers' checkout stands or banks' teller windows. These systems can have queues at each channel or one winding queue where all channels receive customers from one line. The final configuration shown is the *multiple-channel, multiple-phase* queuing system. In this example, customers all receive more than one service in sequence from more than one set or channel of servers. An example here might be a large medical clinic where patients are checked in by one of several assistants, have their vital signs recorded by one of several nurses and receive a medical consultation by one of several doctors.

Another characteristic of the service are the times required to complete each of the services provided. For each phase in the system, service times are described by a mean time and a probability distribution. Frequently, the negative exponential distribution is used to describe the randomness of service time distributions. To determine the probability that the service time, t, will be less than or equal to some specified time, T, the following formula can be used:

$$P(t \leq T) = 1 - e^{-\mu T}$$

where e = 2.71828 (natural log base) and

μ = the average service rate.

Example 12.5 illustrates the use of this formula for calculating the probability of completing service within a specified time period.

For single-channel systems, we can use the average arrival and service rates to calculate average capacity utilization, by dividing the customer arrival rate by the customer service rate. For example, if the arrival rate is three per hour and the service rate is four per hour, then the average capacity utilization is 75 percent. Although, as can be seen in Example 12.4, there will likely be times when utilization for periods during the day approaches or exceeds 100 percent. Now that all of the important elements of

Example 12.5   Service Times at Jay's Quick Lube Shop

Jay's Quick Lube Shop can service an average of four customers per hour or one customer every fifteen minutes, with a crew of three service personnel. The average customer arrival rate on Saturdays is three customers per hour or one customer every twenty minutes. Jay is interested in calculating the probability that actual service time, t, will be within a specific time period, T and he develops a chart showing these probabilities below, using the negative exponential distribution.

SPECIFIC TIME PERIOD	$P(t \leq T \text{ hrs.}) = 1 - e^{-4T}$
15 min. (.25 hrs.)	$1 - e^{-4(.25)} = 0.6321$
20 min. (.33 hrs.)	$1 - e^{-4(.33)} = 0.7329$
30 min. (.5 hrs.)	$1 - e^{-4(.5)} = 0.8647$
40 min. (.67 hrs.)	$1 - e^{-4(.67)} = 0.9314$
45 min. (.75 hrs.)	$1 - e^{-4(.75)} = 0.9502$

Thus, Jay thinks that almost 75 percent of the time, they will be able to service a customer in less than or equal to twenty minutes.

queuing systems have been reviewed, various applications of the models can be discussed and these are presented next.

Queuing System Applications

When using queuing models, managers collect arrival rate and service rate data by observing over time how many customers actually arrive for service and how many customers are actually served. Depending on the service, it may take a number of days or weeks to compile meaningful information. Presented below are applications of the single-channel, single-phase queuing model and the multiple-channel, single-phase queuing model. These are meant only to be introductory applications. Examples for the other queuing systems and applications can be quite complicated and are beyond the scope of this text. Interested readers are encouraged to examine management science or operations research texts for more advanced treatments of this topic. Several references are provided at the end of this chapter for this purpose.

A Single-Channel, Single-Phase Queuing Model Application

This is the most widely used and simplest of all queuing models. The assumptions in using the model are as follows:

- Customers come from an infinite population and are Poisson distributed over time.
- Customers are served in first-come-first-served sequence.
- No balking or reneging occurs.
- Service times are distributed according to the negative exponential distribution.
- The average service rate is greater than the average arrival rate.

The symbols and equations used to determine the operating characteristics for the single-channel, single-phase queuing model are as follows:

λ = average arrival rate
μ = average service rate

$$\rho = \text{average server utilization} = \lambda/\mu$$
$$L_s = \text{expected number of customers in the system} = \lambda/(\mu-\lambda)$$
$$L_q = \text{expected number of customers in the queue} = \lambda^2/[\mu(\mu-\lambda)] = L_s - \lambda/\mu$$
$$W_s = \text{expected waiting time in the system} = 1/(\mu-\lambda) = L_s/\lambda$$
$$W_q = \text{expected waiting time in the queue} = \lambda/[\mu(\mu-\lambda)] = L_q/\lambda$$
$$P_n = \text{probability that there are } n \text{ units in the queuing system}$$
$$= (\lambda/\mu)^n(1-\lambda/\mu)$$

The example below illustrates the calculation of operating characteristics for a single-channel, single-phase service.

Kathy's Sewing Shop is a small neighborhood shop that can serve about five customers per hour. For the past two weeks Kathy has kept track of the customer arrival rate and the average has been four customers per hour. Kathy is interested in calculating the operating characteristics for her store. So she asks one of her customers, a business student at the local university, to help her. The student provides the following information:

$$\lambda = 4 \text{ customers per hour}$$
$$\mu = 5 \text{ customers per hour}$$
$$\rho = 4/5 = 0.8 \text{ or } 80\% \text{ utilization}$$
$$L_s = \lambda/(\mu-\lambda) = 4/(5-4) = 4 \text{ customers}$$
$$L_q = L_s - \lambda/\mu = 4 - 4/5 = 3.2 \text{ customers}$$
$$W_s = L_s/\lambda = 4/4 = 1 \text{ hour} = 60 \text{ minutes}$$
$$W_q = L_q/\lambda = 3.2/4 = 0.8 \text{ hours} = 48 \text{ minutes}$$

Kathy also wants to know how likely it will be that more than four customers will be in her shop at one time. So her student-customer thinks about this and decides that the best way to calculate it is to determine the probabilities of zero, one, two, three and four customers in the shop and then add these and subtract the sum from 1.0. So she provides the following information:

$$\text{For } n = 0 \quad P_0 = (4/5)^0(1-4/5) = 0.200$$
$$n = 1 \quad P_1 = (4/5)^1(1-4/5) = 0.160$$
$$n = 2 \quad P_2 = (4/5)^2(1-4/5) = 0.128$$
$$n = 3 \quad P_3 = (4/5)^3(1-4/5) = 0.102$$
$$n = 4 \quad P_4 = (4/5)^4(1-4/5) = 0.082$$
$$\text{For } n > 4 \quad P_{n>4} = 1- (P_0+P_1+P_2+P_3+P_4)$$
$$= 1 - (.2+.16+.128+.102+.082) = 1- .672 = 0.328$$

So Kathy can expect that there will be more than four people in her shop about 33 percent of the time.

Kathy can also purchase a barcode scanner with an automated cash register that will increase her service rate to ten customers per hour. She wants to know how this will change the average wait time in the queue and in the system. Her student-customer then shows her the very significant change this will make:

$$L_s = \lambda/(\mu-\lambda) = 4/(10-4) = 0.67 \text{ customers}$$
$$W_q = \lambda/[\mu(\mu-\lambda)] = 4/[10(6)] = 0.067 \text{ hours} = 4 \text{ minutes}$$
$$W_s = 1/(\mu-\lambda) = 1/6 \text{ hour} = 10 \text{ minutes}$$

A Multiple-Channel, Single-Phase Queuing Model Application

All of the assumptions shown above still apply for the multiple-channel, single-phase model, except that the number of servers is now greater than one and the queuing system consists of multiple servers serving customers from multiple queues. The operating characteristics of this queuing system are as follows:

λ = average arrival rate

$s\mu$ = average service rate, where s = number of service channels

ρ = average server utilization = $\lambda / s\mu$

P_0 = probability of zero customers in the system

$$= \frac{1}{\sum\limits_{n=0}^{s-1} \frac{(\lambda/\mu)^n}{n!} + \frac{(\lambda/\mu)^s}{s!} \left[\frac{1}{1-(\lambda/s\mu)} \right]} , \text{ for } s\mu > \lambda$$

P_n = probability of n customers in the system

$$= P_0 \frac{(\lambda/\mu)^n}{n!} \text{ for } n \leq s$$

$$= P_0 \frac{(\lambda/\mu)^n}{s! \, s^{n-s}} , \text{ for } n > s$$

L_q = expected number of customers in the queue

$$= P_0 \frac{(\lambda/\mu)^s (\lambda/s\mu)}{s! \, (1-\lambda/s\mu)^2}$$

L_s = expected number of customers in the system

$$= L_q + \lambda/\mu$$

W_q = expected waiting time in the queue

$$= L_q / \lambda$$

W_s = expected waiting time in the system

$$= W_q + 1/\mu$$

The example for the single-channel, single-phase shop is extended below, for the two-channel, single-phase shop, for comparison purposes.

Kathy's Sewing Shop has decided to hire a second worker and buy a second checkout stand with cash register for the shop. Both Kathy and the second worker can serve five customers per hour and the average arrival rate is four customers per hour. Kathy again wants to know all of the operating characteristics of the new configuration. Once again, her student-customer helps her out:

ρ = 4/10 = 0.4, or 40 percent utilization

$$P_0 = \frac{1}{\frac{(4/5)^0}{0!} + \frac{(4/5)^1}{1!} + \frac{(4/5)^2}{2!} \left(\frac{1}{1-(4/10)} \right)}$$

$$= \frac{1}{1+0.8+0.32(1.67)} = \frac{1}{2.33} = 0.428$$

$$L_q = \frac{(4/5)^2(4/10)}{2(1-4/10)^2} (0.428) = 0.152 \text{ customers}$$

$L_s = 0.152 + 4/5 = 0.952$ customers

$W_q = 0.152/4 = .038$ hours, or 2.28 minutes

$W_s = 0.038 + 0.2 = 0.238$ hours, or 14.28 minutes

Note that because of the mean service time and distribution differences, having a two-channel, two-queue system serving customers with an average service rate of five customers per hour per channel is not the same as having a one-channel, one-queue system that serves at a rate of ten customers per hour.

Managing Perceived Waiting Times

The final topic of discussion in waiting line management is the management of **perceived waiting times** (sometimes, customers perceive the wait time to be much longer or shorter than it really is). Even though an admirable job may be done designing a queuing system, there are still likely to be times when demand exceeds the queuing system capacity (recall the mention earlier of the two-hour wait in a doctor's office). For these time periods, service firms must have other tools at their disposal to influence customers' perceptions of the waiting times. In a well-known paper written on the topic of waiting time, David Maister presented some very interesting observations starting with his **First and Second Laws of Service**:[22]

> *Law #1: Satisfaction = perception − expectation*
>
> When customers expect a certain level of service and then perceive the service they actually receive to be higher, they will be satisfied. Conversely, when customers' service expectations are higher than their perceptions once the service has been completed, they are unsatisfied.
>
> *Law #2: It is hard to play catch-up ball*
>
> If customers start out happy when the service is first encountered, it is easy to keep them happy. If they start out disgruntled or become that way during the service, it is almost impossible to turn things around.

Service Law #1 is interesting in that expectations and perceptions are not necessarily based on reality. For example, customer expectations are formed based on previous experiences, marketing campaigns, signs, information from other people and the location, while customer perceptions can be affected during the service encounter by a friendly server, mood music, visually pleasant surroundings and a host of other things. A common practice coming out of Law #1 is to "under-promise and over-deliver." Service Law #2 is good for firms to remember when they are trying to improve service. Investments in service improvements might best be placed at the initial contact or early stages of the service to make sure the service encounter gets off to a good start.

Firms can manage both customer expectations and perceptions by observing and understanding how they are affected when customers wait for service. Waiting time management techniques resulting from this understanding include keeping customers occupied, starting the service quickly, relieving customer anxiety, keeping customers informed, grouping customers together and designing a fair waiting system.[23] Each of these is briefly discussed next.

Keep Customers Occupied

Firms must try to keep customers occupied while waiting in line. This is why magazines, televisions and toys for children to play with are often seen in office waiting areas. Other attention-keepers such as music, windows, mirrors or menus to look at keep customers' minds off the passage of time. In amusement parks such as Disneyland where long lines can be a big problem, customers waiting in line might get entertained by Mickey Mouse, a mime or a juggler, for instance. All these techniques try to lessen the perceived passage of time and influence customer satisfaction with the waiting experience. At the largest pediatric healthcare office in the U.S., Houston's Texas Children's Pediatric Associates serves 250,000 patients with about 160 doctors making queue times a big concern. Internet connectivity allows parents to work while they wait; activity centers and an interactive video wall keep children occupied; and moving from an outer waiting area to an inner one keeps families moving. "Perception is reality," says Kay Tittle, group president.[24]

Start the Service Quickly

Giving waiting customers menus, forms to complete, drinks from the bar or programs to read all act to give customers the impression the service has started. When firms acknowledge receipt of an order via telephone, mail or e-mail, this is another example of beginning the service. If organizations can design preprocess services that begin quickly once a customer encounters a queue, this will act to keep customers occupied and make long waits seem much shorter. The Carphone Warehouse (CPW), a European mobile phone retailer, has turned to Twitter to engage customers quickly and keep them satisfied. They have found it allows them to address complaints more quickly, offer quick feedback on problems and to positively impact customer satisfaction. If a customer wants to know whether a certain city has a retail location, CPW can tweet a link to the store; if a customer wants to know how to remove a SIM card, CPW can tweet the solution.[25]

Relieve Customer Anxiety

Customer anxiety is created in many waiting situations; for example, when customers are afraid they've been forgotten, when they don't know how long their wait is going to be, when they don't know what to do or when they fear they have entered the wrong line. Managers need to observe customers and learn what is likely to cause anxiety and then develop plans to relieve their concerns. These plans might include simply having employees reassure customers, announcing how much longer a caller on hold is likely to wait, announcing the lateness of a plane yet to arrive or using signs to direct customers to the correct line.

Keep Customers Informed

Managers can derail customer anxieties before they even begin by giving customers information as their preprocess and in-process waits progress. When receptionists tell patients that their doctor was called to an emergency, when pilots tell passengers that the plane is waiting to be cleared for gate departure, when work crews place a flashing sign on the road warning drivers to expect delays during a certain period of time and when amusement parks place signs in the queue telling customers the waiting time from that point in line, this information makes waiting customers much more patient because they know that a delay will occur and the reasons for the delay. Consequently, they are much more willing to stay in line, remain satisfied and complete the service.

Group Customers Together

Customers generally prefer waiting together (to commiserate) in queues, rather than waiting alone. Customers act to alleviate their own and others' anxieties, fears and problems while waiting in line by talking to each other, sharing concerns and helping out if possible. This sense of togetherness reduces perceived waiting times and may even add enjoyment to the waiting experience. Managers should think of ways to create or encourage group waiting instead of solo waiting such as closer seating, single queues instead of multiple queues and use of numbered tickets or virtual queues so people don't have to stand in the queue.

Design a Fair Waiting System

"Taking cuts" in a queue is something that can cause significant irritation to others already waiting, particularly if it is seen as unfair. In an emergency room, most people waiting will likely accept that others coming into the queue later might be taken care of first (the queue discipline is most-critical-first-served). Alternately, taking cuts in a long queue at a retail store or amusement park could result in grumbling and shouting from those already waiting. Whenever the queue discipline is something other than first-come-first-served, managers need to be aware of the potential problems this causes and take steps to reduce the feeling of unfairness or segment customers such that the queue discipline is not obvious. Examples include physically separating customers such as in first-class versus economy-class seating on airplanes, taking names and group sizes at a restaurant while concealing the list and putting up signs like "six items or less" at retail checkout stands. In many cases, customers will understand and accept the reasons for using a particular queue discipline if they are informed of it. The next concern of service response logistics is the management of distribution channels.

Managing Distribution Channels

This segment of service response logistics describes several **distribution channels** and strategies a service can use to deliver their services and products to customers. Table 12.2 lists a number of distribution alternatives for a retail store, a bank, an auto repair facility and a university. Many of these distribution alternatives are the traditional ones everyone is used to seeing; however, services today are experimenting with other, nontraditional distribution channels as customer preferences and habits, demographics, technology and competition change.

Some distribution channels have revolutionized the way services do business. For instance, ATMs, debit cards and the Internet have completely changed the financial services industry; many customers almost never set foot inside a bank or stockbroker's office. Today, many people have come to expect these things and many services have responded.

Other distribution strategies have arisen because new technologies made them possible and because customers were asking for them. In the grocery industry, Amazon.com's grocery delivery service AmazonFresh has been operating since 2007 and promises same-day and next-day delivery of groceries (depending on truck availability) to customers in Seattle, Washington. Even though grocery home delivery businesses have failed in the past, materials handling technologies such as robotics and refrigerated totes and the deep pockets of Amazon.com give it a good chance of succeeding this time around.[26] Several of the distribution channel alternatives and issues facing services today are discussed next.

Eatertainment, Entertailing and Edutainment

As service distribution concepts change, new words have been coined to describe these concepts. **Eatertainment** is the combination of restaurant and entertainment elements. Many of these services incorporate elements of local culture or history into their design themes and offer the capabilities of eating, drinking, entertainment and shopping all in one venue. In Forks, Washington, Tim Root and his wife are opening a *Twilight* movie-themed restaurant called The Lodge. They also plan a bar to be called The Dungeon. "The restaurant that [Twilight movie character] Charlie Swan takes Bella to after graduation is referred to as 'the Lodge' so that is the Twilight tie-in," says Root.[27]

Entertailing refers to retail locations with entertainment elements. Many shopping malls are designed today to offer entertainment such as ice skating, rock climbing and amusement park rides. Metreon, in San Francisco, is a high-tech electronics-themed

Table 12.2	Service Distribution Channels
SERVICE	**DISTRIBUTION CHANNEL**
Retail Store	• Freestanding • Mall • Internet • Mail order
Bank	• Main/headquarters • Freestanding branches • Sites in malls • Sites in retail locations • ATMs • Internet • Telephone
Auto Repair Business	• Freestanding • Attached to a large retailer • Franchised outlets • Mobile repair van
University/College	• Public • Private • Specialized/General • Traditional/Adult education • Main campus • Branches • Internet • Day/Evening • Television

retail complex with an IMAX theater, virtual reality games and a 3-D facility. Toy stores such as Toys "R" Us are designed around centers within the stores to allow customers to try out and play with toys. Entertailing developments are designed to hold on to customers longer than the typical 45 minutes, perhaps up to three or four hours. Owners are finding that these customers spend almost twice as much as the typical retail customer on merchandise and services.

Museums, parks and a host of service providers are getting into the act with **edutainment** or **infotainment** to attract more customers and increase revenues. Edutainment combines learning with entertainment to appeal to customers looking for substance along with play. The website www.thegoodfoodfight.com allows visitors to fling food at moving targets while educating them about healthy foods. In the U.S., state and national park employees entertain and inform tourists with indigenous animal lectures and shows or campfire stories in the evenings. Theme parks such as Legoland in San Diego offer attractions that combine fun and education aimed at the two- to twelve-year-old audience. Finally, television shows such as Sesame Street and software aimed at teaching math and foreign languages in an engaging way also fall into this category.

Franchising

Franchising allows services to expand quickly into dispersed geographic markets, protect existing markets and build market share. When the owners have limited financial resources, franchising is a good strategy for expansion. Franchisees are required to invest some of their own capital, while paying a small percentage of sales to the franchiser in return for the brand name, start-up help, advertising, training and assistance in meeting specific operating standards. Many services such as fast-food restaurants, accounting and tax businesses, auto rental agencies, beauty salons, clothing stores, ice cream shops, motels and other small service businesses use franchising as a strategy for growing and competing.

Control problems are one of the biggest issues in franchising. Franchisors periodically perform financial and quality audits on the franchisees along with making frequent visits to facilities to assure that franchisees are continuing to comply with operating standards of the company. The idea of control, however, is something that some new franchisors are experimenting with. The Massachusetts-based Wings Over franchise chain, for instance, lets franchisees make changes to their stores in order to lend an element of uniqueness to each restaurant. The franchise in Washington D.C. is called Wings Over Washington D.C.; several in Florida offer raspberry chipotle wing sauce; and in college towns, many Wings Over restaurants don't open until 4:00 p.m. and they close at 3:00 or 4:00 a.m. This gives franchisees the flexibility to compete with local businesses. It also is viewed as a way to attract franchisees who have many other businesses to select from.

The **microfranchise** is another type of franchising concept and is seen as a good way for economically disadvantaged people to make a living. It offers ready-made, low- risk starter jobs for people with little or no education and little available capital, while giving established companies additional distribution avenues. Drishtee, for example, is an India-based microfranchise. Their small kiosks can be seen in thousands of Indian villages selling basic healthcare products. Drishtee loans franchisees $150 for start-up fees and the kiosks can earn the franchisees about $30 per month in profits. Cellular City, a Philippines-area microfranchise, specializes in new and used cell phones, phone cards and laptops. The start-up costs are higher (about $9,000) but provide $50 to $100 per day in profits for the franchisees.[28]

International Expansion

The search for larger and additional markets has driven services to expand globally. Since the world today has become essentially borderless because of the Internet and other communication mediums, more freedom of movement, greater use of common currencies and the expansion that has already taken place, services today compete in a global economy.

Global service expansion most likely means operating with partners who are familiar with the region's culture, markets, suppliers, competitors, infrastructure and government regulations. For instance, when McDonald's opened its first restaurant in Moscow, an entire food supply chain had to be designed and implemented. McDonald's had to train farmers to produce the type and quality of crops needed to supply the business and then find buyers for the excess food the farmers produced (e.g., the Moscow hotels and embassies).[29]

China's service sector is emerging as a key driver of the Chinese economy—the service sector has now surpassed agriculture in terms of contribution to annual GDP and is growing annually by 14.5 percent. Consequently, many global services are looking to become involved in Chinese markets. For instance, U.S. knowledge services, network services and financial services have been busy setting up operations in China. Giant search engine company Google launched in China in 2006 and has about 30 percent of China's search engine traffic. Lately, Google and the Chinese government have been at odds over Google's diversion of mainland China search traffic to a Hong Kong site to avoid Chinese government censorship. Mapping is one of Google's fastest-growing services in China and it appears that a compromise will soon be reached to allow Google to continue operating in China.[30]

Exposure to foreign currency exchange rate fluctuations can also pose a problem for expanding service firms, requiring them to use financial hedging strategies to reduce exchange rate risk. Firms can operate in several different countries to offset currency problems, since economic downturns in one country can often be offset by positive economic conditions in other countries.

Language barriers, cultural problems and the varying needs of different regional cultures also must be addressed when expanding. Local management must be allowed to vary services, signage and accompanying products to suit local tastes. Restaurants, for instance, typically add local favorites to menus to increase acceptability. Companies must become familiar with language translations in order to properly change the wording on signs and advertisements to increase readability and understanding. The Coca-Cola name in China for example, was initially rendered as "ke-kou-ke-la" on thousands of signs before it was found that the meaning of the phrase was either "bite the wax tadpole" or "female horse stuffed with wax" depending on the regional dialect. Coke personnel eventually studied 40,000 characters to find the phonetic equivalent "ko-kou-ko-le," which translates into "happiness in the mouth." Similarly, Japan's second-largest tourist agency, Kinki Nippon Tourist Co., felt compelled to change its U.S. name after they began getting requests from American customers for unusual sex-oriented trips.[31]

Internet Distribution Strategies

Internet-based "dot com" companies exploded on the scene during the latter part of the 1990s, pushing the NASDAQ to historic highs and promising to enrich anyone with an idea, good or bad, for a website that could generate revenues on the Internet. E-commerce was touted as the coming trillion dollar revolution in retailing. But as it turned out, most of the dot-com companies of that era are gone today. Still, Internet retailing is growing faster than traditional retailing. In 2008, e-commerce accounted for $141 billion in U.S. retail sales or approximately 6 percent of total U.S. retail sales. This reflects an increase of 100 percent from 2005. Online sales are growing by about 13 percent annually, compared to 1 percent for traditional retail sales. Commercial listings on eBay, for instance, have surged so rapidly that their website briefly crashed on November 21, 2009.[32]

One of the primary advantages of the Internet is its ability to offer convenient sources of real-time information, integration, feedback and comparison shopping. Individual consumers use Internet search engines to look for jobs, find and communicate with businesses, find the nearest movie theater, find products, sell things and barter goods. And they can do all this in the privacy of their homes. Globally, approximately 14 billion online searches per month occurred in 2009, for example.[33] Businesses, too, use the Internet to communicate, find and then purchase items from suppliers and sell or provide goods and services to individual consumers and other businesses. Today, most businesses either have a website or are thinking about building one. Many individuals also have their own websites, since domain names can be purchased for as little as $10 per year. Many retailers today sell products exclusively over the Internet (a *pure strategy*), while others use it as a supplemental distribution channel (a *mixed strategy*).

The **pure Internet distribution strategy** can have several distinct advantages over traditional brick-and-mortar services. Internet companies can become more centralized, reducing labor, capital and inventory costs while using the Internet to decentralize their marketing efforts to reach a vastly distributed audience of business or individual consumers. Amazon.com falls into this category. Today, though, the **mixed Internet distribution strategy** of combining traditional retailing with Internet retailing seems to be emerging as the stronger business model. Firms such as JCPenney sell items in retail outlets and also from Internet and store catalogs. Customers can either pick up their purchases at the store or have them delivered. Southwest Airlines was the first airline to establish a home page on the Internet and today approximately 60 percent of its passenger revenue is generated by online bookings via their industry leading website, www.southwest.com.[34]

Developing good customer service capabilities can be challenging, however. JCPenney representatives, for instance, must be able to perform customer service functions over the Internet, in-person and via mail and telephone. Companies are addressing this problem by developing sophisticated **customer contact centers**. These centers integrate their websites and traditional call centers to offer 24/7 support where customers and potential customers can contact the firm and each other using telephone, e-mail, chat rooms and e-bulletin boards. These contact centers allow firms to serve a large number of geographically dispersed customers with a relatively small number of customer service agents.

Just as services have to be concerned with managing service capacity and queues, firms must also invest management efforts in designing the necessary distribution channels to compete in today's marketplaces. The final element of the service response logistics discussion affects all elements of the service itself and the way it is distributed and that is the management of service quality. Although this topic was initially addressed in Chapter 8, the quality management topics geared strictly toward services need further discussion and this topic is presented below.

Managing Service Quality

The fourth and final activity in service response logistics is the management of **service quality**. For services, quality occurs during the service delivery process and typically involves an interaction between a customer and service company employees. Customer satisfaction with the service depends not only on the ability of the firm to deliver what customers want, but on the customers' perceptions of the quality of service received. When customer expectations are met or exceeded, the service is deemed to possess high quality; and when expectations are not met, the perception of quality is poor (recall Maister's First Law of Service). Service quality, then, is highly dependent upon the ability of the firm's employees and service systems to meet or exceed customers' varying expectations. Because of the variable nature of customer expectations, perceptions and happiness, services must continually be monitoring their service delivery systems using the tools described in Chapter 8 while concurrently observing, communicating with and surveying customers to adequately assess and improve quality.

The Five Dimensions of Service Quality

Some of the most highly quoted studies of service quality are those done by Drs. Parasuraman, Zeithaml and Berry.[35] Surveying the customers of a number of different services, they identified **five dimensions of service quality** generally used by customers to rate service quality—reliability, responsiveness, assurance, empathy and tangibles. Reliability was consistently reported in their study as the most important quality dimension.

- *Reliability*: consistently performing the service correctly and dependably.
- *Responsiveness*: providing the service promptly and in a timely manner.
- *Assurance*: using knowledgeable, competent, courteous employees who convey trust and confidence to customers.
- *Empathy*: providing caring and individual attention to customers.
- *Tangibles*: the physical characteristics of the service including the facilities, the servers, equipment and other customers.

Using their survey, the three researchers were able to identify any differences occurring between customer expectations in the five dimensions listed above and customers' perceptions of what was actually received during the service encounter. These differences were referred to as service quality "gaps," and can thus be used to highlight areas in need of improvement for services.

What this research shows is that organizations should develop criteria relating to the five service quality dimensions and then collect data using customer comment cards and mailed or e-mailed surveys of customers' satisfaction with each of the quality dimensions. This will allow them to measure overall service quality performance. Table 12.3 presents criteria that might be used in each of the five quality dimensions. Obviously, these would be expected to vary by industry, products and company. When weaknesses or gaps are encountered in any of the performance criteria, managers can institute improvements in the areas indicated.

World-class service companies realize they must get to know their customers and they invest considerable time and effort gathering information about customer expectations and perceptions. This information is then used to design services and delivery systems that satisfy customers, capture market share and create profits for the firm. These organizations understand that one of the most important elements affecting long-term competitiveness and profits is the quality of their products and services relative to their competitors.

Recovering from Poor Service Quality

There will undoubtedly, from time to time, be occasions when an organization's products and services do not meet a customer's expectations. In most cases, quick recovery from these service failures can keep customers loyal and coming back and may even serve as good word-of-mouth advertising for the firm, as customers pass on their stories of good service recoveries. Most importantly, when service failures do occur, firms must be able to recover quickly and forcefully to satisfy customers. This involves empowering front-line service personnel to identify problems and then provide solutions quickly and in an empathetic way.

Good services offer guarantees to their customers and empower employees to provide quick and meaningful solutions when customers invoke the guarantee. In the U.S., the great majority of retailers offer money-back guarantees if customers are not satisfied and about half offer low-price guarantees where customers are refunded the price

Table 12.3	Examples of Service Quality Criteria
SERVICE QUALITY DIMENSION	**CRITERIA**
Reliability	• billing accuracy • order accuracy • on-time completion • promises kept
Responsiveness	• on-time appointment • timely callback • timely confirmation of order
Assurance	• skills of employees • training provided to employees • honesty of employees • reputation of firm
Empathy	• customized service capabilities • customer recognition • degree of server-customer contact • knowledge of the customer
Tangibles	• appearance of the employees • appearance of the facility • appearance of customers • equipment and tools used

difference for a period of time after purchase.[36] In many cases, quick solutions to service problems are designed into their processes and become part of a service firm's marketing efforts. Firms that anticipate where service failures can occur, develop recovery procedures, train employees in these procedures and then empower employees to remedy customer problems can assure they have the best service recovery system possible.

SUMMARY

Services constitute a large and growing segment of the global economy. Managing the supply chains of services is thus becoming an important part of an overall competitive strategy for services. Since service customers are most often the final consumers of the services provided, successfully managing service encounters involves managing productive capacity, managing queues, managing distribution channels and managing service quality. These four concerns are the foundations of service response logistics and were the primary focus of this chapter.

Service companies must accurately forecast demand, design capacity to adequately meet demand, employ queuing systems to serve customers as quickly and efficiently as possible, utilize distribution systems to best serve the firm's customers and then take steps to assure service quality and customer satisfaction throughout the service process. Provided that managers have selected a good location, designed an effective layout, hired, trained and properly scheduled service personnel and then employed effective service response logistics strategies, firms and their supply chains should be able to maintain competitiveness, market share and profitability.

KEY TERMS

arrival pattern, 424

back-of-the-house operations, 409

balking, 425

Baumol's disease, 405

capacity utilization, 417

chase demand strategy, 418

closeness desirability rating, 411

cost leadership strategy, 406

customer contact centers, 436

demand management, 421

demand source, 423

differentiation strategy, 407

distribution channels, 432

eatertainment, 432

edutainment, 433

entertailing, 432

facilitating products, 413

First and Second Laws of Service, 430

five dimensions of service quality, 437

focus strategy, 408

franchising, 434

front-of-the-house operations, 409

infotainment, 433

level demand strategy, 417

microfranchise, 434

mixed Internet distribution strategy, 436

multiple-channel queuing system, 426

multiple-factor productivity, 405

multiple-phase queuing system, 426

perceived waiting times, 430

pure Internet distribution strategy, 436

pure services, 403

queue discipline, 425

queue management, 418

queue times, 423

queuing systems, 423

reneging, 425

service bundle, 408

service capacity, 417

service delivery systems, 408

service layout strategies, 410

service quality, 415

service response logistics, 416

single-factor productivity, 405

state utility, 403

virtual queues, 425

walk-through service audits, 409

Wal-Mart effect, 405

DISCUSSION QUESTIONS AND EXERCISES

1. Is your university a pure service? Explain.

2. Why is the service sector in the U.S. and other highly developed economies growing more rapidly than the manufacturing sector?

3. Describe the primary differences between goods and service firms.

4. Give an example of a single-factor productivity measure and a multiple-factor productivity measure. Using the formula for productivity, describe all the ways that firms can increase productivity. Which of these ways might be considered risky?

5. Define Baumol's disease and the Wal-Mart effect and how they affect service-oriented economies like the U.S.

6. Discuss the primary issues in the management of global services.

7. What are the three generic strategies that services use to compete? Give examples.

8. When customers purchase a service, they are actually getting a bundle of service attributes. List and describe these attributes using a car-rental agency, a convenience store and a radio station.

9. Provide some examples of front-of-the-house and back-of-the-house service operations.

10. What are some things service firms can do to monitor customer satisfaction?

11. Why are service locations so important?

12. Discuss the principal design objectives for service layouts.

13. How do supply chain management activities differ between services and manufacturing companies? In what ways are these activities alike?

14. What are the four concerns of service response logistics?

15. Define service capacity and provide three examples of it that were not listed in the text.

16. Define capacity utilization. What is an ideal utilization? Can utilization ever be greater than 100 percent? Explain.

17. Describe how you would use a level and a chase demand capacity utilization strategy.

18. What are some alternatives to hiring and laying off workers to vary service capacity as demand varies?

19. Can customers be used to provide extra service capacity? Explain.

20. Describe some demand management techniques that are used when demand exceeds capacity and when capacity exceeds demand.

21. How can firms make use of excess capacity?

22. What are the two elements managers must pay attention to, when managing queues, to maximize customer satisfaction?

23. What are the primary elements to consider when designing any queuing system?

24. Define the terms "balking" and "reneging." How could a firm minimize them?

25. What is a virtual queue? When might one be used?

26. What type of queuing system does a three-channel, four-phase system refer to?

27. What are the advantages and disadvantages of increasing the number of channels?

28. Explain and give examples of Maister's First and Second Laws of Service.

29. If you have designed an effective queuing system, why is it still necessary to practice waiting time management on some occasions?

30. What are the distribution channel alternatives for a weather service? A souvenir shop? A marriage counselor?

31. What is a microfranchise? Would these be good for a developing country? For the U.S.?

32. Describe the important issues in the international expansion of services.

33. Describe and give examples of a pure Internet distribution strategy and a mixed Internet distribution strategy. Find your examples on the Internet.

34. How is service quality related to customer service and satisfaction?

35. Describe the five dimensions of service quality for a dentist's office, how performance in these dimensions might be measured and how recoveries might be handled for failures in each of the service quality dimensions.

36. Can recovery from a poor service quality incident be a good thing? Explain.

PROBLEMS

1. For the previous month, the Ellram Lounge served 1,500 customers with very few complaints. Their labor cost was $3,000; material cost was $800; energy cost was $200; and building lease cost was $1,500. They were open 26 days during the month and the lounge has 20 seats. They are open six hours per day and the average customer stay is one hour.

   a. Calculate the single-factor productivities and the overall multiple-factor productivity. How could they improve the productivity?
   b. Calculate the monthly capacity and the capacity utilization.

2. For the office layout shown below and the accompanying trip and distance matrices, determine the total distance traveled per day. Find another layout that results in a lower total distance traveled per day.

Management (1)	Production (2)	Engineering (3)	Reception (4)
Files (5)	Accounting (6)	Purchasing (7)	Sales (8)

INTERDEPARTMENTAL TRIPS PER DAY							
	(2)	(3)	(4)	(5)	(6)	(7)	(8)
(1)	6	5	2	1	7	6	15
(2)		12	4	5	2	10	5
(3)			2	9	2	10	8
(4)				18	12	4	2
(5)					0	0	0
(6)						6	14
(7)							6

DISTANCES BETWEEN DEPARTMENTS (METERS)							
	(2)	(3)	(4)	(5)	(6)	(7)	(8)
(1)	15	30	45	10	20	35	50
(2)		15	30	20	10	20	35
(3)			15	40	20	10	20
(4)				60	50	30	10
(5)					10	30	50
(6)						20	40
(7)							20

3. For the office layout shown in question number 2, determine the closeness desirability rating using the rating table below. Treat the hallway as if it doesn't exist (i.e., the Production and Accounting Departments touch each other). Can you find a more desirable layout? How could you use both the total distance traveled and the closeness desirability in assessing the layout alternatives? Can you find a layout resulting in relatively good scores using both types of criteria?

CLOSENESS DESIRABILITIES BETWEEN DEPARTMENTS							
	(2)	(3)	(4)	(5)	(6)	(7)	(8)
(1)	2	2	−1	0	1	3	3
(2)		3	0	0	0	3	1
(3)			0	2	0	2	3
(4)				3	1	2	2
(5)					2	2	1
(6)						0	2
(7)							1

4. Oana's Cat Care needs help in her grooming business as shown below for the five-day workweek. Determine a full- and part-time work schedule for the business using the fewest number of workers.

	MONDAY	TUESDAY	WEDNESDAY	THURSDAY	FRIDAY
Workers Required	2	3	3	4	5

5. Given an average service rate of twelve customers per hour, what is the probability the business can handle all the customers when the average arrival rate is ten customers per hour? Use the Poisson distribution to calculate the probabilities for various customer arrivals.

6. With an average service rate of twelve customers per hour and an average customer arrival rate of ten customers per hour, calculate the probability that actual service time will be less than or equal to six minutes.

7. Stella can handle about ten customers per hour at her one-person comic book store. The customer arrival rate averages about six customers per hour. Stella is interested in knowing the operating characteristics of her single-channel, single-phase queuing system.

8. How would Stella's queuing system operating characteristics change for the problem above if she added another cashier and increased her service rate to twenty customers per hour?

INTERNET QUESTIONS

1. Search the Internet for examples of eatertainment, entertailing and edutainment.

2. Search the Internet for examples of microfranchising and report on several.

3. Search the Internet for the terms "McDonald's carbon footprint" or "McDonald's green initiatives," and write a report on this firm's efforts.

4. Write a paper on Wal-Mart's location and layout strategies.

5. Search for examples of virtual queuing systems and report on several of these.

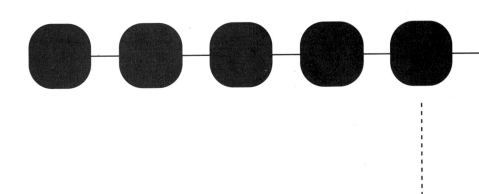

Part 5

Integration Issues in Supply Chain Management

Chapter 13

SUPPLY CHAIN PROCESS INTEGRATION

Use the downturn as an opportunity to collaborate with network partners to find new areas of value. We see strong evidence that supply chain leaders have taken a proactive approach to working with key network constituents to find this value. They simply do not accept economic conditions as an excuse for poor performance and are hard at work finding the next level of savings in their supply chains.[1]

Everyone wants better visibility throughout their supply chains, but the level of integration across supply chains to get that visibility is getting harder.[2]

Learning Objectives

After completing this chapter, you should be able to

- Discuss the overall importance of process integration in supply chain management.
- Describe the advantages of and obstacles to, process integration.
- Understand the important issues of internal and external process integration.
- Understand the role played by information systems in creating information visibility along the supply chain.
- Describe the various processes requiring integration along the supply chain.
- Understand the various causes of the bullwhip effect and how they impact process integration.
- Discuss the various issues associated with supply chain risk and security.

Chapter Outline

The Supply Chain Management Integration Model

Obstacles to Process Integration along the Supply Chain

Managing Supply Chain Risk and Security

Summary

Supply Chain Management in Action

A Panel of Leading Company Managers Discusses Supply Chain Collaboration

Moderator Frank Muschetto, executive vice president and chief procurement officer for Topeo Associates, opened the discussion by noting that his years of experience with McDonald's taught him that the businessperson's definition of collaboration is that it achieves results that cannot be achieved by anyone working alone. He suggested that McDonald's founder Ray Kroc's well-known quote, "None of us is as good as all of us," is a motto for all foodservice companies to live by.

"It's a challenge to find a way not to raise prices to the consumer," said Tad Wampfler, senior vice president of supply chain management for Wendy's International. "We have to find ways to remove costs without taking money from the distributor or the manufacturer." He added that there can be tremendous savings when the supply chain works together. "If we can control costs, it's a win for customers, distributors and manufacturers," he said.

Much of the panel discussion emphasized the critical need for transparency and trust among all channel partners. Otherwise, participants said, it is impossible to achieve any positive results from collaboration. Transparency and trust have not been traditional hallmarks of the foodservice supply chain, noted David Parsley, senior vice president of supply chain management for Applebee's International. "Many people say they want true cooperation, but not everyone can do it," he said. Parsley said one of Applebee's suppliers has collaborated with them for eight years, helping the chain to understand true product costs and working with them on commodity and risk management as well as "anticipatory issues management," such as problems with trans fats. The result has been savings for the operator and increased sales for the supplier.

John Inwright, executive vice president of the commercial division for Nice-Pak Products, also addressed the trust issue. "The more insights we get [into our trading partners' business models], the more we are able to meet their needs," he said. "It's all built on a framework of trust. We are not partners in business; we are trading partners. The basic foundation is how much you value trust."

Stephen Deasey, president and chief executive of The Sygma Network, a division of Sysco Corp., reminded the audience that the operative business model in the past has been "How do we grab a bigger piece of a very small pie?" He pointed out that the model is zero-sum, merely shifting the costs from one party to another. The new collaborative model means that each trading partner shares in a much bigger pie and every party wins.

"Given the level of transparency and trust required for supply-chain collaboration," Muschetto asked, "what are the risks involved?" Jim Lavender, executive vice president of Ben E. Keith Foods, said risks are overstated. Other panelists, however, disagreed, noting that confidentiality is a big issue.

"The better the relationship, the less that risks come into play," Lavender said.

Ben E. Keith was one of a number of competitive distributors who founded Maverick Xchange, an electronic trade platform that later merged with eFS, a similar platform.

"We do more than one-half of our transactions through the electronic platform," Lavender said. "It's unnecessary to have a system all your own."

Lorne Brown, director of supply chain network optimization for McCain Foods USA, said his company historically had kept logistics information "close to the vest." When logistics management network provider Arrowstream first approached McCain asking for complete disclosure of data in order to create a collaborative model, many managers perceived the disclosure risky. Panelists frequently mentioned Arrowstream as an example of a workable collaborative model. Deasey added that, once operators "buy into the logic" of collaboration and have crossed that hurdle, they must develop trust that confidentiality will be maintained by all parties. "The only way to take costs out of the supply chain is to collaborate," he said. "That revelation doesn't happen overnight."

One of the most important steps, Wampfler said, is to work with your partners to identify how you will share in the wealth derived from supply chain collaboration.

"You have to establish that there are savings for everybody and that one party is not trying to squeeze the others by taking it all," he said.

"We've all been guilty of sitting down and deciding what the customer wants without talking to them," Lavender said. "Now we sit down with customers and suppliers to understand what drives their businesses. We've had good success with that."

Source: Anonymous, "Collaborative Supply Cain Model Can Help Control Costs," *Nation's Restaurant News* 42(8), 2008: 20. Used with permission.

Introduction

The ultimate goal in supply chain management is to create value for the services and products provided to end customers, which, in turn, will benefit the firms in the supply chain network. To accomplish this, firms in a supply chain must first integrate their process activities internally and then with their trading partners. Throughout this textbook, the integration of key business processes along the supply chain has been a recurring theme. The term **process integration** means sharing information and coordinating resources to jointly manage a process or processes. We have been introducing and discussing the various processes and issues concerning this time-consuming and somewhat daunting task throughout the text and have been alluding to the idea that key processes must somehow be coordinated, shared or integrated among the supply chain members. In this chapter, some of these issues will be revisited and refined.

Additionally, the advantages, challenges, methods and tools used to achieve process integration both within organizations and among supply chain trading partners will be discussed. Today, process integration remains a significant problem for many organizations. A 2006 survey of U.S. manufacturers, for example, found that 34 percent of the responding companies had no process integration at all with their suppliers and 30 percent had no integration with their customers. And a more recent survey of human resource managers and business executives in 2010 found internal process integration to be one of the most challenging activities to implement and sustain.[3] Generally speaking, since internal integration between departments is considered to be the necessary foundation for successful external integration between trading partners, it can then be understood that problems with internal integration have made external integration even more difficult to achieve.

Specifically, this chapter discusses the key business processes requiring integration, the impact of integration on the bullwhip effect, the importance of internal and external process integration in supply chain management, issues of supply chain risk and security that come about as information is shared and products are moved significant distances and the important role played by information technology (IT).

External process integration can be an extremely difficult task because it requires proper training and preparedness, willing and competent trading partners, trust, compatible information systems, potentially a change in one or more organizational cultures and, as mentioned above, successful internal process integration. However, as described by leading company managers in the chapter opening Supply Chain Management in Action feature, the benefits of collaboration and information sharing between trading partners can be significant: reduced supply chain costs, greater flexibility to respond to market changes, fewer process problems and hence less supply chain safety stock, higher quality levels, reduced time to market and better utilization of resources. It is hoped that this chapter will allow readers to recall and consider all of the previous chapters' topics; their contributions to successful supply chain management; and the means by which collaboration, information sharing and process integration must occur to make supply chain management a core competitive strength.

The Supply Chain Management Integration Model

Figure 13.1 presents a supply chain integration model, starting with the identification of key trading partners, the development of supply chain strategies, aligning the strategies with key process objectives, developing internal process performance measures, internally integrating these key processes, developing external supply chain performance measures for each process, externally integrating key processes with supply chain partners, extending process integration to second-tier supply chain participants and then, finally, re-evaluating the integration model periodically. Each of the elements in the model is discussed next.

Identify Critical Supply Chain Trading Partners

For each of the focal firm's products and services, it is important to identify the critical or **key trading partners** that will eventually enable the successful sale and delivery of end products to the final customers. Over time, companies identify these trading partners through successful business dealings—suppliers that have come to be trusted and that provide a large share of the firm's critical products and services; and repeat, satisfied customers that buy a significant portion of the firm's products. As the focal firm moves out to second- and third-tier suppliers and customers, trading partner numbers increase quite dramatically, which can greatly complicate integration efforts. Identifying only the first-tier primary trading partners allows the firm to concentrate its time and resources on managing important process links with these companies, enabling the larger supply chain to perform better. Including nonessential or supporting businesses will prove counterproductive in terms of successful supply chain management. In a landmark supply chain paper by Lambert, Cooper and Pagh, they define primary or key trading partners as "all those autonomous companies or strategic business units who actually perform operational and/or managerial activities in the business processes designed to produce a specific output for a particular customer or market."[4]

Depending on where within a supply chain the focal firm is physically located (close to its key suppliers, close to end-product customers or somewhere in between), the structure of the network of primary trading partners will vary. Mapping the network of primary trading partners is something that should be done to help the firm decide which

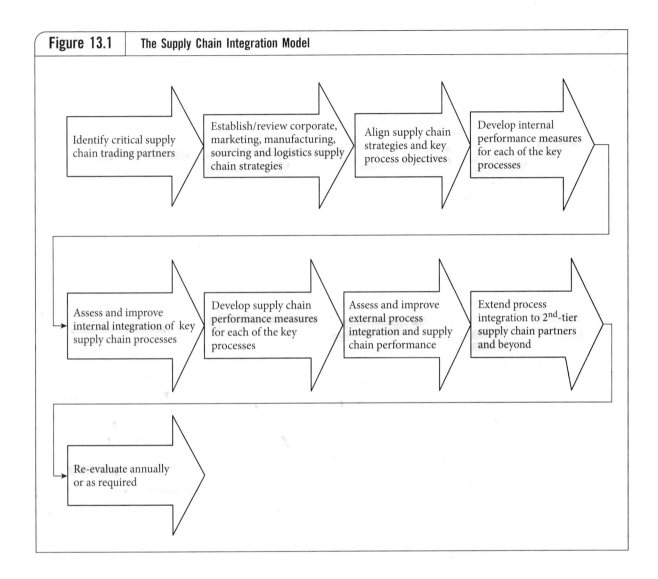

Figure 13.1 | The Supply Chain Integration Model

businesses to include in their supply chain management efforts. For instance, a firm with many key suppliers and customers will most likely limit the number of integrative processes the firm can successfully manage, leading to fewer second-tier relationships. Coordinating processes with its key suppliers was seen as so important to IBM, for example, that in 2006 it moved its global procurement headquarters to Shenzhen, China from the U.S.[5]

Review and Establish Supply Chain Strategies

On an annual basis, management should identify the basic supply chain strategies associated with each of their firm's products and services. If an end product is competing based on quality, then supply chain members should also be using strategies consistent with delivering high quality products at competitive price and service levels. Product strategies should then translate into internal functional policies regarding the types of parts purchased and suppliers used, the manufacturing processes employed, the designs of the products manufactured, the warranty and return services offered and potentially the amount of outsourcing employed. In each of these areas, policies should be geared toward supporting the overall strategy of the supply chain (in this case, high quality).

Similarly, if end products are competing based on sustainability, then strategies and functional policies among each of the supply chain participants must be consistently aimed at achieving favorable environmental impacts or carbon footprints as intermediate products and services are purchased, produced and moved along the supply chain. Supply chain sustainability has become an important issue today as organizations seek better ways to compete. In 2009, for example, Wal-Mart announced plans to initiate a Sustainable Product Index. Their suppliers will be asked to complete a self-assessment that will then become part of a global database of information about product sustainability that will be used to rate products so customers can make better purchase choices. The index will thus create a large incentive among Wal-Mart suppliers to become more aware of the environmental and social impacts of their products.[6]

Align Supply Chain Strategies with Key Supply Chain Process Objectives

Once the primary strategy has been identified for each of the supply chain end products, managers need to identify the important processes linking each of the supply chain partners and establish process objectives to assure that resources and efforts are effectively deployed within each firm, to support the end-product strategy. The key processes and the methods used to integrate and manage process links among supply chain partners will vary based on the internal structure of each firm, the prevailing economic conditions in the marketplace, the degree that **functional silos** exist in any of the trading partners and the nature of existing relationships within the supply chain. In some cases, it may be best to integrate only one key process with one trading partner, while with other partners, more processes would be integrated.

Based on the research of Lambert, Cooper and Pagh, eight processes have been identified as important supply chain business processes. A process can be defined as a set of activities designed to produce a product or service for an internal or external customer. These **key supply chain processes** are shown in Table 13.1. A discussion of each of these processes follows.

Customer Relationship Management

The **customer relationship management process** provides the firm with the structure for developing and managing customer relationships. As discussed in Chapter 10, key customers are identified, their needs are determined and then products and services are developed to meet their needs. Over time, relationships with these key customers are solidified through the sharing of information; the formation of cross-company teams to improve product design, delivery, quality and cost; the development of shared goals; and, finally, improved performance and profitability for the trading partners along with agreements on how to share these benefits. The firm should monitor the impact of customer relationship management efforts in terms of both the financial impact of these efforts and customer satisfaction.

Customer Service Management

The **customer service management process** is what imparts information to customers while also providing ongoing management of any product and service agreements between the firm and its customers. Information can be offered through a number of communication channels including websites, personal interactions, information system linkages and printed media. Objectives and policies are developed to assure proper

Table 13.1	The Eight Key Supply Chain Business Processes[7]
PROCESS	**DESCRIPTION**
Customer Relationship Management	Identifying key customer segments, tailoring product and service agreements to meet their needs, measuring customer profitability and firm's impact on customers.
Customer Service Management	Providing information to customers such as product availability, shipping dates and order status; and administering product and service agreements.
Demand Management	Balancing customer demand with the firm's output capacity; forecasting demand and coordinating with production, purchasing and distribution.
Order Fulfillment	Meeting customer requirements by synchronizing the firm's marketing, production and distribution plans.
Manufacturing Flow Management	Determining manufacturing process requirements to enable the right mix of flexibility and velocity to satisfy demand.
Supplier Relationship Management	Managing product and service agreements with suppliers; developing close working relationships with key suppliers.
Product Development and Commercialization	Developing new products frequently and getting them to market effectively; integrating suppliers and customers into the process to reduce time to market.
Returns Management	Managing used product disposition, product recalls, packaging requirements; and minimizing future returns.

distribution of products and services to customers, to adequately respond to product and delivery failures and complaints and to utilize the most effective means of communication to coordinate successful product, service and information deliveries. The process also includes methods for monitoring and reporting customer service performance, allowing firms to understand the extent that their management efforts are achieving the process objectives. In Auburn University's 2009 State of the Retail Supply Chain study, executives from over 40 retailers thought the primary challenges today for retail supply chains were decreasing costs while improving customer service. To accomplish this, most of the retailers were trying to take innovative approaches to managing their supply chains—they were trying to improve workforce quality, break down internal and external silos, creating more flexible capacities and strengthening their distribution networks.[8]

Demand Management

The **demand management process** is what balances customer demand and the firm's output capabilities. The specific demand management activities include forecasting demand and then utilizing techniques to vary capacity and demand within the purchasing, production and distribution functions. Various forecasts can be used, based on the time frame, the knowledge of the forecaster, the ability to obtain point of sale information from customers and the use of forecasting models contained in many ERP systems. The next step is to determine how to synchronize demand and productive capacity. As discussed in Chapters 5, 6 and 12, a number of effective techniques exist to smooth demand variabilities and increase or decrease capacity when disparities exist between demand and supply. Contingency plans must also be ready for use when demand management techniques fail or when forecasts are inaccurate. Performance measurement systems can prove quite useful here to increase the accuracy of forecasts and to track the success of various demand management activity implementations. After a terrible explosion at a Georgia-based Imperial Sugar refinery destroyed 60 percent of the plant's capacity in 2008, Imperial Sugar was able to rely on its demand management software to show everyone from production to sales, in real time, what could be delivered to which customers, using available inventories. "It was our saving grace," says CIO George Muller.[9]

Order Fulfillment

The **order fulfillment process** is the set of activities that allows the firm to fill customer orders while providing the required levels of customer service at the lowest possible delivered cost. Thus, the order fulfillment process must integrate the firm's marketing, production and distribution plans to be effective. More specifically, the firm's distribution system must be designed to provide adequate customer service levels and their production system must be designed to produce at the required output levels, while marketing plans and promotions must consider the firm's output and distribution capabilities. Related order fulfillment issues are the location of suppliers, the modes of inbound and outbound transportation used, the location of production facilities and distribution centers and the system used for entering, processing, communicating, picking, delivering and documenting customer orders. The order fulfillment process must integrate closely with customer relationship management, customer service management, supplier relationship management and returns management to assure that customer requirements are being met, customer service levels are being maintained, suppliers are helping to minimize order cycle times and customers are getting undamaged, high-quality products.

Manufacturing Flow Management

The **manufacturing flow management process** is the set of activities responsible for making the actual product, establishing the manufacturing flexibility required to adequately serve the markets and designing the production system to meet cycle-time requirements. To be effective, manufacturing flow management activities must be interfaced with the demand management and customer relationship management processes, using customer requirements as inputs to the process. As customers and their requirements change, so too must the supply chain and the manufacturing flow process change to maintain the firm's competitiveness. As was shown in Chapter 8, the flexibility and rapid response requirements in many supply chains result in the firm's use of lean systems in order to continue to meet customer requirements.

Manufacturing flow characteristics also impact supplier requirements. For instance, as manufacturing batch sizes and lead time requirements are reduced, supplier deliveries must become smaller and more frequent, causing supplier interactions and supplier relationships to potentially change. The importance of an adequate material planning system should become evident here, as customer requirements must be translated into production capabilities and supplier requirements. As with other processes, a good set of performance metrics should also be utilized to track the capability of the manufacturing flow process to satisfy demand.

Supplier Relationship Management

The **supplier relationship management process** defines how the firm manages its relationships with suppliers. As was discussed in Chapters 2, 3 and 4 of this textbook, firms in actively managed supply chains seek out small numbers of the best-performing suppliers and establish ongoing, mutually beneficial, close relationships with these suppliers in order to meet cost, quality and/or customer service objectives for key materials, products and services. For other nonessential items, firms may use reverse auctions, bid arrangements or catalogues to select suppliers. Activities in this process include screening and selecting suppliers, negotiating product and service agreements, managing suppliers and then monitoring supplier performance and improvement. Some companies may have a cross-functional team to manage suppliers' progress toward meeting the firm's current and long-term requirements and establishing records of performance improvement over time, while other suppliers may be managed little or not at all, depending on supply chain, company or product requirements. Supplier relationship management personnel routinely communicate with production personnel to obtain feedback on supplier and purchased item performance and with marketing personnel for customer feedback. Additionally, suppliers are frequently contacted for new product development and performance feedback purposes.

Product Development and Commercialization

The **product development and commercialization process** entails developing new products to meet changing customer requirements and then getting these products to market quickly and efficiently. In actively managed supply chains, customers and suppliers are involved in the new product development process to assure that products conform to customers' needs and purchased items meet manufacturing requirements. Activities in the product development and commercialization process include methods and incentives for generating new product ideas; the development of customer feedback mechanisms; the formation of new product development teams; assessing and selecting new product ideas based on financial impact, resource requirements and fit with existing manufacturing and logistics infrastructure; designing and testing new product prototypes; determining marketing channels and rolling out the products; and, finally, assessing the success of each new product. Successful new product development hinges on the involvement of external customers and suppliers and of internal manufacturing, marketing and finance personnel.

Returns Management

The **returns management process** discussed in Chapter 9, can be extremely beneficial for supply chain management in terms of maintaining acceptable levels of customer service and identifying product improvement opportunities. Returns management activities include environmental compliance with substance disposal and recycling, composing operating and repair instructions, troubleshooting and warranty repairs, developing disposition guidelines, designing an effective reverse logistics process and collecting returns data. Returns management personnel frequently communicate with customers and personnel from customer relationship management, product development and commercialization and supplier relationship management during the returns process.

One of the goals of returns management is to reduce returns. This is accomplished by communicating return and repair information to product development personnel, suppliers and other potential contributors to any returns problems, to guide the improvement of future product and purchased item designs. Logistics services may also be included in the returns feedback communication loop.

Gaining momentum in recent years is the idea that sometimes it is best to recycle an item instead of incurring the cost of returning it to the manufacturer. Companies like NYK Logistics operate reverse logistics facilities to sort, test, repair, repackage, part-harvest or recycle returns, which helps to reduce supply costs.[10]

For each of the eight processes identified above, objectives or goals must be developed to help guide the firm toward their supply chain strategy. Additionally, consistent objectives within each functional area of the firm, for each process, help to integrate the processes internally, as well as focus efforts and firm resources on the supply chain strategy.

For instance, if the supply chain strategy is to compete using low pricing, marketing objectives for the customer relationship management process might be to find cheaper delivery alternatives, develop vendor managed inventory (VMI) accounts and automate the customer order process. Production objectives might be to develop bulk packaging solutions consistent with the modes of transportation and distribution systems used, to increase mass production capabilities and to identify the lowest total cost manufacturing sites for specific products, while purchasing objectives might be to identify the cheapest materials and components that meet specifications and to utilize reverse auctions whenever possible. Firms should similarly progress through each of the key processes using teams of employees from each function to develop process objectives.

Develop Internal Performance Measures for Key Process Effectiveness

As alluded to in each of the key processes above (and to be discussed at greater length in Chapter 14), procedures and metrics must be in place to collect and report internal performance data for the eight key processes. Thus, prior to measuring and comparing performance with their supply chain partners, firms must first build good internal performance measurement capabilities across functions. This can prove troublesome given that in a 2006 survey of Canadian manufacturing firms, only about 50 percent were found to have reasonably well-developed performance measurement systems and a study of e-businesses in 2009 had similar findings.[11] Performance measures need to create a consistent emphasis on the overall supply chain strategy and corresponding process objectives. In order to assure that processes are supporting the supply chain strategy, performance should be continuously measured using a set of metrics designed for each process.

Continuing the discussion from the previous section where competing based on low pricing was the supply chain strategy, performance measures for the customer relationship management process would need to be designed for each of the firm's functional areas. The responsibility for designing these measures can also be assigned to the team developing objectives for each of the functional areas. Since the objectives in this case are cost driven, the performance measures should reflect this as well. For the customer relationship management process, performance measures in marketing might be the average delivery cost, the number of new VMI accounts, the average cost of ordering and carrying inventories for the new VMI accounts and the number of new automated order systems over the period of time studied. For production, performance measures might be the average packaging cost per order, the average daily output capability for each product and the average unit cost per order. For purchasing, the performance measures for the customer relationship management objectives might be the average purchasing cost for each of the items purchased and the percentage of time that reverse auctions were used over the period of time studied. Performance measures would similarly be designed for each of the key processes and their corresponding functional objectives. In this way, then, firms have the capability to track the progress toward meeting each of their objectives for each of the key processes.

Assess and Improve Internal Integration of Key Supply Chain Processes

Successful supply chain management requires process coordination and collaboration internally between the firm's functional areas as well as externally between the firm and its trading partners. Achieving process integration within the firm requires a transition from the typical functional silos to one of teamwork and cooperation across business functions. Internal integration has been shown to provide significant benefits for the firm. In a survey of 500 U.S. organizations, for instance, interdepartmental relationships were found to result in reduced cycle times and fewer stockouts.[12] To achieve internal integration, personnel must have management support, resources and empowerment to make meaningful organizational changes to foster the type of cooperation necessary to support the overall supply chain strategy. The formation of cross-functional teams to develop the key process objectives and accompanying performance measures is a good starting point in achieving internal process integration. The Global Perspective feature profiles California-based Blue Coat Systems and their experiences with assessing and improving internal integration between marketing and sales.

Global Perspective

Internal Integration at Blue Coat Systems

Global application delivery network technology provider Blue Coat Systems was struggling with the challenges of rapid growth, outdated systems and a lack of alignment between marketing and sales. "As a company with over $500 million in revenue, trying to achieve our first billion, we had a lot of challenges," said Maxine Graham, senior director-global integrated marketing and operations at Blue Coat. "We are in a high-growth phase. We had a lot of legacy stuff to deal with. We have a global sales force. Our problem was that 'moment of truth' when we realized that sales and marketing were using the same data, but reporting different results," she added.

She listed some of the problems: Marketing and sales data resided in multiple systems and required complex custom reporting; marketing and sales had different definitions for the same terms; and the systems and processes were very North America-centered. After realizing these deficiencies, sales and marketing decided to launch a joint initiative to more closely align the two functions and build common systems and processes, as well as manage and nurture leads.

The goals of the project were to ensure data integrity; build closed-loop systems to track leads from start to finish; develop tighter data integration between sales and marketing automation systems; and establish common definitions, terminology and business processes within sales and marketing. "It was a joint effort between marketing, sales and marketing operations," Graham said. The teams working on the project included marketing and sales operations, field marketing, channel marketing, inside sales, tech reps from sales and marketing automation platforms and executive sponsorship from senior marketing and sales management.

Peter Johnson, senior manager of marketing operations at Blue Coat, said the first step in the process was an internal audit and "gap analysis" of all existing systems and processes within sales and marketing. "First, we needed to understand where we were," he said. The audit included a comprehensive review of Blue Coat's sales force automation and marketing automation platforms; metrics and reporting processes; data integration issues; campaign management; and lead-scoring processes. The company also looked at industry best practices.

The next phase included creating standard terminology between sales and marketing; defining data requirements; developing new business processes (such as getting as much information from sales as possible without asking them to do too much work to provide it); and implementing consistent global reporting systems.

Next, Blue Coat put into place new systems and processes, including data cleansing, a lead-scoring update, a centralized lead-routing structure, shared dashboards for marketing and sales and training for the sales teams. Finally, it monitored, measured and refined the systems. "You have to make a tremendous amount of compromises when you are going through this process," Johnson said. "From the sales operations view, it was a joint project; it was 'socialized' and it was agreed to," he added.

Since implementing the new system, Blue Coat has seen dramatic results. "Now we have lead status reporting - we know what stage a lead is in and who owns it. We have closed-loop metrics from lead to acquisition. We know how many deals are influenced by marketing or sales," Graham said. Pointing to some of the key results, she said marketing-qualified lead conversions were up 108 percent; marketing contribution to the pipeline was up 68 percent; marketing contribution to wins was up 73 percent; and leads to the channel were up 34 percent.

Source: Maddox, K., "Blue Coat Systems Gets Results with Marketing/Sales Integration," *B to B*, V. 95, No. 6 (2010): 7. Used with permission.

The primary enabler of integration, though, is the firm's ERP system. In Chapter 6, the importance and capabilities of ERP systems were described, along with some of the various software applications or modules that are used today. ERP systems provide a view of the entire organization, enabling decision makers within each function to have information regarding customer orders, production plans, work-in-process and finished goods inventory levels, outbound goods in-transit, purchase orders, inbound goods in-transit, purchased item inventories and financial and accounting information. ERP systems thus link business processes and facilitate communication and information sharing between the firm's departments. Since the key business processes overlay each of the functional areas, the firm eventually becomes process oriented rather than functionally oriented as ERP systems are deployed. It is this visibility of information across the organization that allows processes to become integrated within the firm.

To assess the current state of internal integration, firms should first develop an understanding of their **internal supply chains**. Internal supply chains can be complex, particularly if firms have multiple divisions and global organizational structures. Thus, firms should assess the makeup of the teams used in setting process objectives and performance measures—do they include representatives from each of the organization's divisions or business units? These cross-functional teams should adequately represent the firm's internal supply chain.

Once the firm has an understanding of their internal supply chain, they can begin to assess the level of information access across functional boundaries. Does the firm have a single company-wide ERP system linking the functional areas? Are all of the firm's **legacy systems** linked to the ERP system? How easy is it to extract the information needed to make effective decisions? Are centralized **data warehouses** being used to collect data from the various divisions of the firm? Firms that are successfully integrating key business processes are using global ERP systems and data warehouses to make better, informed decisions. Data warehouses store information collected from ERP and legacy systems in one location, such that users can extract information as needed, analyze it and use it to make decisions.

A globally linked ERP system allows the firm to use a common database from which to make product, customer and supplier decisions. Information is captured once, reducing data input errors; information is available in real time, eliminating delays throughout the organization as information is shared; and, finally, information is visible throughout the organization—all transactions taking place can be seen and accessed by everyone on the system. As the firm moves away from legacy systems and toward a fully integrated ERP system, as organization-wide cross-functional teams are created to link key processes to the supply chain strategy and as process performance is monitored and improved, the firm will become more focused on managing the key supply chain processes in an integrated fashion.

Develop Supply Chain Performance Measures for the Key Processes

As was described earlier for internal performance measures, the firm should also develop external performance measures to monitor the links with trading partners regarding the key supply chain processes. And, as with the creation of internal performance measures, teams composed of members from primary trading partners should be created to design these measures to be consistent with overall supply chain strategies.

Continuing with the low-cost supply chain strategy example, trading partners should monitor a number of cost-oriented measures that are averaged across the member firms for each of the key supply chain processes. For the customer relationship management process, examples might include the average delivery cost, rush order cost, VMI carrying cost, finished-goods safety stock costs, returned order costs and spoilage costs. Inbound and outbound logistics costs, in particular, have come under much greater scrutiny over the past few years, because of the rising fuel costs. From 2005 to 2010, for example, gasoline prices increased by more than 50 percent in the U.S.[13] Fuel prices have thus placed increased pressure on trading partners to find cheaper ways to transport goods in a timely fashion and this can be particularly problematic for supply chains following a low-cost strategy. External performance measures should align with internal performance measures, but may vary based on purchasing, production, distribution, customer service and other variations across the participating firms. The topic of external performance measures is discussed further in Chapter 14.

Assess and Improve External Process Integration and Supply Chain Performance

Over time, firms eliminate poor-performing suppliers as well as unprofitable customers while concentrating efforts on developing beneficial relationships and strategic alliances with their remaining suppliers and customers. Building, maintaining and strengthening these relationships is accomplished through use of external process integration. As process integration improves among supply chain partners, so too does supply chain performance. When firms have achieved a reasonably good measure of internal process integration, they are ready to move on to externally integrating key supply chain processes with trading partners.

Supply chain members must be willing to share sales and forecast information, along with information on new products, expansion plans, new processes and new marketing campaigns in order to ultimately satisfy end customers and maximize profits for the entire supply chain membership. Focusing on process integration will enable firms to collaborate and share this information. Again, as with internal process integration, the teams formed to design and organize process performance measures should be viewed as a key resource for external process integration. These teams can set and revise supply chain process objectives and the type of information that must be shared to achieve the objectives. Once the performance metrics are designed for each of the processes, they can be monitored to identify lack of process integration and supply chain competitive weaknesses. Firms should thus periodically, jointly assess their levels of process performance and integration and collaborate on methods to improve both.

Once again, the way information is communicated plays an extremely important role in external process integration. Today, connecting buyers and suppliers via the Internet is the way supply chains are becoming integrated. More generally termed **knowledge-management solutions**, Internet applications tied to desktop applications enable real-time collaboration and flow of information between supply chain partners, the ability to "see" into suppliers' and customers' operations, faster decision making and the collection of supply chain performance metrics. "Today's competitive landscape is defined by companies that are best-in-class in managing their extended end-to-end supply chain," says Lorenzo Martinelli, executive vice-president of E2Open, a California-based provider of supply chain management software.[14]

Supply chain communication and Internet technologies have a number of issues to deal with including handling the flows of goods and information between companies, negotiation and execution of contracts, managing supply and demand problems, making and executing orders and handling financial settlements, all with a high level of security. California-based home textile retailer Anna's Linens uses an Internet portal solution to communicate with over 100 of its key vendors and distributors. The system has enabled Anna's to make opportunistic purchases from other retail closures and immediately interpret global trends using real-time visibility within its supply chain. "Now even our non-EDI capable vendors can accept orders, process orders, print labels and even invoice us electronically," says Miles Tedder, vice-president of supply chain for Anna's.[15]

Extend Process Integration to Second-Tier Supply Chain Partners

As supply chain relationships become more trusting and mature and as the supply chain software used to link supply chain partners' information systems evolves and becomes widely used and relied upon, the tendency will be to integrate processes to second-tier partners and beyond. Today, supply chain software suppliers are developing systems that integrate more easily with other applications, allowing trading partners to exchange ever more complex or detailed information on contracts, product designs, forecasts, sales, purchases and inventories. Using these linkages, companies can, in real time, work with suppliers and customers to compare design ideas, forecasts and order commitments, determine supply/demand mismatches and analyze supplier performance.

Every major software developer today is trying to make its supply chain tools easier to integrate with existing systems and gather data anywhere along a firm's supply chain. One development is the **radio-frequency identification tag (RFID)**, discussed in Chapters 7 and 9. These microchip devices can be attached to pallets or cases to relay information on the products' whereabouts as they move through the supply chain. Thus, a firm's supply chain system can access real-time inventory information and instigate a replenishment order as inventories are drawn down.

The prices of RFID tags vary greatly depending on whether they are *active* or *passive*. **Passive RFID tags** don't contain a power source, require power from a tag reader and cost from $0.07 to $0.15 each, depending on volume, packaging and how the tag is made.

Active RFID tags draw power from an internal battery and are priced in the $20 to $70 range depending on volume required and battery type. Both are finding applications. The passive variety are the ones placed on pallets, cases and even units of product and are used in many warehousing environments; today they are being used by suppliers complying with Wal-Mart's requirement of RFID tags on shipments. The much more costly active tags are being used, for example, to track the whereabouts of expensive equipment or for identification of fleet vehicles in and out of a facility. The U.S. Marines, for example, also use active tags to track container loads on international shipments. The Marines' vision is to have tags talk directly to logistics databases via network access points that will then communicate information to other locations via satellite.[16]

Prior to the development of these supply chain applications, integrating processes beyond first-tier suppliers and customers was somewhat more difficult and time-consuming. As discussed in Chapter 4, firms can develop relationships with their second-tier suppliers and then insist that their direct suppliers use these suppliers. They can also work closely with their key direct suppliers to solve second-tier supplier problems and help them, in turn, to better manage their direct suppliers. To stay on the competitive edge, firms today must use a combination of information system linkages and old-fashioned customer and supplier teamwork to identify and manage second-tier relationships along the supply chain.

Re-evaluate the Integration Model Annually

In light of the dramatic and fast-paced changes occurring with the development of supply chain communication technologies and the frequent changes occurring with new products, new suppliers and new markets, trading partners should revisit their integration model annually to identify changes within their supply chains and to assess the impact these changes are having on integration efforts. New suppliers may have entered the scene with better capabilities, more distribution choices and better resources. Or perhaps the firm may be redesigning an older product, requiring different purchased components or supplier capabilities. Alternatively, the firm may be moving into a new foreign market, potentially requiring an entirely different supply chain. These examples are common and should cause firms to reevaluate their supply chain strategies, objectives, processes, performance measures and integration levels. Computer maker Dell, for example, is switching to use of additional ocean shipping in their supply chains to reduce logistics costs. Currently, Dell's highly regarded supply chain strategy has been to use costly air shipments to enable deliveries of customized computers within days of customer orders. They are shifting now to greater use of retail distribution, requiring more of a forecasting and make-to-stock supply chain, which ultimately will dramatically change their supply chain network and logistics partners. "We will limit the number of configuration choices where appropriate and move more of our products to a low-touch, fixed-configuration [ocean] ship model," explains Dell CFO Brian Gladden.[17]

Obstacles To Process Integration Along The Supply Chain

A number of factors can impede external process integration along the supply chain, causing loss of visibility, information distortion, longer cycle times, stockouts and the bullwhip effect, resulting in higher overall costs and reduced customer service capabilities. Managers must try to identify these obstacles and take steps to eliminate them, resulting in improved profitability and competitiveness for the supply chain's members. Table 13.2 summarizes these obstacles. Each of these is discussed next.

The Silo Mentality

Too often, firms do not consider the impact of their actions on their supply chains and long-term competitiveness and profitability. An "I win, you lose" **silo mentality** can be evidenced when using the cheapest (or hungriest) suppliers, paying little attention to the needs of customers and assigning few resources to new product and service design. Particularly with firms involved in global supply chains, silo mentalities can crop up as a result of cultural differences. The U.K. auto firm Rover is a case in point. In the 1980s, Rover formed a partnership with Japan-based Honda to provide products for its new model program. The arrogance of Rover managers and a lack of a learning culture at Rover prevented them from realizing any benefits from the partnership. Later, when the German firm BMW bought Rover, communications with German managers and political infighting were even worse. The managerial problems that surfaced with Chrysler and Daimler-Benz, leading to dissolution of that partnership, were similar.[18]

Eventually, lack of internal or external collaboration will create quality, cost, delivery timing and other customer service problems that are detrimental to supply chains. In fact, Mr. Wayne Bourne, vice president of logistics and transportation at electronics retailer Best Buy, noted in an interview that the most significant obstacle to overcome in supply chain management was the silo mentality that exists in companies.[19]

Internally, the silo effect might be found between personnel of different departments. The transportation manager, for instance, may be trying to minimize total annual transportation costs against the wishes of the firm's sales department. Delivery inconsistencies caused by use of the cheapest transportation providers might be causing the firm's

Table 13.2	Obstacles to Supply Chain Integration
OBSTACLE	**DESCRIPTION**
Silo mentality	Failing to see the big picture and acting only in regard to a single department within the firm or a single firm within the supply chain.
Lack of supply chain visibility	The inability to easily share or retrieve trading partner information in real time, as desired by the supply chain participants.
Lack of trust	Unwillingness to work together or share information because of the fear that the other party will take advantage of them or use the information unethically.
Lack of knowledge	Lack of process and information system skills and lack of knowledge regarding the benefits of SCM among management and other employees, within the firm and among partners.
Activities causing the bullwhip effect:	
Demand forecast updating	Using varying customer orders to create and update forecasts, production schedules and purchase requirements.
Order batching	Making large orders for goods from suppliers on an infrequent basis to reduce order and transportation costs.
Price fluctuations	Offering price discounts to buyers, causing erratic buying patterns.
Rationing and shortage gaming	Allocating short product supplies to buyers, causing buyers to increase future orders beyond what they really need.

customers to hold extra safety stocks to manage the delivery inconsistencies and potentially leading to shortages and deteriorating customer service levels.

To overcome these and other silo mentalities, firms must strive to align supply chain goals and their own goals and incentives. Functional decisions must be made while considering the impact on the firm's overall profits and those of the supply chain members. Performance reviews of managers should include the ability of their department to integrate processes internally and externally and in meeting overall supply chain goals. Outside the firm, managers must work to educate suppliers and customers regarding the overall impact of their actions on their supply chains and the end customers. This should be an important part of the supply chain partnership creation and management process. Additionally, suppliers should be annually evaluated and potentially replaced if their performance vis-à-vis supply chain objectives does not improve. California-based Sutter Health, a network of physicians, hospitals and other healthcare providers, has long believed integration among all departments is the best and most efficient way to deliver care to patients. In fact, in a study by Dartmouth Medical School's Center for the Evaluative Clinical Sciences, Sutter's physicians, hospitals, home care and hospice services were found to represent a national benchmark.[20]

Lack of Supply Chain Visibility

Lack of **information visibility** along the supply chain is also cited as a common supply chain process integration problem. In global supply chains, information visibility is particularly important. New product safety standards, trade agreements and security mandates are changing almost daily, making information visibility critical for importers and shippers. "Visibility is not just about watching stuff happen," says Melissa Irmen, vice president of products and strategy for North Carolina-based Integration Point, a provider of global trade and regulatory compliance solutions. "Things are changing so fast and to have connectivity to all partners is just critical."[21] In many cases, IT systems are to blame. In a survey of 1,500 pharmaceutical manufacturers, for instance, only one-third thought that their IT systems were providing adequate information visibility, even though most already had spent millions on ERP systems, advanced planning systems and other technologies.[22]

If trading partners have to carve out data from their information systems and then send it to one another where it then has to be uploaded to other systems prior to the data being shared and evaluated, the extra time can mean higher inventories, higher costs, longer response times and lost customers. This is the primary problem that supply chain software producers are working to overcome today. The e-Business Connection feature describes some of Boeing's IT applications and how important they are for keeping track of their suppliers. They, too, have experienced some problems.

e-Business Connection	*Supply Chain Process Integration Is Key to Success at Boeing*

Supply chain execution plays into the intensely competitive tussle for market share taking place between Chicago, Illinois-based Boeing and Toulouse, France-based Airbus. For Boeing, the new 787 Dreamliner aircraft represents a fundamental shift in manufacturing philosophy and approach. Working closely with more than 100 major structural component and systems partners around the world, coordinating the end-to-end supply chain across these various businesses is paramount to the program's success.

It's a capability provided by the Virginia-based Exostar's supply chain management solution and powered by California-based E2open software, which manages the complete order life-cycle and returns process across multiple partner tiers, while also tracking planning schedules and consumption and managing replenishment for Boeing's vendor managed inventory program.

Designed to allow Boeing and its partners to collaborate on planning schedules, issue purchase orders, track purchase order changes, exchange shipping information, manage returns, track shipments and manage inventory consumption across the multiple tiers involved in the manufacturing process, the system also monitors events and process exceptions that occur between partners and evaluates the impact of these events against the master schedule using synchronized, time-sequenced information. "It's crucial that all of the major subassemblies arrive at Boeing for final assembly at the same time," says Lorenzo Martinelli, senior VP at E2open. "If a subassembly is late or missing, there is very little time or space for Boeing to store the other large components. If a partner cannot meet an expected delivery date, then Boeing must adjust the schedule and potentially delay arrival of the other assemblies."

Unfortunately, as any software vendor can tell you, an application can't do all the work for you. Initial assembly instances of the 787 have been plagued by delays in delivery of outsourced work and there have been complaints about lack of transparency into outsourced operations. Moreover, Airbus too has been plagued by assembly problems due to poor communication of design changes impacting work at multiple locations. This only demonstrates that as manufacturing operations become more highly distributed, there will be ongoing demand for supply chain execution solutions that deliver visibility and accountability. And with any fundamentally new business process supported by emerging technology infrastructure, achieving productivity benefits is a change-management and human-capital management project that can be of significant duration.

Source: Wheatley, M., "Supply Chain Execution Proves a Rich Niche for Best-of-Breed Solutions," *Manufacturing Business Technology* 26(5), 2008: 20. Used with permission.

Most of the visibility software applications available allow users to share data among third-party business applications having advanced event management and process integration capabilities. Keeping track of cargo containers for ocean carriers is one such area where supply chain visibility is creating big improvements for the parties involved. For every 100 incoming containers at ports, for instance, only about 45 go out loaded, leaving revenue-generating backhauls on the table. Better supply chain visibility in this case can lead to a better match of loads and containers. International Asset Systems and Trinium Technologies have started a joint venture to create a shipping container data hub linking shipment data from inbound and outbound truckers and ocean carriers, to increase backhaul opportunities.[23]

As businesses expand their supply chains to accommodate foreign suppliers and markets and as outsourcing of manufacturing and logistics services continues, the need to discover tools that extend real-time information to trading partners increases. "It's not good enough to just take the order," says Beth Enslow of Massachusetts-based research company Aberdeen Group. "Now you have to provide a continuous stream of information about its status, feasibility and total cost to customers and partners throughout the world. You don't want customers receiving unexpected transportation expenses or delays in shipments—or worse, receiving them without you knowing about it."[24]

RFID technology can add tremendous real-time information visibility capabilities to supply chains. Users can determine the exact location of any product, anywhere in a supply chain, at any time. Further, RFID tags can capture more accurate, specific and timely data than barcodes, while reducing or eliminating data collection labor time and errors. An RFID tag attached to an automobile seat or engine, for example, can be used to gather and exchange work-in-process data. When a shipment of roses drops below a safe temperature, an RFID system can alert packers to pull those cartons and send them to a closer destination. When a thief tries to break into a shipping container, an RFID-controlled monitor can send an alert to every supply chain partner who needs the information. These are all applications of RFID technology. "When you have bad data, you make bad decisions," says Kaushal Vyas, director of product development at Georgia-based Infor, a business software provider. "You must be able to source and mine data from all the different places in real time, so you can focus on the exceptions that you need to manage in order to boost your performance."[25]

Cloud-based supply chain management is also becoming a reality, as companies seek better ways to outsource manufacturing and services while maintaining necessary information visibility. With high-tech manufacturing, for example, managers want as much information visibility as they can get to reduce risk. Cloud-based supply chain solutions give these managers the ability to quickly scale and compete as the global economy recovers, as well as the ability to automate processes and manage exceptions more effectively. "A typical cloud supply chain already has all of the infrastructure in place," says Mark Woodward, CEO of California-based cloud supply chain provider E2open. "In our case, we have 50,000 suppliers and trading partners already in our network, so when a client comes to us, we are able to connect them to a rich community of partners almost instantaneously." Web portals of the cloud-based supply chains allow trading partners to exchange information and collaborate on a day-to-day basis.[26]

Lack of Trust

Successful process integration between trading partners requires trust and as with the silo mentality and lack of information visibility, the lack of trust is seen as a major stumbling block in supply chain management. Trust develops over time between supply chain trading partners, as each participant follows through on promises made to the other businesses. Even though this sounds cliché, relationships employing trust result in a win-win or win-win-win, situation for the participants. Boeing's 787 Dreamliner, which debuted in July 2007, was the most successful airline launch ever—it resulted in orders for 710 airplanes from 50 companies. Playing a central role in the success of this airliner were Boeing's 70 supplier-partners, who were supplying close to 70 percent of the airplane's parts and assemblies. The trust underlying the partnerships was clearly evident in the fact that Boeing also relied on these suppliers to perform detailed engineering and testing of many of the components supplied for the airliner.[27]

Unfortunately, old-fashioned company practices and purchasing habits don't change overnight. Until managers understand that it is in their firms' best interests to trust each other and collaborate, supply chain management will be an uphill battle. Organizations like the medical treatment innovator Mayo Clinic build a collaborative culture by hiring professionals with collaborative attitudes and a common set of deeply held values regarding care for patients. At computing giant IBM, CEO Sam Palmisano transformed an extremely hierarchical culture based on individualism to one of collaboration by organizing online, town hall-type meetings involving tens of thousands of IBM employees and dozens of trading partners. Collaborative projects are resulting from these meetings. IBM reinforces collaboration with "thanks awards," which are t-shirts, backpacks and other similar gear, emblazoned with the IBM logo and given by IBM employees.[28]

While reciprocal sharing of information among supply chain partners is growing in acceptance, many companies still have a long way to go. "We are early in the cycle, maybe in the second inning," says David Smith, head of human performance practice at Accenture, a global technology services consulting firm. "Companies are beginning to attack it. Very few are getting it right." As a matter of fact, in a 2006 Accenture global survey of 250 executives, 42 percent said knowledge capture and sharing was a significant to severe challenge.[29]

© 2009 Ted Goff

"Just because I was wrong every single time in the past doesn't mean you should gamble with ignoring me now."

Some useful advice for creating collaboration and trust is summed up nicely in an article appearing in *CIO* magazine, a business journal for IT and other business executives. They recommended six ways of "getting to yes:"[30]

1. *Start small*—Begin by collaborating on a small scale. Pick a project that is likely to provide a quick return on investment for both sides. Once you can show the benefits of trust and collaboration, then move to larger projects.

2. *Look inward*—The necessary precondition for establishing trust with outside partners is establishing trust with internal constituents. Break down the barriers to internal communication and integration.

3. *Gather 'round*—The best way to build trust is to meet face-to-face, around a table. Listen to objections, find out the agendas and spring for lunch. Then do it all over again, as people leave and as management changes.

4. *Go for the win-win*—Collaboration is a new way of doing business, where the biggest companies don't bully their partners, but instead help create an environment that optimizes business for all supply chain members.

5. *Don't give away the store*—No one has to share all of their information. Some information should remain proprietary. The simple exchange of demand, purchase and forecast information goes a long way.

6. *Just do it*—One of the best ways to build trust is to simply start sharing information. If all goes well, success breeds trust, allowing partners to progress to bigger things.

Lack of Knowledge

Companies have been slowly moving toward collaboration and process integration for years and it is just within the past few years that technology has caught up with this vision, enabling process integration across extended supply chains. Getting a network of firms and their employees to work together successfully, though, requires managers to use subtle persuasion and education to get their own firms and their trading partners to do the right things. The cultural, trust and process knowledge differences in firms are such that firms successfully managing their supply chains must spend significant time influencing and increasing the capabilities of their own employees as well as those of their trading partners.

Training of supply chain partner employees is also known as **collaborative education** and can result in more successful supply chains and higher partner returns. As technologies change, as outsourcing increases and as supply chains are expanded to foreign sources and markets, the pressure to extend software and management training to trading partners increases. As Rick Behrens, senior manager of supplier development at Boeing Company's Integrated Defense Systems unit, explains, "We look at our suppliers as an extension of Boeing. So since we invest heavily in training and education of our employees, why wouldn't we invest in education and development for our suppliers?" Farm and construction equipment manufacturer John Deere, for example, has established a global learning and development center specifically for training its key suppliers.[31]

Change and information sharing can be threatening to people; they may fear losing control or losing their job, particularly if outsourcing accompanies process integration. Additionally, as firms construct their supply chain information infrastructure, they may find themselves with multiple ERP systems, a mainframe manufacturing application and desktop analysis and design software, that all need to be integrated both internally and externally. Thus, firms must realize that people using the systems must be involved early on in terms of the purchase decision, the implementation process and training.

For all organizations, successful supply chain management requires a regimen of ongoing training. When education and training are curtailed, innovation cannot occur and innovation fuels supply chain competitiveness. Poor decision making and other human errors can have a rippling effect in supply chains, causing loss of confidence and trust and a magnification of the error and correction cost as it moves through the supply chain. Industry trade shows, conferences and expos like the Sensors Expo and Conference, the Symposium on Purchasing and Supply Chain Management or the U Connect Conference can also be valuable sources of learning, exchanging ideas and gathering new information about supply chain management.[32]

Activities Causing the Bullwhip Effect

As discussed in Chapter 1 of this textbook, the **bullwhip effect** can be a pervasive and expensive problem along the supply chain and is caused by a number of factors that supply chain members can control. Recall that even though end item demand may be relatively constant, forecasts of trading partner demand, additions of safety stock and the corresponding orders to suppliers as we move up the supply chain become amplified, causing what is termed the bullwhip effect. These amplified demand levels cause problems with capacity planning, inventory control, workforce and production scheduling and ultimately result in lower levels of customer service, greater overall levels of safety stock and higher total supply chain costs. In an early publication on the bullwhip effect, Dr. Hau Lee and his associates identified four major causes of it. Just recently, Dr. Lee commented that the recent economic downturn has certainly caused a number of bullwhips to again emerge, but that firms could still "tame the bullwhip" with hard work, understanding the causes of demand, gaining visibility and investing in collaboration with partners.[33] The causes of the bullwhip effect and the methods used to counteract it are discussed below.

Demand Forecast Updating

Whenever a buying firm places an order, the supplier uses that information as a predictor of future demand. Based on this information, suppliers update their demand forecasts and the corresponding orders placed with their own suppliers. As lead times grow between orders placed and deliveries, then safety stocks also grow and are included in any orders as they pass up the supply chain. Thus, fluctuations are magnified as orders vary from period to period and as the review periods change, causing frequent **demand forecast updating**. These are major contributors to the bullwhip effect.

One solution to this problem is for the buyer to make their actual demand data available to their suppliers. Better yet, if all point-of-sale data is made available to the upstream tiers of suppliers, all supply chain members can then update their demand forecasts less frequently, using actual demand data. This real demand information also tends to reduce safety stocks among supply chain members, generating even less variability in supply chain orders. Thus, the importance of supply chain information visibility can again be seen.

Using the same forecasting techniques and buying practices also tends to smooth demand variabilities among supply chain members. In many cases, buyers allow some of their suppliers to observe actual demand, create a forecast and determine their resupply schedules—a practice known as **vendor managed inventory** (discussed in Chapters 3 and 4). This practice can generally reduce inventories substantially.

Reducing the length of the supply chain can also lessen the bullwhip effect by reducing the number of occasions where forecasts are calculated and safety stocks are added. Examples of this are Drugstore.com, Amazon.com and other firms that bypass distributors and resellers and sell directly to consumers. Firms can thus see actual end-customer demand, resulting in much more stable and accurate forecasts.

Finally, reducing the lead times from order to delivery will lessen the bullwhip effect. For example, developing just-in-time ordering and delivery capabilities results in smaller, more frequent orders being placed and delivered, more closely matched supply to demand patterns and thus a decreased need for safety stocks.

Order Batching

In a typical buyer–supplier scenario, demand draws down existing inventories until a reorder point is reached wherein the buyer places an order with the supplier. Inventory levels, prior delivery performance and the desire to order full truckloads or container loads of materials may cause orders to be placed at varying time intervals. Thus, the supplier receives an order of some magnitude; then at some indeterminate future time period, another order is received from the buyer, for some quantity potentially much different in size from the prior order. This type of **order batching** amplifies demand variability and adds to the use of safety stock, creating the bullwhip effect.

Another type of order batching can occur when salespeople need to fill end-of-quarter or end-of-year sales quotas or when buyers desire to fully spend budget allocations at the end of their fiscal year. Salespeople may generate production orders to fill future demand and buyers may make excess purchases to spend budget money. These erratic, periodic surges in consumption and production also increase the bullwhip effect. If the timing of these surges is the same for many of the firm's customers, the bullwhip effect can be severe.

As with forecast updating, information visibility and use of more frequent and smaller order sizes will tend to reduce the order batching problem. When suppliers know that large orders are occurring because of the need to spend budgeted monies, for instance, they will not revise forecasts based on this information. Further, when using automated or computer-assisted order systems order costs are reduced, allowing firms to order more frequently. To counteract the need to order full truckloads or container loads of an item, firms can order smaller quantities of a variety of items from a supplier or use a freight forwarder to consolidate small shipments, to avoid the high unit cost of transporting at less-than-truckload or less-than-container load quantities.

Price Fluctuations

When suppliers offer special promotions, quantity discounts or other special pricing discounts, these price fluctuations result in significant **forward buying** activities on the part of buyers, who are stocking up to take advantage of the low price offers. Forward buying occurs between retailers and consumers, between distributors and retailers and between manufacturers and distributors due to pricing promotions at each stage in a supply chain, all contributing to erratic buying patterns, lower forecast accuracies and consequently the bullwhip effect. If these pricing promotions become commonplace, customers will stop buying when prices are undiscounted and buy only when the discount prices are offered, even further contributing to the bullwhip effect. To deal with these surges in demand, manufacturers may have to vary capacity by scheduling overtime and undertime for employees, finding places to store stockpiles of inventory, paying more for transportation and dealing with higher levels of inventory shrinkage as inventories are held for longer periods. ASDA, the fastest-growing grocery and non-food retailer in the U.K., for example, is on pace to overtake Tesco and Sainsbury using an **everyday low pricing (EDLP)** strategy.[34]

The obvious way to reduce the problems caused by fluctuating prices is to eliminate price discounting among the supply chain's members. Manufacturers can reduce forward buying by offering uniform wholesale prices to its customers. Many retailers have adopted this notion of EDLP, while eliminating promotions that cause forward buying. Similarly, buyers can negotiate with their own suppliers to offer EDLP when curtailing promotions.

Rationing and Shortage Gaming

Rationing can occur when demand exceeds a supplier's finished goods available and in this case, the supplier may allocate product in proportion to what buyers ordered. Thus, if the supply of goods is 75 percent of the total demand, buyers would be allocated 75 percent of what they ordered. When buyers figure out the relationship between their orders and what is supplied, they tend to inflate their orders to satisfy their real needs.

This strategy is known as **shortage gaming**. Of course, this further exacerbates the supply problem, as the supplier and, in turn, its suppliers, struggle to keep up with these higher demand levels. When, on the other hand, production capacity eventually equals demand and orders are filled completely, orders suddenly drop to less than normal levels as the buying firms try to unload their excess inventories. This has occurred occasionally in the U.S. and elsewhere around the world—for instance, with gasoline supplies. As soon as consumers think a shortage is looming, demand suddenly increases as people top off their tanks and otherwise try to stockpile gasoline, which itself creates a deeper shortage. When these types of shortages occur due to shortage gaming, suppliers can no longer discern their customers' true demand and this can result in unnecessary additions to production capacity, warehouse space and transportation investments.

One way to eliminate shortage gaming is for sellers to allocate short supplies based on the demand histories of its customers. In that way, customers are essentially not allowed to exaggerate orders. And once again, the sharing of capacity and inventory information between a manufacturer and its customers can also help to eliminate customers' fears regarding shortages and eliminate gaming. Also, sharing future order plans with suppliers allows suppliers to increase capacity if needed, thus avoiding a rationing situation.

Thus, it is seen that a number of rational decisions on the part of buyers and suppliers tend to cause the bullwhip effect. When trading partners use the strategies discussed above to reduce the bullwhip effect, the growth of information sharing, collaboration and process integration occurs along the supply chain. Firms that strive to share data, forecasts, plans and other information can significantly reduce the bullwhip effect.

Managing Supply Chain Risk And Security

As supply chains grow to include more foreign sources and markets, there is a corresponding increase in supply chain disruptions, caused by weather and traffic delays, infrastructural problems, political problems and fears of or actual, unlawful or terrorist-related activities. For example, in just the last few years there have been political upheavals and riots in Thailand, the BP oil well disaster along the U.S. Gulf coastal region, escalating drug wars in Mexico, earthquakes in Chile, China and Haiti, the volcano eruption in Iceland and the Australian wildfire, along with numerous airplane crashes and suicide bombs. Besides the obvious impact on life and limb, these events add elements of greater financial, reputation and customer service risk to global supply chains and the need for enhanced planning, change management and security to mitigate that risk.

So, while lengthening supply chains may have resulted in cheaper labor and material costs, better product quality and greater market coverage, it has also resulted in higher security costs and greater levels of risk, potentially leading to deteriorating profits and customer service levels. Managing risk and security along the supply chain is discussed in detail below.

Managing Supply Chain Risk

In a recent study commissioned by Rhode Island-based commercial insurer Factory Mutual Insurance Co., the three biggest threats facing companies through 2009, according to 500 North American and European company executives, were competition, supply chain disruptions and property-related risks.[35] In yet another study completed in 2006 by global management consulting company Accenture, 73 percent of the responding companies had experienced supply chain disruptions within the past five years and over half had said the impact on customers was moderate to significant. These and other studies point to the fact that as more and more firms penetrate new and emerging markets, **supply chain risk** is increasing. As the global economy emerges from the recent recession, risk management appears to be an even greater concern than ever before to managers. "Clearly, risk mitigation is a high priority for every corporate we speak with. In the U.S., even though the economy may be picking up, this still remains the hot button with virtually all of our clients," says Craig Weeks, managing director of global transaction services at Citibank.[36]

Tom Ridge, the former secretary of Homeland Security in the U.S. and now CEO of risk management consulting firm Ridge Global, says supply chains need to be vetted down to the second, third and fourth tiers. No multinational firm "can afford to let anybody in the supply chain, no matter how far removed, view risk less seriously than it does," he says. The 2010 BP oil disaster in the Gulf of Mexico is a good example. Transocean was the oil rig operator, a supplier for BP in this case. Based on the ongoing finger-pointing in this disaster, Transocean was at least partially responsible for the explosion, rig destruction, worker deaths and oil well blowout. If communication and due diligence can break down as badly as it did between a company and one of its primary direct suppliers, consider the potential financial, reputation and customer service risks posed by the many second- and third-tier suppliers.[37]

A number of steps have been suggested for managing supply chain risk and several good examples exist that highlight successful supply chain risk management. Table 13.3 describes these risk management activities and they are discussed next.

Increase Safety Stocks and Forward Buying

If the firm fears a supply disruption, it may choose to carry some level of safety stock to provide the desired product until a suitable substitute supply source can be found. If the purchased item is readily available from other sources, the desired level of safety stock may be relatively small. On the other hand, if the item is scarce, if the supply disruption is likely to be lengthy or if the firm fears a continued and lengthy price increase, it may decide to purchase large quantities of product, also known as **stockpiling** or **forward buying**. Safety stocks and forward buying should only be viewed as temporary solutions, however, since they can both dramatically increase inventory carrying costs, particularly for firms with large numbers of purchased items.

Table 13.3	Activities Used to Manage Supply Chain Risk[38]
RISK MANAGEMENT ACTIVITY	**DESCRIPTION**
Increase safety stocks and forward buying	Can be costly. A stopgap alternative.
Identify backup suppliers and logistics services	Can create ill will with current partners; requires additional time and relationship building.
Diversify the supply base	Use of suppliers from geographically dispersed markets to minimize the impacts of disruptions.
Utilize a supply chain IT system	Collection and sharing of appropriate information with supply chain partners.
Develop a formal risk management program	Identifies potential disruptions and the appropriate response.

In some cases, though, stockpiling may be viewed as the only short-term solution for managing risk. In 2006, many organizations opted to stockpile the influenza drug Tamiflu to prepare for a potential avian influenza pandemic, since shortages of the drug worldwide had already been experienced. In the U.S., for example, 300 firms along with the government itself had already been engaged in significant stockpiling by the summer of 2006. Since then, supplies of antiviral drugs have increased and the practice of stockpiling has decreased.[39]

Identify Backup Suppliers and Logistics Services

Another very simple strategy for guaranteeing a continuous supply of purchased items and logistics services is to identify suppliers, transportation and warehousing services and other third party services to use in case the preferred supplier or service becomes unavailable. This topic was discussed in relation to the use of sole or single sources in Chapter 2. The disadvantage of this strategy is that it requires additional time to find and qualify sources and to build value-enhancing relationships. Additionally, it may tend to damage existing supplier or logistics provider relationships. The backup source may see limited value in the relationship if they are providing only a small percentage of total demand; their price for the goods or services will likely be higher and the existing firm may view the use of backup companies as a signal that their "piece of the pie" will continue to shrink. Additionally, use of multiple sources may allow proprietary designs or technologies to be copied, creating yet additional risk.

Backup or **emergency sourcing** and multiple sourcing though, may be a sound strategy in specific cases. During the 2002 U.S. West Coast dockworker strikes, airfreight capacity quickly ran out, causing freight rates to skyrocket and firms to be unable to quickly move freight. Companies that had already entered into contracts for emergency airfreight service, though, were able to maintain operations during the port disruptions.[40] Sainsbury's, a U.K. supermarket chain, uses multiple suppliers for the many products they buy as part of their business continuity plan, established in response to events such as the Irish Republican Army's bombing campaigns in the 1990s, the Y2K computer bug, the 2001 fuel shortage and the foot-and-mouth disease outbreaks in the U.K. Additionally, they work closely with key suppliers to assure that they, too, have business continuity plans.[41]

Diversify the Supply Base

Madagascar, one-time provider of half of the world's vanilla supply, saw Cyclone Hudah destroy 30 percent of its vanilla bean vines in 2000. Additionally, a political problem in Madagascar caused their primary port to be closed for many weeks in 2002. These two events caused vanilla prices to skyrocket for an extended period of time until growers in other countries could increase their capacities. Buyers with vanilla supply contracts in multiple countries were able to avoid some of this pricing problem. Eventually, the market for vanilla became more diversified, creating a situation whereby vanilla buyers today have more vanilla sources, outside of Madagascar.[42] The supply of liquid natural gas, LNG, is at risk, since much of the supply of LNG comes from plants in Arabian Gulf countries and Russia. LNG consumers are thus busy trying to diversify their purchases of LNG from other countries such as Norway, Algeria and Libya. Further, new plans for construction of LNG shipping and receiving facilities, additional LNG vessels and LNG regasification facilities will eventually allow for diversification of LNG supply and transportation services.[43] An earthquake in Japan in 2007 halted automobile production at a number of the country's car plants because they were all buying piston rings from Riken, which had sustained damage from the earthquake.[44]

In all of the examples above, concentrating purchases with one supplier was seen as increasing supply risk, while purchasing the same or similar products from geographically dispersed suppliers could have the effect of spreading and hence reducing the risk of supply disruptions from political upheavals, weather-related disasters and other widespread supply problems. Buyers though, must also consider the impact of a geographically dispersed supply base on other supply chain risks. While potentially reducing the risk associated with geographic supply disruptions, the use of suppliers in multiple countries exposes buyers to additional political, customs clearance, exchange rate and security risks.

Utilize a Supply Chain IT System

Chapter 6 discussed the importance of a supply chain communication and information system. Today, as firms expand their supply chains, they find customs clearance requirements and paperwork to be more detailed and complicated than ever. Complying with these regulations requires information and data visibility among supply chain participants and involvement by all key supply chain partners. Accurate data transmissions, as discussed in Chapter 6, can also aid in the reduction of stockouts and the bullwhip effect caused by forecasting and order inaccuracies and late deliveries, which also pose significant risk and cost to supply chains.

Information systems should be designed to help mitigate supply chain risk. As stated by Julian Thomas, head of the supply chain advisory department at global auditing and advisory firm KPMG, "Risk should be on the agenda and as you build your systems, you need to put in place systems to monitor and evaluate risk continuously."[45] Farm and ranch equipment retailer Tractor Supply, headquartered in Tennessee, is a good example of a firm making use of information technologies to support flexible and quick decision making to reduce risk. For example, they use an on-demand transportation management system (TMS), an ERP system and a voice-picking solution for their distribution centers. "In 2005, transportation capacity was really tight after Hurricane Katrina hit, but the way our TMS is configured we have the ability to escalate carrier service from low-cost to high-cost providers and sometimes when all the carriers in a market were taken, we had to take carriers in from another market," says Mike Graham, vice president of logistics at Tractor Supply. "We also have the flexibility within our DC network to react quickly if there is an event and move stores from one DC to another."[46]

Develop a Formal Risk Management Program

By far the most proactive risk management activity is to create a formal risk management plan encompassing the firm and its supply chain participants. Risk management should become an executive-level priority. Potential risks should be identified and prioritized and appropriate responses should be designed that will minimize the disruption to the supply chain. Additionally, mechanisms should be developed to recover quickly, efficiently, with minimal damage to the firm's reputation and customer satisfaction. Finally, performance measures need to be developed to monitor the firm's ongoing risk management capabilities.

A supply chain risk management position should be created to oversee and coordinate the firm's risk management efforts. The risk manager provides guidance and support to department managers, is the interface between the firm and its trading partner risk managers and possesses the knowledge to adequately identify, prioritize and provide a plan to reduce risks. In 2005, Tractor Supply, for example, developed a disaster recovery plan as part of its overall risk management strategy. One year later, their Waco, Texas, distribution center was struck by a tornado in the evening, leaving two to three inches of water standing in the facility and product scattered across the landscape for miles. By the time logistics VP Mike Graham made it to his office the next day, plans were already in place to repair the damage and within several hours all of the customers served by the Waco distribution center were linked to other facilities. "We did not miss a delivery the following week and May is actually a peak season for us," said Mr. Graham.[47]

Richard Sharman, a partner in KPMG's risk advisory services group offers his advice for developing risk management plans: "Companies almost need to ask themselves the stupid questions to think about the full spectrum of business risks and how they would manage them." Another consideration is to know who the firm is doing business with, to assure they are using an appropriate labor force, complying with product safety guidelines and generally using practices that fit with the firm's reputation. "Know your partner. There is no substitute for that," says Brian Joseph, partner at global business consultant PricewaterhouseCoopers.[48] When outsourcing to firms in foreign locales, it is also necessary to have adequate quality controls in place and require suppliers to report periodically to the firm to assure their products meet design requirements.

Managing Supply Chain Security

As supply chains become more global and technologically complex, so does the need to secure them. **Supply chain security management** is concerned with reducing the risk of intentionally created disruptions in supply chain operations including product and information theft and activities seeking to endanger personnel or sabotage supply chain infrastructure. The crash of Pan Am Flight 103 in Lockerbie, Scotland, in 1998 not only tragically illustrated the weaknesses of airline security systems at the time, but it also exposed the dependency of entire supply chains on each member's security capabilities. Pan Am's security processes did not fail in permitting a bomb onto Flight 103—it was Malta Airlines' security system that allowed the luggage carrying the bomb into the baggage handling system.[49] In the U.S., the attacks of September 11, 2001 were a wakeup call to many businesses to begin assessing their needs for supply chain security systems. Prior to that time, most executives were aware that their operations might be vulnerable to security problems; however, most firms (as well as governments) chose to put off improving security practices.

The notion that a supply chain is only as secure as its weakest link is illustrated in the Pan Am example above. It is therefore necessary today for firms to manage not only their own security but the security practices of their supply chain partners as well. Eventually, as supply chains and relationships with trading partners mature, security management will be recognized as an important supply chain process. Supply chain security, though, is an extremely complex problem—security activities begin at the factory where goods are packaged and loaded and then include the logistics companies transporting goods to ports, the port terminals and customs workers, the ocean carriers, the destination ports and customs workers, additional transportation companies, distribution centers and workers and the final delivery companies. And integrating all of these participants are various information systems that also need to be protected.

Security management collaboration should include, for example, contractual requirements for secure systems, "standards of care" for movement and storage of products as they move along the supply chain and the use of law enforcement officials or consultants in security planning, training and incident investigation. James G. Liddy, internationally recognized expert on security, CEO of Virginia-based security firm Liddy International and son of famous Watergate burglar and talk-show host G. Gordon Liddy, says, "Focus on

Table 13.4	Supply Chain Security System Response[51]
LEVEL OF SECURITY SYSTEM RESPONSE	**DESCRIPTION**
Basic initiatives	Physical security measures; personnel security; standard risk assessment; basic computing security; continuity plan; freight protection.
Reactive initiatives	Larger security organization; C-TPAT compliance; supply base analysis; supply continuity plan; limited training.
Proactive initiatives	Director of security; personnel with military or gov't. experience; formal security risk assessment; advanced computing security; participation in security groups.
Advanced initiatives	Customer/supplier collaboration; learning from the past; formal security strategy; supply chain drills, simulations, exercises; emergency control center.

what your real vulnerabilities are and have in place a safety-and-preparedness plan for all hazards. When you enhance your safety procedures and integrate them into your security you create efficiencies."[50]

Table 13.4 describes four increasing levels of supply chain security system preparedness and these are discussed below.

Basic Initiatives

At the most basic level, security systems should include procedures and policies for securing offices, manufacturing plants, warehouses and other physical facilities and additionally, should provide security for personnel, computing systems and freight shipments. Managers should consider use of security badges and guards, conducting background checks on applicants, using anti-virus software and passwords and using shipment tracking technologies.

Today, cargo theft is one of the biggest problems facing global supply chains and some of the basic security approaches can be used to reduce this threat. Loss estimates in the U.S. are tagged at $10 billion to $30 billion per year. And technology and lack of downside risk have enabled thieves to be more sophisticated and daring than ever before. Stolen goods can be moved to a warehouse, off-loaded, repackaged, re-manifested and placed on another vehicle before the theft is even discovered and reported. The existence of online marketers and auction sites even further facilitates the movement and sale of stolen merchandise.[52] Wal-Mart represents a very good example of a network of complex global supply chains—their systems process over 11 million data transfers daily and their annual worldwide product losses top $3 billion.[53]

Corruption is another potential problem organizations must begin to manage. Transparency International, a global group leading the fight against corruption, annually publishes its Corruption Perceptions Index to publicize the degree of corruption existing in a number of countries. The scale ranges from 0 (highly corrupt) to 10 (no corruption). The index combines multiple surveys of public sector employees' perceptions of the level of corruption. In the 2009 ranking, Japan, the U.K. and the U.S. ranked 17th, 18th and 19th respectively. New Zealand, Denmark and Singapore were the top-rated countries, while Myanmar, Afghanistan and Somalia were at the bottom of the 180-country list.[54]

Reactive Initiatives

Reactive security initiatives represent a somewhat deeper commitment to the idea of security management compared to basic initiatives, but still lack any significant efforts to organize a cohesive and firm-wide plan for security management. Many firms in this category, for example, implemented security systems in response to the terrorist attacks of September 11, 2001. These initiatives include becoming C-TPAT compliant, assessing suppliers' security practices, developing continuity plans for various events and implementing specific training and education programs.

C-TPAT or Customs-Trade Partnership Against Terrorism, refers to a partnership among U.S. Customs, the International Cargo Security Council (a U.S. nonprofit association of companies and individuals involved in transportation) and Pinkerton (a global security advising company, headquartered in New Jersey), whereby companies agree to improve security in their supply chain in return for "fast lane" border crossings. This includes conducting self-assessments of the firm's and its partner facilities and updating security policies to meet C-TPAT security requirements and then completing a C-TPAT application. U.S. Customs and Border Protection states that nonparticipants are six times more likely to receive a security-related container inspection at U.S. border crossings.[55] The U.S. government is currently working with other countries to implement similar programs. A number of other government initiatives also fall into the reactive category, such as the "10+2" or Importer Security Filing rule for all shipping containers coming into the U.S. and the Certified Cargo Screening Program (CCSP) regarding all air cargo loaded onto planes in the U.S.

Proactive Initiatives

Proactive security management initiatives venture outside the firm to include suppliers and customers and also include a more formalized approach to security management within the firm. Security activities occurring among firms in this category include the creation of an executive-level position such as director of corporate security; the hiring of former military, intelligence or law enforcement personnel with security management experience; a formal and comprehensive approach to assess the firm's exposure to security risks; the use of cyber-intrusion detection systems and other advanced information security practices; the development of freight security plans in collaboration with 3PLs; and the active participation of employees in industry security associations and conferences. Home Depot, for example, uses a computer risk modeling approach to assess their supply chains' vulnerabilities and design appropriate security measures. "We look at 35 global risk elements and one of those is threat of terrorism," explains Benjamin Cook, senior manager for global trade service for Home Depot. "We use that technique to help us roll out a strategy that is most appropriate to the country we are sourcing from."[56]

Massachusetts-based life insurance company MassMutual wanted to ensure the security of their IT system, spread across a dozen applications, including their website, as well as the 12 million business and individual customer accounts they managed. They named a vice president of information security to direct their information security efforts and they put in place a 50-person security group that included an internal consulting team with specific security item experts, an engineering team that supported firewalls, a security assurance team that analyzed security monitoring devices and a team responsible for identity management. Finally, they purchased a security management software application to help their security team quickly assess and prioritize risks. It creates an aggregate risk score for each application and system MassMutual uses to determine which risks need to be addressed first.[57]

Advanced Initiatives

Firms with advanced security management systems are recognized as industry leaders with respect to their security initiatives. Activities within this category include full collaboration with key suppliers and customers in developing quick recovery and continuity plans for supply chain disruptions, consideration of past security failures of other firms in developing a more comprehensive and effective security system, the design of a complete supply chain security management plan that is implemented by all key trading partners, the undertaking of exercises designed to train participants and test the resilience of the supply chain to security disruptions and the use of an emergency control center to manage responses to unexpected supply chain disruptions.

Industry security leaders like Michigan-based Dow Chemical see supply chain security as simply good business. As Henry Ward, director of transportation security and safety at Dow, offers, "We view security as one of the steps we take to make sure we remain a reliable supplier of goods to the marketplace." Dow's efforts to improve supply chain visibility and security led to a 50 percent improvement in the time it takes to identify and resolve trade transit problems and a 20 percent inventory reduction at receiving terminals. Dow uses RFID and a global positioning system (GPS) to track large intermodal containers as they move from North America to Asia. Dow also sees collaboration with governments and its supply chain partners as crucial to their success. "We take an integrated approach to supply chain security, which means we look at it holistically," says Ward.[58]

As described in this final section, supply chain participants are pulled by opposing objectives—one is to reduce supply chain costs and improve freight handling speed to improve competitiveness and profits; the other is to manage the risk and cost of security breaches. Unfortunately, as supply chains venture into countries in search of cheaper suppliers and implement practices to reduce transit times, the security risks grow. Tim Manahan, a vice president at supply management software provider Procuri, admits, "Very few companies have effective supply chain security systems in place, either for monitoring security issues or for reacting to problems." Managers and government representatives understand the problem much better, though, today, than ten years ago and hopefully, this is beginning to lead to better management of risk and security.

SUMMARY

In this chapter, the topic of integrating processes within the firm and among supply chain partners was discussed, including the steps required to achieve internal and external process integration, the advantages of doing this and the obstacles to overcome. Process integration should be considered the primary means to achieving successful supply chain management, but it is the one thing firms struggle with most when setting out to manage their supply chains. For without the proper support, training, tools, trust and preparedness, process integration most likely will be impossible to ever fully achieve.

The supply chain integration model provides the framework for integrating processes first within the firm and then among trading partners and this model served as the foundation of the chapter. The role played by performance measures in assessing and improving integration was also discussed. Finally, a discussion of supply chain risk and security management outlined the need for firms and their trading partners to collaborate in developing effective strategies for assessing the risk of supply chain disruptions and implementing solutions.

KEY TERMS

active RFID tags, 461

bullwhip effect, 467

cloud-based supply chain management, 465

collaborative education, 467

customer relationship management process, 452

customer service management process, 452

data warehouses, 458

demand forecast updating, 468

demand management process, 453

emergency sourcing, 472

everyday low pricing (EDLP), 469

forward buying, 471

functional silos, 452

information visibility, 463

internal supply chains, 458

key supply chain processes, 452

key trading partners, 450

knowledge-management solutions, 460

legacy systems, 458

manufacturing flow management process, 454

order batching, 469

order fulfillment process, 454

passive RFID tags, 460

process integration, 449

product development and commercialization process, 455

radio-frequency identification tag (RFID), 460

rationing, 469

returns management process, 455

shortage gaming, 470

silo mentality, 462

stockpiling, 471

supplier relationship management process, 454

supply chain risk, 471

supply chain security management, 474

vendor managed inventory, 468

DISCUSSION QUESTIONS

1. What does process integration mean and why is it difficult to achieve?

2. What makes a supplier or customer a key or primary trading partner? Describe why it is important to begin supply chain management efforts with only these key companies.

3. What are the eight key supply chain business processes and why are they important when managing supply chains?

4. What is the difference between the customer service management process and the customer relationship management process?

5. Is it necessary to have internal performance measures for each of the supply chain business processes? Why or why not?

6. Which should come first—internal process integration or external process integration? Why?

7. Why is an ERP system important for both internal and external process integration? What other IT considerations are there?

8. Think of some supply chain (external) performance measures for several of the eight key supply chain business processes, assuming the overall strategy is superior customer service. What if the overall strategy is sustainability?

9. What are knowledge management solutions and how can they support a firm's supply chain integration efforts? Give some examples.

10. How can RFID tags help to enable external process integration?

11. Why is lack of trust an obstacle to supply chain management? How can we overcome this obstacle?

12. Why is visibility so important when integrating processes?

13. Define the bullwhip effect and describe how it impacts supply chain integration or how integration impacts the bullwhip effect.

14. What is cloud-based supply chain management and how might it impact process integration?

15. What is the difference between supply chain management and supply chain process integration?

16. Define the term collaborative education and explain what this has to do with supply chain management.

17. Describe an incidence either personally or at work where you have been involved in shortage gaming.

18. Why should reducing the length of the supply chain also reduce the bullwhip effect?

19. What is everyday low pricing and how does it impact the bullwhip effect?

20. What is the difference between supply chain risk management and supply chain security management? Which do you think is most important?

21. What types of supply chains are most likely to be impacted by risk and security problems? Why?

22. List some steps firms can take to reduce supply chain risk and increase security.

INTERNET QUESTIONS

1. Go to the Institute for Supply Management website, www.ism.ws and find the listing for the latest ISM Annual International Supply Management Conference. Then find

the Conference Proceedings and report on a paper that was presented regarding a topic covered in this chapter.

2. Find the websites of several supply chain security and risk assessment firms and report on their specialties and management experience.

3. Search on the term Customs-Trade Partnership Against Terrorism or C-TPAT and write a paper on the history of C-TPAT and how it is being used today.

4. Search on the term supply chain security problems and write a report on several current problems and how they are being addressed.

Chapter 14

PERFORMANCE MEASUREMENT ALONG THE SUPPLY CHAIN

True incidents are just the tip of the iceberg. What is underwater? You must continue to test the systems, put in place additional measures and evolve the policies and procedures.[1]

Most companies have literally hundreds of supply chain metrics in place. Which ones matter, and what appropriate targets are, will change over time. Are your metrics (still) driving the behavior—and the results—you want and need to succeed?[2]

Learning Objectives

After completing this chapter, you should be able to

- Discuss why managers need to measure and assess the performance of their firms as well as their supply chains.
- Discuss the merits of financial and nonfinancial performance measures.
- List a number of traditional and world-class performance measures.
- Describe how the Balanced Scorecard and the SCOR models work.
- Describe how to design a supply chain performance measurement system.

Chapter Outline

Introduction

Viewing the Supply Chain as a Competitive Force

Traditional Performance Measures

World-Class Performance Measurement Systems

Supply Chain Performance Measurement Systems

The Balanced Scorecard

The SCOR Model

Summary

Supply Chain Management in Action   *Measuring Sustainability in the Chemical Industry*

Sourcing professionals are at a crossroads when working with chemical suppliers. While the typical issues of cost, ontime delivery and quality remain a constant, the issues of sustainability and the green supply chain are quickly altering the equation. Add a complicated global chemical supply chain, often with opaque visibility through second- and third-tier suppliers, and it is no wonder that buyers are a bit more cautious these days when dealing with chemical suppliers. "There is certainly more of a heightened awareness when dealing with chemical suppliers, especially around the areas of regulations, compliance and safety," says Stan Wheeler, the director of global sourcing for the South Carolina-based MWV Specialty Chemicals Division. "Even with ISO 9000 and Responsible Care initiatives, it is important that we keep a close relationship with our domestic and global chemical suppliers."

For the MWV Specialty Chemicals Division, ongoing training and education is an important part of its heightened awareness process. "Courses focusing on corporate social responsibility, monitoring supplier performance and agility and adaptability in supply chain are routinely offered to our sourcing and supply chain staff," says Wheeler. "In the past, when dealing with chemical suppliers, pricing was everything and quality was a given. But these days we need to effectively manage a complicated global supply base where price is just one part of the equation."

Longtime petrochemical sourcing manager Michael Winters says some companies are very concerned about safety and ethical sources of supply, adding that no one wants their name associated with a Bhopal-like disaster. "I look at safety as base table stakes, that is, an implied consideration of well-performing suppliers," says Winters, a board member of the Purchasing Management Association of Boston. "However, in some cases manufacturing considerations such as transport cost, feedstock availability and alternate sources drive sourcing decisions."

The importance of green sourcing is part of broader sustainability processes at the California-based biotechnology company Life Technologies. "Our sourcing decisions are based on compliance to our product specifications as well as quality, cost and service levels," says David Manternach, a member of the strategic sourcing team. "We promote green in our products and we strive for sustainability throughout our global operations."

Life Technologies' sustainability efforts flow to the supply base as well. "We have a global supply chain and we use both domestic and global chemical suppliers to support our international operations, including our manufacturing plants in Scotland, China and India," says Manternach. "Our suppliers are generally receptive to the concepts of sustainability, especially when they see that in many cases the costs to both parties are reduced."

Manternach sees the trend towards a green chemical supply chain accelerating even outside Europe and the U.S. where environmental sensitivity may be less. "Europe is at the forefront of chemical safety with initiatives like REACH [Registration, Evaluation, Authorization & Restriction of Chemicals] but other regions are becoming more receptive and responsive to sustainability efforts. We are a market leader and we want our suppliers to be market leaders as well. Sustainability just makes good business sense."

Source: Weissman, R., "Chemical Supplier Evaluations Go Green," *Purchasing* 139(2), 2010: 26. Used with permission.

Introduction

This chapter discusses the role and importance of performance measurement for both the firm and its supply chains. The old adage "you can't improve what you aren't measuring" is certainly true for firms as well as their supply chains. In fact, a report by the Conference Board of Strategic Performance Management found that companies using performance measurement were more likely to achieve leadership positions in their industry and were almost twice as likely to handle a major change successfully.[3] While several types of performance measures were discussed or suggested in earlier chapters of this textbook, firms need to develop an entire system of meaningful performance measures to become and then remain competitive, particularly when managing supply chains is one of the imperatives.

Performance measurement systems vary substantially from company to company. For example, many firms' performance measures concentrate solely on the firm's costs and profits. While these measures are certainly important, managers must realize that making decisions while relying on financial performance alone gives no indication of the underlying causes of financial performance. Designing standards and then monitoring the many activities or processes indirectly or directly impacting financial performance can provide much better information for decision-making purposes.

Indeed, in recent years as global demand for goods and services has languished, firms have been relying on their supply chain management skills to drive costs out of their supply chains while improving revenues. According to a recent survey of global business managers, three of the activities receiving the most attention during this period have been purchasing, logistics and performance measurement.[4] Always the supply chain innovator, Wal-Mart, for instance, has decided to purchase up to 80 percent of its private label merchandise directly from suppliers within five years, up from 20 percent today, saving them billions of dollars.[5] Supply chain leaders are working closely with their trading partners to seek out and eliminate non-value-creating activities while identifying changing customer requirements and turning these into product and service attributes. And supporting and guiding these activities are good performance measurement systems.

Even for companies like Wal-Mart that rely on low prices to attract customers, cost performance alone is not enough to guarantee success without assuring that products are also available when needed and at acceptable levels of quality. Attaining world-class competitive status requires managers to realize that making process decisions to create or purchase products and services customers want, and then to distribute them in ways that will satisfy customers, requires careful monitoring of cost, quality and customer service performance among all key supply chain trading partners. Achieving adequate performance and then continually improving on those measures are what firms must aim toward. Using an adequate system of performance measures allows managers to pursue that vision. Unfortunately, many firms and their supply chains today are not adequately measuring process performance. According to a survey of Canadian manufacturing firms performed in 2006, for instance, only about 50 percent of the firms had even moderately well-developed performance measurement systems. And in a more recent survey of business technologists, about 75 percent said their firms mainly relied on their suppliers to furnish them with inbound performance information.[6] In other cases, organizations are busy measuring everything in sight and in so doing, they make poor measurements, measure the wrong things and measure things that only make the firm look good—actions that can sometimes lead to misstatements and restatements, loss of confidence and even prove dangerous (Enron and Worldcom might come to mind here). Managers need to realize the importance of creating a good, true set of performance measures, and this is the objective of this chapter.

When managing supply chains, assessing the performance of several tiers of suppliers and customers further complicates an already formidable performance measurement problem. With supply chains, the performance system must become much larger and is complicated by a range of relationships, trust and interactions. Performance at the end-customer level depends on the collective performance among the primary trading companies along the supply chain. Thus, performance measures must be visible and communicated to all participating members of the supply chain while managers continue to collaborate to achieve results that allow all supply chain members to plan ahead, create value and realize benefits. Indeed, it is likely that some member costs will be higher than otherwise would be the case to permit supply chains to offer what end customers want. It is only through cooperation and shared planning and benefits that an effective supply chain-wide performance measurement system can be designed and implemented.

This chapter will discuss the basics of performance measurement including cost-based and other traditional measurements, and then move on to discuss the more effective measurement systems typical of world-class organizations. From there, the discussion will move into measuring the performance of supply chains. Finally, the Balanced Scorecard and the SCOR model methods of performance measurement, which are being utilized effectively in supply chain settings, will be presented and discussed.

Viewing the Supply Chain as a Competitive Force

The eventual and ultimate goal of a supply chain is to successfully deliver products and services to end customers. Traditionally, to meet customer service requirements, firms along the supply chain might simply load their retail shelves, warehouses and factories with finished goods. Today, though, this strategy would ultimately lead to inventory carrying costs and product prices so high that firms would no longer be competitive. For companies to be successful, customers along their supply chains and the end-product users must be satisfied. Thus, firms must invest time and effort understanding supply chain partner and end-customer requirements, and then adjust or acquire supply chain competencies to satisfy the needs of these customers. To obtain the resources to accomplish these tasks, top managers must become involved and support the firm's improvement efforts. Ultimately, well-designed performance measurement systems integrated among key trading partners must be implemented to control and enhance the capabilities of these firms and thus the supply chain.

Understanding End Customers

As discussed in Chapter 10, companies must make efforts to segment customers based on their service needs, and then design production and distribution capabilities to meet those needs. In other words, instead of taking a one-size-fits-all approach to product design and delivery, firms and their supply chains need to look at each segment of the markets they serve and determine the needs of those customers. Companies must look at customer segment needs such as:

- The variety of products required
- The quantity and delivery frequency needed
- The product quality desired
- The level of sustainability sought, and
- The pricing of products.

Obviously, depending on the range of customers the company and its supply chains serve, there will be multiple customer groups and requirements. German company Henkel, for instance, known for its Duck brand duct tape, provides benefits to the customers of retailers like Wal-Mart by designing, branding and marketing household products as the result of analyzing household buying habits and trends. Henkel uses focus groups, expert advisory panels and a consumer hotline to capture consumer ideas. This way, they can build brand loyalty, provide benefits to their retail customers and suggest new products to their supply chain partners.[7]

Understanding Supply Chain Partner Requirements

Once firms understand the end customers' needs, the next step is determining how their supply chains can best satisfy those needs. Supply chain strategies must consider the potential trade-offs existing between the cost, quality, sustainability and service requirements mentioned above. For instance, supply chain responsiveness (meeting due date, lead-time and quantity requirements, and providing high levels of customer service) can come at a cost. To achieve the desired level of responsiveness, companies along the supply chain may also have to become more responsive, potentially requiring investments in additional capacity and faster transportation. Likewise, supply chain quality or reliability may require investments in newer equipment, better technology and higher-quality materials and components among participants in the supply chain.

Conversely, increasing supply chain efficiency (enabling retailers to offer lower prices for goods) creates the need among supply chain partners to make adjustments in the production and delivery capabilities that will lower costs. This may include using slower transportation modes, buying and delivering in larger quantities, and reducing the quality of the parts and supplies purchased. Ultimately, firms within supply chains must collaborate and decide what combination of customer needs their supply chains can and should provide, both today and in the long term. Furniture retailer IKEA, for example, tries to use environmentally and socially responsible suppliers to better satisfy their retail customers. They have developed a code of conduct using life-cycle thinking for their 1,600 suppliers that includes resource use, sustainable forestry practices and proper employee training.[8] The chapter-opening Supply Chain Management in Action feature also provides a discussion of the way the chemical industry is changing to provide better environmental performance for their supply chains.

Adjusting Supply Chain Member Capabilities

With these capability requirements understood, supply chain members can then audit their capabilities and those of their supply chain partners to determine if what they do particularly well is consistent with the needs of the end customers and other supply chain trading partners. Some companies may be well positioned to supply the desired levels of cost, quality and customer service performance, while others may not be as well positioned. Matching or adjusting supply chain member capabilities with customer requirements can be a very difficult task, particularly if the communication and cooperation levels among companies are not excellent, or if companies are serving multiple supply chains and customer segments requiring different sets of capabilities.

In many cases, a dominant company within the supply chain (e.g., Wal-Mart) can use their buying power to leverage demands for supplier conformance to their supply chain requirements. As customer tastes and competition change over time, supply chains can reassess and redesign their strategies for meeting customer requirements and remaining competitive. Use of the Internet, for instance, has become a significant part of many firms' competitive strategies, allowing them to offer much greater product variety and convenience than ever before.

Matching supply chain capabilities to end-customer requirements means that firms and their supply chain partners must be continually reassessing their performance with respect to these changing end-customer requirements. This brings us back to the importance of performance measures and their ability to relay information regarding the performance of each member within the supply chain, along with the performance of the supply chain vis-à-vis their end customers. Now, more than ever before, successful supply chains are those that can continue to deliver the right combination of cost, quality and customer service as customer needs change. Weaknesses in any of these areas can mean loss of competitiveness and profits for all members along the supply chain. Today, the best supply chain performers are more responsive to customer needs, quicker to anticipate changes in the markets and much better at controlling costs, resulting in greater supply chain profits. The next section discusses traditional performance measures.

Traditional Performance Measures

Most performance measures used by firms today continue to be the traditional cost-based and financial statistics reported to shareholders in the form of annual report, balance sheet and income statement data. This information is relied upon by potential investors and shareholders to make stock transaction decisions, and forms the basis for many managers' performance bonuses. Unfortunately, financial statements and other cost-based information don't necessarily reflect the underlying performance of the productive systems of an organization, and as most people witnessed with firms like Texas-based energy company Enron and Mississippi-based long-distance phone company WorldCom a few years ago, cost and profit information can be hidden or manipulated to make performance seem far better than it really was. Enron claimed revenues of $111 billion in 2000. That year, *Fortune* magazine named Enron "America's Most Innovative Company." The very next year, high-profile managers left the company, Enron declared bankruptcy, their fraudulent corporate and accounting practices became public, and by 2004 it had become one of the costliest bankruptcy cases in U.S. history. Thousands of employees lost everything, executives ended up in jail and the Arthur Andersen accounting company, associated with Enron during this period, was dissolved.[9]

As illustrated above, decisions that are made solely to maximize current stock prices don't necessarily mean the firm is performing well or will continue to perform well into the future. Business success depends on the firm's ability to turn internal competencies into products and services that customers want, while providing desired environmental, quality and customer service levels at a reasonable price. Financial performance measures, while important, cannot adequately capture a firm's ability to excel in these areas.

Use of Organization Costs, Revenue and Profitability Measures

These might at first glance seem to be useful types of performance measures, but several problems are associated with using costs, revenues and profits to gauge a firm's performance. Windfall profits that occur when prices rise due to demand increases and supply interruptions, as has been the case in recent years in the oil industry, are one example. When this happens, airlines and other transportation companies suddenly experience much higher costs and reductions in profits while oil companies see suddenly rising profits. Similarly, many tourist destinations like Las Vegas saw dramatic declines in visitor volumes during the recent economic recession, causing hotels and theme parks to report much lower occupancies and profits during this period. These profits, or lack thereof, were not the result of something the firms did or did not do particularly well; they were caused for the most part by uncontrollable environmental conditions. Thus, changes in cost and profit statistics may not accurately reflect the true capabilities of the firm.

Another problem with the use of costs, revenues or profits as performance measures is the difficulty in most cases to attribute cost, revenue or profit contributions to the various functional units or underlying processes of the organization. Many departments and units are interdependent and share costs, equipment, labor and revenues, making it extremely difficult to split out costs and revenues equitably. Additionally, using costs alone as a departmental or business unit performance measure can result in actions that actually raise costs for the organization. For example, rewarding the purchasing department for minimizing their purchasing costs might increase product return rates and warranty repair costs due to low-cost but poor-quality part purchases. Minimizing transportation costs might also look great on financial reports but may result in late deliveries and lower customer service levels, causing a loss of customers. Finally, the practice of allocating overhead costs based on a department's percentage of direct labor hours causes managers to waste time trying to reduce direct labor hours to lower overhead cost allocations when today, direct labor accounts for only a small fraction of total costs. In essence, these overhead costs merely get transferred somewhere else in the firm, leaving the organization no better off, and perhaps in worse shape due to the loss of valuable labor resources.

"We need to cut down on productivity, quality and customer service to save money."

Use of Performance Standards and Variances

Establishing standards for performance comparison purposes can be particularly troublesome and, in some cases, even damaging to an organization. Establishing output standards like 1,000 units/day or productivity standards like 10 units/labor hour establishes an ultimate goal that can drive employees and managers to do whatever it takes to reach their goals, even if it means producing shoddy work or "cooking the books." Additionally, once goals are actually reached, there is also no further incentive to improve.

When standards are not reached, a **performance variance** is created, which is the difference between the standard and actual performance. When organizations hold managers up to performance standards that then create performance variances, managers can be pressured to find ways to make up these variances, resulting in decisions that may not be in the long-term best interests of the firm. Decisions like producing to make an output quota regardless of current finished goods inventory levels, or purchasing unneeded supplies just to use up department budgets, are examples of things that can happen when performance standards are applied without considering the true performance benefits to the organization. When applied at the functional level, these standards act to reinforce the idea of **functional silos**. Departments are then assessed on meeting functional standards instead of optimizing firm or supply chain performance.

Use of Firm-Wide Productivity and Utilization Measures

Overall **total productivity measures** such as *(output)/(costs of labor + capital + energy + material)* and **single-factor productivity measures** such as *(output)/(cost of labor)* are potentially useful but have the same problems as the use of costs and profits for performance measures. These measures, while allowing firms to view the impact of one or any number of the firm's inputs (such as the cost of labor) on the firm's outputs (such as units produced), do not allow the firm to determine the actual performance of any of the resources behind these elements. Decisions made to increase productivity may prove to actually increase a firm's costs and reduce quality or output in the long term, ultimately reducing productivity. For example, a business unit might be tempted to produce at output levels greater than demand to increase productivity, which also increases inventories and inventory carrying costs. Or managers might be inclined to lay off workers and buy the cheapest materials to decrease input costs and thus maximize their productivity without considering the impact on the firm's quality, customer service and employee morale. In these ways, productivity measures can prove to be damaging. Example 14.1 provides a look at calculating productivity and the problems that can arise when making decisions based solely on productivity.

Labor and machine utilization can be shown as *(actual units produced)/(standard output level)* or *(actual hours utilized)/(total hours available)*. These performance measures, when used alone, can encourage the firm, for instance, to reduce labor levels until everyone is overworked, causing queues of work or customers to develop, morale to suffer and quality and customer service levels to erode. Additionally, using the measures discussed above, there is a tendency to continue producing and adding to inventory just to keep machines and people busy. Less time is spent doing preventive maintenance, training and projects that can lead to greater performance and profits in the future. While it is obviously beneficial to meet demand and keep labor costs at optimal levels, maximizing utilization can prove to be very expensive for firms.

Thus, the emphasis on overall performance in terms of generalized criteria such as the firm's financial, productivity or utilization characteristics does not tell the entire story. While it certainly is important for firms to possess financial strength and high levels of productivity and factory utilization, these measures do not reveal in detail the firm's underlying process performance. Using general and internally focused measures like these does not give many clues as to specific problems that may exist or how to go about solving those problems. Managers are left to guess at what types of actions are needed and have no way of knowing if any corrections made actually had the intended effect. What is needed is a set of detailed performance measures throughout the organization and extending to supply chain partners that are consistent with firm and supply chain strategies, allow managers to find root causes of performance failures and, finally, lead managers to reasonable problem solutions.

Example 14.1   Productivity Measures at the Ultra Ski Emporium

The Ultra Ski company makes top-of-the-line custom snow skis for high-end ski shops as well as their own small retail shop, and employs fifteen people. The owner has been adamant about finding a way to increase productivity because his sales have been flat for the past two seasons. Given the information shown below, he has calculated the single-factor and total productivity values as:

Labor productivity = 1000 skis/10,800 hours = 0.093 skis per labor hour

Material productivity = 1000 skis/$18,000 = 0.056 skis per dollar of materials

Lease productivity = 1000 skis/$24,000 = 0.042 skis per lease dollar

INPUTS AND OUTPUTS	LAST YEAR
Skis produced	1,000
Labor hours	10,800
Materials purchased	$18,000
Lease payments	$24,000

He calculates their total productivity by multiplying the labor hours by their average wage of $17 per hour and finds:

Total productivity = 1,000 skis/[10,800($17) + $18,000 + $24,000]
= 0.0044 skis per dollar.

So the owner figures he can get some great improvements in productivity by finding a low-cost supplier, moving to a cheaper location and laying off six workers (reducing his workforce by 40 percent), making his new single-factor productivities:

Labor productivity = 1,000 skis/10,800(.6) hours = 0.154 (a 66 percent increase)
Material productivity = 1,000 skis/$12,000 = 0.083 (a 48 percent increase)
Lease productivity = 1,000/$18,000 = 0.056 (a 33 percent increase)

and his new total productivity:

Total productivity = 1,000 skis/[10,800($17)(.6) + $12,000 + $18,000]
= 0.0071 skis per dollar (a whopping 61 percent increase!)

Consequently, the owner decided to make the changes for the coming year. Unfortunately, they went out of business in six months due to poor-quality materials, a bad location and overworked, low-morale employees.

Traditional performance measures also tend to be short-term oriented. To maximize profits next quarter, firms may focus considerable efforts on delaying capital investments, selling assets, denying new project proposals, contracting out work and leasing instead of purchasing equipment. These actions, while reducing short-term costs, can also significantly reduce a firm's ability to develop new products and remain competitive. New product research, new technology purchases, new facilities and newly trained people all enhance the capabilities of the firm and position it to keep up with ever-changing customer requirements, but these things all initially worsen the performance measures discussed above. Without this infusion of ideas and capital expenditures, though, firms will ultimately perform poorly.

On the other hand, world-class organizations realize that long-term competitive advantage is created when firms' strategies are geared toward continually meeting and exceeding customer expectations of product and service cost, quality, dependability, flexibility and sustainability—in other words, the creation of value. These firms realize that investments to improve their capabilities in these areas will eventually bear fruit and position them to be successful in the long term. Effective performance measurement systems link current operating characteristics to these long-term strategies and objectives. Peoria, Arizona, for example, a city of 150,000 sitting just northwest of Phoenix, has been using performance measures for years and has won numerous awards for their efforts. Their most effective programs have used performance measures along with program descriptions and goals to tell a story. Many of the programs also incorporate satisfaction surveys to measure the extent to which outcomes are valued by customers. They also benchmark performance with some 150 other cities across the U.S.[10]

World-Class Performance Measurement Systems

Businesses respond to increased competitive and marketplace pressures by developing and maintaining a distinctive competitive advantage, which creates the need to develop effective performance measurement systems linking firm strategies and operating decisions to customer requirements. Performance criteria that guide a firm's decision making to achieve strategic objectives must be easy to implement, understand and measure; they must be flexible and consistent with the firm's objectives; and they must be implemented in areas that are viewed as critical to the creation of value for customers. Wisconsin-based Briggs & Stratton Corp., a small-engine manufacturer with about 7,000 employees, has been using an enterprise-wide performance monitoring system for a number of years to help them attain the company's vision of producing low-cost, high-volume, good-quality products. Over 1,500 company users from various departments view and analyze different performance metrics applicable to their side of the business. The company has saved millions of dollars, for instance, by correcting quality problems identified from monitoring warranty claims and costs.[11]

An effective performance measurement system should consist of the traditional financial information for external reporting purposes along with tactical-level performance criteria used to assess the firm's competitive capabilities while directing its efforts to attain other desired capabilities. In fact, in a recent survey of manufacturing and service company executives, the researchers found that in firms with successful lean and Six Sigma programs, there was use of a wider variety of both financial and nonfinancial performance measures.[12] Finally, a good performance measurement system should include measures that *assess what is important to customers*. These measures will vary by company and through time as strategic changes occur to the firm, its products and its supply chains.

Developing World-Class Performance Measures

Creating an effective performance measurement system involves the following steps:[13]

- Identify the firm's strategic objectives.
- Develop an understanding of each functional area's set of requirements for achieving the strategic objectives.
- Design and document performance measures for each functional area that adequately track each required capability.
- Assure the compatibility and strategic focus of the performance measures to be used.

- Implement the new performance monitoring system.
- Identify internal and external trends likely to affect firm and functional area performance over time.
- Periodically re-evaluate the firm's performance measurement system as these trends and other environmental changes occur.

In this way, world-class firms can establish strategically oriented performance criteria among each of the functional areas of the firm within the categories of quality, cost and customer service, and then revisit these measures as problems are solved, competition and customer requirements change and as supply chain and firm strategies change. For instance, the San Diego Zoo in California, a world-class leader in conservation, audits among other things, their waste recycling performance. The zoo initially became interested in recycling waste and other conservation efforts in response to customer and employee suggestions. In 2009, they recovered 74 percent of all waste generated within the facility. Additionally, they found that most of the non-recycled waste was compostable. As a result, new programs have been developed that include composting to further improve their waste recovery performance.[14] Table 14.1 lists a number of performance measures that might be used in different functional areas of the firm to satisfy strategic objectives, enhance the value of the firm's products and services and increase customer satisfaction. As firms become more proactive in managing their supply chains, performance measures must be incorporated into this effort. The next section discusses performance measurement in a supply chain setting.

Supply Chain Performance Measurement Systems

Performance measurement systems for supply chains must effectively link supply chain trading partners to achieve breakthrough performance in satisfying end users. At the local or inter-firm level, performance measures similar to the ones presented in Table 14.1 are required for high-level performance. In a collaborative supply chain setting, these measures must overlay the entire supply chain to assure that firms are all contributing to the supply chain strategy and the satisfaction of end customers. In successful supply chains, members jointly agree on appropriate supply chain performance measures. The focus of the system should be on value creation for end customers, since customer satisfaction drives sales for all of the supply chain's members. While challenging to implement, supply chains are indeed pulling it off. In a major study by the Massachusetts-based Performance Measurement Group that looked at firms and their supply chains from 1995 to 2000, the top supply chain performers were found to be leading the way in terms of responsiveness and reliability performance and total supply chain costs. And, in a 2008 survey of 287 companies and their supply chains conducted by Connecticut-based AMR Research, the most successful supply chains were found to be more centralized, integrated, global and focused on measuring performance.[15]

Electronics retailer Best Buy has been busy for several years now transforming its operations to allow consumer demand to drive its supply chains. Termed **demand-driven supply networks**, the idea is to design supply chains with enough flexibility to respond quickly to changes in the marketplace. One of the cornerstones of Best Buy's supply chain transformation is performance measurement. They have installed an integrated business intelligence system that provides internal users and supply chain members with visibility into its business performance, allowing users to view financial and other performance data and perform trend analyses, for example. Problems can be quickly identified and remedied to reduce costs and improve sales.[16] SAP, the global ERP system

Table 14.1	World-Class Performance Measures
CAPABILITY AREAS	**PERFORMANCE MEASURES**
Quality	1. No. of defects per unit produced and per unit purchased
	2. No. of product returns per units sold
	3. No. of warranty claims per units sold
	4. No. of suppliers used
	5. Lead time from defect detection to correction
	6. No. of workcenters using statistical process control
	7. No. of suppliers who are quality certified
	8. No. of quality awards applied for; no. of awards won
Cost	1. Scrap or spoilage losses per workcenter
	2. Average inventory turnover
	3. Average setup time
	4. Employee turnover
	5. Avg. safety stock levels
	6. No. of rush orders required for meeting delivery dates
	7. Downtime due to machine breakdowns
Customer Service	**Flexibility**
	1. Average number of labor skills
	2. Average production lot size
	3. No. of customized services available
	4. No. of days to process special or rush orders
	Dependability
	1. Average service response time or product lead time
	2. % of delivery promises kept
	3. Avg. no. of days late per shipment
	4. No. of stockouts per product
	5. No. of days to process a warranty claim
	6. Avg. no. of hours spent with customers by engineers
	Innovation
	1. Annual investment in R&D
	2. % of automated processes
	3. No. of new product or service introductions
	4. No. of process steps required per product

provider, uses customer focus groups to get feedback on their existing performance measurement systems, and the customers benefit too—they are able to learn what other firms are doing with the SAP applications. More on this can be found in the Global Perspective feature.

Global Perspective

Competitors Collaborate to Improve Supply Chain Performance

"Business today is all about managing complexity. Supply chain excellence is not an option." That statement from Tom Miller, VP of bottling investments, The Coca-Cola Company, sums up why executives with 33 companies that potentially compete for the same customers convene on a regular basis to share tips for improving supply chain performance.

These companies, which include household names such as Coca-Cola, Kraft Foods, Procter & Gamble, and Johnson & Johnson, make up the SAP Consumer Packaged Goods Customer Advisory Panel, or CPCAC. The group is one of 24 industry panels organized by enterprise software market leader SAP. "The CPAC is a driving force in shaping SAP's product direction," says Emeil van Schaik, SAP's senior VP of manufacturing and consumer industries solutions. "Eighty percent of the work this group does has a direct impact on the SAP product portfolio."

With customers having that type of influence on its product direction, it can be assumed that SAP is developing solutions that are well received in the marketplace. But how do CPAC members benefit from participating in the group, particularly when it requires sharing details about how they use SAP's software to support business processes? "We do talk more about business and business processes than software," Coca-Cola's Miller said of the CPAC meetings. "The value comes from learning from people who already have done some things that you may be trying to do. That's why we're willing to work with our competitors."

Mark Dajani, the Kraft Foods CIO, said there's no reason to worry about sharing information with group members because each company uses the information acquired in the meetings differently. "The idea is to take the best practices and see who executes them best," Dajani said. "The differentiation is in the corporate culture; getting your organization to be the best at executing the best business processes."

For instance, a major issue for all consumer goods companies is how to build a closer bond with consumers. The ultimate goal is gaining a better understanding of what types of products customers want, and how they want to receive them. Hashing out this topic at CPAC meetings led to the conclusion that SAP should beef up the front office portion of its software suite.

When SAP addressed those issues, CPAC members found different ways of applying the new functionality to their own businesses. For global beer producer SABMiller, the new functionality helped improve its ability to execute direct store delivery, which is a crucial element of how SABMiller serves customers in Latin America. "In Columbia, we do direct delivery to 400,000 customers," said Brian Nicholas, head of operations development. "So we need good direct store delivery support." After testing SAP's new functionality with selected customers, Nicholas said, "Now, we're looking at large-scale roll out across the country."

Coke used SAP's improved CRM and supply chain functionality to improve its demand management processes. "Recognizing the need for cost control and improved customer service highlighted the need for improved demand management," Coke's Miller said. In addition to CRM functionality that allows for collecting better customer data, Miller said, the SAP supply chain solutions now have "special algorithms that enable dynamic sales and operations planning." The end result, he said, is "an increased hit rate" when Coke decides which products to send in individual markets.

Kraft Foods has benefited from SAP's improved promotions management capabilities, but Dajani said that's not all the company has gained from participating in CPAC. "What we've done here is break the cycle of looking for software to solve immediate problems," Dajani said. ""We're now looking two years out with SAP and exploring how the software might solve problems we see coming in the future."

Source: Hill, S., "SAP Customer Panel Lets Competitors Collaborate for Mutual Benefit," *Manufacturing Business Technology,* V. 27, No. 6 (2009): 4. Used with permission.

Supply Chain Environmental Performance

Environmental sustainability has been a recurring theme throughout this textbook, and as consumers, governments and business leaders begin to address the need for protecting the environment and reducing greenhouse gas emissions, the demand for products and services will change, along with regulations impacting how supply chains operate. As a result, supply chain performance must begin to include assessments of environmental performance as discussed in the chapter opening Supply Chain Management in Action feature for the chemical industry.

Ultimately, **green supply chain management (GSCM)** is the objective of an effective supply chain environmental performance system. The reach of GSCM extends across the organization and its trading partners, and includes the processes involved in purchasing, manufacturing and materials management, distribution and reverse logistics. GSCM should promote the sharing of environmental responsibility along the supply chain in each of these areas, such that environmentally sound practices predominate, and adverse impacts to global environments are minimized.[17] Perhaps the world's largest green supply chain effort underway is by Wal-Mart and the Sustainability Consortium, a collaborative venture involving a number of companies and universities with the objective of greening Wal-Mart's (and its suppliers') products. While the program is just recently getting started, the environmental requirements that Wal-Mart has distributed to its suppliers have already triggered changes in packaging, distribution and performance tracking.[18]

The design of an effective green supply chain performance system should be discussed by all key supply chain members and be compatible with existing performance monitoring systems. As discussed in earlier chapters, the ISO 14000 environmental management standards, typically associated with one organization's environmental compliance, can be a good starting point for building a green supply chain strategy among supply chain partners. Supply chain members are all beginning to realize that green supply chains are not only becoming a requirement, but they also provide cost savings, additional profits and cheaper prices to the supply chain members and end-product customers. For these reasons, use of environmental sustainability assessments is a concept that is gaining in popularity.

Today, software is available that enables companies to analyze the **carbon footprint** of their supply chains and then evaluate design configurations and various options for reducing total carbon emissions. In many cases, this will also mean lower costs. A number of software suppliers are extending their existing software applications to measure and optimize areas like transportation and inventory management, with explicit consideration for greening the supply chain. Larry Goldenhersch, CEO of California-based green software provider Enviance, explains how this might also help a retailer sell products: "If all screwdrivers cost $1.39, but my screwdriver has 10 pounds of carbon and my competitors have 50 pounds of carbon, I'm going to slap a carbon label on that screwdriver and say, 'Buy my screwdriver. Not only will it turn your screws, but it will save the planet for your kids and your grandkids.'"[19]

Specific Supply Chain Performance Measures

To achieve the type of performance alluded to in this chapter, specific measures must be adopted by supply chain trading partners such that performance can be further aligned with supply chain objectives. A number of these are listed below.[20]

1. *Total Supply Chain Management Costs*: the costs to process orders, purchase materials, purchase energy, comply with environmental regulations, manage inventories and returns and manage supply chain finance, planning and information systems. Leading supply companies are spending from 4 to 5 percent of sales on supply chain management costs, while the average company spends about 5 to 6 percent.

2. *Supply Chain Cash-to-Cash Cycle Time*: the average number of days between paying for raw materials and getting paid for product, for the supply chain trading partners (calculated by inventory days of supply plus days of sales outstanding minus average payment period for material). This measure shows the impact of lower inventories on the speed of cash moving through firms and the supply chain. Top supply chain companies have a cash-to-cash cycle time of about 30 days, which is far less than the average company. These trading partners no longer view "slow-paying" as a viable strategy.

3. *Supply Chain Production Flexibility*: the average time required for supply chain members to provide an unplanned, sustainable 20 percent increase in production. The ability for the supply chain to quickly react to unexpected demand spikes while still operating within financial targets provides tremendous competitive advantage. One common supply chain practice is to maintain stocks of component parts locally for supply chain customers to quickly respond to unexpected demand increases. Average production flexibility for best-in-class supply chains is from one to two weeks.

4. *Supply Chain Delivery Performance*: the average percentage of orders for the supply chain members that are filled on or before the requested delivery date. In the top-performing supply chains, delivery dates are being met from 94 to 100 percent of the time. For average firms, delivery performance is approximately 70 to 80 percent. Updating customers on the expected delivery dates of orders is becoming a common e-service for many supply chains.

5. *Supply Chain Perfect Order Fulfillment Performance*: the average percentage of orders among supply chain members that arrive on time, complete and damage-free. This is quickly becoming the standard for delivery performance and represents a significant source of competitive advantage for top-performing supply chains and their member companies.

6. *Supply Chain e-Business Performance*: the average percentage of electronic orders received for all supply chain members. In 1998, only about 2 percent of all firms' purchase orders were made over the Internet. By 2007, for example, office supply retailer Staples said that 90 percent of their orders came in electronically. Additionally, use of e-procurement can save up to 90 percent of the administrative costs of ordering.[21] Today, supply chain companies are investing heavily in

e-based order-receipt systems, marketing strategies and other forms of communication and research using the Internet.

7. *Supply Chain Environmental Performance*: the percentage of supply chain trading partners that have become ISO 14000 certified; the percentage of supply chain trading partners that have created a director of environmental sustainability; the average percentage of environmental goals met; the average number of policies adopted to reduce greenhouse gas emissions; and the average percentage of carbon footprints that have been offset by sound environmental practices. While these performance indicators may certainly vary by supply chain and industry, the measures here will provide a good starting point for collaboration on supply chain environmental performance.

When combined with the world-class performance measures of Table 14.1, the measures shown above help global supply chain trading partners align themselves with supply chain strategies, creating competencies that lead to dominant positions in their markets. Perhaps most importantly, this type of performance has translated into approximately 75 percent higher profits when compared to the average company.[22]

The Balanced Scorecard

The **Balanced Scorecard (BSC)** approach to performance measurement was developed in 1992 by Drs. Robert Kaplan and David Norton and representatives from a number of companies as a way to align an organization's performance measures with its strategic plans and goals. The BSC thus allowed a firm to move away from reliance on merely financial measures, which effectively improved managerial decision making.[23]

Also referred to as simply **scorecarding**, it has become a widely used model with some 80 percent of large U.S. businesses either using it or having previously used it and a smaller but growing percentage of European businesses using it. Many companies have reported notable successes with the use of the BSC including Mobil Oil, Tenneco, Brown & Root, AT&T, Intel, Allstate, Ernst & Young and KPMG Peat Marwick.[24] According to Shell Canada's human resource director John Hofmeister, "It gives us better and better alignment (between all operating units) and focuses attention on what's important and on results. In addition, the group's reward structure is linked directly to the scorecard."[25] Additionally, in a survey of 1,000 global members of the Institute of Management Accountants, 61 percent of the companies using BSC reported improvements in bottom-line financial results.[26]

There are some indications, though, that BSC use can be problematic, expensive and even unsuccessful. Research from the U.S.-based benchmarking company Hackett Group indicated that while 82 percent of their company database reportedly used scorecards, only 27 percent of the systems were considered "mature." They concluded that most companies were having difficulty taking BSC from concept to reality. John McMahan, senior advisor at Hackett Group, said, "Most companies get very little out of scorecards because they haven't followed the basic rules that make them effective." For example, in the U.S., the average number of measures used is a very high and often confusing 132, while Kaplan and Norton suggest use of 20 to 30 measures.[27] Additionally, consultants are used in many cases to help map the organization's strategy and its effect on performance and to assist in selecting performance measures. Further, information systems may have to be modified, sometimes at great expense, to supply the information necessary for the scorecards. Other weaknesses in the BSC include its inability to show what one's competitors are doing; exclusion of employee, supplier and alliance partner contributions; and its reliance on top-down measures.[28]

Nevertheless, the BSC is widely used in helping organizations track performance and identify areas of weakness. Scorecarding is designed to provide managers with a formal framework for achieving a balance between nonfinancial and financial results across both short-term and long-term planning horizons. The BSC framework consists of four perspectives as shown in Figure 14.1:

- *Financial Perspective*—measures that address revenue and profitability growth, product mix, cost reduction, productivity, asset utilization and investment strategies. Traditional financial measures are typically used.

- *Internal Business Process Perspective*—focuses on performance of the most critical internal business processes of the organization including quality, new product development, flexibility, innovative elements of processes and time-based measures.

- *Customer Perspective*—measures that focus on customer requirements and satisfaction including customer satisfaction ratings, reliability and responsiveness, customer retention, new customer acquisition, customer valued attributes and customer profitability.

- *Learning and Growth Perspective*—measures concentrating on the organization's people, systems, external environment, and including retaining and training employees, enhancing information technology and systems, employee safety and health and environmental sustainability issues.

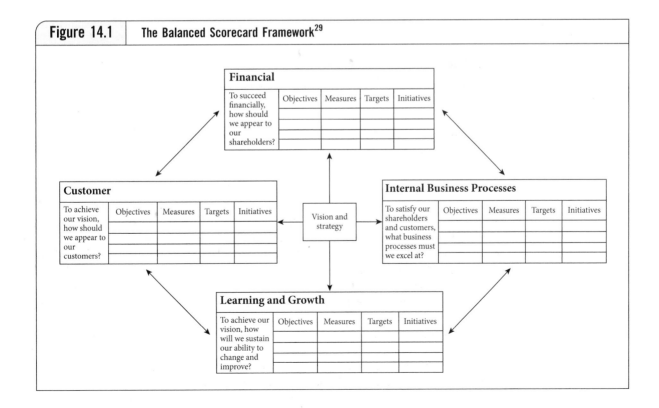

| **Figure 14.1** | **The Balanced Scorecard Framework[29]** |

These perspectives are all linked together using performance measures within each of the four areas. Measurements are developed for each goal in the organization's strategic plan and include both outcome measures and the performance drivers of those outcomes. In doing this, senior managers can channel the specific set of capabilities within the organization toward achieving the firm's goals. A properly constructed scorecard should support the firm's strategy, and consist of a linked series of measures that are consistent and reinforcing. By developing suitable performance measures in each of the perspectives, firms can detect problem areas before they become significant, trace the problem to its root causes and make improvements to alleviate the problem.

The process of developing a BSC begins with defining the firm's strategy. Once that strategy is understood and agreed upon by senior managers, the next step is to translate the strategy's goals into a system of relevant performance measures. Each of the four perspectives in the BSC require four to seven performance measures, resulting in a scorecard with about two dozen measures relating to one single strategy. As alluded to above, the potential for failure does exist if firms are not clear about what they are hoping to achieve and are not focused on ensuring that the best scorecards with the right performance measures linked to firm strategies are used.

The BSC can be also be utilized by firms in a collaborative supply chain setting by expanding the internal perspective of the scorecard to include interfunctional and partnership perspectives that characterize the supply chain. In this way, for instance, the firm's employees are motivated to view their firm's performance vis-à-vis the success of the entire supply chain. Supply chain-oriented performance measures such as the ones described earlier can thus be added to the more internally focused measures traditionally used in a balanced scorecard, to help the firm as well as their supply chains meet their objectives.

Balanced scorecards are being used in the government sector, too, with many positive outcomes. One example is the U.S. Economic Development administration (EDA). The EDA has used the BSC to help develop their world-class performance measurement system. After adoption of the BSC approach, they aligned the organization around a common set of goals, improved the quality of their investments, enhanced efficiencies and created higher-quality jobs. In 2004, they exceeded their target for new investment partners and improved their private sector investment leverage ratio by 500 percent. Today they are recognized as one of the U.S. government's top performers.[30]

Web-Based Scorecards

Today, a number of software applications are available to help design scorecards, which also link via the Web to a firm's enterprise software system. Web-based balanced scorecard applications are also sometimes referred to as **dashboards**. They enable users to retrieve data easily from ERP databases and also enable wide access by users at many locations, while providing desired security features. Today, dashboards are being used to track "big picture" corporate objectives as well as core process performance and more tactical, detailed data. Use of these Web-based dashboards allows managers to see real-time progress toward organizational milestones and helps to ensure that decisions remain in sync with the firm's overall strategies.

Virtually all accounting applications, for example, provide BSC capabilities, including applications offered by Microsoft, SAP, IBM and Oracle. These applications are becoming very popular. According to a 2005 survey by The Data Warehousing Institute, an education and certification organization headquartered in Washington, 74 percent of the respondents stated they used dashboards or were in the process of implementing them.[31] Texas-based petroleum company Valero Energy has been using a Web-based BSC for a few years now. A discussion of their experiences appears in the e-Business Connection feature.

The SCOR Model

One of the more recognized methods for integrating supply chains and measuring trading partner performance is use of the Supply Chain Operations Reference (SCOR) model developed in 1996 by supply-chain consulting firms Pittiglio Rabin Todd &

---

e-Business Connection

Using Dashboards at Valero Energy

It's 7 am in San Antonio, Texas and Rich Marcogliese, chief operating officer at Valero Energy, is holding his usual morning meeting with the plant managers of 16 major refineries throughout the United States and Canada. On the walls of the HQ operations center are a series of monitors centered by a giant screen with a live display of the company's Refining Dashboard. Whether the executives are in the room or connected remotely, all eyes are trained on the web-accessible gauges and charts, which are refreshed with the latest data every five minutes. "They review how each plant and unit is performing compared to the plan," says Valero CIO Hal Zesch, "and if there is any deviation, the manager explains what's going on at their plant."

For Valero, just one dashboard needle moving from green to red might signal millions of dollars at stake. The point of the dashboard isn't to call managers out; it's to give executives timed information so that they can take corrective action. Valero's Refining Dashboard is just the sort of cutting-edge decision-support tool that thousands, if not tens of thousands, of companies are now attempting to create. Those companies have embraced the idea that decisions based on fact will consistently beat those based on gut. Business bestsellers have documented that it's an approach that works. Financial analysts, board members and even the news media increasingly expect sound, data-backed analyses from top management. And when things go wrong, regulators and, in some cases, even district attorneys follow the numbers to trace bad decisions.

Valero rolled out its dashboard in early 2008 at the behest of COO Marcogliese. He had launched a Commitment to Excellence program aimed at improving performance, and he wanted to see real-time data related to plant and equipment reliability, inventory management, safety and energy consumption. A major focus of Valero's Commitment to Excellence program is reducing energy consumption, so the company is rolling out separate dashboards that show detailed statistics on power consumption by unit and plant. "Based on the data, managers can share best practices and make changes in operations to reduce energy consumption while maintaining production levels," CIO Zesch explains. Estimated savings to date: $140 million per year for the seven plants where the dashboards are in use, with expected total savings of $230 million per year once the dashboards are rolled out at all 16 refineries.

The successes have created dashboard-envy within Valero, so IT is working on similar dashboard programs for sales and marketing as well as the strategic sourcing unit.

Source: Henschen, D., "From Gut to Facts," *InformationWeek*, November 16, 2009: 6–10. Use with permission.

McGrath and AMR Research. These firms also founded the Supply-Chain Council, a non-profit global organization with a current membership of over 600 profit and non-profit companies, to manage the **SCOR model**. Today, the Supply-Chain Council has international chapters in North America, Europe, China, Japan, Australia/New Zealand, South East Asia, Brazil and Southern Africa.[32] Their members continuously review and update the SCOR model for use by the membership and others who can purchase the model software. The SCOR model integrates the operations of supply chain members by linking the delivery operations of the seller to the sourcing operations of the buyer, as shown in Figure 14.2.

The SCOR model is used as a supply chain management diagnostic, benchmarking and process improvement tool by manufacturing and service firms in a variety of industries around the globe. Some of the more notable firms to have success using the SCOR model include Intel, IBM, 3M, Cisco, Siemens and Bayer. Striving for the best telecommunications supply chain, Alcatel used SCOR metrics following the economic downturn of 2001 to measure and benchmark its performance. Major improvements were realized in delivery performance, sourcing cycle time, supply chain management cost and inventory days of supply.[33] Cisco set out to revamp their supply chain in 2005 using the SCOR model as a way to monitor their growing global footprint. They eventually appointed a vice president responsible for the SCOR model's functions.[34]

The SCOR model separates supply chain operations into five process categories—plan, source, make, deliver and return, as described below:[35]

- *PLAN*—Demand and supply planning including balancing resources with requirements; establishing/communicating plans for the supply chain; management of business rules, supply chain performance, data collection, inventory, capital assets, transportation and regulatory requirements.

- *SOURCE*—Sourcing stocked, make-to-order and engineer-to-order products including scheduling deliveries, receiving, verifying, and transferring product, authorizing supplier payments, identifying and selecting suppliers, assessing supplier performance, managing incoming inventory and supplier agreements.

- *MAKE*—Make-to-stock, make-to-order and engineer-to-order production execution including scheduling production activities, producing, testing, packaging, staging, and releasing product for delivery, finalizing engineering for engineer-to-order products, managing work-in-process, equipment, facilities and the production network.

Figure 14.2	The SCOR Model Linkages

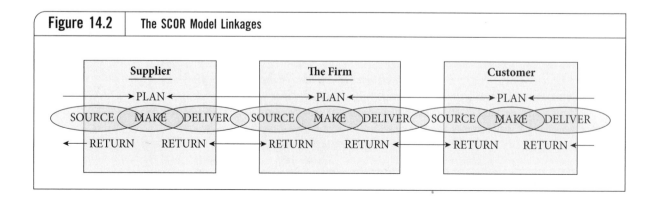

- *DELIVER*—Order, warehouse, transportation and installation management for stocked, make-to-order and engineer-to-order product including all order management steps from order inquiries and quotes to routing shipments and selecting carriers, warehouse management from receiving and picking to loading and shipping product, invoicing customer, managing finished product inventories and import/export requirements.

- *RETURN*—Returns of purchased materials to suppliers and receipt of finished goods returns from customers including authorizing and scheduling returns, receiving, verifying, and disposition of defective or excess products, return replacement or credit, and managing return inventories.

There are three standardized levels of process detail in the SCOR model. At Level 1, users select appropriate process categories from the SCOR configuration toolkit to represent their supply chain and select from thirteen performance attributes as shown in Table 14.2. In Level 2, the SCOR processes are further described by process type. Within each process type are process categories that users specify. The process types and categories are shown in Table 14.3. In Level 3, process flow diagrams are defined with process elements or specific tasks for each of the process categories established in Level 2, showing inputs, process elements and outputs. Additionally, specific performance measures are identified for each of the process elements within the flow diagrams. Some example measures are shown in Table 14.4. Best practices can also be identified at this level. Finally, implementation of supply chain management practices within the company occurs.

As can be seen in the tables, implementing the SCOR model is no simple task and requires a significant investment of time and communication within the firm and among supply chain partners. But the firms that use the model find it very helpful. For instance, Joe Williams, director of global productivity at Mead Johnson Nutritionals, a

Table 14.2	SCOR Level 1 Performance Categories and Attributes
PERFORMANCE CATEGORY	**PERFORMANCE ATTRIBUTE**
Reliability	1. Delivery performance
	2. Fill rates
	3. Perfect order fulfillment
Responsiveness	1. Order fulfillment lead times
Flexibility	1. Supply chain response times
	2. Production flexibility
Cost	1. Supply chain management cost
	2. Cost of goods sold
	3. Value-added productivity
	4. Warranty cost or returns processing cost
Assets	1. Cash-to-cash cycle time
	2. Inventory days of supply
	3. Asset turns

Table 14.3	SCOR Level 2 Process Types and Categories		
SCOR PROCESS TYPE	**CHARACTERISTICS**	**PROCESS CATEGORY**	
Planning	Processes that align expected resources to meet expected demand requirements.	P1: Plan supply chain P2: Plan source P3: Plan make P4: Plan deliver P5: Plan return	
Execution	Processes triggered by planned or actual demand that changes the state of material goods. These are Source (S1–3), Make (M1–3), Deliver (D1–3) and Return (R1–3) processes.	S1: Source stocked product S2: Source MTO product S3: Source ETO product M1: Make-to-stock M2: Make-to-order M3: Engineer-to-order	D1: Deliver stocked product D2: Deliver MTO product D3: Deliver ETO product R1: Return defective product R2: Return MRO product R3: Return excess product
Enable	Processes that prepare, maintain or manage information or relationships on which planning and execution processes rely.	EX1: Establish and manage rules EX2: Assess performance EX3: Manage data EX4: Manage inventory EX5: Manage capital assets EX6: Manage transportation EX7: Manage supply chain configuration EX8: Manage regulatory compliance EX9: Process specific elements (align SC/ financials, supplier agreements)	

Note: X=P,S,M,D,R

Table 14.4	SCOR Level 3 Performance Categories and Measures
PROCESS ELEMENT: SCHEDULE PROCESS DELIVERIES	
PERFORMANCE ATTRIBUTE CATEGORIES	**MEASURES**
Reliability	• % schedules generated within supplier's lead time • % schedules changed within supplier's lead time
Responsiveness	• Average release cycle of changes
Flexibility	• Average days per schedule change • Average days per engineering change
Cost	• Product management and planning costs as a % of product acquisitions costs
Assets	None identified

division of Bristol-Myers Squibb, says the SCOR model is playing a big role in helping their unit measure its supply chain performance against other companies. But getting those measurements "is a big job," he says. "SCOR is definitive in some respects and open to interpretation in others."[36]

Thus, as can be seen by the information presented here, the SCOR model is used to describe, measure and evaluate supply chain configurations. The model is designed to enable effective communication, performance measurement and integration of processes between supply chain members. A standardized reference model helps management focus on management issues, serving internal and external customers and instigate improvements along the supply chain. Using the SCOR software, virtually any supply chain can be configured, evaluated and benchmarked against best practices, leading to continuous improvements and sustainable competitive advantage for the supply chain's participating members. At Nabisco, for instance, the SCOR model is used to link two separate foods divisions. Its U.S. Foods Division ships to warehouses, while its Biscuits Division ships direct to retail outlets. They also use SCOR to see if their handling of returns is keeping up with the industry best practices.[37]

Recently, two additions made to the SCOR model are meant to help further integrate supply chains: the Customer Chain Operations Reference model (CCOR) and the Design Chain Operations Reference model (DCOR). Part of the difficulty of using the SCOR model is that it does not address the processes of sales and marketing, some aspects of service and support processes like human resources and technology development. In response to this, the CCOR model defines the customer part of the supply chain as the integration of Plan, Relate, Sell, Contract, Service and Enable processes. Further, the DCOR model defines the design portion of the supply chain as the integration of Plan, Research, Design, Integrate, Amend and Enable processes.[38]

✸ SCORmark is the newest tool of the Supply-Chain Council, which allows member firms to benchmark performance against selected peer companies using a benchmarking portal at the Supply-Chain Council's website. Benchmark data is supplied by the American Productivity and Quality Center, a Houston-based nonprofit research organization. This has greatly reduced the time it normally takes firms to perform a benchmarking study—from months to weeks and, in some cases, days. The SCORmark portal removes cost barriers for members to obtain accurate and timely benchmark reports. "Our members are now able to use the defined metrics in the SCOR model to set corporate strategy and accurately analyze performance gaps," says Thomas Phelps, the Supply-Chain Council's chairman.[39]

SUMMARY

Measuring the performance of companies and their supply chains is critical for identifying underlying problems and keeping end customers satisfied in today's highly competitive, rapidly changing marketplaces. Unfortunately, many firms have adopted performance measurement systems that measure the wrong things and are thus finding it difficult to achieve strategic goals, and align their goals with those of the other supply chain members and the supply chain as a whole. Good performance measures allow firms to improve their processes, making their supply chains better as well.

Financial performance, while important to shareholders, is argued to provide too little information regarding the firm's underlying ability to provide products and services that satisfy customers. Thus, measures that say something about the firm's quality, productivity, flexibility and customer service capabilities have begun to be used successfully in many organizations. World-class organizations realize how important it is to align strategies with the performance of their people and processes, and performance measurement systems give these firms a means for directing efforts and firm capabilities toward what the firm is trying to do over the long haul—meet strategic objectives and satisfy customers.

As was discussed throughout the chapter, performance measurement systems should be a mix of financial, nonfinancial, quantitative, qualitative, process-oriented, environmentally-oriented and customer-oriented measures that effectively link the actions of the firm to the strategies defined by its executive managers. Firms actively managing their supply chains have an added layer of performance measurement requirements—measures must be added that link the operations of member firms as well as linking the actions of the firms to the competitive strategies of the supply chain. Several performance measurement models were presented and discussed in the chapter that have been successfully used in supply chains to monitor and link supply chain members' performance—namely the Balanced Scorecard and the Supply Chain Operations Reference models.

KEY TERMS

balanced scorecard (BSC), 496

carbon footprint, 494

dashboards, 498

demand-driven supply networks, 491

environmental sustainability, 494

functional silos, 488

green supply chain management (GSCM), 494

performance variance, 488

SCOR model, 500

scorecarding, 496

single-factor productivity measures, 488

total productivity measures, 488

DISCUSSION QUESTIONS

1. Do you think there is a relationship between performance measurement and a firm's competitiveness and profitability? Explain.

2. What do customers have to do with good performance measures?

3. How should performance measures be viewed from a supply chain perspective?

4. In building supply chain competencies, what are the trade-offs that must be considered?

5. What risk do managers take when they view their firm's performance solely in financial terms?

6. List some of the traditional performance measures, and describe their value in today's competitive climate.

7. Discuss the use of performance standards and performance variances. Do schools and universities use them? How can they be damaging to the organization?

8. What is the difference between a total productivity measure and a single-factor productivity measure? Provide an example.

9. List some single-factor and multiple-factor productivity measures for a restaurant, a quick-change oil garage and an overnight delivery service.

10. Using the formula for productivity, (outputs)/(inputs), what are all the ways that productivity can be increased?

11. *Problem:* Cindy Jo's Hair Salon is concerned about their rising costs of supplies, energy and labor, so they are considering investing in better equipment, which hopefully will reduce the time required to perform most hairstyles as well as resulting in better perceived quality by their customers. They predict that the added investment will increase output levels as well as reduce energy costs, since some of the new equipment (hair dryers) use less electricity. Using the following information, determine the current and expected single-factor and total productivity measures. What is the percentage change in total productivity? What other items should be considered before making this capital investment? Do you think the increase in output will overcome the capital costs?

INPUTS AND OUTPUTS	CURRENT (THIS YEAR)	EXPECTED (NEXT YEAR)
Hairstyles per week	250	300
Labor costs per week	$960	$1,010
Energy costs per week	$400	$350
Material costs per week	$300	$325
Capital investment	$0	$12,000

12. What are the advantages and disadvantages of using labor utilization as a performance measure? Do these same arguments apply to machine utilization?

13. How could you increase labor productivity without increasing labor utilization?

14. Using the formulas provided for utilization, calculate the utilization of your classroom.

15. What do you think a good labor utilization would be for a factory? A restaurant? Why?

16. How do world-class performance measures differ from, say, financial performance measures?

17. Using the steps suggested for developing performance measures, create several world-class performance measures for a hotel's front-desk area, maintenance department and room service personnel.

18. How should a firm extend their performance measures to include other supply chain members?

19. What are demand-driven supply networks, and what role do performance measures play in these networks?

20. Why should supply chains begin using green performance measures? Provide some examples of green supply chain performance measures. How would these differ from green performance measures for one firm?

21. What is a carbon footprint, and how can firms reduce theirs?

22. What is perfect order fulfillment? What is cash-to-cash cycle time?

23. Describe the four perspectives of the balanced scorecard. How is this model different from a set of world-class performance measures?

24. What are the steps in developing a balanced scorecard?

25. How is a scorecard different from a dashboard?

26. What are the five process categories of the SCOR model, and which one do you think is most important?

27. Describe what happens as a firm progresses through the standardized levels of process detail in the SCOR model.

28. Which model do you think is best suited to measure supply chain performance—the Balanced Scorecard or the SCOR? Why?

29. What are the latest extensions of the SCOR model, and why are they used?

INTERNET QUESTIONS

1. Go to the U.S. Bureau of Labor Statistics website at www.bls.gov, and report on the labor productivity and total productivity of the U.S. and of other countries listed. How does the U.S. stack up?

2. Go to www.economagic.com and look at capacity utilization numbers for U.S. manufacturers. What is it now? What have the trends been for the past ten years?

3. Find current examples of firms that are using Balanced Scorecards and the SCOR model, and report on their success.

4. What are the current environmental or sustainability performance issues in your area or country? Discuss the companies that are performing well regarding these issues.

APPENDIX 1
Areas under the Normal Curve

This table gives the area under the curve to the left of x, for various Z scores, or the number of standard deviations from the mean. For example, in the figure, if $Z = 1.96$, the value .97500 found in the body of the table is the total shaded area to the left of x.

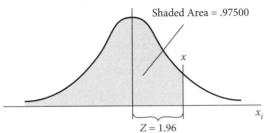

Z	.00	.01	.02	.03	.04	.05	.06	.07	.08	.09
.0	.50000	.50399	.50798	.51197	.51595	.51994	.52392	.52790	.53188	.53586
.1	.53983	.54380	.54776	.55172	.55567	.55962	.56356	.56749	.57142	.57535
.2	.57926	.58317	.58706	.59095	.59483	.59871	.60257	.60642	.61026	.61409
.3	.61791	.62172	.62552	.62930	.63307	.63683	.64058	.64431	.64803	.65173
.4	.65542	.65910	.66276	.66640	.67003	.67364	.67724	.68082	.68439	.68793
.5	.69146	.69497	.69847	.70194	.70540	.70884	.71226	.71566	.71904	.72240
.6	.72575	.72907	.73237	.73536	.73891	.74215	.74537	.74857	.75175	.75490
.7	.75804	.76115	.76424	.76730	.77035	.77337	.77637	.77935	.78230	.78524
.8	.78814	.79103	.79389	.79673	.79955	.80234	.80511	.80785	.81057	.81327
.9	.81594	.81859	.82121	.82381	.82639	.82894	.83147	.83398	.83646	.83891
1.0	.84134	.84375	.84614	.84849	.85083	.85314	.85543	.85769	.85993	.86241
1.1	.86433	.86650	.86864	.87076	.87286	.87493	.87698	.87900	.88100	.88298
1.2	.88493	.88686	.88877	.89065	.89251	.89435	.89617	.89796	.89973	.90147
1.3	.90320	.90490	.90658	.90824	.90988	.91149	.91309	.91466	.91621	.91774
1.4	.91924	.92073	.92220	.92364	.92507	.92647	.92785	.92922	.93056	.93189
1.5	.93319	.93448	.93574	.93699	.93822	.93943	.94062	.94179	.94295	.94408
1.6	.94520	.94630	.94738	.94845	.94950	.95053	.95154	.95254	.95352	.95449
1.7	.95543	.95637	.95728	.95818	.95907	.95994	.96080	.96164	.96246	.96327
1.8	.96407	.96485	.96562	.96638	.96712	.96784	.96856	.96926	.96995	.97062
1.9	.97128	.97193	.97257	.97320	.97381	.97441	.97500	.97558	.97615	.97670
2.0	.97725	.97784	.97831	.97882	.97932	.97982	.98030	.98077	.98124	.98169
2.1	.98214	.98257	.98300	.98341	.98382	.98422	.98461	.98500	.98537	.98574
2.2	.98610	.98645	.98679	.98713	.98745	.98778	.98809	.98840	.98870	.98899
2.3	.98928	.98956	.98983	.99010	.99036	.99061	.99086	.99111	.99134	.99158
2.4	.99180	.99202	.99224	.99245	.99266	.99286	.99305	.99324	.99343	.99361
2.5	.99379	.99396	.99413	.99430	.99446	.99461	.99477	.99492	.99506	.99520
2.6	.99534	.99547	.99560	.99573	.99585	.99598	.99606	.99621	.99632	.99643
2.7	.99653	.99664	.99674	.99683	.99693	.99702	.99711	.99720	.99728	.99736
2.8	.99744	.99752	.99760	.99767	.99774	.99781	.99788	.99795	.99801	.99807
2.9	.99813	.99819	.99825	.99831	.99836	.99841	.99846	.99851	.99856	.99861
3.0	.99865	.99869	.99874	.99878	.99882	.99886	.99889	.99893	.99896	.99900
3.1	.99903	.99906	.99910	.99913	.99916	.99918	.99921	.99924	.99926	.99929
3.2	.99931	.99934	.99936	.99938	.99940	.99942	.99944	.99946	.99948	.99950
3.3	.99952	.99953	.99955	.99957	.99958	.99960	.99961	.99962	.99964	.99965
3.4	.99966	.99968	.99969	.99970	.99971	.99972	.99973	.99974	.99975	.99976
3.5	.99977	.99978	.99978	.99979	.99980	.99981	.99981	.99982	.99983	.99983
3.6	.99984	.99985	.99985	.99986	.99986	.99987	.99987	.99988	.99988	.99989
3.7	.99989	.99990	.99990	.99990	.99991	.99991	.99992	.99992	.99992	.99992
3.8	.99993	.99993	.99993	.99994	.99994	.99994	.99994	.99995	.99995	.99995
3.9	.99995	.99995	.99996	.99996	.99996	.99996	.99996	.99996	.99997	.99997

APPENDIX 2
Answers to Selected End-of-Chapter Problems

Chapter 2

1. 8%

3. 5 times

5. a. 5,500 units, $69,000

   b. buy, $4,000

   c. make, $2,000

Chapter 3

18. The weighted score is 89. Supplier is classified as a Certified Vendor.

Chapter 4

24. 50,000 second-tier suppliers, then reduced to 2,000 second-tier suppliers

Chapter 5

2. (1) 72,567, (2) 71,980, (3) 71,058

Chapter 6

1. a. Chase production strategy

Month	Jan	Feb	Mar	Apr	May	Jun
Demand	2000	3000	5000	6000	6000	2000
Production	2000	3000	5000	6000	6000	2000
Ending inventory	0	0	0	0	0	0
Workforce	20	30	50	60	60	20

   b. Level production strategy

Month	Jan	Feb	Mar	Apr	May	Jun
Demand	2000	3000	5000	6000	6000	2000
Production	4000	4000	4000	4000	4000	4000
Ending inventory	2000	3000	2000	0	-2000	0
Workforce	40	40	40	40	40	40

   (-2000 indicates backlog of 2000 in May).

4. ATP: D

Week		1	2	3	4	5	6	7	8
Model B									
MPS	BI = 20	20	0	20	20	0	20	20	20
Committed customer orders		10	10	10	10	10	0	0	10
ATP:D		20	0	10	0	0	20	20	10

Chapter 7

1. 13.7 times

3. EOQ = 26.18615 (rounded to 5 decimal places)

   Annual holding cost = annual order cost = $11,456.44

   Total annual inventory cost = $3,022,912.88 (including product cost)

8. a. Optimal order quantity = 151 units
   b. Annual purchase cost = $25,200,000.00
   c. Annual holding cost = $405,888.00
   d. Annual order cost = $2,980.13
   e. Total annual inventory cost = $25,608,868.13

11. a. Daily demand = 100 units
    b. Optimal lot size = 750 units
    c. Highest inventory = 600 units
    d. Annual product cost = $2,880,000
    e. Annual holding cost = $7,200
    f. Annual setup cost = $7,200
    g. Total annual inventory cost = $2,894,400
    h. Length of a production period = 1.5 days
    i. Length of each inventory cycle = 7.5 days
    j. Rate of inventory buildup during the production cycle = 400 units/day
    k. The number of inventory cycles per year = 48 times

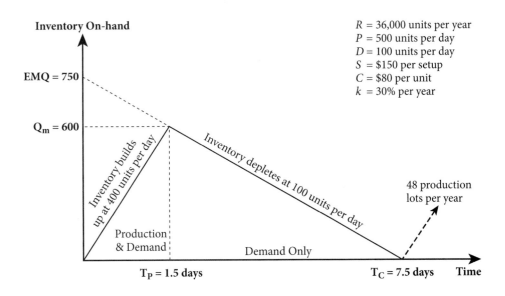

12. Safety stock = 117.6 units, Statistical reorder point = 767.6 units
14. Safety stock = 1,470 units, Statistical reorder point = 4,470 units

Chapter 8

2. It would need to take about 2.3 hours.
3. a. DPMO = 23,214 defects per million rentals
   a. slightly less than 3.5

4. b. $\overline{\overline{X}} = 99.2$ and $\bar{R} = 8.4$

   c. $UCL_x = 105.3$, $LCL_x = 93.1$, $UCL_R = 19.2$, $LCL_R = 0$

6. a. $\bar{P} = .1167$

   b. $\sigma_P = .1015$

   c. $UCL = 0.42$; $LCL = 0$

Chapter 9

16. The starting system has 18,000 total units; $S_2 = 12,728$ units total with three warehouses; and 7,348 units total with one warehouse.

Chapter 10

9. $NPV_A = \$2,639$; $NPV_B = \$2,362$; $NPV_C = \$3,018$

Chapter 11

2. Site A has the highest total weighted score of 84.5 and is the selected site.

Chapter 12

1. a. labor prod. $= 0.5$ cust. per labor $; material prod. $= 1.88$ cust. per mat'l. $; energy prod. $= 7.5$ cust. per energy $; mult. fact. prod. $= 0.38$ cust. per $

   b. monthly capacity $= 3120$ customers; capacity utilization $= 48.1$ %

2. Distance traveled $= 5,545$ m/day; you could put Depts. 4 and 5 closer together (switch 5 and 8), so the new distance $= 3805$ m/day.

3. 19 points; try switching Depts. 5 and 8

4. 2 full-time and 3 part-time workers would fill the requirements.

6. Probability $= 0.7$

7. $L_s = 1.5$ customers; $L_q = 0.9$ customers

8. $P_0 = 1/(1 + .6 + .18(1.43)) = 0.538$; $L_q = .538(.36(.3) / 2(.7^2)) = .059$ customers

Chapter 14

11. Current total productivity $= 250/\$1,660 = 0.151$ haircuts/dollar
Expected total productivity $= 300/\$1,685 = 0.178$ haircuts/dollar (an 18% increase)

Glossary

A

ABC inventory control system A useful technique for determining which inventories should be managed more closely and which others should not (A-items are the most important).

ABC inventory matrix A diagram that illustrates whether a firm's physical inventory matches its inventory usage. It is derived by plotting an ABC analysis based on inventory usage classification on the vertical axis and an ABC analysis based on physical inventory classification on the horizontal axis.

acceptance sampling In purchasing, it is a statistical screening technique that can be used to determine whether or not a shipment will be accepted, returned to the supplier or used for billback purposes when defects are fixed or units are eliminated by the buyer.

active RFID tags An RFID tag that is equipped with an onboard power supply to power the integrated circuits and broadcast its signal to the reader.

aggregate production plan (APP) A long-range production plan; it sets the aggregate output rate, workforce size, utilization, inventory and backlog levels for a plant.

air carrier A carrier using airliners for transportation; one of the five modes of transportation .

airline security Protection that is provided for airlines against terrorist attacks and other illegal activities.

analytic SRM A method that allows the company to analyze the complete supplier base.

application service provider (ASP) A company that offers website services for a fee, such as self-serve reverse auction websites.

arrival pattern The frequency with which customers arrive at a business.

assignable variations Process variations that can be traced to a specific cause. Assignable variations are created by causes that can be identified and eliminated and thus become the objective of statistical process control efforts.

Association of Southeast Asian Nations (ASEAN) An economic and geopolitical organization created in 1967 that today comprises the following countries in the Southeast Asian region: Brunei, Cambodia, Indonesia, Laos, Malaysia, Myanmar, the Philippines, Singapore, Thailand and Vietnam. The primary objective of ASEAN is to promote economic, social and cultural development of the region through cooperative programs.

assignable variations These are process variations that can be traced to a specific cause.

Assignable variations are created by causes that can be identified and eliminated and thus become the objective of statistical process control efforts.

attribute data Yes/no kinds of data. These indicate the presence of some attribute such as color, satisfaction, workability or beauty (for instance, determining whether or not a car was painted the right color, if a customer liked the meal, if the lightbulb worked or if the dress was pretty).

available-to-promise (ATP) quantity The uncommitted portion of a firm's planned production. It is used to promise new customer orders.

B

back-of-the-house operations Those services that do not require customer contact.

backsourcing Bringing back in-house some activities that had been previously outsourced; also called *insourcing*.

backward vertical integration The process of acquiring upstream suppliers.

balanced scorecard (BSC) A management system developed in the early 1990s by Robert Kaplan and David Norton that helps companies to continually refine their vision and strategy. The balanced scorecard uses a set of measures to provide feedback on internal business performance in order to continually improve strategic performance.

balanced scorecard framework Refers to the method used to complete the balanced scorecard (the types of data used).

balking Refusing to join a queue once it is seen how long it is.

barter The complete exchange of goods and/or services of equal value without the exchange of currency. The seller can either consume the goods and/or services or resell the items.

Baumol's disease A productivity growth problem named after noted U.S. economist William Baumol in the 1960s. For most services, automation can be a troublesome issue, and the labor content per unit of output can be quite high relative to manufactured goods. These two things can lead to a declining productivity growth rate as a nation's economy becomes less manufacturing oriented and more service oriented.

benchmarking The practice of copying what other businesses do best; studying how things are done well in other firms to potentially make use of the same methods.

best-of-breed solution An ERP system that picks the best application or module for each individual function.

bid bonds Bonds posted by bidders to ensure that the successful bidder will fulfill the contract as stated.

bill of materials (BOM) An engineering document that shows an inclusive listing of all component parts and assemblies making up the final product.

billback penalty A fee charged back to the supplier for services or products not received by the customer.

blank check purchase order A small value purchase order with a signed blank check attached, usually at the bottom of the purchase order.

blanket order release A form used to release a specific quantity against a prenegotiated blanket purchase order.

blanket purchase order A purchase order that covers a variety of items and is negotiated for repeated supply over a fixed time period, such as quarterly or yearly.

breakbulk The process of breaking down large quantity shipments so that items can be combined into specific customer orders and then shipped out.

break-even analysis A technique that uses the fixed and variable costs to determine the quantity where the total costs are equal between two or more alternatives. It is a handy tool for computing the cost-effectiveness of sourcing decisions, when cost is the most important criterion. Breakeven occurs when revenues equal fixed plus variable costs. Can also refer to when one cost curve intersects another.

break-even model See *break-even analysis*.

bullwhip effect A term referring to ineffective communication between buyers and suppliers and infrequent delivery of materials, combined with production based on poor forecasts along a supply chain that results in either too little or too much inventory at various points of storage and consumption. Simply, it causes an amplification of the variation in the demand pattern along the supply chain.

business clusters According to Dr. Michael Porter, "clusters are geographic concentrations of interconnected companies and institutions in a particular field. Clusters encompass an array of linked industries and other entities important to competition."

business cycle Alternating periods of expansion and contraction in economic activity.

business ethics The application of ethical principles to business situations.

business process reengineering (BPR) A radical rethinking and redesigning of business processes that seeks to reduce waste and increase performance. The goal is to create significant changes through assessments of current processes, design of better processes using modeling techniques, implementation of the new processes, and continuing performance assessments.

Buy American Act Legislation mandating that U.S. government purchases and third-party purchases that utilize federal funds must buy domestically produced goods, if the price differential between the domestic product and an identical foreign-sourced product does not exceed a certain percentage amount.

C

C charts A statistical process control technique that is used to monitor the total number of defects per unit.

C-TPAT compliant An assessment of suppliers' security practices, the development of continuity plans for various events and the implementation of specific training and education programs.

call centers or **customer contact centers** Customer service departments that integrate all of the methods customers can use to contact a business, including telephone, mail, comment cards, email, and website messages and chat rooms.

capacity The output capabilities of a firm's labor and machine resources.

capacity planning A hierarchical planning process that is used to determine the capacity needed for a specific production level.

capacity requirements planning (CRP) A short-range capacity planning technique that is used to check the feasibility of the material requirements plan.

capacity utilization A ratio equal to capacity used/capacity available per period; indicates the level at which the firm utilizes its available capacity.

carbon footprint A firm's or supply chain's total carbon emissions.

carbon-neutral The state achieved when a firm can offset the carbon footprint of its operations— for example, by planting trees.

cause-and-effect diagram Also called *fishbone diagram* or *Ishikawa diagram*. A method that is used to aid in brainstorming and isolating the causes of a problem. Typically there are four causes of problems (the 4-Ms).

cause-and-effect forecasting A forecasting method that uses one or more factors (independent variables) that are related to demand to predict future demand.

centralized–decentralized purchasing structure A hybrid purchasing structure that is centralized at the corporate level but decentralized at the individual business unit level.

centralized purchasing The single purchasing department, usually located at the firm's corporate office, that makes all the purchasing decisions for the entire corporation.

change management An organized approach to manage the change from the current state to the desired state.

channel equity The value for a firm embodied in its distribution channel.

channel integration Collaborating with, or taking over suppliers and customers (vertical channel integration); or doing the same with competitors (horizontal channel integration).

chase demand strategy A strategy that is used when the amount of capacity varies with demand. See also *chase production strategy*.

chase production strategy A production strategy that adjusts output to match the demand pattern during each production period.

check sheet A sheet listing a number of potential problems that receive a check mark every time the problem occurs.

Civil Aeronautics Act of 1938 Legislation that promoted the development of the air transportation system, air safety, and airline efficiency by establishing the Civil Aeronautics Board to oversee market entry, establish routes with appropriate levels of competition, develop regional feeder airlines and establish reasonable rates. The Civil Aeronautics Administration was also established to regulate air safety.

class rates The transportation rates based on the particular class of the product transported; some products have higher published class rates than others.

clickstream A record of the items that a specific customer clicks on when visiting a website.

closed-loop MRP An MRP-based manufacturing planning and control system that incorporates aggregate production planning, master production scheduling, material requirements planning and capacity requirements planning.

closeness desirability rating A scale used to rate how desirable it is to have two departments close together. The objective is to design a layout that maximizes the desirability rating for the entire facility.

cloud-based supply chain management When trading partners make use of software solutions readily available from Internet providers for a subscription fee, allowing them to create a global presence on the Internet very quickly.

cloud computing When shared resources and other information are made available to users over the Internet, usually for a subscription fee. It allows small businesses, for example, to make use of sophisticated software without actually making the purchase; also termed *on-demand computing*.

co-managed inventories A somewhat more collaborative form of VMI; can also refer to JIT II.

co-sourcing The sharing of a process or function between internal staff and an external

supplier; when a firm both makes and buys a good; also referred to as *selective sourcing*, or *partial outsourcing*.

coal slurry Pulverized coal that is suspended in water.

collaboration Working together through information sharing with suppliers and customers on various activities.

collaborative education Providing training for supply chain partner employees.

collaborative negotiations The process that occurs when both sides work together to maximize the joint outcome, or to create a win-win result; also referred to as *integrative negotiations*.

collaborative planning, forecasting, and replenishment (CPFR) According to the Voluntary Interindustry Commerce Standards (VICS) Association, CPFR is "a business practice that combines the intelligence of multiple trading partners in the planning and fulfillment of customer demand. CPFR links sales and marketing best practices, such as category management, to supply chain planning and execution processes to increase availability while reducing inventory, transportation and logistics costs."

collaborative relationships The win-win supplier-buyer-customer relationships that supply chain companies strive to achieve.

collaborative transportation management Logistics providers and shippers working together and sharing forecasting, planning and replenishment information to optimize transportation vehicle usage.

commodity rates Rates that apply to minimum quantities of specified products that are shipped between two specified locations.

common carriers Transportation providers that offer services to all shippers at published rates between designated locations.

Common Market of Eastern and Southern Africa (COMESA) A customs union established to foster economic growth among the member countries of Burundi, Comoros, D. R. Congo, Djibouti, Egypt, Eritrea, Ethiopia, Kenya, Libya, Madagascar, Malawi, Mauritius, Rwanda, Seychelles, Sudan, Swaziland, Uganda, Zambia, and Zimbabwe.

competitive bidding A process whereby suppliers offer bid prices to buyers, to get business. The purchase contract is usually awarded to the *lowest priced bidder*, determined to be a responsive and responsible supplier by the buyer.

concurrent engineering Designing the manufacturing process or service delivery system simultaneously with the design of the product.

consolidation warehouses Warehouses that collect large numbers of LTL shipments from nearby regional sources of supply, then deliver in TL or CL quantities to a manufacturer.

consumer's risk The risk assumed when a buyer accepts a shipment of poor-quality units because the sample *did* meet the acceptance standard; this results in a type-II error.

consumer survey forecast A questionnaire that seeks input from customers on important issues such as future buying habits, new product ideas and opinions about existing products. The survey is administered through telephone, mail, Internet or personal interviews. Data collected from the survey are analyzed using statistical tools and judgments, to derive a set of meaningful results.

container-on-flatcar (COFC) A form of intermodal transportation; standardized shipping containers are transported via rail flatcar, and they can also be placed on a truck chassis or on an ocean-going container ship.

continuous improvement Constantly seeking improvements in all processes. The cornerstone of TQM and Six Sigma quality efforts.

continuous review system An inventory management system where the physical inventory levels are counted on a continuous or daily basis.

contract carriers For-hire carriers that are like common carriers but are not bound to serve the general public.

Contracts for the International Sale of Goods (CISG) A set of rules established by the United Nations to govern the international transactions in goods.

contributor factory A manufacturing facility that plays a greater strategic role than a server factory by getting involved in product development and engineering, production planning, making critical procurement decisions and developing suppliers.

control charts A method that monitors process variabilities and then collects and plots sample measurements of the process over time. The means of these sample measures are plotted on the control charts.

corporate purchasing card A credit card issued to authorized employees to purchase goods, usually small value purchases, directly from suppliers without the need to go through the purchasing department.

corporate social responsibility The practice of business ethics.

cost leadership strategy A business approach that requires a large capital investment in automated, state-of-the-art equipment, significant efforts in the areas of controlling and reducing costs, doing things right the first time, standardizing services and aiming marketing efforts at cost-conscious consumers.

cost-of-service pricing A pricing strategy used when carriers desire to establish prices that vary based on their fixed and variable costs.

counterpurchase A trade arrangement whereby the original exporter either buys or finds a buyer to purchase a specified quantity of unrelated goods and/or services from the original importer.

countertrade A global sourcing process in which goods and/or services of domestic firms are exchanged for goods and/or services of equal value or in combination with currency from foreign firms. This type of arrangement is sometimes used by countries where there is a shortage of hard currency or as a means to acquire technologies.

critical-to-quality (CTQ) characteristics Those characteristics related to customers and their service or product requirements that are critical to achieving customer satisfaction.

crossdocking A continuous replenishment logistics process at a distribution center, where incoming goods are sorted and/or consolidated, and then shipped out to their final destinations, without the need to store the goods. Cross-docking generally takes place within 24 hours, sometimes less than an hour, after shipment arrivals and is used to replenish high-demand inventories.

cross-selling Purchasing that occurs when customers are sold additional products as the result of an initial purchase.

customer chain operations reference (CCOR) model A model that defines the customer part of the supply chain as the integration of Plan, Relate, Sell, Contract, Service and Enable processes.

customer churn The rate at which customers leave or stop using a firm.

customer contact centers See *call centers.*

customer defection analysis Information that analyzes why customers stop using a particular business.

customer lifetime value (CLV) Assigning a profit figure to each customer by summing the margins of all the products and services purchased over time, less the cost of marketing to and maintaining that customer, such as the costs of direct mail and sales calls and the service costs for each customer. Additionally, the firm forecasts future purchased quantities, profit margins, and marketing costs for each customer, discounts these back to the current date and then adds this projected profit quantity to the current profit amount. Also known as *customer value* or *customer profitability.*

customer relationship management (CRM) Managing a firm's customer base such that customers remain satisfied and continue to purchase goods and services. Sometimes it also refers to CRM software applications.

customer service The provision of information, help, and/or technical support to customers in a way that meets or exceeds customer expectations.

customer service management process A process that provides information to customers while also providing ongoing management of any product and service agreements between the firm and its customers.

customer value See *customer lifetime value.*

customs brokers Global logistics intermediaries that move international shipments through customs for companies as well as handle the necessary documentation required to accompany the shipments.

Customs-Trade Partnership Against Terrorism (C-TPAT) program A partnership between U.S. Customs, the International Cargo Security Council (a U.S. nonprofit association of companies and individuals involved in transportation) and Pinkerton (a global security advising company, headquartered in New Jersey), whereby companies agree to improve security in their supply chain in return for "fast lane" border crossings.

cycle counting A commonly used technique in which physical inventory is counted on a periodic basis to ensure that physical inventory matches current inventory records.

cyclical variations Wavelike movements (in demand) that last longer than one year and are influenced by macroeconomic and political factors.

D

dashboards Web-based balanced scorecard applications that allow users to retrieve data easily from ERP databases and also enable wide access by users at many locations, while providing desired security features.

data privacy The desire of customers to keep personal information from becoming compromised or being shared with other companies to generate income.

data warehouses Information system structures used to store data that was collected from the various divisions of the firm.

decentralized–centralized purchasing structure A hybrid purchasing structure that is decentralized at the corporate level but centralized at the individual business unit level.

decentralized purchasing A system where individual, local purchasing departments, such as at the plant or field-office level, make their own purchasing decisions.

deep-sea transportation Ocean-going shipping vessels, primarily carrying containers.

defects per million opportunities (DPMO) A Six Sigma quality metric.

Delphi method forecast A qualitative forecasting method in which a group of experts are surveyed during several rounds to gain consensus on future events. Because the group members do not physically meet, they thus avoid the scenario where one or a few experts could dominate a discussion.

demand-driven supply networks A system that designs supply chains with enough flexibility to respond quickly to changes in the marketplace.

demand forecast updating Changing the method used to calculate a forecast.

demand management A set of activities that range from determining or estimating the demand from customers through converting specific customer orders into promised delivery dates to help balance demand with supply.

demand management process The activities that try to balance customer demand and the firm's output capabilities.

demand source That part of the input process that deals with customer arrivals.

demand time fence A firmed planning segment that is used with the MRP application; it usually stretches from the current period to a period several weeks into the future.

Department of Defense (DOD) A major public buyer within the United States government.

Department of Transportation Act Legislation that created the Department of Transportation (DOT) in 1966 to coordinate the executive functions of all government entities dealing with transportation related matters.

dependent demand The internal demand for parts based on the demand of the final product in which the parts are used.

design chain operations reference (DCOR) model A model describing the design portion of the supply chain that includes integration of the Plan, Research, Design, Integrate, Amend and Enable processes.

differentiation strategy A business approach that is based on creating a product or service that is considered unique. Usually associated with high quality.

direct costs Costs that are directly traceable to the unit produced, such as the amount of materials and labor used to produce a unit of the finished good.

direct offset A form of countertrade that usually involves coproduction, or a joint venture, and exchange of related goods and/or services.

distribution center A warehouse that performs breakbulk activities and then forms outbound specific product assortments that are then shipped to the customer.

distribution channels The network through which products and services are delivered to customers.

distribution network The organization of a distribution system that ensures successful product delivery.

distribution requirements planning (DRP) A time-phased finished goods inventory replenishment plan in a distribution network.

distributive negotiations A negotiating objective that seeks an outcome that primarily favors the interests of one side.

E

e-procurement Electronic or computerized purchasing.

early supplier involvement (ESI) A process involving key suppliers during the product design and development stage to take advantage of their knowledge and technologies.

eatertainment The combining of restaurant and entertainment elements.

economic manufacturing quantity (EMQ) or production order quantity (POQ) A variation of the classic EOQ model, used to determine the most economical number of units to produce.

economic order quantity (EOQ) model The classic independent demand inventory system that computes the optimal order quantity to minimize total inventory costs.

economies of scale A theory stating that the cost per unit decreases as the number of units purchased, produced or transported increases.

edutainment The combining of learning with entertainment to appeal to customers looking for substance along with play.

effective performance measurement system A system that encompasses the traditional financial information for external reporting purposes along with tactical-level performance criteria used to assess a firm's competitive capabilities while directing its efforts to attain other desired capabilities.

efficient consumer response (ECR) Another term referring to JIT. ECR concepts are intended to make the firm more flexible and responsive to customer requirements and changes.

80/20 rule A theory originating from Pareto analysis, which suggests that most of a firm's problem "events" (80 percent) are accounted for by just a few (20 percent) of the problems; can also be applied to other areas, such as ABC inventory control, which says that 80 percent of the inventory dollars come from 20 percent of the inventory items. See also *Pareto analysis.*

electronic data interchange (EDI) A computer-to-computer exchange of business documents such as purchase orders, order status inquiries and reports, promotion announcements and shipping and billing notices.

electronic invoice presentment and payment (EIPP) A billing process that sends and receives invoices and payments online. Representing one of the most commonly used B2B transactions; it is designed to create greater efficiencies among the companies using the technology.

electronic product code (EPC) A widely used RFID standard managed by EPCglobal, Inc.

emergency sourcing The act of maintaining a backup source of supply available to provide purchased items when the primary source has temporarily become unavailable.

enterprise resource planning (ERP) A packaged business software system that lets a company automate and integrate the majority of its business processes, share common data and practices across the enterprise and produce and access information in a real-time environment.

entertailing The combining of retail locations with entertainment elements—such as offering ice skating, rock climbing and amusement park rides at a shopping mall.

environmental management system (EMS) The practices put in place by a firm to try to reduce environmental waste and improve environmental performance.

environmental sustainability The need to continually protect the environment and reduce greenhouse gas emissions.

ethical sourcing The practice of purchasing from suppliers that are governed by social and ethical practices.

Ethical Trading Initiative (ETI) An alliance of organizations seeking to take responsibility for improving working conditions and agreeing to implement the ETI Base Code, a standard for ethical practices for the firms and its suppliers.

European Union (EU) A European international trade organization designed to reduce tariff and nontariff barriers among member countries. Set up after the Second World War, the EU was officially launched on May 9, 1950, with France's proposal to create a European federation consisting of six countries: Belgium, Germany, France, Italy, Luxembourg, and the Netherlands. A series of accessions resulted in a total of 27 member states in 2007. Currently, the EU has added Croatia, Former Yugoslav Republic of Macedonia, Turkey, and Iceland as candidate countries.

event-based marketing A marketing strategy that offers the right products and services to customers at the right time.

everyday low pricing (EDLP) A method that keeps prices as low as possible to reduce the need to have promotions, which leads to more bullwhip effect.

exception rates Published rates that are lower than class rates for specific origin-destination locations or volumes.

exempt carriers For-hire carriers that are exempt from the regulations of services and rates.

expediting The act of contacting the supplier to speed up an overdue shipment.

exponential smoothing forecasting A forecasting technique in which the forecast for next period's demand is the current period's forecast adjusted by a fraction of the difference between the current period's actual demand and forecast.

F

facilitating products Products such as computers, furniture, and office supplies that are not part of the services sold but rather are consumed inside the firm and must also be managed.

fair trade product A product manufactured or grown by a disadvantaged producer in a developing country that receives a fair price for its goods.

Federal Acquisition Regulation (FAR) The primary set of rules issued by the U.S. government to govern the process through which the government purchases goods and services.

Federal Acquisition Streamlining Act (FASA) A federal act signed by President Clinton in October 1994 to remove many restrictions on government purchases that do not exceed $100,000.

Federal Aviation Act of 1958 Legislation that replaced the Civil Aeronautics Administration with the Federal Aviation Administration (FAA) and gave the FAA authority to prescribe air traffic rules, make safety regulations and plan the national airport system.

financial performance measures Performance measures that concentrate on cost, profits and sales figures.

finished goods Completed products ready for shipment.

First and Second Laws of Service Two laws proposed by David Maister in a well-known paper written on the topic of waiting time: (1) Satisfaction = perceptions − expectations, and (2) It is hard to play catch-up ball.

first-tier customers A firm's direct customers.

first-tier suppliers A firm's direct suppliers.

fishbone diagram A method that can be used to aid in brainstorming and isolating the causes of a problem.

five dimensions of service quality Five categories used by customers to rate service quality: reliability, responsiveness, assurance, empathy, and tangibles.

five-Ss Five Japanese words, coming originally from Toyota, that relate to industrial housekeeping. The idea is that by implementing the five-Ss, the workplace will be cleaner, more organized and safer, thereby reducing processing waste and improving productivity.

fixed costs Costs that are independent of the output quantity.

fixed order quantity models Independent demand inventory models that use fixed parameters to determine the optimal order quantity to minimize total inventory costs.

flow diagrams Tools that use annotated boxes representing process action elements and ovals representing wait periods, connected by arrows to show the flow of products or customers through the process.

FOB destination pricing A price quotation that includes transportation to the buyer's location when products are purchased from a supplier.

FOB origination pricing A price quotation in which the buyer may decide to purchase goods and provide the transportation to the shipping destination; in this case, the supplier quotes are lower.

focal firm The firm used in an example; the subject firm.

focus strategy A business approach incorporating the idea that a firm can serve a narrow target market or niche better than other firms that are trying to serve a broad market.

follow-up A proactive act to contact the supplier to ensure on-time delivery of the goods ordered.

forecast bias A measure of the tendency of a forecast to be consistently higher (negative bias) or lower (positive bias) than the actual demand.

forecast error The difference between actual demand and the forecast.

foreign freight forwarders Service providers that move goods for companies from domestic production facilities to foreign customer destinations, using surface and air transportation and warehouses. They consolidate small shipments into larger TL, CL or container shipments, decide what transportation modes and methods to use, handle all of the documentation requirements and then disperse the shipments at their destination.

foreign trade zones (FTZs) Secure sites within the U.S. under the supervision of the U.S. Customs Service. These are where materials can be imported duty-free as long as the imports are used as inputs to production of goods that are eventually exported.

forward buying Activities that occur when buyers stock up to take advantage of low price offers.

forward vertical integration The process of acquiring downstream customers.

fourth-party logistics provider (4PL) Outside agents that manage all of a firm's worldwide 3PL providers; also termed a *lead logistics provider*.

franchising A business practice that allows services to expand quickly in dispersed geographic markets, protect existing markets and build market share. Franchisees are required to invest some of their own capital, while paying a small percentage of sales to the franchiser in return for the brand name, start-up help, advertising, training and assistance in meeting specific operating standards.

Free and Secure Trade Program (FAST) A U.S. Customs' security program; the overall goal is to ensure the security of international supply chains and international trucking in particular. To participate in FAST, motor carriers must become C-TPAT certified and their commercial drivers must complete an application and undergo a background check.

freight forwarders Firms that consolidate a large number of small shipments to fill entire truck trailers or rail cars that transport items at truckload or carload prices.

front-of-the-house operations Operations that are involved with interactions with customers, such as front desk operations.

functional products MRO items and other commonly purchased items and supplies. These items are characterized by low profit margins, relatively stable demands and high levels of competition.

functional silos Departments in a firm that are only concerned with what is going on in their department and not what is in the best interests of the firm.

G

general freight carriers The carriers transporting the majority of goods shipped in the U.S.; includes common carriers.

General Services Administration (GSA) A U.S. federal agency that is responsible for most federal purchases. It is based in Washington, D.C., and has 11 regional offices throughout the U.S.

global sourcing Purchasing from non-domestic suppliers.

global supply chains Supply chains with foreign trading partners.

global sustainability index Wal-Mart's creation of an index that rates the environmental and sustainable aspects of products and their suppliers using a survey designed to help suppliers evaluate their own sustainability efforts in four areas: energy and climate, natural resources, material efficiency and people and community.

global trade management systems Software that enables shippers and carriers to submit the correct import/export documents as goods are moved between countries.

granger laws Midwestern U.S. laws that established maximum rates, prohibited discrimination and forbade mergers for railroads.

green development The implementation of environmentally friendly development.

green logistics A philosophy of understanding and working to reduce the ecological impact of logistics in both the forward and reverse supply chain.

green power Electricity products that include large proportions of electricity generated from renewable and environmentally preferable energy sources such as wind and solar energy.

green purchasing A practice aimed at ensuring that purchasing personnel include environmental considerations and human health issues when making purchasing decisions; also termed *green sourcing* and *sustainable procurement*.

green reverse logistics programs Systems that focus on reducing the environmental impact of certain modes of transportation used for returns, reducing the amount of disposed packaging and product materials by redesigning products and processes, and making use of reusable totes and pallets.

green sourcing See *green purchasing*.

green supply chain management An organizational approach that extends the concept of green logistics to include activities related to environmentally responsible product design, acquisition, production, distribution, use, reuse and disposal by partners within the supply chain.

greenwashing Making environmental claims for products that are exaggerated or misleading.

H

high-speed trains Passenger trains that typically average 70 miles per hour or greater.

holding or **carrying costs** The costs incurred for holding inventory in storage.

hybrid centralized distribution system A system using IT applications to combine a more decentralized warehousing system with a central control of purchased items.

hybrid purchasing organization A firm that uses either a centralized–decentralized or decentralized–centralized purchasing structure.

I

ICC Termination Act of 1995 Legislation that eliminated the Interstate Commerce Commission.

implosion A DRP logic where demand information is gathered from a number of field distribution centers and aggregated in the central warehouse, and eventually passed onto the manufacturing facility.

import broker A firm that is set up to import goods for customers for a fee. An import broker does not take title to the goods.

import merchant A firm that imports and takes title to the good, and then resells them to a buyer.

incoterms (International Commercial Terms) A uniform set of rules created by the International Chamber of Commerce to simplify international transactions of goods with respect to shipping costs, risks and responsibilities of the buyer, seller and shipper.

indented bill of materials Indentations are used to present the level number within the

bill of materials; also known as the *multilevel bill of materials*.

independent demand The demand for final products and service parts. It has a demand pattern that is affected by trends, seasonal patterns and general market conditions.

indirect costs Those costs that cannot be traced directly to the unit produced and are synonymous with manufacturing overhead.

indirect offset A form of countertrade that involves an exchange of goods and/or services unrelated to the initial purchase.

industrial buyers Buyers with a primary responsibility of purchasing raw materials for conversion purposes.

information visibility The degree that information is communicated and made available to various constituents, typically on the Internet.

infotainment The combining of learning with entertainment to appeal to customers looking for substance along with play; also called *edutainment*.

innovative products Newly developed products characterized by short product life cycles, volatile demand, high profit margins and relatively less competition.

insourcing To begin performing in-house some activity that was formerly outsourced.

integrated logistics When two companies share logistics processes.

integration A shared-process view of the supply chain that spans multiple departments, processes and software applications for internal users and external partners.

integrative negotiations Also referred to as *win–win negotiations*.

intermediately positioned strategy A location strategy that places warehouses midway between the sources of supply and the customers.

intermodal marketing companies (IMCs) Companies that act as intermediaries between intermodal railroad companies and shippers.

intermodal transportation Two or more modes of transportation that combine to deliver a shipment of goods.

internal control An internal operational system that prevents, for example, abuse of purchasing funds.

internal supply chain An organization's network of internal suppliers and internal customers. Internal supply chains can be complex, particularly if the firm has multiple divisions and organizational structures around the globe.

international purchasing Buying raw materials from overseas suppliers. It is also referred to as *global sourcing*.

Interstate Commerce Act of 1887 The 1887 act created the Interstate Commerce Commission (ICC), required rail carriers to charge reasonable rates, to publish rates, file them with the

ICC and make these available to the public, and prohibited discriminatory practices (charging some shippers less than others for the same service). The act also prohibited agreements between railroads to pool traffic or revenues.

inventory costs The purchase cost, order cost and carrying cost.

inventory turnover The number of times a firm's inventory is utilized and replaced over an accounting period, such as a year.

inventory turnover ratio or **inventory turnovers** A widely used measure to analyze how efficiently a firm uses its inventory to generate revenue.

inventory visibility The ability of supply chain companies to see inventory quantities of the various members, typically using the Internet.

invitation for bid (IFB) A request for qualified suppliers to submit bids for a contract. Suppliers are asked to bid, given certain opening and closing dates of the bid. The basis for awarding a contract is preset and binding.

Ishikawa diagram A tool for brainstorming causes of problems; also called a *fishbone diagram*.

ISO 9000 A series of management and quality assurance standards in design, development, production, installation and service developed by the International Organization for Standardization (ISO).

ISO 14000 A family of international standards for environmental management developed by the International Organization for Standardization (ISO).

J

JIT warehousing The process of moving inventory more quickly through inbound and outbound warehouses and distribution centers. As firms develop their supply chain management capabilities, warehouses and distribution centers will develop more JIT capabilities, like cross-docking; also termed *lean warehousing*.

jury of executive opinion forecast A qualitative forecasting method in which a group of experts collectively develop a forecast.

Just-in-Time (JIT) Originally associated with Toyota managers like Taiichi Ohno and his kanban system, JIT encompasses continuous problem solving to eliminate waste. Today it is also referred to as *lean* or *lean thinking*.

Just-in-Time (JIT) production system See *Toyota Production System* and *lean production*.

K

kaizen A Japanese word for "continuous improvement."

kanban A Japanese word for "card"; it is a visual tool used in lean production.

keiretsu relationships Partnership arrangements between Japanese manufacturing firms and their suppliers.

key suppliers The firm's most important, strategic suppliers.

key supply chain processes The eight processes that are most important to integrate in the supply chain.

key trading partners The most important companies in a supply chain that enable the successful sale and delivery of end products to the final customers.

knowledge-management solutions A system that uses Internet applications tied to desktop applications that enable real-time collaboration and flow of information between supply chain partners.

knowledge-management system A system that is able to capture the accumulated knowledge of experienced sales staff and other skilled personnel if they leave an organization.

L

lag capacity strategy A reactive approach that adjusts capacity in response to demand.

lead capacity strategy A proactive approach that adds or subtracts capacity in anticipation of future market condition and demand.

lead factory A source of product and process innovation and competitive advantage for the entire organization.

lead logistics provider (LLP) Outside agents that manage all of a firm's 3PLs; also termed a 4PL.

lead management system A tool that allows sales reps to follow prescribed sales tactics when dealing with sales prospects or opportunities, to aid in closing the deal with a client.

lean layouts Arrangements that reduce wasted movements of workers, customers and/or work-in-process (WIP), and achieve smooth product flow through the facility.

lean manufacturing See *lean production*.

lean production Organizing work and analyzing the level of waste existing in operating machinery, warehouses and systems to fit a lean process flow. The goals are to reduce production throughput times and inventory levels, cut order lead times, increase quality and improve customer responsiveness with fewer people and other assets.

Lean Six/Lean Six Sigma A new term used to describe the melding of lean production and Six Sigma quality practices.

lean supply chain relationships The relationships that occur when the focal firm, its suppliers and its customers begin to work together to identify customer requirements, remove waste, reduce cost and improve quality and customer service

lean thinking See *JIT*.

lean warehousing See *JIT warehousing*.

legacy MRP system A broad label used to describe an older information system that

usually works at an operational level to schedule production within a single facility.

legacy systems A firm's existing software applications.

legal forms of transportation For-hire transportation service companies are classified legally as either common, contract, exempt or private carriers.

less-than-truckload (LTL) carriers Carriers that move small packages or shipments taking up less than one truckload; the shipping fees are higher per hundred weight (cwt) than TL fees, since the carrier must consolidate many small shipments into one truckload, then break the truckload back down into individual shipments at the destination for individual deliveries.

level demand strategy A theory for managing capacity that occurs when a firm utilizes a constant amount of capacity regardless of demand variations.

level production strategy A production strategy that relies on a constant output rate and capacity while varying inventory and backlog levels to handle the fluctuating demand pattern.

leveraging purchase volume The concentration of purchase volume to create quantity discounts, less-costly volume shipments and other more favorable purchase terms.

line haul rates The charges for moving goods to a nonlocal destination; these can be further classified as *class rates, exception rates, commodity rates* and *miscellaneous rates.*

linear trend forecast A forecasting method in which the trend can be estimated using simple linear regression to fit a line to a time series of historical data.

load brokers Firms that bring shippers and transportation companies (mainly truckers) together. The load broker is legally authorized to act on the shipper's or carrier's behalf and typically these companies are hired because of their extensive knowledge of the many transportation alternatives available or the many shippers needing transportation; also referred to as *transportation brokers.*

logistics The practice of moving and storing goods to meet customer requirements for the minimum cost.

logistics audit A periodic audit of a firm's logistics system, with the objective of finding an optimal mix of both cost and customer service.

long-range planning horizon A planning horizon that covers a year or more.

M

maintenance, repair, and operating (MRO) supplies Materials and supplies that are used internally when producing products but are not parts of the products.

make or buy (materials or components) A strategic decision that can impact an organization's competitive position.

make-to-order manufacturing firms Firms that make custom products based on orders from customers, resulting in long lead times and higher unit costs.

make-to-stock manufacturing firms Firms that typically emphasize immediate delivery of off-the-shelf, standard goods at relatively low prices compared to the chase strategy.

manufacturing cells or **work cells** Cells that are designed to process similar parts or components, saving duplication of equipment and labor as well as centralizing the area where units of the same purchased part are delivered.

manufacturing flow management process The set of activities responsible for making the actual product, establishing the manufacturing flexibility required to adequately serve the markets, and designing the production system to meet cycle time requirements.

manufacturing resource planning (MRP-II) An outgrowth and extension of the original closed-loop MRP system.

market dominance The firm with the dominant position in the market, selling the most units of product.

market positioned strategy A location strategy that places warehouses close to customers, to maximize customer service and to allow the firm to generate transportation economies by using inbound TL and CL deliveries to each warehouse location.

master production schedule (MPS) A medium-range production plan that is more detailed than the aggregate production plan.

match or **tracking capacity strategy** A moderate strategy that adjusts capacity in small amounts in response to demand and changing market conditions.

material requirements planning (MRP) A software application that has been available since the 1970s; it performs an analysis of the firm's existing internal conditions and reports back what the production and purchase requirements are for a given finished product manufacturing schedule.

material requisition (MR) An internal document initiated by the material user to request materials from the warehouse or purchasing department.

mean absolute deviation (MAD) An indicator of forecast accuracy based on an average of the absolute value of the forecast errors over a given period of time. The measure indicates, on average, how many units the forecast is off from the actual data.

mean absolute percentage error (MAPE) An indicator of forecast accuracy based on the true magnitude of the forecast error. The monthly absolute forecast error divided by actual demand is summed, then divided by the number of months used in the forecast to derive an average, and lastly multiplied by 100. The measure indicates, on average, what percent the forecast is off from the actual data.

mean square error (MSE) An indicator of forecast accuracy. The forecast errors are squared and then summed and divided by the number of periods to determine the mean square error. The measure penalizes large errors more than small errors.

merchants Firms that buy goods in large quantities for resale purposes. Wholesalers and retailers are examples of merchants.

microfranchise A type of franchising concept that offers ready-made, low-risk starter jobs to people with no education and little available capital while giving established companies additional distribution avenues.

micro-purchases Government purchases of less than $2,500.

miscellaneous rates Contract rates that are negotiated between two parties involving shipments containing a variety of products (in the typical case, the rate is based on the overall weight of the shipment).

mixed Internet distribution strategy The combining of traditional retailing with Internet retailing.

mobile marketing An advertising technique that places advertising messages on mobile phones.

Motor Carrier Act of 1935 Legislation that brought motor carriers under ICC control, thus controlling entry into the market, establishing motor carrier classes of operation, setting reasonable rates, requiring ICC approval for any mergers or acquisitions, and controlling the issuance of securities.

motor carriers Trucks; the most flexible mode of transportation, accounting for almost one-third of all U.S. for-hire transportation.

muda A Japanese word meaning waste or anything that does not add value.

multiple channel queuing system A system in which multiple servers act in parallel.

multiple-factor productivity Inputs that can be represented by the sum of labor, material, energy and capital costs.

multiple phase queuing system A system in which multiple servers act in series.

multiple regression forecast A forecast technique using multiple regression.

N

naïve forecast A forecasting approach where the actual demand for the immediate past period is used as a forecast for next period's demand.

natural variations Variations that are random and uncontrollable with no specific cause; also termed *environmental noise* or *white noise*.

negotiated pricing Transportation pricing that is agreed upon by both parties.

non-vessel operating common carriers (NVOCC) Carriers that operate very similarly to international freight forwarders but normally use scheduled ocean liners.

nontariffs Import quotas, licensing agreements, embargoes, laws and other regulations that are imposed on imports and exports.

North American Free Trade Agreement (NAFTA) Legislation that began on January 1, 1994, and will eventually remove most barriers to trade and investment among the U.S., Canada and Mexico.

O

Ocean Shipping Reform Act of 1998 Legislation that eliminated the requirement for ocean carriers to file rates with the Federal Maritime Commission.

offset An exchange agreement for industrial goods and/or services as a condition of military-related export. It is also commonly used in the aerospace and defense sectors.

offshore factory A firm that manufactures products at low cost with minimum investment in technical and managerial resources in low labor cost countries, then exports all of its finished goods.

on-demand computing See *cloud computing*.

on-demand CRM Outsourced or externally hosted online CRM services.

open-end purchase order A purchase order that covers a variety of items and is negotiated for repeated supply over a fixed time period, such as quarterly or yearly. Additional items and expiration dates can be renegotiated in an open-end purchase order.

open-source CRM products Free online CRM applications and user forums.

operating exposure The risk caused by fluctuating exchange rates that affect production, warehousing, purchasing and selling price.

opportunities for a defect to occur (OFD) The number of activities or steps in a process wherein a defect could occur. Used in the DPMO calculation.

optimization The highest level of processes and decision-making that occurs through enhanced analytical tools such as On-Line Analytical Processing (OLAP) tools. The method determines the best number of units to produce, store or purchase, among other things, given cost and service considerations.

option overplanning Raising the final requirements of component parts beyond 100 percent in a super bill of materials to cover uncertainty.

order batching A type of inventory control that occurs when small orders are combined into one large order. This amplifies demand variability and adds to the use of safety stock, creating the bullwhip effect.

order costs Direct variable costs associated with placing an order with a supplier.

order cycle The activities involved in ordering and receiving purchased items.

order fulfillment process The set of activities that allows a firm to fill customer orders while providing the required levels of customer service at the lowest possible delivered cost.

outsource The process that occurs when a firm purchases materials or products instead of producing them in-house.

outpost factory A manufacturing facility that is set up in a location with an abundance of advanced suppliers, competitors, research facilities and knowledge centers to get access to the latest information on materials, components, technologies and products.

P

P charts A chart that monitors the *percent defective* in each sample.

Pareto analysis A graphic technique that prioritizes the most frequently occurring problems or issues. The analysis recommends that problems falling into the most frequently occurring category be assigned the highest priority and managed closely.

Pareto charts A useful method for organizing applications of data in many formats; based on the work of Vilfredo Pareto, a nineteenth-century economist.

part families Similarly processed parts in a group of components.

passive RFID tags RFID tags that are without an internal power source and require power from a tag reader.

payment bonds Bonds posted by the bidders to protect the buyer against any third-party liens not fulfilled by the successful bidder.

perceived waiting times An aspect of queue management that occurs when customers think the wait time is much longer or shorter than it really is.

perfect order fulfillment A process that allows orders to arrive on time, complete and damage free. A *perfect order* is thus an order that did arrive on time, complete and damage free.

performance bonds Bonds posted by the bidders to guarantee that the work done by the successful bidder meets specifications and is completed in the time specified.

performance scorecards A type of balanced scorecard or other form of scorecarding, where a formal approach to develop and use performance measures is undertaken.

performance variance The difference between the standard and actual performance.

periodic review system A review of physical inventory at specific points in time.

petty cash A small cash reserve maintained by a midlevel manager or clerk.

piggyback service A type of intermodal transportation involving the loading of shipping containers or truck trailers on a rail flatbed car; also known as *container-on-flat-car (COFC)* and *trailer-on-flat-car (TOFC)*.

pipeline carriers One of the five modes of transportation; carries oil, natural gas, coal slurry and other liquids/gases.

place utility A situation that is created when customers get things delivered to the desired location.

planned order releases The bottom line of an MRP part record. It designates when the specific quantity is to be ordered from the supplier or to begin being processed. These quantities also determine the gross requirements of the dependent or "children" parts going into this higher level part or product.

planning factor A calculation showing the number of units of a specific component required to make one unit of a higher-level part.

planning time fence A period typically stretching from the end of the firmed segment to several weeks farther into the future; also known as the *tentative segment*.

point of sale information Cash register sales data.

poka-yoke Error- or mistake-proofing.

posttransaction costs Customer service costs that occur after the sale.

posttransaction elements Customer service activities that occur after a sale.

pretransaction elements Customer service activities that occur before a sale.

price break point The minimum quantity required to receive a quantity discount.

private carrier A form of transportation owned by a company, such as a fleet of trucks, which is used to ship that company's goods only.

private cloud A data center that is owned by the firm and managed in-house.

private warehouses Warehouses that are owned by the firm storing the goods.

process diagram A tool that is the necessary first step to evaluating any manufacturing or service process; a drawing showing how products or people flow through a process; also called *process map*.

process integration The sharing of information and coordinating resources to jointly manage a process.

procurement credit card A credit card issued to authorized employees to purchase goods, usually small value purchases, directly from suppliers without the need to go through the purchasing department; also known as *corporate purchasing card*.

producer's risk The risk that occurs when a buyer rejects a shipment of good-quality units because the sample quality level *did not* meet the acceptance standard.

product development and commercialization process The development of new products to meet changing customer requirements and then getting these products to market quickly and efficiently.

product family A group consisting of different products that share similar characteristics, components or manufacturing processes.

product positioned strategy A location strategy that places warehouses close to the sources of supply, to enable the firm to collect various goods and then consolidate these into TL or CL quantities for shipment to customers.

production kanban A visual signal such as a light, flag or sign that is used to trigger production of certain components.

profit-leverage effect A purchasing performance measure that calculates the impact of a change in purchase spend on a firm's profit before taxes, assuming gross sales and other expenses remain unchanged.

public procurement or public purchasing The management of the purchasing and supply management function of the government and nonprofit sector, such as educational institutions, charitable organizations and the federal, state and local governments.

public warehouse An independent warehouse that is operated as a for-profit business.

pull system An operating system where synchronized work takes place only upon authorization from another downstream user in the system rather than strictly to a forecast. JIT systems or lean systems are typically referred to as pull systems.

purchase order (PO) A contractual commercial document issued by the buying firm to a supplier, indicating the type, quantities and agreed prices for products or services that the supplier will provide to the buying firm.

purchase requisition An internal document initiated by the material user to request the purchasing department to buy specific goods or services.

purchasing spend The money spent by an organization in buying goods and services.

pure Internet distribution strategy Selling goods or services strictly over the Internet.

pure services Services that offer few, if any, tangible products to customers.

Q

QR codes A form of mobile marketing that involves the use of the camera function on a smart phone and installing a QR code reader on the phone.

qualitative dimensions Nonquantitative assessments, such as closeness desirability, when assessing how close to position departments in a layout.

qualitative forecasting methods Forecasts based on opinions and intuition.

quality-of-life factors Those issues that contribute to "a feeling of well-being, fulfillment or satisfaction resulting from factors in the external environments."

quality The ability of a product or service to satisfy customer expectations. This definition is echoed by the American Society for Quality when it states: "Quality is defined by the customer through his/her satisfaction."

quantitative forecasting methods Forecasts based on mathematical models and relevant historical data.

quantity discount model or **price break model** A variation of the classic EOQ model, wherein purchase price is allowed to vary with the quantity purchased.

queue discipline The order in which customers are served.

queue management A demand management strategy that is used to deal with excess customers.

queue times The period of time encountered while waiting for a service.

queuing systems The processes used to align, prioritize and serve customers.

quick response (QR) See *JIT*.

R

R-chart A chart that is used to track sample ranges, or the variation of the measurements within each sample.

radio frequency identification (RFID) A technology that enables huge amounts of information to be stored on chips (called tags) and read at a distance by readers, without requiring line-of-sight scanning.

radio frequency identification tag The chips used to store information about a specific product or carton using RFID.

rail carriers A carrier using trains for transport.

Railroad Revitalization and Regulatory Reform Act Commonly known as the 4-R Act; this legislation was passed in 1976 and made several regulatory changes to help the railroads.

Railway Passenger Service Act Legislation passed in 1970 that created Amtrak.

random variations Changes due to unexpected or unpredictable events such as natural disasters (hurricanes, tornadoes, fire), strikes and wars.

rationing A strategy that can occur when demand exceeds a supplier's finished goods available. In such cases, the supplier may allocate product in proportion to what buyers ordered.

raw materials Unprocessed purchased inputs or materials that are used to manufacture finished goods.

real-time location systems (RTLS) WiFi-enabled radio frequency identification (RFID) tags used on rail cars to allow tracking of rail cars (and their assets) in real-time.

Reed-Bulwinkle Act Legislation passed in 1948 that gave groups of carriers the ability to form rate bureaus or conferences wherein they could propose rate changes to the ICC.

regional trade agreements Trade agreements between countries, as in the EU.

relationship marketing or **permission marketing** An extension of target marketing; letting customers select the type and time of communication with organizations.

reneging Leaving a queue before receiving the service.

reorder point (ROP) The lowest inventory level at which a new order must be placed to avoid a stockout during the order cycle time period.

request for proposal (RFP) A formal request for a project or product proposal issued by the buyer to qualified suppliers. The use of RFPs allows the supplier to develop part specifications based on their own knowledge of the materials and technology needed.

request for quotation (RFQ) A formal request for pricing from a supplier; commonly used when the purchasing requirements are clear.

resource requirements planning (RRP) A long-range capacity planning module that is used to check whether aggregate resources are capable of satisfying the aggregate production plan.

responsible bid A supplier that is capable and willing to perform the work as specified.

responsive bid A submitted bid that conforms to the invitation to bid.

return on assets (ROA) A financial ratio, calculated as after-tax income divided by total assets also referred to as *return on investment.*

returns management process A process that manages product returns. This can be extremely beneficial for supply chain management in terms of maintaining acceptable levels of customer service and identifying product improvement opportunities.

returns management systems Systems that develop and implement efficient methods for transporting and storing returns while seeking

to recover some value, if possible, from the returned items. Returns management activities include environmental compliance with substance disposal and recycling, composing operating and repair instructions, troubleshooting and warranty repairs, developing disposal guidelines, designing an effective reverse logistics process and collecting returns data.

reverse auctions An online bidding arrangement whereby suppliers try to under-bid each other to win a purchase order.

reverse logistics A unique form of inbound logistics where returned goods are properly disposed with an attempt to recover some of their original value.

rewarding suppliers Giving suppliers more business when their performance is deemed to be excellent.

right-shoring The combining of on-shore, near-shore and far-shore operations into a single, flexible, low-cost approach to supply chain management.

rights and duties A theory stating that some actions are right in themselves without regard for the consequences.

right-to-work laws State legislation that provides employees with the right to decide whether to join or support a union financially.

risk pooling The relationship between the number of warehouses, inventory and customer service; it can be explained intuitively as follows: when market demand is random, it is very likely that higher-than-average demand from some customers will be offset by lower-than-average demand from other customers.

road trains Trucks pulling more than two trailers; these are commonly seen in Australia where trucks are used instead of railroads in low population areas.

ROROs Roll-on-roll-off containerships that allow truck trailers and containers to be directly driven on and off the ship, without use of cranes.

rough-cut capacity plan (RCCP) A plan that is used to check the feasibility of the master production schedule.

running sum of forecast errors (RSFE) A measure of forecast bias—that is, whether the forecast tends to be consistently higher or lower than actual demand.

S

sales activity management system A management tool that reduces errors and improves customer satisfaction and productivity; typically refers to a software application.

sales agent The authorized sales representative of an overseas supplier that assists the supplier to conduct business in a foreign country.

sales force automation (SFA) A sales tool software application that is used for documenting field activities, communicating with the home office and retrieval of sales history and other company-specific documents in the field.

sales force composite forecast A forecast in which field sales personnel are asked to estimate their customers' purchases for the period in question. These are then summed, to achieve the forecast.

sales order A supplier's offer to sell goods and services at the supplier's terms and conditions. The sales order becomes a legally binding contract when accepted by the buyer.

sales territory management systems Software applications that allow sales managers to obtain current information and reporting capabilities regarding each salesperson's activities on each customer's account, total sales in general for each sales rep, their sales territories and any ongoing sales initiatives.

scorecarding A performance measure design technique such as the Balanced Scorecard that uses the scorecard model.

sealed bid A bid for business by a supplier in response to an invitation for bid sent by a buyer. The bid is kept sealed until all bids are received, whereupon they are opened and the low bidder is typically awarded the purchase contract.

seasonal variations Peaks and valleys in demand that repeat over a consistent interval such as hours, days, weeks, months, years or seasons.

second-tier suppliers and customers A supplier's suppliers and a customer's customers.

segment customers Placing customers in a behavioral class, such as males/females, age brackets and profitability, so as to better design marketing campaigns for each segment.

selective sourcing The sharing of a process or function between internal staff and an external provider; also referred to as *co-sourcing.*

server factory A manufacturing facility that is set up primarily to take advantage of government incentives, minimize exchange risk, avoid tariff barriers and reduce taxes and logistics costs to supply the regional market where the factory is located.

service bundle A group of attributes that are offered to customers when purchasing services, including the explicit service itself, the supporting facility, facilitating goods and implicit services. Successful services are designed to deliver this bundle of attributes in the most efficient way, while still satisfying customer requirements.

service capacity The number of customers per day that a firm's service delivery systems are designed to serve, although it could also be some other period of time such as customers per hour or customers per shift.

service delivery system A continuum of services that may range from mass-produced, low-customer-contact systems at one extreme (such as ATMs) to highly customized, high-customer-contact systems at the other (such as expensive beauty salons).

service layout strategies A method that works in combination with location decisions to further support the overall business strategies of differentiation, low cost or market focus. Office layouts tend to be departmentalized; commercial airliner layouts segment customers; casino layouts are designed to get customers in quickly and then keep them there by spacing out the attractions; and self-serve restaurant buffet layouts are designed to process customers quickly.

service level The in-stock probability.

service quality The satisfaction or perceived level of quality a customer experiences with regard to a service. It includes many elements—for example, because of health and safety concerns, pharmacies are under intense pressure to provide high quality services to customers.

service response logistics The management and coordination of an organization's activities that occur while the service is being performed.

setup The activity required to change products on an assembly-line.

setup costs The costs associated with setting up machines and equipment to produce a batch of product; the term is often used in place of *order costs*.

seven Rs rule Having the *right* product, in the *right* quantity, in the *right* condition, at the *right* place, at the *right* time, for the *right* customer, at the *right* cost.

seven wastes A concept that encompasses things such as excess wait times, inventories, material and people movements, processing steps, variabilities and any other non-value-adding activity.

shippers' associations Nonprofit membership cooperatives that make domestic or international arrangements for the movement of members' cargo.

Shipping Act of 1984 Legislation that allowed ocean carriers to pool or share shipments, assign ports, publish rates and enter into contracts with shippers.

shortage gaming A strategy that occurs when buyers figure out the relationship between their orders and what is supplied, and they then tend to inflate their orders to satisfy their real needs.

sigma drift A theory that assumes process variations will grow over time, as process measurements drift off target.

silo effect An organizational issue that causes a firm to be reactive and short-term-goal oriented. At this stage, no internal functional integration is occurring.

silo mentality See *silo effect.*

simple exponential smoothing forecast A sophisticated weighted moving average forecasting technique in which the prediction for the next period's demand is the current period's forecast adjusted by a fraction of the difference between the current period's actual demand and forecast.

simple linear regression model Similar to the *linear trend forecast*. The difference is that the independent variable is no longer time but an explanatory variable of demand.

simple moving average forecast A method that uses historical data to generate a forecast; it works well when the demand is fairly stable over time.

simplification A reduction of the number of components, supplies or standard materials used in the product or process during product design.

Single-factor productivity measures Output measure that are divided by a single input measure, such as labor cost.

single integrator solution An ERP system that uses all the desired applications from the same vendor.

single sourcing Buying from one supplier when multiple suppliers are available.

Six Sigma A system that stresses a commitment by top management to enable a firm to identify customer expectations and excel in meeting and exceeding those expectations. A type of TQM method devised by Motorola.

social media Online services such as LinkedIn, Twitter and Facebook.

social sustainability Exhibiting long-term concern for worker safety, hourly wages, working conditions, child workers and basic human rights.

software-as-a-service model (SaaS model) Also referred to as an *application service provider* (*ASP*) and *cloud computing provider*. Perhaps as many as 50 percent of all CRM programs are now designed and maintained for clients by ASPs. In many cases, firms do not have the time, knowledge or infrastructure to buy and build an effective CRM program, so they use Internet on-demand CRM services provided by an ASP. These providers also offer high levels of data security, which many firms find very attractive.

sole sourcing Typically, the situation when the supplier is the only available source.

source factory A manufacturing facility that has a broader strategic role than an offshore factory, with plant management heavily involved in supplier selection and production planning.

sourcing Purchasing.

Southern Common Market (MERCOSUR) A regional trade agreement among Argentina, Brazil, Paraguay and Uruguay, formed in March 1991.

specialized carriers Carriers that transport liquid petroleum, household goods, agricultural commodities, building materials and other specialized items.

square root rule A rule suggesting that the system average inventory (impacted by adding or deleting warehouses) is equal to the old system inventory times the ratio of the square root of the new number of warehouses to the square root of the old number of warehouses.

Staggers Rail Act of 1980 Legislation aimed at improving finances for the rail industry.

standards for performance Specific performance requirements or objectives set by top management.

state utility A situation that occurs when services do something to things that are owned by the customer, such as transport and store their supplies, repair their machines, cut their hair or provide their healthcare.

statistical process control (SPC) A method that allows firms to visually monitor process performance, compare the performance to desired levels or standards and take corrective steps quickly before process variabilities get out of control and damage products, services and customer relationships.

stockless buying or **system contracting** An extension of the blanket purchase order.

stockpiling To set aside or hoard purchased items, if it is thought that prices will soon increase.

strategic alliance development Improving the capabilities of key trading partners.

strategic partnerships A close working relationship that develops among trading partner relationships.

strategic sourcing Strategically managing a firm's external resources and services to improve cost, quality, delivery, performance and competitive advantage.

strategic supplier alliances The creation of partnerships with key suppliers.

strategic 3PL alliances Partnerships with third-party logistics providers.

subcontracting The process of entering into a contractual agreement with a supplier to produce goods and/or services according to a specific set of terms and conditions.

super bill of materials Another type of bill of materials that is useful for planning purposes.

supplier certification Defined by the Institute of Supply Management as "an organization's process for evaluating the quality systems of key suppliers in an effort to eliminate incoming inspections."

supplier co-location Placing a supplier's employee within a buyer's firm, to perform purchasing activities. A type of VMI; also referred to as *JIT II*.

supplier development   The efforts of a buying firm to improve the capabilities and performance of specific suppliers to better meet its needs.

supplier evaluation   A key activity in supplier management that determines the current capabilities of suppliers.

supplier management   One of the most crucial issues within the topic of supply management—getting suppliers to do what the buyer's firm wants them to do.

supplier partnerships   A commitment over an extended time to work together to the mutual benefit of both parties, sharing relevant information and the risks and rewards of the relationship.

supplier relationship management (SRM) Accenture defines SRM as "the systematic management of supplier relationships to optimize the value delivered through the relationship over their life cycle."

supplier relationship management process   A process by which the firm manages its relationships with suppliers.

supply base or **supplier base**   The list of suppliers that a firm uses to acquire its materials, services, supplies and equipment.

supply base rationalization, supply base optimization, or **supply base reduction**   Getting rid of poorly performing suppliers.

supply chain   A network of trading partners that make products and services available to consumers, including all of the functions enabling the production, delivery and recycling of materials, components, end products and services.

supply chain integration   Collaborating with or sharing key supply chain process activities with supply chain trading partners.

supply chain management (SCM)   The integration of key business processes regarding the flow of materials from raw material suppliers to the final customer.

Supply Chain Operations Reference (SCOR) model   A theory developed in 1996 by supply chain consulting firms Pittiglio Rabin Todd & McGrath and AMR Research, to formalize the attainment of supply chain management.

supply chain performance measurement Determining the performance of an entire supply chain.

supply chain responsiveness   The capability of firms to link together all of the supply chain participants' information and communication systems using the latest technologies.

supply chain risk management   Managing the risks in supply chains, such as the weather, traffic delays and political risks.

supply chain security management   A method that is concerned with reducing the risk of intentionally created disruptions in supply chain operations including product and information theft and activities seeking to endanger personnel or sabotage supply chain infrastructure.

supply chain visibility   The ability of supply chain members to see what is happening to inventories up and down the supply chain.

supply management   The identification, acquisition, access, positioning and management of resources the organization needs or potentially needs in the attainment of its strategic objectives.

surety bonds   Bonds posted by bidders to ensure that the successful bidder will accept the contract.

sustainable development   A development that meets the needs of the present without compromising the ability of future generations to meet their own needs.

sustainable procurement or **sustainable sourcing**   See *green purchasing*.

sustainable supply chain   A supply chain that demonstrates commitment to green practices and environmental responsibility.

sustainability   A commitment to environmental responsibility.

system nervousness   A situation where a small change in the upper- level production plan causes a major change in the lower-level production plan.

T

target marketing   Targeting specific customer segments, with respect to promotional efforts.

tariff   An official list or schedule showing the duties, taxes or customs imposed by a host country on imports or exports.

third-party logistics services (3PLs)   For-hire outside agents that provide transportation and other services including warehousing, document preparation, customs clearance, packaging, labeling and freight bill auditing.

time series forecasting   A prediction technique based on the assumption that the future is an extension of the past and that historical data can thus be used to forecast future demand.

time utility   A state of well-being that is created when customers get products delivered at precisely the right time, not earlier and not later.

total cost of ownership or **total cost of acquisition**   The unit price of the material, payment terms, cash discount, ordering cost, carrying cost, logistical costs, maintenance costs and other more qualitative costs that may not be easy to assess.

total productivity measure   A measure of total outputs divided by total inputs.

Toyota Production System   A methodology created by Toyota Motor Company in the 1950s. The idea is to make the best use of an organization's time, assets and people in all processes in order to optimize productivity. Also known as *JIT* and *lean production*.

tracking signal   A tool used to check the forecast bias.

trade secrets   Proprietary information owned by the firm–financial, business, scientific, technical, economic or engineering information, including patterns, plans, compilations, programmed devices, formulas, designs, prototypes, methods, techniques, processes, procedures, programs or codes, whether tangible or intangible.

trading company   A firm that puts buyers and sellers from different countries together and handles all of the export/import arrangements, documentation and transportation for both goods and services.

trailer-on-flatcar service (TOFC)   Point-to-point pick-up and delivery service using motor carriers and flatcars that carry truck trailers.

transaction elements   Activities that occur during the sale of a product or service.

transactional SRM   A system that enables an organization to track supplier interactions such as order planning, order payment and returns. The volume of transactions involved may result in independent systems maintained by geographic region or business lines. Transactional SRM tends to focus on short-term reporting.

Transportation Act of 1920   Legislation that instructed the ICC to ensure that rates were high enough to provide a fair return for the railroads each year.

Transportation Act of 1940   Legislation that further extended the Interstate Commerce Act of 1887, establishing ICC control over domestic water transportation.

Transportation Act of 1958   Legislation that established temporary loan guarantees to railroads, liberalized control over intrastate rail rates, amended the rule of rate making to ensure more intermodal competition and clarified the differences between private and for-hire motor carriers.

transportation brokers   Legally authorized intermediaries that bring shippers and transportation companies (mainly truckers) together.

transportation deregulation   The laws that seek to reduce government regulation in the transportation industry, allowing market forces to dictate services offered.

transportation intermediaries   For-hire agencies that bring shippers and transportation providers together.

transportation management systems   Software applications that allow firms to select the best mix of transportation services and pricing to determine the best use of containers or truck trailers, to better manage transportation contracts, to rank transportation options, to clear customs and to track fuel usage, product movements and carrier performance.

transportation regulation The laws that protect consumers in areas of monopoly pricing, safety and liability.

transportation security Protection that is provided to transportation companies against unlawful activities such as terrorism.

Transportation Worker Identification Credential (TWIC) A transportation security initiative mandated by the Maritime Transportation Security Act of 2002 and the Safe Port Act of 2006.

traveling requisition A material requisition that is used for materials and standard parts that are requested on a recurring basis.

trend variations Increasing or decreasing movements over time that are due to factors such as population growth, population shifts, cultural changes and income shifts. Common trends are linear, S-curve, exponential or asymptotic.

truckload (TL) carriers Trucks that move shipments that take up one full truckload.

Type-I error When a process is mistakenly thought to be out of control and an improvement initiative is undertaken unnecessarily.

Type-II error When a process is thought to be exhibiting only natural variations and no improvement is undertaken, even though the process is actually out of control.

U

Uniform Commercial Code (UCC) Legislation that governs the purchase and sale of goods.

U.S. Baldrige Quality Award Legislation enacted in 1987, named in honor of Malcolm Baldrige, President Ronald Reagan's Secretary of Commerce, that seeks to recognize U.S. companies for service or product quality.

utilitarianism A theory that maintains an ethical act creates the greatest good for the greatest number of people.

V

value engineering A method that uses various design techniques to reduce production and usage costs as much as possible, so as to maximize profitability.

value-of-service pricing A strategy that allows carriers to price their services at competitive levels the market will bear.

variable costs Expenses that vary as a function of the output level.

variable data Measurable data, such as weight, time and length (as in the weight of a box of cereal, the time to serve a customer or the length of a steel girder).

vendor managed inventory (VMI) A progressive partner-based approach to controlling inventory and reducing supply chain costs. Customers provide information to the key supplier, including historical usage, current inventory levels, minimum and maximum stock levels, sales forecasts and upcoming promotions, who then takes on the responsibility and risk for planning, managing and monitoring the replenishment of inventory. The supplier may even own the inventory until the product is sold.

vertically integrated firm A firm whose business boundaries include one-time suppliers and/or customers.

virtual inventory Inventory information that is shared on one online database.

virtual queues A queuing system in which customers' places in the queue are tracked by a computerized system that allows customers to roam the premises until their names are called.

visibility Information and process flows in and between organizations. Views are customized by role and aggregated via a single portal.

W

waiting times The time spent by customers who are waiting for service.

walk-through service audits A method of monitoring a service system that is performed by management and covers service system attributes from the time customers initially encounter the service until they leave.

Wal-Mart effect A theory postulating that the booming growth in information technology has allowed many big-box retailers such as Wal-Mart to realize large productivity growth rates.

warehouse management systems Software applications facilitating the proper storage and movement of inventory and minor

manufacturing such as assembly or labeling activities within the warehouse, and movement of shipments onto the transportation carrier.

water carrier A carrier using ships for transportation.

Web-based CRM CRM applications that are available online.

Web-based scorecards Online databases that allow managers to see real-time progress toward organizational milestones and help to ensure that decisions remain in sync with the firm's overall strategies.

website self-service Self-service applications on a company's website.

weighted-factor rating model A method commonly used to compare the attractiveness of several locations along a number of quantitative and qualitative dimensions.

weighted moving average forecast A technique that allows greater emphasis to be placed on more recent data to reflect changes in demand patterns.

withdrawal kanban A visual signal such as a light, flag or sign that indicates a container of parts can be moved from one work cell to another.

work-in-process (WIP) Materials that are partially processed but not yet ready for sales.

world-class performance measures Performance measures used by the most successful global firms.

World Trade Organization (WTO) The only international organization dealing with the rules of trade between nations. Its functions include administering the WTO agreements, providing a forum for trade negotiations, handling trade disputes, monitoring national trade policies, providing technical assistance and training programs for developing countries and cooperating with other international organizations.

X

chart A control chart that tracks the central tendency of the sample means for variable data.

Z

zone of rate freedom A regulation that allows carriers to charge fees over their variable costs, up to a set limit.

References

CHAPTER 1

Burgess, R., "Avoiding Supply Chain Management Failure: Lessons from Business Process Reengineering," *The International Journal of Logistics Management* 9(1), 1998: 15–24.

Chopra, S. and P. Meindl. *Supply Chain Management: Strategy, Planning and Operation.* Upper Saddle River, NJ: Prentice Hall, 2001.

Frazelle, E. *Supply Chain Strategy: The Logistics of Supply Chain Management.* New York: McGraw-Hill, 2002.

Hammer, M. and J. Champy. *Reengineering the Corporation.* London: Nicholas Brealey, 1993.

Handfield, R. B. and E. L. Nichols. *Introduction to Supply Chain Management.* Upper Saddle River, NJ: Prentice Hall, 1999.

Lambert, D. M., M. C. Cooper and J. D. Pagh, "Supply Chain Management: Implementation Issues and Research Opportunities," *The International Journal of Logistics Management* 9(2), 1998: 1–19.

Lee, H. L., V. Padmanabhan and S. Whang, "Information Distortion in a Supply Chain: The Bullwhip Effect," *Management Science* 43(4), 1997: 546–58.

Simchi-Levi, D., P. Kaminsky and E. Simchi-Levi. *Designing and Managing the Supply Chain.* New York: McGraw-Hill, 2000.

Stevens, G. C., "Integrating the Supply Chain," *International Journal of Physical Distribution and Logistics Management* 19(8), 1989: 3–8.

Tan, K. C., "A Framework of Supply Chain Management Literature," *European Journal of Purchasing and Supply Management* 7(1), 2001: 39–48.

Webster, S. *Principles & Tools for Supply Chain Management,* New York: McGraw-Hill/Irwin, 2008.

CHAPTER 2

Burt, D. N., D. W. Dobler and S. L. Starling. *World Class Supply Management: The Key to Supply Chain Management,*" 7th ed. New York: McGraw-Hill/Irwin, 2003.

Leenders, M. R., P. F. Johnson, A. E. Flynn and H. E. Fearon. *Purchasing and Supply Management,* 13th ed. New York: McGraw-Hill/Irwin, 2006.

Monczka, R., R. Handfield, L. C. Giunipero and J. L. Patterson. *Purchasing and Supply Chain Management,* 4th ed. Florence, KY: Cengage Learning, 2009.

Prahalad, C. K. and G. Hamel. "The Core Competence of the Corporation," *Harvard Business Review* 68(3), 1990: 79–91.

Wisner, J. D. and K. C. Tan. "Supply Chain Management and Its Impact on Purchasing," *Journal of Supply Chain Management* 36(4), 2000: 33–42.

CHAPTER 4

Anderson, M. and P. Katz, "Strategic Sourcing," *International Journal of Logistics Management* 9(1), 1998: 1–13.

Burt, D., D. Dobler and S. Starling. *World Class Supply Management: The Key to Supply Chain Management,* 7th ed. New York: McGraw-Hill/Irwin, 2003.

Kaplan, N. and J. Hurd, "Realizing the Promise of Partnerships," *Journal of Business Strategy* 23(3), 2002: 38–42.

Lummus, R., R. Vokurka and K. Alber, "Strategic Supply Chain Planning," *Production and Inventory Management Journal* 39(3), 1998: 49–58.

Simchi-Levi, D., P. Kaminsky and E. Simchi-Levi. *Designing and Managing the Supply Chain: Concepts, Strategies and Case Studies,* 2d ed. New York: McGraw-Hill/Irwin, 2003.

Vonderembse, M., "The Impact of Supplier Selection Criteria and Supplier Involvement on Manufacturing," *Journal of Supply Chain Management* 35(3), 1999: 33–39.

CHAPTER 6

Chopra, S. and P. Meindl. *Supply Chain Management.* 4th ed. Upper Saddle River, NJ: Prentice Hall, 2010.

Duffy, R. J. and M. Gorsage, "Facing SRM and CRM," *Inside Supply Management* 13(8), August 2002: 30–37.

Fogarty, D. W., J. H. Blackstone and T. R. Hoffmann. *Production and Inventory Management*. 2nd ed. Cincinnati: South-Western Publishing, 1991.

Hopp, W. J. and M. L. Spearman, "To Pull or Not to Pull: What Is the Question?" *Manufacturing & Service Operations Management* 6(2), 2004: 133–148.

Jacobs, F. R. and R. B. Chase. *Operations and Supply Management*. 12th ed. Boston: McGraw-Hill, 2009.

Orlicky, J. *Material Requirements Planning: The New Way of Life in Production and Inventory Management*. New York: McGraw-Hill, 1975.

Simchi-Levi, D., P. Kaminsky and E. Simchi-Levi. *Designing and Managing the Supply Chain*. 3rd ed. Boston: McGraw-Hill/Irwin, 2008.

Vollmann, T. E., W. L. Berry, D. C. Whybark and F. R. Jacobs. *Manufacturing Planning and Control for Supply Chain Management*. 5th ed. Boston: McGraw-Hill/Irwin, 2005.

Wagner, B. J. and E. F. Monk. *Enterprise Resource Planning*. 3rd ed. Boston: South-Western Cengage Learning, 2009.

CHAPTER 7

Chase, R. B., F. R. Jacobs and N. J. Aquilano. *Operations Management for Competitive Advantage*. 11th ed. Boston: McGraw-Hill/Irwin, 2006.

EPCglobal, "EPCglobal Tag Data Standards Version 1.3 Ratified Specification," EPCglobal Inc., March 8, 2006.

EPCglobal, "The EPCglobal Architecture Framework EPCglobal Final Version 1.2," EPCglobal Inc., September 10, 2007.

Fogarty, D. W., J. H. Blackstone and T. R. Hoffmann, *Production & Inventory Management*. 2nd ed. Cincinnati: South-Western, 1991.

Hax, A. and D. Candea. *Production and Inventory Management*. Englewood Cliffs, NJ: Prentice-Hall, 1984.

Krajewski, L. J., L. P. Ritzman and M. J. Malhorta. *Operations Management: Process and Value Chains*. 8th ed. Reading, MA: Prentice-Hall. 2007.

Vollmann, T. E., W. L. Berry, D. C. Whybark and F. R. Jacobs. *Manufacturing Planning and Control for Supply Chain Management*. 5th ed. Boston: McGraw-Hill/Irwin, 2005.

CHAPTER 8

Burt, D. N., D. W. Dobler and S. L. Starling. *World Class Supply Management: The Key to Supply Chain Management*. 7th ed. New York: McGraw-Hill, 2003.

Crosby, P. B. *Quality Is Free*. New York: McGraw-Hill, 1979.

Crosby, P. B. *Quality without Tears*. New York: McGraw-Hill, 1984.

Deming, W. E. *Out of the Crisis*. Cambridge, MA: MIT Center for Advanced Engineering Study, 1986.

Evans, J. R. and W. M. Lindsay. *The Management and Control of Quality*. 4th ed. Cincinnati: South-Western, 1999.

Heizer, J. and B. Render. *Principles of Operations Management*. 4th ed. Upper Saddle River, NJ: Prentice-Hall, 2000.

Jacobs, F. and R. Chase. *Operations and Supply Management: The Core*. New York: McGraw-Hill/Irwin, 2008.

Juran, J. and A. Godfrey. *Juran's Quality Handbook*. New York: McGraw-Hill, 2000.

Krajewski, L., L. Ritzman and M. Malhotra. *Operations Management: Processes and Value Chains*. 8th ed. Upper Saddle River, NJ: Pearson/Prentice-Hall, 2007.

Lucier, G. and S. Seshadri, "GE Takes Six Sigma Beyond the Bottom Line," *Strategic Finance* 82(11), 2001: 40–46.

Smith, G. *Statistical Process Control and Quality Improvement*. New York: Macmillan, 1991.

Vokurka, R. J. and R. R. Lummus, "The Role of Just-in-Time in Supply Chain Management." *International Journal of Logistics Management* 11(1), 2000: 89–98.

CHAPTER 9

Bloomberg, D. J., S. LeMay and J. B. Hanna. *Logistics*. Upper Saddle River, NJ: Prentice Hall, 2002.

Coyle, J. J., E. J. Bardi and C. J. Langley. *The Management of Business Logistics*. St. Paul, MN: West Publishing, 1996.

Lambert, D. M., J. R. Stock and L. M. Ellram. *Fundamentals of Logistics Management*. New York: McGraw-Hill, 1998.

Sampson, R. J., M. T. Farris and D. L. Shrock, *Domestic Transportation: Practice, Theory and Policy*. 5th ed. Boston: Houghton Mifflin, 1985.

Stock, J. R. and D. M. Lambert, *Strategic Logistics Management*. 4th ed. New York: McGraw-Hill, 2001.

CHAPTER 10

Barnes, J. G. *Secrets of Customer Relationship Management*. New York: McGraw-Hill, 2001.

Bergeron, B. *Essentials of CRM: A Guide to Customer Relationship Management*. New York: John Wiley & Sons, 2001.

Bloomberg, D. J., S. LeMay and J. B. Hanna. *Logistics*. Upper Saddle River, NJ: Prentice Hall, 2002.

Dyché, J. *The CRM Handbook: A Business Guide to Customer Relationship Management*. Upper Saddle River, NJ: Addison-Wesley, 2002.

Fitzsimmons, J. and M. Fitzsimmons. *Service Management for Competitive Advantage*. New York: McGraw-Hill, 1994.

Lawrence, F. B., D. F. Jennings and B. E. Reynolds. *eDistribution*. Mason, OH: South-Western, 2003.

Metters, R., K. King-Metters and M. Pullman. *Successful Service Operations Management*, Mason, OH: South-Western, 2003.

CHAPTER 11

Arend, M. "Manufacturing Is On the Move." *Site Selection Magazine* (November 2002).

Barnes, N. G., A. Connell, L. Hermenegildo and L. Mattson. "Regional Differences in the Economic Impact of Wal-Mart." *Business Horizons* (July/August 1996).

Barros, A. I. *Discrete and Fractional Programming Techniques for Location Models*. Dordrecht: Kluwer Academic Publishers, 1998.

Beckmann, M. J. *Lectures on Location Theory*. Berlin, New York: Springer-Verlag, 1999.

Bolton, J. and E. Chu, "Global Sourcing for High Performance: Leading practices and the emerging role of international procurement organizations in China" 11/22/2006; available from http://www.accenture.com/Countries/Netherlands/Research_and_Insights/By_Industry/Consumer_Goods_and_Services/GlobalSourcingHighPerformance.htm

Brown, G. and A. McMahon. "The MATRIX: Here's the Smartest Way to Compare Factors and Narrow Your Location Choices." *Business Facilities* (April 2002). Available from http://www.facilitycity.com/busfac/bf_02_04_cover.asp

Clapp, D. "Making the Move: A Paradigm Shift in the Far East." *Business Facilities* (September 2002). Available from http://www.facilitycity.com/busfac/bf_02_09_move.asp

Clapp, D., M. E. McCandless and K. Khan. "The World's Most Competitive Locations." *Business Facilities*, (September 2001). Available from http://www.facilitycity.com/busfac/bf_01_09_cover.asp

Devan, J., E. Carr, I. Ho, S. Yiannouka and J. A. Pantangc. "Doing business in China: A McKinsey Survey of executives in Asia," *The McKinsey Quarterly* (7 March 2007).

Drezner, Z. and H. W. Hamacher. *Facility Location: Applications and Theory*. Springer-Verlag, 2004.

Ferdows, K. "Making the Most of Foreign Factories." *Harvard Business Review* (March–April 1977): 73–88.

Greenhut, M. L. *Location Economics: Theoretical Underpinnings and Applications*. Aldershot, UK; Brookfield, Vt, US: Edward Elgar Publishing Limited, 1995.

Hack, G. D. *Site Selection for Growing Companies*. Westport, Conn.: Quorum Books, 1999.

Hagel, J. III and M. Singer. "Unbundling the Corporation." *Harvard Business Review* (March–April 1999): 133–41.

Jensen, K. and G. Pompelli. "Manufacturing Site Location Preferences of Small Agribusiness Firms." *Journal of Small Business Management* (July 2002).

Khan, K. "Project Persuasion." *Business Facilities* (July 2000). Available from http://www.facilitycity.com/busfac/bf_02_07_cover.asp

Lee, H., V. Tummala and R. Yam. "Manufacturing Support for Hong Kong Manufacturing Industries in Southern China." Available from http://www.ism.ws/ResourceArticles/2000/winter00p35.cfm

MacCormack, A., D. Lawrence, J. Newmann III and D. B. Rosenfield. "The New Dynamics of Global Manufacturing Site Location." *Sloan Management Review* (Summer 1994): 69–79.

MacKay, S. "The New Rules for G7 Site Selection." *Business Facilities* (September 2002). Available from http://www.facilitycity.com/busfac/bf_02_09_cover.asp

Magretta, J. "The Power of Virtual Integration: An Interview with Dell Computer's Michael Dell." *Harvard Business Review* (March–April 1998): 72–84.

Mallot, J. "Quality of Life: How to Know It When You See It." *Business Facilities* (September 2002). Available from http://www.facilitycity.com/busfac/bf_02_11_cover2.asp

Porter, M. "Clusters and Competition: New Agenda for Companies, Government and Institutions." *Harvard Business School Press Chapter* (7 June 1999).

Porter, M. "Clusters and the New Economics of Competition." *Harvard Business Review* (1 November 1998).

Rufinni, F. "The New Face of Logistics: Technology and e-Commerce Have Reshaped the Horizons of Today's Largest Distribution Hubs." *Business Facilities* (September 2002). Available from http://www.facilitycity.com/busfac/bf_02_09_special1.asp

Scott, B. R. *Country Analysis in a "Global Village."* Harvard Business School Note #9-701-073 (12 January 2001).

"Taming the Dragon: Mastering China's Growth Dynamics" July 2005; available from http://www.accenture.com/Global/Netherlands/Research_and_Insights/policy_And_Corporate_Affairs/TamingTheDragonDynamics.htm

CHAPTER 12

Anderson, D., D. Sweeney and T. Williams. *An Introduction to Management Science*. Mason, OH: South-Western, 2003.

Davis, M., N. Aquilano and R. Chase. *Fundamentals of Operations Management*. New York: McGraw-Hill, 1999.

Drazen, E., R. Moll and M. Roetter. *Logistics in Service Industries*. Oak Brook, IL: Council of Logistics Management, 1991.

Fitzsimmons, J. and M. Fitzsimmons. *Service Management for Competitive Advantage*. New York: McGraw-Hill, 1994.

Heizer, B. and B. Render. *Principles of Operations Management*. Upper Saddle River, NJ: Prentice Hall, 2001.

Markland, R., S. Vickery and R. Davis. *Operations Management*. Mason, OH: South-Western, 1998.

Metters, R., K. King-Metters and M. Pullman. *Successful Service Operations Management*. Mason, OH: South-Western, 2003.

Rodriguez, C. *International Management: A Cultural Approach*. Mason, OH: South-Western, 2001.

Taha, H. A. *Operations Research: An Introduction*. Upper Saddle River, NJ: Prentice Hall, 2003.

Taylor, B. *Introduction to Management Science*. Upper Saddle River, NJ: Prentice Hall, 2002.

CHAPTER 13

Chopra, S. and P. Meindl. *Supply Chain Management: Strategy, Planning and Operation*. Upper Saddle River, NJ: Prentice Hall, 2001.

Croxton, K. L., S. J. Garcia-Dastugue, D. M. Lambert and D. S. Rogers, "The Supply Chain Management Processes," *International Journal of Logistics Management* 12(2), 2001: 13–36.

Handfield, R. B. and E. L. Nichols. *Supply Chain Redesign: Transforming Supply Chains into Integrated Value Systems*. Upper Saddle River, NJ: Financial Times Prentice Hall, 2002.

Lambert, D. M., M. C. Cooper and J. D. Pagh, "Supply Chain Management: Implementation Issues and Research Opportunities," *International Journal of Logistics Management* 9(2), 1998: 1–19.

Simchi-Levi, D., P. Kaminsky and E. Simchi-Levi. *Designing and Managing the Supply Chain*. New York: McGraw-Hill/Irwin, 2003.

CHAPTER 14

Kaplan, R. S. and D. P. Norton, "Linking the Balanced Scorecard to Strategy," *California Management* Review 39(1), 1996: 53–79.

Evans, J. R. and W. M. Lindsay. *The Management and Control of Quality*. Mason, OH: South-Western, 2002.

Metters, R., K. King-Metters and M. Pullman. *Successful Service Operations Management*. Mason, OH: South-Western, 2003.

Nicholas, J. M. *Competitive Manufacturing Management*. New York: McGraw-Hill, 1998.

Wisner, J. D. and S. E. Fawcett, "Linking Firm Strategy to Operating Decisions through Performance Measurement," *Production and Inventory Management Journal* 32(3), 1991: 5–11.

Endnotes

CHAPTER 1

1. Quote by John Langley, PhD, supply chain executive forum director of the supply chain & logistics institute at Georgia Tech, in Terreri, A., "Supply Chain Trends to Watch," *World Trade* 23(7), 2010: 16–21.

2. Quote by Janice Lindsay, vice president of supply chain operations for Florida-based radio manufacturer Harris Corp., in Cable, J., "Positioned for Growth," *Industry Week* 259(4), 2010: 46.

3. Carbone, J., "Supply Chain Manager of the Year: Steve Darendinger Champion of Change," *Purchasing* 135(13), 2006: 37.

4. Listed in the CSCMP Terms and Glossary at www.cscmp.org, on August 13, 2010.

5. Found in the ISM Glossary of Key Supply Management Terms at www.ism.ws on August 13, 2010.

6. Found in the LSCMS SCM Dictionary at www.lcms.org on August 13, 2010.

7. Zieger, A., "Don't Choose the Wrong Supply Chain Partner," *Frontline Solutions* 4(6), 2003: 10–14.

8. Tan, K., S. Lyman, and J. Wisner, "Supply Chain Management: A Strategic Perspective," *International Journal of Operations and Production Management* 2(6), 2002: 614–31.

9. U.S. Census Bureau information found at www.census.gov/manufacturing/asm/index.html.

10. Poirier, C., M. Swink, and F. Quinn, "Progress Despite the Downturn," *Supply Chain Management Review* 13(7), 2009: 26.

11. Keith, O., and M. Webber, "Supply-Chain Management: Logistics Catches Up with Strategy," *Outlook* (1982), cit. Christopher, M.G., "Logistics," *The Strategic Issue*. London: Chapman and Hall, 1992.

12. Shaw, A. *Some Problems in Market Distribution*. Cambridge, MA: Harvard University Press, 1915.

13. Smith, J., "The Adam Smith of Supply Chain Management," *World Trade* 19(9), 2006: 62.

14. Avery, S., "Supply Chain Management Is Key to Meeting Requirements of Demanding Customers," *Purchasing* 136(1), 2007: 56.

15. Cable, J., "What You Can't See Can Hurt You," *Industry Week* 259(1), 2010: 44.

16. Dudlicek, J., "Winning the West," *Dairy Foods* 110(12), 2009: 55–60.

17. Cable, J. "Positioned for Growth," *Industry Week* 259(4), 2010: 46–47.

18. Mishra, D., "Optimizing the Supply Chain," *Dealerscope* 49(2), 2007: 1.

19. Anonymous, "Sizing Up the Elephant," *Industry Week* 259(2), 2010: 35.

20. Robinson, A., and D. Schroeder, "The Role of Front-Line Ideas in Lean Performance Improvement," *The Quality Management Journal* 16(4), 2009: 27–40.

21. Hannon, D., "3PL Helps Fashion Retailer Turnaround Its Supply Chain," *Purchasing* 135(17), 2006: 24.

22. Braddock, R., "FreshDirect's Secret Ingredient: Customer Focus," *Customer Relationship Management* 13(12), 2009: 24–25.

23. Mishra, D., "Everyone's Business," *Dealerscope* 48(13), 2006: 164–65.

24. Phillips, Z., "Outsourcing Overseas Cuts Costs, Raises Risks," *Business Insurance* 44(31), 2010: 11–12.

25. Ramirez, S., "The Art and Science of Supply Management," *World Trade* 23(4), 2010: 26–30.

26. Lapide, L., "Is it Possible to Have Predictive Metrics?" *Supply Chain Management Review* 13(8), 2009: 4.

27. Burnson, P., "Shipper Profile: HP Traces Outsourcing Back to Its Roots," *Logistics Management* 48(8), 2009: 56–57.

28. Anonymous, "Backshoring Gains Momentum," *Machine Design* 82(12), 2010: 36.

29. Bonney, J., "Logistics Cost Measure Fell to Record Low in 2009," *Journal of Commerce*, June 9, 2010: 1.

30. Wright, J., "Sourcing Successfully in the New China," *Logistics Management* 48(9), 2009: 34.

31. Shacklett , M., "Mobile Technology and the Supply Chain," *World Trade* 23(7), 2010: 22–25.

32. Anonymous, "Meeting Compliance Mandates Requires a Good Look at the Shop Floor," *Manufacturing Business Technology* 25(2), 2007: 16.

33. Tieman, R., "Plan for the Future from Fork to Farm," *Financial Times*, January 27, 2010: 6.

34. Sowinski, L., "Why Green Matters More," *World Trade* 23(5), 2010: 7.

35. Dutton, G., "Staples Nails Sustainability," *World Trade* 22(8), 2009: 34–37.

36. Quinn, B., "Keeping Green Claims Accurate," *Pollution Engineering* 42(1), 2010: 15.

37. Hoffman, W., "CEOs Catch Logistics," *Traffic World*, March 6, 2006: 1.

38. McCrea, B., "TMS: Your Key to the New Economy," *Logistics Management* 49(2), 2010: 38; Anonymous, "Ariba, Inc.: MWBrands Reels in Savings with Ariba," *Economics Week*, December 4, 2009: 18.

39. Copyright © 1994 President and Fellows of Harvard College (the Beer Game board version) and © 2002 The MIT Forum for Supply Chain Innovation (the Beer Game computerized version). Interested students can visit http://beergame.mit.edu to learn more about the Beer Game and to play the computerized version. Students can also read Hammond, J. H., "The Beer Game: Board Version," Harvard Business School case #9-694-104, rev. October 27, 1999, for more information.

CHAPTER 2

1. UNLV Purchasing Department, http://purchasing.unlv.edu/about/, accessed February 19, 2010.

2. Arnseth, L. "Calculating TCO for Intangibles," *Inside Supply Management* 20(10) October 2009: 30.

3. Tan, K. C. "The Key to an Effective Purchasing System: Is It Technology or Supplier Relationship Management?" *Practix: Good Practices in Purchasing & Supply Chain Management* 11, September 2007: 1–8.

4. "2006 Statistics for All Manufacturing by State," *Annual Survey of Manufactures*, U.S. Census Bureau, November 18, 2008, www.census.gov/manufacturing/asm/historical_data/index.html.

5. ISM Glossary of Key Supply Management Terms, www.ism.ws/glossary, accessed February 27, 2010.

6. Tan, K.C., and Dajalos, R., "Purchasing Strategy in the 21st Century: E-Procurement", *Practix: Best Practices in Purchasing & Supply Chain Management*, 4(3), 7–12.

7. Pomfret, J. and K. Soh, "For Apple Suppliers, Loose Lips Can Sink Contracts," *Reuters*, February 17, 2010, www.reuters.com/assets/print?aid=USTRE61G3XA20100217, accessed March 14, 2010; Dean, J, "The Forbidden City of Terry Gou," *The Wall Street Journal*, August 11, 2007, http://online.wsj.com/article/SB118677584137994489.html#printMode, accessed September 3, 2010.

8. Hannon, D., "P-card Program Expansion Is a Global Challenge," *Purchasing* 138(12), 53–55, December 19, 2009; Anonymous, "P-card Program's Success requires Careful Planning," *Purchasing* 138(8), 16–17, August 2009.

9. World Trade Organization. "International Trade Statistics 2009," WTO Publications, Geneva, www.wto.org/english/res_e/statis_e/its2009_e/its2009_e.pdf.

10. Hornbeck, J. F. "CRS Report for Congress—NAFTA at Ten: Lessons from Recent Studies," February 13, 2004.

11. Case, S., and D. Arnold. "Greening Federal Purchasing," *Government Procurement*, August 2005: 18–26.

12. U.S. Department of Energy, "Guide to Purchasing Green Power, Renewable Electricity, Renewable Energy Certificates and On-Site Renewable Generation," EPA430-K-04-015, September 2004.

13. Pomfret, J. and K. Soh. "For Apple Suppliers, Loose Lips Can Sink Contracts," *Reuters*, February 17, 2010, www.reuters.com/assets/print?aid=USTRE61G3XA20100217, accessed March 14, 2010.

CHAPTER 3

1. Arnseth, L. "The Power of Balanced Partnerships," *Inside Supply Management* 20(11), November 2009: 26.

2. Edmisten, B. E., "Collaboration Counts," *Inside Supply Management* 20(10), October 2009: 10.

3. "ISM Glossary of Key Supply Management Terms: Supplier Partnership," Institute of Supply Management, www.ism.ws/Glossary/GlossaryTermDetail.cfm?TermID=2559.

4. Stundza, T., "Ford Has a Better Idea," *Purchasing*, September 7, 2006.

5. Treece, J. B., "Ford Adds 13 to Preferred Suppliers List," *Automotive News*, April 24, 2010, www.autonews.com/apps/pbcs.dll/article?AID=/20100424/OEM01/100429894/1254/OEM05.

6. Ohmae, K., "The Global Logic of Strategic Alliances," *Harvard Business Review*, March-April 1989: 143–152.

7. Lewis, Jordan D., *Trusted Partners: How Companies Build Mutual Trust and Win Together*. New York: The Free Press, 1999: 7.

8. "Buyers Target Strategic Partners," *Purchasing*, April 5, 2001.

9. "Supplier Selection & Management Report," March 2002, Institute of Management and Administration (IOMA).

10. Covey, S.R., "Steven Covey Quotes and Sayings"; available from www.bestinspirationalquotes.com/success-leaders/stephen-covey.htm

11. MacDonald, M., "Managing Change: A Matter of Principle," *Supply Chain Management Review*, January/February 2002, www.manufacturing.net/scm/.

12. Atkinson, W. "Whirlpool's Procurement Takes the Lead in Outsourcing," *Purchasing Magazine Online*, March 1, 2007.

13. Drab, D., "Economic Espionage and Trade Secret Theft: Defending Against the Pickpockets of the New Millennium," Xerox Corporation, www.xerox.com/downloads/wpaper/x/xgs_business_insight_economic_espionage.pdf.

14. Hannon, D., "Best Practices: Hackett Group Outlines the World-Class Procurement Organization," *Purchasing*, December 8, 2006.

15. "Accenture Builds High Performance in Supplier Relationship Management with mySAP SRM Solutions," Accenture, www.accenture.com/NR/rdonlyres/D7E62F38-EC79-4D04-82B3-3E055BEE386C/41337/SRM_BuildingHighPerformace6.pdf.

16. Babineaux, F. M., "Measuring Supplier Performance (How to Get What You Measure and Other Intentional Consequences)," 87th Annual International Supply Management Conference, 2002 International Conference Proceedings, May 2002.

17. McGinnis, M. A., "Building Better Performance Measures," *NAPM Insights*, May 1, 1995: 50–53.

18. Russell, P. G., and W. C. Kropf, "Hewlett-Packard's Packaging Supplier Evaluation Process and Criteria," Hewlett-Packard Web site, packaging.hp.com/procurement/paper.doc.

19. Gunasekaran, A., C. Pate, and E. Tirtiroglu., "Performance Measures and Metrics in a Supply Chain Environment," *International Journal of Operations & Production Management* 21(1/2), 2001: 71–87.

20. Ellram, L. M., "A Structured Method for Applying Purchasing Cost Management Tools," www.ism.ws/ResourceArticles/1996/jwinter962.cfm.

21. "ISM Glossary of Key Supply Management Terms: Total Cost of Ownership," Institute of Supply Management.

22. Kelly, K. M., "Lessons from the Toy Aisle," *Automotive Design & Production* 119(10), October 2007: 8.

23. Finstad, R., "Total Recall: A Flawed System of Trade," *Far Eastern Economic Review* 70(9), November 2007, 46–50.

24. Honeywell Supplier Portal, www.supplier.honeywell.com/servlet/com.honeywell.supplier.MainServlet.

25. Honeywell Supplier Scorecard Training Module, www.supplier.honeywell.com/docs/ssc/help/scorecard_viewlet_swf.html.

26. "Supplier Certification: A Continuous Improvement Strategy," Tompkins Associates—M-49, www.tompkinsinc.com/publications/monograph/monographList/M-49.PDF.

27. "Glossary of Key Supply Management Terms: Supplier Certification," Institute of Supply Management Web site.

28. ISO – ISO 9000/ISO 14000: Quality Management Principles, www.iso.org/iso/iso_catalogue/management_standards/iso_9000_iso_14000/qmp.htm.

29. The ISO Survey 2008, www.iso.org/iso/survey2008.pdf.

30. Ibid.

31. ISO – ISO 9000/ISO 14000: In the Global Economy, www.iso.org/iso/iso_catalogue/management_ standards/iso_9000_iso_14000/in_the_global_economy.htm.

32. Handfield, R. B., D. R. Krause, T. V. Scannell, and R. M. Monzka., "Avoid the Pitfalls in Supplier Development," *Sloan Management Review*, Winter 2000: 37–49.

33. Ibid.

34. "Supplier Continuous Quality Improvement (SCQI) Program"; https://supplier.intel.com/static/quality/ scqi.htm.

35. "Supplier Continuous Quality Improvement (SCQI) Program", https://supplier.intel.com/static/quality/ SCQI_Program_Brochure.pdf.

36. Honeywell Six Sigma Plus, www51.honeywell.com/aero/AboutUs/SixSigmaPlus3/Six-Sigma-Plus.html? c=12.

37. "Doing Business with Boeing," The Boeing Company; www.boeingsuppliers.com/index.html.

38. Ibid.

39. Media, The Boeing Company, http://boeing.mediaroom.com/index.php?s=43&item=1161.

40. "Nikon Named Recipient of Prestigious Intel SCQI Award", www.nikonprecision.com/newsletter/ spring_2009/article_05.html.

41. "Hormel Foods Corporation Announces Supplier Awards", www.hormelfoods.com/newsroom/press/ 20060927a.aspx.

42. "Hormel Foods Honors 58 Suppliers with Spirit of Excellence Awards," www.hormelfoods.com/ newsroom/press/20100415.aspx.

43. Barling, B., "The Five Tenets of SRM," *AMR Research*, June 10, 2002, www.amrresearch.com.

44. "Accenture Builds High Performance,"op. cit.

45. "A Study of Emerging Issues and Cutting-edge Knowledge," SAS Institute Inc., www.sas.com/ solutions/sci/special_report.pdf.

46. Ibid.

47. Barling, B., op cit.

CHAPTER 4

1. "Ethical Sourcing at Starbucks," www.starbucks.com/sharedplanet/ethicalSourcing.aspx.

2. "Sustainable Forestry: Benefits of Sustainable Sourcing,"www.rainforest-alliance.org/forestry.cfm? id=sustainable_sourcing.

3. Ellinor, R., "Taking a Larger Slice of the Market," *Supply Management* 11(1), 2006: 15.

4. Murray, S., "Profile: Ethical Sourcing Highlights Cadbury's Commitment," *FT.com*, June 9, 2009.

5. Worthington, I., M. Ram, H. Boyal, and M. Shah, "Researching the Drivers of Socially Responsible Purchasing: A Cross-National Study of Supplier Diversity Initiatives," *Journal of Business Ethics* 79(3), 2008: 319–331.

6. Berthiaume, D., "Reebok's Sourcing Strategy Places Ethics First," *Chain Store Age*, January 2006: 32A.

7. Boggan, S., "Nike Admits Mistakes Over Child Labor," *Independent/UK*, October 20, 2001, www.independent.co.uk; Levenson, E., "Citizen Nike," *CNNMoney.com*, November 17, 2008, www.cnnmoney.com/2008.

8. Coleman, F., "In Search of Ethical Sourcing," *Directorship* 33(2), 2007: 38–39; Cooper, B., "Perspectives on the Ethical Sourcing Debate in the Clothing Industry," *Just-Style*, November 2007: 21.

9. Murray, S., "Confusion Reigns Over Labeling Fair Trade Products," *Financial Times*, June 13, 2006: 2. Also see: www.fairtrade.net, www.wfto.com.

10. Allen, B., "In Pursuit of Responsible Procurement," *Summit* 9(4), 2006: 7.

11. Tighe, C., "Rubber Gloves Form Next Fair Trade," *Financial Times*, April 13, 2009: 17.

12. "Global Fairtrade Sales Increase by 22%," www.fairtrade.net, June 4, 2009.

13. For more information, see the Goldman Environmental Prize Web page: www.goldmanprize.org.

14. See, for example, Androich, A., "Get Your Green On," *RealScreen*, July/August 2007: 14; Watson, T., "Environmental Pioneer Dies," *USA Today*, November 7, 2000: 24A.

15. To visit the Institute for Supply Management, go to www.ism.ws.

16. Turner, M., and P. Houston, "Going Green? Start with Sourcing," *Supply Chain Management Review* 13(2), 2009: 14–20.

17. Pinchot, G., *The Conservation of Natural Resources*. Washington DC: U.S. Dept. of Agriculture, 1908. (Farmers' Bulletin, 327) NAL Call no.: 1 Ag84F no.327; also see Beatley, T., "Sustainability 3.0 Building Tomorrow's Earth-Friendly Communities," *Planning* 75(5), 2009: 16–22.

18. Anonymous, "Getting Leaner—Ahead of the Pack: Suppliers Adjust to New Packaging Priorities," *Retailing Today*, Fourth Quarter, 2006: 16.

19. Ibid.

20. Mulani, N., "Sustainable Sourcing: Do Good While Doing Well," *Logistics Management* 47(7), 2008: 25–26.

21. Ibid.

22. Lim, S., "Backers Don't Buy 'Friendly' Palm Oil," *Wall Street Journal*, July 15, 2009: C14.

23. Snell, P., "Struggle with Sustainability," *Supply Management* 11(23), 2006: 7.

24. Beatley, T., "Sustainability 3.0 Building Tomorrow's Earth-Friendly Communities," *Planning* 75(5), 2009: 16–22.

25. Ellinor, R., "Costing the Earth," *Supply Management* 12(2), 2007: 24.

26. Same as reference Beatley, T.

27. Kuranko, C., "The Green Standard," *The American City & County* 123(9), 2008: 40–43.

28. For more information, see the TerraChoice Web site: www.terrachoice.com.

29. Fisher, M. "What Is the Right Supply Chain for Your Product?" *Harvard Business Review* 75(2), 1997: 105–116.

30. Snell, P., "Chrysler Ups Spend on Low-Cost Sourcing," *Supply Management* 12(5), 2007: 8.

31. Reeve, T., and J. Steinhausen, "Sustainable Suppliers, Sustainable Markets," *CMA Management* 81 (2), 2007: 30–33.

32. Murphy, A., C. Satterthwaite, D. Grounsell, and M. Chandra, "As the Recession Eases Should Sustainability Become a Priority?" *Marketing*, October 14, 2009: 24.

33. Morrissey, H., "Be a Top Flight Customer," *Supply Management* 11(7), 2006: 30.

34. Gooch, F., "Playing Fair in Hard Times," *Supply Management* 13(24), 2008: 42–44.

35. The interested reader is invited to navigate the ISO site: www.iso.org.

36. Alpert, B., "Do-Gooders Who Could Do Better," *Barron's* 87(46), 2007: 40–41.

37. Anonymous, "Integrity Interactive Corporation, New Integrity Interactive Service," *Business & Finance Week*, April 14, 2008: 195.

38. For more information, see "Cross-Industry Report of Standard Benchmarks," at www.capsresearch .org.

39. Young, I., "Sustainable Logistics and Supply Chains: How Europe Provides a Role Model," *Chemical Week* 171(23), 2009: 38.

40. Weil, N., "What Price Innovation?" *CIO* 21(2), 2007: 1–6.

41. Whitten, D., and D. Leidner, "Bringing IT back: An Analysis of the Decision to Backsource or Switch Vendors," *Decision Sciences* 37(4), 2006: 605–622.

42. Atkinson, W., "Chevron Leverages Buyers in Outsourcing Decisions," *Purchasing* 135, no. 5(2006): 20.

43. Forth, K., "Insourcing to Improve Output," *FDM* 78(5), 2006: 30–35.

44. "Job Insourcing Is on the Rise," *Oxford Analytica Daily Brief Service*, September 8, 2009: 1–3.

45. "Bringing IT back: An Analysis of the Decision to Backsource or Switch Vendors," *Decision Sciences* 37(4), 2006: 605–622.

46. Bailor, C., "Making a Clear Connection," *Customer Relationship Management* 9(5), 2005: 30–35.

47. Atkinson, W., "Novellus Realizes Benefits of Early Supplier Involvement," *Purchasing* 137(4), 2008: 15.

48. Purdum, T., "VMI: Size Matters," *Industry Week* 256(3), 2007: 19–29.

49. Shister, N., "Applying the Ides of the Wal-Marts of the World to Smaller Companies," *World Trade* 19 (3), 2006: 26–29.

50. Albright, B., "No More Label Worries," *Frontline Solutions* 3(9), 2002: 54.

51. Atkinson, W., "Does JIT II Still Work in the Internet Age?" *Purchasing* 130(17), 2001: 41–42.

52. "Chrysler Embarks on 'Most Advanced Supplier Colocation Project,'" *MSI* 22(11), 2004: 48; Kelly, K., and B. Visnic, "A New Relationship," *Ward's Auto World* 40(9), 2004: 37–38.

53. Deierlein, B., "JIT: Zero Tolerance for Late Deliveries," *Fleet Equipment* 26(1), 2000: 36–39.

54. Avery, S., "Linking Supply Chains Saves Raytheon $400 Million," *Purchasing* 130(16), 2001: 27–31.

55. See, for example, Langfield-Smith, K., and D. Smith, "Management Control Systems and Trust in Outsourcing Relationships," *Management Accounting Research* 14(3), 2003: 381–307, and Ertel, D., "Alliance Management: A Blueprint for Success," *Financial Executive* 17(9), 2001: 36–41.

56. Dyer, J., P. Kale, and H. Singh, "How to Make Strategic Alliances Work," *Sloan Management Review* 42(4), 2001: 37–43.

57. Gyves, S., and E. O'Higgins, "Corporate Social Responsibility: An Avenue for Sustainable Benefit for Society and the Firm?" *Society and Business Review* 3(3), 2008: 207–218.

58. Tavi, J., "Learning from Global World-Class e-Procurement Practices," *Strategic Finance* 89(10), 2008: 24–29.

59. Cameron, S., "Making a Difference," *Supply Management* 12(13), 2007: 50–52.

60. Anonymous "Tech Briefs," *Supply Management* 13(9), 2008: 11.

61. Anonymous "GreenWizard Opens Its Online Green-Product Database," *Economics Week*, January 8, 2010: 58.

62. Fosdick, G., and M. Uphoff, "Adopting Cross-Industry Best Practices for Measurable Results," *Healthcare Executive* 22(3), 2007: 14–19.

63. See, for instance, Andersen, B., T. Fagerhaug, S. Randmael, J. Schuldmaier, and J. Prenninger, "Benchmarking Supply Chain Management: Finding Best Practices," *Journal of Business and Industrial Marketing* 14(5/6), 1999: 378–89; Carr, A., and L. Smeltzer, "The Relationship among Purchasing Benchmarking, Strategic Purchasing, Firm Performance, and Firm Size," *Journal of Supply Chain Management* 35(4), 1999: 51–60; Ellram, L., and G. Zsidisin, S. Siferd, and M. Stanly, "The Impact of Purchasing and Supply Management on Corporate Success," *Journal of Supply Chain Management* 38(1), 2002: 4–17; and Krause, D., S. Vachon, and R. Klassen, "Special Topic Forum on Sustainable Supply Chain Management," *Journal of Supply Chain Management* 45 (4), 2009: 18–25.

64. Anonymous, "Third-Party Logistics: Kings of Networking," *Logistics Management* 48(8), 2009: 46.

65. Biederman, D., "The Unpaved Path to Growth," *Journal of Commerce*, January 18, 2010: 1.

66. Anonymous, "Management Update," *Logistics Management* 48(3), 2009: 1.

67. Sowinski, L., "Green Is Here for Good," *World Trade* 21(12), 2008: 44–47.

68. Stokes, S., and G. Aimi, "The Green Logistics Factor," *Inside Supply Management* 20(4), 2009: 34.

69. Avery, S., "Today's Travel Procurement Professional Knows How to Manage Supplier Relationships," *Purchasing* 138(2), 2009: 54.

CHAPTER 5

1. www.vics.org/docs/committees/cpfr/Interview_with_Larry_Smith_West_Marine_Oct_8_2003.pdf.

2. Fisher, M., J. Hammond, W. Obermeyer, and A. Raman, "Making Supply Meet Demand in an Uncertain World," *Harvard Business Review*, May–June 1994: 83–93.

3. The Institute for Supply Management's *Manufacturing and Non-Manufacturing Report on Business* is available at, www.ism.ws/ISMReport/content.cfm?ItemNumber=10743&navItemNumber=12944.

4. "May 2010 Manufacturing ISM *Report On Business*"; available from, www.ism.ws/ISMReport/MfgROB.cfm?navItemNumber=12942.

5. "Apple: 600,000 iPhone Preorders Crashed Systems," June 16, 2010, ZDNet; available from www.zdnet.com/blog/btl/apple-600000-iphone-preorders-crashed-systems/35899?tag=mantle_skin;content.

6. N. Knox, "A380 Makes Massive Debut," *USA TODAY*; available from www.usatoday.com/money/biztravel/2005-01-16-a380-usat_x.htm.

7. Airbus A380; from Wikipedia, the free encyclopedia; available from http://en.wikipedia.org/wiki/Airbus_A380.

8. Boeing 787; from Wikipedia, the free encyclopedia; available from http://en.wikipedia.org/wiki/Boeing_787.

9. M. Fisher, J. Hammond, W. Obermeyer, and A. Raman, "Making Supply Meet Demand in an Uncertain World," *Harvard Business Review* (May–June 1994): 83–93.

10. C. L. Jain, "Forecasting Process at Wyeth Ayerst Global Pharmaceuticals," *Journal of Business Forecasting*, Winter 2001–02: 3–4, 6.

11. 2010 Eruptions of Eyjafjallajökull; available from http://en.wikipedia.org/wiki/2010_eruptions_of_Eyjafjallajökull.

12. 2010 Haitian Earthquake; available from http://en.wikipedia.org/wiki/2010_Haiti_earthquake.

13. Chaman, L. Jain, "Benchmarking Forecasting Models," *The Journal of Business Forecasting* 25(4), Winter 2006/2007: 14–17.

14. Duncan, R., "Quality Forecasting Drives Quality Inventory at GE Silicones," *Industrial Engineering* 24 (1), 1992: 18–21.

15. Lawrence, M., M. O'Conner, and B. Edmundson, "A Field Study of Forecasting Accuracy and Processes," *European Journal of Operational Research* 22(1), April 1, 2000: 151–60.

16. "The CPFR Model," Voluntary Industry Commerce Standards (VICS) Association, available from www.vics.org/committees/cpfr/cpfr_model_faqs/.

17. Supply Chain Management Terms and Glossaries—Council of Supply Chain Management Professionals; available from http://cscmp.org/digital/glossary/document.pdf.

18. Global Commerce Initiative website: www.gci-net.org.

19. "VICS Collaborative Planning, Forecasting and Replenishment (CPFR): An Overview," 18 May 2004, found at www.vics.org/docs/committees/cpfr/CPFR_Overview_US-A4.pdf.

20. Ibid.

21. Smith, L., "West Marine: A CPFR Success Story"; available from www.scmr.com/article/CA6317964.html.

22. Ibid.

23. "CPFR Pilot Project Overview," VICS CPFR; available from www.cpfr.org/documents/pdf/07_4_0_CPFR_pilot_Overview.pdf.

24. i2 Demand Planner; available from www.autobox.com/pdfs/dp.pdf.

25. Case Study: Medtronic Sofamor Danek; available from www.i2.com/view.cfm?id=open-casestudy&caid=122

26. J. Uchneat, "CPFR's Woes Not Related to Trust," *Computerworld*, July 22, 2002; available from www.computerworld.com/news/2002/story/0,11280,72834,00.html.

27. "John Galt Solutions Selected as Top Innovator by Supply & Demand Chain Executive Magazine"; available from www.johngalt.com/News_&_Events/pr_Demand_Inventory_Management_SDC.shtml.

28. i2 Demand Planning Solutions; available from www.i2.com/view.cfm/demand-planning/.

29. Cloud Computing; available from http://en.wikipedia.org/wiki/Cloud_computing.

CHAPTER 6

1. Chaneski, W. S., "Planning Your Resources Wisely," *Modern Machine Shop* 82(9), February 2010: 30–32.

2. Kelly, C., "Analytics Drives Strategic Sourcing," *APICS Best Practices*, www.apics.org, March 30, 2010.

3. Fogarty, D. W., J. H. Blackstone, and T. R. Hoffmann. *Production & Inventory Management.* 2nd ed. Cincinnati: South-Western, 1991.

4. Field, A.M., "Stretching the Limits of ERP," *The Journal of Commerce* 8, January 2007: 76–78.

5. Roberto, M., "ERP Enters Age of Infrastructure," *Manufacturing Business Technology* 25(7), July 2007: 24–25.

6. Curt, B., "The ERP Edge," *Multichannel Merchant* 3(7), July 2007: 50–54.

7. Jutras, C., "The ERP in Manufacturing Benchmark Report," *Aberdeen Group, Inc.*, August 2006: 1–31.

CHAPTER 7

1. Friedman, D., "Inventory Management That Counts," *Electrical Wholesaling* 89(9), September 2008: 59–60.

2. www.gs1.org/epcglobal. "The Global Language of Business: EPCglobal" accessed on December 28, 2010.

3. Anonymous, "Wal-Mart, DOD Start Massive RFID Rollout; Is Everybody Ready?" *Inventory Management Report* 05(01) January 2005: 1, 10–12.

4. Songini, M. L., "Procter & Gamble: Wal-Mart RFID Effort Effective," *ComputerWorld* 41(9), February 26, 2007: 14.

5. Fish, L.A. and W. C. Forrest, "A Worldwide Look at RFID," *Supply Chain Management Review* 11(3), April 1, 2007: 48–55; Hoffman, W., "Wave of the Future: Changes in Technology, Industry Consolidation, Global Standards Begin to Raise RFID's Profile," *Journal of Commerce* 9(35), Sept 8, 2008: 44; Wu, N., H. H. Tsai, Y. S. Chang, and H. C. Yu, "The Radio Frequency Identification Industry Development Strategies of Asian Countries," *Technology Analysis & Strategic Management* 22(4), May 2010: 417–431; http://en.wikipedia.org/wiki/ Image:EPC-RFID-TAG.jpg, accessed May 30, 2010.

6. Narsimhan, S., D. W. McLeavey, and P. Billington. *Production Planning and Inventory Control.* 2nd ed. Saddle River, NJ: Prentice Hall, 1995.

CHAPTER 8

1. Anonymous, "Going Lean with Large-Part Machining," *Manufacturing Engineering* 143(6), 2009: 65–68.

2. Apology by Mr. Akio Toyoda, the president of Toyota, regarding the recall of millions of Toyota automobiles; in Kageyama, Y. "Toyota Recalls Prius Cars Worldwide." *Las Vegas Review Journal*, February 9, 2010: D1.

3. Reed, J., and B. Simon, "Toyota's Long Climb Comes to an Abrupt Halt," *Financial Times*, February 6, 2010: 9.

4. Information in this profile came from Anonymous, "Toyota Overtakes GM in Global Vehicle Sales," Associated Press news release, Apr. 24, 2007, found at www.msnbc.com/id/18286221; Anonymous, "CTS Comments on Toyota's January 21 Safety Voluntary Recall," CTS Corp. news release, Jan. 27, 2010, found at www.ctscorp.com; Reed, J., and B. Simon, "Toyota's Long Climb Comes to an Abrupt Halt," *Financial Times*, February 6, 2010: 9; Kageyama, Y., "Toyota Recalls 437,000 Priuses, Hybrids Globally," AP news release, February 9, 2010, found at www.news.yahoo.com/s/ap/20100209/ap_on_bi_ge/toyota_recall_102; Kim, S., "Timeline—Toyota's Rise and Run-up to Its Recall Crisis," Reuters Detroit news bureau, February 9, 2010, found at www.reuters.com/article/idAFN0920267420100209?rpc=44; Thomas, K., "Accelerator Complaints Climb," *Las Vegas Review-Journal*, February 16, 2010: D1.

5. For histories of lean and the Toyota Production System see, for instance, Becker, R. "Learning to Think Lean: Lean Manufacturing and the Toyota Production System," *Automotive Manufacturing & Production* 113(6), 2001: 64–5; Dahlgaard, J., and S. Dahlgaard-Park. "Lean Production, Six Sigma Quality, TQM and Company Culture," *TQM Magazine* 18(3), 2006: 263–77.

6. Information on the Ford manufacturing system was found at www.lean.org.

7. Arndorfer, J., C. Atkinson, J. Bloom, and M. Cardona, "The Biggest Moments in the Last 75 Years of Advertising History," *Advertising Age* 76(13), 2005: 12–15; and Reed and Simon, ref. 3.

8. Manivannan, S. "Error-Proofing Enhances Quality," *Manufacturing Engineering* 137(5), 2006: 99–105.

9. Nakamoto, M. and J. Reed. "Toyota Claims Global Top Spot from GM," *FT.com*, April 24, 2007: 1.

10. Womack, J., D. Jones, and D. Roos. *The Machine That Changed the World*. New York, NY: Maxwell MacMillan International, 1990.

11. Minter, S. "Measuring the Success of Lean," *Industry Week* 259(2), 2010: 32.

12. Waurzyniak, P., "Lean Automation," *Manufacturing Engineering* 142(2), 2009: 65–71.

13. Ben-Tovim, D., J. Bassham, D. Bolch, and M. Martin, "Lean Thinking Across a Hospital: Redesigning Care at the Flinders Medical Centre," *Australian Health Review* 31(1), 2007: 10–15.

14. Anonymous, "A Small Company Makes Big Gains Implementing Lean," *Management Services* 50(3), 2006: 28–31.

15. Roughead, G., "Featured Company: U.S. Navy," *ASQ Six Sigma Forum Magazine* 8(3), 2009: 40.

16. Manrodt, K., K. Vitasek, and R. Thompson, "The Lean Journey/Part II: Putting Lean to Work," *Logistics Management* 47(8), 2008: 74.

17. Albright, D., and A. Lo, "Transportation Management's Role in Supply Chain Excellence," *Logistics Management* 48(10), 2009: 44.

18. Anonymous, "Taking Lean Beyond the Plant Floor," *Industry Week* 257(8), 2008: 15.

19. Jargon, J., "Latest Starbucks Buzzword: 'Lean' Japanese Techniques," *Wall Street Journal*, August 4, 2009: A1.

20. Kerr, J. "What Does 'Lean' Really Mean?" *Logistics Management* 45(5), 2006: 29–33.

21. Fitz, T., "The Greening of the GPO," *Graphic Arts Monthly* 81(12), 2009: 26.

22. Kempfer, L., "The Safety Mosaic," *Material Handling Management* 62(4), 2007: 44–45.

23. Anonymous, "Tool for Productivity, Quality, Throughput, Safety," *Management Services* 50(3), 2006: 16–18; Becker, J., "Implementing 5S: To Promote Safety & Housekeeping," *Professional Safety* 46(8), 2001: 29–31.

24. Sedam, S., "Lean Serves as Recession-Buster for Builder," *Professional Builder* 75(2), 2010: 19.

25. Avery, S., "Suppliers Are Continuing Source of Innovation for P&G," *Purchasing* 138(8), 2009: 14.

26. Shaw, M., "Customers Drive End-Product Attributes, Technology Choices at MeadWestvaco Mill," *Pulp Paper* 78(1), 2004: 40.

27. Varley, P., "All-Inclusive Deal," *Supply Management* 4(21), 1999: 40–41.

28. Anonymous, "Going Deep with a Four-Way Valve," *Manufacturing Engineering* 142(5), 2009: 39–42.

29. Harriman, F., "Origins of the Term 'KANBAN' from Conversations with Chihiro Nakao." Found at www.fredharriman.com/resources/OriginsofKanban, February 22, 2010.

30. Anonymous, "Improvements Drilled Through," *Works Management* 59(10), 2006: 38–39.

31. Robinson, A., and D. Shroeder, "The Role of Front-Line Ideas in Lean Performance Improvement," *The Quality Management Journal* 16(4), 2009: 27–40.

32. King, A., and M. Lenox, "Lean and Green? An Empirical Examination of the Relationship Between Lean Production and Environmental Performance," *Production and Operations Management* 10(3), 2001: 244–56.

33. Blanchard, D., "Diagnosis: Green and Lean," *Industry Week* 255(9), 2006: 13.

34. Smith, M., "Going Green Drives Sales," *Printing Impressions* 49(10), 2007: 60–61.

35. Jusko, J., "Putting Waste to Work," *Industry Week* 257(10), 2008: 41–43.

36. Phillips, E., "Six Sigma: The Breakthrough Management Strategy Revolutionizing the World's Top Corporations," *Consulting to Management* 13(4), 2002: 57–59. Also see the SSA & Co. Web site: www.ssaandco.com.

37. Information about Six Sigma and sigma drift can be found at multiple locations; for example, www.isixsigma.com, or www.wikipedia.org/Six_Sigma.

38. Blanchard, D., "Diagnosis: Green and Lean," *Industry Week* 255(9), 2006: 13.

39. See, for example, *CRN*, June 4, 2007: 12; and Phillips, E., "Six Sigma: The Breakthrough Management Strategy Revolutionizing the World's Top Corporations," *Consulting to Management* 13 (4), 2002: 57–59.

40. "Business Brief—Primary PDC Inc.: Joint Bankruptcy Plan Filed to Dissolve Former Polaroid," *Wall Street Journal*, January 17, 2003: B-3.

41. "Six Sigma and Lean: A Marriage in the Making," *Business Credit* 108(10), 2006: 35.

42. See, for example, Brodshy, R. "Deep-Sixing Waste," *Government Executive* 41(12), 2009: 19–20; Kucner, R., "Staying Seaworthy," *Six Sigma Forum Magazine* 8(2), 2009: 25–31; and Westervelt, R., "Clariant Rebuilds Momentum," *Chemical Week* 171(10), 2009: 41.

43. Harbert, T., "Lean, Mean, Six Sigma Machines," *Electronic Business* 32(6), 2006: 38–42.

44. Gilbert, J., and J. Wisner., "Mattel, Lead Paint, and Magnets: Ethics and Supply Chain Management," *Ethics & Behavior* 20(1), 2010: 33–46.

45. See the Automotive Industry Action Group's website, www.aiag.org, for this and other industry information.

46. Deming, W. E. *Out of the Crisis*. Boston: MIT Press, 1986.

47. See www.deming.org for more information.

48. *Quality Is Free* is out of print; Crosby, P. B. *Quality Without Tears*. New York: McGraw-Hill, 1984.

49. Juran, J. M., and A. B. Godfrey. *Juran's Quality Handbook*. Milwaukee: ASQ Quality Press, 1999.

50. Butman, J., and J. Roessner. *An Immigrant's Gift: The Life of Quality Pioneer Joseph M. Juran*. PBS Documentary Video, produced by Howland Blackiston.

51. Baldrige information was obtained from the official website, www.baldrige.nist.gov.

52. ISO information was obtained from the organization's website, www.iso.org.

53. Information found in www.ge.com/sixsigma.

54. Descriptions found in www.isixsigma.com, www.asq.org, and www.xlp.com.

55. Adapted from Table 27 of the ASTM STP 15D ASTM *Manual on Presentation of Data and Control Chart Analysis*, © 1976 American Society for Testing and Materials, Philadelphia, PA.

CHAPTER 9

1. Varma, A. and A. Clayton. "Moving Goods Sustainably in Surface Transportation," *Institute of Transportation Engineers ITE Journal* 80(3), 2010: 20–24.

2. Minsk, R., "Plugging Cars into the Grid: Why the Government Should Make a Choice," *Energy Law Journal* 30(2), 2009: 317–376.

3. Council of Supply Chain Management Professionals, www.cscmp.org/aboutcscmp/definitions.

4. Berman, J., "ATA Chairman: Truckers Should Look at How they Do Business," *Logistics Management* 49(2), 2010: 18; Hasbrouck, E., "FAQ about Airline Bankruptcies," *The Practical Nomad*, found at www.hasbrouck.org/articles/bankruptcy.html; Keeton, A., "Corporate News: Air Industry Faces Grim Year Ahead," *Wall Street Journal*, September 16, 2009: B3.

5. Found at www.airlineworld.wordpress.com/2010/01/24, March 12, 2010.

6. Horowitz, S., "Wal-Mart to the Rescue: Private Enterprise's Response to Hurricane Katrina," *The Independent Review* 13(4), 2009: 511–528.

7. "Swift Currents, Debris Slow Recovery Effort," found at www.npr.org, August 13, 2007.

8. Cassidy, W., "Big LTL Carriers Getting Smaller," *Journal of Commerce*, March 4, 2010: 1.

9. Material for road trains came from www.outback-australia-travel-secrets.com/australian-road-trains.html, www.truckersnews.com/riding-the-down-under-express and www.ourterritory.com/katherine_region/road_trains.htm.

10. Material for the Shinkansen train came from www.japaneselifestyle.com.au/travel/shinkansen_nozomi.htm, www.japan-guide.com/e/e2018.html and www.railway-technology.com/projects/shinkansen.

11. Material for the Antonov An-225 came from Spaeth, A., "When Size Matters," *Air International*, December 2009: 29; www.theaviationzone.com/factsheets/an225.asp; www.airbususa380.tripod.com/id6.html; and www.antonov.com/products/air/transport.html.

12. Material for the largest water carriers came from www.globalsecurity.org/military/systems/ship/jahre-viking.html; www.blupulzz.com/?Id=2245; and www.emma-maersk.info.

13. Material for the largest pipelines came from "Russia's Putin Launches Pacific Oil Terminal," *Reuters.com*, December 28, 2009; "Pipeline Re-routed in Russia's Far East, Endangered Leopard Habitat Spared," March 13, 2007, found at www.panda.org/what_we_do/successes/?96640/World's-longest-oil-pipeline-re-route; Wise, J., "World's Longest Underwater Pipeline Will Tap the Sea," *Popular Mechanics*, June 2007, found at www.popularmechanics.com/science/extreme_machines.

14. Trebilcock, B., "RTLS: Find a Needle in a Haystack," *Modern Materials Handling* 61(7), 2006: 42.

15. "Acela Express, USA", found at www.railway-technology.com/projects/amtrak/.

16. Conkey, C. and A. Roth, "U.S. News: U.S. Commits $13 Billion to Aid High-Speed Rail," *Wall Street Journal*, April 17, 2009: A5; Sanchanta, M. and J. Mitchell, "Corporate News: High-Speed Rail Approaches Station," *Wall Street Journal*, January 26, 2010: B3; and Sanchanta, M. and Y. Takahashi, "JR Central Chairman Aims to Bring Shinkansen to U.S," *Wall Street Journal (Online)*, February 16, 2010.

17. Macklem, K., "Is There a Fast Train Coming?" *MacLean's* 116(8), 2003: 24–25; Hood, C., "Biting the Bullet: What We Can Learn from the Shinkansen," *Electronic Journal of Contemporary Japanese Studies*, May 23, 2001. Discussion paper No. 3.

18. See www.boeing.com and www.antonov.com.

19. Thuermer, K., "Air Cargo's Painfully Slow Climb," *Logistics Management* 49(1), 2010: 43.

20. Hibbert, L., "Out of the Backwater," *Professional Engineering* 15(7), 2002: 26–27; British Waterways publication, "New Freight on Inland Waterways," found at www.british-waterways.co.uk/images/BWFBroc1_tcm6-71390.pdf.

21. Singhj, B., "The World's Biggest Ship," *The India Tribune* (online edition), www.tribuneindia.com/1999/99jul11/sunday/head3.htm, July 11, 1999.

22. Information found at en.wikipedia.org/wiki/Container_ship.

23. BNSF website: www.bnsf.com.

24. Atlantic Container Line website: www.aclcargo.com.

25. Richardson, H., "Pricing/Costing Series Part III—Pricing: Carriers Calculate Their Risks," *Transportation & Distribution* 35(3), 1994: 29–31.

26. Cassidy, W., "Arrow Trucking Owes Nearly $100 Million," *Journal of Commerce*, March 23, 2010: 1; Clark, P., "A Longer Range," *Financial Times*, March 2, 2010: 6; and Leach, P., "Angels to the Rescue," *Journal of Commerce*, February 22, 2010: 1.

27. See www.southwest.com earnings reports.

28. See www.nmfta.org.

29. Anonymous, "DHS Rolls Out Airport Body Scanners," *Informzationweek—Online*, March 5, 2010.

30. Karp, A., "Cargo Screening's: 'Serious Challenges,'" *Air Transport World* 46(6), 2009: 45–47.

31. Staff, "This Week," *Journal of Commerce*, March 29, 2010: 1.

32. Edmonson, R., "DHS Scans 98 Percent of Imports for Radiation," *Journal of Commerce*, July 22, 2009: 1.

33. See the following: Edmonson, R., "TWICs Technology Challenge," *Journal of Commerce*, February 22, 2010: 1; Staff, "Risk of Train Terror Attack Reduced: DHS IG," *Journal of Commerce*, March 2, 2009: 1.

34. Jerman, R. and R. Anderson, "Regulatory Issues: Shipper Versus Motor Carrier," *Transportation Journal* 33(3), 1994: 15–23.

35. See, for instance, Dempsey, P., "The Disaster of Airline Deregulation," *Wall Street Journal*, May 9, 1991: A15; Leonard, W., "Airline Deregulation: Grand Design or Gross Debacle?" *Journal of Economic Issues* 17(2), 1983: 453–465; O'Brian, B. and C. Solomon, "Braniff Files for Protection from Creditors," *Wall Street Journal*, September 29, 1989: 1; Staff, "Texas Air Provides $10 Million in Aid to People Express," *Wall Street Journal*, October 16, 1986: 1; and Staff, "Business Brief—Texas Air Corp," *Wall Street Journal*, June 7, 1990: A1.

36. Cassidy, W., "Bigger Faster," *Journal of Commerce*, June 23, 2008: 1.

37. Kator, C., "Warehouse Giants," *Modern Materials Handling* 61(12), 2006: 31.

38. Feare, T., "Jazzing Up the Warehouse," *Modern Material Handling* 56(7), 2001: 71–72.

39. Gregor, A., "Precious Works Housed in Armour," *Financial Times*, November 4, 2008: 10.

40. Terreri, A., "The Course to Outsource," *Warehousing Management* 8(9), 2001: 35–38.

41. Biederman, D., "3PLs Put Pedal to the Metal," *Journal of Commerce*, March 8, 2010: 1.

42. Brown, M., "The Slow Boat to Europe," *Management Today*, June 1997: 83–86.

43. Maister, D. H., "Centralization of Inventories and the 'Square Root Law,'" *International Journal of Physical Distribution and Materials Management* 6(3), 1976: 124–134.

44. Warnenburg, C. M., trans. and P. Hall, ed., *Von Thunen's Isolated State*. Oxford, UK: Pergamon Press, 1966.

45. Friedrich, C. J., trans. *Alfred Weber's Theory of the Location of Industries*. Chicago: University of Chicago Press, 1929.

46. Hoover, E. M. *The Location of Economic Activity*. New York: McGraw-Hill, 1948.

47. Greenhut, M. L. *Plant Location in Theory and in Practice*. Chapel Hill: University of North Carolina Press, 1956.

48. Trebilcock, B., "Distribution Evolution at PDS," *Modern Materials Handling* 65(2), 2010: 14–15.

49. Fabey, M., "Changing Trade Winds," *Traffic World* 263(8), 2000: 41–42.

50. MacDonald, A., "What Business Leaders Need to Know About: Atlantic Maritime," *World Trade* 19(4), 2006: 42–48.

51. Terreri, A., "Delivering Supply Chain Excellence," *World Trade* 23(3), 2010: 24–28.

52. Blanchard, D., "When You'd Rather Not Do It Yourself," *Material Handling Management*, October 2009: 48.

53. Thuermer, K., "Tweaking the Supply Chain to Optimize Value and Minimize Cost," *World Trade* 21(10), 2008: 24–27.

54. Hannon, D., "GM Hatches Plan to Cut 70 Days from Order Cycle Time," *Purchasing* 130(13), 2001: 61–62.

55. Schulz, J., "GM Buys Out Vector SCM, Brings Logistics Back In-House," *Logistics Management Online*, August 1, 2006; found at www.logisticsmgmt.com/index.asp?layout=articlePrint&articleID=CA6365036.

56. Kerr, J., "What's the Right Role for Global 3PLs?" *Logistics Management* 45(2), 2006: 51–54.

57. See, for example, Abshire, R., and S. Premeaux, "Motor Carrier Selection Criteria: Perceptual Differences Between Shippers and Carriers," *Transportation Journal* 31(1), 1991: 31–35; Bardi, E., P. Bagchi, and T. Raghunathan,"Motor Carrier Selection in a Deregulated Environment," *Transportation Journal* 29(1), 1989: 4–11; Foster, J., and S. Strasser, "Carrier/Modal Selection Factors: The Shipper/Carrier Paradox," *Transportation Research Forum* 31(1), 1990: 206–212; and Murphy, P., J. Daley, and P. Hall, "Carrier Selection: Do Shippers and Carriers Agree, or Not?" *Transportation Research* 33E(1), 1997: 67–72.

58. Mejza, M. C., and J. D. Wisner, "The Scope and Span of Supply Chain Management," *The International Journal of Logistics Management* 12(2), 2001: 37–56; Tan, K. C., and J.D. Wisner, "A Comparison of the Supply Chain Management Approaches of U.S. Regional and Global Businesses," *Supply Chain Forum* 2(2), 2001: 20–28.

59. Terreri, A., "Delivering Supply Chain Excellence," *World Trade* 23(3), 2010: 24–28.

60. Field, A., "Spirit of Cooperation," *Journal of Commerce*, October 2, 2006: 1.

61. Dutton, G., "Collaborative Transportation Management," *World Trade* 16(2), 2003: 40–43.

62. Schulz, J., "Cutting LTL Costs: Going to the Bench," *Logistics Management* 48(2), 2009: 35.

63. Gallagher, T., "FedEx Trade Opens Six Offices," *Journal of Commerce*, February 12, 2010: 1.

64. Biederman, D., "Visibility into Compliance," *Journal of Commerce*, April 5, 2010: 1.

65. Sechler, B., "Transport Broker Thrives," *Wall Street Journal* (Eastern edition), July 1, 2009: 1.

66. Obtained from the following sites: www.redbooktrucking.com, www.freightquote.com and www.direct-freight.com.

67. Information obtained from www.midwestshippers.com.

68. Information obtained from www.hubgroup.com and Boyd, J., "Intermodal Takes Separate Tracks," *Journal of Commerce*, February 22, 2010: 1.

69. Kerr, J., "Macy's Maneuver to Fill Empty Miles," *Logistics Management* 49(3), 2010: 24–28.

70. See www.epa.gov/smartway.

71. See www.responsibletrans.org.

72. Trepins, D., "European Logistics: Meeting the Challenge of Climate Change," *Logistics Management* 48(11), 2009: 60–61.

73. Fitzgerald, T., T. Brown, and E. Stewart, "Subway's Journey to Green," *Logistics Management* 48(4), 2009: 22–23.

74. McCrea, B., "8th Annual Software Survey: Spending Remains Flat," *Logistics Management* 49(4), 2010: 46–47.

75. Hannon, D., "American Railcar Uses TMS to Shine Light on Inbound Supply Chain," *Purchasing* 139(3), 2010: 13.

76. McCrea, B., "WMS: Prompt Payback," *Logistics Management* 48(5), 2009: 40.

77. Andel, T. "No Failure to Communicate," *Modern Materials Handling* 64(10), 2009: 15.

78. McCrea, B., "GTM Has Arrived," *Logistics Management* 49(1), 2010: 34.

79. Anonymous, "Management Dynamics; Brunzl Distribution USA Implements Global Trade Management Platform," *Economics Week*, September 4, 2009: 13.

80. Russell, S., "'Robust' Security for Crossborder Trucking," *Traffic World*, July 2, 2007: 1.

81. Simon, B., "Border Snarls Put Brakes on Canada Trade," *Financial Times*, September 4, 2007: 24.

82. See, for instance, Cassidy, W., "House Members Rip Cross-Border Trucking," *Journal of Commerce*, April 14, 2010: 1; MacDonald, A., "NAFTA: A Delicate Balance," *World Trade* 22(10), 2009: 30–33; and Moens, A., "The Peace Bridge Project and the Need to Harmonize Canada–US Border Security," *The Canadian Manager* 32(2), 2007: 20–22.

83. Anonymous, "Freight Forwarders Best Foreign Performance," *Logistics Management* 48(8), 2009: 44.

84. U.S. Dept. of Commerce website: www.ita.doc.gov/td/oetca/staff.html.

85. See Anonymous, "National Association of Foreign-Trade Zones Promotes Benefits of FTZs," *Economics Week*, September 25, 2009: 29; and the U.S. Dept. of Commerce Foreign-Trade Zones Board website: http://ia.ita.doc.gov/ftzpage/index.

86. NAFTA information was obtained from the U.S. Trade Representative website: www.ustr.gov.

87. Bedell, D., "Can NAFTA Fill the Gap?" *Global Finance* 24(3), 2010: 30–32; Schot, J., "North American Free Trade Agreement (NAFTA)," *The Princeton Encyclopedia of the World Economy* 2, 2009: 851–55.

88. Lawrence, D., "China Issues Food, Toy Recall Rules to Tighten Safety," *Bloomberg.com News*, August 31, 2007, www.bloomberg.com/apps/news?pid=20601080&sid=asUaOAct_vrc&refer=asia.

89. Rogers, L., "Going in Reverse to Move Forward," *Modern Materials Handling* 64(9), 2009: 28.

90. Gallagher, T., "GENCO Contracts for Dell Remanufacturing," *Journal of Commerce*, July 22, 2009: 1; and www.content.dell.com/us/en/corp/d/press-releases.

91. Blanchard, D., "Moving Ahead by Mastering the Reverse Supply Chain," *Industry Week* 258(6), 2009: 58.

92. Martinez, R., "Best Practices in Returns Management," *Multichannel Merchant* 26(12), 2010: 29.

93. Hoffman, W., "Reversing Returns," *Journal of Commerce*, November 17, 2008: 1.

94. Rogers, L., "Going in Reverse to Move Forward," *Modern Materials Handling* 64(9), 2009: 28.

95. More information on this case can be found at http://web.indstate.edu/recycle/9505.html.

96. Trowbridge, P., "A Case Study of Green Supply-Chain Management," *Greener Management International*, Autumn 2001: 121–35.

CHAPTER 10

1. Cuddeford-Jones, M., "Online Retail: This Time It's Very Personal," *Marketing Week*, May 28, 2009: 26.

2. Lager, M., "Pint of View," *Customer Relationship Management* 14(4), 2010: 42.

3. Burns, M., "CRM Survey 2010," *CA Magazine* 143(3), 2010: 11.

4. Jack, L., "Industry Attitudes: Investment the Only Guarantee of Bright Future," *Marketing Week*, December 3, 2009: 26–30.

5. Dyché, J. *The CRM Handbook: A Business Guide to Customer Relationship Management.* Upper Saddle River, NJ: Addison-Wesley, 2002.

6. Bergeron, B. *Essentials of CRM: A Guide to Customer Relationship Management,* New York, NY: John Wiley & Sons, 2002.

7. Ragins, E., and A. Greco., "Customer Relationship Management and e-Business: More than a Software Solution," *Review of Business* 24(1), 2003: 25–30.

8. Hoffman, J., "A Better Way to Design Loyalty Programs," *Strategy & Leadership* 36(4), 2008: 44.

9. Foss, B., "What Makes for CRM System Success—Or Failure?" *Journal of Database Marketing & Customer Strategy Management* 15 (2), 2008: 68–79.

10. Anonymous, "E-Business Disaster: Why an Ambitious and Expensive Project Failed," *Strategic Direction* 25(5), 2009: 21–22.

11. Dickie, J., "Fueling the CRM Engine," *Customer Relationship Management* 11(4), 2007: 10.

12. Goldenberg, B., "Your People Are Half the Battle," *Customer Relationship Management* 14(4), 2010: 6.

13. Anonymous, "NMA @ 10: Secrets of Success," *New Media Age*, June 16, 2005: 18.

14. Chilton, D., "CRM Masters," *Marketing* 111(21), 2006: S19–20.

15. Rigby, E., "Tesco Adds Extra 100 Discount Lines," *Financial Times*, February 13, 2009: 19.

16. Mukerjee, K., and K. Singh., "CRM: A Strategic Approach," *IUP Journal of Management Research* 8(2), 2009: 65–82.

17. Bailor, C., "Elder Effect," *Customer Relationship Management* 10(11), 2006: 36–40.

18. Ostroff, J., "Internet Ad Trends Favor Consumers," *KiplingerForecasts.com*, May 9, 2008: 1.

19. Fernando, A., "Start Talking in Code!" *Communication World* 27(1), 2010: 8–9.

20. The Toyota Yaris MySpace page is: www.myspace.com/yaris.

21. Goldwyn, C., "E-Mail: The Upside/Downside," *Restaurant Hospitality* 93(6), 2009: 30.

22. Hintze, J., "A Wealth of Progress," *USBanker* 120(4), 2010: 32–33.

23. Anonymous, "Maximizing Growth and Retention with Cross-Selling," *Texas Banking* 98(11), 2009: 24.

24. Kanu, K "Get In or Get Left Behind," *Black Enterprise* 39(4), 2008: 76–80.

25. Ragins, E., and A. Greco., "Customer Relationship Management and e-Business: More than a Software Solution," *Review of Business* 24(1), 2003: 25–30.

26. Nadeem, M., "How e-Business Leadership Results in Customer Satisfaction and Customer Lifetime Value," *The Business Review, Cambridge* 6(1), 2006: 218–24.

27. Helms, M., and D. Mayo, "Assessing Poor Quality Service: Perceptions of Customer Service Representatives," *Managing Service Quality* 18(6), 2008: 610–18.

28. Bailor, C., "Not Fade Away," *Customer Relationship Management* 11(2), 2007: 22–26.

29. Collier, S., and P. Heckman, "Another Way to Look at 'Member Value'," *Credit Union Magazine* 73(1), 2007: 9A.

30. Fuhrman, E., "Bottler of the Year: Coca-Cola Bottling Co. Consolidated," *Beverage Industry* 101(1), 2010: 30–35.

31. Hosford, C., "AmerisourceBergen Saves with Automated Sales Info," *B to B* 91(13), 2006: 18.

32. Dahl, J., "Save the Smarts," *Credit Union Magazine* 75(9), 2009: 68–69.

33. Shaprio, R. D., and J. L. Heskett, *Logistics Strategy: Cases and Concepts*. St. Paul, MN: West Publishing Co., 1985.

34. Lichtenstein, G., "Best Airlines 2009 in US, Canada," *Senior Travel*, September 3, 2009: 1.

35. Anonymous, "Air New Zealand," *Air Transport World* 47(2), 2010: 24.

36. Aho, K., "10 Companies That Treat You Right," *MoneyCentral MSN.com*, May 18, 2010: 1.

37. Farfan, B., "Retail Companies on Business Week's 2010 Customer Service Champ List," *About.com Guide* found at http://retailindustry.about.com/od/customerservicebests/a/retail_customer_service_champs_2010_ business_week.htm.

38. Anonymous, "Cox Communications," *Marketing Weekly News*, October 3, 2009: 116.

39. Wojcik, J., "UnitedHealthcare," *Business Insurance* 43(41), 2009: 14.

40. Aho, K., "10 Companies We Love to Hate," *MoneyCentral MSN.com*, May 18, 2010: 1.

41. Paczkowski, J., "AT&T Ranked Last in Consumer Reports' Best Cellphone Service Survey," *AllThingsDigital.com*, December 1, 2009.

42. Aho, K., "10 Companies We Love to Hate," *MoneyCentral MSN.com*, May 18, 2010: 1.

43. Lauber, M., "Charter Cable Rated as Worst Again by Consumer Reports," found at www.wsaw.com/home/headlines/81028247.html, January 8, 2010.

44. Aho, K., "10 Companies We Love to Hate," MoneyCentral MSN.com, May 18, 2010: 1.

45. Levin, G., "The Viability of Virtual Queuing Tools," *Call Center Magazine* 19(10), 2006: 29.

46. Anonymous, "Special Report: Telemarketing's True Calling," *Marketing Week*, September 21, 2006: 39.

47. Klie, L., "Satisfaction with Automation Increases Only Slightly," *Speech Technology* 12(5), 2007: 10–11.

48. Fox, A., "The Ins and Outs of Customer Contact Centers," *HRMagazine* 55(3), 2010: 29–31.

49. Ali, S., "Leadership (A Special Report): If You Want to Scream, Press ... Do Call Centers Have to Be So Infuriating?" *Wall Street Journal*, October 30, 2006: R4.

50. Adams, J., "Self-Service: Curse or Competitive Advantage?" *Supply House Times* 52(6), 2009: 14; Lamont, J., "KM Past and Future: Closing the Knowledge Loop," *KM World* 19(1), 2010: 8–10.

51. Wisner, J. D., and W. J. Corney, "Comparing Practices for Capturing Bank Customer Feedback," *Benchmarking: An International Journal* 8(3), 2001, 240–50.

52. Anonymous, "Lessons from the Domino's Turnaround," *Restaurant Hospitality* 94(6), 2010: 30.

53. Lager, M., "Smooth Sailing," *Customer Relationship Management* 13(7), 2009: 45.

54. Shum, P., L. Bove, and S. Auh, "Employees' Affective Commitment to Change: The Key to Successful CRM Implementation," *European Journal of Marketing* 42(11/12), 2008: 1346–71; Lassar, W., S. Lassar, and N. Rauseo, "Developing a CRM Strategy in Your Firm," *Journal of Accountancy* 206(2), A2008: 68–73.

55. Many of these references can be found at the American CRM Directory, or www.american-crm-directory.com.

56. Dyché, J. *The CRM Handbook: A Business Guide to Customer Relationship Management.* Upper Saddle River, NJ: Addison-Wesley, 2002.

57. Keenan, C., "In Search of Wallet Share," *USBanker* 120(3), 2010: 20–25.

58. Dickie, J., "Don't Confuse Implementation with Adoption," *Customer Relationship Management* 13(5), 2009: 10.

59. Goldenberg, B., "A CRM Initiative's Bermuda Triangle," *Customer Relationship Management* 11(5), 2007: 10.

60. Prosch, M., "Preventing Identity theft Throughout the Data Life Cycle," *Journal of Accountancy* 207(1), 2009: 58–63; and Ball, D., and D. Gauthier-Villars, "France Got Stolen HSBC Data," *The Wall Street Journal*, March 12, 2010: C1.

61. Tsai, J., "New Social Media Not Helping Sales," *DestinationCRM.com*, April 8, 2009: 1.

62. Kaser, D., "Plotting Social Media's Bottom Line," *Information Today* 26(9), 2009: 16.

63. Musico, C., "Innovation Picks Up Static," *Customer Relationship Management* 14(1), 2010: 18–19.

64. Hoover, J., "Jive Blends Wiki, Social Networking into One," *InformationWeek*, March 16, 2009: 22.

65. McCarthy, C., "After Facebook Backlash, Nestle Steps Up Sustainability," *The Social CNET News*, May 17, 2010: 1.

66. McKay, L., "Strategy and Social Media: Everything's Social (Now)," *Customer Relationship Management* 13(6), 2009: 24–28.

67. Wasserman, T., "Why Micro-Blogging Is What's Good for General Motors," *Brandweek* 51(7), 2010: 29.

68. Company information from www.salesforce.com; also see Pombriant, D., "The Man Who Moved a Paradigm," *Customer Relationship Management* 13(11), 2009: 6.

69. Whiting, R., "The Right SaaS Pitch for SMBs," *CRN*, February 1, 2010: 12.

70. Veverka, M., "Sky's the Limit," *Barron's* 90(1), 2010: 19–21.

71. Anonymous, "Interpop: Domino's Mulls Microsoft Cloud," *Informationweek Online*, April 26, 2010: 1.

CHAPTER 11

1. Global Location Trends—Annual Report, IBM Global Business Service, October 2009; available from ftp://public.dhe.ibm.com/common/ssi/sa/wh/n/gbl03009usen/GBL03009USEN.PDF.

2. M. Porter, "Clusters and the New Economics of Competition," *Harvard Business Review*, November–December 1998.

3. "Honda Chooses Indiana for US$400 mil. Factory"; available from www.globalinsight.com/SDA/SDADetail6236.htm

4. Global Location Trend—Annual Report, IBM Global Business Service, October 2009; available from ftp://public.dhe.ibm.com/common/ssi/ecm/en/gbl03009usen/GBL03009USEN.PDF.

5. Amazon Investor Relations; available at http://phx.corporate-ir.net/phoenix.zhtml?p=irol-irhome&c=97664.

6. 2009 Amazon.com Annual Report; available from http://phx.corporate-ir.net/External.File?item=UGFyZW50SUQ9Mzc2NjQyfENoaWxkSUQ9Mzc1Mjc3fFR5cGU9MQ==&t=1.

7. Shah, J. "Fedex's Hub of Supply Chain Activity – At Its Own Operation, the Logistics Company Has Made an Art Out of the Science of Supply Chain Management," *EBN*, April 30, 2001: 1.

8. K. Ferdows, "Making the Most of Foreign Factories," *Harvard Business Review*, March–April 1997: 73–88.

9. Ibid.

10. Ibid.

11. Ibid.

12. What Is the WTO? available from www.wto.org/english/thewto_e/whatis_e/whatis_e.htm.

13. Regional Trade Agreements; available from .www.wto.org/english/tratop_e/region_e/region_e.htm.

14. "The European Union at a Glance, Member States of the EU"; available from http://europa.eu/abc/european_countries/index_en.htm.

15. North American Free Trade Agreement (NAFTA)—Office of the United States Trade Representative; available from .www.ustr.gov/trade-agreements/free-trade-agreements/north-american-free-trade-agreement-nafta.

16. MERCOSUR; available from http://en.wikipedia.org/wiki/Mercosur.

17. Association of South East Asian Nations (ASEAN); available from www.aseansec.org/about_ASEAN.html.

18. Common Market for Eastern and Southern Africa (COMESA); available from www.comesa.int/.

19. Ibid.

20. D. Clapp, M. E. McCandless, and K. Khan, "The World's Most Competitive Locations," *Business Facilities*, September 2001; available from www.facilitycity.com/busfac/bf_01_09_cover.asp.

21. IMD World Competitiveness Yearbook; available from www.imd.ch/research/publications/wcy/index.cfm.

22. World Competitiveness Report, Methodology and Principles of Analysis; available from www.imd.ch/research/publications/wcy/upload/methodology.pdf.

23. Global Competitiveness Report 2009-2010, World Economic Forum; available from www.weforum.org/pdf/GCR09/GCR20092010fullreport.pdf.

24. Grier, P., "An Economic Vision: Silicon States," *Christian Science Monitor*, V. 91, No. 61(1999): 1.

25. 2006 Amazon.com Annual Report; available from http://media.corporate-ir.net/media_files/irol/97/97664/2006AnnualReport.pdf.

26. Objectives—North American Agreement on Environmental Cooperation; available from www.cec.org/Page.asp?PageID=122&ContentID=2730&SiteNodeID=567&BL_ExpandID=.

27. "Trade and Environment," World Trade Organization; available from www.wto.org/english/tratop_e/envir_e/environment.pdf.

28. Ibid.

29. John F. Wasik, "The Surprising Success of the Green Supply Chain," *CNNMoney.com*; available from http://money.cnn.com/2010/08/13/news/companies/corporate_sustainability.fortune/index.htm.

30. "Balancing Market Access and Supplier Proximity"; available from http://rightsite.asia/en/article/balancing-market-access-and-supplier-proximity.

31. "The Supercenter Era: 1992 to 2002," *DSN Retailing Today* (New York), August 6, 2002: pp. 27–31.

32. Malkin, E., "Manufacturing Jobs Are Exiting Mexico," *New York Times*, November 5, 2002: 1.

33. J. Mallot, "Quality of Life: How to Know It When You See It," *Business Facilities*, November 2002; available from www.facilitycity.com/busfac/bf_02_11_cover2.asp.

34. Indicators—Quality of Life Progress Report, Jacksonville Community Council Inc.; available from www.jcci.org/jcciwebsite/pages/indicators.html.

35. "Right-to-Work States"; available from www.nrtw.org/rtws.htm.

36. About Mapping Analytics; available from www.mappinganalytics.com/about/about.html.

37. Ibid.

38. M. Porter, "Clusters and the New Economics of Competition," *Harvard Business Review*, (November-December 1998), 77–90.

39. "Business Clusters in the UK—A First Assessment"; available from www.dti.gov.uk/clusters/map/graphics/forintro.pdf.

40. Brody, B., "High-Tech Clusters Span the Globe," *Business Facilities*, March 2001; available from www.facilitycity.com/busfac/bf_01_03_global.asp.

41. The World Commission on Environment and Development (the Brundtland Commission) Definition of Sustainable Development; available from www.unngosustainability.org/CSD_Definitions SD.htm.

42. "Sustainable Development Discussions to Focus on Smart Use of Resources," Economic and Social Council of UN; available from www.un.org/News/Press/docs/2010/envdev1123.doc.htm.

43. The United Nations Framework Convention on Climate Change; available from http://unfccc.int/2860.php.

44. Kyoto Protocol; available from http://unfccc.int/kyoto_protocol/items/2830.php.

45. "Sustainable Development"; available from http://en.wikipedia.org/wiki/Sustainable_development.

CHAPTER 12

1. Griswold, D., "What America Makes Best," *Barron's* 89(45), 2009: 46.

2. Quotes by Tom Hoch, owner of restaurant design firm. In D. Berta's "Versatility Adds Value," *Nation's Restaurant News* 44(6), 2010: 20.

3. Cetron, M., and O. Davies., "Trends Shaping Tomorrow's World: Economic and Social Trends and Their Impacts.," *The Futurist* 44(3), 2010: 35–52.

4. Griswold, D. "What America Makes Best," *Barron's* 89(45), 2009: 46.

5. Cetron, M., and O. Davies, "Trends Shaping Tomorrow's World: Economic and Social Trends and Their Impacts," *The Futurist* 44(3), 2010: 35–52.

6. Blackstone, B., "Is Productivity Growth Back in Grips of Baumol's Disease?" *Wall Street Journal*, August 13, 2007: A2.

7. Cain, R., "Finding the Right Fit," *Journal of Commerce*, May 10, 2010: 1.

8. Pollitt, D., "Warehouse Team Develops IT Skills One Stage at a Time," *Training & Management Development Methods* 23(3), 2009: 525–30.

9. Anonymous, "Iconic Brands Combine to Create Full-Service Restaurant Company," *Franchising World* 42(5), 2010: 91; Betts, P., and M. Nakamoto, "Solar Impulse Takes Flight Towards the Impossible," *Financial Times*, April 9, 2010: 17; and Scholtes, S., "Capco Eyes North America Expansion," *Financial Times*, September 17, 2009: 27.

10. Porter, M. *Competitive Strategy: Techniques for Analyzing Industries and Competitors.* New York: The Free Press, 1980.

11. Paul, C., "LCC Dogfight Over India," *Air Transport World* 47(5), 2010: 28.

12. Bailor, C., "Buying into the Customer Experience." *Customer Relationship Management* 11(6), 2007: 15.

13. Hoffman, W., "Building the Little Guy," *Traffic World*, September 3, 2007: 1.

14. Ainlay, T., and J. Gabaldon, *Las Vegas: The Fabulous First Century.* Mt. Pleasant, SC: Arcadia Publishing, 2003; Land, B., and M. Land. *A Short History of Las Vegas.* Reno: University of Nevada Press, 2004.

15. Anonymous, "Fiat Group Brazil Honors Ryder as a 2007 Top Supplier," *Traffic World*, June 4, 2008: 1; Anonymous, "Toyota Honors Ryder with 2006 Excellent Award for Value Improvement," *Traffic World*, May 1, 2007: 1.

16. Levin, A., "Green Gets Going," *Foodservice Equipment & Supplies* 62(3), 2010: 18.

17. Warren, M., "Simply Irresistible," *Profit* 29(3), 2010: 68–69.

18. Drazen, E. L., R. E. Moll, and M. F. Roetter. *Logistics in Service Industries.* Oak Brooks, IL: Council of Logistics Management, 1991: 34.

19. Brin, D., "Express Scripts Tries Self-Service Kiosks," *The Wall Street Journal*, November 11, 2009: 1.

20. Li, H., "Charging Cars for Pennies," *Canadian Business* 82(19), 2009: 24.

21. Anonymous, "Lavi Industries Inc.," *Marketing Weekly News*, March 27, 2010: 200; Anonymous, "North Asia Office Carat China, Shanghai," *Media*, December 17, 2009: 36.

22. Maister, D., "The Psychology of Waiting Lines," In J. A. Czepiel, M. R. Solomon, and C. F. Surprenant, *The Service Encounter.* Lexington, MA: Lexington Books, D.C. Heath & Co., 1985.

23. Ibid.

24. Okie, S., "Form Follows Function: A Redesigned Pediatric Office," *Health Affairs* 29(5), 2010: 979–81.

25. Petouhoff, N., "The Social Customer Economy," *Customer Relationship Management* 14(3), 2010: 14.

26. Andel, T., "Can Amazon Succeed at Grocery Delivery?" *Modern Materials Handling* 62(9), 2007: 15. Also see their website: http://fresh.amazon.com.

27. Anonymous, "Come in for a Bite," *Nation's Restaurant News* 44(1), 2010: 5.

28. Flandez, R., "New Franchise Idea: Fewer Rules, More Difference," *Wall Street Journal*, September 18, 2007: B4; Jones, L., D. Lehr, and J. Fairbourne, "A Good Business for Poor People," *Stanford Social Innovation Review* 8(3), 2010: 44–49.

29. Byrne, H., "Welcome to McWorld," *Barron's* 74(35), 1994: 25–28.

30. Britton, E., and V. Rossi, "The Future of China's Service Sector," *The China Business Review* 34(3), 2007: 42–47; Chao, L., "Corporate News: Google Seeks Beijing License," *Wall Street Journal*, June 11, 2010: B2; Hille, K., "Google Searches for Truce in China," *FT.com*, June 29, 2010: 1.

31. Hoffman, G., "On Foreign Expansion," *Progressive Grocer* 75(9), 1996: 156.

32. Anonymous, "Business: Bleak Friday; Retail v e-tail in America," *The Economist* 393(8659), 2009: 69.

33. Pinkerton, J., and A. Gray, "Retail in a Google World," *Dealerscope* 49(1), 2007: 46–51; also see www.goftp.com/how many searches per day in 2009.

34. Rooney, K., "Consumer-Driven Healthcare Marketing: Using the Web to Get Up Close and Personal," *Journal of Healthcare Management* 54(4), 2009: 241–51.

35. See, for instance, Parasuraman, A., V. A. Zeithaml, and L. L. Berry, "SERVQUAL: A Multiple-Item Scale for Measuring Consumer Perceptions of Service Quality," *Journal of Retailing* 64(1), 1988: 12–40; Parasuraman, A., V. A. Zeithaml, and L. L. Berry, "Conceptual Model of Service Quality and Its Implications for Future Research," *Journal of Marketing* 49, Fall 1985: 41–50.

36. McWilliams, B., and E. Gerstner, "Offering Low Price Guarantees to Improve Customer Retention," *Journal of Retailing* 82(2), 2006: 105.

CHAPTER 13

1. Poirier, C., M. Swink, and F. Quinn, "Progress Despite the Downturn," *Supply Chain Management Review* 13(7), 2009: 26.

2. Krizner, K., "Supply Chain Visibility and Efficiency Gets a Boost," *World Trade* 23(1), 2010: 22–25.

3. Blanchard, D., "Too Many Supply Chains are Failing to Integrate," *Industry Week* 255(11), 2006: 45–46; Anonymous, "Talent Management Must Mesh with Business Goals for Post-Recession Success," *HR Focus* 87(1), 2010: 8.

4. Lambert, D., M. Cooper, and J. Pagh, "Supply Chain Management: Implementation Issues and Research Opportunities," *International Journal of Logistics Management* 9(2), 1998: 1–19.

5. Siu, S., "CargoSmart Ltd," *Journal of Commerce*, January 8, 2007: 1.

6. Quinn, B., "Walmart's Sustainable Supply Chain," *Pollution Engineering* 41(9), 2009: 24.

7. These processes are discussed in detail in Lambert, D. M., M. C. Cooper, and J. D. Pagh, "Supply Chain Management: Implementation Issues and Research Opportunities," *International Journal of Logistics Management* 9(2), 1998: 1–19; and in Croxton, K. L., S. J. Garcia-Dastugue, and D. M.

Lambert, "The Supply Chain Management Processes," *International Journal of Logistics Management* 12(2), 2001: 13–36.

8. Anonymous, "Report: Retailers Turning to SCM," *Modern Materials Handling* 65(1), 2010: 9.

9. Overby, S., "Managing Demand After Disaster Strikes," *CIO* 23(9), 2010: 1.

10. Anonymous, "Sustainability at Sea and in Northwest Arkansas," *Retailing Today*, June/July 2009: 24–25.

11. Henri, J., "Are Your Performance Measurement Systems Truly Performing?" *CMA Management* 80(7), 2006: 31–35; Hinton, M., and D. Barnes, "Discovering Effective Performance Measurement for e-Business," *International Journal of Productivity and Performance* 58(4), 2009: 329–40.

12. Wilding, R., "Playing the Tune of Shared Success," *Financial Times*, November 10, 2006: 2.

13. www.eia.doe.gov/oil_gas/petroleum/data_publications.

14. DiBenedetto, B., "Thinking Lean," *Journal of Commerce*, May 21, 2007: 1.

15. Wilson, M., "A Blanket Solution," *Chain Store Age* 86(1), 2010: 39.

16. See, for instance, www.rfidinc.com; www.rfidjournal.com; Andel, T., "RFID: The Only Thing Passive about the Marines," *Modern Materials Handling* 62(8), 2007: 61; Fink, R., J. Gillett, and G. Grzeskiewicz, "Will RFID Change Inventory Assumptions?" *Strategic Finance* 89(4), 2007: 34–39; and Joch, A., "'Active' Assistance," *Hospitals & Health Networks* 6(3), 2007: 36–37.

17. Armbruster, W., "Dell Looks to the Ocean," *Journal of Commerce*, April 26, 2010: 1.

18. Lester, T., "Masters of Collaboration—How Well Do U.K. Businesses Work Together," *Financial Times*, June 29, 2007: 8.

19. Trunick, P., "It's Crunch Time," *Transportation & Distribution* 43(1), 2002: 5–6.

20. Anonymous, "Robert Reed on Hospital-Physician Integration," *Healthcare Financial Management* 64 (6), 2010: 30.

21. Biederman, D., "Visibility into Compliance," *Journal of Commerce*, April 5, 2010: 1.

22. Geller, S., "The Pharmaceutical Industry Looks to Reduce Waste by Getting Lean," *Pharmaceutical Technology* 31(3), 2007: 130.

23. Hoffman, W., "Linking the Chain," *Traffic World*, April 23, 2007: 1.

24. Beasty, C., "The Chain Gang," *Customer Relationship Management* 11(10), 2007: 32–36.

25. Field, A., "Sound the Alarm," *Journal of Commerce*, May 7, 2007: 1.

26. Shaklett, M., "Is Supply Chain Management Emerging from the Clouds?" *World Trade* 23(4), 2010: 34–37.

27. Avery, S., "At Boeing, Supplier Collaboration Takes Off," *Purchasing* 136(13), 2007: 1.

28. Maccoby, M., "Creating Collaboration," *Research Technology Management* 49(6), 2006: 60–62.

29. Roberts, B., "Counting on Collaboration," *HR Magazine* 52(10), 2007: 47–51.

30. Paul, L., "Suspicious Minds: Collaboration among Trading Partners Can Unlock Great Value," *CIO* 16 (7), 2003: 74–82.

31. Maylett, T., and K. Vitasek, "For Closer Collaboration, Try Education," *Supply Chain Management Review* 11(1), 2007: 58.

32. Infiormation about these annual conferences can be found at www.sensorsexpo.com, www.ism.ws and www.uconnect.gs1us.org.

33. Lee, H., V. Padmanabhan, and S. Whang, "The Bullwhip Effect in Supply Chains," *Sloan Management Review* 38(3), 1997: 93–102; Lee, H., "Taming the Bullwhip," *Journal of Supply Chain Management* 46(1), 2010: 7.

34. Rigby, E., "Netto Seen as Significant 'Step-Change' for ASDA," *Financial Times*, May 28, 2010: 20.

35. Hofmann, M., "Financial Executives Rate Top Challenges through 2009," *Business Insurance* 41 (21), 2007: 4–5.

36. O'Connell, O., "Americas Trade & Supply Chain: Lessons Learned," *Trade Finance*, April 2010: 1.

37. Anonymous, "A BP Lesson: Supply-Chain Risk," *Institutional Investor*, June 2010: 1.

38. Field, A., "How 'Free' Is Free Trade?" *Journal of Commerce*, December 18, 2006: 1–3; Kline, J., "Managing Emerging Market Risk," *Logistics Management* 46(5), 2007: 41–44; Swaminathan, J., and B. Tomlin, "How to Avoid the Risk Management Pitfalls," *Supply Chain Management Review* 11(5), 2007: 34–43.

39. Esola, L., "Employers Questioned on Pandemic Drug Plan," *Business Insurance* 40(49), 2006: 4–5.

40. Swaminathan, J., and B. Tomlin, "How to Avoid the Risk Management Pitfalls," *Supply Chain Management Review* 11(5), 2007: 34–43.

41. Anonymous, "Supply Disruption Discussed," *Business Insurance* 37(22), 2003: 17.

42. Swaminathan, J., and B. Tomlin, "How to Avoid the Risk Management Pitfalls," *Supply Chain Management Review* 11(5), 2007: 34–43.

43. Anonymous, "Supply Diversity Cuts Risk Exposure," *Oil & Gas Journal* 105(17), 2007: 65–68.

44. Tieman, R., "It's About Common Sense," *Financial Times*, September 10, 2007: 5.

45. Ibid.

46. Anonymous, "Flexing Supply Chain Muscle," *Chain Store Age* 83(9), 2007: 10A.

47. Ibid.

48. Felsted, A., "Lessons from Barbie World," *Financial Times*, September 10, 2007: 1.

49. Rice, J., "Rethinking Security," *Logistics Management* 46(5), 2007: 28.

50. Terreri, A., "How Do You Balance Shipment Speed with a Secure Supply Chain?" *World Trade* 19 (11), 2006: 18–22.

51. Rice, J., "Rethinking Supply Chain Security," *Logistics Management*, May 1, 2007.

52. Anderson, B., "Prevent Cargo Theft," *Logistics Today* 48(5), 2007: 37–38.

53. McCourt, M., "Supply Chains: Get a Global View and Find the Weakest Link," *Security* 44(8), 2007: 8.

54. Information found at www.transparency.org.

55. See, for example, the website www.cargosecurity.com/ncsc/education-CTPAT.asp.

56. Terreri, A., "How Do You Balance Shipment Speed with a Secure Supply Chain?" *World Trade* 19 (11), 2006: 18–22.

57. Greenemeier, L., "MassMutual Gets Control of Its Security Data," *InformationWeek*, September 17, 2007: 108–09.

58. Michel, R., "Profit from Secure Supply Chains," *Manufacturing Business Technology* 24(11), 2006: 1.

CHAPTER 14

1. Zalud, B., "Every Link in the Chain," *Security* 47(5), 2010: 28–30. Quote by Bill Anderson, Director of International Safety, Ryder Systems.

2. Fraser, J., "Performance Measures Must Change to Reflect Current Business," *Manufacturing Business Technology* 27(5), 2009: 30–31.

3. Adams, B., "Performance Measures and Profitability Factors of Successful African-American Entrepreneurs: An Exploratory Study," *Journal of American Academy of Business* 2(2), 2003: 418–24.

4. Poirier, C., M. Swink, and F. Quinn, "Progress Despite the Downturn," *Supply Chain Management Review* 13(7), 2009: 26.

5. Biederman, D., "The Customer Is King, Again," *Journal of Commerce*, May 10, 2010: 1.

6. Henri, J., "Are Your Performance Measurement Systems Truly Performing?" *CMA Management* 80(7), 2006: 31–35; Biddick, M., "Time for a SaaS Strategy," *InformationWeek*, January 18, 2010: 27–30.

7. Blackwell, R., and K. Blackwell, "The Century of the Consumer: Converting Supply Chains into Demand Chains," *Supply Chain Management Review*, Fall 1999: 22–32.

8. Balkau, F., and G. Sonnemann, "Managing Sustainability Performance through the Value-Chain," *Corporate Governance* 10(1), 2010: 46–56.

9. Fusaro, P., and R. Miller. *What Went Wrong at Enron: Everyone's Guide to the Largest Bankruptcy in U.S. History*. Hoboken, NJ: Wiley, 2002.

10. Christensen, P., and K. Gregory, "Becoming a Data-Driven Organization: City of Peoria, Arizona," *Government Finance Review* 26(2), 2010: 57–59.

11. Katz, J., "Beyond the Executive Branch," *Industry Week* 256(1), 2007: 20A.

12. Debusk, G., and C. Debusk, "Characteristics of Successful Lean Six Sigma Organizations," *Cost Management* 24(1), 2010: 5–10.

13. Adapted from Nicholas, J. M. *Competitive Manufacturing Management*. New York: McGraw-Hill, 1998; and Wisner, J., and S. Fawcett, "Linking Firm Strategy to Operating Decisions through Performance Measurement," *Production and Inventory Management Journal* 32(3), 1991: 5–11.

14. Hae, E., and D. Ballou, "Raising the Recycling Rate at World-Class Zoo," *BioCycle* 50(10), 2009: 31–33.

15. Geary, S., and J. Zonnenburg, "What It Means to Be Best in Class," *Supply Chain Management Review*, July 2000: 42–50; Aquino, D., and K. O'Marah, "What Makes Modern Supply Chain Professional?" *Supply Chain Management Review*, May 2009: 12–13.

16. Mishra, D., "Feeding Best Buy," *Dealerscope* 48(12), 2006: 82.

17. Hervani, A., M. Helms, and J. Sarkis, "Performance Measurement for Green Supply Chain Management," *Benchmarking* 12(4), 2005: 330–54.

18. See www.walmartstores.com/sustainability and www.sustinabilityconsortium.org.

19. Anonymous, "IT Helps Firms Go Green, Save Money," *Industry Week* 258(11), 2009: 11.

20. Adapted from Geary, S., and J. P. Zonnenburg, "What It Means to Be Best in Class," *Supply Chain Management Review*, July 2000: 42–50.

21. Varmazis, M., "What to Look for in Online Office Supply Catalogs," *Purchasing* 136(11), 2007: 33.

22. Geary, S., and J. P. Zonnenburg, "What It Means to Be Best in Class," *Supply Chain Management Review* July 2000: 42–50.

23. See, for example, DeBusk, G., and A. Crabtree, "Does the Balanced Scorecard Improve Performance?" *Management Accounting Quarterly* 8(1), 2006: 44–48; Kaplan, R. S., and D. P. Norton, "The Balanced Scorecard—Measures That Drive Performance," 70(1), 1992: 71–79; Lester, T., "Measure for Measure, the Balanced Scorecard Remains a Widely Used Management Tool," *Financial Times*, October 6, 2004: 6; and Lawson, R., W. Stratton, and T. Hatch, "Scorecarding in the Public Sector: Fad or Tool of Choice?" *Government Finance Review* 23(3), 2007: 48–52.

24. Chow, C. W., D. Ganulin, K. Haddad, and J. Williamson, "The Balanced Scorecard: A Potent Tool for Energizing and Focusing Healthcare Organization Management," *Journal of Healthcare Management* 43(3), 1998: 263–80.

25. Lester, T., "Measure for Measure, the Balanced Scorecard Remains a Widely Used Management Tool."

26. DeBusk, G., and A. Crabtree, "Does the Balanced Scorecard Improve Performance?" *Management Accounting Quarterly* 8(1), 2006: 44–48.

27. Lester, T., "Measure for Measure, the Balanced Scorecard Remains a Widely Used Management Tool."

28. Alsyouf, I., "Measuring Maintenance Performance Using a Balanced Scorecard Approach," *Journal of Quality in Maintenance Engineering* 12(2), 2006: 133–43.

29. Kaplan, R. S., and D. P. Norton, "Linking the Balanced Scorecard to ~~~~~ ~fornia Management Review* 39(1), 1996: 53–79.

30. Bush, P., "Strategic Performance Management in Government: Usin~~~~~~~~~~~ ~card," *Cost Management* 19(3), 2005: 24–31.

31. Stephens, Jr., T., "Drive Your Business Performance: Getting Starte~~~~~ Catalyst, July/August 2007: 22–24.

32. Interested readers can visit www.supply-chain.org for more information about the Supp~~~~~ ~ouncil.

33. Taken from the online proceedings of the Supply-Chain World—Latin America 2002 conference, Mexico City, Mexico (www.supplychainworld.org/la2002/program.html).

34. Harbert, T., "Why the Leaders Love Value Chain Management," *Supply Chain Management Review* 13(8), 2009: 12–16.

35. Printed with permission from the Supply-Chain Council, www.supply-chain.org.

36. Stedman, C., "Users Eye Standard for Supply Chain," *Computerworld News*, June 1, 1998 issue. Web page: www.computerworld.com/news/1998.

37. Saccomano, A., "Keeping SCOR," *Traffic World* 255(13), 1998: 27–28.

38. Bolstorff, P., "How to Make Your Supply Chain More Valuable," *Logistics Today* 46(6), 2005: 19–21.

39. DiBenedetto, B., "Keeping SCOR," *Journal of Commerce*, April 23, 2007: 1.

Author Index

Subject Index

Note: Figures, tables, and examples are indicated by page numbers including f, t, and e.